Philosophy

Philosophy
A Text with Readings

THIRD EDITION

MANUEL VELASQUEZ
Santa Clara University

VINCENT BARRY
Bakersfield College

WADSWORTH PUBLISHING COMPANY
Belmont, California
A Division of Wadsworth, Inc.

PHILOSOPHY EDITOR: Kenneth King
PRODUCTION EDITOR: Sandra Craig
DESIGNER: MaryEllen Podgorski
PRINT BUYER: Karen Hunt
COPY EDITOR: Evelyn Mercer Ward
ART RESEARCHER: Toni Haskell
COVER DESIGNER: Vargas/Williams/Design
COVER PHOTOGRAPH: Guy Montil of West Light
COMPOSITOR: Graphic Typesetting Service
SIGNING REPRESENTATIVE: Kay Chamberlain

Printed in the United States of America   19

3 4 5 6 7 8 9 10—92 91 90 89

LIBRARY OF CONGRESS CATALOGING-IN-PUBLICATION DATA

Velasquez, Manuel G.
    Philosophy, a text with readings / Manuel Velasquez, Vincent Barry.
       p.   cm.
    Rev. ed. of: Philosophy, a text with readings / Vincent Barry. 2nd ed. 1983.
    Includes index.
    ISBN 0-534-08526-1
    1. Philosophy—Introductions.   I. Barry, Vincent E.   Philosophy,
a text with readings.   II. Title.
BD21.V4 1988
100—dc19   87-21757
                                                      CIP

Contents

PART II

Metaphysics   93

CHAPTER 3

Philosophy and God   94

CHAPTER 4   Reality and Being   161

PART III

Epistemology   223

CHAPTER 5   The Nature of Knowledge   224

CHAPTER 6   Truth   265

Brief Selections Included Within the Chapters

CHAPTER 5   The Nature of Knowledge

Preface to the
Third Edition

Although a significant number of new features have been added to this edition of *Philosophy: A Text with Readings*, it continues to have four main objectives: (1) to introduce readers to traditional philosophical problems in a way that will help them define and shape their own lives; (2) to expose readers to philosophical argumentation in such a way that they will feel confident in handling abstract concepts; (3) to help readers recognize philosophical problems in everyday contexts and to deal with everyday problems philosophically; and (4) to provide readers with a representative sampling of primary philosophical writings and philosophical fiction.

ORGANIZATION

The material in this edition continues to be organized around the notion of self-discovery. Each chapter returns to this notion and links the material discussed to the reader's growth in self-knowledge. The chapters are sufficiently self-contained, however, that instructors can use them in whatever order they choose and omit whatever chapters they wish.

Because this book has remained useful to a wide audience, this revision has retained the main contents and features of the central chapters from earlier editions, with the exception of the first chapter, which has been completely rewritten. The first chapter now contains a major section on Socrates as a primary example of the philosophical task and

includes substantial selections from the Socratic dialogues. Chapter 2 focuses on human nature. Succeeding chapters then introduce the following topics in order: God and religious experience, reality and being, the nature of knowledge, truth, ethics, and social philosophy. Absent from this edition are two topics that were present in earlier editions but that instructors generally omitted: philosophy of art and philosophy of science. Also new in this edition is the division of each chapter into several sections to facilitate the reader's assimilation of the materials.

SPECIAL FEATURES

Among the many features that make this text unique are the following:

1. Coverage of all the core philosophical issues, including human nature, metaphysics, epistemology, ethics, and social philosophy. Also covered are selected topics in Eastern philosophy, which impart a cross-cultural flavor.

2. Substantial summaries of the thought of one or two major philosophers at the end of every chapter. Called Historical Showcases, each summary contains large selections from the writings of one or two philosophers who raise issues treated in the chapter. Arranged in chronological order, the Historical Showcases provide an overview of the history of philosophy and encourage students to see philosophy as a "great conversation" across centuries. Socrates is treated in the main text of Chapter 1, and thereafter Showcases include: the Pre-Socratics, Plato, Aristotle, Aquinas, Descartes, Hobbes, Berkeley, Hume, Kant, Mill, Nietzsche, Marx, and Rawls.

3. End-of-chapter selections from philosophical fiction. These selections, culled from outstanding

classical and contemporary literature, dramatize the immediacy of philosophy in our lives and glitter with philosophical insights.

4. Numerous Philosophy and Life inserts scattered throughout the text. These inserts show philosophy's impact on everyday life or its interesting connections to other current topics, such as science, psychology, the law, sociobiology, animal rights, and medical dilemmas. For example, an insert in Chapter 1 relates Socrates' views on obeying the law as expressed in the *Crito* to the views of participants in the sanctuary movement; an insert in Chapter 5 relates the topic of knowledge to Heisenberg's uncertainty principle. Over a dozen new Philosophy and Life inserts have been added to those of the previous edition.

5. Fictional dialogues. The purpose of these informal conversations is to make abstract and theoretical concepts more accessible and less intimidating to the neophyte.

6. Boxed quotations. Scattered throughout the text are short quotations taken from a wide range of writers and sources which relate to the topics under discussion. These quotations are meant to expand on the topics or to suggest a provocative new slant on the issues.

7. Substantial selections from primary sources. Primary source material is included not only in all the Historical Showcases but is liberally introduced into the main text, where it is always carefully explained. To make these materials accessible to beginning undergraduates, new, highly simplified translations of several texts (of Plato, Aristotle, Aquinas, and others) have been prepared, and several standard translations (such as Max Mueller's translation of Kant) have been simplified and edited. These primary source selections also introduce those philosophers (such as Anselm, Locke, Sartre, Rousseau, Moore, Blanshard, James, Kierkegaard, Russell) who are significant but who could not be treated in a separate Historical Showcase.

8. Section on logic. A brief treatment of some of the major aspects of logic has been included as an appendix to Chapter 1.

9. Chapter bibliographies. At the end of each chapter there is a list of works that expand on the topics discussed in that chapter.

10. End-of-section exercises. To aid students, questions and exercises are provided at the end of every section within a chapter.

11. Main points. Each chapter begins with a summary of the main points that will be covered. These serve as overviews of the chapters and are helpful as reviews after the chapter is completed.

REVISIONS

In all chapters major sections have been extensively rewritten to update and improve the materials as well as to correct a few errors that have become evident during the many years this text has been in use. Some of the major revised sections include: the entire Chapter 1; the section on Buddhism in Chapter 2; the section on the design argument in Chapter 3; the section on Descartes in Chapter 5; the section on Humean skepticism in Chapter 7; and the section on Rawls in Chapter 8.

Users who are familiar with earlier editions will notice that two chapters have been omitted (the chapters on philosophy of art and on philosophy of science) and that the others have been arranged in a new order. The chapters on ethics and social philosophy have been moved to the end of the book, and the chapters on God, reality, and knowledge have been moved forward. The two original introductory chapters have retained their place at the beginning of the book. This order has been adopted because readers find religious issues inherently interesting to discuss at the beginning of the course and because the new arrangement allowed the Historical Showcases to be placed in chronological order.

ACKNOWLEDGMENTS

We would like to thank the following reviewers for their contributions to the Third Edition: Ronald L. Burr, University of Southern Mississippi; Angie

Cooksey, Ball State University; Zvi Edelson, Community College of Allegheny County, Boyce Campus; Wesley Henry, Tennessee Technology University; Brooks McDaniel, Illinois Central College; Merrill Proudfoot, Park College; Alex Von Schoenborn, University of Missouri—Columbia; and John Velasquez, Santa Ana College.

PART I   Introduction

The word *philosophy* comes from the Greek words *philein*, meaning "to love," and *sophia*, meaning "wisdom." Philosophy is the love of wisdom. It is the pursuit of wisdom about what it means to be a human being, what the fundamental nature of God and reality are, what the sources and limits of our knowledge are, and what is good and right in our lives and in our societies.

This book is divided into four parts. In this first part we devote the initial chapter to looking more closely at what philosophy is and the second chapter to discussing what it is to be a human being. We begin with these topics because they raise fundamental issues that affect our overall approach to the study of philosophy. Part II contains chapters examining our basic beliefs about God and reality. The third part is composed of a chapter on knowledge and a chapter on truth. And the final part contains a chapter on ethics and one on the normative issues raised by life in society.

CHAPTER 1

The Nature
of Philosophy

*The feeling of wonder is the mark of the philosopher,
for all philosophy has its origins in wonder.*

PLATO

*Philosophy traditionally has been nothing less than the
attempt to ask and answer, in a formal and
disciplined way, the great questions of life that
ordinary men put to themselves in reflective
moments.*

TIME MAGAZINE, 7 JANUARY 1966

Introduction

The Thinker, Auguste Rodin. "We have all been touched and moved by the feelings and questions of wonderment from which all philosophy derives."

Philosophy begins with wonder. Although many of us may lack a knowledge of the jargon and history of philosophy, we have all been touched and moved by the feelings of wonderment from which all philosophy derives. We wonder about who we really are; whether God exists; why pain, evil, and sorrow exist; why a close friend was killed; whether science tells us all there really is to know about the universe; whether there is life after death; what true happiness, love, and friendship are; whether standards of taste in music and art are only individual likes and dislikes; whether moral right and wrong are based merely on personal opinion; and whether suicide, abortion, or euthanasia are ever justified. This wonderment and questioning is at the heart of philosophy and begins early in our lives. Almost as soon as children learn to talk, they ask: Where did I come from? Where do people go when they die? What's beyond the sky? How did the world start? Who made God? Why is one and one two and not three? Virtually from the beginning of life, every human being becomes familiar with the questions that form the subject matter of philosophy.

But although philosophy begins with wonder and questions, it does not end there. Philosophy tries to go beyond the conventional answers to these questions that we may have received when we were too young to think through our own answers. The goal of philosophy is to enable us to decide the answers to these questions for ourselves—to make up our own minds about our self-identity, life, knowledge, art, religion, and morality without solely depending on the authority of parents, peers, television, teachers, or society. Many of our religious, political, and moral beliefs are beliefs that we accepted as children long before we had the ability to question them or explain to ourselves the reasons behind them. Philosophy examines these beliefs, not necessarily to reject them but to learn why we hold them and to ask whether there are good reasons to continue holding them. In this way our basic beliefs about reality and life become *our own*: We accept them because we have examined their rationales, not because we have been conditioned by our parents, peers, and society. We thus gain a kind of independence and freedom, or what some modern philosophers call "autonomy." The goal of philosophy, then, is autonomy: the freedom of being able to decide for yourself what you will believe in by using your own reasoning abilities.

MAIN POINTS

This opening chapter aims to dispel much of the anxiety that students have about philosophy by communicating some of philosophy's fun and excitement and showing that philosophy is not to be feared but rather to be cultivated and relished. This chapter considers the meaning of philosophy, examines some of its characteristics, and introduces some of the earliest philosophers and their writings. Most important, it addresses the question: What is the value of philosophy? The main points in this chapter are as follows:

1. Philosophy, which literally means "love of wisdom," begins with wonder about our most basic beliefs. Its goal is to help us achieve autonomy by making us more aware of our own beliefs and encouraging us to reason and think through issues for ourselves.

2. The "Allegory of the Cave" is one of the best-known passages in *The Republic*, a work of the Greek philosopher Plato. The allegory describes the philosopher's climb from the dark cave of ignorance up into the light of knowledge.

3. Philosophy is the critical and rational examination of the most fundamental assumptions that underlie our lives.

4. The three main fields of philosophy are epistemology, metaphysics, and ethics.

5. Epistemology deals with questions of knowledge (including the structure, reliability, extent, and kinds of knowledge); truth, validity, and logic; and a variety of linguistic concerns. An example is the philosopher Bertrand Russell's question of whether we can really know the external world.

6. Metaphysics addresses questions of reality (including the meaning and nature of being); the nature of mind, self, and human freedom; and some topics that overlap with religion, such as the existence of God, the destiny of the universe, and the immortality of the soul. An example is the question of whether human beings are free or determined.

7. Ethics is the study of our values and moral principles and how they relate to human conduct and to our social and political institutions. For example, do we have a moral obligation to avoid inflicting pain on other living creatures or is our only obligation to ourselves?

8. Philosophy also includes several fields usually referred to as "the philosophy of . . . ," including the philosophy of science, the philosophy of art, and the philosophy of education. These fields of philosophy examine the basic assumptions underlying particular areas of human knowledge or activity.

9. Socrates is usually considered the "father of philosophy" although he was preceded by a group of earlier philosophers, the pre-Socratics. Socrates was put to death for persistently examining the unques-

> **We can help one another to find out the meaning of life, no doubt. But in the last analysis the individual person is responsible for living his own life and for "finding himself." Others can give you a name or a number, but they can never tell you who you really are. That is something you yourself can only discover from within.**
>
> THOMAS MERTON

tioned assumptions of his fellow Athenians. The views of Socrates are preserved by his disciple, Plato, in his early dialogues, including *Euthyphro, The Apology,* and *Crito.*

10. *Euthyphro* shows Socrates questioning traditional religious beliefs; *The Apology* shows Socrates at his trial explaining his life-long commitment to philosophy; *Crito* shows Socrates awaiting death and questioning his own beliefs about the authority of the state.

11. The use of the dialogue form is intended to convey the idea that philosophy develops through conversation.

12. Philosophy can help satisfy "actualizing needs" (the need for self-fulfillment, realization of one's potential) by (1) helping us develop our own opinions and beliefs, (2) increasing our self-awareness, (3) equipping us to deal with uncertainty, (4) eliciting creativity, and (5) aiding us in clearly conceptualizing our value systems.

13. In studying philosophy we risk having our personal and cultural beliefs and assumptions exposed, but this risk is worth taking considering the value of philosophy.

14. The pre-Socratics, including Thales, Parmenides, and Heraclitus, were the first philosophers. Although their views were sometimes naive, they raised some of the basic questions with which we still struggle.

THE MEANING OF PHILOSOPHY

Plato, one of the earliest and greatest philosophers, illustrated how philosophy aims at freedom through a famous parable called the "Allegory of the Cave," which he described in *The Republic,* a classic philosophical work on the nature of justice. It is included here in an edited and simplified translation from the Greek.

And now let me describe the human situation in a parable about ignorance and learning. Imagine there are men living at the bottom of an underground cave whose entrance is a long passageway that rises up through the ground to the

Plato is philosophy and philosophy Plato.

RALPH WALDO EMERSON

light outside. They have been there since childhood and have their legs and necks chained so that they cannot move. Their heads are held by the chains so that they must sit facing the back wall of the cave and cannot turn their heads to look up through the entrance behind them. At some distance behind them, up nearer the entrance to the cave, a fire is burning, and objects pass in front of the fire so that they cast their shadows on the back wall where the prisoners see the moving shadows projected as if on a screen. All kinds of objects are paraded before the fire, including statues of men and animals whose shadows dance on the wall in front of the prisoners.

Those prisoners are like ourselves. The prisoners see nothing of themselves or each other except for the shadows each one's body casts on the back wall of the cave. Similarly, they see nothing of the objects behind them, except for their shadows moving on the wall.

Now imagine the prisoners were able to talk with each other, and suppose their voices echoed off the wall so that the voices seemed to be coming from their own shadows. Then wouldn't they talk and refer to these shadows as if the shadows were real? For the prisoners, reality would consist of nothing but the shadows.

But next imagine that one of the prisoners was freed from his chains. Suppose he was suddenly forced to stand up and face toward the entrance of the cave and then forced to walk up toward the burning fire. The movement would be painful, and the glare from the fire would blind him so that he would not see clearly the real objects whose shadows he used to watch. What would he think if someone explained that everything he had seen before was an illusion and that now he was nearer to reality and that his vision was actually clearer?

Imagine he was then shown the objects that had cast their shadows on the wall and he was asked to name each one—wouldn't he be at a complete

Plato: "And the climb upward out of the cave into the upper world is the ascent of the mind into the domain of true knowledge."

loss? Wouldn't he think the shadows he saw before were more true than these objects?

Next imagine he was forced to look straight at the burning light. His eyes would hurt and the pain would make him turn away and try to escape back to things he could see more easily, convinced that they really were more real than the new things he was being shown.

But suppose that once more someone takes him and drags him up the steep and rugged ascent from the cave and forces him out into the full light of the sun. Won't he suffer greatly and be furious at being dragged upward? As he approaches the light his eyes will be dazzled and he won't be able to see any of that world we ourselves call reality. Little by little he will have to get used to looking at the upper world. At first he will see shadows on the ground best, next perhaps the reflections of men and other objects in water, and then maybe the objects themselves. After this he would find it easier to gaze at the light of the moon and the stars in the night sky than to look at the daylight sun and its light. Last of all he will be able to look at the

sun and contemplate its nature—not as it appears reflected in water but as it is in itself and in its own domain. He would come to the conclusion that the sun produces the seasons and the years and that it controls everything in the visible world. He will understand that it is in a way the cause of everything that he and his fellow prisoners used to see.

Suppose the released prisoner now recalled the cave and what passed for wisdom among his fellows there. Wouldn't he be happy about his new situation and feel sorry for them? They might have been in the habit of honoring those among themselves who were quickest to make out the shadows and those who could remember which usually came before others so that they were best at predicting the course of the shadows. Would he care anything for such honors and glories or would he envy those who won them? Wouldn't he rather endure anything than go back to thinking and living like they did?

Finally, imagine that the released prisoner was taken from the light and brought back into the cave to his old seat. His eyes would be full of darkness. Now he would have to compete in discerning the shadows with the prisoners who had never left the cave while his own eyes were still dim. Wouldn't he appear ridiculous? Men would say of him that he had gone up and had come back down with his eyesight ruined and that it was better not even to think of ascending. In fact, if they caught anyone trying to free them and lead them up to the light, they would try to kill him.

I say, now, that the prison is the world we see with our eyes; the light of the fire is like the power of our sun. And the climb upward out of the cave into the upper world is the ascent of the mind into the domain of true knowledge.[1]

This intriguing parable, which Plato recounted well over two thousand years ago, highlights several crucial aspects of what philosophy is. First, in the parable philosophy is the *activity* of ascending upward from the cave to the light. That is, philosophy is an activity. In this respect philosophy differs from most other academic subjects, and unlike other subjects, it does not consist of a lot of infor-

---

1. Plato, *The Republic*, bk. 7, trans. Manuel Velasquez (Copyright © 1987 by Manuel Velasquez).

Philosophy is not a theory but an activity.

LUDWIG WITTGENSTEIN

mation or theories. Although it is true that philosophers have developed many theories and views, these are the *products* of philosophy, not philosophy itself. Philosophy is an activity, not a body of facts, names, or views to be memorized. While studying philosophy, of course, you will be asked to learn the names and theories of several important philosophers, not for the sake of memorizing them but to aid you in learning how to "do" philosophy. By seeing how the best philosophers have "done" philosophy and by considering their views and theories, you can better understand what philosophizing involves, and you can use their insights to shed light on your own philosophical journey.

Second, as Plato makes clear in the parable, philosophy is a difficult activity. The journey upward is arduous because it involves questioning the most basic beliefs that everyone accepts about himself and the universe. This means, as the parable suggests, that philosophy sometimes may lead you in directions that society does not support and toward views that others reject. Philosophy is also arduous because it requires that we reason critically, consistently, and carefully about our fundamental beliefs. We may rebel against being asked to systematically and logically question and criticize views that we have always accepted. But climbing out of the cave requires intellectual discipline and the hard work of thinking things through as rationally and precisely as we can. That is why someone taking the first steps in philosophy can be aided by a teacher who, as Plato says, will "drag him up the steep and rugged ascent from the cave and force him out into the full light of the sun," requiring him to ask himself in a careful and reasoned manner the hard questions he is reluctant to ask.

Third, as Plato indicates and as we have already suggested, the aim of philosophy is freedom. Philosophy intends to break the chains that imprison and hold us down, the chains we often do not even know are there. Like the prisoners in the cave, we uncritically accept the beliefs and opinions of those around us, and this leads us to see the world in narrow, rigid ways. Philosophy aims at breaking these chains, at helping us break out of the prejudices and unthinking habits we have long absorbed and move toward more reflective views that are truly our own.

And fourth, Plato's parable intimates that the subject matter of philosophy—the beliefs philosophy examines—consists of those matters that are most basic to human existence. Like the prisoner who is led to look at the real objects that project the shadows he assumed were real, the person who does philosophy seeks to examine the basic values and realities that underlie the natural and social world we know. The word *philosophy* itself suggests this, since it is derived from two Greek words: *philein*, which means "to love," and *sophia*, which means "wisdom." To do philosophy is to love wisdom. And since wisdom is an understanding of the most fundamental aspects of human living, to love wisdom (to do philosophy) is to seek to understand and grapple with those underlying issues that are most fundamental and basic to our lives. Philosophy examines, for example, the basic ideas that underlie religion when it asks: Is there a God? Is there an afterlife? What truth is there in religious experience? It examines the basic ideas that underlie science when it asks: Are there limits to what the scientific method can tell us about reality? Are scientific theories merely useful approximations, or do they impart real truths about the universe? What is truth? Philosophy examines the basic values that

Philosophy means liberation from the two dimensions of routine, soaring above the well known, seeing it in new perspectives, arousing wonder and the wish to fly.

WALTER KAUFMANN

underlie our relations with each other when it asks: What is justice? What do we owe each other? What is love? And it examines the basic notions that underlie our views about reality when it asks: Is human freedom possible, or is everything determined by outside forces? Do things operate by chance, or is there some purpose to the universe? Are the ordinary objects we experience all there is to reality, or is there something more ultimate beyond the world of appearances? To do philosophy, then,

Philosophy is the thoughts of men about human thinking, reasoning and imagining, and the real values in human existence.

CHARLES W. ELIOT

Philosophy is man's quest for the unity of knowledge: it consists in a perpetual struggle to create the concepts in which the universe can be conceived as a *universe* and not a *multi*verse.

WILLIAM HALVERSON

is to examine the basic and most important assumptions that underlie our human lives.

We can perhaps distill much of our discussion up to this point in the following, somewhat complicated definition: Philosophy is the activity of critically and rationally examining the reasons behind the most fundamental assumptions of our human lives.

PHILOSOPHY AND LIFE 1.1

Philosophical Issues

Virtually every activity and every profession raises philosophical issues. Science, theology, psychology, the practice of law and medicine, and even taxation all involve questions that more or less directly force us to address philosophical issues. Mark Woodhouse invites us to consider the following examples:

1. A neurophysiologist, while establishing correlations between certain brain functions and the feeling of pain, begins to wonder

SOURCE: Mark D. Woodhouse, *A Preface to Philosophy* (Belmont, Calif.: Wadsworth, 1984), 1–2, 26–27. Used by permission.

whether the "mind" is distinct from the brain.

2. A nuclear physicist, having determined that matter is mostly empty space containing colorless energy transformations, begins to wonder to what extent the solid, extended, colored world we perceive corresponds to what actually exists and which world is more "real."

3. A behavioral psychologist, having increasing success in predicting human behavior, questions whether any human actions can be called "free."

4. Supreme Court justices, when framing a law to distinguish

obscene and nonobscene art forms, are drawn into questions about the nature and function of art.

5. A theologian in a losing battle with science over literal descriptions of the universe (or "reality") is forced to redefine the whole purpose and scope of traditional theology.

6. An anthropologist, noting that all societies have some conception of a moral code, begins to wonder just what distinguishes a moral from a nonmoral point of view.

7. A linguist, in examining the various ways language shapes our view of the world, declares that there is no one "true reality"

QUESTIONS

1. Ask about six friends what they think philosophy is. Is there any agreement?

2. Would it be accurate to say that every profession has its own philosophy? What does this mean? How would you characterize the educational philosophy of the institution that you are attending?

3. The text suggests that in Plato's "Allegory of the Cave," the climb from the cave represents the climb "from the dark cave of ignorance up into the light of knowledge." Can you suggest other reasonable interpretations of Plato's myth?

4. Suppose someone objected, "If philosophy is an ongoing process, what's the point of engaging in it? You'll never get any certain answers; your search will never end. Such a prospect is thoroughly depressing." How would you respond to this criticism?

The Traditional Divisions of Philosophy

Another way of understanding what philosophy means is to ask how it has traditionally been approached: What are its main questions and major issues? Traditionally, philosophy has sought an organized understanding of reality and our place in

because all views of reality are conditioned and qualified by the language in which they are expressed.

8. A perennial skeptic, accustomed to demanding and not receiving absolute proof for every view encountered, declares that it is impossible to know anything.

9. A county commissioner, while developing new zoning ordinances, begins to wonder whether the *effect* or the *intent* (or both) of zoning laws makes them discriminatory.

10. An IRS director, in determining which (religious) organizations should be exempted from tax, is forced to define what counts as a "religion" or "religious group."

11. A concerned mother, having decided to convert her Communist son, is forced to read the *Communist Manifesto* and to do some thinking about Marxist and capitalist ideologies.

And, as Woodhouse also suggests, philosophical questions are continually raised in our everyday life and conversations. Consider, for example, the following statements, which all involve philosophical issues: Sociology is not a science. Drugs reveal new levels of reality. History never repeats itself. Every religion has the same core of truth. We should all be left free to do our own thing, as long as we don't hurt anyone else. All truth depends on your point of view. The most important thing you can do is find out who you are. This could all be a dream.

QUESTIONS

1. Are there any areas of life that do not involve philosophical issues?

2. What are your views on the issues Woodhouse lists?

3. How would the issues Woodhouse lists be resolved?

4. What kinds of reasons would count for or against a given position on these issues?

5. Can these issues be resolved?

it: an understanding of how we ought to live, including the bases for our personal and social moral values, and an understanding of what knowledge and truth are. Of course, philosophers approach these general concerns in many ways, each emphasizing some particular aspect of our human concerns. Thus, one philosophy, termed *analytic philosophy*, approaches these questions by concentrating on our use of language. Analytic philosophers, for example, ask: What do "reality" and "morally good" mean in our language? Another philosophy, called *pragmatism*, stresses the need to find solutions to the problems of our social existence. The pragmatic philosopher might ask: What role do "reality" and "truth" play in our social life? Still another philosophy, *existentialism*, is concerned with making life meaningful for each individual. The existentialist might ask: What meaning does the individual give to his own reality, his own morality, and his own truth?

The variety of approaches notwithstanding, philosophy in general has been concerned with three broad questions: What is knowledge? What is real? What is right and good? Although these questions cannot be considered in isolation and although the distinction between them is sometimes blurred, almost all philosophical issues can be categorized as being concerned with one of these three inquiries.

These traditional concerns suggest the three categories under which philosophical topics are usually grouped: knowledge, reality, and value. The fields of philosophy that explore these topics are generally termed *epistemology, metaphysics,* and *ethics.*

Epistemology literally means the study of knowledge. A variety of problems are usually discussed as part of epistemology: the structure, reliability, extent, and kinds of knowledge we have; the meaning of truth (including definitions of truth and validity); logic and a variety of strictly linguistic concerns; and the foundations of all knowledge, including whether real knowledge is even possible.

To get a fuller idea of what epistemology is, we can consider the words of a modern philosopher who suggests the kinds of questions that epistemology addresses. In the following passage, Bertrand Russell, an early twentieth-century philoso-

Bertrand Russell: "Is there any knowledge in the world which is so certain that no reasonable man could doubt it?"

pher, raises the question of whether we can be certain our senses give us any real knowledge even of the physical world around us.

Is there any knowledge in the world which is so certain that no reasonable man could doubt it? . . . In the search for certainty it is natural to begin with our present experiences. . . . It seems to me that I am now sitting in a chair, at a table of a certain shape, on which I see sheets of paper with writing or print. By turning my head I see out of the window buildings and clouds and the sun. . . . Yet all this may be reasonably doubted.

To make our difficulties plain, let us concentrate attention on the table. To the eye it is oblong, brown and shiny, to the touch it is smooth and cool and hard; when I tap it, it gives out a wooden sound. It might seem as if no difficulty would arise; but as soon as we try to be more precise our troubles begin. Although I believe that the table is "really" of the same color all over, the parts that reflect the light look much brighter than the other parts, and some parts look white because of reflected light. I know that, if I move, the parts

The first step towards philosophy is incredulity.

DENIS DIDEROT

that reflect the light will be different, so that the apparent distribution of colors on the table will change. It follows that if several people are looking at the table at the same moment, no two of them will see exactly the same distribution of colors, because no two can see it from exactly the same point of view. . . . This color is not something which is inherent in the table, but something depending upon the table and the spectator and the way the light falls on the table. . . .

The same thing applies to the texture. With the naked eye one can see the grain, but otherwise the table looks smooth and even. If we looked at it through a microscope, we should see roughnesses and hills and valleys, and all sorts of differences that are imperceptible to the naked eye. Which of these is the "real" table?

Similar difficulties arise when we consider the sense of touch. The sensation we obtain depends upon how hard we press the table and also upon what part of the body we press with; thus the various sensations due to various pressures or various parts of the body cannot be supposed to reveal *directly* any definite property of the table, but at most to be *signs* of some property which perhaps *causes* all the sensations, but is not actually apparent in any of them. And the same applies still more obviously to the sounds which can be elicited by rapping the table.

Thus it becomes evident that the real table, if there is one, is not the same as what we immediately experience by sight or touch or hearing. The real table, if there is one, is not *immediately* known to us at all, but must be an inference from what is immediately known. Hence two very difficult questions at once arise; namely, (1) Is there a real table at all? (2) If so, what sort of object can it be?[2]

In this somewhat difficult passage, Russell is trying to show by logical arguments that the knowledge we have of the world around us comes from the sensations we have. Because we have these sensations, we *infer* that there is a world outside of us that *causes* the sensations we have. But how do we know? How can we know that there is anything outside of us? For all we know, we could be like a hallucinating or dreaming person who has sensations of things that are not there. How can we ever really know, then, that there is a world beyond our sensations and that we are correct when we "infer" there is? And what knowledge can we have of what that world is really like? Out of these puzzling questions arises the field of epistemology, of philosophers' attempts to rationally determine what we can know and how we can come to know it.

Metaphysics, the second major area of philosophy, is the study of the most general or ultimate characteristics of reality or existence. Some of the issues that fall under metaphysics are the place of humans within the universe; the purpose and nature of reality; and the nature of mind, self, and consciousness. Also included are issues related to religion, such as the existence of God, the destiny of the universe, and the immortality of the soul.

One of the core questions of metaphysics—one that gives us an idea of what metaphysics is about—is this: Is everything in the universe determined by outside causes or are humans, at least, freely able to choose for themselves? Again, learning how some philosophers have treated this issue will give us a better understanding of what metaphysics is about.

One important position in metaphysics is "determinism," the view that all things in reality, including human beings, are unfree. Paul Henri d'Holbach, who wrote in the eighteenth century, held such a view.

In whatever manner man is considered, he is connected to universal nature, and submitted to the necessary and immutable laws that she imposes on all beings she contains. . . . He is born without his own consent; his [physical and mental] organization does in no way depend on himself; his ideas come to him involuntarily; and his habits are in the power of those who cause him to have them.

2. Bertrand Russell, *The Problems of Philosophy* (New York: Oxford University Press, 1959), 7–11. Reprinted by permission of Oxford University Press.

He is unceasingly modified by causes, whether visible or concealed, over which he has no control and which necessarily regulate his existence, color his way of thinking, and determine his manner of acting. . . .

His will is necessarily determined by the qualities, good or bad, agreeable or painful, of the object or the motive that acts upon his senses or which he retains in his memory. In consequence, he acts necessarily, his action is the result of the impulse he receives either from the motive, from the object, or from the idea which has modified his brain or disposed his will. When he does not act according to this impulse, it is because there comes some new cause, some new motive, some new idea, which modified his brain in a different manner, gives him a new impulse, and determines his will in another way. . . . In all this he always acts according to necessary laws from which he has no means of emancipating himself. . . .

In short, the actions of man are never free; they are always the necessary consequence of his temperament, of the ideas he has received, including his true or false notions of happiness, and of those opinions that are strengthened by example, by education, and by daily experience. . . . Man is not a free agent in any instant of his life.[3]

But many contemporary philosophers deny this deterministic picture of all reality. Viktor Frankl, for example, a Jewish philosopher-psychologist who suffered terrible degradations while imprisoned by the Nazis who had murdered his entire family, argues that the popularity of determinism is a kind of mental illness, a "collective neurosis." His experiences of how people responded to the terror-filled hell holes of the German prison camps proved to him, he claims, that human beings are ultimately free.

Man is *not* fully conditioned and determined; he determines himself whether to give in to conditions or stand up to them. In other words, man is ultimately self-determining. Man does not simply exist, but always decides what his existence will be, what he will become in the next moment. By the same token, every human being has the freedom to change at any instant. . . .

A human being is not one thing among others. *Things* determine each other, but *man* is ultimately self-determining. What he becomes—within the limits of endowment and environment—he has made out of himself. In the concentration camps, for example, in this living laboratory and on this testing ground, we watched and witnessed some of our comrades behave like swine while others behaved like saints. Man has both potentialities within himself. Which one is actualized depends on decisions but not on conditions.[4]

Which of these two views is supported by the strongest reasons: the view that all reality (including ourselves) is causally determined or the view that human beings are ultimately free to make of themselves what they choose to become? This is one of the fundamental questions of metaphysics.

Ethics, the third major area of philosophy, refers to the study of our values and moral principles and how these relate to our conduct and to our social institutions. Ethics includes the nature of moral obligation; what is good for human beings and basic moral principles; the nature and justification of social structures and political systems; and the morality of various kinds of behavior and social policies that involve crucial human interests.

The specific issues discussed in ethics vary widely and include questions such as: Are abortion, suicide, and euthanasia ever morally right? Is capitalism or communism a better form of life? Should the law permit or prohibit adultery, pornography, capital punishment, or homosexuality? Again, some examples may make these kinds of inquiries a bit clearer, and perhaps the best place to start is with the statement of Albert Schweitzer, a philosopher who held that humans have a duty to avoid inflicting pain and suffering on any living creature.

The great fault of all ethics hitherto has been that they believed themselves to have to deal only with the relations of man to man. In reality, however, the question is what is his attitude to the world and all life that comes within his reach. A man is ethical only when life, as such, is sacred to him, that of plants and animals as that of his fel-

---

3. Baron Paul Henri d'Holbach, *System of Nature* (London: Dearsley, 1797).

4. Victor Frankl, *Man's Search for Meaning* (New York: Washington Square Press, 1963), 206, 213.

low men, and when he devotes himself helpfully to all life that is in need of help.[5]

But not everyone agrees with such lofty sentiments. Many philosophers, in fact, have reasoned that ethics is a sham. Harry Browne, for example, concludes that morality is really a kind of trap if it is taken to mean that people should put the happiness of others ahead of their own. Selfishness, he holds, is and should be everyone's policy.

> Everyone is selfish; everyone is doing what he believes will make himself happier. The recognition of that can take most of the sting out of accusations that you're being "selfish." Why should you feel guilty for seeking your own happiness when that's what everyone else is doing, too? . . .
>
> To find constant, profound happiness requires that you be free to seek the gratification of your own desires. It means making positive choices.
>
> If you slip into the Unselfishness Trap, you'll spend a good part of your time making negative choices—trying to avoid the censure of those who tell you not to think of yourself. . . .
>
> If someone finds happiness by doing "good works" for others, let him. That doesn't mean that's the best way for you to find happiness.
>
> And when someone accuses you of being selfish, just remember that he's only upset because you aren't doing what *he* selfishly wants you to do.[6]

Browne's view that morality is a sham because humans always try to satisfy themselves and therefore their actions are always selfish is called "egoism." The contemporary philosopher James Rachels strongly questions this view in the following passage:

> Why should we think that merely because someone derives satisfaction from helping others this makes him selfish? Isn't the unselfish man precisely the one who *does* derive satisfaction from helping others, while the selfish man does not? Similarly, it is nothing more than shabby sophistry to say, because Smith takes satisfaction in helping his

friend, that he is behaving selfishly. If we say this rapidly, while thinking about something else, perhaps it will sound all right; but if we speak slowly, and pay attention to what we are saying, it sounds plain silly.[7]

Which of these views is correct: that morality is a sham or that we have a duty, as Schweitzer says, to respect and help all life that needs our help? These questions, too, are important, and they are the kinds of inquiries that form the subject matter of ethics, the third major area of philosophy.

Finally, there is a wide range of philosophical inquiries that are usually referred to as "the philosophy of . . .". These include, for example, the philosophy of science, the philosophy of art, and the philosophy of education. Each of these areas of philosophy attempts to question and analyze the basic or fundamental assumptions of the subject. The philosophy of science, for example, asks what the "scientific method" is, whether it is valid, and whether the theories it produces are merely useful mental constructs or objective descriptions of reality. The philosophy of education asks what education is, what it is for, and what its proper place is in the broader structure of society. And the philosophy of art asks what art itself is, what its meaning and point is, and whether there are objective standards of art or whether all art is merely a matter of fads and tastes.

QUESTIONS

1. Read through the various passages quoted as examples of philosophical writings in epistemology, metaphysics, and ethics. What makes these *philosophical* writings? What reasons are provided in support of a philosophical position? How does philosophy differ from the natural sciences? The social sciences? Literature?

2. Think of as many philosophical questions as you can and then place each under one or more of the three major philosophical categories.

---

5. Albert Schweitzer, *The Philosophy of Civilization* (New York: Macmillan, 1950), 310.

6. Harry Browne, "The Morality Trap," from *How I Found Freedom in an Unfree World* by Harry Browne (New York: Macmillan, 1937).

---

7. James Rachels, "Egoism and Moral Skepticism," from *A New Introduction to Philosophy*, ed. Steven M. Cahn (New York: Harper & Row, 1971.)

3. List the philosophical concerns you wish to learn about during your introductory philosophy course. Try to be specific. Suppose, for example, you'd like to learn something about religion. Exactly what would you like to learn? Try to formulate a question that will direct your study, such as "Is there any reason to believe that God exists?" or "If God is all good and all powerful, how can evil exist?"

> **The adjusted American lacks self-approval; that is to say, he has not developed a self-image that he can believe is both accurate and acceptable. The culture abounds with misdirections, which the adjusted American acquires. . . . Perhaps above all he learns to seek self-acceptance indirectly, by seeking to substitute the good opinions of others for self-approval. It is thus that he becomes "other directed."**
>
> GAIL and SNELL PUTNEY

An Example of Philosophy: Socrates

The best way of getting an understanding of philosophy is to consider a philosopher in action. And the best place to begin is with the philosopher who is sometimes called the "father of philosophy," the Greek thinker Socrates. We should note, however, that Socrates was not the first philosopher: He was preceded by a group of philosophers called the pre-Socratics. The pre-Socratics were the first thinkers who questioned religious authority and who tried to provide nonreligious explanations of nature. (For more information, see the showcase about the pre-Socratics at the end of this chapter.) Nevertheless, Socrates' life and views best exemplify the meaning of philosophy, so we will look at his work.

Socrates was born in 469 B.C. in Athens, Greece. Athens by that time was a flourishing and remarkably vigorous city-state. The Greek theater had already produced the noted dramatist Aeschylus and would soon see the comedies of Aristophanes and the tragedies of Sophocles and Euripedes. The Greek armies had defeated the much larger nation of Persia, and Athens was on the verge of attaining naval control of the Aegean Sea.

As he grew older, Socrates was led to question the conventional beliefs held by his fellow Athenians. We are told that he would haunt the streets of Athens, buttonholing powerful men and asking them irreverent questions about their opinions. To those who pretended to know about justice, for example, he would ask: What is justice? What does it mean? What do all just acts have in common? Similarly, he would probe ideas about virtue, knowledge, morality, and religion. By continual questioning, Socrates would plumb a person's system of beliefs, deflating cherished certainties and exposing their emptiness. Although Socrates' persistent questioning of traditional habits of thought left many puzzled, many more reacted with anger.

Even as he engaged in this irritating practice of questioning the beliefs of his fellows, Socrates saw Athens rise to its glory under the great statesman Pericles, who presided over a splendid golden age of democracy, an age of great architectural, artistic, and literary advances arising from the powerful military and economic forces commanded by Athens. But all this came to an end when a proud Athens was defeated in war and became embroiled in a disastrous thirty-year civil war. Plague broke out in Athens, inflation struck its economy, and intense class struggles erupted between the rich old aristocratic families and their poorer fellow citizens. In the end, the defeated, desperate, and frustrated Athenians searched for scapegoats. They blamed their troubles on Socrates and his habit of questioning everything, which, they said, had helped weaken the traditional values and beliefs that once had made Athens strong.

Since Socrates left no writing, most of what we know about him comes from the *Dialogues* written by Socrates' disciple Plato. The *Dialogues* are short dramas in which the character of Socrates plays a major role. Although there is some controversy over how accurately Plato's *Dialogues* reflect the real conversations of Socrates, most experts today agree that the first dialogues Plato wrote (for example, *Euthyphro, The Apology,* and *Crito*) are more-or-less faithful representations of Socrates' views, even when they do not represent Socrates' actual words.

One of these early dialogues, *Euthyphro*, presents a marvelous example of how Socrates questions almost to the point of irritation. In fact, as you read through the dialogue, you will probably start feeling irritated and asking why Socrates doesn't get past the questions and start giving *answers*. He gives no answers because all he wants is for you to realize that you, too, do not have any good answers to his questions. The dialogue opens in front of the court of the king. Socrates is there to learn more

Socrates: "The unexamined life is not worth living."

about an indictment for "unholiness" that has been brought against him for questioning traditional beliefs. He sees an old friend arrive, a priest named Euthyphro. Here, again in a simplified and edited translation, is their dialogue as Plato wrote it.

EUTHYPHRO: Socrates! What are you doing here at the court of the King?

SOCRATES: I am being impeached, Euthyphro, by a young man I hardly know named Meletus. He accuses me of making up new gods and denying the existence of the old ones.

EUTHYPHRO: I am sure you will win your case, Socrates, just like I expect to win mine.

SOCRATES: But what is your suit, Euthyphro?

EUTHYPHRO: I am charging my father with murder, Socrates. One of my slaves in a drunken fit killed a fellow slave. My father chained up the culprit and left him in a ditch unattended several days to await the judgment of a priest. But the cold, the hunger, and the chains killed him. So now I am charging my father with murder, against the ignorant wishes of my family who do not know what true holiness requires of a priest like me.

SOCRATES: Good heavens, Euthyphro! Do you have such a clear knowledge of what holiness is that you are not afraid you might be doing something unholy in charging your own father with murder?

EUTHYPHRO: My most valued possession, Socrates, is the exact knowledge I have of these matters.

SOCRATES: You are a rare friend, Euthyphro. I can do no better than take you as my teacher so that I can defend myself against Meletus who is accusing me of being unholy. Tell me, then, what is holiness and what is unholiness?

EUTHYPHRO: Holiness is doing what I am doing: prosecuting anyone who is guilty of murder, sacrilege, or of any similar crime—whether he be your father or mother, or whoever, it makes no difference—and not to prosecute them is unholiness.

SOCRATES: But wouldn't you say, Euthyphro, that there are many other holy acts?

EUTHYPHRO: There are.

SOCRATES: I was not asking you to give me *examples* of holiness, Euthyphro, but to identify the characteristic which makes all holy things be holy. There must be some characteristic that all holy things have in common, and one which makes unholy things unholy. Tell me what this characteristic itself is, so that I can tell which actions are holy, and which unholy.

EUTHYPHRO: Well, then, holiness, is what is loved by the gods, and what is not loved by them is unholy.

SOCRATES: Very good, Euthyphro! Now you have given me the sort of answer I wanted. Let us examine it. A thing or a person that is loved by the gods is holy, and a thing or a person that the gods hate is unholy. And the holy is the opposite of the unholy. Does that summarize what you said?

EUTHYPHRO: It does.

SOCRATES: But you admit, Euthyphro, that the gods have disagreements. So some things are hated by some gods and loved by other gods.

EUTHYPHRO: True.

SOCRATES: Then upon your view the same things, Euthyphro, will be both holy and unholy.

EUTHYPHRO: Well, I suppose so.

SOCRATES: Then, my friend, you have not really answered my question. I did not ask you to tell me which actions were both holy and unholy; yet that is the outcome of your view. In punishing your father, Euthyphro, you might be doing what is loved by the god Zeus, but hateful to the god Cronos.

EUTHYPHRO: But Socrates, surely none of the gods would disagree about the rightness of punishing an injustice.

SOCRATES: Both men and gods would certainly agree on the general point that unjust acts should be punished. But men and gods might disagree about whether this particular act is unjust. Is that not true?

EUTHYPHRO: Quite true.

SOCRATES: So tell me, my friend: How do you know that all the gods agree on this particular act: that it is just for a son to prosecute his father for chaining a slave who was guilty of murder and who died in chains before the religious authorities said what should be done with him? How do you know that all the gods love this act?

EUTHYPHRO: I could make the matter quite clear to you, Socrates, although it would take me some time.

SOCRATES: Euthyphro, I will not insist on it. I will assume, if you like, that all the gods here agree. The point I really want to understand is this: Do the gods love what is holy because it is holy, or is it holy because they love it? What do you say, Euthyphro? On your definition whatever is holy is loved by all the gods, is it not?

EUTHYPHRO: Yes.

SOCRATES: Because it is holy? Or for some other reason?

EUTHYPHRO: No, that is the reason.

SOCRATES: Then what is holy is loved by the gods because it is holy? It is not holy because it is loved?

EUTHYPHRO: Yes.

SOCRATES: Then, Euthyphro, to be loved by the

gods cannot be the same as to be holy. And to be holy cannot be the same as to be loved by the gods.

EUTHYPHRO: But why, Socrates?

SOCRATES: Because, Euthyphro, when I asked you for the essence of holiness, you gave me only a quality that accompanies holiness: the quality of being loved by the gods. But you have not yet told me what holiness itself is [the quality *because of which* the gods love what is holy]. So please, Euthyphro, do not hide your treasure from me. Start again from the beginning and tell me what holiness itself is.

EUTHYPHRO: I really do not know, Socrates, how to express what I mean. Somehow or other our arguments seem to turn around in circles and walk away from us.

SOCRATES: Then I will help you instruct me, Euthyphro. Tell me—Is it not true that everything that is holy is also just?

EUTHYPHRO: Yes.

SOCRATES: Does it follow that everything that is just is also holy? Or is it rather the case that whatever is holy is just, but only some just things are holy while others are not? For justice is the larger notion of which holiness is only a part. Do you agree in that?

EUTHYPHRO: Yes; that, I think, is correct.

SOCRATES: Then, since holiness is a part of justice, let us ask what part.

EUTHYPHRO: I know, Socrates! Holiness is that part of justice which involves service to the gods, while the other part of justice involves service to our fellow men.

SOCRATES: Very good, Euthyphro. But there is still one small point on which I need your help: What

do you mean by "service"? Is not service always designed to benefit or improve those who are served?

EUTHYPHRO: True.

SOCRATES: So does holiness, which is a kind of service, benefit or improve the gods? Would you say that when you do a holy act you make the gods better?

EUTHYPHRO: Good heavens, no!

SOCRATES: Then what is this service to the gods that is called holiness?

EUTHYPHRO: It is the kind that slaves show their masters.

SOCRATES: I understand. A sort of ministering to the gods.

EUTHYPHRO: Exactly.

SOCRATES: And now tell me, my good friend, about this ministering to the gods: What activities does it involve?

EUTHYPHRO: It would be difficult to learn them all, Socrates. Let me simply say that holiness is learning how to please the gods by prayers and sacrifices.

SOCRATES: And sacrificing is giving to the gods, while prayer is asking of the gods?

EUTHYPHRO: Exactly, Socrates.

SOCRATES: But real giving involves giving them something they want from us, does it not? For surely it would be pointless to give someone what they do not want.

EUTHYPHRO: Very true, Socrates.

SOCRATES: But then tell me, what benefit comes to the gods from our gifts? Clearly they are the givers of every good thing we have. So how we can give any good thing to them in return is puzzling.

EUTHYPHRO: But Socrates, you do not imagine that any benefits come to the gods from the gifts we give them?

SOCRATES: If not, Euthyphro, then what sort of gifts can these be?

EUTHYPHRO: What else but praise and honor and whatever is pleasing to them.

Many talk like philosophers and live like fools.

H. G. BOHN

SOCRATES: Holiness, then, is doing what is pleasing to the gods, and not what is beneficial to them?

EUTHYPHRO: I would say that holiness, above all, is doing what is loved by the gods.

SOCRATES: Does it surprise you our arguments go in circles? Surely you must remember that a few moments ago we concluded that to be holy is not the same as to be loved by the gods?

EUTHYPHRO: I do.

SOCRATES: Then either we were wrong in that admission or we are wrong now.

EUTHYPHRO: Hmm. I suppose that is the case.

SOCRATES: Then we must begin again and ask, "What is holiness?" If any man knows, you must. For if you did not know the nature of holiness and unholiness I am sure you would never have charged your aged father with murder and run the risk of doing wrong in the sight of the gods. Speak, then, my dear Euthyphro, and do not hide your knowledge from me.

EUTHYPHRO: Perhaps some other time, Socrates. Right now I am in a hurry to be off somewhere.

SOCRATES: My friend! Will you leave me in despair? And here I had hoped that you could teach me what holiness itself is.[8]

In this dialogue Socrates is involved in the kind of critical questioning that characterizes philosophy. With careful, logical reasoning and in a systematic manner, he probes some of the fundamental religious beliefs on which Euthyphro bases his life and actions. Socrates brings logic and reason to bear on those issues that are most important both to Euthyphro and to himself, since he himself is being accused of acting against religion.

Moreover, Socrates' method reveals that Euthyphro—and we ourselves—does not really understand the basic things he takes for granted. Socrates questions Euthyphro's easy assumption that he knows what his religious duty is, that he knows what it means for something to be religiously just,

and that he knows what it is to serve the gods and why the gods want to be served through certain acts and not others. At every turn, Euthyphro finds that he does not really understand the conventional religious beliefs he has been brought up to hold. He does not even know what makes an action pleasing to the gods. All he can say is that he believes the gods approve of certain acts, but he has no idea why they approve of those acts and not others. Euthyphro might be you or I. Are we so sure about our own most basic religious beliefs? Do those of us who believe in God really know why God approves and commands certain acts and not others? What makes an act right? As Socrates might ask: Do we believe that actions are right because God (or society) approves of them, or do we believe that God (or society) approves of certain acts because they are right? Do we really know what right action itself is, or do we merely know one of its accompanying characteristics? If Socrates' method of questioning without arriving at answers seems frustrating, it is so partly because it exposes our own lack of wisdom.

Socrates' relentless and, to some, infuriating questioning of his fellow citizens eventually led to his death. Shortly after the scene described in *Euthyphro*, Socrates was in fact indicted by Meletus and others and brought to trial. The speech Socrates delivered in his defense was summarized by Plato in his brilliant work *The Apology*. The speech is especially fascinating because it provides a summary of Socrates' life and of his devotion to philosophical questioning. Socrates is standing in court, facing the jury composed of five hundred Athenian citizens that has just heard the testimony of his accusers, who charge him with corrupting the youth of Athens and with not believing in the gods of the state.

I do not know, my fellow Athenians, how you were affected by my accusers whom you just heard. But they spoke so persuasively they almost made me forget who I was. Yet they hardly uttered a word of truth.

But many of you are thinking, "Then what is the origin of these accusations, Socrates?" That is a fair question. Let me explain their origins. Some of you know my good friend Chaerephon.

---

8. Plato, *Euthyphro*, ed. and trans. Manuel Velasquez (Copyright © 1987 by Manuel Velasquez).

Before he died he went to Delphi and asked the religious oracle there to tell him who the wisest man in the world was. The oracle answered that there was no man wiser than Socrates.

When I learned this, I asked myself, "What can the god's oracle mean?" For I knew I had no wisdom. After thinking it over for a long time, I decided that I had to find a man wiser than myself so I could go back to the god with this evidence. So I went to see a politician who was famous for his wisdom. But when I questioned him, I realized he really was not wise, although many people—he especially—thought he was. So I tried to explain to him that although he thought himself wise, he really was not. But all that happened was that he came to hate me. And so did many of his supporters who overheard us. So I left him, thinking to myself as I left that although neither of us really knew anything about what is noble and good, still I was better off. For he knows nothing, and thinks that he knows, while I neither know nor think that I know. And in this I think I have a slight advantage.

Then I went to another person who had even greater pretensions to wisdom. The result was exactly the same: I made another enemy. In this way I went to one man after another and made more and more enemies. I felt bad about this and it frightened me. But I was compelled to do it because I felt that investigating god's oracle came first. I said to myself, I must go to everyone who seems to be wise so I can find out what the oracle means.

My hearers imagine that I myself possess the wisdom which I find wanting in others. But the truth is, Men of Athens, that only god is wise. And by his oracle he wanted to show us that the wisdom of men is worth little or nothing. It is as if he was telling us, "The wisest man is the one who, like Socrates, knows that his wisdom is in truth worth nothing." And so I go about the world obedient to god. I search and question the wisdom of anyone who seems to be wise. And if he is not wise, then to clarify the meaning of the oracle I show him that he is not wise. My occupation completely absorbs me and I have no time for anything else. My devotion to the god has reduced me to utter poverty.

There is something more. Young men of the richer classes, who do not have much to do, follow me around of their own accord. They like to hear

pretenders exposed. And sometimes they imitate me by examining others themselves. They quickly discover that there are plenty of people who think they know something but who really know nothing at all. Then those people also get angry at me. "This damnable Socrates is misleading our youth!" they say. And if somebody asks them, "How? What evil things does he do or teach them?" they cannot say. But in order not to appear at a loss, these people repeat the charges used against all philosophers: that we teach obscure things up in the clouds, that we teach atheism, and that we make the worst views appear to be the best. For people do not like to admit that their pretensions to knowledge have been exposed.

And that, fellow Athenians, is the origin of the prejudices against me.

But some of you will ask, "Don't you regret what you did since now it might mean your death?" To these I answer, "You are mistaken. A good man should not calculate his chances of living or dying. He should only ask himself whether he is doing right or wrong—whether his inner self is that of a good man or of an evil one."

And if you say to me, "Socrates, we will let you go free but only on condition that you stop your questioning," then I will reply, "Men of Athens, I honor and love you. But I must obey god rather than you, and while I have life and strength I will never stop doing philosophy." For my aim is to persuade you all, young and old alike, not to think about your lives or your properties, but first and foremost to care about your inner self. I tell you that wealth does not make you good within, but that from inner goodness comes wealth and every other benefit to man. This is my teaching, and if it corrupts youth, then I suppose I am their corrupter.

Well, my fellow Athenians, you must now decide whether to acquit me or not. But which-

---

Philosophy is at once the most sublime and the most trivial of human pursuits.

WILLIAM JAMES

ever you do, understand that I will never change my ways, not even if I have to die many times. To talk daily about what makes us good, and to question myself and others, is the greatest thing man can do. For the unexamined life is not worth living.

[At this point Socrates rested his case. The jury debated among themselves and then, in a split vote, they reached their final verdict.]

Men of Athens, you have condemned me to death. To those of you who are my friends and who voted to acquit me let me say that death may be a good thing. Either it is a state of nothingness and utter unconsciousness, or, as men say, it is merely a migration from this world to another. If it is complete unconsciousness—like a sleep undisturbed even by dreams—then death will be an unspeakable gain. And if it is a journey to another world where all the dead live, then it will also be a great good. For then I can continue my search into true and false knowledge: In the next world, like in this one, I can continue questioning the great people of the past to find out who is wise and who merely pretends to be. So do not be saddened by death. No evil can happen to a good man either in this life or in death.

Well, the hour of departure has arrived, and we must each go our ways. I to die, and you to live. Which is better only god knows.[9]

Again Socrates' speech provides a remarkable example of what philosophy is. Philosophy is the quest for wisdom: an unrelenting devotion to uncover the truth about what matters most in one's life. It is a quest for wisdom that is undertaken in the conviction that a life based on an easy, uncritical acceptance of the conventional beliefs we have had since our childhood is an empty life. As Socrates puts it, "The unexamined life is not worth living." Philosophy is a quest that is difficult, not only because it requires hard thinking but also because it sometimes requires taking positions that are unpopular and not shared by others.

Socrates was jailed immediately after his trial. There, while awaiting his execution, he continued his avid questioning. But his questions then focused more on his own beliefs about right and wrong, good and evil. In one of his final conversations recorded in the dialogue *Crito*, Socrates considered whether he had the courage to face death for his beliefs. The day before his execution he awoke to find his close friend Crito sitting in his jail cell next to him.

SOCRATES: Crito! What are you doing here at this hour? It must be quite early.

CRITO: Yes, it is.

SOCRATES: What time is it?

CRITO: The dawn is breaking.

SOCRATES: I am surprised the jailer let you in. Did you just get here?

CRITO: No, I came some time ago.

SOCRATES: Then why did you sit and say nothing? Why have you come here so early?

CRITO: Oh my dear friend, Socrates! Let me beg you once again to take my advice and escape from here. If you die I will not only lose a friend who can never be replaced, but people who do not know us will think that I could have saved you but was not willing to pay the necessary bribes. And you would be betraying your children since they will surely meet the unhappy fate of orphans.

SOCRATES: Dear Crito, your zeal is invaluable, if it is right. But if wrong, the greater the zeal, the greater the evil. I have always been guided by reason. I cannot turn away now from the principles I have always tried to honor. So let us look carefully at the issues before us. Shall we begin with your views about what people will think? Tell me, were we right long ago when we said that not all the opinions of men should be valued? Consider the athlete: Should he follow the advice and opinions of every man? Or should he listen to one man only—his doctor or trainer?

CRITO: He should follow the one man's advice.

SOCRATES: He should train in the way that seems good to the one man who has understanding rather than listen to the opinions of the many?

CRITO: True.

---

9. Plato, *The Apology*, ed. and trans. Manuel Velasquez (Copyright © 1987 by Manuel Velasquez).

SOCRATES: Doesn't the same principle hold, Crito, in the matter we are discussing: which course of action is right and good and which is wrong and evil? In this matter should we follow the opinions of the many or of the one who has understanding? If the athlete follows the advice of men who have no understanding, he will destroy his body, won't he?

CRITO: Yes.

SOCRATES: And is the body better than that inner part of ourselves—the soul—that is concerned with right and wrong, good and evil?

CRITO: Certainly not.

SOCRATES: Then, Crito, you are wrong to suggest that we should listen to the opinions of the many about right and wrong or good and evil. The values you bring up—money, loss of reputation, and educating children—are based on the opinions of the many. They do not concern the only real issue before us: Is it right or wrong for me to escape against the wishes of the Athenians? So follow me now in my questioning.

CRITO: I will do my best, Socrates.

SOCRATES: Is it true that we should never intentionally do wrong?

CRITO: It certainly is.

SOCRATES: And what about returning evil for evil—which is the morality of the many—is that right or not?

CRITO: It is not right.

SOCRATES: But in leaving this prison against the will of the Athenians, am I doing evil to anyone?

CRITO: I am not sure, Socrates.

SOCRATES: Well, imagine that just as I was about to escape, the laws of our society arrived and asked me, "Socrates, what are you trying to do? Do you want to destroy us? Won't society fall if its law has no power and if private citizens can set the law aside whenever they want?"

How will I answer them, Crito? Perhaps I could respond, "Yes, but society injured me: It sentenced me unjustly." Is that what I should say?

CRITO: Definitely, Socrates!

SOCRATES: Then what if the laws reply, "But didn't you agree to obey our judgments, Socrates?"

And if I show astonishment at this reply, the laws might add, "Do not be surprised, Socrates. You, who are always asking questions, answer us now. Long ago we gave you birth when your father married your mother by our aid and conceived you. Do you object to our marriage laws?"

"No," I would have to reply.

"Then do you object to the laws under which you were raised and which provided for your education?"

"They were fine," I would say.

"Well, then," they would conclude, "We gave you birth. And we raised and educated you. Can you deny then that you are like our son and should obey us? Is it right to strike back at your father when he strikes you?"

"Moreover, after we brought you into the world, and after we educated and provided you with many benefits, we proclaimed that you and all Athenians were free to leave us with all your goods when you came of age. But he, who had experienced how we administer our society and freely chose to stay, entered into an implied contract that he would obey us.

"So he who disobeys us, we maintain, wrongs us in three ways: First, because in disobeying us he is disobeying his parents; second, because in disobeying us he is disobeying those who gave him the benefits of an education; third, because he agreed to obey us and now he neither obeys nor does he show us where we were wrong. But are we right in saying that you agreed to be governed by us?"

How shall I answer that question, Crito? Must I not agree?

CRITO: There is no other way, Socrates.

SOCRATES: Then the laws will say, "Then, Socrates, in escaping you are breaking the agreement you made with us. So listen to us and not to Crito. Think not of life and children first and of justice afterwards. Put justice first."

This, Crito, is the voice I seem to hear quietly murmuring nearby, like a mystic who thinks he hears a flute playing in his ears. That voice is humming in my ears, and it prevents me from hearing

The Death of Socrates, Jacques-Louis David.

any other. Still, if you have anything more to add, Crito, speak up.

CRITO: I have nothing more to say, Socrates.

SOCRATES: Then, Crito, let me do what I must, since it is the will of god.[10]

The next morning, after saying farewell to his family and friends, Socrates drank the poison hemlock and died.

Here again, then, on the eve of his death, we find Socrates engaged in the task of philosophy. But now he brings his skills to bear on his own assumptions and his own life. He reasons that where morality is concerned, he should disregard the "opinions of the many"; that is, moral right and wrong do not depend on what most in our society believe. Instead, moral right and wrong depend on reasoning correctly about whether one is inflicting evil on others. Socrates says that if he escapes he would inflict evil on society because he has an obligation to obey its laws. He has this obligation because society, like a parent, deserves obedience, because it has bestowed important benefits on him, and because he has tacitly agreed to obey. Other considerations, he claims, are irrelevant. And so he concludes that it is wrong for him to escape.

But now the reader might well question Socrates' own beliefs. Is it true that moral right and wrong do not depend on what our society believes? Do we really have an obligation to obey the laws of society? Even to the death? If we do have such an obligation, do we have it because we must "repay" society through our unwavering obedience? Have

10. Plato, *Crito*, trans. Manuel Velasquez (Copyright © 1987 by Manuel Velasquez).

we really made some kind of promise to obey society? Must we obey any command of the law no matter how terrible?

The answers to these questions are not clear, although they are obviously important to our own lives. We must each decide for ourselves what morality is and which moral principles we will choose to live by. We must each decide for ourselves whether we have an obligation to obey the law or whether there are some laws that we are free to disobey. And we must each decide what, if anything, we owe society for what it has done for us. The reader should ponder these questions himself or herself. Although we will not spend any more time on them

PHILOSOPHY AND LIFE 1.2

Sanctuary and the Law

In January 1985 sixteen people, including two Roman Catholic priests, a Presbyterian minister, and three nuns, were charged with illegally smuggling and sheltering Central American refugees in the United States. The refugees were people fleeing from torture and virtually certain death in their own war-torn countries. The sixteen people charged with illegally helping the refugees argued that giving sanctuary to the refugees was a matter of conscience and that they were obligated to obey their conscience rather than the law. Several newspapers carried the story.

Tucson, Arizona—In direct defiance of immigration statutes, the Rev. John Fife and his compatriots in the sanctuary movement help transport Central American refugees across the Mexican border into the United States. They find food and shelter for them, often in churches, and then transport their wards through relays to cities such as Chicago, Los Angeles, Cincinnati and Seattle.

Two hundred churches publicly have declared their status as sanctuaries,

and the pastors, priests, rabbis and lay workers who have joined the movement speak freely about their work. . . .

"When you hear about the fear and the violence and the torture these people face at home, you have little choice but to help," said Jill Levis of Christ Church Presbyterian in Burlington, Vt. *"The Bible says that God takes sides and he tells us to take the side of the needy."*

"We are acting out our faith," said Peggy Hutchison, who was charged in the same federal indictment as Fife and fourteen other sanctuary workers. *"We believe very strongly in what we are doing."*

Fife said, *"You have to help the refugees or else you lose your soul."*

Ruth Anne Myers, district director in Arizona for the Immigration and Naturalization Service, insists that "the government's position is simply that it is against the law to smuggle, harbor or transport aliens into the United States.

"The law doesn't say if good people are doing it, it's OK, or if the people doing it think the law is wrong, it's OK," Myers added. *"It's like the bombing of abortion clinics. These are people who take the law into their own hands for religious reasons."*

Sanctuary activists argue that it is too difficult for most Central Ameri-

cans to prove to the satisfaction of the INS that they will be murdered or tortured if they return home.

All of the Arizona activists facing trial have said they will not suspend their sanctuary activity as long as they are free. Twenty-five unindicted co-conspirators, from places such as Seattle, Germantown, Pa., and Rochester, N.Y., have said they will continue their work and plan to refuse to testify against their indicted friends.

Even if all the charged activists are jailed, Fife said, the movement will not stop. "They can put Jim and I away for years, and sanctuary will go like gang busters," he said. *"No one runs this movement. It runs by itself, on faith."*

QUESTIONS

1. Is it wrong for the workers in the sanctuary movement to break the law? Is it wrong to refuse to testify against sanctuary workers who have broken the law? Is it wrong to continue to break the law once the courts have reached a decision on the sanctuary cases?

2. How would Socrates respond to the sanctuary movement workers? Would you agree with Socrates?

3. Is civil disobedience ever justified?

SOURCE: "Answering to a Higher Obligation," *San Jose Mercury News,* 1 January 1985, p. 1. Used by permission.

now, we will return to them later. At this point what is important is the realization that the activity of answering these kinds of questions is what philosophy is all about. Socrates' own willingness to grapple with these questions even in the face of death provides us with a priceless and still powerful example of what philosophy means.

Plato's dialogues of Socrates all take the form of a conversation. The use of this "dialogue form" is intended to convey a final important feature of philosophy: Philosophy develops through conversation. As Socrates develops his philosophical views by engaging in reflective dialogue with his fellows, so also can you develop your own views in dialogue with your peers, teachers, and the many philosophers you will meet in this book. In fact, some characterize philosophy as "a great conversation" with philosophers of the past. These thinkers view philosophers of the past as debating with each other through their writings and us as participants in this debate when we read and discuss these philosophers' views. Philosophy, then, is a kind of dialogue, which is why the dialogue format is perfect for presenting philosophy. This format will be used repeatedly in the chapters that follow. Within each chapter you will find several twentieth-century dialogues composed by one of the authors of this text. The purpose of these dialogues is to emphasize that philosophy develops through conversation and to show how philosophical issues are raised in a twentieth-century context. We cannot hope that our dialogues will duplicate the ingenious drama and cleverness found in Plato's dialogues. But we hope that like Plato's dialogues, ours will also move you to question and systematically think about those issues that are most basic to our human lives. We hope, in short, that they will lead you into doing philosophy.

QUESTIONS

1. Have you known bright people who weren't wise? Why weren't they wise? Make two lists, one containing the characteristics of intelligent people, the other the characteristics of wise people. How much overlapping is there? What kind of wisdom would you like to possess?

2. Are actions right because God or society says they are right? When you are unsure whether an action is right, do you try to determine its rightness or wrongness by trying to find out what God or society holds? Take some action that you believe is clearly right or clearly wrong and show that it is right or wrong. How is the rightness or wrongness of an action established?

3. It is sometimes said that the admission of ignorance is the beginning of wisdom. Why? Does Socrates' self-defense indicate this belief?

4. Do you have an obligation to obey the law? What is the basis of this obligation? How far does it extend? Could you ever have an obligation to *disobey* the law? What makes these questions *philosophical* questions?

5. What exactly is the meaning of Socrates' maxim, "The unexamined life is not worth living"? How does it relate to philosophy?

6. Construct a dialogue between two people discussing the nature of beauty. One person insists that beauty lies in the eye of the beholder. The other person attempts to get the first person to analyze this claim, to clarify and crystallize the concept.

The Significance of Philosophy

WHY PHILOSOPHY?

But we have not yet addressed a question that a person studying philosophy for the first time may have: Why should I spend the time and effort to study philosophy? It is clear, perhaps, why one should spend time studying those subjects that will provide the knowledge and skills needed to get a job or succeed in a career. We each need a job or a career to get along, to earn our living and meet our basic needs. But what needs does philosophy meet?

When people talk about getting along, they generally mean satisfying what psychologists often term *maintenance needs*, the physical and psychological needs that people must satisfy in order to maintain themselves as human beings: food, shelter, security, social interaction, and so on. Little wonder, then, that most of us have no trouble understanding the need for job preparation courses: They clearly help in satisying maintenance needs.

Some modern psychologists, Abraham Maslow among them, point out that humans have needs other than maintenance ones, which they term *actualizing needs*. While more difficult to describe than maintenance needs, actualizing needs appear to be associated with self-fulfillment, creativity, self-expression, realization of your potential, and, in a word, being everything you can be. Why mention these? Because evaluating the worth of courses and disciplines in terms of their job preparation value is to take a narrow view of what human beings

need. It completely overlooks higher-level needs. This doesn't mean, of course, that studying philosophy will necessarily lead to self-actualization. But philosophy assists by promoting the ideal of self-actualization, or what psychotherapist Carl Rogers terms the "fully functioning person."

Consider some characteristics of the self-actualized or fully functioning person. One is the ability to form one's own opinions and beliefs. Self-actualized people don't automatically go along with what's "in" or what's expected of them. Not that they are necessarily rebels; they just make up their own minds. They think, evaluate, and decide for themselves. What could better capture the spirit of philosophy than such intellectual and behavioral independence?

A second characteristic is profound self-awareness. Self-actualized people harbor few illusions about themselves and rarely resort to easy rationalizations to justify their beliefs and actions. If anything, philosophy is geared to deepen self-awareness by inviting us to examine the basic intellectual foundations of our lives.

A third characteristic is flexibility. Change and uncertainty don't devastate self-actualized people. Indeed, they exhibit resilience in the face of disorder, doubt, uncertainty, indefiniteness, even chaos. But they are not indifferent or uncaring. Quite the opposite. They are much involved in their experiences. Because of their resilience, they not only recognize the essential ambiguity of human affairs but also develop a high ambiguity tolerance. They are not upended by a lack of definite answers or of concrete solutions. When seriously undertaken, the study of philosophy often promotes what some have termed a philosophical calm, the capacity to persevere in the face of upheaval. This stems in part from an ability to put things in perspective, to see the "big picture," to make neither too much nor too little of events.

A fourth characteristic of self-actualized or fully functioning people is that they are generally creative. They are not necessarily writers, painters, or musicians, for creativity can function in many ways and at various levels. Rather, such people exhibit creativity in all they do. Whether spending leisure time or conversing, they seem to leave their own distinctive mark. Philosophy can help in this process by getting us to develop a philosophical perspective on issues, problems, and events. This means, in part, that we no longer see or experience life on the surface. We engage it on deeper levels, and we interact with it so that we help fashion our world. In another way, because philosophy exercises our imaginations, it invites a personal expression that is unique and distinctive.

Finally, self-actualized or fully functioning people have clearly conceptualized, well-thought-out value systems in morality, the arts, politics, and so on. Since a fundamental concern of philosophy is values and since philosophy often deals directly with morals, art, politics, and other value areas, it offers an opportunity to formulate viable assessments of worth and find meaning in our lives. For some psychologists, the search for meaning and values constitutes the human's primary interest (see Philosophy and Life 1.3).

PHILOSOPHY AND LIFE 1.3

Viktor Frankl's Logotherapy

Dr. Viktor E. Frankl is one psychologist who believes that the search for meaning is the human's primary interest. Frankl, professor of psychiatry and neurology, spent three years at Auschwitz and other Nazi concentration camps. He then gained his freedom, only to learn that almost all his family had been wiped out. During those years of incredible suffering and degradation, which he in part describes in his *Man's Search for Meaning*, Frankl developed a theory of psychotherapy termed *logotherapy*.

Logotherapy is derived from the Greek word *logos*, which denotes "meaning." Logotherapy focuses on the meaning of human existence as well as on humans' search for such meaning. According to Dr. Frankl and other logotherapists, the striving to find meaning in their lives is the primary motivational force in humans. He writes:

Man's search for meaning is a primary force in his life and not a "secondary rationalization" of instinctual drives. This meaning is unique and specific in that it must and can be ful-
filled by him alone; only then does it achieve a significance that will satisfy his own will to meaning. There are some authors who contend that meaning and values are "nothing but defense mechanisms, reaction formation and sublimation." But as for myself, I would not be willing to live merely for the sake of my "defense mechanisms," nor would I be ready to die merely for the sake of my "reaction formations." Man, however, is able to live and even to die for the sake of his ideals and values!

Logotherapy, therefore, considers humans as beings whose primary concerns are fulfilling a meaning and actualizing values, rather than the mere gratification and satisfaction of drives and instincts.

Dr. Frankl contends that the human search for meaning and value may arouse inner tensions rather than inner equilibrium. But he feels that these tensions are an indispensable prerequisite to mental health. There is nothing that would so effectively help one survive even the worst conditions, as the knowledge that there is a meaning in one's life. As evidence, he recalls his prison experiences, in which he witnessed that those who believed that there was a task waiting for them, a meaning, were the most likely to survive. In a word, for Dr. Frankl mental health is based in part on the tension that's inherent in humans who recognize the gap between what they are and what they should become.

QUESTIONS

1. Can the study of philosophy be related to the principles of logotherapy?

2. Is there any wisdom in the following words of the German philosopher Friedrich Nietzsche (1844–1900): "He who has a *why* to live for can bear almost any *how*"?

3. What, if any, meaning do you currently find in your life?

SOURCE: Frankl, *Man's Search for Meaning*, 154–155.

Some philosophers have shared this particular psychological insight, although expressing it differently. Perhaps the best example is found in the thought of Aristotle, who developed his view of self-realization by distinguishing among bodily goods (such as health), external goods (such as wealth), and spiritual (that is, psychological) goods (such as virtue). In his masterly analysis of happiness, *Nicomachean Ethics* (bk. 1, chs. 4–13; bk. 10, chs. 6–9), Aristotle says that happiness, which is the end or goal of all human beings, does not consist in any action of the body or senses. In the language of Maslow, happiness does not consist in satisfying maintenance needs. Rather, happiness involves the satisfaction of higher-level needs, in what Aristotle calls action of what is noblest and best in us: our reason. But happiness is not the activity of practical reason, for this is full of care and trouble in meeting basic needs. In contrast, happiness is the activity of speculative and theoretical reason; it is the life of the intellectual virtues, the chief of which is philosophic wisdom, which equips us for contemplating the highest truth and good. In brief, for Aristotle, health, maturity, education, friends, and worldly goods (all of which serve to satisfy maintenance needs) should be made subordinate aids to the truly happy life, which consists in a self-realization that takes root in the contemplative life.

So it seems safe to say that part of philosophy's value lies in its assisting us to satisfy higher-level needs, which often arise when maintenance needs have been met. At the same time, philosophy also contributes to the satisfaction of some maintenance needs. We mentioned previously the need for security. People acquire insurance policies and often go to extreme measures to avoid anxiety-inducing situations. But security needs show up on other levels. People seek to make sense out of their world in a variety of ways: through allegiance to religious beliefs, adherence to political systems, commitment to causes, and participation in clearly defined ways of seeing things and living. In part, such loyalties and behavior betray the human need for the security that stems from having ordered our universe, from having made sense out of things. Can philosophy help?

In fact, it's hard to imagine a better place to begin this ordering process than with the study of philosophy. One of the goals of philosophy is the integration of experience into a unified, coherent, systematic world view. Studying philosophy exposes you not only to world-view alternatives but also to how philosophers have ordered the universe for themselves. Stated another way, at the personal level, philosophy aims to integrate thought, feeling, and action in a meaningful way. As a result, philosophy extends the range of personal alternatives. Perhaps we believe things or have outlooks primarily because of our acculturation. We've never really thought about these beliefs or perspectives, having adopted them as an intellectual backdrop. We all have such taken-for-granted beliefs. But optional life-styles may exist that are more suitable for us. Or we may not fully understand and appreciate the worth of our own taken-for-granted ideas. Either way, philosophy offers the opportunity to test various beliefs, outlooks, and life-styles.

Other things make the study of philosophy worthwhile. Consider, for example, the importance of awareness. In part, personal freedom depends on awareness of self and the world. To a large degree, we are only as free as we are aware of the significant influences on our lives. In helping us deepen our awareness, philosophy gives us the ability to deal with and perhaps to slough off encumbrances to freedom.

What's more, philosophy exposes us to the history of thought. By portraying the evolutionary nature of intellectual achievement, it provides a perspective on the continuing development of human thought. As we confront the thought of various philosophers, we realize that one outlook is not necessarily true and another false; the value of any attitude lies chiefly in its usefulness within a given context. A merit of this exposure is that it breeds humility. We realize that if today's view has proved yesterday's inadequate, then tomorrow's may so prove today's. As a result, we become more tolerant, more receptive, and more sympathetic to views that compete or conflict with our own. We're less biased, provincial, ingrown; more open-minded and cosmopolitan.

Also, the study of philosophy helps us refine

our powers of analysis, our abilities to think critically, to reason, to evaluate, to theorize, and to justify. As we said earlier, these skills are the tools of philosophy. Exposure to the great ideas of extraordinary thinkers is likely to hone our own powers of analysis, hopefully enough to apply them constructively to our own affairs.

In conclusion, we might relate the value of philosophy to what we earlier noted as one of its distinctive characteristics: the absence of a body of definitely ascertainable knowledge. For many, rather than a value of philosophy, its uncertainty suggests that philosophy is of little worth. Is this so? Or is philosophy's uncertainty its strength?

Those critical of philosophy on this point should ask themselves: What in life is certain? Death and taxes, replied that great American humorist and writer Mark Twain. Were he alive today, advances in organ transplant, the advent of cryonics, and the rumble of taxpayer revolt might give Twain pause. The point is that very little, if anything, can be considered certain. Indeed, some, like Bertrand Russell, would insist that the only thing that is certain is uncertainty itself. Thus, Russell contended that the value of philosophy is its uncertainty. It seems fitting, then, that we should conclude this overview of the value of philosophy with a passage from Russell's *The Problems of Philosophy*, in which he explains his contention. Notice how Russell, after making this point, goes on to discuss what he considers to be philosophy's chief value, the nature of the subjects that it contemplates.

When a speculative philosopher believes he has comprehended the world once and for all in his system, he is deceiving himself; he has merely comprehended himself and then naively projected that view upon the world.

CARL G. JUNG

The value of philosophy is, in part, to be sought largely in its very uncertainty. The man who has no tincture of philosophy goes through life imprisoned in the prejudices derived from common sense, from the habitual beliefs of his age or his nation, and from convictions which have grown up in his mind without the cooperation or consent of his deliberate reason. To such a man the world tends to become definite, finite, obvious; common objects rouse no questions, and unfamiliar possibilities are contemptuously rejected. As soon as we begin to philosophize, on the contrary, we find . . . that even the most everyday things lead to problems to which only very incomplete answers can be given. Philosophy, though unable to tell us with certainty what is the true answer to the doubts which it raises, is able to suggest many possibilities which enlarge our thoughts and free them from the tyranny of custom. Thus, while diminishing our feeling of certainty as to what things are, it greatly increases our knowledge as to what they may be; it removes the somewhat arrogant dogmatism of those who have never traveled into the region of liberating doubt, and it keeps alive our sense of wonder by showing familiar things in an unfamiliar aspect.

Apart from its utility in showing unsuspected possibilities, philosophy has a value—perhaps its chief value—through the greatness of the objects which it contemplates, and the freedom from narrow and personal aims resulting from this contemplation. The life of the instinctive man is shut up within the circle of his private interests: family and friends may be included, but the outer world is not regarded except as it may help or hinder what comes within the circle of instinctive wishes. In such a life there is something feverish and confined, in comparison with which the philosophic life is calm and free. The private world of instinctive interests is a small one, set in the midst of a great and powerful world which must, sooner or later, lay our private world in ruins. Unless we can so enlarge our interests as to include the whole outer world, we remain like a garrison in a beleaguered fortress, knowing that the enemy prevents escape and that ultimate surrender is inevitable. In such a life there is no peace, but a constant strife between the insistence of desire and the powerlessness of will. In one way or another, if our life is to be great and free, we must escape this prison and this strife.

One way of escape is by philosophic contemplation. Philosophic contemplation does not, in its widest survey, divide the universe into two hostile camps—friends and foes, helpful and hostile, good and bad—it views the whole impartially. Philosophic contemplation, when it is unalloyed, does not aim at proving that the rest of the universe is akin to man. All acquisition of knowledge is an enlargement of the Self, but this enlargement is best attained when it is not directly sought. It is obtained when the desire for knowledge is alone operative, by a study which does not wish in advance that its objects should have this or that character, but adapts the Self to the characters which it finds in its objects.[11] *

Before we conclude this chapter, it is useful to observe a recurring problem in any introduction to philosophy. That problem concerns focus. Because so much material is and must be covered, the overall treatment may lack focus; the student may be left confused or with only a most superficial understanding. While there is no easy solution to this problem, one useful device is to take a more in-depth look at important figures in the material being covered. This book will use this strategy. Since the purpose of this technique is to exhibit the writings and thoughts of philosophers, an appropriate term for it is *showcase*. Each showcase not only includes an overview of the philosophy of important figures but also includes edited selections from their writings so that the student can have the opportunity to read the philosophers' own words. Moreover, taken together, the showcases in the text are intended to provide a feeling for the history of philosophy. Consequently, the showcases, for the most part, are in historical order. Since we are beginning philosophy, our first showcase will spotlight the pre-Socratics, the philosophers who preceded Socrates. To Socrates, the "father of philosophy," we have already been introduced. Examining the pre-Socratics will also give us a better idea of the historical significance of philosophy. These first philosophers had a remarkable impact on how we today view reality and ourselves, an impact that philosophy continues to have through the ages.

QUESTIONS

1. What indications of actualizing needs do you currently see in your life?

2. What evidence suggests that your college curriculum was devised in part with something like actualizing needs in mind?

3. It's not uncommon for "successful" people to be bored. Indeed, many academically successful students express profound boredom with school. What, in your mind, is the nature of boredom? Can it be related to actualizing needs? Can philosophy in any way combat boredom?

4. Can you think of any people whom you consider self-actualized? What traits do they show?

5. Give an example of how increasing your awareness has made you freer.

6. Exactly what is the difference, if any, between approaching reality through poetry and approaching reality philosophically?

7. What is the difference, if any, between approaching reality through the methods of the natural sciences and approaching reality philosophically?

CHAPTER SUMMARY AND CONCLUSIONS

We began by observing that while some people do not approach philosophy as a field of study, everyone nevertheless philosophizes in daily life when wondering about basic beliefs. Philosophy, as the love of wisdom, is pictured by Plato as a climb from darkness to light in the pursuit of wisdom. We noted that the philosophical enterprise is an activity characterized by asking and answering questions for ourselves through critical, persistent analysis. The wisdom that philosophy seeks is the cultivation of critical habits, the search for truth, the questioning of the obvious. In general, philosophical concerns are today grouped around three themes: epistemology, metaphysics, and ethics. The pre-Socratics

---

11. Russell, *Problems of Philosophy*, 158–159. Reprinted by permission of Oxford University Press.

were the first philosophers, but Socrates, the "father of philosophy" best exemplifies the search for wisdom as he is portrayed in the dialogues of his disciple Plato. The dialogues also exemplify another important characteristic of philosophy: Philosophy develops through conversation. As for the value of studying philosophy, philosophy can help satisfy the higher-level human needs. It also seems to satisfy some maintenance needs, such as the need for security. Furthermore, it liberates through increasing awareness, deepens tolerance and broadens our capacity to receive the disclosures of the world, refines our powers of analysis, helps us deal with the uncertainties of living, and enlarges us through the nature of the subjects that it contemplates. Finally, while the study of philosophy entails definite intellectual risks, in the last analysis these are justified by the rewards that philosophy promises.

There are no free lunches, not even in philosophy. If you want what philosophy offers, you must pay a price. Part of the price is long, painstaking study and careful examination and reexamination of ideas, outlooks, and assertions. Another part is the realization that this process is endless; we will not reach a point where all questions are resolved, all doubt eliminated. But potentially the highest price to be paid for the rewards of philosophical study is the risks that we will run; for in subjecting beliefs to the critical questioning that makes up an important part of the philosophical enterprise, we risk unmasking personal and cultural assumptions. Doubtless, the collapse of a cherished belief, like the loss of a loved one, can deeply wound and pain. Not surprisingly, we resist having challenged those ideas that we take for granted. So, as we begin our adventure into the exciting, though disturbing, world of great philosophical ideas, it's important to ponder this question: Can individuals or societies progress without intellectual suffering?

It seems not, though it might take many pages and volumes to illustrate and demonstrate this belief. Enough here to suggest that in many ways, if not all, we are better off today than our primitive ancestors were. But so-called civilization and all that it implies have not come easily. Many along the way have suffered enormous intellectual agony.

> **Philosophers play a strange game. They know very well that one thing alone counts: Why are we born on this earth? And they also know that they will never be able to answer it. Nevertheless, they continue sedately to amuse themselves.**
>
> JACQUES MARITAIN

We met one such person in this chapter, Socrates, who ultimately paid with his life for what he believed. Consider how profoundly impoverished we would be, personally and collectively, had Socrates been unwilling to pay the price. He, like countless others, paid his intellectual dues and, to a large extent, ours as well.

But a considerable debt is still outstanding, for neither as individuals nor as a species do we have all the answers, the whole truth, the full meaning. And isn't that, after all, what we seek? Isn't it what we've always sought? If so, then let's press on, convinced that the goal we seek is well worth the risks.

In the pages ahead, as we consider many of the enduring philosophical questions, uppermost in each of our minds will be the question: Who and what am I? We could call this the unifying theme that draws together what may appear to be disparate philosophical concerns. We'll see that the study of philosophy can help us in answering this question, for ultimately a human being is many things: a moral being, a social and political animal, an appreciator of art and beauty, a perceiver and knower, a scientist, a religionist. As we now know, all these aspects of humanity and self are areas of intense philosophical concern and speculation. Our adventure into the world of philosophy, therefore, is more than an encounter with great ideas, thinkers, systems, and movements. It's a voyage into ourselves. It's a quest for self-definition and understanding.

The Pre-Socratics

Western philosophy began with the question the Greek thinker Thales asked around 585 B.C.: What is the ultimate reality of which everything is made? Thales' answer will strike you as a bit funny and prosaic. He answered, "Everything ultimately is made of water!"

But Thales' answer is unimportant. What is significant is that he was the first to take a radically new "philosophical" approach to reality. Thinkers before Thales were content to explain reality as the whimsical work of mythical gods. The Greek poet Hesiod (ca. 776 B.C.), for example, explains how the sky came to rain on the earth by describing the sky as a male god who was castrated by his son while sleeping with the goddess Earth.

Great Heaven came at night longing for love.
He lay on Earth spreading himself full on her.
Then from an ambush, his own son stretched out his
    left hand,
And wielding a long sharp sickle in his right,
He swiftly sliced and cut his father's genitals.
Earth received the bloody drops that all gushed forth,
And she gave birth to the great Furies and mighty
    giants.
Now when chaste Heaven desires to penetrate the
    Earth,
And Earth is filled with longing for this union,
Rain falling from her lover, Heaven, impregnates her,
And she brings forth wheat for men and pastures for
    their flocks.[12]

---

12. Hesiod, *The Theogony*, pt. 11, lines 177–185, trans. Manuel Velasquez (Copyright © 1987 by Manuel Velasquez).

Thales departed in three ways from this mythological and poetic approach to reality. First, he had the idea that although reality is complex, it should be explainable in terms of one or a few basic elements. Second, he decided that reality should be explained in terms of natural, observable things (like water) and not by poetic appeals to unobservable gods. Third, he rejected the idea that reality should be explained through the authority of religious myths from the past that could neither be proved nor disproved. Instead, he tried to provide a literal and factual explanation that others could evaluate for themselves through reasoning and observation.

Thus, although Thales' theory—that water is the basic stuff out of which everything is made—seems naive, he was the first to break away from religious myth and strike out on a new path that used human reason and observation to explore the universe. Taking this momentous and daring step marks him as a genius. In fact, today we continue to travel the road Thales showed us. Much of our basic scientific research is still devoted to finding the simplest elemental forces out of which everything in the universe is made, and we still proceed by proposing literal theories or "hypotheses" that can be proved or disproved through reason and observation. It took the genius of Thales to set Western civilization on this amazingly fruitful path of discovery.

But it was two other early Greek philosophers, Heraclitus (ca. 554–484 B.C.) and Parmenides (ca. 480–430 B.C.), who proposed the most interesting and radical of the early philosophical views of reality. Both philosophers left the question of what things are made of and turned their attention to the problem of *change*—whether change is a basic reality or a mere illusion, real or merely appearance.

Heraclitus, in a remarkable series of sayings, proposed that change is the fundamental reality. He asserted that like a fire's flame, "All reality is changing." Like a flowing river, everything in the universe changes from moment to moment so we can never touch or perceive the same thing in two different moments. The only enduring realities are the recurring patterns (like the seasons) of change itself.

In the same rivers we step and yet we do not step; we ourselves are the same and yet we are not. You cannot step in the same river twice, for other waters are ever flowing on. The sun is new every day. The living and the dead, the waking and sleeping, the young and the old, these are changing into each other; the former are moved about and become the latter, the latter in turn become the former. Neither god nor man shaped this universe, but it ever was and ever shall be a living Fire that flames up and dies in measured patterns. There is a continual exchange: all things are exchanged for Fire and Fire for all things. Fire steers the universe. God changes like Fire.[13]

Parmenides, convinced that Heraclitus was completely mistaken, proposed a theory that was the exact opposite. Parmenides held that change is an illusion and that the universe in reality is a frozen unchanging object. "We can speak and think only of what exists. And what exists is uncreated and imperishable, for it is whole and unchanging and complete. It was not nor shall be different since it is now, all at once, one and continuous."[14] How was Parmenides led to this view? He argued that nothingness or "nonbeing" cannot be real, since we cannot even think of nothingness. Yet change requires nonbeing or nothingness. For if something changes, it must change into something that did not exist before: Something must come into being out of nonbeing. But nonbeing does not exist. So nothing can come from nonbeing. Therefore, change cannot exist: The universe has no beginning, and nothing in it changes.

> For what beginning of the universe could you search for? From what could it come? I will not let you say or think "From what was not" because you cannot even conceive of "what is not." Nor will true thinking allow that, besides what exists, new things could also arise from something that does not exist. How could what exists pass into what does not exist? And how can what does not exist come into existence? For if it came into existence,

then it earlier was nothingness. And nothingness is unthinkable and unreal.[15]

Parmenides' strange view received additional support from one of his students, Zeno, who agreed that change was an illusion. Zeno argued that "A runner cannot move from one point to another. For to do so, he must first get to a point half-way across, and to do this, he must get half-way to the half-way point, and to do this he must get half-way to that point, and so on for an infinite number of spaces."[16]

Since an infinite number of spaces cannot be crossed (at least not in a finite length of time), Zeno concluded that no object moves: Motion is an illusion of our senses!

In spite of—or perhaps because of—their unusual views, the pre-Socratic philosophers (that is, philosophers who lived before Socrates) made several crucial contributions to our thinking. They got us to rely on our reason and to search for new ways of looking at reality instead of relying on the authority of the past. They introduced us to the problem of "the one and the many": Can the many things of our experience be explained in terms of one or a few fundamental constituents? They introduced the problem of "appearance and reality": Does a more basic reality underlie the changing world that appears before us? Moreover, the views they proposed continue even today to have followers. Twentieth-century "process philosophers," for example, hold that change or "process" is the fundamental reality, while some twentieth-century British philosophers have held that change is an illusion.

---

15. Ibid., 8.
16. Aristotle, *Physics*, 239b11, trans. Manuel Velasquez.

---

13. Diels-Kranz, *Fragments of the Presocratics*, Heraclitus, 49, 12, 6, 88, 30, 90, 64, 67, trans. Manuel Velasquez.
14. Ibid., Parmenides, 7.

VOLTAIRE

Story of a Good Brahman

Among history's most satiric and philosophical storytellers ranks the Frenchman Voltaire (1694–1778). Best known for his ironic classic Candide, *Voltaire wrote numerous shorter, perhaps less familiar works that are often as provocative if not as dazzling as his masterpiece. "Story of a Good Brahman" is one. With few but well-chosen words, Voltaire presents the paradox that is at once the curse and blessing of the philosophically minded: Why persist in asking unanswerable questions when all they do is make us unhappy? His reply: The alternative, not asking them, is more appalling. Voltaire seems to say that, in the long run, the peace and comfort that philosophers experience must derive from knowing that they exercise the human's noblest quality—curiosity—even though being curious may preclude contentment.*

I met on my travels an old Brahman, a very wise man, full of wit and very learned; moreover he was rich, and consequently even wiser; for, lacking nothing, he had no need to deceive anyone. His family was very well governed by three beautiful wives who schooled themselves to please him; and when he was not entertaining himself with his wives, he was busy philosophizing.

Near his house, which was beautiful, well decorated, and surrounded by charming gardens, lived an old Indian woman, bigoted, imbecilic, and rather poor.

The Brahman said to me one day: "I wish I had never been born."

I asked him why. He replied:

"I have been studying for forty years, which is forty years wasted; I teach others, and I know nothing; this situation brings into my soul so much humiliation and disgust that life is unbearable to me. I was born, I live in time, and I do not know what time is; I find myself in a point between two eternities, as our sages say, and I have no idea of eternity. I am composed of matter; I think, and I have never been able to find out what produces thought; I do not know whether my understanding is a simple faculty in me like that of walking or of digesting, and whether I think with my head, as I take with my hands. Not only is the principle of my thinking unknown to me, but the principle of my movements is equally hidden from me. I do not know why I exist.

SOURCE: *Voltaire: Candide, Zadig and Selected Stories*, trans. Donald M. Frame (Copyright © 1961 by Donald M. Frame). Reprinted by arrangement with The New American Library.

However, people every day ask me questions on all these points; I have to answer; I have nothing any good to say; I talk much, and I remain confounded and ashamed of myself after talking.

"It is much worse yet when they ask me whether Brahma was produced by Vishnu or whether they are both eternal. God is my witness that I don't know a thing about it, and it certainly shows in my answers. 'Ah! Reverend Father,' they say to me, 'teach us how it is that evil inundates the whole world.' I am as much at a loss as those who ask me that question; I sometimes tell them that all is for the very best, but those who have been ruined and mutilated at war believe nothing of it, and neither do I; I retreat to my house overwhelmed with my curiosity and my ignorance. I read our ancient books, and they redouble the darkness I am in. I talk to my companions: some answer that we must enjoy life and laugh at men; the others think they know something, and lose themselves in absurd ideas; everything increases the painful feeling I endure. I am sometimes ready to fall into despair, when I think that after all my seeking I know neither where I come from, nor what I am, nor where I shall go, nor what shall become of me."

The state of this good man caused me real pain; no one was either more reasonable or more honest than he. I perceived that the greater the lights of his understanding and the sensibility of his heart, the more unhappy he was.

That same day I saw the old woman who lived in his vicinity: I asked her whether she had ever been distressed not to know how her soul was made. She did not even understand my question: she had never reflected a single moment of her life over a single one of the points that tormented the Brahman; she believed with all her heart in the metamorphoses of Vishnu, and, provided she could sometimes have some water from the Ganges to wash in, she thought herself the happiest of women.

Struck by the happiness of this indigent creature, I returned to my philosopher and said to him:

"Aren't you ashamed to be unhappy at a time when right at your door there is an old automaton who thinks of nothing and who lives happily?"

"You are right," he answered; "I have told myself a hundred times that I would be happy if I was as stupid as my neighbor, and yet I would want no part of such a happiness."

This answer of my Brahman made a greater impression on me than all the rest. I examined myself and saw that indeed I would not have wanted to be happy on condition of being imbecilic.

I put the matter up to some philosophers, and they were of my opinion.

"There is, however," I said, "a stupendous contradiction in this way of thinking."

For after all, what is at issue? Being happy. What matters being witty or being stupid? What is more, those who are content with their being are quite sure of being content; those who reason are not so sure of reasoning well.

"So it is clear," I said, "that we should choose not to have common sense, if ever that common sense contributes to our ill-being."

Everyone was of my opinion, and yet I found no one who wanted to accept the bargain of becoming imbecilic in order to become content. From this I concluded that if we set store by happiness, we set even greater store by reason.

But, upon reflection, it appears that to prefer reason to felicity is to be very mad.

Then how can this contradiction be explained? Like all the others. There is much to be said about it.

QUESTIONS

1. Why, do you think, does Voltaire call his Brahman "good"? Why didn't he entitle his story "Story of a Brahman"?

2. Why doesn't the Brahman desire the happiness of the old woman?

3. Voltaire seems to say that you can be either a reasoning or a happy creature, but not both. Do you agree?

4. Which of the two would you prefer to be: the Brahman or the old woman? Why?

5. Which of the two, the Brahman or the old woman, would you say is more in harmony with the nature of a human being?

6. Voltaire describes the woman in his story as "poor." Do you think, however, that you would mischaracterize the story if you saw the discrepancies in life orientations exclusively in economic terms?

SUGGESTIONS FOR FURTHER READING

Adler, Mortimer J. *The Conditions of Philosophy.* New York: Dell, 1967. One of the great humanistic thinkers of our time presents a clear, readable account of the nature of philosophy. Adler's paperback contains several suggestions about what's needed to make philosophy more applicable to the modern world.

Allen, E. L. *From Plato to Nietzsche.* New York: Ballantine Books, 1983. A paperback presenting a simple overview of the thoughts of the great philosophers.

Bontempo, Charles I., and S. Jack Odell, eds. *The Owl of Minerva.* New York: McGraw-Hill, 1975. This collection of original articles by eighteen leading contemporary philosophers explains what the authors find attractive and fulfilling about their work.

Copleston, F. C. *History of Philosophy.* 8 vols. Garden City, N.Y.: Doubleday, 1965. This series of paperbacks provides the most comprehensive and authoritative treatment of Western philosophers in the English language.

Cornman, James W., and Keith Lehrer. *Philosophical Problems and Arguments.* 2d ed. New York: Macmillan, 1974. Several examples of how contemporary analytic philosophers examine philosophical issues.

De George, Richard T. *The Philosopher's Guide to Sources, Research Tools, Professional Life, and Related Fields.* Lawrence: The Regents Press of Kansas, 1980. A complete guide to books, journals, and other sources of information about philosophy and particular philosophers.

Durant, Will. *The Story of Philosophy.* New York: Pocket Books, 1953. An immensely readable account of the development of philosophy. Full of anecdotes and informative asides, Durant's paperback book charms while it enlightens.

Edwards, Paul, ed. *The Encyclopedia of Philosophy.* 8 vols. New York: Macmillan and Free Press, 1967. A basic source of information on virtually every conceivable subject in philosophy. Some of the articles are heavy going, but all are excellent.

Emmet, E. R. *Learning to Philosophize.* Harmondsworth, England: Penguin, 1968. This paperback presents a straightforward explanation of several philosophical questions and how they can be critically examined.

Friedman, Maurice. *The Hidden Human Image*. New York: Dell, 1974. Friedman's paperback book is especially helpful in exploring contemporary human concerns. It is philosophically stimulating without being pedantic or stuffy. A good book to ignite philosophical thinking and debate.

Jones, W. T. *History of Western Philosophy*. 2d ed. New York: Harper & Row, 1976. A four-volume readable history of philosophy that provides historical and cultural background on each of the great philosophers.

Jung, Carl. *The Undiscovered Self*. New York: New American Library (Mentor Books), 1957. In this short paperback, the renowned psychoanalyst discusses the psychic forces dividing the world, underscoring the need for personal integrity and freedom to counter the dehumanization of contemporary society. Reason without self-knowledge, he writes, is humanly disastrous.

Korner, Stephan. *Fundamental Questions in Philosophy*. London: Penguin, 1971. A good paperback introduction to the basic questions of philosophy. Korner's work traces the changes that have occurred in philosophy over the years. The author emphasizes the importance of logic.

Lavine, T. Z. *From Socrates to Sartre: The Philosophic Quest*. New York: Bantam Books, 1984. The very readable paperback text of an extremely interesting PBS television series on the great philosophers.

O'Connor, D. J. *A Critical History of Western Philosophy*. New York: Free Press, 1964. Concise articles on the central philosophical views of the major Western philosophers.

Persig, Robert. *Zen and the Art of Motorcycle Maintenance*. New York: Bantam Books, 1980. This enjoyable novel raises interesting philosophical questions about the nature of reality and our way of looking at reality.

Philips, Michael, ed. *Philosophy and Science Fiction*. Buffalo, N.Y.: Prometheus Books, 1984. A fascinating examination of philosophical themes in science fiction. This paperback contains seventeen science fiction stories that raise interesting philosophical questions.

Plato. *The Last Days of Socrates*. Translated by Hugh Tredennick. Baltimore, Md.: Penguin Books, 1969. A paperback translation of the full text of four Socratic dialogues: *Euthyphro, The Apology, Crito, Phaedo*.

Rorty, Richard. "Philosophy in America Today," in *The American Scholar* 51 (Spring 1982):183–200. A contemporary philosopher looks at the place academic philosophy has today and suggests that it is not as distinctive as some people think.

Runes, Dagobert D., ed. *Dictionary of Philosophy*. 15th ed. Paterson, N.J.: Littlefield Adams, 1964. A handy little book that provides definitions of most philosophical terms.

Russell, Bertrand. *The Problems of Philosophy*. New York: Oxford University Press, 1959. This short and simple little paperback is a fascinating introduction to the main problems of philosophy. Intended for nonexperts, it will be perfectly clear to the beginner.

Stumpf, Samuel Enoch. *Socrates to Sartre: A History of Philosophy*. 3d ed. New York: McGraw-Hill, 1982. Stumpf provides an easy but accurate synopsis of the central views of the major Western philosophers.

Taylor, A. E. *Socrates*. New York: Doubleday Anchor, 1959. This short paperback is still one of the most informative and readable books about the life of Socrates.

Woodhouse, Mark B. *A Preface to Philosophy*. 3d ed. Belmont, Calif.: Wadsworth, 1984. A good introduction to the nature of philosophy and to methods of philosophical reasoning.

APPENDIX

A Look at Logic

Philosophy should not be confused with mere speculation. There are significant differences between mere speculation and philosophy. When we merely speculate, we dream up grand ideas and visions about how things might be. We might speculate, for example, that "All this might be a dream!" Philosophy does more than this, however. Philosophy is the attempt to *prove* that certain ideas or visions are true. That is, philosophy is the attempt to *give reasons* for the views and positions we propose. Philosophizing requires that you try to reach the truth through logical reasoning. Without logical reasoning, there is no philosophy but only mere speculation.

Because philosophy requires logical reasoning, logic is a basic tool of the philosopher. So we provide here some fundamental ideas about what logical reasoning is.

Logic is the skill of distinguishing valid arguments from invalid ones. An argument in philosophy, of course, is not a quarrel but a group of statements or "premises" that are supposed to prove or establish a person's conclusions. Thus every argument has two parts: (1) a group of premises and (2) a conclusion. Here, for example, is a simple argument.

PREMISES

    (1) If a good God existed, then there would be no evil in the world.

    (2) But obviously, there is evil in the world.

CONCLUSION

    (3) So a good God does not exist.

Philosophers usually divide arguments into two kinds: deductive and inductive. The argument above is a deductive argument. We will begin our examination of logic by looking first at "deductive arguments." Once we have a good idea of what deductive arguments are, we will briefly look at how "inductive arguments" work.

DEDUCTIVE ARGUMENTS

In a good or valid argument, the conclusion logically follows from the premises. This means that, in a valid *deductive* argument, *if* the premises are true the conclusion also *must* be true. So if you accept the premises of a valid deductive argument, then you *must* also accept the conclusion. The argument above, for example, is a valid deductive argument. So *if* (1) and (2) were both true, then (3) would also have to be true.

The most common form of argument is the syllogism: an argument containing two premises and a conclusion. One important kind of syllogism is the "categorical syllogism," which consists of "categorical" statements, that is, statements about classes (or "categories") of things. Each of the premises and the conclusion of a categorical syllogism states that one class of things is or is not included in another class, either in part or wholly. For example, here are two valid categorical syllogisms.

All abortions are murders.	All A are M.
All murders are immoral.	All M are I.
So all abortions are immoral.	All A are I.
Some acts of civil disobedience are violent.	Some A are V.
No violent acts are justified.	No V are J.
So some acts of civil disobedience are not justified.	Some A are not J.

And here are three examples of invalid categorical syllogisms.

All perverts love pornography.	All P are L.
Joe loves pornography.	All J are L.
So Joe is a pervert.	All J are P.

All cruel and unusual punishments are unconstitutional.

All C are U.

No traffic fines are cruel and unusual punishments.

No T are C.

So no traffic fines are unconstitutional.

No T are U.

Some rich people are not boorish.

Some R are not B.

Some students are not rich.

Some S are not R.

So some students are not boorish.

Some S are not B.

What distinguishes the valid categorical syllogisms from the invalid ones? There are four easy rules that can be used to determine whether a categorical syllogism is valid. But to understand these, we first have to know some simple terminology. First, as the reader can see, there are only four kinds of categorical statements, depending on whether a statement is "universal" (like 1 and 2 below) or "particular" (like 3 and 4) and on whether it is "affirmative" (like 1 and 3) or "negative" (like 2 and 4). Second, every categorical statement contains two "terms," A and B, each of which refers to a class of things and each of which can be "distributed" or "undistributed." A term is "distributed" if the sentence makes a statement that includes *all* the members of the class or (in the case of negative statements) that excludes *all* the members of the class; otherwise the term is "undistributed." For example, in statements of the form 1 below, A is distributed and B is undistributed; in those of form 2, A and B are both distributed; in 3, A and B are both undistributed; in 4, A is undistributed and B is distributed.

1. All A are B (universal affirmative; A distributed, B undistributed).

2. No A are B (universal negative; A and B both distributed).

3. Some A are B (particular affirmative; A and B both undistributed).

4. Some A are not B (particular negative; A undistributed, B distributed).

Now we can state the four rules for validity. A categorical syllogism is valid if and only if it satisfies all four rules; it is invalid if it violates one or more.

1. The middle term (the term present in both premises and absent from the conclusion) must be distributed at least once.

2. If a term is distributed in the conclusion, it must also be distributed in the premises.

3. At least one premise must be affirmative.

4. If one premise is negative, the conclusion must be negative.

For instance, the first of the three examples of invalid syllogisms above violates rule 1; the second violates rule 2; the third violates rule 3. On the other hand, the two valid syllogisms do not violate any of the rules.

A second important kind of argument is the "hypothetical syllogism." Hypothetical syllogisms contain "hypothetical statements," that is, statements in which two simpler sentences are connected with the words *If-then*. Here are some examples of hypothetical statements.

If it's raining, then the ground is wet.

If you study, then you'll get a good grade.

If Sue is late, then she must be sick.

If we keep building bombs, then we'll use them someday.

The first simple sentence in a hypothetical statement is called the "antecedent," while the second is called the "consequent." The antecedents in the examples above are "it's raining," "you study," "Sue is late," and "we keep building bombs." The consequents are "the ground is wet," "you'll get a good grade," "she must be sick," and "we'll use them someday."

The most common kind of hypothetical syllogisms are arguments whose premises consist of one hypothetical statement and one simple sentence and whose conclusion is a simple sentence. Here is an example of a valid hypothetical syllogism.

(a) If it's raining, then the ground is wet.　　If R, then W.

(b) But it's raining.　　But R.

(c) So the ground is wet.　　Therefore, W.

Notice that in this *valid* hypothetical syllogism, the simple premise (b) *affirms the antecedent* of the hypothetical premise (a), and the conclusion (c) affirms its consequent. Consider now a second example of a hypothetical syllogism that is also valid.

(d) If it's raining, then the ground is wet.　　If R, then W.

(e) But the ground is not wet.　　But not W.

(f) Therefore it's not raining.　　Therefore, not R.

In this *valid* hypothetical syllogism, the simple premise (e) *denies the consequent* of the hypothetical premise (d), and the conclusion denies its antecedent.

Now here are two examples of *invalid* hypothetical syllogisms. In the first invalid example, the simple premise incorrectly affirms the consequent, while in the second invalid example, the simple premise incorrectly denies the antecedent.

(g) If it's raining, then the ground is wet.

(h) But the ground is wet.

(i) Therefore it's raining.

(j) If it's raining, then the ground is wet.

(k) But it's not raining.

(l) Therefore the ground is not wet.

A little reflection will show that in both of these examples, the conclusion does not logically follow from the premises. In the first example, the fact that the ground is wet may be due to something other than rain (maybe someone left the sprinklers on). In the second example, the fact that it's not raining does not rule out that the ground is wet

(again, even if it's not raining someone might have turned the sprinklers on).

We can now state an easy rule for knowing whether a hypothetical syllogism is valid or not, but first we will need a more careful definition of hypothetical syllogisms. A hypothetical syllogism consists of exactly two premises and a conclusion of the following kinds:

1. One premise is a hypothetical statement.

2. One premise affirms or denies the antecedent or the consequent of the hypothetical.

3. The conclusion affirms or denies the consequent or the antecedent of the hypothetical.

Now we can say that a hypothetical syllogism is valid if one premise affirms the antecedent and the conclusion affirms the consequent, or if one premise denies the consequent and the conclusion denies the antecedent; otherwise it is invalid.

A third important kind of syllogism is the "hypothetical chain argument." Hypothetical chain arguments may contain more than two premises. In hypothetical chain arguments, all the premises and the conclusion are hypothetical statements. Here is an example of a hypothetical chain argument.

If you study hard, then you will pass the exam.　　If S, then P.

If you pass the exam, then you will get an A.　　If P, then A.

If you get an A, then you will graduate.　　If A, then G.

If you graduate, then you will be happy.　　If G, then H.

So if you study hard, then you will be happy.　　So if S, then H.

The rule for determining the validity of a hypothetical chain argument is simple. A hypothetical chain argument is valid if the consequent of one premise is the antecedent of a second premise, the consequent of that premise is the antecedent of a third, and so on, while the antecedent of the conclusion is the antecedent of the first premise and the consequent of the conclusion is the consequent of the last premise.

A fourth and last important kind of argument is the disjunctive syllogism. The disjunctive syllogism contains a disjunctive statement. A disjunctive statement is a sentence that states that either one thing will happen or another will, but not both. Here are several disjunctive statements.

(m) Either the sun will shine, or it will be cloudy.

(n) Either I will study, or I will flunk.

(o) Either God exists, or Christianity is wrong.

The two simpler parts of a disjunctive statement are called "disjuncts." In example (m), one disjunct is "the sun will shine" and the other is "it will be cloudy"; in example (n), the two disjuncts are "I will study" and "I will flunk"; in example (o), the disjuncts are "God exists" and "Christianity is wrong."

A disjunctive syllogism is an argument with two premises and a conclusion in which one premise is a disjunctive statement, one premise affirms or denies one of the disjuncts, and the conclusion affirms or denies the other disjunct. Here are two examples of disjunctive syllogisms: The first is valid, the second is invalid.

Either they married, or they broke up.

But they didn't break up.

_____

So they married.

Either Jones ate pumpernickel, or Mary did.

But Jones ate pumpernickel.

_____

So Mary did not.

The rule for determining the validity of a disjunctive syllogism is simple. A disjunctive syllogism is valid if one premise denies one disjunct and the conclusion affirms the other; otherwise it is invalid.

Now that you have a better idea of what valid deductive arguments are, we can briefly list some of the major *fallacies*. A fallacy is an attempt to establish a conclusion without using good logic. There are many kinds of fallacies, but the following are some of the most common:

Appeal to Emotion One common fallacy is the attempt to establish a claim, not by providing good reasons for the claim but by appealing to the passions and prejudices of the audience.

Appeal to Authority Another common fallacy is the attempt to establish a claim by appealing to an unqualified expert or an irrelevant authority.

Ad Hominem Argument This is an argument that attacks the *person making a claim* instead of addressing the issue. I use an ad hominem argument, for example, when someone argues that God does not exist, and I reject his argument on the grounds that "He's an evil person anyway."

Argument from Ignorance This is an argument that claims that since there is no evidence that *P* is false, *P* must be true. For example, I am arguing from ignorance if I say that since you cannot prove that God does not exist, God must exist.

Begging the Question I beg the question when I give a circular argument, that is, when the premises I use to prove a conclusion already assume that the conclusion is true. For example, if I say, "What he claims must be true because he always speaks the truth," then I am begging the question.

False Cause A false cause argument is an argument that claims that since A occurred before B, A must be the *cause* of B. For example, a person is using a false cause argument when she says that since a black cat crossed her path before she had an accident, the black cat must have caused the accident.

Equivocation An argument is based on equivocation when a word or expression changes its meaning in the course of the argument. Here is an example: "Since I saw nobody in the room and you saw nobody in the room, we both saw the same person, Nobody."

Amphiboly An argument is based on amphiboly when it uses a grammatical construction that is ambiguous because it can be understood in two ways.

Misplaced Accent An argument based on misplaced accent is one that is misleading because it emphasizes a word or expression that is designed to mislead or because it omits relevant information.

Composition The fallacy of composition is the fallacy of attributing the characteristics of the parts of a thing to the whole thing itself. Here is an example: "If every book in the library is good, it must be a good library."

Division The fallacy of division is the fallacy of attributing the characteristics of a whole thing to one or more of its parts. For example: "Since it is a good library, each book in it must be good."

INDUCTIVE ARGUMENTS

Inductive arguments, unlike deductive arguments, do not guarantee that the conclusion *must* be true if the premises are true. Instead, inductive arguments provide evidence that shows merely that the conclusion is probably true or that it is reasonable to accept the conclusion on the basis of the evidence. Court trials in which the court's final decision is based on "circumstantial evidence" normally use inductive arguments. Suppose, for example, that hair of the accused was found at the scene of the crime, that the accused earlier had boasted he would commit the crime, and that the accused was seen in the vicinity where the crime occurred shortly before it was committed. Then the jurors might conclude that the accused committed the crime. Their reasoning would be based on an inductive argument: an argument that supports the conclusion by making it *probable* but not certain.

The most important kind of inductive argument is an argument that generalizes from several instances. When scientists, for example, observe that all the members of a certain species they have examined have certain markings, they may conclude that all members of that species have those markings. This kind of argument, in fact, characterizes much of what natural scientists do.

Like deductive reasoning, inductive reasoning is also subject to several fallacies. Some of the more important kinds of mistakes one can make when using inductive arguments are the following:

Hasty Generalization This is the fallacy of basing a generalization on an inadequate number of instances or observations.

Forgetful Generalization This is the fallacy of drawing a conclusion without taking into account relevant data that would affect the conclusion.

Lazy Induction This is the fallacy of failing to draw as strong a conclusion as the evidence allows.

Of course, it is always possible that an inductive argument may be wrong even though one has tried to avoid all fallacies and mistakes, for inductive aruments only make their conclusions probable. It is therefore always possible that the conclusion of a careful and well-founded inductive argument may still be false.

EXERCISES

Examine the following arguments and determine whether they are deductive or inductive, valid or invalid, and if invalid whether they make one or more of the fallacies identified above.

1. If there were a God, then there would be an afterlife, but since there is no God, there must be no afterlife.

2. None of the students we talked to has taken philosophy, so there must be no philosophy offered at this school.

3. Since we know that Plato was a homosexual, his arguments and claims about morality cannot be correct.

4. Surely anyone who has ever held a newborn baby must realize that the fetus is human and therefore that abortion is murder.

5. " 'I'm all for women having equal rights,' said Bullfight Association president Paco Camino. 'But I repeat, women shouldn't fight bulls because a bullfighter is and should be a man.' "[17]

6. "Mysticism is one of the great forces of the world's history. For religion is nearly the most important thing in the world, and religion never remains for long altogether untouched by mysticism." John McTaggart and Ellis McTaggart.

7. If there is no single correct moral standard, then different societies will have different moral beliefs. But obviously, different societies have different moral beliefs, so there is no single correct moral standard.

8. If violence is never morally justified, then wars are always unjust. But wars are not always unjust, so violence is sometimes morally justified.

9. If morality depends on what my society approves, then "this act is morally right" would mean "my society approves of this act." But if "this act is morally right" means "my society approves of this act," then whatever acts my society approves of must be morally right. If whatever acts my society approves of must be morally right, then I am not justified in saying that my society approves of some immoral actions. But I am justified in saying that my society approves of some immoral actions, so morality does not depend on what my society approves of.

10. McEnroe and Conners are the two best tennis players in the world, so they'd make the best doubles team.

---

17. *San Francisco Chronicle*, 28 March 1972.

CHAPTER 2   Human Nature

*Indeed it is of the essence of man . . . that he can
lose himself in the jungle of his existence, within
himself, and thanks to his sensation of being lost can
react by setting energetically to work to find himself
again.*

JOSÉ ORTEGA Y GASSET

Introduction

The most basic question in philosophy is this: What am I? It is also a question that presses in on us continually in our everyday concerns. Not long ago there was a popular expression that described the effort to define oneself: "Getting your act together." Perhaps you've heard a friend say, "I've got to get my act together," or maybe you've said it. Events often seem more than we can bear. Demands at home, school, and work can build until we fear that we are losing touch with who and what we are. Or tragedy may strike near to us and leave us wondering about the meaning of life. Or we may find ourselves reacting to situations with violence or hatred. At moments like these we ask, "What am I about?" "What am I?" "What does it mean to be human?"

The question "What am I?" is closely related to the question "What is a human being?" or "What is human nature?" For if I view human nature as essentially good, rational, and free, I'm inclined to see myself that way too. If I consider human nature basically evil, irrational, and unfree, I'm likely to see myself that way. So the issue of who and what I am is inseparable from the question of what human nature is.

This chapter examines various views of human nature. We begin our philosophical journey with this issue because it is so basic. In fact, some philosophers have held that *all* philosophy is nothing more than an attempt to answer the question: What is the human being? Questions about what we can know, what reality is, and what we ought to do,

they hold, can only be answered in terms of what we humans are. What we can know depends on the powers of knowledge that humans have; our views about what reality is depend on how we humans experience the universe; and what we ought to do depends on what is proper for the kinds of creatures that we humans are. Almost all philosophical issues, then, are related to the question: What is the nature of the human being? For this reason, we will begin with this question. Moreover, we will continually return to this question throughout the chapters that follow as we explore different views of reality, knowledge, and ethics. All of these philosophical approaches shed light on the basic personal question: What am I?

MAIN POINTS

The main points of this chapter are the following:

1. Human nature refers to what it means to be a member of our species, what makes us different from anything else. The social sciences provide conflicting definitions of human nature, some viewing humans as cruel, selfish and evil and others viewing humans as peace loving, cooperative, and good.

2. Essentialist views of human nature consider all humans to have the same immaterial (not physically observable) property that defines the essence of every human self. Descartes, for example, held that each human self (each "I") has the same essential property: the property of being a thinking thing. Some essentialist views refer to this immaterially defined self as the "soul."

3. One important essentialist view of human nature sees each human self as a rational being. This view (of which Descartes is a later representative), which dates from the ancient Greeks, contends that humans are primarily reasoning creatures. This view

Philosophy is doubt.

MONTAIGNE

> **Of all created creatures man is the most detestable. Of the entire brood he is the only one that possesses malice. Also he is the only creature that has a nasty mind.**
>
> MARK TWAIN

fosters a concept of the self as something existing apart from and above the objective world and as capable of discovering truth, beauty, and goodness. It also fosters a view of freedom as self-awareness.

4. A second important essentialist view, the Judeo-Christian religious view of the human, claims that humans are unique because they are made in the image of God, their Creator, who has endowed them with self-consciousness and an ability to love. This concept fosters a view of self as being purposeful, moral, and possessing free will.

5. Although scientific views agree that all humans have the same nature, several scientific views refuse to define this human nature in terms of an immaterial property. A strict scientific view reduces humans to observable physiochemical processes. Even though the social sciences don't share this highly materialistic view, they can be as reductionist. Twentieth-century psychological behaviorism makes no essential distinction between body and mind or between humans and the rest of nature. Concepts such as purpose, morality, and will are, say the behaviorists, the results of prescientific thinking. Everything is determined, and there is no personal freedom.

6. Existentialist views deny that all humans have the same fixed nature. Instead, existentialists claim that each human creates his or her own nature. Unlike strict scientific views, however, the existentialist view holds that we are not mere products of our environment. Existentialism asserts that although there is no fixed human nature, there is

still an existing self and that the self is a freely choosing, self-creating, active agent.

7. Several Eastern views not only deny that all humans have the same fixed nature, they also deny that the self exists, holding that the concept of a fixed human nature and of a self are imaginary and arise from deep-seated cravings.

THE VARIETY OF VIEWS OF HUMAN NATURE

Anthropology, psychology, sociology, and philosophy provide definitions and descriptions of human nature that frequently differ and conflict; these differences can leave us uncertain about our *precise nature*. Some social scientists, for example, have championed the view that humans are essentially cruel, selfish, and evil—unreasoning creatures molded by social forces. In his *On the Origin of Species by Means of Natural Selection* (1859), Charles Darwin (1809–1882) presented a picture of nature as a battlefield for an unforgiving war of survival in which the fittest survived. The thought and work of Sigmund Freud (1856–1939) also support this view. As an illustration, consider his predatory view of human nature presented in *Civilization and Its Discontents*:

> Men are not gentle, friendly creatures wishing for love, who simply defend themselves if they are attacked, but . . . a powerful measure of desire for aggressiveness has to be reckoned as part of their instinctual endowment. The result is that their neighbor is to them not only a possible helper or sexual object, but also a temptation to them to gratify their aggressiveness . . . to seize his possessions, to humiliate him, to cause him pain, to torture and to kill him. . . .
>
> Anyone who calls to mind the atrocities of the early migrations, of the invasion of the Hun or the so-called Mongols under Genghis Khan and Tamerlane, of the sacks of Jerusalem by the pious crusaders, even indeed the horrors of the last world-war, will have to bow his head humbly before the truth of this view of man.[1]

---

1. Sigmund Freud, *Civilization and Its Discontents* (London: Hogarth, 1930), 85–86.

Sigmund Freud: "Men are not gentle, friendly creatures wishing for love, but [possess] a powerful measure of desire for aggressiveness."

Others have agreed with this view, including Konrad Lorenz,[2] Carl Jung,[3] and Robert Ardrey.[4]

On the other side, a large group of psychologists and social scientists view human nature as being unaggressive, peace loving, cooperative, and good; people are rational creatures with a significant amount of control over their lives and destinies. Thus, some years back, after he had considered all the available evidence, psychologist Gordon Allport drew this conclusion about human nature in his monumental study of prejudice: "Normal men everywhere reject in principle and by preference the path of war and destruction. They like to live

in peace and friendship with their neighbors, they prefer to love and be loved rather than to hate and be hated. . . . While wars rage, yet our desire is for peace and while animosity prevails, the weight of mankind's approval is on the side of affiliation."[5]

More recently, Carl Rogers drew similar conclusions from his exhaustive study of clients in psychotherapy: "One of the most revolutionary concepts to grow out of clinical experience is the growing recognition that the inmost core of man's nature, the deepest layers of his personality, the base of his 'animal nature,' is positive in nature—is basically socialized, forward moving, rational, and realistic."[6]

The studies of some anthropologists support this optimistic view. Margaret Mead, for example, found a primitive New Guinea tribe to be entirely peace loving and convinced that all humans were naturally unaggressive, self-denying, and ultimately concerned with nurturing children.[7] Of course, she found other tribes that were aggressive in the extreme. Most recently, social scientist Ashley Montagu has attacked the aggressionist view in his *The Nature of Human Aggression*.[8]

Today the debate about human nature has re-emerged in the light of the life sciences. The reality of test-tube babies, the creation of androids, and the possibility of understanding and controlling the genetic code all raise fundamental questions about what it means to be a human. Since a view of human nature relates to how we see ourselves and our place in the world, the impact of these developments is most personal.

Given the present proliferation of views, it might be hard to imagine that individuals were once quite certain about what kind of beings they were. There have been times when people felt little doubt about the essential nature of human beings and thus likely felt little if any confusion about their self-concepts. As an example, consider the view expressed in the

2. Konrad Lorenz, *On Aggression* (New York: Harcourt Brace Jovanovich, 1966).
3. Carl Jung, "Relations Between the Ego and the Unconscious," in *Collected Works,* trans. R. F. C. Hull (Princeton, N.J.: Princeton University Press, 1953).
4. Robert Ardrey, *African Genesis* (New York: Delta, 1961). Robert Ardrey, *The Territorial Imperative* (New York: Atheneum, 1966).

5. Gordon Allport, *The Nature of Prejudice* (Boston: Beacon Press, 1954), xiv.
6. Carl Rogers, *On Becoming a Person: A Therapist's View of Psychotherapy* (Boston: Houghton Mifflin, 1961), 90–91.
7. Margaret Mead, *From the South Seas: Studies of Adolescence and Sex in Primitive Societies* (New York: Morrow, 1939).
8. Ashley Montagu, *The Nature of Human Aggression* (New York: Oxford University Press, 1976).

seventeenth century by the first great philosophical figure of the modern age, René Descartes (1596–1650). Notice in this selection from his most famous work, *Meditations on First Philosophy*, that Descartes leaves no question that the essential nature of a human inheres in one property: that it thinks.

But what, then, am I? A thinking thing, it has been said. But what is a thinking thing? It is a thing that doubts, understands (conceives), affirms, denies, wills, refuses, that imagines also, and perceives. Assuredly it is not little, if all these properties belong to my nature. But why should they not belong to it? Am I not that very being who now doubts of almost everything; who, for all that, understands and conceives certain things; who affirms one alone as true, and denies the others; who desires to know more of them, and does not wish to be deceived; who imagines many things, sometimes even despite his will; and is likewise percipient of many, as if through the medium of the senses? Is there nothing of all this as true as that I am, even although I should be always dreaming, and although he who gave me being employed all his ingenuity to deceive me? Is there also any one of these attributes that can be properly distinguished from my thought, or that can be said to be separate from myself? For it is of itself so evident that it is I who doubt, I who understand, and I who desire, that it is here unnecessary to add anything by way of rendering it more clear. And I am as certainly the same being who imagines; for, although it may be (as I before supposed) that nothing I imagine is true, still the power of imagination does not cease really to exist in me and to form part of my thought. In fine, I am the same being who perceives, that is, who apprehends certain objects as by the organs of sense, since, in truth, I see light, hear a noise, and feel heat. But it will be said that these presentations are false, and that I am dreaming. Let it be

so. At all events it is certain that I seem to see light, hear a noise, and feel heat; this cannot be false, and this is what in me is properly called perceiving, which is nothing else than thinking. From this I begin to know what I am with somewhat greater clearness and distinctness than heretofore.[9]

Some students of philosophy term such a view as Descartes's *essentialist*.[10] By this they mean a view that holds that all humans have a self that is of the same nature (the same kind of thing) as all other human selves, and, moreover, the nature of this human self is defined by an immaterial property (a property that is not physically observable). Descartes, for example, asserts in the passage above that he has a self—an "I"— and he implies that all humans have the same kind of self. He then goes on to specify the nature or essence of this self: The human self is a particular kind of thing, namely, a "thinking thing." In later passages he claims that this property—the property of thinking—is not physically observable, it is immaterial. Thus all humans have a self that is of the same fixed nature or essence, and this essence is defined in terms of an immaterial property. As we will see, some essentialist views refer to this immaterially defined self as the "soul."

We will organize our discussion in this chapter by categorizing views of human nature as "essentialist" or "nonessentialist." Specifically, we'll consider two of the most influential essentialist doctrines in Western civilization: the rational and the religious views. Just as important, we'll look at three alternative views that deny, each in a different way, that the human self has an immaterially defined nature. These can be termed the *scientific, existential,* and *Eastern* views. Each has grown in influence and popularity in the Western world in this century.

For coherence and unity, we'll consider these doctrines' perspectives on human goodness, rationality, and freedom. In this way we can understand

Man is but a reed, the weakest thing in nature, but he is a thinking reed.

BLAISE PASCAL

9. René Descartes, *The Method, Meditations and Philosophy of Descartes*, trans. John Veitch (New York: Tudor, 1901), 188–190. Reprinted by permission.
10. See Walter L. Fogg and Peyton E. Richter, *Philosophy Looks to the Future* (Boston: Holbrook Press, 1974), 196–198.

how these doctrines can and do affect us: how we see ourselves, interact with others, and live.

While these views are important philosophical outlooks, they are far from mere abstractions. They have immediate and significant impact on our own identities. Indeed, in the course of our study, we will continually see that the great philosophical ideas always affect us personally.

QUESTIONS

1. In your judgment, are humans basically selfless or selfish? Would humans tend to take advantage of each other or would they tend to help each other if there were no social restraints (such as legal restraints and the police)? In your judgment, do our social institutions tend to corrupt a fundamentally good human nature or do they tame a fundamentally evil human nature? Explain your answers.

2. Make a list of the fundamental properties that you think define a human being. Your list should enable you to distinguish humans from other kinds of creatures.

3. Are there basic emotional and psychological differences between men and women? Are any such differences the result of their nature or does society instill such differences through early training, education, and child-rearing practices?

What then is man? The smallest part of nothing.

EDWARD YOUNG

Essentialist Views of Human Nature

THE RATIONAL VIEW

One highly influential theory of human nature, held by the ancient Greeks, views the human primarily as a thinker capable of reasoning. This view is well illustrated in the thought and writings of a man considered by some to be the greatest philosopher—Plato. Although Plato did not consider reason to be the sole constituent of human nature, he did hold that it was the highest part of human nature. Conversing in *The Republic*, Socrates and Glaucon present Plato's view by discussing the question: What is the self? Notice in the following passage the recurrence of the word *soul*, a common translation of Plato's term *psyche*. Since Plato did not intend all the theological connotations that we frequently place on the word *soul*, it would be wiser to substitute *inner self* for *soul*.

SOCRATES: Isn't it sometimes true that the thirsty person [who wants to drink] also, for some reason, may want not to drink?

GLAUCON: Yes, often.

SOCRATES: What can we say, then, if not that in his soul there is a part that desires drink and another part that restrains him? This latter part is distinct from desire and usually can control desire.

GLAUCON: I agree.

SOCRATES: And isn't it true in such cases that such control originates in reason, while the urge to drink originates in something else?

GLAUCON: So it seems.

SOCRATES: Then we can conclude that there are in us two distinct parts. One is what we call "reason," and the other we call the nonrational "appetites." The latter hungers, thirsts, desires sex, and is subject to other desires.

GLAUCON: Yes, that is the logical conclusion.

SOCRATES: But what about our emotional or spirited element: the part in us that feels anger and indignation? . . . Anger sometimes opposes our appetites as if it is something distinct from them. . . . Yet this emotional part of ourselves is [also] distinct from reason.[11]

To understand Plato's view, consider this illustration. Suppose you are very thirsty. Before you is a glass of poisoned water. One part of yourself, what Plato called Appetite—located in the abdomen—invites you to drink. By Appetite he meant thirst and hunger, as well as sexual and other physical desires. But a second part of yourself, Reason, forbids you to drink. By Reason Plato meant the uniquely human capacity for thinking reflectively and drawing conclusions—the ability to follow relationships from one thought to another in an orderly and correct way. This rational part of the self, said Plato, has its center in the brain. In this illustration a conflict rises between Appetite and Reason. But Plato claimed conflict could rise in another way, as when our emotions flare up.

Suppose someone cuts you off on the highway. You become enraged; you begin to blow your horn and shake your fist at the driver. You are even tempted to tailgate for a few miles just to vent your spleen. But what good would that do? Besides, it would be dangerous. Plato would say that the conflict here is not between Reason and Appetite, but between Reason and what he variously calls anger, indignation, and Spirit. Spirit is like self-assertion or self-interest; according to Plato, it resides in the breast.

Thus, in Plato's view, Reason, Spirit, and Appetite are the three defining parts of the human self

11. Plato, *The Republic*, bk. 4, trans. and ed. Manuel Velasquez (Copyright © 1987 by Manuel Velasquez).

Man is a rational animal who always loses his temper when he is called upon to act in accordance with the dictates of reason.

OSCAR WILDE

---

or "soul." Depending on which part dominates, we get three kinds of people, whose main desires are knowledge, success, and gain. But Plato leaves no doubt about which element should dominate: Reason. True, each element plays a part, but Spirit and Appetite have no knowledge with which to order themselves and must be brought under the control of Reason. Through Reason we can discover the truth about how we ought to live, and when Spirit and Appetite are subordinate to Reason, we will live according to this truth. This truth, according to Plato, involves knowledge of Ideals that exist in another dimension of reality, which only Reason can apprehend. (For a much fuller discussion of Plato's view of human nature, see the showcase on Plato at the end of this chapter.)

For Plato's student Aristotle (384–322 B.C.) reason is also the human's highest power. Although Aristotle's views were quite different from Plato's, Aristotle, too, held that human reason is able to discover the truth about human nature and how we ought to live. But while Plato held that the truth about human nature involved knowledge of another realm of reality, Aristotle held that the truth about human nature required only knowledge of our own world. (For a fuller discussion of Aristotle's views, see the showcase on Aristotle at the end of this chapter.) In any case, Aristotle agreed that our ability to reason is the characteristic that sets the human self apart from all other creatures of nature. Likewise, the Stoics, members of a school of thought founded by Zeno 308 B.C., regarded the ideal person as able to suppress passion and emotion through reason. Only in this way could humans discover knowledge and be in harmony with cosmic reason, or **logos**.

Although the views of Plato, Aristotle, and the Stoics differ in many ways, they all stress reason as the human's most important feature. They generally would have us see the self as a body and a mind. The body is physical and subject to the laws that govern matter. The mind is immaterial; it is conscious and characterized by reasoning. Unlike the body, the mind has no extension; it is not part of the world of matter and thus is not subject to its laws.

We might even view ourselves as fields of conflict between these two aspects of our nature. Furthermore, since we are the only creatures with a rational mind, we would likely experience conflict with nature; we might see ourselves as distinct from the matter of the world and as potential masters of

---

PHILOSOPHY AND LIFE 2.1

Lana, Seeker of Truth

Sara of USC, Washoe and Lucy of Oklahoma, Nim of Columbia, Lana of Yerkes—all names well known to those who study human language. They're all chimpanzees.

Separately and together, these chimps have demonstrated the ability to converse with humans, to combine acquired words in order to describe new objects or situations, to distinguish difference and sameness, to understand "if-then" concepts, to describe their moods, to lie, to choose and use words in syntactical order, to express desires, to anticipate future events, to seek signed communications with others of their species, and, at least in one instance, to extract the truth from a lying human. This last remarkable occurrence is recorded by Duane Rumbaugh of the Yerkes Primate Center in Atlanta in *Language Learning by a Chimpanzee: The Lana Project*.

Human Tim, Rumbaugh recalls, had entered chimp Lana's room with a bowl of monkey chow, which Lana had requested be loaded into her food machine. But instead of honoring her request, Tim loaded the machine with cab-

bage, then told Lana that chow was in the machine. Rather than asking the machine for her chow, as was her custom, Lana asked Tim, "You put chow in machine?" Tim lied that he had.

LANA: Chow in machine?

TIM: (still lying) Yes.

LANA: No chow in machine (which was true).

TIM: What in machine (repeated once)?

LANA: Cabbage in machine (which was true).

TIM: Yes, cabbage in machine.

LANA: You move cabbage out of machine.

TIM: Yes (whereupon he removed the cabbage and put in the monkey chow).

LANA: Please machine give piece of chow (repeatedly until all was obtained).

In 1637 René Descartes wrote: "There are no men so dull and stupid that they cannot put words together in a manner to convey

their thoughts. And this proves not merely that animals have less reason than man, but they have none at all, for we see that very little is needed to talk." Experiences with chimps like Lana and gorillas like Koko at Stanford, who has exhibited a learned vocabulary of 300 words and an IQ of around 85, would strongly call such an easy distinction between human and beast into question.

QUESTIONS

1. If chimps and apes have access to language, can they be expected to reason?

2. Primatologists currently suspect that there's no significant distinction between the ape's capacity for language and our own. Would this in any way affect our concept of human nature? Our responsibilities to animals?

3. Might Descartes counter that it's not so much whether chimps can use language, but whether they mean what they say, know what they mean, and have self-awareness—as indicated by language?

it. In short, our mind enables us to stand apart from our environment, to find meaning and sense in the events around us. We gain freedom through self-awareness, by becoming conscious of the forces that have shaped us and the influences that have made us what we are. Freedom is a function of self-awareness; ignorance is bondage. Through reason we can also discover how we ought to live. The way to truth is through reason, which leads to moral knowledge.

So the implications of the rational view for our own image of what we are are vast. In the rational view we see ourselves as reasoning, free, moral beings. Our reason can and should control our emotions and our appetites. This classical view is one of the most influential theories in Western civilization. We still largely accept some version of it, despite many recent and fascinating experiments with primates (see Philosophy and Life 2.1). Of equal importance, however, is the religious view.

THE RELIGIOUS VIEW

According to the Judeo-Christian tradition, humans are made in the image of God. They are essentially divine beings, because they contain something of the self-consciousness and ability to love that characterize their Creator.

This ability to love is the distinguishing characteristic of the Judeo-Christian view. Whereas the Greeks held that only those capable of attaining theoretical and moral knowledge could realize the purpose of living, the divine view contends that the two purposes of life—loving God and serving God—are open to all regardless of intelligence. As Saint Paul writes, "If I understand all mysteries and all knowledge . . . but have not love, I am nothing" (2 Cor. 13:2). Being given by God, this love is divine, and so allows humans to share in divinity.

At the same time, the divine view is hardly a denial of the rational view. On the contrary, Plato strongly influenced Christian thought through philosophers such as the Roman Plotinus (205?–270?) and the early Christian Saint Augustine (354–430). We observe in their philosophies a similar dualism of mind and body and a belief in the uniqueness of the human mind. But the divine view also holds

Adam and Eve. In his idealized figures of the first man and woman being tempted by Satan, the fifteenth-century Christian artist Albrecht Dürer (1471–1528) attempted to portray humans as rational, loving beings made in the image of God but capable of great good and evil.

that a single personal God created humans in His own image; that is, He endowed His creation with self-consciousness and the ability to love. This ability is what makes human beings unique.

What views of self is this divine view likely to foster? First, since the universe is the expression of an intelligent mind (God), believers may see themselves as part of a universe whose meaning and purpose they personally share through fellowship with God. One's purpose in life, therefore, is found in serving and loving God.

For the Christian, the way to serve and love God is by emulating the life of Jesus of Nazareth. In the life of Jesus we find an expression of the highest virtue: love. We love when we perform selfless acts as Jesus did, developing a keen sense of social mindedness and realizing that people are creatures of God and are thereby worthwhile. Thus, Jesus said, "Love one another as I have loved you."

For the Jew, one serves and loves God primarily through expressions of justice and righteousness. One also develops a sense of honor that is derived from a commitment to the ideals of truth, humility, fidelity, and kindness. This commitment also produces a sharp sense of responsibility to family and community.

The religious view also fosters the concept of a moral self: Each of us is capable of great good, but also of great evil. When we refuse to serve and love God, we commit our greatest evil. This refusal is expressed in various ways: injustice, vanity, pride, and dishonesty. Whenever we commit these offenses to God, we lose touch with ourselves by retreating from our alliance with Him. In contrast to the Greek belief that we must develop our rational powers to perceive the moral order in the universe, the divine view holds that intelligence is no prerequisite for a moral sense. We do good when we make God the center of our lives; we do wrong when we retreat from this commitment. Yes, we are rational, but what makes us unique is our divine likeness.

That we can make moral decisions implies that we are *free* to make them. Moral freedom, then, is another feature of the self fostered by the divine view. As divine creations, we are supposedly free to choose a course that will bring us closer to or take us further from our Creator. As a result, we bear full responsibility for our moral choices and cannot blame external factors for our failure to love and serve God.

As noted, the views of the human as a rational and as a divine being have been the most influential in Western civilization. In them we find the intellectual emphasis of the Greeks and the religious emphasis of the Jews and Christians. From them we inherit the view that an essential human nature is shared by all individuals. In this sense human nature precedes any particular human being; the universal human prototypes (Adam and Eve) precede the individual human experience.

In the twentieth century two other views have arisen, both of which deny a fixed human nature

that is immaterially defined. As a result, their influences on one's self-concept differ from those of the rational and divine views. One view sees human nature in the material terms of science, the other holds that the human self is an existential being with no fixed nature. Apart from the shared belief that there is no immaterial human nature, these two views are quite unlike. In recent years the Western world has experienced a burgeoning interest in still another nonessentialist view, that of Eastern religion and philosophy. This nonessentialist view not only denies that there is a fixed human nature but it also denies that there is such a thing as a human self. In the next section we'll consider these three challenges to essentialist views.

QUESTIONS

1. Some people argue that because nonhuman animals can think, humans are not unique at all. What is the difference between thinking and reasoning? What mental states indicate a thinking process? Would you say that reasoning presumes thinking but that thinking does not presume reasoning?

2. What historical evidence indicates that we are rational animals? What evidence indicates that we are not?

3. How do the rational and religious views foster a concept of the human as being at odds with nature? Does history indicate that Westerners have lived up to this concept? Does contemporary experience confirm or challenge the wisdom of this concept?

4. Do you think that religions have generally not emphasized the God-given capacity to love as much as other concepts, such as sinful human nature, reward and punishment, and adherence to dogma?

Challenges to Essentialist Views

SCIENTIFIC VIEWS

Science's increasing impact has created a marked tendency to view the human "scientifically." However, what this means depends very much on what scientific perspective you take.

For example, one strict scientific view claims that people can be explained by the natural sciences. True, humans are more complex than other entities, but ultimately they can be reduced to observable physical and chemical phenomena. There is no essential human nature in the classical or religious sense. There is no immaterial mind or ability to love that makes us unique. The mind and thinking are simply the electrochemical activities of the brain.

Those who maintain this view, that complex processes like life and thought can be explained wholly in terms of simpler physical and chemical processes, are often called *reductionists* or *mechanists*. Reductionism is the idea that one kind of reality can be completely understood in terms of another kind. Reductionists take something that is commonly thought to be real and reduce it to an appearance of something else. Thus, the strictly scientific view we've sketched holds that science reaches no further than observable facts. Human nature can be attributed or reduced to such facts.

However, not all scientific views reduce human nature to a physiochemical process. Since the nineteenth century, a number of sciences have emerged that deal directly with human beings, society, and the relationships between them. These include anthropology, economics, political science, sociology, and psychology. These sciences have amassed an impressive collection of facts and material that describe people and human relationships. Social scientists do not study the human as a strictly physical object, as do the natural sciences. Nonetheless, many of them have advanced the theory that people can best be understood as an integrated system of observable responses resulting from genetics and environment, that individuals are basically passive objects—things that are acted upon and that really cannot help acting as they do. Even a cursory reading of social science literature discloses a widespread belief that humans are driven beings, moved by outer and inner needs or urges. Historically, debate has centered over what these needs are.

Political philosopher Karl Marx (1818–1883) rejected the primacy of reason and the divine origins of humankind. Material forces, said Marx, produce both human nature and societal tendencies. What changes social structure is the production and reproduction of life; the primary need is survival. How we make a living is therefore of utmost importance, for the basic social characteristic that motivates humans is their productive capacity. We can influence our lives and history somewhat by altering our living conditions, but this capacity does not reside in our brains, wills, ideas, or desires. It exists mainly in the means of production and the class dynamics of society. Marx's view, then, is not strictly scientific but psychosocial.

An example of the psychosocial approach in psychology is the work of Sigmund Freud. Freud held that nothing we do is haphazard or coinci-

---

One of the gross deficiencies of science is that it has not yet defined what sets man apart from other animals.

RENÉ DUBOS

---

dental; everything results from mental causes, most of which we are unaware of. According to Freud, the mind is not only what is conscious or potentially conscious but also what is unconscious. This unconsciousness is a reservoir of human motivation comprised of instincts. In general, most of what we think, believe, and do is the result of unconscious urges, especially those developed in the first five years of life in response to traumatic experiences.

Marx and Freud both evidence some reductionism and do not support the notion of a basic immaterial human nature. Indeed, as the social sciences have continued to grow and as the influence of the natural sciences has increased, the belief in an essential human nature has steadily declined.

As a result, today there is a tendency to view humans in a more strictly scientific way. This view has received impetus from psychological **behaviorism**, a school of psychology that restricts the study of humans to what can be observed—namely human behavior.

Founded by John B. Watson and advanced by B. F. Skinner, behaviorism is not concerned with human motives, goals, purposes, or actions. As Watson put it, a human being is simply "an assembled organic machine ready to run." Behaviorists view all humans as empty organisms having identical neural mechanisms that await conditioning and programming. Concepts such as will, impulse, feelings, and purpose have no place. We are, in effect, mechanisms that are shaped and controlled

PHILOSOPHY AND LIFE 2.2

Is Selflessness Real?

Several contemporary biologists have argued that apparently selfless human behavior is actually a kind of selfish activity that our genes impel us to carry out. Desmond Morris, for example, suggests that when a man rushes into a burning house to save his daughter—or if an old friend or even a complete stranger rescues the child—he is actually saving an organism that contains or, in the case of the friend or stranger, probably contains his own genes. We have developed these protective behaviors so that our genes can survive and be passed on to future generations. Thus, helping behaviors are

SOURCE: Desmond Morris, *Manwatching, A Field Guide to Human Behavior* (New York: Harry N. Abrams, 1977), 153–154.

genetically selfish: They are mechanisms that our genes have evolved to ensure *their own* survival.

The man who risks death to save his small daughter from a fire is in reality saving his own genes in their new body-package. And in saving his genes, his act becomes biologically selfish, rather than altruistic.

But supposing the man leaping into the fire is trying to save, not his daughter, but an old friend? How can this be selfish? The answer here lies in the ancient history of mankind. For more than a million years, man was a simple tribal being. . . . [T]he chances were that every member of your own tribe was a relative of some kind. . . . [In saving your old friend] you would be helping copies of your own genes. . . . Again . . . genetic selfishness.

[Moreover, when man] was tribal, . . . any inborn urge to help his fellow

men would have meant automatically that he was helping gene-sharing relatives. . . . But with the urban explosion, man rapidly found himself in huge communities, surrounded by strangers, and with no time for his genetic constitution to alter to fit the startlingly new circumstances. So his altruism inevitably spread to include [complete strangers].

QUESTIONS

1. What do theories of evolution such as that proposed by Desmond Morris imply about our human nature?

2. Could all human behavior be explained in terms of genes?

3. If Morris is right, does it make sense to say that humans are or are not selfish?

by our environment. By facing this fact, say behaviorists, we will be better able to cope with the human condition by concentrating on the external factors that mold our behavior.

Skinner has argued that a new, improved social order is needed that is based on scientific principles of design and control. The basis of this prescription is his view that humans are not free and self-governing agents who can do what they please; they are the products of conditioning. Such a view has deep implications, as the selection below from his widely read *Beyond Freedom and Dignity* suggests. You'll notice Skinner's frequent use of the word *contingencies*. By this word Skinner means the contingencies of reinforcement, which are relationships among (1) the occasion on which a response occurs, (2) the response itself, and (3) the reinforcing consequences. Here's a simple example. A child just beginning to talk utters many babbling sounds. Eventually the child babbles "mamma." On this occasion the mother beams and embraces the child. The child associates its act of saying "mamma" with the positive attention and the reinforcing consequences that follow it. This is a signal event in the child's life: an experience of the satisfying fact that producing a particular verbal sound brings attention and approval from mother. So the child repeats the word and utters others, eventually becoming a competent communicator.[12]

A contingency of reinforcement, then, is a sequence of events in which some key act is necessary in order to receive a reward. This concept is central to Skinner's psychology and philosophy, which are captured in the following selection:

> A self is a repertoire of behavior appropriate to a given set of contingencies. A substantial part of the conditions to which a person is exposed may play a dominant role, and under other conditions a person may report, "I'm not myself today," or, "I couldn't have done what you said I did, because that's not like me." The identity conferred upon a self arises from the contingencies responsible for the behavior. Two or more repertoires generated

B. F. Skinner: "The hypothesis that man is not free is essential to the application of scientific method to the study of human behavior."

> by different sets of contingencies compose two or more selves. A person possesses one repertoire appropriate to his life with his friends and another appropriate to his life with his family, and a friend may find him a very different person if he sees him with his family or his family if they see him with his friends. The problem of identity arises when situations are intermingled, as when a person finds himself with both his family and his friends at the same time.
>
> Self-knowledge and self-control imply two selves in this sense. The self-knower is almost always a product of social contingencies, but the self that is known may come from other sources. The controlling self (the conscience or superego) is of social origin, but the controlled self is more likely to be the product of genetic susceptibilities to reinforcement (the id, or the Old Adam). The controlling self generally represents the interests of others, the controlled self the interests of the individual.
>
> The picture which emerges from a scientific analysis is not of a body with a person inside, but

12. See Finley Carpenter, *The Skinner Primer* (New York: Free Press, 1974), 6.

of a body which *is* a person in the sense that it displays a complex repertoire of behavior. [13]

According to the behaviorist view, the self is not primarily the mind, and it certainly is not unique. Rather, everyone is essentially the same kind of empty organism that awaits the input of environmental forces. In effect, the individual's behavior is not free, but determined.

Determinism is the theory that everything in the universe is totally ruled by causal laws. Stated in another and perhaps more accurate way, every event has a prior condition, and all events are at least theoretically predictable if all the prior conditions are known. In the strictly scientific world, it is generally assumed that everything is determined by natural laws. The universe and its parts participate in and are governed by an orderly causal sequence. Events follow conditions with predictable regularity. With the growth of the social sciences, the doctrine of determinism has extended beyond the natural and physical sciences to the biological and social sciences. In fact, Skinner makes one of the strongest contemporary cases for determinism.

He views freedom as a myth. All our responses, he argues, are the result of past contingencies of conditioning and reinforcement. He doesn't deny that we *feel* free, but he does maintain that this feeling is itself a conditioned response.

> The use of such concepts as individual freedom, initiative, and responsibility has, therefore, been well reinforced. When we turn to what science has to offer, however, we do not find very comforting support for the traditional Western point of view. The hypothesis that man is not free is essential to the application of scientific method to the study of human behavior. The free inner man who is held responsible for the behavior of the external biological organism is only a prescientific substitute for the kinds of causes which are discovered in the course of a scientific analysis. All these alternatives lie *outside* the individual. [14]

---

13. B. F. Skinner, *Beyond Freedom and Dignity* (New York: Knopf, 1971), 190. Reprinted by permission.
14. B. F. Skinner, *Science and Human Behavior* (New York: Macmillan, 1953), 447–448.

Man is a biodegradable but nonrecyclable animal blessed with opposable thumbs capable of grasping at straws.

BERNARD ROSENBERG

In sum, scientific views like Skinner's generally tend to be reductionist and to deny any essential immaterial human nature. They reject personal freedom and any inherent rational force in the human makeup and view people as innately neither good nor evil but neutral, highly educable creatures that can be markedly influenced or even controlled by environmental conditions.

Another twentieth-century view that denies any essential immaterial human nature insists that humans are ultimately free of their genetic and environmental influences and actively control what and who they will be. This is the existential view.

THE EXISTENTIAL VIEW

The theory that humans actively determine their nature appears full-blown in our century in a philosophy called **existentialism**. Existentialists focus on individual existence and its problems. They deny any essential human nature in the traditional rational or religious sense, insisting that individuals create their own characters through free, responsible choices and actions. Humans are active participants in the world, not determined mechanisms. Although they recognize outside influences, existentialists insist that each self determines its own human nature.

While existentialism continues to be popular among religious thinkers, we'll confine our remarks to atheistic existentialism, since its view provides a unique concept of human nature and self. The chief exponent of atheistic existentialism is Jean-Paul Sartre (1905–1980), who sees humans as "condemned to be free." We are free because we can rely neither on a God (who doesn't exist) nor on society to justify our actions or to tell us what we essentially are. We are condemned because without absolute guidelines we must suffer the agony of our own decision making and the anguish of its consequences.

Although he believes that there are no true universal statements about what humans ought to be, Sartre does make at least one general statement about the human condition: We are free. This freedom consists chiefly of our ability to envisage additional possibilities to our state, to conceive of what is not the case, to suspend judgment, and to alter our condition. We should, therefore, make individual choices, fully aware that we are doing so. We must take full responsibility not only for our actions but also for our beliefs, feelings, and attitudes. To illustrate, many people believe that we have little or no control over our emotions. If we're depressed, we're depressed, and there's little we can do about it. Sartre argues that if we're depressed, we've chosen to be. Emotions, he says, are not moods that come over us but ways in which we freely choose to perceive the world, to participate in it. It is the consciousness of this freedom and its accompanying responsibilities that cause our anguish. The most anguishing thought of all is that we are responsible for ourselves. Sometimes we escape this anguish by pretending we are not free, as when we pretend that our genes or our environment is the cause of what we are, or that we are spectators rather than participants, passive rather than active. When we so pretend, says Sartre, we act in "bad faith."

Self-deception or bad faith is the attempt to avoid anguish by pretending to ourselves that we are not free. There are various ways we do this: by trying to convince ourselves that our nature is determined by outside influences, forces beyond our control, unconscious mental states, or by anything but ourselves. One graphic example of self-deception provided by Sartre involves a young woman sitting with a man who, she knows, is bent on seduction. He takes her hand. In order to avoid the painful necessity of making a decision to accept or reject the man, the woman pretends not to notice, leaving her hand in his. The bad faith here lies in the woman's pretending to be a passive object, a being-in-itself, rather than what she really is: con-

scious and, therefore, a free being. Here's Sartre's account of the incident, as he develops it in *Being and Nothingness*.

Take the example of a woman who has consented to go out with a particular man for the first time. She knows very well the intentions which the man who is speaking to her cherishes regarding her. She knows also that it will be necessary sooner or later for her to make a decision. But she does not want to realize the urgency; she concerns herself only with what is respectful and discreet in the attitude of her companion. She does not apprehend this conduct as an attempt to achieve what we call "the first approach"; that is, she does not want to see possibilities of temporal development which his conduct presents. She restricts this behavior to what is in the present; she does not wish to read in the phrases which he addresses to her anything other than their explicit meaning. If he says to her, "I find you so attractive!" she disarms this phrase of its sexual background; she attaches to the conversation and to the behavior of the speaker, the immediate meanings, which she imagines as objective qualities. The man who is speaking to her appears to her sincere and respectful as the table is round or square, as the wall coloring is blue or gray. The qualities thus attached to the person she is listening to are in this way fixed in a permanence like that of things, which is no other than the projection of the strict present of the qualities into the temporal flux.

Man will do nothing unless he has first understood that he must count on no one but himself; that he is alone, abandoned on earth in the midst of his infinite responsibilities; without help, with no other aim than the one he sets himself, with no other destiny than the one he forges for himself on this earth.

JEAN-PAUL SARTRE

This is because she does not quite know what she wants. She is profoundly aware of the desire which she inspires, but the desire cruel and naked would humiliate and horrify her. Yet she would find no charm in a respect which would be only respect. In order to satisfy her, there must be a feeling which is addressed wholly to her *personality*—i.e., to her full freedom—and which would be a recognition of her freedom. But at the same time this feeling must be wholly desire; that is, it must address itself to her body as object. This time then she refuses to apprehend the desire for what it is; she does not even give it a name; she recognizes it only to the extent that it transcends itself toward admiration, esteem, respect and that it is wholly absorbed in the more refined forms which it prc duces, to the extent of no longer figuring anymore as a sort of warmth and density. But then suppose he takes her hand. This act of her companion risks changing the situation by calling for an immediate decision. To leave the hand there is to consent in herself to flirt, to engage herself. To withdraw it is to break the troubled and unstable harmony which gives the hour its charm. The aim is to postpone the moment of decision as long as possible. We know what happens next; the young woman leaves her hand there, but she *does not notice* that she is leaving it. She does not notice because it happens by chance that she is at this moment all intellect. She draws her companion up to the most lofty regions of sentimental speculation; she speaks of Life, of her life, she shows herself in her essential aspect—a personality, a consciousness. And during this time the divorce of the body from the soul is accomplished; the hand rests inert between the warm hands of her companion—neither consenting nor resisting—a thing.

We shall say that this woman is in bad faith, but we see immediately that she uses various procedures in order to maintain herself in this bad faith. She has disarmed the actions of her companion by reducing them to being only what they are.[15]

Existentialism obviously emphasizes the individual. The self in this view is not necessarily rational, divine, or mechanical. It is neither a crea-

ture of God nor a kind of empty organism. It is instead a project that possesses a subjective life; it is the sum total, not of everything that happens to it, but of everything it ever does. In the end, we are our choices; to be human means to be free.

In his *Existentialism and Humanism*, Sartre vigorously expresses the existential view of human nature. Notice in the selection that follows the primacy that Sartre gives to existence. Existence is prior to essence, he believes; humans exist first, then they make something of themselves. In this fact lies the human condition.

> Atheistic existentialism, of which I am a representative, declares . . . that if God does not exist there is at least one being whose existence comes before its essence, a being which exists before it can be defined by any conception of it. That being is man. . . . What do we mean by saying that existence precedes essence? We mean that man first of all exists, encounters himself, surges up in the world—and defines himself afterwards. If man as the existentialist sees him as not definable, it is because to begin with he is nothing. He will not be anything until later, and then he will be what he makes of himself. Thus, there is no human nature, because there is no God to have a conception of it. Man simply is. Not that he is simply what he conceives himself to be, but he is what he wills.[16]

Clearly, existentialism gives the inner life and experience a new emphasis. Whereas those seeing the self as a response to stimuli ignore the inner world of feelings, sensations, moods, and anxieties, existentialists focus on it. Indeed, this inner life is precisely what the self experiences, and thus it is the self. In it are found our feelings of despair, fear, guilt, and isolation, as well as our uncertainties, especially about death. There we confront the meaninglessness that is at the core of existence and thus discover a truth that enables us to live fully conscious of what being human means.

Despite existentialism's assertion of self and its wide contemporary influence, many argue that the self is really an illusion and that attachment to this

---

15. Jean-Paul Sartre, *Being and Nothingness*, trans. Hazel E. Barnes (New York: Philosophical Library, 1956), 55–56. Copyright © 1956 by Philosophical Library, Inc. Reprinted by permission of Philosophical Library, Inc.

---

16. Jean-Paul Sartre, *Existentialism and Humanism*, trans. Philip Mairet (London: Methuen, 1949), 85.

illusion causes existential sorrow, anguish, and ultimate absurdity. Psychological behaviorists would probably so argue. But this reaction has become increasingly popular in the West with the spread of Eastern philosophies and religions that deny the existence of the self.

EASTERN VIEWS

When we speak of Eastern philosophy, we refer to those systems of thought, belief, and action espoused by many peoples in the Near and Far East. Because Eastern thought offers many views of human nature, it is impossible to mention them all. Buddhism's view is particularly noteworthy for several reasons. First, it represents a large number of Eastern thinkers. Second, many Westerners have been converted to Buddhism. Third, it contrasts sharply with most Western views. At the same time, we must acknowledge the rich diversity of Buddhist sects: Theravada, Mahayana, Bodhisattva and Pure Land, and Zen. The treatment of Buddhism and Eastern thought in this book will likely prove too cursory for most Westerners, but our intention is not to exhaust the subject but to provide a vital transcultural perspective as well as evidence of the global view of philosophy.

Buddha, the founder of Buddhism, was the son of a chief of a hill tribe in India. At the age of twenty-nine, Buddha gave up his family life for the life of an ascetic and eventually became the leader of a small group of followers who practiced a "middle way" between an extreme asceticism and an indulgent worldly life. He is said to have gained enlightenment under a pipal tree at Bihar and to have devoted his life to teaching a little group of followers. He died at the age of eighty in the fifth century B.C.

About a century after his death, Buddha's growing group of followers split into two groups: a group of dissenters named the "Mahasanghikas" and a group, the "Theravada," who claimed to remain true to the original teachings of Buddha's first followers. By the end of the third century B.C., a body of doctrines had emerged that formed the essentials of this Theravada. It is uncertain how many of the legends and sermons attributed to Buddha by the

Buddha: "It is simply the mind clouded over by impure desires and impervious to wisdom, that obstinately persists in thinking of 'me' and 'mine'."

Theravada are really his and how many are the later work of his followers. But for our purposes the doctrines of the Theravada can be accepted as the core doctrines of Buddhism.

Basic to the doctrines of Buddhism are the "Four Noble Truths": First, from birth to death all life inevitably involves suffering (although it may be temporarily avoided with youth, health, and riches) in every aspect of our lives that is tied to our individuality. Second, we suffer because we desire or crave things: pleasure, life, power. Our desires keep us returning to this transient world through successive "rebirths." The more we try to satisfy our cravings, the worse they become, making us suffer even more. Third, release from suffering can only be gained by putting an end to our craving. Finally, craving can only be ended by following the Noble Eightfold Path.

> And this is the Noble Truth of Sorrow. Birth is sorrow, age is sorrow, disease is sorrow, death is sorrow; contact with the unpleasant is sorrow, separation from the pleasant is sorrow, every wish unfulfilled is sorrow—in short, all the five components of individuality are sorrow.
>
> And this is the Noble Truth of the Arising of Sorrow. It arises from craving, which leads to rebirth, which brings delight and passion, and seeks pleasure now here, now there—the craving for sensual pleasure, the craving for continued life, the craving for power.
>
> And this is the Noble Truth of the Stopping of Sorrow. It is the complete stopping of that craving, so that no passion remains, leaving it, being emancipated from it, being released from it, giving no place to it.
>
> And this is the Noble Truth of the Way which leads to the Stopping of Sorrow. It is the Noble Eightfold Path—[having] Right Views, Right Resolve, Right Speech, Right Conduct, Right Livelihood, Right Effort, Right Mindfulness, and Right Concentration.[17]

Also central to Buddhist thought is the belief that all things are composite and transient. All things are aggregates composed of elements that inevitably change over time. There is, therefore, nothing that abides permanently as an individual. Everything, including the gods and all living things, is characterized by constant movement and change as well as by sorrow.

The self, like everything else, is also in a state of constant flux, and it too is nothing more than a composite of constantly changing elements: our form and matter, our sensations, our perceptions, our psychic dispositions, and our conscious thought. But these are never the same from moment to moment. What we call the self, then, either considered as the body or considered as the mind, is utterly transient. It is a new aggregate from one moment to the next that cannot even control its own dissolving changes. The self, then, as a permanently abiding individual entity does not exist. According to the Buddha, the idea of self is an illusory belief that produces harmful thoughts of "me," "mine," desire, vanity, egoism, and ill will.

> If the body were an ego-personality, it could do this and that as it would determine. [But] a king . . . becomes ill despite his intent and desire, he comes to old age unwillingly, and his fortune and his wishes often have little to do with each other.
>
> If the mind were an ego-personality it could do this and that as it would determine, but the mind often flies from what it knows is right and chases after evil unwillingly.
>
> If a man believes that such an impermanent thing [as the body], so changeable and replete with suffering, is the ego-personality, it is a serious mistake. The human mind is also impermanent and suffering; it has nothing that can be called an ego-personality.
>
> Therefore, both body and mind . . . are far apart from both the conceptions of "me" and "mine." It is simply the mind clouded over by impure desires and impervious to wisdom, that obstinately persists in thinking of "me" and "mine."[18]

Unless one grasps that everything including the self is transient, one cannot find salvation. If one resists the pervasive flux of phenomena and desires permanence where none exists, the inevitable result is the sorrow that we indicated above. Only by gradually abandoning all sense of individuality through the Noble Eightfold Path and losing oneself completely in an ineffable state called "Nirvana" (which means "blowing out") can one hope to find salvation. Buddha himself is said to have found this state sitting beneath the pipal tree at Bihar.

It is clear that the Buddhist conception of the self conflicts with the traditional Western idea that humans are selves with a fixed nature. It conflicts even with the existentialist view that holds that humans are enduring selves even though they have

---

17. William Theodore de Bary, *Sources of Indian Tradition*, vol. 1, from *Samyutta Nikaya* (New York: Columbia University Press, 1958), 99.

18. *The Teaching of Buddha*, rev. ed. (Tokyo: Bukkyo Deudo Kyokai, 1976).

The supreme ideal of Greece is to save the ego from anarchy and chaos. The supreme ideal of the Orient is to dissolve the ego into the infinite and to become one with it.

KIMON FRIAR

no determined nature. Not only is there no fixed nature in the Buddhist conception but also, because everything is in flux, there is not even an enduring self.

This Buddhist conception of the self also implies another important contrast with Western views. The Western conceptions of the self we reviewed above all assume that the self is an enduring entity with its own individuality and that we should protect the interests of this individuality in its struggle against the world. Existentialism, with its claim that each person must "make" himself, is one example of this assumption in action, as is the very Western idea of the primacy of the individual and the Western idea of legitimate self-interest and the importance of striving for personal success and fulfillment. The Buddhist conception, however, advocates giving up this attempt to bolster our own individuality: We should reject the assumption that our individuality is a reality that we should strive to support and enhance. On the contrary, Buddhism suggests that salvation is achievable only by giving up the craving for self-identity. We should give up the idea of striving for personal success and self-fulfillment altogether!

QUESTIONS

1. Psychological behaviorists claim that the human can be measured experimentally. Are there any human characteristics that contradict this claim? What human qualities cannot be measured?

2. Behaviorists also argue that techniques and engineering practices can be used to shape behavior so that people will function harmoniously for everyone's benefit. What questions would you raise about such a proposal?

3. Sartre's existentialism leaves us with our moral rules or behavioral guidelines, yet it ultimately holds us responsible for all our choices. Do you find such a view appealing? Contradictory? Unsettling? Liberating?

4. To what degree and in what ways, if any, do you experience your life as free, as Sartre describes freedom?

5. Contrast the Buddhist approach to human nature with the rational, religious (Judeo-Christian), scientific, and existentialist views.

6. Does the view of no self have anything to offer the Western world? In what areas?

Observations and Conclusions

SOME OBSERVATIONS

In examining any one view, there is a tendency to see it as excluding others. But these theories rarely do that. The rational, religious, and existential views, for example, all agree on the human's essential freedom. The scientific and Buddhist views agree that the self does not exist in the way that traditional Western thought would have it.

You yourself might hold a traditional view that the human is a combination of mind and body. You might consider the mind immaterial and immortal, the body material and mortal. You would probably view yourself, then, from the rational and scientific perspectives. So these traditions do overlap, and combined views are not only common but seemingly necessary to account for the full range of human experience. Differences in views are more often differences of emphasis than of content.

Thinkers obviously disagree about which aspect of the human experience deserves the most emphasis. Differences in emphases have produced these different positions about human nature. Each offers a different aspect of what it means to be human, and none completely describes that phenomenon. Nevertheless, in recent decades, the scientific and existential perspectives have grown increasingly dominant.

In the last analysis, no one theory can fully describe and explain human nature. The most reasonable position seems to be one that does not distort and ignore aspects of human experience beyond its own focus and that can accommodate additional data about the human condition. The most plausible view of human nature is one that is sufficiently rich in categories and concepts to allow theorists to formulate a variety of theories. This position accords significance to all phenomena, particularly subjectivity.

Although we cannot say which view fulfills these requirements, the acceptance or rejection of a particular view influences our lives and how we interpret issues. The issue of freedom, to which we have already referred, is a good example. Whether we consider ourselves free, partially free, or not free at all depends to a large extent on what our view of human nature is. This attitude toward freedom in turn influences how we live. Thus, our view of human nature affects our lives.

Also, our experiences affect our views of human nature because of the intimacy between our experiences and our self-concepts. Obviously, we can sail along smoothly in life buoyed up by unexamined assumptions, such as that we are free. Then something happens; we run aground. A crisis forces us to evaluate what we take for granted, and we wonder whether we are really free. Our inquiry, if pursued with philosophical zest, leads to far-reaching questions about what kind of being we are. As a result, we may even modify our particular view. To illustrate the interplay between these theoretical constructs and our personal lives and identities, consider the case of Doris.

Having grown up in a religious environment, Doris has assumed that everyone possesses free will, that is, the God-given capacity to make voluntary decisions, to choose freely from alternatives. Taking this for granted, she has lived with the comfortable belief that she is the responsible ruler of her life.

Then, Doris begins college and starts thinking about what she will do with her life. Had she lived a generation or two ago, she would not even have posed the question—she would have become a wife and mother without too much thought. But times have changed and circumstances are different. "It's just not that simple anymore," she tells her tradition-minded parents, who still are not convinced that college is the proper place for their daughter.

"Why not take something practical, like business or nursing?" they ask. A woman can always find work as a secretary or nurse, they tell her, or perhaps as an elementary school teacher.

Doris is majoring in elementary school education, but she is dissatisfied. She finds the curriculum unchallenging and the prospect of life in a classroom unattractive. Lately she has begun to think about engineering. She has always been extremely good at math and science, and she enjoys working with machinery. However, studying engineering hardly seems practical: It is expensive and grueling. Even if she does succeed, she still worries about the future for a female engineer. Prospects are improving, but they are still uncertain. And what about the pressure along the way? Already many of her friends are married; others are set on traditional female professions.

It's very important for Doris to make her own choice. Most of all she wants to feel that she alone is deciding, not her parents, friends, or society. She is convinced that making the decision is tough enough without feeling that someone else is actually making it. Doris's problem cuts to the very assumption on which she has based her life, which springs from the religious view of human nature.

Feeling the pinch of her dilemma, Doris seeks advice from a friend, Jane. Jane does not believe in the religious concept of free will. She considers herself primarily a thinker who, through commitment to thought and reason, tries to solve her problems as a rational being. Let us see what advice Jane gives to Doris, using a form we have already seen: the form of a philosophical dialogue.

DORIS: I'm going to be a teacher.

JANE: Are you sure that's what you want to do?

DORIS: No, but I'm tired of weighing the pros and cons. It's decided, and that's the end of it.

JANE: *It's* decided? A second ago you said *you* decided.

DORIS: I mean me. *I* have decided.

JANE: Okay, why do you want to be a teacher?

DORIS: Look, Jane, I really don't want to go through all this again.

> **To be a philosopher is not merely to have subtle thoughts, nor even to found a school, but so to love wisdom as to live according to its dictates, a life of simplicity, independence, magnanimity, and trust.**
>
> HENRY DAVID THOREAU

JANE: I think you should.

DORIS: But what good will it do?

JANE: It might stop you from doing something you'll regret.

DORIS: Whatever I do I'm going to regret.

JANE: Okay, so you have unpleasant alternatives. By examining them, at least you'll know why you made the decision.

DORIS: Is that so important—to know *why*?

JANE: Sure it is. If you don't know why you're choosing something, how do you know *you* are choosing it? Remember when you bought your car?

DORIS: Yes.

JANE: Did you know why you bought it?

DORIS: Of course. I needed transportation.

JANE: And you wanted something small, cheap, and dependable.

DORIS: Right.

JANE: You knew why you were buying the car. And if someone asked, you could have told them.

DORIS: So?

JANE: So isn't this choice as important as buying a car?

DORIS: Of course it is.

JANE: Then why do you want to be a teacher?

DORIS: For a lot of reasons. For one, my parents think it's a good idea.

JANE: Sure they do, but for *their* reasons.

DORIS: What do you mean?

JANE: Well, *they're* not becoming a teacher—*you* are. *They're* not the ones who must spend the rest of their professional lives in a classroom—*you* are.

DORIS: You make them sound terrible.

JANE: I don't mean to. I'm just trying to help you see sides of the question that you don't seem to be aware of.

DORIS: Do you really believe I'm not being honest with myself about this?

JANE: I don't know. But if *you* are really going to choose, you should be aware of *why* you're choosing. Otherwise you're having the choice made for you. And that's what's really going to hurt over the long haul—much more than if you make the so-called right choice.

DORIS: You know, Jane, you've got me thinking.

JANE: In what way?

DORIS: Well, I'm just wondering how many things that I'm not even aware of are influencing this choice.

JANE: Right. Now you're taking charge. You've taken the first step toward choosing for yourself.

DORIS: I don't know if that's so good. After all, I can never be aware of everything.

JANE: Of course not. But you can become aware of the important influences.

Because Jane views the human as a reasoning being, she encourages Doris to think and reflect, to develop insightful awareness. Just as important, she offers an alternative to Doris's own view of personal freedom and perhaps to her view of human nature. Jane sees herself as someone who is free only to the degree that she is aware of the factors affecting her choices. The less aware, the less free; the more aware, the more free. In Jane's view, then, freedom is always contingent on self-awareness. If she's right, then individually we carry the heavy burden of developing insights into the factors that influence our lives. Otherwise we remain imprisoned by them.

So Jane seems to be saying that Doris must somehow *learn* to be free. But can Doris do this? After all, many factors affect her decision. Perhaps these factors are also affecting how well she can learn and how much awareness she can have. How much self-insight can she actually develop? Suppose that Doris was never encouraged to be self-aware, that self-awareness was not a value in her upbringing. Can she suddenly develop it? Such a question asks exactly what kind of being Doris is and, by extension, any of us is. Are we essentially free to alter the conditions that have affected us? Are we to become self-aware just for the sake of self-awareness? We still must decide what to do.

Taking Jane's advice to think, introspect, and become self-aware, Doris examines the factors bearing on her choice. She discovers a whole list of influences: parents, home life, education, friends, and so forth.

For example, she recalls how as a little girl she was given dolls and dollhouses to play with, encouraged to think of marriage and family, and sheltered from considering professions such as medicine, engineering, or law. In fact, she can't think of a single instance when someone asked her, "What are you going to be when you grow up?" although she recalls that they often asked that of her brother. What she would be seemed a foregone conclusion: a wife and mother.

Such considerations set her to thinking about just how free any person is in view of all the environmental and hereditary influences affecting us. She wonders if we can behave any differently from the way in which we are programmed. Thinking along this line, Doris suspects that she cannot help acting as she will, for her past is determining her future.

Discontent with the idea that she is not at all free, Doris confides in another friend, Fred. Fred sees humans existentially, as active participants in the world around them. They are by nature free to choose and direct their lives. Although this sounds like the concept of free will, Fred's sense of freedom poses no God from whom freedom springs. Rather, freedom is an integral part of being human.

Doris cannot quite believe that she is free in the way that Fred believes. She asks him whether, if she introspects enough, she will discover the right

Girl Before a Mirror, Pablo Picasso. 1932. "In the last analysis, the question 'What is a human?' is one of the most important that we can ask. . . . Life's meaning and purpose, what we ought to do, what we can hope to accomplish—all are profoundly affected by what we consider human nature."

thing to do. Fred points out that it isn't a question of the right thing to do: If there were a right decision to be made, we would be under an obligation to discover it. But obligations are the opposite of freedom; they restrict and limit rather than liberate. Her job, Fred tells Doris, is not to discover the

so-called right decision but to *make* it; in making it, she will make herself. Doris doesn't understand.

"Right now," says Fred, "you're like an empty canvas that sits waiting for you, the artist, to put color and form on it for meaning. It sits awaiting its real identity."

"But the paints, what about the paints? Aren't they just everything that's ever happened to me? Aren't they what give me meaning?"

"No. It's the painter who does that. What paints are used are left to the artist—to you in this case. And if no painting ever appears on the canvas, that too is up to the artist, up to you."

Fred sees Doris as an agent engaged in her own self-definition. He admits that the past influences the present and the present the future. But humans are not mechanical; they are not objects. They are subjects: They are acted upon, but they act as well. It is this dimension, the "I" as agent, that provides us with freedom. Simply by being, we are free. This freedom allows us to determine what we will be, to fashion meaning out of experience. There are no mechanical laws that bind us to something not of our own making. We exist, and how we exist is

---

PHILOSOPHY AND LIFE 2.3

Koestler and James

Does it really matter which view of human nature you believe? Sure, they carry different implications. Some hold we're free, others that we're not; some say that we have a divine destiny, others that we don't. But in the last analysis, such claims raise unanswerable philosophical questions. So, what difference does it make what view you hold?

Author and outspoken opponent of behaviorism Arthur Koestler (1905–1983) thinks it does make a difference. In his autobiography, *Arrow in the Blue*, Koestler recalls how his own belief in free will significantly affected his decision to abandon his studies in engineering for the uncertain career of an author. Writes Koestler:

I had no plans except "to lead my own life." In order to do that I had to "get off the track." This metaphorical track I visualized very precisely as an

endless stretch of steel rails on rotting *sleepers. You were born onto a certain track, as a train is put on its run according to the timetable; and once on the track, you no longer had free will. Your life was determined . . . by outside forces; the rail of steel, stations, shunting points. If you accepted that condition, running on rails became a habit which you could no longer break. The point was to jump off the track before the habit was formed, before you became encased in a rattling prison. To change the metaphor: reason and routine kept people in a straitjacket which made their living flesh rot beneath it.*

For Koestler, then, the belief in his own personal freedom led him to the conviction that he could "jump off the track" chosen for him by others, that he could lead his own life.

Koestler's account is reminiscent of the crisis that the American philosopher and psychologist William James (1842–1910) once faced. James had suffered throughout his life from a variety of emotional disorders that left him feeling profoundly alienated. Then, like Koes-

tler, James seemingly took a giant step toward resolving his problems when he was able to satisfy himself that he was free. James captures the moment in a letter to his father: "I think that yesterday was a crisis in my life. I finished the first part of Renouvier's second 'Essais' and see no reason why his definition of Free Will—'the sustaining of a thought because I choose to when I might have other thoughts'—need be the definition of an illusion. At any rate, I will assume for the present—until next year—that it is no illusion. My first act of free will shall be to believe in free will."

QUESTIONS

1. Illustrate how the belief in one or more of the views of human nature is concretely expressed in your life.

2. Have you ever felt or found yourself "blocked" because of how you saw yourself or what you believed you were or were capable of being?

SOURCES: Arthur Koestler, *Arrow in the Blue* (New York: Macmillan, 1952), 32. Henry James, ed., *The Letters of William James* (Boston: Atlantic Monthly Press, 1920), 148.

up to each of us. The whole meaning of our lives lies in creating our own being. Whatever Doris does with her life, *she* is responsible—not any external forces.

What has occurred here? A question of intense personal concern has evoked philosophical ponderings about human nature. In the last analysis, the question "What is a human?" is one of the most important that we can ask, for much hinges on its answer. Life's meaning and purpose, what we ought to do, what we can hope to accomplish—all are profoundly affected by what we consider human nature (see Philosophy and Life 2.3). If we truly are children of God, then God's purpose for our existence defines us, informs us what to do. But if we are ultimately the product of society, then our happiness and welfare are bound up with social conditions, and presumably we should work to improve them. If we are fundamentally free and can't avoid individual choice, then seemingly the only sensible approach toward life is to accept our lot and make our choices with full awareness of what we're doing. Thus, while at times seeming to float in the ether of abstraction, these views of human nature vitally affect our lives. What's more, we can use the stuff of our experience to gain a firmer grasp of these views and their influences.

QUESTIONS

1. Political polls and projections are often said to influence the outcome of elections. What control, if any, does a forecast exercise over an event (for example, the astrological prophecies of Jeane Dixon)? If the existence of God is assumed, and if He already knows how things are going to turn out, can any of us alter that result? If we cannot alter something, are we free?

2. In *Crito*, Plato shows Socrates refusing to escape from jail, even though he has been imprisoned unjustly, because such an action would violate the principles of a life dedicated to upholding the law. As a result, Socrates drinks the hemlock and dies. Was he free to choose differently? Was he a victim of his past?

3. Jane claims, "By examining [the alternatives],

at least you'll know why you made the decision. . . . If you don't know why you're choosing something, how do you know *you* are choosing it?" Relative to the problem of self, how important would you say it is to know *why* you do something? In what sense are you less yourself by not knowing? Can you think of an instance in which it may be better not to know why you're doing something? Would it be better in the long term as well as the short?

4. Point to examples in your own life that show you doing things for other people's reasons. Perhaps your choice to be in school or to study a particular subject would be a good place to begin. How susceptible to peer pressure do you think you are? Do you detect the pressure affecting the views you hold? In what area of life do you feel you can truly express yourself?

5. Doris suggests that the very faculty of self-awareness may be a victim of the same influences that Jane claims are affecting Doris's decision. Can you illustrate Doris's suggestion?

6. Are we strictly mechanical, as Doris suspects? Can you think of qualities we possess that computers do not? Are they qualities computers *can never* possess, or qualities they do not possess now but could in the future?

7. Fatalism is the belief that events are fixed, that nothing we can do will alter them—what will be, will be. Is Doris a fatalist? Are you? Do scientific views necessitate fatalism? Is fatalism consistent with the doctrine of free will? Is it consistent with the view of the human as thinker? As an existential being?

8. If Fred believed that the right decision lay buried in us like a treasure to be discovered, he could not believe that we were truly free to make our own decisions. Why?

9. The difference between "making" yourself and "finding" yourself is partly chronological. Does making yourself precede or follow your coming into existence? Does finding yourself suggest that something precedes your existence? Relate your explanations to each of the five views.

10. Can you think of any instance in which you

would have no freedom at all? If we are essentially free, how does this freedom lead to uncertainty?

CHAPTER SUMMARY AND CONCLUSIONS

We opened the chapter by raising the issue of human nature as it applies to personal identity: Who and what am I? How we see ourselves has been influenced by at least five theories of human nature: the rational view, the religious view, the scientific view, the existential view, and the Eastern view. Although it is impossible to say which theory is most accurate, we frequently interpret aspects of our lives, such as personal freedom, through these theories. They do not exist in isolation, but often melt into one another. We seldom find ourselves acting exclusively according to one school of thought; more often we must act under the influences of several. They should provoke some personal reflections about what we believe and why.

But freedom, rationality, and goodness are only three issues describing who and what we are. There are others: what we know, what we consider to be ultimately real, what we cherish as objects of ultimate loyalty, what we hold to be morally right, what we regard as beautiful, and so on. All are fundamental expressions of how we see ourselves. As is the case with the issue of personal freedom, our beliefs in these areas betray many influences. We will explore these influences in further chapters, for these subjects are among those that constitute the study of philosophy.

Over two thousand years ago Socrates claimed that "the unexamined life is not worth living." When humans begin to examine life, they begin to philosophize. Philosophers are persons who perceive to some degree how the many experiences and insights of their existence form a pattern of meaning. Philosophy, as we saw in Chapter 1, is a journey undertaken by those who are deeply concerned with who and what they are and what everything means. We have taken the first steps on that journey by reflecting on the most basic question of philosophy: What is human nature? Although we will now leave our direct reflections on this question, the question will stay with us indirectly

throughout the rest of this book. For, as we suggested, all of philosophy can be considered an attempt to answer the question: What am I? Consequently, in each of the chapters that follow, we will continually return to this issue to see what additional light can be shed on it.

Before we close we should note that this philosophical concern with knowing what I am is not new. In *The Apology*, from which we quoted in the first chapter, we read that Socrates' own philosophical journey began with an oracle from the god at Delphi in Greece. History tells us that at the entrance to the temple at Delphi was the inscription, "Know thyself!" Socrates' philosophical journey is thus often interpreted as a quest for self-knowledge. Our own philosophical journey can likewise be seen as a journey toward self-knowledge.

The familiar lament, "I don't know who I am," once thought to belong only to the crisis of adolescence, to be resolved by the adult stage, is heard not only from teenagers but from adults of all ages. Education, status, "success," material security or lack of it, seem to have little bearing upon the unhappiness and loneliness in the life of those who have found no focus of identity or pattern of meaning in their existence.

AARON UNGERSMA

Every man has a wild beast within him.

FREDERICK THE GREAT

Plato and Aristotle

The preceding discussion was intended to provide an array of overviews of human nature, and thus has certain pitfalls. One might conclude from the discussion that philosophy is merely a catalogue of diverse opinions; that engaging an issue such as human nature, philosophy ultimately does little more than serve up a smorgasbord of opinions. Moreover, focusing on a single issue as we have just done inevitably dislodges the portion from the mosaic of interrelated pieces which, taken together, make up a full-scale philosophy. In fact, one cannot fully appreciate a position on an issue without understanding how it fits in with an entire outlook. In order to avoid these pitfalls and give the preceding material a sharper focus, we will now take a more in-depth look at two philosophers: Plato and Aristotle.

PLATO

Plato was born in 427 B.C. into a wealthy family of the nobility of Athens, Greece. As a teenager he met and became well acquainted with Socrates, eventually adopting him as an informal teacher. Plato admired Socrates deeply, feeling that Socrates' reliance on reason was the key to the solution of the many political and cultural problems that then plagued Athens. Since the death of the great Athenian statesman Pericles, Athens had been engaged in an unending series of wars that Pericles himself had initiated and that ended with the defeat of Athens at the hands of the city-state of Sparta.

But after peace was restored, the Athenians condemned Socrates to death, accusing him of undermining the Athenian culture and thus being responsible for its many troubles. Shocked and disillusioned by Socrates' execution, Plato withdrew from public life and devoted himself to philosophy until his death in 347 B.C.

In the philosophical theories that he elaborated, Plato fashioned a distinctive view of human nature, a view, in fact, that came to have a crucial formative influence on all future theories of human nature. An important twentieth-century philosopher, Alfred North Whitehead, in fact, asserted that "all philosophy is nothing more than a footnote to Plato." Whitehead was referring to the fact

Plato: "If, as we say, perfect beauty and goodness and every ideal exist, then it is a necessary inference that just as these ideals exist, so our souls existed before we were born."

69

that Plato was the first philosopher to develop philosophical notions of human nature, human knowledge, and metaphysics and was also the first to pose the basic questions about these topics that all future philosophers would continue to ask. Plato's views on human nature, then, are important not only for themselves but also because of their enduring influence on all subsequent philosophical thought.

Most of what we know about Plato's philosophy is based on the many dialogues he wrote in which the character of Socrates appears as the major speaker. In his "early" dialogues, Plato more or less faithfully reported Socrates' original views. But as Plato grew older and his own theories began to develop, the character of Socrates increasingly became the mouthpiece for Plato's own views. In what are called the "middle" and "late" dialogues, in fact, the views expressed by the character Socrates are entirely those of Plato.

The most fundamental contribution Plato made to philosophy was the distinction he drew between the changing physical objects we perceive with our senses and the unchanging ideals we can know with our minds. One of the clearest examples of this distinction that Plato gives is drawn from the science of geometry with which he was familiar. Plato pointed out that we use our minds in geometry to discover unchanging exact truths about ideally perfect lines, squares, and circles. Yet the physical objects in the visible world are never perfectly straight, square, or circular and they are continually changing. At best, physical objects are imperfect replicas of the ideal objects we contemplate in geometry. As Plato put it: "Those who study geometry use visible figures and reason about them. But they are not thinking of these, but of the ideals which they resemble. They are thinking of a perfect square or a perfect line, and so on, and not of the imperfect figures they draw. . . . The visible figures they draw are merely replicas and what they are seeking is to understand the ideals which can be known only by the mind."[19]

Plato pointed out that this distinction between a perfect ideal and its imperfect replicas also applies to art and morality. With our minds we are able to think about the ideal of perfect beauty and perfect goodness. But in addition to these two ideals there are the many physical objects we see with our senses and which are only imperfectly beautiful and imperfectly good. The following dialogue, in which Plato put his own ideas into the mouth of Socrates, expressed the matter in this way:

SOCRATES: We say there are many objects that are beautiful and many objects that are good and similarly many objects that are instances of something specific.

GLAUCON: Yes, indeed.

SOCRATES: And, in addition, we say there is perfect beauty itself and perfect goodness itself. And a similar thing may be said about any definite ideal which has many instances. Each of the many instances is related to its perfect ideal insofar as each shares in that ideal and each gets its name from that ideal.

GLAUCON: Very true.

SOCRATES: The many objects are visible but they are not the objects we know [with our minds], while the ideals are the objects we know [with our minds] but they are not visible to the eye.[20]

As the quote above suggests, Plato realized that his distinction between a perfect ideal and its many imperfect physical replicas actually extended to every class of things "of which there are many instances." The many human beings we see, the many oak trees, and the many tables are more or less imperfect replicas of what we think of as the ideal human being, the ideal oak tree, and the ideal table. Again, in Plato's words as expressed by Socrates in dialogue:

Philosophy is the highest music.

PLATO

---

19. Plato, *The Republic*, bk. 6, 510, trans. Manuel Velasquez (Copyright © 1987 by Manuel Velasquez).
20. Ibid., bk. 6, 507.

SOCRATES: Don't we usually assume that when there are many things that have the same name, there is also an ideal that corresponds to them? You understand, don't you?

GLAUCON: I do.

SOCRATES: Consider any such group of many things. For example, there are many things we call beds and many tables.

GLAUCON: Yes, there are.

SOCRATES: And these have ideals corresponding to them. Two, in fact: one of the bed and one of the table.[21]

To these ideals Plato gave the name "Forms." He came eventually to hold that a separate Form exists for each kind of thing. For example, for things that are good, there is the Form of Goodness; for things that are human, there is the Form of Humanness; for things that are triangular, there is the Form of Triangle. The Form of a certain class of objects consists of those characteristics that make those objects be the kind of objects they are. For example, the Form of Horse consists of those characteristics that make each horse be a horse. But the visible objects in our world never perfectly embody their Forms: Visible objects are only imperfect and changing reflections of the invisible, perfect, and unchanging Forms. The visible world is like an imperfect mirror of the perfect Forms, and visible objects are like so many imperfect images of these Forms. Each of the many horses in our world, for example, is an imperfect duplicate or copy of the one perfect Form of Horse, just as each human is a replica of the one perfect Form of Human Being.

To a large extent, Plato's theory of Forms was inspired by the questioning of his teacher Socrates. Socrates, the reader may recall, often would ask his hearers for "the characteristic that makes a thing be what it is." For example, in the dialogue *Euthyphro* Socrates says, "I was not asking you to give me *examples* of holiness, Euthyphro, but to identify the characteristic that makes all holy things be

holy. There must be some characteristic that all holy things have in common, and one which makes unholy things unholy. Tell me what this characteristic itself is." In a similar manner, Socrates searched for the characteristic that makes a thing be Just, and the characteristic that makes a thing be Beautiful. Plato felt that his Forms were the "characteristics" for which Socrates had been searching, since the Form of a thing is what "makes it be what it is." Thus, Plato felt that in discovering the Forms, he had discovered the objects for which Socrates had searched all his life.

All sciences, Plato felt, must be based on these ideals we know with our minds and not on their visible, changing, and imperfect replicas. As geometry is about ideal figures and morality is about ideal goodness, so also each science is about the ideal forms that pertain to a certain class of things. The science of medicine, for example, is based on the doctor's knowledge of the ideally perfect human body. Because visible objects are continually changing and imperfect, Plato felt, they cannot be what a science studies, for science, like geometry, tries to state laws and truths that are exact and do not change from moment to moment.

However, Plato's discovery that the mind knows perfect ideals that comprise the sciences but that are not found in the visible world created a problem. Since they do not exist in the visible world, are these perfect ideals merely arbitrary creations of the mind? Are they mental figments that have no reality outside the mind? Plato saw that if the ideals that comprise geometry, morality, and the other sciences have no reality, then all of these sciences are worthless, because geometry, morality, and all sciences would be about unreal objects.

Because Plato had a passionate faith that our scientific and moral knowledge was concerned with reality, he drew the only conclusion possible: The perfect ideals with which geometry, morality, and the sciences are concerned must be real. That is, these perfect ideals, or Forms, really exist outside the mind. Since they do not exist in the visible world around us, they must exist in a world that is not visible to us. Plato concluded that there are two real worlds: the nonvisible world of unchanging perfect Forms and the visible world that con-

---

21. Ibid., bk. 10, 595.

tains their many changing replicas. In fact, Plato held, the Forms are *more* real than their replicas, since somehow (Plato suggested that God was responsible) the Forms are the basic models according to which their imperfect replicas are made. As he put it: "These ideals are like patterns that are fixed into the nature of things. Each of the many things is made in the image of its ideal and is a likeness to it. The many replicas share in the ideal insofar as they are made in its image."[22]

But how do we acquire our knowledge of the perfect ideals if they do not exist in the visible world? Plato's solution to this problem was ingenious. He argued that since we do not see the perfect ideals in our present world and since we obviously have knowledge of these ideals and investigate them in the sciences, we must have acquired this knowledge in a previous life. This shows, he held, that we have souls and that our souls must be immortal. Thus Plato's theory of Forms directly influenced his views on human nature, as Plato's own words, expressed by the character Socrates, reveal.

SOCRATES: Tell me, Simmias, do we think that there is such a thing as perfect justice?

SIMMIAS: We certainly do.

SOCRATES: And perfect beauty as well as perfect goodness?

SIMMIAS: Of course.

SOCRATES: Well, did you ever see these with your eyes?

SIMMIAS: Certainly not. . . .

SOCRATES: And do we say there is such a thing as perfect equality? I do not mean the imperfect equality of two lengths of wood or two stones, but something more than that: absolute equality.

SIMMIAS: We most certainly say there is. . . .

SOCRATES: But when did we come to think about perfect equality? Didn't we do so when we saw the imperfect equality of stones and pieces of wood and this brought to mind something else, namely perfect equality?

SIMMIAS: Certainly.

SOCRATES: Now when we see one thing and it brings to mind something else, that is what we call remembering, is it not?

SIMMIAS: Surely. . . .

SOCRATES: Do we agree, then, that when someone sees something that he recognizes as an imperfect instance of some other thing, he must have had previous knowledge of that other thing? . . .

SIMMIAS: We must agree. . . .

SOCRATES: Then we must have had a previous knowledge of perfect equality before we first saw the imperfect equality of physical objects and recognized it fell short of perfect equality. . . .

SIMMIAS: Yes.

SOCRATES: Then before we began to see or hear or use the other senses, we must somewhere have gained a knowledge of perfect equality. . . .

SIMMIAS: That follows necessarily from what we have said before, Socrates.

SOCRATES: And we saw and heard and had the other senses as soon as we were born?

SIMMIAS: Certainly.

SOCRATES: Then it appears that we must have acquired our knowledge of perfect equality before we were born.

SIMMIAS: It does.

SOCRATES: Now if we acquired that knowledge before we were born, and . . . lost it at birth, but afterwards by the use of our senses regained the knowledge which we had previously possessed, would not the process which we call learning really be recovering knowledge which we had? And shouldn't we call this recollection?

SIMMIAS: Assuredly.

SOCRATES: Then, Simmias, the soul existed previously, before it was in a human body. It existed apart from the body and had knowledge. . . . If, as we say, perfect beauty and goodness and every ideal exists, and if we compare to these whatever objects we see, then it is a necessary inference that

---

22. Plato, *Parmenides*, 132, trans. Manuel Velasquez (Copyright © 1987 by Manuel Velasquez).

just as these ideals exist, so our souls existed before we were born. . . .

SIMMIAS: Yes, Socrates. You have convinced me that the soul existed before birth. . . . But perhaps Cebes here still has doubts. . . .

SOCRATES: Well, these ideals or Forms, which are true reality, are they always the same? Consider perfect equality or perfect beauty or any other ideal. Does each of these always remain the same perfect form, unchanging and not varying from moment to moment?

CEBES: They always have to be the same, Socrates.

SOCRATES: And what about the many individual objects around us—people or horses or dresses or what have you—which we say are equal to each other or are beautiful? Do these always remain the same or are they changing constantly and becoming something else?

CEBES: They are continually changing, Socrates.

SOCRATES: These changing objects can be seen and touched and perceived with the senses. But the unchanging Forms can be known only with the mind and are not visible to the senses. . . . So there are two kinds of existing things: those which are visible and those which are not. . . . The visible are changing and the invisible are unchanging.

CEBES: That seems to be the case. . . .

SOCRATES: Now which of these two kinds of things is our body like?

CEBES: Clearly it is like visible things. . . .

SOCRATES: And what do we say of the soul? Is it visible or not?

CEBES: It is not visible.

SOCRATES: Then the soul is more like the invisible and the body like the visible?

CEBES: That is most certain, Socrates.

SOCRATES: Recall that we said long ago that when the soul relies on its bodily senses—like sight or hearing or the other senses—it is dragged by the body toward what is always changing. Then the soul goes astray and is confused as it staggers around drunkenly among these changing things.

CEBES: Very true.

SOCRATES: But when the soul turns within and reflects upon what lies in herself [knowledge of the Forms], she finds there the perfect, eternal, immortal, and unchanging realm that is most like herself. She would stay there forever if it were possible, resting from her confused wanderings. So long as she continues to reflect upon the unchanging [Forms], she herself is unchanging and has what we call wisdom.

CEBES: That is well and truly said, Socrates.

SOCRATES: So which kind of thing is the soul most like?

CEBES: The soul is infinitely more like what is unchanging. . . .

SOCRATES: And the body is more like the changing?

CEBES: Yes.

SOCRATES: One more thing: When soul and body are united, it is the nature of the soul to rule and govern and of the body to obey and serve. Which of these two functions is like god and which is like a mortal? Is it not true that what rules is like god and what is ruled is like a mortal?

CEBES: True. . . .

SOCRATES: Then, Cebes, does it not follow that the soul is most akin to what is divine, immortal, intellectual, perfect, indissoluble, and unchanging, while the body is most like what is mortal, unintellectual, dissoluble, and ever changing?

CEBES: That cannot be denied.[23]

Plato's view of human nature, then, is a direct consequence of his theory of Forms. Because we know the Forms, it follows that we have souls and that our souls existed apart from our bodies before we were born into this world. While our bodies are visible, changing, and subject to decay, our souls are like the Forms and so they are invisible, eternal, immortal, and godlike.

Having come to the conclusion that our souls—our inner selves—existed before we were born and would continue to exist after our deaths, Plato felt

---

23. Plato, *Phaedo*, trans. and ed. Manuel Velasquez (Copyright © 1987 by Manuel Velasquez), 72–80.

that it was imperative to care for our souls. He held that the soul within us consists of three parts that sometimes struggle against each other.

SOCRATES: But does our soul contain . . . three elements or not? . . . Do we gain knowledge with one part, feel anger with another, and with yet a third desire food, sex, drink, and so on? This is a difficult question.

GLAUCON: I quite agree.

SOCRATES: Let us approach the question in this way. It is clear that the same parts of a single thing cannot move in two opposing directions. So if we find that these three elements oppose each other, we shall know that they are distinct parts of ourselves.

GLAUCON: Very well. . . .

SOCRATES: Now consider a thirsty man. Insofar as he is thirsty, his soul craves drink and seeks it.

GLAUCON: That is clear. . . .

SOCRATES: Yet isn't it sometimes true that the thirsty person [who wants to drink] also, for some reason, may *not* want to drink?

GLAUCON: Yes, often.

SOCRATES: In his soul there is a part that desires drink and another part that restrains him. This latter part then is distinct from desire and usually can control desire. . . . Doesn't such control originate in reason, while the urge to drink originates in something else? . . .

GLAUCON: So it seems.

SOCRATES: Then we can conclude that there are in us two distinct parts. One is what we call "reason," and the other we call the nonrational "appetites." The latter hungers, thirsts, desires sex, and is subject to other desires. . . .

GLAUCON: Yes, that is the logical conclusion.

SOCRATES: So there are at least two distinct elements in us. But what about our emotional or spirited part: the part in us that feels anger and indignation?

GLAUCON: Perhaps we should say that it is part of our appetites.

SOCRATES: Maybe. But think about this story which I think is true. Leontius was walking up from Piraeus one day when he noticed the bodies of some executed criminals on the ground. Part of him was overcome with a desire to run over and look at the bodies, while another part felt angry at himself and tried to turn away. He struggled with himself and shut his eyes, but at last the desire was too much for him. Running up to the bodies, he opened his eyes wide and cried, "There, damn you! Feast yourselves on that lovely sight!"

GLAUCON: I'm familiar with that story.

SOCRATES: The point of the story is that anger sometimes opposes our appetites as if it is something distinct from them. And we often find that when our appetites oppose our reason, we become angry at our appetites. In the struggle between appetite and reason, our anger sides with reason. . . .

GLAUCON: That is true. . . .

SOCRATES: Yet this emotional part of ourselves is distinct from reason. The poet Homer, for example, . . . describes people whose reason inclines them to choose the better course, contrary to the impulses of anger.

GLAUCON: I entirely agree.

SOCRATES: So . . . the soul has three distinct parts.[24]

Plato thought that his discovery of the three-part soul provided us with the key to happiness and virtue. Personal happiness and virtue, Plato held, can be achieved only when the three parts of our soul are in harmony with each other and are properly subordinated to each other. Happiness is possible only if reason rules the emotions and desires and both the emotions and desires have been trained to be led harmoniously by reason. We become unhappy when the three parts of ourselves are constantly fighting against each other so that we lack inner harmony, and we fall victim to vice when we are ruled by our emotions or desires. Plato writes:

---

24. Plato, *The Republic*, trans. Manuel Velasquez (Copyright © 1987 by Manuel Velasquez), 437–441.

SOCRATES: A man is just when . . . each part within him does what is proper for it to do. . . .

GLAUCON: Indeed.

SOCRATES: Isn't it proper for reason to rule since it can acquire knowledge and so can know how to care for the whole soul; and isn't it proper that the emotions should obey and support reason?

GLAUCON: Certainly. . . .

SOCRATES: When reason and the emotions have been trained and each has learned its proper function, they should stand guard over the appetites . . . lest the appetites grow so strong that they try to enslave and overthrow them.

GLAUCON: Very true. . . .

SOCRATES: In truth, justice is present in a man . . . when each part in him plays its proper role. The just man does not allow one part of his soul to usurp the function proper to another. Indeed, the just man is one who sets his house in order, by self-mastery and discipline coming to be at peace with himself, and bringing these three parts into tune like the tones in a musical scale. . . . Only when he has linked these parts together in well-tempered harmony and has made himself one man instead of many will he be ready to go about whatever he may have to do, whether it be making money, satisfying his bodily needs, or engaging in affairs of state. . . .

GLAUCON: That is perfectly true, Socrates. . . .

SOCRATES: Next we must consider injustice. That must surely be a kind of war among the three elements, whereby they usurp and encroach upon one another's functions. . . . Such turmoil and aberration we shall, I think, identify with injustice, intemperance, cowardliness, or the other vices.

GLAUCON: Exactly. . . .

SOCRATES: Virtue, then, seems to be a kind of health and beauty and strength of the soul, while vice is like a kind of disease and ugliness and weakness in the soul.[25]

To train the emotions and appetites so that they will readily obey reason was crucial for Plato. He likens our emotions and appetites to two winged steeds that can either drag our reason downward into the confusions and illusions of the visible changing world or can help carry our reason upward to comtemplate the world of unchanging perfect Forms through the study of the sciences and the acquisition of wisdom. In a beautiful image Plato compared the three-part soul to a chariot, with the charioteer driving a white-winged horse and a black-winged horse.

> Let me speak briefly about the nature of the soul by using an image. And let the image have three parts: a pair of winged horses and a charioteer. . . . One of the horses is of a noble breed, the other ignoble and the charioteer controls them with great difficulty. . . . The vicious steed goes heavily, weighing down the charioteer to the earth when it has not been thoroughly trained. . . . Above them . . . in the heaven above heaven . . . there abides the true reality with which real knowledge is concerned: the Forms which are visible only to the mind and have no color, shape, or hardness. . . . It is the place of true knowledge . . . where every soul which is rightly nourished feeds upon pure knowledge, rejoicing at once again beholding true reality. . . . There souls can behold perfect justice and temperance . . . not in things which change, but in themselves. The souls that are most like god are carried up there by their charioteer . . . , although troubled by their steeds and only with difficulty beholding true being. Other souls rise only to fall again, barely glimpsing it and then altogether failing to see because their two steeds are too unruly.[26]

As this passage suggests, Plato held that we could be completely virtuous only if our reason knows the Forms. In particular, our reason must know the Form of the Good, since only by grasping what Goodness is can we know what the three parts of the soul must do to be good. Thus for Plato complete virtue can be achieved only by coming

25. Ibid., 441–445.

26. Plato, *Phaedrus*, trans. and ed. Manuel Velasquez (Copyright © 1987 by Manuel Velasquez), 246–248.

to have knowledge of the Form of the Good, which exists unchanging in a world of Forms separate from ours.

Plato held that the best ruler, the perfect king, would be a person—male or female—whose soul was self-disciplined enough to enable him or her to contemplate true being in the perfect Forms. Such a person, Plato wrote, would be a true "philosopher," which in Greek means "lover of wisdom." So the king must be a philosopher.

SOCRATES: If a man believes there are many things which are beautiful but does not know beauty itself . . . is he awake or is his life nothing but a dream?

GLAUCON: I would say he is dreaming.

SOCRATES: And if a man knows beauty itself and can distinguish it from its many replicas, and does not confuse beautiful things with beauty itself . . . is he dreaming or awake?

GLAUCON: He is awake. . . .

SOCRATES: If people look at the many visible things which are beautiful, but do not know beauty itself, . . . and similarly see things which are just but do not know justice itself, then they merely have opinions and do not have real knowledge of these things. . . . While those who know the real unchanging [Forms] have true knowledge . . . and are philosophers. . . .

GLAUCON: By all means.

SOCRATES: Well, are not those who have no knowledge of true being any better than blind men? They have no true models in their souls to illuminate things. They cannot fix their eyes on true reality nor can they refer to it when they lay down their laws regarding what is beautiful, just and good. . . . So should we make them rulers? Or should we establish as rulers those who know true reality and who are virtuous?

GLAUCON: Obviously the latter.[27]

The ruler, even more than the ordinary citizen, then, must keep his mind fixed on the unchanging ideals or Forms—especially the Form of the Good—

and his emotions and appetites under the control of reason. Only in this way will he rule the state in such a way that, like the virtuous individual, it will have harmony and happiness.

Plato's theory of Forms, then, which he developed under the influence of Socrates' teaching, was the basis for his influential view of human nature. All future philosophers would struggle with Plato's problem: How can we account for the fact that our mind comprehends perfect ideals that this world only imperfectly duplicates? Many twentieth-century philosophers (such as Kurt Godel, J. McTaggart, A. N. Whitehead, and Bertrand Russell) have agreed that only Plato's theory of Forms can adequately account for our knowledge of certain ideals, especially mathematical ideals. And many philosophers who have rejected Plato's theory of Forms have agreed, nevertheless, with Plato's claims concerning the soul and the body. Plato's philosophy remains very much alive today.

ARISTOTLE

Although Aristotle was the student of Plato, his approach to human nature was very different from Plato's. Son to a physician of a Macedonian king, Aristotle was born in 384 B.C. at Stagira in northern Greece. When he was seventeen his father sent him to Athens to study in Plato's Academy, the ancient equivalent of a modern-day university. There he found in Plato an inspiring teacher, whom he later described as a man "whom bad men have not even the right to praise, and who showed in his life and teachings how to be happy and good at the same time." Aristotle stayed on as a teacher at the Academy until Plato's death twenty years later. After leaving the Academy, Aristotle was asked by King Philip II of Macedonia, the new conqueror of the Greeks, to tutor his young son, the future Alexander the Great. Three years later when his pupil Alexander ascended the throne, Aristotle returned to Athens to set up his own school, the Lyceum. There he taught and wrote for twelve years until the death of Alexander, his protector, released a tide of pent-up anger the Greeks had long harbored toward their Macedonian conquerors and their friends. Under threat of death, Aristotle fled Ath-

27. Plato, The Republic, 476–485.

ens and took refuge in a Macedonian fort, saying that he did not want "the Athenians to sin twice against philosophy" by killing him as they had killed Socrates. He died there one year later.

As a young man Aristotle seems to have been a close follower of Plato, holding fast to the doctrine of Forms and to Plato's view that the immortal soul apprehended the Forms in an earlier existence. But as Aristotle grew older, he came to have increasing doubts about Plato's views. Plato held that physical objects were replicas of unchanging Forms that exist in a separate world: For each class of things, such as the class of horses, there is a Form that serves as their model and that contains their essential characteristics. The Form of Horse, for example, contains the essential characteristics that make a thing be a horse, and each physical horse in our material world is modeled on this otherworldly Form.

Aristotle agreed with Plato's view that there are forms, since he agreed that each class of things has certain essential characteristics—its "form." But unlike Plato, Aristotle did not believe that Forms exist in some separate world apart from the visible things around us. Instead, he held, the forms of visible things exist in the visible things themselves. How is this possible?

According to Aristotle, those characteristics that make a thing be what it is and that all things of that kind have in common are the "form" of a thing. For example, the form of roundness consists of those characteristics that all round things have in common and that make a thing round. The form of a horse consists of those characteristics that all horses have in common and that make a thing a horse and not, say, a cow. Although we can distinguish *in our minds* between roundness and visible round things, this does not mean that, besides the visible round things around us, there also exists *in reality* a *separate* ideal object called "Roundness." Roundness only exists in round things, and horseness only exists in the horses we see around us.

Once Aristotle realized that the world could be explained without a separate world of ideal Forms, he began to develop a new view of reality that was much closer to common sense than Plato's. The changing world around us, Aristotle held, can be

Aristotle: "In all our activities there is an end which we seek for its own sake, and everything else is a means to this end. . . . Happiness is [this] ultimate end. It is the end we seek in all that we do."

explained by using his new concept of form together with three other kinds of "causes": the material cause, or the stuff out of which things are made; the efficient cause, or the agent who brings about a change; and the final cause, or the purpose of the change.

Consider, for example, how a lump of marble can be changed into a statue of Socrates by a sculptor. If we ask *why* the marble changed as it did, we can give four kinds of explanations. First, we can explain why the marble statue came to have some of its characteristics by identifying its form, or "formal cause": Because it has the form of a statue of Socrates, it came to be shaped like Socrates. Second, we can explain why the statue has other characteristics by identifying the matter out of which it is made, or the "material cause": Because it is made out of marble, it is hard and white. Third, we can explain why the marble changed as it did by identifying the agent who made the statue, or the "efficient cause": Because the artist chiseled the marble, it gradually came to be shaped like Socrates. And fourth, we can explain why the statue came to be by identifying the purpose for which it was made, or the "final cause": The artist made the statue because he was trying to please a patron. Thus, things can be explained completely in terms of their causes in this world without having to theorize Forms from some other world as Plato did. Aristotle explained his four causes in these words.

> Next we must examine explanations or "causes," and state clearly the number and kinds of explanations there are. For we are seeking knowledge of things and we know a thing only when we can explain why it is as it is. And we explain something by identifying its basic causes. So, obviously, if our aim is to know the changing and perishing objects of nature, we will have to know their basic causes and use them to explain things.
> One kind of explanation [the material cause] is provided by identifying the material of which a thing is made and which remains present in the thing. For example, the bronze of which a statue is made or the silver of a bowl. . . .
> A second kind of explanation [the formal cause] is provided by identifying the form or plan of a thing, that is, by stating the essential characteristics that define a thing. . . .
> A third kind of explanation [the efficient cause] is provided by identifying the agent who produced or changed something. For example, an advisor is the efficient cause of the changes he advises, a father is the efficient cause of the children he produced, and generally whatever produces or changes anything is the efficient cause of what is produced or changed.
> Finally, a kind of explanation [the final cause] is also provided when we give the end or purpose of a thing. For example, health can explain taking a walk, as when we ask, "Why is he taking a walk?" and reply, "For the sake of his health" and thereby feel that we have given an explanation.[28]

Aristotle held, then, that everything in the universe has a certain form, is made out of a certain matter, is produced by certain efficient causes, and is made to serve a certain purpose or function. We explain a thing fully when we have identified its form, matter, efficient causes, and specific functions. The purpose of science is to explain the many things in the universe by identifying their four causes. It is pointless, Aristotle held, to bring in a separate world of unchanging perfect forms as Plato did. Instead, we should pay attention to *this* changing, visible world in which we live, and science should study the individual things in *this* world to identify their various causes instead of spending time thinking about an invisible world of Forms.

Not only did Aristotle reject Plato's views on a separate world of unchanging Forms, he also rejected his views on the soul. Plato had argued that the soul is a separate thing within us that can exist apart from the body and that in an earlier existence had acquired knowledge of the Forms, which it remembered in this life. Aristotle rejected this view because here, too, he felt that we must adhere to the four causes, which involve our experience in this world only. Therefore, Aristotle noted, to say that something has a soul is to say that it is alive. Consequently, the human soul is nothing more than those characteristics that distinguish a living human from a dead one. The soul, he declared, is nothing more than the *form* that our body has when it is alive. This meant that the soul is not a separate entity that can exist apart from the body and that survives death.[29] The soul is merely the form of a living human—those essential characteristics that make each of us a living human being—and like other forms, it cannot exist apart from the visible things in this world.

> Let us leave behind, then, the theories of the soul that have come down to us from our predecessors and let us make a fresh start by trying to define what the soul is. . . .
> As I have said, the individual things in the world are composed in part of the matter [out of which they are made] . . . , and in part of a form

---

28. Aristotle, *Physics*, bk 2, ch. 3, trans. and ed. Manuel Velasquez (© 1987 by Manuel Velasquez).

29. However, Aristotle may have thought that *part* of the soul—what he called the "active intellect"—survived death. In some passages he seems to hint at this, but scholars still debate his meaning.

which makes them be the kind of thing that they are. . . .

The most common individual things are physical bodies, especially the natural physical bodies from which everything else is made. Now some physical bodies have life, and some do not. . . . Every natural physical body that has life is an individual thing and so it, too, must be composed of matter and form. . . . Now a physical body itself, when it has life, cannot be a soul. For the body is what *has* attributes [such as life or soul] and is not itself an attribute. The body is rather the matter [of which the living being is made]. The soul, therefore, must be the form of a physical body that has the power of living. . . .

It is as pointless, therefore, to ask whether the body and the soul are identical, as to ask whether the wax and its shape are identical, or, in general, to ask whether the matter of a thing is identical with its form. . . .

So we now have the definition of the soul. The soul is the form or the essential characteristics of a body that has the power of living. . . . Clearly, then, the soul is not separable from the body.[30]

But if the soul does not preexist (as Plato had suggested), how then do we come to have knowledge of the forms of things? Aristotle's answer to this question was straightforward. We can know the forms of things—the essential characteristics of things—because through repeated experience, our minds come to know the essential characteristics of physical things and can consider them apart from these physical things. For example, after seeing many round things, we become capable of thinking about the characteristic of roundness itself, and after studying many horses, we become capable of thinking about horseness itself. In this way our minds are able to "abstract" or mentally separate the form of a thing from the thing itself and thereby come to know it. Through this process of abstraction, then, the mind forms the ideal concepts with which the sciences deal. For instance, by considering many imperfect circles, lines, and squares, we "abstract" the idea of the perfect circle, the

perfect line, and the perfect square and reason about these in the science of geometry. The sciences deal with these ideal essences of things. Thus, Aristotle concluded, although the sciences deal with the ideal forms of things as Plato had realized, this does not require us to posit another world where these ideal forms exist. The forms of things are real enough because the real objects in our visible world embody these forms. And the sciences deal with these forms when our minds abstract them and consider them as ideals separate from the visible objects in our world. But although we *think* of them as separate, they do not *exist* as separate.

Aristotle also departed from Plato's views on happiness and virtue. Plato held that we could achieve full happiness and virtue only by coming to know the perfect forms that exist in another world. Aristotle rejected this view and held, instead, that happiness and goodness had to be found in *this* world. "Even if there were a perfect Good that existed apart from the many things in our world which are good, it is evident that this good would not be anything that we humans can realize or attain. But it is an attainable good that we are now seeking."[31]

To discover what kind of goodness is attainable in this life, Aristotle proceeded by examining the various pursuits and activities in which we actually engage. In doing this, of course, he was following the method required by his theory of the four causes: Everything is to be explained in terms of the causes things have in *this* world. Aristotle began by pointing out that when we do something, we are usually trying to achieve some other aim or good. Our "highest good" or "highest end," then, would be whatever we are ultimately seeking in everything we do in this world. He wrote:

Every art and every inquiry, and likewise every activity, seems to aim at some good. This is why the good is defined as that at which everything aims.

But sometimes the end at which we are aiming

30. Aristotle, *De Anima*, bk. 2, ch. 1, trans. and ed. Manuel Velasquez (© 1987 by Manuel Velasquez).

31. Aristotle, *Nicomachean Ethics*, bk. 1, ch. 6, trans. Manuel Velasquez.

is the activity itself while other times the end is something else that we are trying to achieve by means of that activity. When we are aiming at some end to which the activity is a means, the end is clearly a higher good than the activity. . . .

Now if in all our activities there is some end which we seek for its own sake, and if everything else is a means to this same end, it obviously will be our highest and best end. Clearly there must be some such end since everything cannot be a means to something else since then there would be nothing for which we ultimately do anything and everything would be pointless. Surely from a practical point of view it is important for us to know what this ultimate end is so that, like archers shooting at a definite mark, we will be more likely to attain what we are seeking [in all our actions].[32]

Since human beings are in continual search of something, it is obviously important for us to be clear about what this "something" is. This "something," of course, would be the "final cause" that explains *why* we humans do what we do. Aristotle tries to identify this "highest end," or "final cause," in the following passage in which he remains true to his view that we must look for the causes of things by examining what happens in *this* world.

Some people think our highest end is something material and obvious, like pleasure or money or fame. One thinks it is this, and another thinks it is that. Often the same person changes his mind: When he is sick, it is health; when he is poor, it is wealth. And realizing they are really ignorant, such men express great admiration for anyone who says deep-sounding things that are beyond their comprehension. . . .

Most people think the highest end is pleasure and so they seek nothing higher than a life of pleasure. . . . They reveal their utter slavishness in this for they prefer [as their highest end] a life that is attainable by any animal. . . . Capable and practical men think the highest end is fame, which is the goal of a public life. But this is too superficial to be the good we are seeking since fame depends on those who give it. . . . Moreover, men who pursue fame do so in order to be

assured of their own value. . . . Finally, some men devote their lives to making money in a way that is quite unnatural. But wealth clearly is not the good we are seeking since it is merely useful as a means to something else. . . . What, then, is our highest end?

As we have seen, there are many ends. But some of them are chosen only as a means to other things, for example, wealth, musical instruments, and tools [are ends we choose only because they are means to other things]. So it is clear that not all ends are ultimate ends. But our highest and best end would have to be something ultimate. . . .

Notice that an end that we desire for itself is more ultimate than something we want only as a means to something else. And an end that is never a means to something else is more ultimate than an end that is sometimes a means. And the most ultimate end would be something that we always choose for itself and never as a means to something else.

Now happiness seems more than anything else to answer to this description. For we always choose happiness for itself and never for the sake of something else. For happiness is something we always choose for its own sake and never as a means to something else. But fame, pleasure, . . . and so on, are chosen partly for themselves but partly also as a means to happiness, since we believe that they will bring us happiness. Only happiness, then, is never chosen for the sake of these things or as a means to any other thing.

We will be led to the same conclusion if we start from the fact that our ultimate end would have to be completely sufficient by itself. . . . By this I mean that by itself it must make life worth living and lacking in nothing. But happiness by itself answers this description. It is what we most desire even apart from all other things. . . .

So, it appears that happiness is the ultimate end and completely sufficient by itself. It is the end we seek in all that we do.[33]

Having finally arrived at the conclusion that in everything we do we are seeking happiness, Aristotle then turned to the question: What must we do to achieve happiness? His teacher Plato had

---

32. Ibid., bk. 1, chs. 1–2.

33. Ibid., bk. 1, chs. 4–5, 7.

said that we will be happy only if we achieve knowledge of those Forms that exist in another world. Aristotle rejected this suggestion. Human happiness must be achievable in this life, through our activities in this world. But how, then, is happiness achieved? Aristotle felt that to discover the path to happiness, we must first know what the specific purpose of humanity is: What is it that human nature is meant to do and that nothing else can do? Here is Aristotle's answer.

> The reader may think that in saying that happiness is our ultimate end we are merely stating a platitude. So we must be more precise about what happiness involves.
>
> Perhaps the best approach is to ask what the specific purpose or function of man is. For the good and the excellence of all beings that have a purpose—such as musicians, sculptors, or craftsmen—depend on their purpose. So if man has a purpose, his good will be related to this purpose. And how could man not have a natural purpose when even cobblers and carpenters have a purpose? Surely, just as each part of man—the eye, the hand, the foot—has a purpose, so also man as a whole must have a purpose. What is this purpose?
>
> Our biological activities we share in common even with plants. So these cannot be the purpose or function of man since we are looking for something specific to man. The activities of our senses we also plainly share with other things: horses, cattle, and other animals. So there remain only the activities that belong to the rational part of man. . . . So the specific purpose or function of man involves the activities of that part of his soul that belongs to reason, or that at least is obedient to reason. . . .
>
> Now the function of a thing is basic, and its good is something added to this function. For example, the function of a musician is to play music, and the good musician is one who also plays music but who in addition does it well. So, the good for man would have to be something added to his function of carrying on the activities of reason; it would be carrying on the activities of reason but doing so well or with excellence. But a thing carries out its proper functions well when it has the proper virtues. So the good for man is carrying out those activities of his soul [which belong

to reason] and doing so with the proper virtue or excellence.[34]

Human happiness, then, is to be found by doing well what humans are best able to do: live their lives with reason. And to do something well is to act with virtue. So human happiness is achieved by acquiring the virtues that will enable us to use our reason well in living our lives. But what is human virtue? What does it mean to have the *"virtue"* of using our reason well in living our lives? Aristotle replies that human virtue requires learning what "the mean" is: learning what it is to achieve "the mean" in our feelings and actions. We have virtue when our reason knows what the mean is and when we live according to this knowledge.

> Since our happiness, then, is to be found in carrying out the activities of the soul [that belong to reason], and doing so with virtue or excellence, we will now have to inquire into virtue, for this will help us in our inquiry into happiness. . . .
>
> To have virtue or excellence, a thing (1) must be good and (2) must be able to carry out its function well. For example, if the eye has virtue, then it must be a good eye and must be able to see well. Similarly, if a horse has its virtue, then it must be all that it should be and must be good at running, carrying a rider, and charging. Consequently, the proper virtue or excellence of man will consist of those habits or acquired abilities that (1) make him a good man and (2) enable him to carry out his activities well. . . .
>
> Now the expert in any field is the one who avoids what is excessive as well as what is deficient. Instead he seeks to hit the mean and chooses it. . . . Acting well in every field is achieved by looking to the mean and bringing one's actions into line with this standard of moderation. For example, people say of a good work of art that nothing could be taken from it or added to it, implying that excellence is destroyed through excess or deficiency but achieved by observing the mean. The good artist, in fact, keeps his eyes fixed on the mean in everything he does. . . .
>
> Virtue, therefore, must also aim at the mean.

---

34. Ibid., bk. 1, ch. 7.

For human virtue deals with our feelings and actions, and in these we can go to excess or we can fall short or we can hit the mean. For example, it is possible to feel fear, confidence, desire, anger, pity, pleasure, . . . and so on, either too much or too little—both of which extremes are bad. But to feel these at the right times, and on the right occasions, and towards the right persons, and with the right object, and in the right fashion, is the mean between the extremes and is the best state, and is the mark of virtue. In the same way, our actions can also be excessive or can fall short or can hit the mean.

Virtue, then, deals with those feelings and actions in which it is wrong to go too far and wrong to fall short but in which hitting the mean is praiseworthy and good. . . . It is a habit or acquired ability to choose . . . what is moderate or what hits the mean as determined by reason.[35]

The path to human happiness, then, is by living according to the moderation that our reason discovers. By using our reason, Aristotle is saying, we can know what it means not to go to excess in our feelings and actions. To the extent that we live according to this knowledge, we have virtue and will be happy in this world. Aristotle provides several specific examples of what virtue is.

But it is not enough to speak in generalities. We must apply this to particular virtues and vices. Consider, then, the following examples.

Take the feelings of fear and confidence. To be able to hit the mean [by having just enough fear and just enough confidence] is to have the virtue of courage. . . . But he who exceeds in confidence has the vice of rashness, while he who has too much fear and not enough confidence has the vice of cowardliness.

The mean where pleasure . . . is concerned is achieved by the virtue of temperance. But to go to excess is to have the vice of profligacy, while to fall short is to have the vice of insensitivity. . . .

Or take the action of giving or receiving money. Here the mean is the virtue of generosity. . . . But

the man who gives to excess and is deficient in receiving has the vice of prodigality, while the man who is deficient in giving and excessive in taking has the vice of stinginess. . . .

Or take one's feelings about the opinion of others. Here the mean is the virtue of proper self-respect, while the excess is the vice of vanity, and the deficiency is the vice of small-mindedness. . . .

The feeling of anger can also be excessive, deficient, or moderate. The man who occupies the middle state is said to have the virtue of gentleness, while the one who exceeds in anger has the vice of irascibility, while the one who is deficient in anger has the vice of apathy.[36]

Our human nature, then, is capable of achieving happiness in this world. Although we do not have an immortal soul as Plato argued, nevertheless we do have reason and can use our reason to control our feelings and actions. To live according to reason by being moderate in our feelings and actions is to acquire human virtue. And this kind of virtue will produce the happiness that our human nature seeks in everything we do.

Thus, although Aristotle's views of human nature grew out of the views of his teacher Plato (much like Plato's views grew out of those of his teacher Socrates), Aristotle's final theories were quite different from Plato's (as different as Plato's were from Socrates'). Where Plato looked to some other world of unchanging Forms to explain human nature, Aristotle looked for the "four causes" of things completely within this world. As a result, Aristotle looked only to this world to explain how our human nature can achieve knowledge and happiness. Where Plato explained human knowledge by saying it was acquired in some earlier life when the soul existed without the body, Aristotle held that we acquire all of our knowledge in this life and that the soul cannot exist apart from the body. And where Plato believed that happiness is acquired by coming to know the Forms that exist in another world, Aristotle held that happiness is acquired by being moderate in our feelings and actions in this world.

---

35. Ibid., bk. 1, ch. 13; bk. 2, ch. 6.

36. Ibid., bk. 2, ch. 7.

QUESTIONS

1. Why is Plato's philosophy sometimes said to be "poetic?" Is this a good or bad quality for philosophy?

2. Mathematicians often make statements such as "There exist two primes between x and y." What kind of existence are they talking about? How does Plato explain this kind of existence?

3. What is the source of the ideas we have about ideals that are not encountered in our physical world (such as Beauty, Justice, Goodness)?

4. "If each person derived her ideas of mathematics by generalizing from her personal experience, then the laws of mathematics would differ from person to person: For one person, two plus two would equal four, and for another, it would not. If mathematical ideas were constructed by society, then the laws of mathematics would differ from society to society: In America, two plus two would equal four, but in other societies, it might not. The fact that the laws of mathematics must be the same for every person and every society proves that numbers and their laws exist independently of any person or society. And this shows that Plato was right." Evaluate this argument.

5. Compare Plato's theory of the soul to Freud's view that the human psyche contains three parts— an irrational id, a conscious ego, and an unconscious superego, each of which can be distinguished from the others by the psychological conflicts that arise among them.

6. Do you agree with Plato's view that appetite and emotion (at least anger) must be subject to reason? Why or why not?

7. Does Aristotle's theory of abstraction account for the knowledge we have of mathematical laws, which must be the same for all persons and all societies (see question 4 above)? Does Plato or Aristotle best account for our knowledge of mathematics and our knowledge of ideals such as Beauty, Goodness, and Justice?

8. Do you agree with Aristotle's view that all moral virtue is a mean between the extremes of excess and deficiency? What about the virtues of honesty and love?

9. Does Aristotle's theory imply that only a virtuous person can be happy? Do you agree that happiness without virtue is impossible? Explain.

10. Is there any difference between doing what is morally right and doing what will make one happy?

JOHN BARTH

Night-Sea Journey

What's the wildest thing you can imagine? Contact with extraterrestrial life? Living forever?
Unending happiness? No doubt the list could go on and on. It's not likely, though, that your list
would include a philosophical spermatozoon. But author John Barth asks us to imagine exactly
this in his captivating short story "Night-Sea Journey."

A few years ago Woody Allen played a similar motif for laughs in one of his films. But
Barth, one of our most inventive storytellers,[37] *is dead serious. In developing his metaphor, he*
raises profound philosophical questions about life, God, the universe, human nature, and the
human condition. In short, Barth uses the microcosmic world of reproduction to launch a philo-
sophical inquiry about the cosmos, the human's place in it, and the world beyond.[38]

"One way or another, no matter which theory of our journey is correct, it's myself I address; to whom I rehearse as to a stranger our history and condition, and will disclose my secret hope though I sink for it.

"Is the journey my invention? Do the night, the sea, exist at all, I ask myself, apart from my experience of them? Do I myself exist, or is this a dream? Sometimes I wonder. And if I am, who am I? The Heritage I supposedly transport? But how can I be both vessel and contents? Such are the questions that beset my intervals of rest.

"My trouble is, I lack conviction. Many accounts of our situation seem plausible to me—where and what we are, why we swim and whither. But implausible ones as well, perhaps especially those, I must admit as possibly correct. Even likely. If at times, in certain humors—stroking in unison, say, with my neighbors and chanting with them 'Onward! Upward!'—I have supposed that we have after all a common Maker, Whose nature and motives we may not know, but Who engendered us in some mys-

SOURCE: John Barth, *Lost in the Funhouse*. (Copyright © 1966 by John Barth). Reprinted by permission of Doubleday and Company.

37. Other Barth titles: *Giles Goat-Boy, The Sot-Weed Factor, The End of the Road,* and *The Floating Opera.* "Night-Sea Journey" can be found in his collection of experimental short stories *Lost in the Funhouse,* in which Barth explores ways to use the disembodied authorial voice metaphorically.

38. My thanks to Professor David Long of California State University at Sacramento for suggesting this selection and insights into it.

terious wise and launched us forth toward some end known but to Him—if (for a moodslength only) I have been able to entertain such notions, very popular in certain quarters, it is because our night-sea journey partakes of their absurdity. One might even say: I can believe them *because* they are absurd.

"Has that been said before?

"Another paradox: it appears to be these recesses from swimming that sustain me in the swim. Two measures onward and upward, flailing with the rest, then I float exhausted and dispirited, brood upon the night, the sea, the journey, while the flood bears me a measure back and down: slow progress, but I live, I live, and make my way, aye, past many a drownèd comrade in the end, stronger, worthier than I, victims of their unremitting *joie de nager*. I have seen the best swimmers of my generation go under. Numberless the number of the dead! Thousands drown as I think this thought, millions as I rest before returning to the swim. And scores, hundreds of millions have expired since we surged forth, brave in our innocence, upon our dreadful way. 'Love! Love!' we sang then, a quarter-billion strong, and churned the warm sea white with joy of swimming! Now all are gone down—the buoyant, the sodden, leaders and followers, all gone under, while wretched I swim on. Yet these same reflective intervals that keep me afloat have led me into wonder, doubt, despair—strange emotions for a swimmer!—have led me, even, to suspect . . . that our night-sea journey is without meaning.

"Indeed, if I have yet to join the hosts of the suicides, it is because (fatigue apart) I find it no meaningfuller to drown myself than to go on swimming.

"I know that there are those who seem actually to enjoy the night-sea; who claim to love swimming for its own sake, or sincerely believe that 'reaching the Shore,' 'transmitting the Heritage' (*Whose* Heritage, I'd like to know? And to whom?) is worth the staggering cost. I do not. Swimming itself I find at best not actively unpleasant, more often tiresome, not infrequently a torment. Arguments from function and design don't impress me: granted that we can and do swim, that in a manner of speaking our long tails and streamlined heads are 'meant for' swimming; it by no means follows— for me, at least—that we *should* swim, or otherwise endeavor to 'fulfill our destiny.' Which is to say, Someone Else's destiny, since ours, so far as I can see, is merely to perish, one way or another, soon or late. The heartless zeal of our (departed) leaders, like the blind ambition and good cheer of my own youth, appalls me now; for the death of my comrades I am inconsolable. If the night-sea journey has justification, it is not for us swimmers ever to discover it.

"Oh, to be sure, 'Love!' one heard on every side: 'Love it is that drives and sustains us!' I translate: we don't know *what* drives and sustains us, only that we are most miserably driven and, imperfectly, sustained. *Love* is how we call our ignorance of what whips us. 'To reach the Shore,' then: but what if the Shore exists in the fancies of us swimmers merely, who dream it to account for the dreadful fact that we swim, have always and only swum, and continue swimming without respite (myself excepted) until we die? Supposing even that there *were* a Shore—that, as a cynical companion of mine once imagined, we rise from the drowned to discover all those vulgar super- stitions and exalted metaphors to be literal truth: the giant Maker of us all, the Shores of Light beyond our night-sea journey!—whatever would a swimmer do there? The fact is, when we imagine the Shore, what comes to mind is just the opposite of our condition: no more night, no more sea, no more journeying. In short, the blissful estate of the drowned.

" 'Ours not to stop and think; ours but to swim and sink. . . .' Because a moment's thought reveals the pointlessness of swimming. 'No matter,' I've heard some say, even as they gulped their last: 'The night-sea journey may be absurd, but here we swim, will-we nill-we, against the flood, onward and upward, toward a Shore that may not exist and couldn't be reached if it did.' The thoughtful swimmer's choices, then, they say, are two: give over thrashing and go under for good, embrace the absurdity; affirm in and for itself the night-sea journey; swim on with neither motive nor destination, for the sake of swimming, and compassionate moreover with your fellow swimmer, we being all at sea and equally in the dark. I find neither course acceptable. If not even the hypothetical Shore can justify a sea-full of drownèd comrades, to speak of the swim-in-itself as somehow doing so strikes me as obscene. I continue to swim—but only because blind habit, blind instinct, blind fear of drowning are still more strong than the horror of our journey. And if on occasion I have assisted a fellow-thrasher, joined in the cheers and songs, even passed along to others strokes of genius from the drownèd great, it's that I shrink by temperament from making myself conspicuous. To paddle off in one's own direction, assert one's independent right-of-way, overrun one's fellows without compunction, or dedicate oneself entirely to pleasures and diversions without regard for conscience—I can't finally condemn those who journey in this wise; in half my moods I envy them and despise the weak vitality that keeps me from following their example. But in reasonabler moments I remind myself that it's their very freedom and self-responsibility I reject, as more dramatically absurd, in our sense-less circumstances, than tailing along in conventional fashion. Suicides, rebels, affirm-ers of the paradox—nay-sayers and yea-sayers alike to our fatal journey—I finally shake my head at them. And splash sighing past their corpses, one by one, as past a hundred sorts of others: friends, enemies, brothers; fools, sages, brutes—and nobodies, million upon million. I envy them all.

"A poor irony: that I, who find abhorrent and tautological the doctrine of survival of the fittest (*fitness* meaning, in my experience, nothing more than survival-ability, a talent whose only demonstration is the fact of survival, but whose chief ingredients seem to be strength, guile, callousness), may be the sole remaining swimmer! But the doctrine is false as well as repellent: Chance drowns the worthy with the unworthy, bears up the unfit with the fit by whatever definition, and makes the night-sea journey essentially *haphazard* as well as murderous and unjustified.

" 'You only swim once.' Why bother, then?

" 'Except ye drown, ye shall not reach the shore of Life.' Poppycock.

"One of my late companions—that same cynic with the curious fancy, among the first to drown—entertained us with odd conjectures while we waited to begin our journey. A favorite theory of his was that the Father does exist, and did indeed make us and the sea we swim—but not a-purpose or even consciously; He made us, as it were, despite Himself, as we make waves with every tail-thrash, and may be unaware of our existence. Another was that He knows we're here but doesn't care what happens to us, inasmuch as He creates (voluntarily or not) other seas and swimmers at more or less regular intervals. In bitterer moments, such as just before he drowned, my friend even supposed that our Maker wished us unmade; there was indeed a Shore, he'd argue, which could save at least some of us from drowning and toward which it was our function to struggle—but for reasons unknowable to us He wanted desperately to prevent our reaching that happy place and fulfilling our destiny. Our 'Father,' in short, was our adversary and would-be killer! No less outrageous, and offensive to traditional opinion, were the fellow's speculations on the nature of our Maker: that He might well be no swimmer Himself at all, but some sort of monstrosity, perhaps even tailless; that He might be stupid, malicious, insensible, perverse, or asleep and dreaming; that the end for which He created and launched us forth, and which we flagellate ourselves to fathom, was perhaps immoral, even obscene. Et cetera, et cetera: there was no end to the chap's conjectures, or the impoliteness of his fancy; I have reason to suspect that his early demise, whether planned by 'our Maker' or not, was expedited by certain fellow-swimmers indignant at his blasphemies.

"In other moods, however (he was as given to moods as I), his theorizing would become half-serious, so it seemed to me, especially upon the subjects of Fate and Immortality, to which our youthful conversations often turned. Then his harangues, if no less fantastical, grew solemn and obscure, and if he was still baiting us, his passion undid the joke. His objection to popular opinions of the hereafter, he would declare, was their claim to general validity. Why need believers hold that *all* the drownèd rise to be judged at journey's end, and non-believers that drowning is final without exception? In *his* opinion (so he'd vow at least), nearly everyone's fate was permanent death; indeed he took a sour pleasure in supposing that every 'Maker' made thousands of separate seas in His creative lifetime, each populated like ours with millions of swimmers, and that in almost every instance both sea and swimmers were utterly annihilated, whether accidentally or by malevolent design. (Nothing if not pluralistical, he imagined there might be millions and billions of 'Fathers,' perhaps in some 'night-sea' of their own!) However—and here he turned infidels against him with the faithful—he professed to believe that in possibly a single night-sea per thousand, say, one of its quarter-billion swimmers (that is, one swimmer in two hundred fifty billions) achieved a qualified immortality. In some cases the rate might be slightly higher; in others it was vastly lower, for just as there are swimmers of every degree of proficiency, including some who drown before the journey starts, unable to swim at all, and others created drownèd, as it were, so he imagined what can only be termed impotent Creators, Makers unable to Make, as well as uncommonly fertile ones and all grades between. And it pleased him to deny any necessary relation between a Maker's productivity and His other virtues—including, even, the quality of His creatures.

"I could go on (*he* surely did) with his elaboration of these mad notions—such as that swimmers in other night-seas needn't be of our kind; that Makers themselves might belong to different *species*, so to speak; that our particular Maker mightn't Himself be immortal, or that we might be not only His emissaries but His 'immortality,' continuing His life and our own, transmogrified, beyond our individual deaths. Even this modified immortality (meaningless to me) he conceived as relative and contingent, subject to accidental or deliberate termination: his pet hypothesis was that Makers and swimmers *each generate the other*—against all odds, their number being so great—and that any given 'immortality-chain' could terminate after any number of cycles, so that what was 'immortal' (still speaking relatively) was only the cyclic process of incarnation, which itself might have a beginning and an end. Alternatively he liked to imagine cycles within cycles, either finite or infinite: for example, the 'night-sea,' as it were, in which Makers 'swam' and created night-seas and swimmers like ourselves, might be the creation of a larger Maker, Himself one of many, Who in turn et cetera. Time itself he regarded as relative to our experience, like magnitude: who knew but what, with each thrash of our tails, minuscule seas and swimmers, whole eternities, came to pass—as ours, perhaps, and our Maker's Maker's, was elapsing between the strokes of some supertail, in a slower order of time?

"Naturally I hooted with the others at this nonsense. We were young then, and had only the dimmest notion of what lay ahead; in our ignorance we imagined night-sea journeying to be a positively heroic enterprise. Its meaning and value we never questioned; to be sure, some must go down by the way, a pity no doubt, but to win a race requires that others lose, and like all my fellows I took for granted that I would be the winner. We milled and swarmed, impatient to be off, never mind where or why, only to try our youth against the realities of night and sea; if we indulged the skeptic at all, it was as a droll, half-contemptible mascot. When he died in the initial slaughter, no one cared.

"And even now I don't subscribe to all his views—but I no longer scoff. The horror of our history has urged me of opinions, as of vanity, confidence, spirit, charity, hope, vitality, everything—except dull dread and a kind of melancholy, stunned persistence. What leads me to recall his fancies is my growing suspicion that I, of all swimmers, may be the sole survivor of this fell journey, tale-bearer of a generation. This suspicion, together with the recent sea-change, suggests to me now that nothing is impossible, not even my late companion's wildest visions, and brings me to a certain desperate resolve, the point of my chronicling.

"Very likely I have lost my senses. The carnage at our setting out; our decimation by whirlpool, poisoned cataract, sea-convulsion; the panic stampedes, mutinies, slaughters, mass suicides; the mounting evidence that none will survive the journey—add to these anguish and fatigue; it were a miracle if sanity stayed afloat. Thus I admit, with the other possibilities, that the present sweetening and calming of the sea, and what seems to be a kind of vasty presence, song, or summons from the near upstream, may be hallucinations of disordered sensibility. . . .

"Perhaps, even, I am drowned already. Surely I was never meant for the rough-and-tumble of the swim; not impossibly I perished at the outset and have only imaged the night-sea journey from some final deep. In any case, I'm no longer young, and it is we spent old swimmers, disabused of every illusion, who are most vulnerable to dreams.

"Sometimes I think I am my drownèd friend.

"Out with it: I've begun to believe, not only that *She* exists, but that She lies not far ahead, and stills the sea, and draws me Herward! Aghast, I recollect his maddest notion: that our destination (which existed, mind, in but one night-sea out of hundreds and thousands) was no Shore, as commonly conceived, but a mysterious being, indescribable except by paradox and vaguest figure: wholly different from us swimmers, yet our complement; the death of us, yet our salvation and resurrection; simultaneously our journey's end, mid-point, and commencement; not membered and thrashing like us, but a motionless or hugely gliding sphere of unimaginable dimension; self-contained, yet dependent absolutely, in some wise, upon the chance (always monstrously improbable) that one of us will survive the night-sea journey and reach . . . Her! *Her*, he called it, or *She* which is to say, Other-than-a-he. I shake my head; the thing is too preposterous; it is myself I talk to, to keep my reason in this awful darkness.

There is no She! There is no You! I rave to myself; it's Death alone that hears and summons. To the drowned, all seas are calm. . . .

"Listen: my friend maintained that in every order of creation there are two sorts of creators, contrary yet complementary, one of which gives rise to seas and swimmers, the other to the Night-which-contains-the-sea and to What-waits-at-the-journey's-end: the former, in short, to destiny, the latter to destination (and both profligately, involuntarily, perhaps indifferently or unwittingly). The 'purpose' of the night-sea journey—but not necessarily of the journeyer or of either Maker!—my friend could describe only in abstractions: *consummation, transfiguration, union of contraries, transcension of categories.* When we laughed, he would shrug and admit that he understood the business not better than we, and thought it ridiculous, dreary, possibly obscene. 'But one of you,' he'd add with his wry smile, 'may be the Hero destined to complete the night-sea journey and be one with Her. Chances are, of course, you won't make it.' He himself, he declared, was not even going to try; the whole idea repelled him; if we chose to dismiss it as an ugly fiction, so much the better for us; thrash, slash, and be merry, we were soon enough drownèd. But there it was, he could not say how he knew or why he bothered to tell us, any more than he could say what would happen after She and Hero, Shore and Swimmer, 'merged identities' to become something both and neither. He quite agreed with me that if the issue of that magical union had no memory of the night-sea journey, for example, it enjoyed a poor sort of immortality; even poorer if, as he rather imagined, a swimmer-hero plus a She equaled or became merely another Maker of future night-seas and the rest, at such incredible expense of life. This being the case—he was persuaded it was—the merciful thing to do was refuse to participate; the genuine heroes, in his opinion, were the suicides, and the hero of heroes would be the swimmer who, in the very presence of the Other, refused Her proffered 'immortality' and thus put an end to at least one cycle of catastrophes.

"How we mocked him! Our moment came, we hurtled forth, pretending to glory in the adventure, thrashing, singing, cursing, strangling, rationalizing, rescuing, killing, inventing rules and stories and relationships, giving up, struggling on, but dying all, and still in darkness, until only a battered remnant was left to croak 'Onward, upward,' like a bitter echo. Then they too fell silent—victims, I can only presume, of the last frightful wave—and the moment came when I also, utterly desolate and spent, thrashed my last and gave myself over to the current, to sink or float as might be, but swim no more. Whereupon, marvelous to tell, in an instant the sea grew still! Then warmly, gently, the great tide turned, began to bear me, as it does now, onward and upward will-I nill-I, like a flood of joy—and I recalled with dismay my dead friend's teaching.

"I am not deceived. This new emotion is Her doing; the desire that possesses me is Her bewitchment. Lucidity passes from me; in a moment I'll cry 'Love!' bury myself in her side, and be 'transfigured.' Which is to say, I die already; this fellow transported by passion is not I; *I am he who abjures and rejects the night-sea journey!* I. . . .

"I am all love. 'Come!' She whispers, and I have no will.

"You who I may be about to become, whatever You are: with the last twitch of my real self I beg You to listen. It is *not* love that sustains me! No; though Her magic makes me burn to sing the contrary, and though I drown even now for the blasphemy, I will say truth. What has fetched me across this dreadful sea is a single hope, gift of my poor dead comrade: that You may be stronger-willed than I, and that by sheer force of concentration I may transmit to You, along with Your official Heritage, a private legacy of awful recollection and negative resolve. Mad as it may be, my dream is that some unimaginable embodiment of myself (or myself plus Her if that's how it must be) will come to find itself expressing, in however garbled or radical a translation, some reflection of these reflections. If against all odds this comes to pass, may You to whom, through whom I speak, do what I cannot: terminate this aimless, brutal business! Stop Your hearing against Her song! Hate love!

"Still alive, afloat, afire. Farewell then my penultimate hope: that one may be sunk for direst blasphemy on the very shore of the Shore. Can it be (my old friend would smile) that only utterest nay-sayers survive the night? But even that were Sense, and there is no sense, only senseless love, senseless death. Whoever echoes these reflections: be more courageous than their author! An end to night-sea journeys! Make no more! And forswear me when I shall forswear myself, deny myself, plunge into Her who summons, singing . . .

" 'Love! Love! Love!' "

QUESTIONS

1. The following terms recur in the story: *night, sea, night-sea, swimmer, shore, She.* Keeping in mind the reproduction metaphor, what would these terms stand for? What meaning do they carry beyond the reproduction metaphor? (For example, a swimmer might stand for a spermatozoon, but also for any individual human being.)

2. The narrator/night-sea swimmer says: "My trouble is, I lack conviction." What does this mean, and how does the swimmer's lack of resolve correlate with the human condition?

3. Why can the night-sea swimmer believe the common Maker view of human nature while holding it absurd?

4. What does the night-sea swimmer mean by "Another paradox: it appears to be these recesses from swimming that sustain me in the swim"? Can the recesses in any way be compared with philosophy and philosophizing?

5. What does the night-sea swimmer understand by "love"? Would you agree?

6. Why does even the possibility of the Shore leave the night-sea swimmer with misgivings?

7. What alternative religious views of human nature does the night-sea swimmer suggest?

8. Why does the night-sea swimmer reject the survival-of-the-fittest view?

9. Does the night-sea swimmer at any point seem to reject the existential view? Why?

10. What is the night-sea swimmer's ultimate wish?

SUGGESTIONS FOR FURTHER READING

Adler, Mortimer. *Aristotle for Everybody*. New York: Macmillan, 1980. In this short paperback, Adler explains Aristotle's basic ideas for the beginning reader of philosophy.

Barret, William. *Death of the Soul: From Descartes to the Computer*. Garden City, N.Y.: Doubleday, 1987. An interesting discussion of how philosophy has affected and been affected by our cultural views of human nature.

Ellison, Ralph. *Invisible Man*. New York: Vintage, 1951. Launching this novel with an explosive opening chapter, Ellison has written a compelling tale of the quest for self-discovery.

Erickson, Erik. *Identity, Youth and Crisis*. New York: Norton, 1968. In this classic on the quest for self-identity, psychoanalyst Erickson relates issues of individual identity to the historically changing patterns of social organization.

Green, Marjorie. *Introduction to Existentialism*. Chicago: Chicago University Press, 1976. This is an excellent introduction to existentialist thought.

Plato. *Great Dialogues of Plato*. Translated by W. H. D. Rouse. New York: New American Library (Mentor Books), 1956. This paperback contains readable translations of the major works of Plato.

Sanders, Steven, and David R. Cheney, eds. *The Meaning of Life*. Englewood Cliffs, N.J.: Prentice-Hall, 1980. An anthology of writings discussing the value of life.

Sartre, Jean-Paul. *Nausea*. New York: New Directions, 1964. In this novel Sartre illustrates his views on freedom, ambiguity, anxiety, and nothingness.

Skinner, B. F. *Walden II*. New York: Macmillan, 1962. Psychologist Skinner presents his behaviorist utopia, governed by principles of stimulus and response, positive reinforcement, and aversive conditioning. The novel is a good introduction to the ideas spelled out in Skinner's *Beyond Freedom and Dignity*.

Stevenson, Leslie. *Seven Theories of Human Nature*. London: Clarendon, 1974. This fine book examines the philosophical views of seven philosophers on human nature. Includes discussions of Plato, Jesus, Marx, Freud, Sartre, Skinner, and Lorenz.

Taylor, A. E. *The Mind of Plato*. Ann Arbor, Mich.: Ann Arbor Paperbacks, 1960. This introduction to Plato's thought is written by a convinced Platonist and is considered by many to be still the best introduction to Plato.

Thoreau, Henry David. *Walden and Other Writings*. Edited by Joseph Wood Krutch. New York: Bantam, 1971. Thoreau's classic autobiographical statement of how he avoided a life of "quiet desperation" and found personal freedom and identity in nature.

Warner, Rex. *The Greek Philosophers*. New York: New American Library (Mentor Books), 1958. This readable paperback presents a nice overview of the thoughts of the ancient philosophers.

Watts, Alan. *The Book: On the Taboo Against Knowing Who You Are*. New York: Collier, 1966. In a thoroughly readable work, Watts examines what he considers to be the West's mistaken focus on ego and self. He argues for the Eastern position of no self and interdependence of all things. In addition, Watts raises questions of love, suffering, death, and the meaning of existence.

PART II   Metaphysics

The term *metaphysics* (meaning "after" or "beyond" physics) has a curious origin. It arises with Aristotle, who wrote a series of essays on fundamental problems about the classifications or categories of being. Early librarians listed these essays after Aristotle's works on physics. Later philosophers noticed this ordering, and these essays came to be called in Greek *ta meta ta physika biblia*, that is, "the books that come after the physics." Subsequently, this was shortened to *The Metaphysics*, and the topics dealt with in these essays were called "metaphysics." Eventually, metaphysics came to be associated with subjects that transcend physics—the supernatural, the occult, and the mysterious.*

Actually, metaphysics does not refer exclusively to a single field or discipline. It encompasses a number of problems whose implications are so broad that they affect just about every other field of philosophy. Specifically, metaphysics is an inquiry into the first principles of being, that is, the attempt to discover the most pervasive characteristics that underlie all our knowledge of, and reasoning about, existence.† Metaphysics also refers to subjects that are nonempirical and nonscientific.

A number of problems traditionally fall under metaphysics. Among them are: the structure and development of reality viewed in its totality; the meaning and nature of being; the nature of mind, self, and consciousness; the existence of God, the destiny of the universe, and the immortality of the soul. The next two chapters, entitled "Philosophy and God" and "Reality and Being," engage a number of these issues.

---

*Robert Paul Wolff, *About Philosophy* (New York: Prentice-Hall, 1976), 262.
†See Eugene A. Troxell and William S. Snyder, *Making Sense of Things: An Invitation to Philosophy* (New York: St. Martin's Press, 1976), 171–172.

CHAPTER 3

Philosophy and God

The highest that man can attain in these matters is wonder.

GOETHE

Introduction

In the West there has probably been no greater influence on one's view of self than religion, which has fostered the view of the human as a divine being. The Judaic and the Christian religious traditions share the belief that what makes humans unique is that they have a divine nature by virtue of possessing consciousness and the ability to love. We are creatures who stand midway between nature and spirit. We are on the one hand finite, bound to earth, and capable of sin. On the other, we are able to transcend nature and to achieve infinite possibilities. Primarily because of Christianity, we view ourselves as beings with a supernatural destiny, as possessing a life after death, as being immortal, and as uniquely valuable.

But religion has fostered beliefs, attitudes, and feelings not only about a supernatural dimension but also about this world. Thus, religious positions commonly circulate concerning various political, educational, and even economic questions. These positions are influential in molding public opinion. In recent years, in fact, religions have become so socially directed that many traditionalists feel that religions are undergoing secularization—that is,

---

If God did not exist it would be necessary to invent him.

VOLTAIRE

---

becoming worldly. Whether or not this charge is justified, *religion* is becoming increasingly difficult to define. However, we should attempt to do so before examining precisely how religion relates to the issue of self. Here are the main points we will make in this chapter.

MAIN POINTS

1. Traditionally, religion refers to a belief in God that is institutionalized and incorporated in the teachings of some religious body, such as a church or synagogue. Today, emphasis is on deep personal experience with the object of one's chief loyalty.

2. Theism is the belief in a personal God who has created the world and is immanent in its processes, and with whom we may come into intimate contact.

3. Three traditional arguments for a theistic God are the ontological argument (such as Saint Anselm's), the cosmological argument (such as Saint Thomas Aquinas's), and the argument from design (such as William Paley's). Each of these arguments has its critics.

4. Besides the traditional objections made to these arguments, critics have raised other objections to theism:
a. How can so much apparent evil emanate from an all-good and all-powerful God?
b. How can God be all-knowing and yet not suffer along with us?
c. How can God be unchanging and yet have perfect knowledge of our changing world?

5. Pantheism argues that everything is God and God is everything.

6. Panentheism argues that everything is in God, who is both fixed and changing, unity and diversity, inclusive of all possibilities.

7. William James called the acquisition of religious belief a live, forced, and momentous option.

8. Many people, unable to find religious belief or experience in a theistic God, find both in a deep personal encounter with a divine dimension.

9. Mysticism claims direct and immediate awareness that is not dependent on direct sense experience or on reason. The mystical experience is inexpressible and noetic.

10. Radical theology, as presented by Søren Kierkegaard and Paul Tillich, has mystical overtones. It appeals to deep personal experience as justification for belief. Tillich's God is being itself, the "God above God," the "ground of all being."

11. The psychedelic experience can resemble mystical states of consciousness.

12. Eastern religious views, such as Hinduism, Buddhism, and Zen Buddhism, are highly sympathetic to claims of personal religious experience.

RELIGION

When you hear the word *religion*, what do you think of? A church? A synagogue? A belief? Religion includes many things: prayer, ritual, institutional organization, and so on. To define *religion* precisely is difficult. Traditionally, the word has referred to a belief in God that is institutionalized and incorporated in the teachings of some body, such as a church or synagogue. Some people, however, hold that religion need not imply a belief in God. Buddhism, for example, although usually considered a religion, contains no belief in a personal God like the God of the Judaic and Christian traditions. Others claim that whatever anyone holds as the most important value in life is a religion, which frequently finds expression outside religious institutions.

It is a little easier to note features of religion than to define it, although qualifications are still necessary. Religion continues to be one of humankind's dominant interests. Unlike science, it stresses personal commitment based on a meaningful relationship with the sacred, which is often a Supreme Being. Such commitment is generally founded on belief, although most religionists claim that belief divorced from feeling is misguided. Feeling and emotion seem prominent in religion, although these too can mislead. Religion frequently finds expression through institutionalized ritual. Recent trends indicate, however, that many people feel that the emphasis on a symbolic object of devotion, ritualized through an organizational structure, has blurred religion's real import: a deep and personal experience with the object of one's chief loyalty.

In the last analysis, religion is not just an institution, a collection of doctrines, or a stylized ritual. Without exception, religious leaders have spoken in terms of personal commitment, experience, and need. In so doing they have recognized the roots from which religion has sprung: our unending search for meaning and fulfillment. In this sense they have emphasized religious belief rather than religion, religious practice rather than theology.

Literally speaking, **theology** means simply "the rational study of God." In practice, however, the term is usually reserved for the rational study of religious beliefs by scholars committed to those beliefs. A "theologian," for example, is a person who studies God and the religious beliefs of a community but who does so with the assumption that God exists and that those religious beliefs are true. By contrast, philosophers approach God and religious beliefs without these assumptions: For the philosopher, these assumptions must themselves be proved.

Theology (and philosophy) has not always touched the faithful in a direct way. The devoted need little theology. Indeed, early Christian history testifies to the priority of faith over knowledge—thus, Saint Anselm's aphorism "I believe in order to understand." We mention this to emphasize that for the vast majority of people, religious belief is more important than any formal theology, and it should therefore be distinguished from theology.

In this chapter we shall have numerous occasions to speak of **religious belief**, which we'll use in its most general sense: the belief that there is an unseen order and that we can do no better than to be in harmony with this order. Likewise, when we use the term *religious experience*, we shall be referring to an experience of this unseen order and our individual place in this order. Having found this place, people feel an intense personal relationship with the rest of creation, perhaps even with a Creator. In this respect, we all seek a religious experience; we all search for an internal peace resulting from a harmonious personal relationship with all other living things. Religious belief and experience continue to be of intense philosophical interest. They are also intimately joined with the issue of self.

Where do we find religious experience today? Some find it in traditional religious concepts, such as the existence of a personal God who listens to and answers prayer, who rewards the faithful and punishes the unworthy. Others, finding such a belief irrational, relate to the divine without relating to a Supreme Being. They claim that religious experience is an intimately personal encounter with the basis of all being, with the source of all reality. Still others find religious experience through the expansion of consciousness—that is, the experience of reality in an unaccustomed manner. And there are many who turn to Eastern thought—Hinduism and Buddhism, for example.

In this chapter we shall explore these and related concerns by thinking philosophically about religion. That is what the philosophy of religion is about. Although such a study ordinarily includes

---

PHILOSOPHY AND LIFE 3.1

Defining Religion

Sometimes the most ordinary things create tremendous bafflement. Everyone knows what religion is. But can you define it? Here are several attempts:

Religion is concern *about experiences which are regarded as of supreme value;* devotion *towards a power or powers believed to originate, increase, and conserve these values; and some* suitable expression *of this concern and devotion, whether through symbolic rites or through other individual and social conduct.* Edgar S. Brightman

Any activity pursued in behalf of an ideal and against obstacles and in spite of threats of personal loss because of conviction of its general and enduring value is religious in quality. John Dewey

Religion is the ritual cultivation of socially accepted values. J. Fischer

Religion is a propitiation of, and dependency on, superior powers which are believed to control and direct the course of nature and human life. Sir James G. Frazer

Religion is a theory of man's relation to the universe. S. P. Haynes

Religion is a sense of the sacred. Sir Julian Huxley

Religion is (subjectively regarded) the organization of all duties as divine commands. Immanuel Kant

Religion consists in the perception of the infinite under such manifestations as are able to influence the moral character of man. Max Muller

Religion is one's attitude toward whatever he considers to be the determiner of destiny. James Bissett Pratt

The essence of religion is the feeling of utter dependence upon the infinite reality, that is, upon God. F. Schleiermacher

Religion is man's ultimate concern for the Ultimate. Paul Tillich

Religion, as a minimum, is the belief in spiritual beings. E. B. Taylor

Religion is a belief in an ultimate meaning of the universe. Alfred R. Wallace

A religion, on its doctrinal sides, can thus be described as a system of general truths which have the effect of transforming character when they are sincerely held and vividly apprehended. Alfred North Whitehead

Obviously, the very definition of this pervasive phenomenon is controversial. Even today there is no widespread agreement about how to define religion, although everyone seems to know exactly what it is.

QUESTION

1. How would you define religion?

many aspects of religion, including God, immortality, salvation, creation, and all particular religions, we shall focus instead on the nature and varieties of religious experience, on the many ways in which individuals claim to discover their place in the cosmos.

QUESTIONS

1. Explain the difference between "religious belief" and "formal theology."

2. Evaluate this statement: "For many people belief in science has achieved the status of a religion." Can "science" be a "religion"? Explain.

3. What kinds of beliefs or behavior would a person have to adopt before you would be willing to say that the person is a "religious" person? What does the term mean to you?

Monotheism

The most common way for people of a Judeo-Christian culture to find their place in the scheme of things is through a relationship with a personal God—through theistic belief. **Theism** is a belief in a personal God who is creator of the world and immanent in its processes and with whom we may come into intimate contact.[1] **Monotheism** is the belief that there is only one God. Most of us have been raised to accept a theistic concept of God, which forms the basis for our religious feelings and experiences. This God is the basis for the view of the human as divine, as having an immortal soul and a supernatural destiny.

This concept has perhaps never been under greater attack than it is today. Even theologians are asking whether the believer can any longer believe in this traditional God: a single, all-powerful, all-knowing, and all-good God who, having created life, actively participates in the lives of His creatures by listening to and answering prayer. They are questioning an assumption that has centuries of tradition behind it, that is a cornerstone of the lives of many people today, and that has produced not only our religious beliefs but also our ways of perceiving ourselves and the world around us.

Wilbur Daniel Steele, in his short story "The Man Who Saw Through Heaven," portrays the dimensions of the problem facing the contempo-

---

1. Harold H. Titus and Marilyn S. Smith, *Living Issues in Philosophy*, 6th ed. (New York: D. Van Nostrand, 1974), 334.

rary theistic believer. In it he depicts Herbert Diana, a self-educated man, who like many theists has accepted a conventional amount of scientific facts as more proof of "what God can do when He puts His mind to it." Intellectually, Diana has accepted the fact of a spherical earth speeding through space, but deep down in his heart he knows "that the world lay flat from modern Illinois to ancient Palestine, and that the sky above it, blue by day and by night festooned with guiding stars for wise men, was the nether side of a floor on which the resurrected trod."[2] How would a man of such simple faith react to a vision of the heavens that he has never believed possible, to a look through an incredibly powerful telescope into an ink black sky that he has always viewed as the floor of heaven, to a vision of the enormity of the universe? How would his simple belief in a personal God stand up to the sudden realization that He must also be personally and completely involved in an infinity of galactic universes and lives? For the first time in his life, Herbert Diana's faith is tested. His well-ordered medieval world concept has to deal with twentieth-century realities. His simple ideas of a heaven "up there" and a hell "down there," of a God who is personally concerned with each person's immortal destiny, and of the infinite importance of a single soul and of what that soul chooses to do—all these beliefs suddenly shrink in the vastness of what his eyes have seen and his mind cannot forget.

In a sense we are all Dianas, for we live in a period that pits traditional religious concepts against the growing weight of scientific fact. Can we, *should* we believe in the God of theism, or must we modify this belief and perhaps abandon it? Consider, as Diana must, the millions of solar systems that we view as stars. Imagine how many millions of satellites must have supported organic life at some time. Imagine how many millions of creatures, perhaps grotesque by our standards, but creatures nonetheless. Then consider clusters of universes apart from ours. And consider further that "all these,

The Ancient of Days, William Blake. "Theism is a belief in a personal God who is creator of the world and with whom we may come into intimate contact. This God is the basis for the view of the human as divine, as having an immortal soul and a supernatural destiny."

all the generations of these enormous and microscopic beings harvested through a time beside which the life span of our earth is as a second in a million centuries: all these brought to rest for an eternity to which the time in itself is a watch tick—all crowded to rest pellmell, thronged, serried, packed to suffocation in layers unnumbered light-years deep."[3] Do we know the God who rules over such universes?

Today science has brought many of us, like Herbert Diana, to ask not only if we believe in a traditional God but also if there is any God at all.

2. Wilbur Daniel Steele, "The Man Who Saw Through Heaven," in *The Search for Personal Freedom*, 3d ed., eds. Neal Cross, Leslie Lindou, and Robert Lamm (Dubuque, Iowa: W. C. Brown, 1968), 27.

3. Ibid., 28.

Nevertheless, despite the rise of science and the decay of traditional religious forms, religion thrives in this country. In other words, while rational arguments might have an impact on the beliefs of people like Herbert Diana, in general they have little effect on most people's beliefs. In fact, this is why Diana is ultimately able to return to his "simple faith"—not because he had new evidence, but because he *chose* to believe rather than not to believe. Believing in a personal God was his way of locating himself in the scheme of things. Such people don't believe on the basis of scientific evidence, which may or may not support their belief.

Interestingly, some philosophers have held that God's existence is so obvious that it hardly needs proof. During the Middle Ages, Saint Augustine and Saint Anselm (whose "ontological argument" we will examine below), for example, held that we have within our minds a conception of God that compels us to believe that God exists. Several centuries later, the seventeenth-century French philosopher René Descartes held that we have in our minds an idea of a perfect God that we could not have made up ourselves. The perfection of the God we have in mind, he argued, compels us to acknowledge that God must exist. In fact, Descartes held, we could not know *anything* with certitude if there were no God to guarantee that our

---

PHILOSOPHY AND LIFE 3.2

Religion and Science

For many people the growth of science has made the so-called truths of religion increasingly difficult to maintain. Some, however, have found science not so different from religious belief. Contemporary Christian philosopher Étienne Gilson is a good example.

Gilson argues that, contrary to the traditional distinction between science and religion, the language of modern science and the questions it asks are fundamentally nonscientific. For example, Gilson cites the English astronomer Sir James Jeans's description of the emergence of life as "highly improbable," of human existence as "accidental," and of the entire creation as "surprising." In Gilson's view such descriptions, strictly speaking, are not scientific. He suggests, therefore, that in facing the most basic questions, such as the origin of the universe, science, like religion, must operate on a

kind of faith or belief and not on established fact.

He then observes that in its attempt to explain the origin of things, science shows a markedly nonscientific or metaphysical bent. The reason is that such investigations imply a search for the first cause or causes of things, a subject that traditionally has been addressed by metaphysics. More to the point, in attempting to account for things, some scientists appeal to chance. Others, while assuming the operation of mechanical laws of nature, nonetheless propose a self-made, spontaneously arising universe. Such explanations, says Gilson, are essentially no different from, say, Thomas Aquinas's cosmological argument that premises a cause for every event and concludes with an uncaused cause.

In brief, then, Gilson's view is that the more scientific we become, the more metaphysical we

must be—and the more religious. In the end, he sees much of contemporary science as providing a methodological basis for demonstrating the efficacy of religious truths.

QUESTIONS

1. Do you agree that the distinction between science and metaphysics is not clear-cut?

2. Investigation of the microcosmic reality and the astrophysical macrocosm seems to produce in many scientists a humility and sense of reverence that borders on the religious. A long line of scientists, including Einstein, have seen the universe as God's "sensorium." What do you think they mean by this?

3. Are there any facts of science that make you more inclined to religious belief? Less inclined?

knowledge is generally accurate. Thus, for Descartes, God is the foundation on which all our scientific knowledge is built. (For a fuller discussion of Descartes's philosophy, see the showcase at the end of this chapter.)

Others find in science a new basis for religious belief. In fact, appeals to reason and experience have figured prominently in the history of Christian theology. For example, numerous theologians have advanced arguments for the existence of a personal God, as we shall shortly see. But it is vital to recognize the purpose of these arguments: to advance the quest to understand God. Knowledge of God was and continues to be one of the most significant topics occupying thinkers from Saint Augustine onward. And the arguments advanced for God's existence were one element in the centuries-long attempt to determine the extent to which humans could have rational knowledge of God and to which philosophy had a bearing on theological matters. Certainly every thinker of note considered arguments, but they didn't emphasize them. Thomas Aquinas (1225–1274), for example, was not trying to use his arguments to convince anyone of God's existence. Their appearance in his monumental *Summa Theologica* was largely pedagogical. The theological summary was intended for believers whose main task was to know the theological tradition for their work as students and as masters.

We will begin our overview of philosophy and religion with some of these arguments for the existence of God. We present them as illustrations of a traditional way by which people have fortified their religious convictions, strengthened their relationship with a personal God, and discovered something about that God. In reading these arguments, notice their reliance on reason and sense experience, on rationalism and empiricism and keep in mind the contrasting approach, which is essentially nonrational. We will see how this latter approach has been revitalized and how for many people today it serves as the basis for religious belief and experience. In reading this chapter, then, you will begin to mine two rich veins in the development of religious thought, the rational and nonrational.

Saint Anselm: "There is, then, so truly a Being that which nothing greater can be conceived, that It cannot even be conceived not to exist; and this being Thou art, O Lord, our God."

THE ONTOLOGICAL ARGUMENT

There are many arguments propounding God's existence in Saint Augustine, but they are not as formalized and as self-conscious as the ones asserted in the eleventh century by Saint Anselm. He offered one argument that relied on reason alone. Later arguments would be based on the experience of the things of the world, but Anselm held that the mind by itself could arrive at such a realization.

God, Anselm reasoned, is "that than which none greater can be conceived." Now, what if God were just an idea? If he were, we could easily conceive of something greater: a God who actually existed. Therefore, Anselm concluded, if God is "that than which none greater can be conceived," then God must exist. This is about as distilled a version of Anselm's ontological argument as one is likely to get. To appreciate it fully, you must follow its development in Anselm's most important philosophical work, the *Proslogion*. In reading the following passage, keep in mind the impulse behind it: "*Credo ut intelligam*"—"I believe in order that I may understand." Thus, without belief, one can have no understanding of God.

> Truly there is a God, although the fool hath said in his heart, there is no God.
>
> And so, Lord, do thou, who dost give understanding to faith, give me, so far as thou knowest it to be profitable, to understand that thou art as we believe; and that thou art that which we believe. And, indeed, we believe that thou art a being than which nothing greater can be conceived. Or is there no such nature, since the fool hath said in his heart, there is no God? (Psalms xiv.1). But, at any rate, this very fool, when he hears of this being of which I speak—a being than which nothing greater can be conceived—understands what he hears, and what he understands in his understanding; although he does not understand it to exist.
>
> For, it is one thing for an object to be in the understanding, and another to understand that the object exists. When a painter first conceives of what he will afterwards perform, he has it in his understanding, but he does not yet understand it to be, because he has not yet performed it. But after he has made the painting, he both has it in his understanding, and he understands that it exists, because he has made it.
>
> Hence, even the fool is convinced that something exists in the understanding, at least, than which nothing greater can be conceived. For, when he hears of this, he understands it. And whatever is understood, exists in the understanding. And assuredly that, than which nothing greater can be conceived, cannot exist in the understanding alone. For, suppose it exists in the understanding alone: then it can be conceived to exist in reality; which is greater.
>
> Therefore, if that, than which nothing greater

The very impossibility in which I find myself to prove that God is not, discloses to me His existence.

JEAN DE LA BRUYÈRE

> can be conceived, exists in the understanding alone, the very being, than which nothing greater can be conceived, is one, than which a greater can be conceived. But obviously this is impossible. Hence, there is no doubt that there exists a being, than which nothing greater can be conceived, and it exists both in the understanding and in reality.
>
> And it assuredly exists so truly, that it cannot be conceived not to exist. For, it is possible to conceive of a being which cannot be conceived not to exist; and this is greater than one which can be conceived not to exist. Hence, if that, than which nothing greater can be conceived, can be conceived not to exist, it is not that, than which nothing is greater can be conceived. But this is an irreconcilable contradiction. There is, then, so truly a being than which nothing greater can be conceived to exist, that it cannot even be conceived not to exist; and this being thou art, O Lord, our God.
>
> So truly, therefore, dost thou exist, O Lord, my God, that thou canst not be conceived not to exist; and rightly. For, if a mind could conceive of a being better than thee, the creature would rise above the Creator; and this is most absurd. And, indeed, whatever else there is, except thee alone, can be conceived not to exist. To thee alone, therefore, it belongs to exist more truly than all other beings, and hence in a higher degree than all others. For, whatever else exists does not exist so truly, and hence in a less degree it belongs to it to exist. Why, then, has the fool said in his heart, there is no God (Psalms xiv.1), since it is so evident, to a rational mind, that thou dost exist in the highest degree of all? Why, except that he is dull and a fool?[4]

Anselm has had his supporters over the years. But more people have attacked the ontological argument. Immanuel Kant was one. He claimed that the concept of an absolutely necessary being is not proved by the fact that reason apparently requires it.

To understand Kant's criticism, ask yourself this: Under what conditions will a triangle have three sides? Obviously, when and where there is a tri-

---

4. Saint Anselm, *Saint Anselm: Basic Writings*, trans. S. N. Deane (La Salle, Ill.: Open Court Publishing, 1962). Reprinted by permission.

angle. In other words, *if* there is a triangle, it has three sides. But *if* is conditional: that is, what follows it may not be. "If there is a triangle" does not imply that there necessarily *is* a triangle. Likewise, "*If* there is a perfect being, then a perfect being exists" does not mean a perfect being does exist. Kant claims that Anselm is defining God into existence—that he is asking us to form a concept of a thing in such a way as to include existence within the scope of its meaning. Undoubtedly, Anselm would object that it is contradictory to posit a triangle and yet reject its three sides. Kant would agree. But he would add that there is no contradiction in rejecting the triangle *along with* its three sides. "Likewise of the concept of an absolutely necessary being. If its existence is rejected, we reject the thing itself with all its predicates; and no question of contradiction can then arise."

But a perfect being is unique. Because Anselm thought nonexistence was an imperfection and therefore inconsistent with the nature of a perfect being, he argued that a perfect being must exist. And he was right, assuming that existence adds to a thing. But imagine a perfect companion. Attribute to it all the properties that will make it perfect. Then ask yourself, "Does its existence add anything to the concept?" The point is that to assert existence is not to add a property but to assert a relationship between the thing conceived and the world. In other words, you do not add anything to the creature of your fantasy by positing its existence; you merely establish its relationship to other things. This is what Kant meant when he wrote: "When I think of a being as the supreme reality, without any defect, the question still remains whether it exists or not."

THE COSMOLOGICAL ARGUMENT

After Anselm's ontological argument, the next important attempt to justify God's existence was made by the greatest of all the rational theologians, the thirteenth-century Christian philosopher Saint Thomas Aquinas (1225–1274). His arguments are systematically organized and stated in Aristotelian language. In his monumental *Summa Theologica*, Aquinas offers five proofs, only one of which will

> **The celestial order and the beauty of the universe compel me to admit that there is some excellent and eternal Being, who deserves the respect and homage of men.**
>
> CICERO

concern us here. (For the other proofs and a fuller discussion of his philosophy, see the showcase on Aquinas at the end of this chapter.) This proof begins with an observation about the physical world, and thus it is "cosmological" in that it results from a study of the universe.

Aquinas's argument originates in the observed fact that things in this universe are caused: Their existence is caused by other things. Aquinas then reasons that these observed effects are the last in a chain of such effects. This chain, however, must not go back endlessly, because it then would have no beginning: The chain must start somewhere. It must start, says Aquinas, with a being who itself is uncaused. Such a being he terms *God.* This argument is elaborated in the following passage from his *Summa Theologica*:

> [One] way [of proving God's existence] is based on the nature of efficient causes. In the world we see around us, there are ordered lines of efficient causes [in which each member of the line produces the next member]. But nothing can be its own efficient cause, since then it would have to exist prior to itself and this is impossible. Now it is not possible for a line of efficient causes to extend to infinity. For in any line of efficient causes, the first is the cause of the intermediate ones, and the intermediate ones cause the last one. Now if we remove any of the causes, we remove all the remaining effects. So if there were no first cause then there would be no last cause nor any intermediate ones. But if a line of efficient causes extended back to infinity, then we would find no first cause. Consequently, if the line of causes extended back to infinity, there would be no intermediate causes nor any last causes in existence in

the universe. But we know this is false. So it is necessary to admit that there is a first efficient cause. And this we call God.[5]

There are two key objections to this cosmological argument. The first concerns its contention that there can be no infinite regress in the causal sequences of the universe. Aquinas reasoned that an infinite regress might account for the individual links in the causal chain, but not for the chain itself. Is he right?

Suppose a friend visits you at college. You wish to show her around the campus. So, you take her to the library, the humanities building, the science labs, the cafeteria, and so on, until she sees the entire college. After this tour, she asks, "But where is the college?" You might find that a silly question, since you had already shown her the college by showing her its parts. In a similar way David Hume questioned Aquinas's cause argument: "Did I show you the particular causes of each individual in a collection of twenty particles of matter, I should think it very unreasonable, should you afterwards ask me, what was the cause of the whole twenty. For this is sufficiently explained in explaining the cause of the parts."[6] Hume is arguing that the individual links in the causal chain find cause in their immediate predecessors. This fact is enough to account for the chain itself. The same kind of logic might be applied to events and contingent beings (beings that are not necessary). In other words, if Hume's argument has merit, there is no need or any logical justification for positing a first mover, a first cause, or a necessary being. Of course, this objection relies on a commitment to mechanism and hence a denial that the whole is greater than the sum of its parts. If this assumption is rejected, an explanation is required for both the parts and the whole.

The second objection is that the argument's conclusion is contradicted by its premise. To illustrate, Aquinas insists that every event must have a cause. But if this is so, why stop with God? The notion of an uncaused cause seems to contradict the assumption that everything has a cause. And even if there is an uncaused cause, why must it be God? Arthur Schopenhauer expresses this objection succinctly when he writes that the law of universal causation "is not so accommodating as to let itself be used like a cab for hire, which we dismiss when we have reached our destination."[7]

A number of contemporary Thomists (thinkers who generally agree with Thomas Aquinas) have modified this first-cause argument. For them, the endless series that the argument dismisses is not a regress of events in time but a regress of explanations. As John Hick interprets the position: "If fact A is made intelligible by its relation to fact B, C and D (which may be antecedent to or contemporary with A), and if each of these is in turn rendered intelligible by other facts, at the back of the complex there must be a reality which is self-explanatory, whose existence constitutes the ultimate explanation of the whole. If no such reality exists, the universe is a mere unintelligible brute fact."[8] But how do we know that the universe is not "a mere unintelligible brute fact"? Hick's argument appears to present a dilemma: Either a first cause exists or the universe makes no sense. But can't the universe make sense as something that is simply there?

THE DESIGN ARGUMENT

The most popular of the arguments of God's existence has been the proof from design, often called the teleological argument. Simply put, the order and purpose manifest in the working of things demand a God. Even when evolutionists offer an explanation for such apparent order, supporters of the design argument reply, "Yes, but why did things evolve in this way and not in some other?" Traditionally a prominent argument for God's exis-

5. Saint Thomas Aquinas, *Summa Theologica*, I, q.2, a.3, trans. and ed. Manuel Velasquez.
6. David Hume, *Dialogues Concerning Natural Religion*, ed. N. Kemp Smith (Edinburgh: Nelson, 1947), 18.

7. Quoted in C. J. Ducasse, *A Philosophical Scrutiny of Religion* (New York: Ronald Presss, 1953), 335.
8. John Hick, *Philosophy of Religion* (Englewood Cliffs, N.J.: Prentice-Hall, 1963), 21. Reprinted by permission.

tence, the design proof has currency even among some biologists today, such as Edmund W. Sinnot, and some theologians, such as Robert E. D. Clark.

In 1802 theologian William Paley presented one of the best known expositions of the design proof. Comparing natural organisms to the mechanism of a watch, Paley argued that just as the design of a watch implies the existence of a maker, so the design evidenced by natural organisms implies the existence of a "Divine Agency."

In crossing a heath, suppose I pitched my foot against a *stone*, and were asked how the stone came to be there. I might possibly answer, that for anything I knew to the contrary, it had lain there for ever: nor would it perhaps be very easy to show the absurdity of this answer. But suppose I had found a *watch* upon the ground, and it should be inquired how the watch happened to be in that place; I should hardly think of the answer which I had before given, that for anything I knew the watch might have always been there. Yet why should not this answer serve for the watch as well as for the stone? Why is it not as admissible in the second case as in the first? For this reason, and for no other, viz. that when we come to inspect the watch, we perceive (what we could not discover in the stone) that its several parts are framed and put together for a purpose, e.g., that they are so formed and adjusted as to produce motion, and that motion so regulated as to point out the hour of the day; that if the different parts had been differently shaped from what they are, of a different size from what they are, or placed after any other manner, or in any other order, than that in which they are placed, either no motion at all would have been carried on in the machine, or none which would have answered the use that is now served by it. . . . This mechanism being observed . . . the inference, we think, is inevitable, that the watch must have had a maker; that there must have existed, at some time, and at some place or other, an artificer or artificers, who formed it for the purpose which we find it actually to answer; who comprehended its construction and designed its use. . . .

[E]very indication of contrivance, every manifestation of design, which existed in the watch, exists in the works of nature; with the difference, on the side of nature, of being greater and more,

and that in a degree which exceeds all computation. I mean, that the contrivances of nature surpass the contrivances of art, in the complexity, subtlety, and curiosity, of the mechanism; and still more, if possible, do they go beyond them in number and variety; yet, in a multitude of cases, are not less evidently mechanical, not less evidently contrivances, not less evidently accommodated to their end, or suited to their office, than are the most perfect productions of human ingenuity. . . .

Every observation which was made [above] concerning the watch, may be repeated with strict propriety concerning the eye, concerning animals, concerning plants, concerning, indeed, all the organized parts of the works of nature. . . .

Were there no example in the world of contrivance, except that of the *eye*, it would be alone sufficient to support the conclusion which we draw from it, as to the necessity of an intelligent Creator. . . . If there were but one watch in the world, it would not be less certain that it had a maker. . . . So it is with the evidences of a Divine agency.[9]

As was the custom of religious thinkers of his day, Paley called on a long list of examples from the sciences (especially biology) to demonstrate his argument. The migration of birds, the instincts of other animals, the adaptability of species to various environments, and the human's ability to forecast based on probable causation all suggested a plan and a planner.

Many contemporary writers have agreed. How, they wonder, can we otherwise explain our continued safety from the two zones of high-intensity particulate radiation trapped in the earth's magnetic field and surrounding the planet? As one writer says, "The ozone gas layer is mighty proof of the Creator's forethought. Could anyone attribute this device to a chance evolutionary process? A wall which prevents death to every living thing, just the right thickness, and exactly the correct defense, gives every evidence of plan."[10]

But critics have asked, "Does the appearance

---

9. William Paley, *Natural Theology*, in *The Works of William Paley* (Philadelphia: Crissy & Markley, 1857), 387–485.
10. Arthur I. Brown, *Footprints of God* (Findlay, Ohio: Fundamental Truth Publishers, 1943), 102.

of order necessitate conscious design?" The order in the universe, they say, could have occurred by chance through an incredibly long period of evolution. Hume argues that in an infinite amount of time, a finite number of particles in random motion must eventually effect a stable order. After all, it is impossible to imagine a universe without some design. In fact, by definition, a universe must have design.

As Darwin later contended, the life around us has won in the "struggle for survival"—the fit have survived and the unfit have perished. Through a process of natural selection, in which those that can adapt survive and the rest die, a stability in things comes to pass. Concerning our safety under an ozone umbrella, both Hume and Darwin would point out that it is not explained by a God who made things and then shielded them but by an evolutionary fact: that only life that adjusted to the precise level of ultraviolet radiation penetrating this ozone has survived. In other words, life has adjusted to the ozone; ozone has not sustained life.

OBJECTIONS TO THEISM: THE PROBLEM OF EVIL

The traditional proofs for God's existence, as we've seen, are claimed to have obvious flaws. There are additional objections, of which the major is the problem of evil.

Clearly humans continue to be beset by all kinds of problems: sickness, poverty, suffering, and death. Yet theism insists that there is an all-good, all-powerful Creator. Is this not at least paradoxical? How is evil compatible with an all-good Creator? If God is all-powerful, surely He could destroy all evil. If He doesn't, why not? Is He really not all-powerful? Or is it that He's unwilling? But if God is unwilling, then He seems to have evil intentions, which certainly aren't consistent with the nature of an all-good God.

In his *Dialogues Concerning Natural Religion*, a three-person discussion of the chief arguments for God's existence, Hume considers this question of evil. His conclusion, in the words of one of his characters, Philo, is that one's experience in the world argues against the existence of an all-good, all-powerful being.

My sentiments, replied Philo, are not worth being made a mystery of; and, therefore, without any ceremony, I shall deliver what occurs to me with regard to the present subject. It must, I think, be allowed that, if a very limited intelligence whom we shall suppose utterly unacquainted with the universe were assured that it were the production of a very good, wise, and powerful being, however finite, he would, from his conjectures, form *beforehand* a different notion of it from what we find it to be by experience; nor would he ever imagine, merely from these attributes of the cause of which he is informed, that the effect could be so full of vice and misery and disorder, as it appears in this life. Supposing now that this person were brought into the world, still assured that it was the workmanship of such a sublime and benevolent being, he might, perhaps, be surprised at the disappointment, but would never retract his former belief if founded on any very solid argument, since such a limited intelligence must be sensible of his own blindness and ignorance, and must allow that there may be many solutions of those phenomena which will forever escape his comprehension. But supposing, which is the real case with regard to man, that this creature is not antecedently convinced of a supreme intelligence, benevolent, and powerful, but is left to gather such a belief from the appearances of things—this entirely alters the case, nor will he ever find any reason for such a conclusion. He may be fully convinced of the narrow limits of his understanding, but this will not help him in forming an inference concerning the goodness of superior powers, since he must form that inference from what he knows, not from what he is ignorant of. The more you exaggerate his weakness and ignorance, the more diffident you render him, and give him the greater suspicion that such subjects are beyond the reach of his faculties. You are obliged, therefore, to reason with him merely from the known phenomena, and to drop every arbitrary supposition or conjecture.[11]

Hume is saying that if we presuppose an all-good, all-powerful God, then we, in effect, ration-

---

11. Hume, *Dialogues Concerning Natural Religion*, pt. XI.

alize away the evil that we experience as being something beyond our ability to comprehend. But if we don't presuppose such a being, then our experience in the world lends no support to the claim that an all-good, all-powerful being exists. If we don't take God's existence for granted, then the experience of "vice and misery and disorder" in fact argues against a theistic God.

There have been a number of attempts to deal with the problem of evil. Augustine, for one, argues that evil is a negative thing—that is, the absence of that good that is due a creature. To be real, said Augustine, is to be good. Since only God is perfectly good, only God is wholly real. God's creation, therefore, being finite and limited, must contain incomplete goodness—that is, evil. But this argument seems to dodge the issue. Call sickness lack of health, if you wish, and suffering lack of peace—the fact remains that people experience pain and suffering, which they commonly regard as evil. Why does an all-powerful God allow such "absences of good"?

Others argue that evil is necessary for good, that only through evil can good be achieved. It is true that in many instances good seems to depend on evil, as in the case of having to suffer surgical pain to rid one's body of disease. But to say that God can bring about good in no other way than through inflicting pain seems to deny God's omnipotence.

But the most common and serious attempt to escape the problem of evil is to claim human freedom as the cause of evil. Since we are free, we are free to do evil as well as good. Even an omnipotent God could not make us free in all other respects but not free to do evil, since this would be contradictory. Therefore, evil results from free human choice.

But there are several problems with this argument. First, it does not account for natural evils: earthquakes, droughts, and tornadoes. Humans apparently exercise no control over these. So the argument can pertain only to moral evils—that is, those perpetrated by humans on other creatures: war, murder, and torture. Undoubtedly we are free to do this evil, but why did an all-powerful God enable us to do such terrible things? After all, if He is all-powerful, He could have made us differently. Already we are vulnerable, limited creatures. Why not make us unable to do evil? Perhaps we do not really understand the nature of evil; what we perceive as evil may in God's eyes be good. But if this is so, even more complex questions arise concerning the nature and morality of the Supreme Being. We are also left puzzled about what goodness itself really is.

John Hick (1922–), lecturer in divinity at Cambridge University, has taken a novel approach to the problem of evil. In his *Philosophy of Religion*, Hick suggests that a world without suffering would be unsatisfactory. Consistent with the thinking of early Hellenistic fathers of the Christian church, such as Irenaeus, Hick seems to argue that while humans are made in the image of God, they have not yet been brought as free and responsible agents into the finite likeness of God as revealed in Christ. The world, then, "with all its rough edges," becomes the sphere in which this stage of the creative process takes place.

> I see little evidence in this world of the so-called goodness of God. On the contrary, it seems to me that, on the strength of His daily acts, He must be set down a most stupid, cruel and villainous fellow.
>
> H. L. MENCKEN

Suppose, contrary to fact, that this world were a paradise from which all possibility of pain and suffering were excluded. The consequences would be very far-reaching. For example, no one could ever injure anyone else: the murderer's knife would turn to paper or his bullets to thin air; the bank safe, robbed of a million dollars, would miraculously become filled with another million dollars (without this device, on however large a scale, proving inflationary); fraud, deceit, conspiracy, and treason would somehow always leave the fabric of society undamaged. Again, no one would ever be injured by accident: the mountain-climber, steeplejack, or playing child falling from a height would float unharmed to the ground; the reckless driver would never meet with disaster. There would be no need to work, since no harm could result from avoiding work; there would be no call to be concerned for others in time of need or danger, for in such a world there could be no real needs or dangers.

To make possible this continual series of individual adjustments, nature would have to work by "special providences" instead of running according to general laws which men must learn to respect on penalty of pain or death. The laws of nature would have to be extremely flexible: sometimes gravity would operate, sometimes not; sometimes an object would be hard and solid, sometimes soft. There could be no sciences, for there would be no enduring world structure to investigate. In eliminating the problems and hardships of an objective environment, with its own laws, life would become like a dream in which, delightfully but aimlessly, we would float and drift at ease.

One can at least begin to imagine such a world. It is evident that our present ethical concepts would have no meaning in it. If, for example, the notion of harming someone is an essential element in the concept of a wrong action, in our hedonistic paradise there could be no wrong actions—nor any right actions in distinction from wrong. Courage and fortitude would have no point in an environment in which there is, by definition, no danger of difficulty. Generosity, kindness, the *agape* aspect of love, prudence, unselfishness, and all other ethical notions which presuppose life in a stable environment, could not even be formed. Consequently, such a world, however well it might promote pleasure, would be very ill adapted for the development of the moral qualities of human personality. In relation to this purpose it would be the worst of all possible worlds.

It would seem, then, that an environment intended to make possible the growth in free beings of the finest characteristics of personal life, must have a good deal in common with our present world. It must operate according to general and dependable laws; and it must involve real dangers, difficulties, problems, obstacles, and possibilities of pain, failure, sorrow, frustration, and defeat. If it did not contain the particular trials and perils which—subtracting man's own very considerable contribution—our world contains, it would have to contain others instead.[12]

Persons of faith may be largely indifferent to evil as an issue, since they "know" their God beyond rationality and can easily say that we can't begin to fathom God's mystery. In the last analysis, evil may be a problem only for those whose tolerance of mystery is minimal. The rationalist or empiricist must explain away mystery rather than confronting it and getting intimations of the divine and the holy. But for many people, evil just isn't a problem. The same can be said of the other criticisms made of theism.

One of those criticisms concerns God's all-knowing nature. If God is all-knowing, He is aware of what is going on. But can He be aware of our travail without suffering with us? Some say that is precisely why God became man. But how can the timeless and unchanging become incarnate in our world of change? In addition, God's knowledge of our changing world is said to be itself unchanging. How is this possible? Traditional theism, furthermore, speaks of a God that transcends creation; God is said to be different from and superior to what He made. But isn't perfect knowledge contingent on knowing something "inside out"? A parent never completely knows its offspring, for it can never fully know what that offspring feels, thinks, and desires. If God has perfect knowledge, isn't He then a composite of the many things that make up reality? But if this is so, how can God at the same time be separate and distinct from His creation? These questions have led some reflective theists to argue for pantheism and panentheism in place of traditional monotheism. Others reject theism completely.

QUESTIONS

1. Anselm argues that a perfect being must exist because the lack of existence is an imperfection. Could you argue that, on the contrary, a perfect

---

12. Hick, *Philosophy of Religion*, 45–46.

being must not exist because existence is an imperfection? Explain.

2. If you believe in God, do you believe on the basis of Anselm's ontological argument? If you do not believe in God, do you disbelieve because you consider the ontological argument inadequate?

3. Explain the difference between these two statements: "If there is a perfect being, then a perfect being exists" and "If there can be a perfect being, then a perfect being exists." Which represents the ontological argument? Which is the objection to it? With which do you agree, and why?

4. Evaluate these statements.
a. God was the first event.
b. God caused the first event.
c. God is an uncaused cause.
d. A mind without a body, God, created matter, including bodies.

5. Do you agree that if there is no first cause, the universe makes no sense? Is an infinite regress nonsensical?

6. If you believe in God, do you believe because of the argument from cause? If you do not believe in God, do you disbelieve because of the inadequacy of the argument from cause?

7. Aquinas's proofs are based on analogical reasoning, in which he compares what we have experienced directly with what we have not. What is the source of his analogy in the cause argument? Is the analogy a good one?

8. Explain what Hume means when he says, "A universe by definition must appear designed, for it shows design."

9. In what ways would you say organic evolution is compatible with the account of creation given in Genesis? In what ways is it incompatible?

10. If you believe in God, do you believe because of the argument from design? If you do not believe in God, do you disbelieve because of the inadequacies in the argument from design?

Alternatives to Monotheism

Pantheism means literally "all God." It is the belief that everything is God and God is everything. In brief, God and the universe are identical. Pantheists see God as an immense, interconnected system of nature, in much the same way as did philosopher Baruch Spinoza (1632–1677). Spinoza reasoned that if God is all-powerful, all-knowing, and all-present, as traditionalists claim, then God must be everything. If God is everything, He can't be separate from anything. If God is all-powerful, there can be no world outside God. Hence, all of nature, everything that is, must be God. But how can God be constituted of incomplete, changing parts, as we see manifest in nature? Spinoza's pantheism perceives things as necessary—that is, as incapable of being otherwise. If this is so, what happens to free choice? What happens to the human as an experience-confronting, choice-making entity?

Peculiar to the twentieth century is a brand of theism known as **panentheism**, which attempts to

Has God any dwelling-place save earth and sea, the air of heaven and virtuous hearts? Why seek the Deity futher? Whatever we see is God, and wherever we go.

LUCAN

merge theism and pantheism. Rather than believing that all is God, panentheists hold that all is *in* God. God interpenetrates everything, as in pantheism, but God is also transcendent. Developed by G. T. Fechner, Friedrich von Schelling, and Charles Peirce, panentheism sees God as a Supreme Being whose original nature is fixed, unchanging, and inclusive of all possibilities. But at the same time God has a historical nature that exists in time as a growing, changing, expanding dimension. God, therefore, is a unity of diversity, being and becoming, the one and the many. He contains all contrast with Himself.

Still, problems of logic remain. How can such a fusion of opposites occur? Did God create His temporal nature? What precisely is the relationship between God's finite nature and His infinite nature? Was God "compelled" to exist in time? Panentheism may be more coherent than theism or pantheism, but it seems to raise further complexities that require an almost mystical grounding to be accepted.

The problems of establishing a panentheistic, pantheistic, or theistic God have led many to disbelieve God's existence. Such disbelief generally takes the form of atheism or agnosticism.

ATHEISM

Atheism denies the major claims of all varieties of theism. In the words of atheist Ernest Nagel (1937–), "Atheism denies the existence . . . of a self-consistent, omnipotent, omniscient, righteous and benevolent being who is distinct from and independent of what has been created."[13] Philosophical atheists today generally share a number of characteristics. First, although they often differ on how to establish claims to knowledge, they agree that sense observation and public verification are instrumental and that scientific method is the measure of knowledge and truth. As Nagel states, "It is indeed this commitment to the use of an empirical method which is the final basis of the atheistic

13. Quoted in Ramona Cormier, Ewing Chinn, and Richard Lineback, eds., *Encounter: An Introduction to Philosophy* (Glenview, Ill.: Scott, Foresman, 1970), 224.

God does not know everything and never has known everything.

MAURICE MAETERLINCK

critique of theism." Thus, by means of respectable methodology, the atheist claims to explain what theists can account for only through introducing an unverifiable hypothesis about a deity.

Atheists reject **animism**—the belief that supernatural creatures in the form of spirits exist and exercise control over the natural world. On the contrary, atheists deal exclusively with the natural, physical world. If we are to make any progress, they say, we must focus our attention on the properties and structures of identifiable objects located in space. The variety of things that we experience in the universe can be accounted for in terms of the changes that things undergo when relating with other things. At the same time, there is no discernible unifying pattern of change. "Nature," says Nagel, "is ineradicably plural, both in respect to the individuals occurring in it as well as in respect to the processes in which things become involved." In short, "An atheistic view of things is a form of materialism."

With their emphasis on empiricism and the physical world, atheists generally accept a utilitarian code of ethics. Such a code holds that total social consequences determine the moral action. There is no code of morality apart from the results of human actions. The final standard o moral evaluation is no commandment, no divinely inspired code of conduct, but the satisfaction of the complex needs of the human creature.

As a result of these viewpoints, atheists focus directly on the world here and now, and they generally resist authoritarianism and stress individualism. Traditionally, they have opposed moral codes that try to repress human impulses in favor of some otherworldly ideal. At the same time, this stress on the individual has not made atheists forget the role that institutions can play in advancing human goals. Because atheists cannot fortify their moral positions with promises of immortality, threats of damnation, or guarantees of righteous recompense, they must rely on what Nagel calls "a vigorous call to intelligent activity—activity for the sake of realizing human potentialities and for eliminating whatever stands in the way of such realization." But there are objections to atheism.

Objections to Atheism

One objection to atheism is that its claim that God does not exist can no more be proved than can the theistic claim that God does exist. Atheists counter that there's insufficient evidence, in quantity and quality, to claim that God exists. However, perhaps a statement like "God exists" cannot be handled like a scientific statement. Furthermore, we are especially susceptible to a subjective interpretation of evidence for God's existence. This interpretation is based on various assumptions about knowledge and the world. These assumptions are open to question. Why are the epistemological bases of atheism sound and those of theism not?

But most people are not so analytical. Instead, they charge atheism with abandoning humankind to its own devices and with ignoring the persistent belief in a force superior to humankind, a force that often leaves us with hope, confidence, faith, and love in the face of apparently insurmountable troubles. To strip us of these qualities is to leave us both ill equipped to cope with life and, more importantly, morally bankrupt.

Finally, consider this observation about atheism, which is more of an insight related to the first objection than a criticism. Atheism, to use Nagel's own word, involves a "commitment," in much the way that theism or monotheism does. In other words, empirically minded atheists erect their position as much on a commitment of faith as those who hold religious positions. All the characteristics of atheism that Nagel cites are founded as much on a categorical commitment as are the characteristics of the religionists. The commitments obviously differ: The religionist's commitment is to nonrational, nonempirical ways of knowing; the atheist's is to empiricism. If this is so, we should ask the atheist for empirical-rational reasons for committing oneself to empirical-rational standards and subsequently to atheism. Lacking these reasons, by what criterion can we judge the empiricist-atheistic commitment of faith to be more sound than the theistic commitment?

AGNOSTICISM

Having studied the arguments for and against the existence of God, many thinkers claim that neither side is convincing. As a result, they say they just don't know whether God exists—a position known as **agnosticism**.

The nineteenth-century English scientist Thomas Huxley was a well-known agnostic. For Huxley, agnosticism expressed absolute faith in the validity of the principle "that it is wrong for a man to say that he is certain of the objective truth of any proposition unless he can produce evidence which logically justifies that certainty."[14] Huxley would find sympathy among contemporary linguistic analysts, who go further and assert that the propositions "God exists" and "God does not exist" are meaningless because there is no possible way of verifying these claims. The linguistic analyst, however, is much harsher than Huxley ever intended to be. For Huxley the statements were at least meaningful, if insoluble. So he suspended judgment, as he did on the real nature of such ultimates as matter and mind. The agnostic position implies ignorance of the nature of such things. As Huxley puts it, "We have not the slightest objection to believe anything you like, if you will give us good grounds for belief; but, if you cannot, we must respectfully refuse, even if that refusal should wreck morality and insure our damnation several times over. We are quite content to leave the decision of the future. The course of the past has impressed us with the firm conviction that no good ever comes of falsehood, and we feel warranted in refusing even to experiment in that direction."[15]

---

14. Quoted in Cormier, Chinn, and Lineback, *Encounter*, 227.
15. Quoted in Cormier, Chinn, and Lineback, *Encounter*, 230.

Objections to Agnosticism

Agnosticism, unlike atheism, need not prove any claim, for it makes none that demands verification. But it is still open to all the other objections to atheism. In addition, one can validly wonder whether one can suspend judgment on the question of whether God exists.

To suspend judgment on whether unicorns exist is one thing, but to do so on whether God exists is quite another. Unicorns make no difference in our lives, but this cannot be said of God. Consider how much is tied up in our belief or disbelief in God's existence. For many, absolute proof for or against God's existence would mean a different lifestyle—a different way of thinking, seeing, and behaving. But whatever position we take, we are probably assuming it as if there were absolute evidence for it, even though we admit there is none. And in all likelihood we are trying to live according to this position. To suspend judgment on the question seems to be avoiding the issue, because the question evidently does not allow such a response. In short, critics of agnosticism argue that we are faced not with a false dilemma but with a genuine one: We must either believe that God exists or not believe it. We'll see this position developed fully later in James's "The Will to Believe."

In the last analysis, the existence or nonexistence of a theistic God cannot yet be proved. But lack of certain evidence does not make the question any less important, any more than our not knowing what to study in college makes the issue of an academic major unimportant. The point is that, lacking sufficient evidence, most of us still believe or disbelieve. And the position we take affects how we see ourselves. Whether we see ourselves as surviving after death—as being immortal, being reborn, or experiencing resurrection—is a good example. It is a question of fundamental concern that we will examine next.

QUESTIONS

1. What implications does pantheism have for the question of who you are? Does this attract you to or repel you from the idea of pantheism? What could count as proof for or against pantheism?

2. In your view, is atheism more or less rational than agnosticism? Is atheism more or less virtuous than agnosticism?

3. Do you agree with the seventeenth-century French philosopher Blaise Pascal who suggested that atheism is not a good bet: "Let us weigh the gain and loss in betting that God exists: if you win, you win everything; if you lose, you lose nothing. You should unhesitatingly bet that He exists!"

Most intellectual people do not believe in God, but they fear him just the same.

WILHELM REICH

Traditional Religious Experience

BELIEF IN IMMORTALITY

Any person who is conscious of death has wondered: Will I continue to live in some way after I die? This question has occupied humankind from earliest times and perhaps penetrates the issue of self more deeply than any other. For if we continue to live after death, we must wonder about the state, form, and condition of that existence; we must wonder whether our present life will affect those aspects of the next life, whether the departed currently live among us, and whether contact between this world and the next is possible. The belief in survival after death is closely connected with a belief in God: If we believe God exists, it is easier to accept this belief.

When speaking of personal survival after death, the term *immortality* inevitably comes up. We can speak of immortality in several ways. There is biological immortality, which is the continuance of germ plasm after death. In this sense, we are immortal. We are also immortal in the sense that we leave behind us a social legacy or contribution by which we are remembered. Some people also speak of an impersonal immortality in which, upon physical death, the self merges with the unity of all things, a world soul. Versions of this belief are popular in Eastern religions, in which the self assumes a different form after death—as a human, an animal, even an insect. Plato subscribed to the doctrine of transmigration of souls, or **metempsychosis**, the passing of the soul into another body

after death. But these beliefs are not what people in the West generally mean by immortality. Rather, they view survival after death as the continuance of personal identity in some other world or realm. The issue, then, is whether the conscious self persists after death.

Although they generally agree on the existence of some kind of personal survival after death, religious leaders are divided over its nature. The source of the division stems from two traditions: the Greek and the Judeo-Christian.

The Greek influence originates primarily from Plato, who first attempted to prove the existence of the soul, or reason. As we saw in an earlier showcase, Plato argued that the body belongs to the world known to us through our physical senses and shares the nature of this world: change, impermanence, and death. On the other hand, the soul, or reason, is related to the permanent, unchanging realities that we are aware of when contemplating not particular things but universal, eternal Ideals. Related to this higher and lasting realm, the soul, unlike the body, is immortal. After death, the souls of those who have contemplated the eternal realities will gravitate to the world of eternal Ideals, despite their bodies' turning to dust.

The Judeo-Christian tradition, in contrast, has generally emphasized resurrection along with immortality, although Judaism de-emphasizes, even declines in some sects, resurrection. Whereas Plato considered only the soul immortal, the Jewish and Christian view, as found occasionally in the Old Testament and more often in the New Testament, is that the complete human—soul and body—may be resurrected by God. This belief posits the direct intervention of a theistic God and a special divine

---

Death is the true inspiring genius, or the muse of philosophy . . . . Indeed, without death men could scarcely philosophize.

ARTHUR SCHOPENHAUER

---

act of recreation. The human is utterly dependent on the love of God for survival after death. Christians argue that there is evidence for resurrection in the New Testament. But the belief is also justified as a necessary part of the purpose of God. It is argued that God would be contradicting Himself to have created humans for fellowship with Himself, only to have them extinguished and this purpose unfulfilled.

Apart from its religious aspects, the question of life after death has recently received new attention with the growing interest in **extrasensory perception**, the phenomenon of having experiences without relying on the normal senses. Although there are many facets of ESP, the one relevant to this discussion is **telepathy**, the name given to the phenomenon of a thought in one person's mind evidently causing a similar thought in another person's mind without normal means of communication. For example, one person will draw a geometric pattern and then transmit a mental impression of it to someone in another room, who then creates a similar pattern. Experiments have ruled out chance in instances of telepathy. S. G. Soal, for example, has reported experimental results demonstrating that the probability of chance operating in such cases ranges from 100,000 to 1 to billions to 1.[16]

Just how telepathic communication works is unknown. So far, only negative conclusions have been reached. Telepathy does not seem to consist of physical radiation, such as radio waves, for distance has no effect. Nor does the thought leave the sender's consciousness to enter the receiver's, for frequently the senders are not even aware of the thought until it is brought to their attention, and receivers often receive just a fragment of it. As a result, some believe that, although our minds are exclusive of one another on the conscious level, we are constantly influencing one another on the unconscious level. It is at this level that telepathy is believed to occur, particularly through the link of emotion or common interest that may exist between two especially close people. Telepathy sometimes is used as evidence of survival after death, although it seems to be questionable evidence.

The Proceedings of the Society for Psychical Research in London contains many documented cases of people who had recently died appearing to people who were still unaware of their deaths. The Society for Psychical Research is a well-established institute with rigorous standards and an impressive membership list of scholars.

In the case of "ghosts"—apparitions of the dead—it has been established that there can be "meaningful hallucinations" through telepathic sources. The classic example is the woman who, while sitting by a lake, witnessed the figure of a man running toward the lake and throwing himself in. A few days later a man killed himself by doing precisely this. Presumably, as the man contemplated his suicide, his thought was telepathically projected onto the scene by the woman's mind.[17]

The Society for Psychical Research also reports that minds that operate in mediumistic trances, alleging to be the spirits of the departed, frequently provide information that the medium could not possibly know. How is this possible? Again, one currently popular theory is that the communication really results from telepathic contact between the medium and the client. This theory is dramatized in the case of two women who decided to test the spirits by assuming the personality of a completely imaginary character in an unpublished novel written by one of the women. Having filled their minds with all the characteristics of this fictitious person, they went to a medium, who proceeded to describe accurately the fictitious character as a spirit from the beyond and to report appropriate messages from him.[18] Thus, although ESP is opening fascinating vistas on the mind, it is doing little to support the contention that there is an afterlife or other world. This, of course, does not mean that one does not exist.

The belief in an afterlife, inspired by religious conviction, will undoubtedly persist, and many

---

16. S. G. Soal, *The Experimental Situation in Psychical Research* (London: The Society for Psychical Research, 1947).

17. Hick, *Philosophy of Religion*, 106.
18. Ibid., 105.

If only God would give me some clear sign! Like making a large deposit in my name at a Swiss bank.

WOODY ALLEN

people will continue to live their lives with one eye on this world and one on the next. Although there is no conclusive evidence to resolve the question of God's existence, we live as if there is, incorporating corollary beliefs and ways of viewing ourselves and the world. Do we have any real basis for such beliefs? Lacking certain evidence, are those who believe in God irrational, or are they justified in perhaps allowing their hearts to rule their heads? Since this question of religious belief is so influential in our lives, it seems appropriate now to examine it fully.

RELIGIOUS BELIEF

Whether or not the existence of God is an issue today, the question of whether or not to *believe* in a divine dimension is. Is the cosmos far-flung matter that originated in chance and is propelled by accident? Or is it, scientific explanations notwithstanding, something sacred, something divine? How we answer these questions will greatly affect our self-concepts and consequently our lives. In this case, the belief is as important a question as the fact.

A simple example will illustrate the influence of belief in our lives. Suppose at some point in college you begin to question whether you should actually be there. You are finding it neither interesting nor manageable. Besides, you have a pretty good job that you like and, if you work full-time, you can make enough money to get married. On the other hand, limiting your education might restrict your personal and professional opportunities. What should you do: Stay in school or quit? You must choose; there is no escaping the issue.

Obviously, there is no certain answer. The best you can do is open-mindedly collect and weigh the data and decide. But whatever your choice, you will undoubtedly *believe* you are doing the right thing. In fact, that belief will help make the decision, which will have important consequences for your life. The decision might be reversible, but it will steer your life in a certain direction. That direction will be full of experiences that another direction might have lacked, experiences that will help shape you. So, in believing you should choose that direction, you have really decided to a degree what you will become.

Like the dilemma of whether to stay in school, the answer to the question of God's existence is inconclusive. But the question of *belief* in a divine dimension—whether theism, pantheism, or panentheism—is not. Although you cannot resolve this question, you can decide whether to believe in some kind of divine dimension. And that belief, if you are true to it, will affect your life, because through it you relate yourself to the world and everything in it.

There are many responses to the question of God's existence. One is to become so overwhelmed by the question that one gives up hope of ever believing anything. But this reaction is a decision—a decision to remain uncommitted. Another possibility is to avoid the anguish of decision making by choosing whatever belief is conventional, popular, acceptable, or fashionable—in effect, to choose to become one of the statistics that we allow to formulate our beliefs. On the other hand, we might face up to the anguish of decision making, consider its implications, choose to believe or not to believe, then live that decision. The decision is ours to make.

There are many paths to God, my son. I hope yours will not be too difficult.

LEW WALLACE

William James: "To say, 'Do not decide, but leave the question open,' is itself a decision,—just like deciding yes or no,—and is attended with the same risk of losing the truth."

Aside from whether a theistic God exists, is there any basis for religious belief? Do we have any grounds for believing in a divine dimension of any sort? Perhaps religious belief ultimately is not based and cannot be based on any evidence. Perhaps it must be a personal decision made with the heart. In a classic address entitled "The Will to Believe," American philosopher William James confronted this issue. After delivering the speech, he wrote that he wished he had entitled it "The Right to Believe."

"The Will to Believe"

The thrust of James's address is captured in the following argument: "Our passional nature not only lawfully may, but must, decide an option between propositions, whenever it is a genuine option that cannot by its nature be decided on intellectual grounds; for to say, under such circumstances, 'Do

not decide, but leave the question open,' is itself a decision—just like deciding yes or no,—and is attended with the same risk of losing the truth."[19] Without understanding the terms as James understands them, we can easily misconstrue what he is saying.

First, consider the word *option*. By this James means a choice between two hypotheses, a *hypothesis* being anything that may be proposed for our belief. "There is a divine dimension to the universe" would be a hypothesis; so would "There is no divine dimension to the universe." Some hypotheses are *live*; a live hypothesis "appeals as a real possibility to him to whom it is proposed." For example, the proposal that you believe in the Mahdi (the Islamic messiah) would probably not be appealing to you because of your Western acculturation and perhaps ignorance of Islam. The hypothesis would be a *dead* one. On the other hand, to an Arab it would probably be very much live. The deadness or liveness of any hypothesis, then, is not a quality inherent in the proposal but a quality determined by the individual thinker. It is an indication of our willingness to act; a hypothesis is most live when we are willing to act irrevocably—that is, to believe.

James further points out that there are several kinds of options: (1) living or dead, (2) forced or avoidable, and (3) momentous or trivial. A genuine option is living, forced, and momentous.

By a *living* option, James means one in which both hypotheses are live ones. For example, the proposal, "Be a theosophist or be a Muhammadan" would probably be a dead option, because neither proposal is likely to be a live one for you. On the other hand, "Be a Christian or be an atheist" would probably be a living option, because both choices are probably live for you.

Now, suppose someone proposed "Either love me or hate me." You could avoid a decision by remaining indifferent to the person. Likewise, if someone proposed "Either vote for me or vote for my opponent," again you could avoid the decision

---

19. William James, "The Will to Believe," in *Encounter*, eds. Ramona Cormier, Ewing Chinn, and Richard Lineback, 236.

by not voting at all. Options like these are not forced; they are *avoidable*. On the other hand, if someone said "Either accept this proof or go without it," you would be forced to make a choice. When there is no way to avoid a decision, the option is *forced*.

Finally, an option is *momentous* when the opportunity is unique, when the stakes are significant, and when the decision is irreversible. For example, a friend comes by one night with some "surefire" stock. The once-in-a-lifetime opportunity, she promises, will yield incredible riches. To accept her offer or reject it would be a momentous option. On the other hand, whether to wear jeans or slacks to school would be a *trivial* option, because it is not unique, attended by high stakes, or irreversible.

Now, what does James mean by "our passional nature"? As an empiricist, James forsakes an objective certainty. He claims that we can never be absolutely sure of anything except that consciousness exists. But he does *not* abandon the quest for truth itself; he still believes that truth exists. This belief springs more from desire and feeling than from reason; it is more passional than rational. This belief provides the best chance of attaining truth, "by systematically continuing to roll up experiences and think." His point is that, since we can never know with certainty, there will inevitably be a nonintellectual, nonrational element to what we choose to believe—a passional element. James writes, "Instinct leads, intelligence only follows." The first two tasks of this passional element are knowing the truth and avoiding error.

Choosing between these two "commandments," we could end up affecting our lives in completely different ways. For example, suppose you regarded the avoidance of error as paramount and the search for truth as secondary. Since there is very little if anything for which there is incontrovertible evidence, you would probably draw no conclusions. The result would be life-long intellectual suspension. Imagine a child who cannot choose one of thirty-one ice cream flavors for fear that his choice may not live up to his expectations or that he will regret his choice. James is suggesting that when we are more committed to avoiding error

than to chasing the truth, we necessarily lose the truth, since there will never be absolute supporting evidence. But to make such a choice is to be "like a general informing his soldiers that it is better to keep out of battle forever than to risk a single wound. Not so are victories either over enemies or over nature found."[20] Or, we might add, over the self.

It is easy to misunderstand James. He is not saying that avoiding error should always be subordinate to attaining truth. In options that are not momentous, James claims that we can save ourselves from believing a falsehood by not deciding until all the evidence is in. This approach would apply to most of the scientific questions and human issues that we are likely to face. In other words, in most choices the need to act is seldom so urgent that it is better to act on a false belief than on no belief at all. But he also argues that there are forced and momentous choices that we cannot ("as men who may be interested at least as much in positively gaining truth as in merely escaping dupery") always wait to make. As he puts it, "In the great boardinghouse of nature, the cakes and the butter and the syrup seldom come out so even and leave the plates so clean."

Granted, for some people religious belief is not a hypothesis that could possibly be true. But for most it is a live option. To these people, James says that religious belief is a momentous option. They stand to gain much by their belief and to lose much by their nonbelief. It is also a forced option. If they choose to wait in order to avoid error, they risk losing the chance of attaining the good that religious belief promises. "It is as if a man should hesitate indefinitely to ask a certain woman to marry him because he was not perfectly sure that she would prove an angel after he brought her home. Would he not cut himself off from that particular angel-possibility as decisively as if he went and married someone else?" Or, more simply, should the ice cream shop close while the child is debating his choice, the result would be the same as if he had chosen to have no ice cream. On a question

---

20. William James, *The Varieties of Religious Experience* (New York: Longmans, Green, 1929), 74.

that cannot be answered on intellectual grounds, James argues that we not only can but *should* allow our "passional nature" to decide it. We must choose to chase truth, not to avoid possible error; for in fearing to be duped, we exclude the possibility of being right.

James's argument has relevance not only for those who believe in a personal God but also for those whose innermost feelings detect a divine dimension at work in the cosmos, but not necessarily a Supreme Being such as the one of traditional theism. Because he relies on the importance of personal experience in religious belief, James is providing a philosophical basis for a personal encounter with the sacred, whatever we may experience that to be. Just what constitutes a personal experience of the divine is a complex question, but individuals often use it as their source of or justification for religious belief.

Personal Experience of the Divine

We said earlier that religious belief, in its most general terms, is the belief that there is an unseen order and that we can do no better than to be in harmony with this order. Our religious attitudes spring from this belief. But this belief need not be rooted in objects present to our senses. On the contrary, the *belief* in a thing's existence can evoke in us as powerful a reaction as the thing itself. As an example, consider this dialogue between a young man and a young woman who meet in a park.

YOUNG MAN: Do you come here often?

YOUNG WOMAN: Whenever I need to feel the presence.

YOUNG MAN: The presence?

YOUNG WOMAN: Haven't you ever felt a void, an emptiness?

YOUNG MAN: A quiet desperation?

YOUNG WOMAN: That, too.

YOUNG MAN: It's not something one can easily speak of.

YOUNG WOMAN: True.

YOUNG MAN: And coming here helps?

YOUNG WOMAN: It stills the loneliness.

YOUNG MAN: But there's no one here.

YOUNG WOMAN: There's the sunshine and sometimes the rain. And almost always the breeze.

YOUNG MAN: I guess nature *can* be therapeutic.

YOUNG WOMAN: No, it's the *presence* that brings me here.

YOUNG MAN: The presence of what?

YOUNG WOMAN: Of something greater than myself.

YOUNG MAN: God?

YOUNG WOMAN: If you want. I'd rather not name it, because words are so misleading. But I know there's something there. . . . Why are you looking around? You won't see it, you know. But it's there, all the same.

This young woman feels a sense of reality that is deeper and more real to her than her sense experiences. She cannot fully communicate what she experiences. It cannot be defined, it does not consist of sensation, it does not consist of specific hypotheses based on such facts. Yet what she feels is more convincing than those truths arrived at through rational methods.

Rationalism gives a small and sketchy account of the nonspecific, nonlearned parts of our mental lives. True, reason and logic can be used to argue, point out flaws, and refute. But in the presence of what James calls "dumb intuitions," rationalism invariably loses the fight. Thus, something in this woman absolutely *knows*, despite any rationalistic argument to the contrary.

The apparent weakness of rationalistic thinking shows up dramatically in discussions of religious belief, particularly in the issue of God's existence. Very few of us today believe in God because of rational proofs. Similarly, few do not believe or have stopped believing because the arguments are flawed. Many people, perhaps most, do not need any rational proof for their religious belief, any more than they need proof that they feel joyful or loving. Others might point out innumerable reasons for not feeling joyful or loving, but to those experiencing these feelings, such arguments bend like straws in the wind. It is this kind of personal, direct, nonrational experience that frequently characterizes the sense of a divine presence that is not the personal God of traditional theism. On the contrary, this experience often takes the form of mysticism.

MYSTICISM

YOUNG MAN: Can you describe what you feel when you experience the presence?

YOUNG WOMAN: Not really. Words are really inadequate, and I think it all sounds very foolish to someone who thinks more than feels.

YOUNG MAN: But I'd like for you to try. You see, what you say may touch my life. And it would be terrible to lose that possibility because you thought I'd ridicule what you say.

YOUNG WOMAN: All right. I'll try to describe what happened last week on this very spot. At first I was frightened. I was losing myself, I thought, perhaps losing my mind. Then suddenly I had a vivid impression of something indescribable—call it God if you wish. At that moment when I felt most abandoned, I became one with this infinite power, this spirit of infinite peace. Through my attachment to this prodigious power, I sensed myself as I never have before. I felt one with everything: trees, birds, insects. I gloried in my existence, of being part of it all—part of the blades of grass, the bark of trees, the drops of rain. It was as if my thoughts were piercing the great veil of confusion and ignorance that I had always looked through. Suddenly I saw why we suffer, why it's necessary to suffer, why there will always be suffering. I also saw the thread of love that weaves through nature and makes it all one. I saw all the terrible hatred as love and the love as potential hatred, the one serving as counterpoint to the other, the two together producing the song of the universe, a cosmic harmony that left me in a divine ecstasy. There was more, much more; but even now I feel the inadequacy of words, and I'd rather not reduce my experiences any further.

The young woman appears to have had a mystical experience. One problem in trying to speak of such experiences is that, by nature, they defy verbalization. Religious belief often finds its origins in such mystical states of consciousness.

In his *Varieties of Religious Experience*, James proposes two characteristics by which an experience may be termed mystical. First is *ineffability*; that is, the state defies expression. Like the young woman, the experiencer feels that the mystical experience cannot be adequately reported. Second, there is a *noetic quality* about these experiences: To the individual they appear to be knowledge. They provide insight into the depths of human experience that no amount of intellectualizing can plumb. They are revelations and illuminations that are full of meaning, truth, and importance.

Mysticism, then, is the experience of a reality more inclusive than that which we are generally conscious of. According to mysticism, we can truly know only when we surrender our individual selves and sense a union with the divine ground of all existence. Certainly, mystical experiences vary in content, but like the young woman's experience, they often involve an acute awareness of a divine presence and of a direct communion with divinity, although this divinity is more likely to be an incomprehensible entity than a theistic deity.

Like most people, mystics have sensed within themselves a desire or longing that goes beyond the imperfect world of which they are a part. They may feel an urge for something permanent and free that transcends sorrow and is of everlasting value. They may feel airborne, looking for a place to land. Most Westerners try to quell such feelings and desires by seeking outside themselves, but mystics believe that the outward search is a race on a treadmill.

Mystics turn to the self to still these uneasy inner feelings. What occurs is impossible to describe—it must be experienced. But the writings of mystics indicate that, above everything else, the inner way leads to an understanding that all is one and one is all; that the self is one continuous process with God, the cosmos, or whatever term a particular culture or individual chooses to call ultimate and eternal reality. Such an inner experience has been termed "religious experience," "mystical experience," and "cosmic consciousness." But none of these terms captures the nature of such experi-

Ecstasy of Saint Teresa, Giovanni Lorenzo Bernini. "**A fourth character of the numinous is bliss. References to heaven, paradise, salvation, and love all suggest a feeling of supreme fulfillment and satisfaction. The numinous satisfies the most profound yearnings of the human heart.**"

ences, any more than the phrase "in love" describes what we experience in that state. The philosophy of religion employs the term *numinous* to describe these mystical states.

The Numinous

Peter Koestenbaum lists several characteristics of the numinous experience.[21] One is a feeling of infinite dependence, of the experiencer and the mundane world being insignificant. Values change, and

a new sense of reality supplants the old. Thus, Thomas Aquinas, a consummate rational theologian, underwent a mystical experience after completing his major work. As a result, he was led to describe his previous efforts as so much straw compared with what he'd experienced. He never wrote another line.

Another aspect of the numinous is mystery. Mystery is closely related to James's ineffability and to what the young woman in the park is experiencing. Since our language is designed to handle ordinary experience in the ordinary world, a numinous experience is often described simply as a mystery or miracle. You will recall from Chapter 1 that in his famous "Allegory of the Cave," Plato writes about a prisoner who escapes the cave prison where humankind is condemned to watch shadows on a screen, which it then takes for reality. Having escaped and contemplated the real world, the prisoner returns to the cave and attempts to enlighten his cavemates, but in vain. Their points of reference and his are different, and so he cannot convey his experience. A similar communication gap faces the mystic.

Terror is a third characteristic of the numinous. This results from the total annihilation of our world of experience as we know it, the removal of all stability and substance from our existence. Numerous Old Testament passages evidence the kind of dread that accompanies the numinous. Speaking through one of His prophets, the God of the Old Testament says, "Their slain shall also be cast out, and their stink shall come up out of their carcasses and the mountains shall be melted with their blood" (Isa. 34:3) and "For the indignation of the Lord is upon all nations, and his fury upon all their armies: he hath utterly destroyed them, he hath delivered them to the slaughter" (Isa. 34:2). Literally interpreted, these references suggest that God must be capable of evil. But viewed analogically, they represent the element of terror in the numinous.

A fourth character of the numinous is bliss. References to heaven, paradise, salvation, and love all suggest a feeling of supreme fulfillment and satisfaction. The numinous satisfies the most profound yearnings of the human heart. Thus, Saint Catherine of Genoa writes, "If of that which my

---

21. Peter Koestenbaum, *Philosophy: A General Introduction* (New York: Van Nostrand Reinhold, 1968), 140–147.

Reason refuses its homage to a God who can be fully understood.

M. F. TUPPER

heart is feeling one drop were to fall into hell, hell itself would become life eternal."[22]

As Koestenbaum points out, there are many other characteristics of the numinous. The key point is that religion may be approached through a numinous interpretation. In fact, the mystical tradition in both Judaism and Christianity parallels the evolution of rational theology, and it is even generally supported by it. In the 1960s and 1970s there was an intense and unprecedented interest in what we can call the transformation of consciousness, much of which sprung from a sense of personal estrangement from the world. Many felt out of touch and tried to locate themselves in the scheme of things. The result was that more and more people rejected the traditional institutional prescriptions for inner peace and contentment and instead followed their own vague but pressing sense of what was good for them. This pursuit took many forms—"self-healing," "consciousness expansion," "positive growth potential," and "survival experiments"—but all had nonrational, mystical overtones. It is impossible to discuss all these movements, but we can introduce three phenomena that, although quite different in content and methodology, are similar in their attempts to gain religious experience through a mystical transformation of consciousness. These are radical theology, the use of psychedelic drugs, and the study of Eastern religious thought.

QUESTIONS

1. Is an irrefutable proof or evidence of life after death possible in this life? Why or why not? What kind of evidence would you find absolutely irrefutable?

2. Can you give some examples from your own life of what James means by "a live hypothesis"?

3. Have you ever had what you would call a "personal religious experience"? What made it religious and different from other more ordinary experiences? Could one have religious experiences without believing in God? Explain. Could one have a "personal religious experience" that was false? How would one distinguish the real from the false experience?

4. Is mysticism necessarily in conflict with institutionalized religion? Is it necessarily in conflict with rationality?

5. Can you describe the view of reality that mysticism requires? What view of human nature does mysticism require? Do you believe these views are correct? Why or why not?

6. Some varieties of mysticism emphasize feelings at the expense of reason. Is there any reason to accept feelings when they conflict with reason? Is this question self-contradictory? How would the mystic justify his feelings?

7. Evaluate this statement of seventeenth-century French philosopher Blaise Pascal: "If we submit everything to reason, our religion will have nothing in it mysterious or supernatural. If we violate the principles of reason, our religion will be absurd and ridiculous." Are we forced to accept this dilemma?

---

22. Quoted in Koestenbaum, *Philosophy*, 146.

Nontraditional Religious Experience

Søren Kierkegaard: "If God does not exist, it would of course be impossible to prove it; and if he does exist it would be folly to attempt it."

RADICAL THEOLOGY

The nagging questions about the existence and nature of a Supreme Being have spawned a school of theology that deviates from traditional theism more radically than do pantheism and panentheism. Such "radical theologians," as these thinkers are often termed, perceived God not as a being among other beings but as an aspect of reality. As a result, they feel that our relationship with God is more experiential than rational. The modern roots of this view can be traced to thinkers like the Danish philosopher Søren Kierkegaard (1813–1855).

The society into which Kierkegaard was born was thoroughly Christian. Everyone believed the same dogmas, although few gave much thought to their beliefs. By the same token, all attended the same Lutheran churches and church social functions, and mechanically mouthed the doctrines that they were raised to espouse. While this behavior passed for Christianity, Kierkegaard believed that it was anything but that. In his view, such behavior lacked passion, and so did the Christians who displayed the behavior. Where they should have felt fear, these people were complacent; where they should have shown intensity, they were secure. To put it bluntly, Kierkegaard was revolted by these self-professed pillars of the Christian community. Appropriately enough, then, in works such as *Philosophical Fragments* and *Concluding Unscientific Postscript*, Kierkegaard spent most of his short life

expostulating a view of Christianity and of being a Christian that was at once new and yet very old.

Central to Kierkegaard's religious thought is his distinction between the objective and subjective thinker, which is essentially a distinction between reason and faith. In Kierkegaard's view, the objective thinker is one who strikes an intellectual, dispassionate, scientific pose toward life. In effect, the objective thinker adopts the view of an observer.

In contrast, the subjective thinker is passionately and intensely involved with truth. Truth for the subjective thinker is not just a matter of accumulating evidence to establish a viewpoint, but something of profound personal concern. Because questions of life and death, of the meaning of one's human existence, of one's ultimate destiny, often preoccupy subjective thinkers, Kierkegaard sometimes calls them existential thinkers.

While it is true that Kierkegaard is primarily concerned with subjective thinking, he never denies that objective thinking has its place. He simply asserts that not all of life's concerns are open to objective analysis. Indeed, from Kierkegaard's view, it would be fair to say life's most important questions defy objective analysis. A good example, which also happens to be Kierkegaard's preoccupation as a religious thinker, is religious faith. Religious faith, says Kierkegaard, is not open to objective thinking because it involves a relationship with God. Stated another and more exact way, religion and religious faith are a confrontation with the unknown, not something knowable. In the following passage from *Philosophical Fragments*, Kierkegaard demonstrates what he means.

> But what is this unknown something with which the Reason collides when inspired by its paradoxical passion, with the result of unsettling even man's knowledge of himself? It is the Unknown. It is not a human being, in so far as we know what man is; nor is it any other known thing. So let us call this unknown something: *the God.* It is nothing more than a name we assign to it. The idea of demonstrating that this unknown something (the God) exists, could scarcely suggest itself to the Reason. For if the God does not exist it would of course be impossible to prove it; and if he does exist it would be folly to attempt it. For at the very outset, in beginning my proof, I would have presupposed it, not as doubtful but as certain (a presupposition is never doubtful, for the very reason that it is a presupposition), since otherwise I would not begin, readily understanding that the whole would be impossible if he did not exist. But if when I speak of proving the God's existence I mean that I propose to prove that the Unknown, which exists, is the God, then I express myself unfortunately. For in that case I do not prove anything, least of all an existence, but merely develop the content of a conception. . . .
>
> The works from which I would deduce God's existence are not directly and immediately given. The wisdom in nature, the goodness, the wisdom in the governance of the world—are all these manifest, perhaps, upon the very face of things? Are we not here confronted with the most terrible temptations to doubt, and is it not impossible finally to dispose of all these doubts? But from such an order of things I will surely not attempt to prove God's existence; and even if I began I would never finish, and would in addition have to live

> constantly in suspense, lest something so terrible should suddenly happen that my bit of proof would be demolished. From what works then do I propose to derive the proof? From the works as apprehended through an ideal interpretation, i.e., such as they do not immediately reveal themselves. But in that case it is not from the works that I make the proof; I merely develop the ideality I have presupposed, and because of my confidence in *this* I make so bold as to defy all objections, even those that have not yet been made. In beginning my proof I presuppose the ideal interpretation, and also that I will be successful in carrying it through; but what else is this but to presuppose that the God exists, so that I really begin by virtue of confidence in him?[23]

From this passage it is clear that Kierkegaard condemns the "proofs" for God's existence, as well as other attempts to "know" God. The reason is that, by Kierkegaard's account, God cannot be known; God is not subject to rational, objective analysis. But if the point of religion and religious faith is not to know God, then just what is their point? To *feel*, rather than to know.

In the end, rational thinking, which is the religious expression of objective thinkers, points to the existence of God but gives individuals little on which to erect a relationship with God. "I contemplate the order of nature," says Kierkegaard, "in the hope of finding God, and I see omnipotence and wisdom; but I also see much else that disturbs my mind and excites anxiety. The sum of all this is objective uncertainty." Faced with objective uncertainty, with the inconclusiveness of objective analysis and rational debate and the "proofs," we are anguished. This anguish, this suffering, is all compounded by the anticipation of our own death and our feeling of smallness and insignificance in the face of the eternal order of things. The debates go on, our lives ebb away. We must make a decision. This decision is what Kierkegaard calls the "leap of faith," which consists of a commitment to a rela-

---

23. Søren Kierkegaard, *Philosophical Fragments*, trans. David Swenson (Copyright 1936, © 1962 by Princeton University Press). Excerpt reprinted by permission of Princeton University Press.

Paul Tillich: "Depth is what the word God means, the source of your being, of your ultimate concern, of what you take seriously without any reservation. 'Life has no depth. Life is shallow. Being itself is surface only.' If you could say this in complete seriousness, you would be an atheist; but otherwise you are not. He who knows the depth knows about God."

tionship with God that defies objective analysis. Of course, we may choose not to make the leap of faith; we may, instead, try to minimize the suffering through professional understanding and knowledge, through objective analysis. But for this alternative, Kierkegaard has only sarcasm: *"The two ways,"* he says; "One is to suffer; the other is to become a professor of the fact that another suffered."

The chief exponent of radical theology in our time has been protestant theologian Paul Tillich (1886–1965). Tillich, an existentialist, contends that traditional theism has erred in viewing God as *a* being and not *being itself*, an error that he believes the proofs for God's existence, discussed earlier, have fostered. As a result, we have bound God to our subject-object structure of reality. *He*—notice the sexualization—is an object for us as subjects, becoming the target for our prayers, worship,

and supplications. He becomes almost some *thing* to which we direct our lives. At other times we make ourselves object for Him as subject. Because theism posits an all-knowing, all-powerful God, and because we are neither, the relationship must therefore be one of superior (God) to inferior (us), controller to controlled, subject to object. An antagonistic tension results. As Tillich says, "He deprives me of my subjectivity because he is all-powerful and all-knowing. I revolt and try to make him into an object, but the revolt fails and becomes desperate. God appears as an invincible tyrant, the being in contrast with whom all other things are without freedom and subjectivity."[24] This image of God as "invincible tyrant," he feels, is a much more telling blow to theological theism than all the objections to the traditional proofs for God's existence. Tillich believes that his criticism is justified, for God as tyrant is "the deepest root of the Existentialist despair and the widespread anxiety of meaninglessness in our period." Notice that Tillich rejects traditional theism not on empirical but on theological grounds. For Tillich, theism is just bad theology.

If Tillich and other radical theologians reject the theistic concept of God, what do they offer as a substitute? What kind of God do they believe in? Tillich's God is a "God above God," "the ground of being." This God transcends the God of theism and so dissipates the anxiety of doubt and meaninglessness. This ground of being is not proved, because it cannot be. It is neither an object nor a subject. It is present, although hidden, in every divine-human encounter. Tillich grants that this notion is paradoxical. But he notes that Biblical religion and Protestant theology are already studded with paradoxes. Consider the "paradoxical character of every prayer of speaking to somebody to whom you cannot ask anything because he gives or gives not before you ask, of saying 'thou' to somebody who is nearer to the I than the I is to itself." Indeed, it is paradoxes like these, says Tillich, that "drive the religious consciousness toward

---

24. This and all other Tillich quotes are from: Paul Tillich, *The Courage to Be* (New Haven, Conn.: Yale University Press, 1952). Reprinted by permission.

a God above the God of theism, a God that is the Ground of our very being."

The "ground of being" is only one of Tillich's many slippery concepts. "Depth" is another. "Depth is what the word God means," he writes, but still we ask what depth is. The word seems to have no meaning. "If the word has not much meaning for you, translate it," advises Tillich, "and speak of the depths of your life, of the source of your being, of your ultimate concern, of what you take seriously without any reservation." Atheists might reply, "That there is no God—now *that* I take seriously, without any reservation." But Tillich would say that this is impossible, for to call themselves atheists they would have to forget everything traditional that they ever learned about God, maybe even the word itself. The only people who can rightly call themselves atheists are those who can say, "Life has no depth. Life is shallow. Being itself is surface only. If you could say this in complete seriousness, you would be an atheist; but otherwise you are not. He who knows the depth knows about God."

Like many existentialists, Tillich is not easy to understand. But clearly he believes that traditional theism has erred in making God an object. It does so in its definitions of Him and in its proofs of His existence. God cannot be proved, as if He were an equation or a laboratory specimen. Such "objectivation" not only limits the deity but also raises the very kinds of inconsistencies that are leading to a loss of faith. Tillich's God, therefore, defies traditional definitions and proofs. His God is closer to the concept attained by the mystic but still significantly different. Where the mystic would eschew sense experience and reason when taken as ultimate, and through intuition alone move to a knowledge of God, Tillich confronts the world of experience and its nagging questions. He is no escapist, no dodger of doubt. On the contrary, he faces the concrete world of finite values and meanings and uses all its imperfections, skepticism, and meaninglessness to confront what is ultimately real: being. And in this ground of all being he experiences God. Everyone does "who knows the depth."

Objections to Radical Theology

Besides having many elusive concepts, Tillich's theology provokes other objections. He seemingly says that those who do not recognize his God, the ground of all being, are not ultimately concerned. Suppose you tell an unaccomplished violinist that the reason she failed to become a virtuoso is that she never practiced long enough. "Long enough!" she protests. "Are you kidding? Why, I have practiced every day of my life!" "Obviously, it wasn't long enough," you reply, "because you never became a virtuoso." Clearly, by "long enough" you mean "until one becomes a virtuoso." Your directive to the would-be virtuoso, then, was nothing more than "Practice until you become a virtuoso, and you will become a virtuoso." In logic, a statement whose predicate repeats its subject, as this one does, is called a **tautology**. Is Tillich's argument tautological? Has he, as Anselm evidently did, defined something into existence? When Tillich says, "He who knows about the depth knows about God," he seems to be saying, "He who knows about God knows about God." When he argues, "If one is ultimately concerned or has the courage to be, then one knows God," he appears to say, "If one knows God or knows God, then one knows God."

Tillich also claims to have an experience of divine presence, of a merging with some fundamental reality. No one may question his experience; it is as personal as a headache or a hunger pang. But his interpretation of his experience can be questioned. We can and should, it seems, ask for verification when he interprets that experience as resulting from contact with the ground of all being. Tillich must verify the reality of the ground of all being and establish it as the cause of his transcendent experiences.

Tillich would probably reply that the knowl-

A man's religion is the truth he lives habitually, subconsciously and consciously.

BENJAMIN C. LEEMING

edge of his God is a completely different kind of knowledge from that which we customarily speak of. Taking his departure from psychology or from religious or mystical experience, areas open to all, he would argue that his knowledge transcends empirical data and defies scientific verification. It is knowledge whose source is much closer to mystical intuition than to senses or reason, although the latter are instrumental in generating the intuitive response. This knowledge is similar to the mystical knowledge of the young woman in the dialogue, who knows in her heart that what she feels plumbs the depths of reality. This knowledge is rooted in a personal experience, traditionally induced through prayer and meditation. However, some seek a similar experience in less traditional ways.

ALTERED MENTAL STATES AND RELIGIOUS EXPERIENCE

The word *psychedelic* is defined as "of or pertaining to or generating hallucinations, distortions of perception, and, occasionally, psychotic-like states." It is true that the five principal psychedelic drugs—LSD-25, mescaline, psilocybin, dimethyl-tryptamine (DMT), and marijuana—when used indiscriminately have produced these characteristics in certain people. But the same characteristics frequently accompany the so-called mystical or religious experience, the numinous.

Raynor Johnson, in his excellent collection of accounts of mystical experiences *Watcher on the Hills*,[25] lists some states of consciousness that mystical experiences invariably involve, all of which also characterize psychedelic experiences. First is a sense of timelessness. Mystics as well as psychedelic drug users frequently describe a loss of the sense of time. A minute may seem like an hour, an hour like a minute. Both groups fall into a state of such utter relaxation that they become oblivious to temporal affairs. Often accompanying these feelings is

an acute realization that the purpose of life is to live and experience every moment as fully as possible.

Because of these similarities between drug use and mystical experience, the young man in our dialogue, who once used marijuana, can understand the woman's seemingly unintelligible mystical experience.

YOUNG MAN: Funny, but as I've been listening to you describe your experience I've had a feeling of déjà vu.

YOUNG WOMAN: Then you know what I'm trying to describe.

YOUNG MAN: I think I do. But let me ask you something. Did you have the feeling that time slowed down?

YOUNG WOMAN: Not only did it slow down, but it was as if I were anchored in the present. Every pore seemed to open to what was occurring *now*.

YOUNG MAN: The past didn't exist.

YOUNG WOMAN: Nor the future.

YOUNG MAN: You had none of the normal concerns about the future?

YOUNG WOMAN: I had neither anxiety about it nor anticipation of it. It simply didn't exist.

YOUNG MAN: I once felt that way—that I had crossed the time barrier between the finite and the infinite, that time was just an illusion. And then I experienced something strangely wonderful, something very difficult to explain, and that was that everything was somehow integrated. Somehow, having broken through the bubble of time, I experienced the oneness of everything, things that before had somehow been separated by time.

YOUNG WOMAN: And spatial relationships.

YOUNG MAN: Yes, time and space—they both struck me as illusions.

YOUNG WOMAN: And as long as we're committed to those illusions, we persist in perceiving reality in terms of opposing forces: good and bad, love and hate, right and wrong.

YOUNG MAN: But there are no opposites. I felt this more strongly than I've ever felt anything. That

25. Raynor Johnson, *Watcher on the Hills* (London: Hodder and Stoughton, 1959). See also Charles Tart, *Altered States of Consciousness* (New York: Doubleday, 1972).

all things are interconnected and intertwined with everything else.

Here is another principal feature of the mystical and psychedelic experience: the loss of a sense of polarity. What we commonly view as opposites are seen as different sides of the same coin. There is an interdependence among all things, such as between heads and tails or between up and down.

Self necessitates other; good, bad; solid, space; saints, sinners. In this state the mystic and sometimes the psychedelic drug user realize that each thing in existence can have meaning and definition only in terms of something else. There is, then, just oneness.

Such a loss of conventional classification labels can produce a heightened sense of the interdependence among all parts of creation.

PHILOSOPHY AND LIFE 3.3

Distinguishing Between the Drug- and Non-Drug-Induced Religious Experience

In his widely read essay "Do Drugs Have Religious Import?" professor of philosophy Huston Smith recounts an intriguing experiment he once conducted among a group of Princeton students. He provided the students with accounts of two religious experiences. One occurred under the influence of drugs, the other without their influence. The students were asked to distinguish between them. Here are the two accounts.

Suddenly I burst into a vast, new, indescribably wonderful universe.

SOURCES: Huston Smith, "Do Drugs Have Religious Import?" *Journal of Philosophy* 61 (1964): 517–530. The first account: Anonymous, in "The Issue of the Consciousness-Expanding Drugs," *Main Currents in Modern Thought* 20 (1963): 10–11. (Experienced under the influence of drugs.) The second account: R. M. Bucke, quoted in William James, *The Varieties of Religious Experience* (New York: Modern Library, 1902), 390–391. (Not experienced under the influence of drugs.)

Although I am writing this over a year later, the thrill of the surprise and amazement, the awesomeness of the revelation, the engulfment in an overwhelming feeling-wave of gratitude and blessed wonderment, are as fresh, and the memory of the experience is as vivid, as if it had happened five minutes ago. And yet to concoct anything by way of description that would even hint at the magnitude, the sense of ultimate reality . . . this seems such an impossible task. The knowledge which has infused and affected every aspect of my life came instantaneously and with such complete force of certainty that it was impossible, then or since, to doubt its validity.

All at once, without warning of any kind, I found myself wrapped in a flame-colored cloud. For an instant I thought of fire . . . the next, I knew that the fire was within myself. Directly afterward there came upon me a sense of exultation, of immense joyousness accompanied or immediately followed by an intellectual illumination impossible to describe.

Among other things, I did not merely come to believe, but I saw that the universe is not composed of dead matter, but is, on the contrary, a living Presence; I became conscious in myself of eternal life. . . . I saw that all men are immortal: that the cosmic order is such that without any peradventure all things work together for the good of each and all; that the foundation principle of the world . . . is what we call love, and that the happiness of each and all is in the long run absolutely certain.

In Smith's experiment, twice as many students (forty-six) answered incorrectly as answered correctly (twenty-three).

QUESTIONS

1. Which account do you think reflects a drug-induced experience?

2. Does a difficulty in distinguishing between the drug-induced experience and the non-drug-induced experience argue for or against Watts's thesis about societal proscriptions against drug usage?

YOUNG WOMAN: I recall becoming engrossed in watching a tiny ant that was moving across my foot.

YOUNG MAN: Did you wonder at the ant's universe?

YOUNG WOMAN: Really! I thought that the ant must think of itself as I think of myself, although it sounds silly to speak of an ant thinking. But then I recognized that I couldn't even begin to speak of myself thinking if it weren't for the ant, if it weren't for the apparent difference between us.

YOUNG MAN: Without the ant you would lack self-definition.

YOUNG WOMAN: In a sense I would. And without everything else I stand in relation to, I would melt away, evaporate.

YOUNG MAN: The thought terrifies me.

YOUNG WOMAN: And it did me, but then I was filled with marvel at this cosmic order that finds a place for everything and somehow ordains a role for each.

The young woman seems to be describing an experience of the relativity of all things, an experience similar to one that the young man experienced under the influence of marijuana. Such an experience frequently reveals a sense of the self as a link in an infinite chain that connects each life to all other lives. This hierarchy of processes and beings ranges from subatomic particles through bacteria and insects to human beings and supernatural beings.

There is a final feature that frequently accompanies both experiences. Some describe it as the awareness of eternal energy.

YOUNG MAN: I think the most marvelous part of my experience was the sense of incredible strength that I had.

YOUNG WOMAN: A kind of energy.

YOUNG MAN: Yes, you could call it that.

YOUNG WOMAN: I remember seeing an almost blinding light.

YOUNG MAN: Did you feel that this light was the source of all life, of all being?

YOUNG WOMAN: More than that. I felt that the light was me.

YOUNG MAN: Yes, that the concentrated energy was your own being.

YOUNG WOMAN: That I was the source of all life, that it all flowed from me, that I was . . .

YOUNG MAN: Divine?

Accompanying such experiences is the profound recognition that the totality of existence is a single energy. But even more often this energy is one's own being: It is a realization that the individual is the divinity and the divinity is all that is.

Obviously, not everyone under the influence of psychedelic drugs will experience these states of consciousness. Nor should everyone seeking a religious experience try psychedelic drugs. In too many cases, excessive and indiscriminate use ends tragically. Nevertheless, the similarity between the mystical and psychedelic experiences in altering states of consciousness raises philosophical curiosity about why society disapproves of drug use.

First, it is obvious that society disapproves of psychedelics because of their often deadly effects. But if their effect can be strikingly similar to that of a religious or mystical experience, are we, in effect, disapproving of that as well? Zen scholar Alan Watts, in his fascinating essay "Psychedelic and Religious Experience,"[26] says we are. He gives a number of reasons, two of which are noteworthy here.

Like the psychedelic experience, the mystical experience is not logical. Because it defies common sense, it runs counter to empirical and rational knowledge, the basis of Western epistemology. Such experiences are inconsistent with how we relate ourselves to the universe—that is, as separate, individual egos confronting an external and often alien world. Religious, mystical, and psychedelic experiences, then, are truly revolutionary. They suggest ways of seeing and knowing that contradict most of what we have grown up to accept.

---

26. Alan Watts, "Psychedelic and Religious Experience," *California Law Review* 56 (1968): 74.

Even more important, when we claim consciousness of oneness with God or with the universe, we fly in the face of our society's concept of religion. Our Jewish and Christian origins do not sanction the individual's claim to identity with the Godhead, even though this identity may have been peculiarly true of Jesus Christ. For anyone to claim that he or she is the all-powerful and all-knowing ruler of the world has traditionally been considered blasphemy.

Watts is suggesting, then, that the prohibition against such drugs, even in controlled scientific studies, is really a prohibition against questioning traditional secular and religious values. As evidence, he records how suspicious institutional religion has always been of mystical claims and how persecutive it has been, as in the case of Johannes "Meister" Eckhart, whose claims of equality with God resulted in his condemnation as a heretic. Western mystics who have received church acceptance, such as Saint Teresa of Avila and Saint John of the Cross, have always acknowledged a distinction between themselves and their God.

The Eastern philosophical and religious traditions, on the other hand, have always been sympathetic to mystical claims and experiences. For this reason many may seek the source of their religious experiences not in drugs or in radical theology but in these traditions.

EASTERN RELIGIOUS TRADITIONS

As we mentioned in Chapter 2, Eastern philosophy refers to those systems of thought, belief, and action espoused by many peoples of the Near and Far East. It is neither our intention nor within our capabilities to mention all of these, let alone discuss them adequately. But we should mention at least two of the principal religions to which many Westerners are turning for meaningful religious experience: Hinduism and Buddhism.

Hinduism

One of the oldest of Eastern traditions is Hinduism, which has been practiced by hundreds of millions of people for about five thousand years. Hin-

Dancing Ganesha, India, ninth century. "To understand enlightenment you must understand the law of karma, the law of sowing and reaping. . . . The wheel of existence turns until we achieve enlightenment, after which we are released from this series of rebirths."

duism has many divisions and subdivisions, and no leader or belief is accepted by every Hindu sect. In fact, so diversified is Hinduism that it is very difficult to describe it as a whole. Any attempt at description is bound to be an oversimplification. A further complication is the fact that our language has no precise equivalents for certain Indian terms and concepts.

Aware of these limitations, let us begin with the literary source of Hindu teaching. Although many texts form the body of Hindu scripture, one has influenced Hindu thought more than any other: the *Bhagavad-Gita*, the Song of the Lord, which is part of the great epic *Mahabharata*. Reading the Gita will introduce you to the principal concepts of Hinduism, as well as to beautiful poetry.

One concept common to all expressions of Hinduism is the oneness of reality. This oneness is the absolute, or Brahman, which the mind can never fully grasp or words express. Only Brahman is real; everything else is an illusory manifestation of it. A correlative belief is the concept of **atman**, or no self. What we commonly call I or the self is an illusion, for each true self is one with Brahman. When we realize this unity with the absolute, we realize our true destiny.

Also common to all Hindu thought are four primary values. In order of increasing importance, they may be roughly translated as wealth, pleasure, duty, and enlightenment. The first two are worldly, which when kept in perspective are good and desirable values. Duty, or righteousness, refers to patience, sincerity, fairness, love, honesty, and similar virtues. The highest spiritual value is enlightenment, by which one is illuminated and liberated and, most importantly, finds release from the wheel of existence. Repeated existence is the destiny of those who do not achieve enlightenment.

To understand enlightenment you must understand the law of **karma,** the law of sowing and reaping. All of us, through what we do or do not do, supposedly determine our destiny. If we are particularly evil, we may find ourselves reborn as subhumans. If we are noble, we may be reborn as especially favored humans. This wheel of existence turns until we achieve enlightenment, after which we are released from this series of rebirths.

Sri Sarvepalli Radhakrishnan, in *A Source Book in Indian Philosophy*,[27] lists characteristics common

to all Indian thought. First is an emphasis on the spiritual. It is the spiritual that endures and is ultimately real. Second is the realization that our philosophy and our life are inextricably enmeshed. What we believe is how we live; if our beliefs are in error, our lives will be unhappy. Third is a preoccupation with the inner life. The road to enlightenment stretches not outward but inward. To understand nature and the universe we must turn within. Fourth is an emphasis on the nonmaterial oneness of creation. There are no polarities; a unity of spirit provides cosmic harmony. Fifth is the acceptance of direct awareness as the only way to understand what is real. Unlike the user of psychedelic drugs, the Indian believer finds this direct perception through spiritual exercises, perhaps through the practice of yoga. Reason is of some use, but in the last analysis we know only through an inner experience of oneness with all of creation. Sixth is a healthy respect for tradition, but never a slavish commitment to it. The past can teach but never rule. Finally, Indian thought recognizes the complementary nature of all systems of belief. Hinduism is not rooted in any single doctrine, nor does it claim a monopoly on truth or wisdom. It preaches tolerance of all sincere viewpoints and includes many of these within its own spiritual teachings.

Buddhism

Another major Eastern tradition is Buddhism, contained in the teachings of Siddhartha Gautama (563 B.C.–?), its founder. Since Gautama found no evidence for a belief in a personal god, his teachings are a diagnosis of and a prescription for the "disease" of living.

He preached the Four Noble Truths, which we mentioned in Chapter 2. It might be useful to show how they compare with some of Tillich's ideas. The First Noble Truth, concerned with the suffering that we experience in living, Tillich might call "existential despair," although he would attribute it to theism. The Second Noble Truth identifies the cause of this suffering or, more accurately, this frustration: clinging or grasping based on **avidya,** ignorance and unawareness. This unawareness is characterized by commitment to the world of things

---

27. Sarvepalli Radhakrishnan and Charles A. Moore, eds., *A Source Book in Indian Philosophy* (Princeton, N.J.: Princeton University Press, 1957), xx–xxvi.

and illusion, maya, and not to the concrete world of reality. This unawareness is also characterized by a doomed attempt to control oneself and the environment, which can lead only to a futile grasping that results in self-frustration and the viciously circular pattern of life called **samsara,** the round of birth and death. Tillich might see this as the false subject-object distinction that we customarily make. The Third Noble Truth concerns the ending of samsara, called **nirvana,** release or liberation. It is the way of life that results when we stop grasping and clinging. Tillich would call it experiencing the "depth," the "ground of all being"; in the nirvana state we are released from the round of incarnations and enter a state that defies definition. The Fourth Noble Truth describes the Eightfold Path of the Buddha's **dharma**—that is, the doctrine whereby self-frustration is ended. We outlined this in Chapter 2.

Zen Buddhism

Japanese scholar D. T. Suzuki, who has marvelously rendered the philosophy of Zen Buddhism to the Western mind, shows in "Zen Buddhism" how Zen has established itself firmly on a teaching that claims to be

> A special transmission outside the Scripture;
> No dependence on words or letters;
> Direct pointing at the Mind of Man;
> Seeing into one's Nature and the attainment of
>   Buddhahood.[28]

These four lines, says Suzuki, describe the essentials of Zen Buddhism and provide insight into its religious impulses.

Suzuki points out that the first line does not imply the existence of an esoteric Buddhist teaching that came to be known as Zen. Quite the opposite is true. "A special transmission outside the Scripture" is understood by reference to the second line, which asserts Zen's lack of dependence on words and letters. "Words and letters" and "the Scripture" stand for conceptualism and all that the

term implies. Zen abhors and eschews words and concepts, as well as the reasoning based on them. It views a preoccupation with ideas and words as an empty substitution for experience.

In contrast, Zen upholds the direct experience of reality. It does not brook secondhand accounts or authoritative renderings of reality. Zen followers aspire to drink from the fountain of life rather than to listen to accounts of it. The ultimate truth is a state of inner experience achieved by means of wisdom. This state is beyond the realm of words and discriminations. To discriminate is to be caught in the endless cycle of birth and death with no hope of emancipation, attainment of nirvana, or realization of Buddhahood.

How, then, are we emancipated? How does Zen help one to achieve nirvana or Buddhahood? In answering this, Zen reminds us that we live in a world of dualities, of contradictory opposites. To be emancipated from the world may mean to leave or to deny it. Some people have taken this to mean self-destruction, but Suzuki suggests that this is a misinterpretation of Zen teaching. It is the mere amassing of knowledge, the storing of shopworn concepts, that is self-destructive. Rather, emancipation consists of recognizing the inadequacy of explanations and discriminations, of rejecting the notion that an explanation of a thing or fact exhausts the subject. For Zen there is no better explanation than actual experience, and actual experience is all that is needed to attain Buddhahood.

Let's turn to the last two lines: "Direct pointing at the Mind of Man; / Seeing into one's Nature and the attainment of Buddhahood." To grasp the meaning here, we must understand what is meant by *Mind, Nature,* and *Buddhahood.*

Mind does not refer to our ordinary functioning mind, the mind that thinks according to the laws of logic and psychological explanations. It is the mind that lies beneath all of these thoughts and feelings. For the Zen Buddhist, the Mind is also known as Nature, that is, reality. We may look on the Mind as the last point that we reach when we dig down psychologically into the depths of a thinking and feeling subject. Nature is the limit of objectivity. But the natural objective limit is the psychological subjective limit, and vice versa. When

---

28. Daisetz T. Suzuki, "Zen Buddhism," in *The Essentials of Zen Buddhism,* ed. Bernard Phillips (New York: Dutton, 1962), 73.

we reach the one, we find ourselves in the other. True, in each case we start differently: We go out to Nature, we go in to ourselves. But in the end there's a confluence of the two, a point of merging. When we have the Mind, we have Nature. When we understand Nature, we understand the Mind. They are one and the same.

Now we can speak of enlightenment, of Buddhahood. The person who has a thorough understanding of the Mind and whose movements are at one with Nature is the Buddha, the enlightened one. Nature personified is the Buddha. In effect, then, Mind, Nature, and Buddha are three different points of reference. The ideal of Zen, then, as expressed in the four lines, is to seize reality without the interference of any agency—intellectual, moral, or ritualistic.

The direct holding of reality is the awakening of **prajñā,** transcendental wisdom. Transcendental wisdom answers all questions that we can formulate about our spiritual life. Thus, wisdom is not the intellect in the ordinary sense. It transcends dialectics of all kinds. It is not analytical reasoning but a leap over the intellectual impasse, and in this it is an act of will. At the same time, it sees into nature. There is a noetic quality about it. It is both will and intuition. Zen is associated with willpower, because avoiding the tendency to analyze and intellectualize requires an act of will. This requires individual effort. Outsiders can only help by reminding us that all outside help is futile.

The literature of Zen glitters with anecdotal reminders of this. An especially graphic story involves a Zen Buddhist monk who is asked about the depths of the Zen River while he is walking over a bridge. At once he seizes the questioner and would have hurled him into the rapids had others not frantically interceded. The monk wanted the questioner to go down to the bottom of the river and to take its measure.

The basic principle of Zen is the growth or self-maturing of the inner experience. People used to intellectual exercises, moral persuasion, and devotional exercises will find Zen a disarming if not heretical teaching. But this is precisely what makes Zen unique in the history of religion. It proposes that we look within a thing in order to understand it. In contrast, we usually describe a thing from the outside in order to understand it; we speak of it in objective terms. While this objective method has its place and value, Zen proposes a method that for millions gives the key to an effective and all-satisfying understanding.

Obviously, there is much more to Hinduism, Buddhism, and Zen than we have outlined. Nevertheless, these sketches illustrate major differences between Eastern and Western thought. Let's consider these differences more closely.

DIFFERENCES BETWEEN EAST AND WEST

First, the East rejects the West's "objectified" God. There is no claim of a personal, all-knowing, all-good, all-powerful, and all-loving God, as there is in the Western tradition. As a result, Eastern thinkers have never debated God's existence. As a corollary, Buddhism does not share the Western view that there is a moral law, enjoined by God or by nature, which it is our duty to obey. In contrast, Western religions frequently, if not always, include behavioral proscriptions that if violated may lead to eternal damnation. In short, our tradition presents a God who expects us to behave in a certain way. In contrast:

> The Buddha's precepts of conduct—abstinence from taking life, taking what is not given, exploitation of the passions, lying, and intoxication— are voluntarily assumed rules of expedience, the intent of which is to remove the hindrances to clarity of awareness. Failure to observe the precepts produces bad *"karma"* not because *karma* is a law or moral retribution, but because all motivated and purposeful actions, whether conventionally good or bad, are *karma* insofar as they are directed to the grasping of life. Generally speaking, the conventionally "bad" actions are rather more grasping than the "good."[29]

Finally, whereas the thrust of Western religion traditionally has been to align us with our divine

---

29. Alan Watts, *The Way of Zen* (New York: Pantheon, 1957), 61. Reprinted by permission.

creator, Eastern thought, like Tillich's emphasis on being, aims to ground us in what is real. To do so, Eastern thought generally prescribes discipline, self-control, moderation, and detachment. Although these values are frequently observed in Western religious practice, they are just as frequently seen as means to an end: salvation and reward. While they are ways of attaining wisdom and truth, they are also ways of avoiding damnation.

Perhaps these differences explain why, since the middle 1960s, there has been a growing interest in the United States in Eastern thinking and religions. Many people are turning away from traditional faiths in favor of Zen Buddhism, Yoga, transcendental meditation, the International Society for Krishna Consciousness, Vedanta, and so on. Obviously, converts to Eastern religions have not stopped asking about their places in the scheme of things. One the contrary, they are asking perhaps more intensely than ever. Apparently, the traditional Western answers no long work for them. The traditional concepts of self, subject-object distinction, Judeo-Christian dogma, the egocentric emphasis on one's personal relationship with a theistic God, and the dismissal of nonhuman natural objects as essentially inferior and alien—perhaps all have conspired to send these seekers in other directions. Many features characterize these new directions: the emphasis on the workings of the mind and inner growth; the importance of discipline, practice, and method; a distrust of doctrines and dogmas; and hope for integrating body and intellect, feelings, and reason through a personal philosophy. But central to these features seem

to be a reevaluation and a redefinition of one's traditional concept of the divine and one's relationship to it.

QUESTIONS

1. In your own words, what is Tillich's objection to traditional or theological theism?

2. Are you sympathetic to Tillich's objections? If so, cite instances to illustrate that your sympathy is grounded in experience.

3. Anglican bishop John Robinson has said, "The traditional material is all true, no doubt, and one recognizes it as something one ought to be able to respond to, but somehow it seems to be going on around one rather than within. Yet to question it openly is to appear to let down the side, to be branded as hopelessly unspiritual, and to cause others to stumble." First interpret this statement, then explain it from the viewpoint of a church leader. Finally, ask yourself if it has any meaning for you.

4. Anselm's ontological argument claimed that existence was a necessary part of the meaning of a perfect being. Is Tillich similarly claiming that God is a necessary part of the meaning of "ultimately concerned"? Is he defining God into existence?

5. Some people claim that the mere fact that Tillich interprets his own knowledge of the "depth" as an experience of God does not make it so. Neither does it guarantee the existence of God. Are such critics distinguishing between belief and knowledge? How?

6. Some people compare Tillich's claim that experience of the "ground of all being" is an experience of God to the claim "I have a toothache because some mad genius has possessed my body and is causing the pain." Evaluate this analogy.

7. Do you think that Tillich's claims need public verification, as critics say they do? Is Tillich talking about a completely different kind of knowledge, a knowledge that transcends empirical data? In what ways is this a mystical knowledge?

8. Would you say that James's two characteristics of a mystical experience would also apply to a psychedelic-induced state of consciousness?

All religions pronounce the name of God in their particular language. As a rule it is better for a man to name God in his native tongue rather than in one that is foreign to him.

SIMONE WEIL

---

9. If through fasting, meditation, and prayer someone induced in himself a conscious state similar to a psychedelic-induced one, do you think society would react as it does to the user of psychedelics? If not, why not?

10. A common objection to the use of psychedelics is that the user loses touch with reality. What does such an objection assume? Do you think that the validity of this objection depends on the circumstances under which the drug is used?

11. What would you say are the main sources of attraction for Westerners in Eastern thought?

12. What obstacles would you note that many Westerners might face in adjusting to Eastern thought?

CHAPTER SUMMARY AND CONCLUSIONS

We opened this chapter by noting that all religions speak of personal commitment and experience and of our need to find our place in the cosmic scheme of things. Traditionally in the West, these phenomena have been sought through a relationship to a personal, theistic God, and many arguments have been assembled for God's existence. Seeing weaknesses in the theistic position, many have adopted pantheism or panentheism, others atheism or agnosticism. Whether or not God exists, the question of religious belief persists and affects our lives. For many, this decision involves a relationship not to a personal God but to a divine dimension to the universe, which they sense through personal experience. There has been a growing emphasis on this kind of personal experience as the basis of religious belief. In this connection we examined mysticism and movements with mystical overtones, such as radical theology, psychedelic drug use, and Eastern religious thought.

Clearly, the philosophy of religion has had a long and illustrious history that continues to unfold. The concept of religious experience is inextricably linked with a psychology of self, for religious experience is one way that we can integrate our personalities and lives and thereby achieve wholeness. Perhaps this wholeness is what psychologist Abra-

ham Maslow means when he speaks of "peak experiences," vivid moments in our lives when everything seems to fall into place, when our vision is clear, our lives meaningful, and our place in the order of things certain.[30]

Up until very recently, it was thought that the experiences that Maslow describes happened only to saints, mystics, artists, and poets, but certainly not to average people. Maslow suggests the contrary and offers a constructive insight into religious experience that might provide common ground for different viewpoints.

The moments that Maslow describes seem linked to feelings of self-fulfillment, achievement, and creativity. Thus, they can happen to anyone. But we must allow them to happen; we must open ourselves to them. This element of personal receptivity has always been an integral part of religious teaching, of the numinous, but it is often buried under pomp and ceremony.

The growth of interest in humanistic psychology suggested ways of getting in touch with the self and thereby with religious impulses. It spurred interest in expanding our awareness of self by increasing our creativity, improving our health, enhancing our learning and problem solving, and, most important, providing ecstatic experiences. A number of mind and brain investigations that attempt to see the human from all sides resulted, which led to new concepts of self that originate in a kind of religious experience, in which we experience self and reality in a new and different way.

Rather than viewing humans as a bundle of responses to stimuli, we now accept the richness and complexity of the human and the importance of each individual. Central to this emphasis on the individual is a recognition of wholeness. The centuries-old split between mind and body has been abandoned for the *holistic* approach, which recognizes the inseparability of mind and body and the influence of each on the other. Appropriately, there is more recognition of the roles that emotions and spiritual feelings play in our lives and of the limi-

---

30. See Abraham Maslow, *Toward a Psychology of Being* (New York: D. Van Nostrand, 1968).

tations of logic and rationality. As a result, subjective experience is gaining respect in scientific circles, a place heretofore reserved for objective experience. The realization that science and individual experience are not incompatible is growing. In addition, whereas we once had presumed ourselves to be objects of Freud's subconscious forces, we have now found a belief in our own capacity for growth, self-transcendence, or what Maslow calls "self-actualization."

The potential for what we have been calling religious experience is staggering. In the future, areas of conscious awareness that we hardly dream of today may open up. This awareness will no doubt be accompanied by a deep and reverent sensitivity to the profound mystery of life and our wondrous part in it.

HISTORICAL SHOWCASE

Aquinas and Descartes

In this chapter we have examined a broad range of philosophical issues raised by belief in God. But we have tended to treat these issues in isolation from other philosophical questions. For most major philosophers, however, questions about God cannot be addressed in isolation. Most major philosophers have felt that questions about God are deeply related to other important philosophical issues. For this reason, philosophers' views on God have profoundly influenced their positions on other philosophical questions.

In this historical section we will showcase two philosophers whose views about God determine their views on other important philosophical issues: Aquinas and Descartes. By examining their work, we will also get an idea of how these two major philosophers incorporate God into a large philosophical system. Thus, becoming acquainted with these two philosophers will give us an idea of how one's position on one philosophical issue can dramatically affect and interact with one's views on other issues in philosophy.

AQUINAS

No period of history was more preoccupied by religion than the medieval era, and the greatest of the medieval thinkers was Thomas Aquinas. Although Aquinas was influenced by the writings of Aristotle (whom we showcased in the last chapter), he was also deeply influenced by the events of the fifteen centuries (322 B.C. to A.D. 1225) that separated

Thomas Aquinas: "There must be something which is the cause of the Being, Goodness, and other perfections of things, and this we call God. . . . The eternal law is the plan in God's mind in accordance with which every motion of the universe is governed."

him from Aristotle, Plato, and the other Greek philosophers. Those centuries saw the Roman Empire (ca. 300 B.C. to ca. A.D. 500) rise and spread over Europe and also witnessed the birth of Christianity at the very height of the Empire's power. They also saw the collapse of civilization, as barbarian tribes repeatedly invaded the Empire until, after centuries of battering, the Empire was destroyed and Europe descended into the Dark Ages. During the Dark Ages most philosophy ceased while men and women turned to coping with the tasks of surviving in the barbaric world that Europe had become and in which Christianity was gradually spreading. It was not until Aquinas's time that conditions in Europe once again became conducive to philosophical activities and that new centers of learning—the first "universities"—were established. But the Europe that emerged from the Dark Ages had become completely Christianized, and, conse-

quently, philosophy tended to focus on the religious concerns that dominated discussion in the new universities. It was only natural that Thomas Aquinas's thinking should focus on the philosophical problems raised by the religion that now dominated Europe.

Born in 1225 to a wealthy family of the Italian nobility, Saint Thomas Aquinas was raised to hold high office in the Roman Catholic Church, a position that his family hoped would prove advantageous to their political fortunes. In preparation for this career, the family sent him at the age of five to study in a Benedictine monastery, where he remained until he entered the University of Naples at the age of fourteen. At Naples, Thomas came into contact with the Dominicans, an inspiring Order of monks dedicated to poverty and to service through teaching. In spite of the vigorous opposition of his family, Thomas entered the Dominican Order in 1241, dashing his family's hopes for his ecclesiastical career. Four years later the Order sent him to the new University of Paris to study under Albert the Great, a scholar of towering intellect already famous for his knowledge of Aristotle's doctrines. Under his influence, Thomas began to draw heavily on Aristotle's teachings, gradually producing a brilliant synthesis of Christian theology and Aristotelian philosophy. Aquinas remained a dedicated Christian scholar and teacher throughout his life, churning out a prodigious number of writings until his death in 1274. In his two greatest works, the *Summa Contra Gentiles* and the *Summa Theologica*, Thomas addresses virtually every philosophical issue raised by Christianity and resolves it in a way that many feel is philosophically sound yet true to the Christian faith. Aquinas's philosophy, in fact, often has been called the "Christian philosophy" and is still held by a large number of Christians.

Aquinas did not confuse religious faith with philosophy. With great care he distinguished between truths that are known by faith, truths that are known by reason, and truths that are known by both faith and reason. Philosophy, he held, consists of truths that our unaided reason can discover by reflecting on our natural experience in the world. Theology, on the other hand, begins with truths that have been revealed by God through scripture and accepted by faith and from these revealed truths draws further religious truths. There is some overlap between philosophy and theology, however, because there are some truths that can be discovered by our unaided reason and have also been revealed by God. In his own words:

> Some truths about God exceed the capacity of our human reason. An example of this is the truth that God is three persons in one. But there are some truths that reason by its very nature is also able to discover. Examples of these are the truths that God exists, that there is only one God, and similar truths. In fact, these truths about God have been proved by several philosophers who have relied completely on the light of their natural reason.[31]

Aquinas's philosophy begins with his famous five proofs for the existence of God (one of which we saw in our discussion of "cosmological" proofs), some of which were influenced by Aristotle's views on "causes." Each of the proofs proceeds by pointing to some aspect of the world we experience: its motion, its causality, its contingency, its imperfection, or its unthinking order. Each proof then argues that this aspect of the world cannot account for itself: Each aspect demands the existence of something—of a Divine Being—that is utterly different from the objects we experience. The motion of objects demands the existence of an unmoved mover; the causality we see at work demands the existence of something that is uncaused; the contingency of objects demands the existence of something that is noncontingent; the existence of imperfect objects demands the existence of something that is perfect; and the existence of order among objects that do not think demands the existence of something that thinks and that produces that order. The five proofs of Aquinas proceed as follows:

✳ That God exists can be proved in five ways.
The first and clearest way is the argument from motion. It is certain and evident to our senses that some things in the world are in motion. Now if

something is moved, it must be moved by something else. . . . For nothing can change from being potentially in motion to being in a state of actual movement unless something else that is in actual movement acts on it. . . . So whatever is moving must be moved by something else. Now if that by which it is moved is itself moving, then it, too, must be moved by something else, and that by something else again. But this cannot go on to infinity because then there would be no first mover. And if there were no first mover, then nothing would move since each subsequent mover will move only to the extent that it is moved by the motion imparted by the first mover. The [other] parts of a staff, for example, will move only to the extent that the [top of the] staff is moved by the hand. Therefore, there must be a first mover that is not moved. And this first unmoved mover is what we mean by God.

The second way is based on the nature of efficient causes. In the world we see around us, there are ordered lines of efficient causes [in which each member of the line produces the next member]. But nothing can be its own efficient cause, since then it would have to exist prior to itself and this is impossible. Now it is not possible for a line of efficient causes to extend to infinity. For in any line of efficient causes, the first is the cause of the intermediate ones, and the intermediate ones cause the last one. Now if we remove any of the causes, we remove all the remaining effects. So if there were no first cause then there would be no last cause nor any intermediate ones. But if a line of efficient causes extended back to infinity, then we would find no first cause. Consequently, if the line of causes extended back to infinity, there would be no intermediate causes nor any last causes in existence in the universe. But we know this is false. So it is necessary to admit that there is a first efficient cause. And this we call God.

The third way is based on contingency and necessity. It proceeds as follows. We find in nature things that are contingent. These are things that are generated and that can corrupt, and which therefore can exist or can cease to exist. Now it is impossible for such contingent things to exist forever. For if it is possible for something to cease existing, then eventually a moment will come when it will cease to exist. Therefore, if everything were contingent, then eventually everything would have ceased existing. If this happened, then

---

31. Saint Thomas Aquinas, *Summa Contra Gentiles*, I, q.3, a.2, trans. and ed. Manuel Velasquez.

even now nothing would exist, because something can start to exist only through the action of something that already exists. It follows that not everything is contingent, that is, some things must exist necessarily, that is, forever. Now every necessary thing is caused to exist forever either by something else or not by anything else. But as we proved above, it is impossible for a line of causes to be infinite. So there must exist something which derives its necessary existence from itself and not from something else, and which causes the existence of all other necessary beings. This is what we all mean by God.

The fourth way is based on the degrees of perfection that we find in things. Among the objects in our world some are more and some less good, true, noble, and the like. But to say that a thing has more or less of a certain perfection is to say that it resembles to a greater or lesser degree something which perfectly exemplifies that perfection. . . . So there must be something which is most perfectly true, most perfectly good, most perfectly noble, and, consequently, which most perfectly exists (since, as Aristotle shows, those things that are perfectly true also exist perfectly). Now that which most perfectly exemplifies some quality, also causes other things to have that quality to a greater or lesser degree. Fire, for example, which most perfectly exemplifies the quality of heat, is the cause of the heat in hot things. Therefore, there must be something which is the cause of the being, goodness, and every other perfection in things. And this we call God.

The fifth way of proving God's existence is based on the order in the universe. We see that things which lack knowledge, such as natural objects, act for an end. That is, their activity is always or nearly always aimed at achieving the best result. It is clear, therefore, that their activity is not produced by chance but by design. Now things which lack knowledge cannot move unerringly toward an end unless they are directed toward that end by some being that has knowledge and intelligence much like an arrow is directed toward its target by an archer. Therefore there must exist an intelligent Being Who directs all natural things toward their respective ends. This Being we call God.[32]

According to Aquinas, each of the five proofs for the existence of God tells us something about God. The first proof implies that unlike anything in the universe, God imparts motion to everything without Himself moving and therefore without Himself being in time and without being material. The second implies that unlike anything we know, God is the uncreated creator that causes everything to exist. The third tells us that—again unlike anything in our experience—God cannot cease existing because His existence does not depend on anything else. The fourth tells us that unlike anything in the universe, God is perfect goodness, perfect truth, perfect nobility, and perfect existence. And the fifth tells us that God is the supremely wise intelligence in whom all the order in the universe originates.

Nevertheless, Aquinas cautions, there is such a vast gulf between ourselves and God that the knowledge of God that we can glean from the five proofs is very imperfect. Each of the proofs merely tells us that some aspect of the universe we experience requires the existence of something else that is *unlike* anything in that universe and therefore *unlike* anything in our experience. Aquinas expresses this idea by asserting that although the proofs show us *that* God is, they do not tell us *what* God is. The proofs give us what Aquinas calls a "negative way" of knowing God. They do not give us a positive conception of God but lead us to *remove* certain ideas from our conception of God: God is *not* in motion, God is *not* created, God is *not* dependent, God is *not* imperfectly good, God is *not* guided by blind instinct.

But does this "via negativa"—this negative approach—provide us with the only knowledge we have of God? Are we doomed to know only what God is *not* and doomed never to have any positive knowledge of God? At first sight it would seem that we could never have any positive knowledge of God, for all of our positive knowledge is based on our experience of the universe around us. But God is unlike anything in our experience. So it would seem that we could never have any experience on which we could base our knowledge of God. However, Aquinas responds, there is an imperfect kind of positive knowledge of God that is open to us.

---

32. Saint Thomas Aquinas, *Summa Theologica*, I, q.2, a.3, trans. Manuel Velasquez. © 1978 by Manuel Velasquez.

This is what he calls "knowledge by analogy" or "analogical knowledge" of God.

Aquinas explains analogical knowledge as follows: He points out that there are certain words—such as *good, wise,* and *loving*—that we apply both to God, whom we do not experience, and to human creatures, whom we do experience. We say for example, that God is good, wise, and loving, and we say that this or that person of our experience is good, wise, or loving. We could conceivably be applying such words to both God and humans in any of three ways. First, the words could have a *univocal* meaning: That is, they could have exactly the same meaning when applied to God whom we do not experience as when applied to the humans we do experience. But this is impossible since God and humans are so unlike that the goodness, wisdom, and love of God must be different from the goodness, wisdom, and love we experience in humans.

> It is impossible for a word to be applied univocally to both God and the creatures he produces. For when an effect is not equal to the power of the cause that produced it, the effect receives only an imperfect likeness of the cause: that is, the effect will be like the cause only to an imperfect degree. . . . Thus, when the word "wise" is applied to human beings, the word in a way comprehends and includes in its meaning the thing to which it refers [i.e., imperfect wisdom as we experience it and as God produced it]. But this is not so when the word is applied to God. For when the word "wise" is applied to God it refers to something [perfect wisdom] that exceeds the meaning of the word and which is not comprehended.[33]

Second, then, words applied to both God and creatures could have an *equivocal* meaning: They could mean something totally different when applied to each. But this, too, is inadequate, Aquinas insists. If the words we use changed their meaning when we applied them to God, then we could not say anything at all about God. For we would never know what our words meant when we applied them to God since their meaning derives entirely from our experience of creatures.

Neither can we say that words that are applied to God and creatures have a purely equivocal sense, although some thinkers have held this view. If words that applied to both God and creatures were purely equivocal, then our experience of creatures would not allow us to know anything about God nor to prove anything about God. For the words we used in our reasoning would always be exposed to the fallacy of equivocation. [They would have one meaning in part of our reasoning and another meaning in another part.] Now this is contrary to the procedure of some philosophers, such as Aristotle, who managed to prove many things about God. It also contradicts scripture which says "The invisible things of God are clearly seen, being understood from the things that He created."[34]

Humans, then, must reflect God's nature to some degree since they are His creation: The goodness, wisdom, and love of humans that we experience must reflect imperfectly the perfect goodness, wisdom, and love of God in whom they originate. So, Aquinas concludes, the third and correct way in which we apply to God certain words whose meaning is based on our experience of humans is *by analogy.* Words such as *wise, good,* or *loving* are applied both to God and humans with an *analogical* meaning: The words do not have a completely different meaning when applied to each, but their meaning is also not exactly the same.

> We have to conclude that these words are applied to both God and creatures in an *analogous* sense, that is, with a meaning that is based on a relationship. . . . For example, the word "healthy" can be applied to a medicine as well as to an animal because of the relationship the medicine has to the health of the animal: the medicine is the cause of the animal's health. In a similar way, words can be applied to both creatures and to God in an analogous and not in a purely univocal nor in a purely equivocal sense. Consider that we can apply to God only words whose meanings we draw from our experience of creatures. Consequently, when we apply a word to both God and creatures, its meaning has to be based on the relationship that creatures have to God: they are related to

---

33. Ibid., I, q.13, a.5.

34. Ibid.

God as to their origin and their cause in whom all their perfections pre-exist in a way that excels their existence in creatures. Now this kind of common possession of perfections is the basis of a kind of meaning that is midway between pure univocation and pure equivocation. When a word is applied analogically in this way to two different beings its meaning does not remain completely identical as with univocal uses, nor does it have completely different meanings as in equivocal uses.[35]

Our experience of humans, then, gives us an imperfect but positive knowledge of attributes that exist in God in a perfect way. We can never fully comprehend God's own unique and perfect goodness, wisdom, and love, which are quite different from our imperfect and partial goodness, wisdom, and love. So *good, wise,* and *loving* do not have exactly the same meaning when applied to God and humans. Nevertheless, we do experience the partial goodness, wisdom, and love of humans and know that it reflects the perfect goodness, wisdom, and love of God from whom they derive. This knowledge allows us to say that there is some similarity of meaning between *good, wise,* and *loving* when used of both God and humans.

The universe that God created, Aquinas holds, is governed by laws that are imposed by God. Aquinas calls this law the "eternal law," and he likens God to a ruler or a craftsman who fashions the law of the universe.

Before any craftsman makes something, he must have in his mind an idea of what he will make. Similarly, before a ruler governs his subjects, he must have in his mind some idea of what his subjects are to do. The craftsman's idea of what he will make constitutes a plan of the object to be made (it is also part of what we call his skill). And the ruler's idea of what his subjects are to do constitutes a kind of law. . . . Now since God is the wise creator of the universe, He is like a craftsman who makes something. And He is also like the ruler since He governs every act and motion of every single creature. Consequently, the idea in God's wise mind, according to which everything

was created, can be called a plan (or an ideal model, or even a part of God's skill); and since everything is also governed according to this same idea, it can also be called a law. So the eternal law is nothing more than a plan in God's mind, in accordance with which every act and motion of the universe is directed.[36]

The laws that order the universe govern creatures through the natural forces and inclinations that were made part of their natures when they were created. As part of that universe, human beings are also subject to the eternal law of God through the natural inclinations within us that move us toward our own ends and activities. Unlike other creatures, however, human beings use their reason to direct themselves toward their ends.

It is clear from the preceding article that the eternal law is the guide and standard for everything that is subject to God's provident direction. Clearly, therefore, the activities of all creatures are equally determined by the eternal law. Their activities are determined by the natural forces and inclinations that were made part of their natures when they were created [by God]. These natural forces and inclinations cause creatures to engage in their appropriate activities and attain their appropriate ends.

Now rational creatures [such as humans] are also subject to God's provident direction, but in a way that makes them more like God than all other creatures. For God directs rational creatures by instilling in them certain natural inclinations and [reasoning] abilities that enable them to direct themselves as well as other creatures. Thus human beings also are subject to the eternal law and they too derive from that law certain natural inclinations to seek their proper ends and proper activities. These inclinations of our nature constitute what we call the "natural law" and they are the effects of the eternal law imprinted in our nature.

Thus, even scripture suggests that our natural ability to reason (by which we distinguish right from wrong) in which the natural law resides, is nothing more than the image of God's own reason imprinted on us. For Psalm Four asks, "Who will show us what is right?" and it answers, "The light

---

35. Ibid.

36. Ibid., I–IIae, q.93, a.1.

of Thy Mind, O Lord, which has been imprinted upon us."[37]

Aquinas argued that morality is based on these "natural inclinations" or "natural law" that God instilled within us. Our reason perceives as goods those things toward which we are naturally inclined and perceives as evil whatever is destructive of those goods. It is morally right to pursue the goods toward which we are naturally inclined and morally wrong to pursue what is destructive of those goods. Thus, the natural law is the basis of morality.

A thing is good if it is an end that we have a natural inclination to desire; it is evil if it is destructive of what our nature is inclined to desire. Consequently, those kinds of things that our nature is inclined to desire are perceived by our reason as good for our human nature. And our reason will conclude that those kinds of things ought to be pursued in our actions. But if our reason sees a certain type of thing as destructive of what human nature is inclined to desire, it will conclude that that type of thing ought to be avoided.

We can therefore list the basic [moral] precepts of the natural law by listing the kinds of things that we naturally desire. First, like every other nature, human nature is inclined to desire its own survival. Consequently it is a natural [moral] law that we ought to preserve human life and avoid whatever is destructive of life. Secondly, like other animals, human nature is inclined to desire those things that nature teaches all animals to desire by instinct. For example, all animals have an instinctive desire to come together in a union of male and female, and an instinctive desire to care for their young. [So it is morally right to pursue these things.] Thirdly, human nature is inclined to desire those goods that satisfy our intellects. This aspect of our nature is proper to human beings. Thus, human nature is inclined to desire knowledge (for example, to know the truth about God) and to desire an orderly social life. Consequently, it is a natural [moral] law that we ought to dispel ignorance and avoid harming those among whom we live.[38]

Thus, for Aquinas, the God whose existence is implied by an imperfect universe is also the God who creates the moral laws that we come to know by reflecting on our basic human inclinations. God is not only the foundation of the existence of the universe, He is also the foundation of morality.

DESCARTES

The role that God plays in the philosophy of Descartes is uniquely different from the role He plays in other philosophies such as that of Aquinas. For Aquinas as well as for other philosophers, God's existence is a conclusion we reach by coming to know the world around us. For Descartes, however, God is the One who guarantees that we can come to know the world around us. For Descartes, God is not a Being whom we come to know about *after* we know the world around us: Instead, God is a Being whom we must first know about *before* we can know anything for certain about the world around us. God does not come at the end of knowledge but at the beginning!

But there are many other differences between Descartes and Aquinas, symptomatic, perhaps, of the fact that in the three and a half centuries that elapsed between these philosophers, Europe had changed a great deal. No longer was Europe dominated by a single religion: Protestantism had appeared to compete with Catholicism. The physical sciences were emerging under the impetus of the new discoveries and theories of Galileo and Copernicus. Many of the new modern nations of Europe had already established themselves with their own particular languages, governments, and cultures. The New World of the Americas was being explored. And everywhere fresh minds were bubbling with new ideas and disputing the old medieval views—including those of Aquinas—that had so long dominated European intellectual life.

René Descartes was born in 1596 in Touraine to a councillor of the Parliament of Brittany. A brilliant young man, he was sent in 1604 to study in the Jesuit college of La Fleche where, although he was impressed by the precision of mathematics, he was deeply distressed by the disputes and doubts that surrounded all other realms of knowledge,

---

37. Ibid., I–IIae, q.91, a.2.
38. Ibid., I–IIae, q.94, a.2.

René Descartes: "I noticed that while I wished to think all things false, it was absolutely essential that the 'I' who thought this should be something, and remarking that this truth, 'I think, therefore I am' was so certain that all the extravagant suppositions of the sceptics were incapable of shaking it, I came to the conclusion that I could receive it as the First Principle of the philosophy I was seeking."

especially philosophy. The end of school, in 1612, left him feeling unsettled and dissatisfied. As he later wrote in his *Discourse on Method*, a short philosophical work in which he described how he came to formulate his own philosophy:

As soon as I had completed the entire course of study at the close of which one is usually received into the ranks of the learned, . . . I found myself embarrassed with so many doubts and errors that it seemed to me that the effort to instruct myself had no effect other than the increasing discovery of my own ignorance. And yet I was studying at one of the most celebrated Schools in Europe. . . . I was delighted with Mathematics because of the certainty of its demonstrations and the evidence of its reasoning. . . . On the other hand, . . . I shall not say anything about Philosophy, but that,

[although] it has been cultivated for many centuries by the best minds that have ever lived, . . . nevertheless no single thing is to be found in it which is not subject to dispute, and in consequence which is not dubious. . . . [A]s to the other sciences, inasmuch as they derive their principles from Philosophy, I judged that one could have built nothing solid on foundations so far from firm.[39]

Disillusioned, Descartes at the age of seventeen resolved to leave school, join the army, and begin to travel, hoping that by studying "the great book of the world" he would find more truth than he had found in school.

This is why, as soon as age permitted me to emerge from the control of my tutors, I entirely quitted the study of letters. And resolving to seek no other knowledge than that which could be found in myself, or at least in the great book of the world, I employed the rest of my youth in travel, in seeing courts and armies, in speaking with men of diverse temperaments and conditions, in collecting varied experiences, in proving myself in the various predicaments in which I was placed by fortune, and under all circumstances bringing my mind to bear on the things which came before it, so that I might derive some profit from my experience.[40]

But the young Descartes found himself as dissatisfied by the many conflicting opinions he encountered on his travels with the army as he had been by his formal studies in school. And this led him one fateful winter day to resolve to see whether he could reach the truth on his own by turning to study his own inner being.

[During the time] I only considered the manners of other men I found in them nothing to give me settled convictions; and I remarked in them almost as much diversity as I had formerly seen in the opinions of philosophers. . . . But after I had employed several years in thus studying the book of the world and trying to acquire some experi-

39. René Descartes, *Discourse on Method*, trans. Elizabeth S. Haldane and G. R. T. Ross, in *The Philosophical Works of Descartes*, vol. 1 (Cambridge: Cambridge University Press, 1911), 83, 85, 87.
40. Ibid., 86.

ence, I one day formed the resolution of also making myself an object of study and of employing all the strength of my mind in choosing the road I should follow. . . . I was then in Germany, . . . returning from the coronation of the Emperor to rejoin the army, [when] the setting in of winter detained me in a quarter where, since I found no society to divert me, while fortunately I had also no cares or passions to trouble me, I remained the whole day shut up alone in a stove-heated room where I had complete leisure to occupy myself with my own thoughts.[41]

There in his quiet little "stove-heated room," Descartes thought back to the careful method of reasoning that he had found in the mathematics he had studied and admired in school. This method, Descartes felt, begins with "simple" truths that are so "clearly and distinctly perceived" that they cannot be doubted and proceeds to the more complex truths that rest on the simple truths. Perhaps this method of reasoning could be used in other fields to establish all truth with certitude.

Those long chains of reasoning, simple and easy as they are, of which geometricians make use in order to arrive at the most difficult demonstrations, had caused me to imagine that all those things which fall under the cognizance of man might very likely be mutually related in the same fashion; and that, provided only that we abstain from receiving anything as true which is not so, and always retain the order which is necessary in order to deduce the one conclusion from the other, there can be nothing so remote that we cannot reach to it, nor so recondite that we cannot discover it. . . . Considering also that of all those who have hitherto sought for the truth in the Sciences, it has been the mathematicians alone who have been able to succeed in . . . producing reasons which are evident and certain, I did not doubt that it had been by means of a similar method that they carried on their investigations.[42]

Convinced that by turning to mathematics he had found an instance of the only reliable method for discovering truth, Descartes summarized his new method in four rules.

The first of these was to accept nothing as true which I did not clearly recognize to be so: that is to say, carefully to avoid precipitation and prejudice in judgments, and to accept in them nothing more than what was presented to my mind so clearly and distinctly that I could have no occasion to doubt it.

The second was to divide up each of the difficulties which I examined into as many parts as possible, and as seemed requisite in order that it might be resolved in the best manner possible.

The third was to carry on my reflections in due order, commencing with objects that were the most simple and easy to understand, in order to rise little by little, or by degrees, to knowledge of the most complex. . . .

The last was in all cases to make enumerations so complete and reviews so general that I should be certain of having omitted nothing.[43]

Feeling he now had a method for pursuing the truth, Descartes left his little room and again took up his travels. Nine years passed before felt ready to apply his method to philosophical issues.

Inasmuch as I hoped to be able to reach my end more successfully in converse with man than in living longer shut up in the warm room where these reflections had come to me, I hardly awaited the end of winter before I once more set myself to travel. And in all the nine following years I did nothing but roam hither and thither. . . . Nine years thus passed away before I had taken any definite part in regard to the difficulties as to which the learned are in the habit of disputing, or had commenced to seek the foundation of any philosophy. . . . [Then I] resolved to remove myself from all places where any acquaintances were possible, and to retire to this country [Holland, where] . . . I can live as solitary and retired as in deserts the most remote.[44]

Here, in solitude, Descartes began a long series of "meditations" during which he slowly built a philosophy that, he was convinced, was as solid

41. Ibid., 87.
42. Ibid., 91–92.

43. Ibid., 92.
44. Ibid., 98–100.

and certain as mathematics because it relied on the same method. He began by putting his first rule into practice by "rooting out of my mind" all opinions that were the least bit doubtful. Through this "method of doubt" Descartes came upon the basic truth that was to serve as the "simple" principle from which he would "rise to the most complex."

I do not know that I ought to tell you of the first meditations there made by me, for they are so metaphysical and so unusual that they may perhaps not be acceptable to everyone. . . . Because I wished to give myself entirely to the search after Truth, I thought that it was necessary for me to take an apparently opposite course, and to reject as [if] absolutely false everything as to which I could imagine the least ground of doubt, in order to see if afterwards there remained anything in my belief that was entirely certain. Thus, because our senses sometimes deceive us, I wished to suppose that nothing is just as they cause us to imagine it to be; and because there are men who deceive themselves in their reasoning and fall into fallacies, even concerning the simplest matters of geometry, and judging that I was as subject to error as was any other, I rejected as [if] false all the reasons formerly accepted by me as demonstrations. And since all the same thoughts and conceptions which we have while awake may also come to us in sleep without any of them being at that time true, I resolved to assume that everything that ever entered into my mind was no more true than the illusions of my dreams.

But immediately afterwards I noticed that while I thus wished to think all things false, it was absolutely essential that the "I" who thought this should be something, and remarking that this truth, "I think, therefore I am" was so certain and so assured that all the most extravagant suppositions brought forward by the skeptics were incapable of shaking it, I came to the conclusion that I could receive it without scruple as the first principle of the Philosophy which I was seeking.

And then, examining attentively that which I was, I saw that I could conceive that I had no body, and that there was no world nor place where I might be; but yet that I could not for all that conceive that I was not. On the contrary, I saw from the very fact that I thought of doubting the truth of other things, it very evidently and certainly followed that I was. On the other hand if I

had only ceased from thinking, even if all the rest of what I had ever imagined had really existed, I should have no reason for thinking that I had existed. From that I knew that I was a substance the whole essence or nature of which is to think, and that for its existence there is no need of any place, nor does it depend on any material thing; so that this "me," that is to say, the soul by which I am what I am, is entirely distinct from body, and is even more easy to know than is the latter; and even if body were not, the soul would not cease to be what it is.

After this I considered generally what in a proposition is requisite in order to be true and certain; for since I had just discovered one which I knew to be such, I thought that I ought also to know in what this certainty consisted. And having remarked that there was nothing at all in the statement, "I think, therefore I am" which assures me of having thereby made a true assertion, excepting that I see very clearly that to think it is necessary to be, I came to the conclusion that I might assume, as a general rule, that the things which we conceive very clearly and distinctly are all true—remembering, however, that there is some difficulty in ascertaining which are those that we distinctly conceive.

Following upon this, and reflecting on the fact that I doubted, and that consequently my existence was not quite perfect (for I saw clearly that it was a greater perfection to know than to doubt), I resolved to inquire whence I had learnt to think of Something more perfect than I myself was. And I recognized very clearly that this conception must proceed from some Nature which was really more perfect. As to the thoughts which I had of many other things outside of me, like the heavens, the earth, light, heat, and a thousand others, I had not so much difficulty in knowing whence they came, because, remarking nothing in them which seemed to render them superior to me, I could believe that, if they were true, they were dependencies upon my nature, in so far as it possessed some perfection; and if they were not true, that I held them from nothing, that is to say, that they were in me because I had something lacking in my nature. But this could not apply to the idea of a Being more perfect than my own, for to hold it came from nought would be manifestly impossible; and because it is no less contradictory to say of the more perfect that it is what results from and depends on the less perfect, than to say that there is something which proceeds from nothing, it was equally impossible that I should hold it from myself. In this way it could not but follow that it had been placed in me by a Nature which was really more perfect than mine could be, and which even had within itself all the perfections of which I could form any idea—that is to say, to put it in a word, which was God. To which I added that since I knew some perfections which I did not possess, I was not the only being in existence; but there was necessarily some other more perfect Being on which I depended, or from which I acquired all that I had.[45] ✴

Thus, Descartes was led by his method to realize that he existed, that he had a soul, and, most important, that God existed, for, as Descartes reasoned, God is the foundation of all truth. God is not a deceiver and God ensures that whatever we "clearly and distinctly" understand is true. Error arises only when we pass judgment on matters that are not clearly and distinctly understood.

For, first of all, I recognize it to be impossible that He should ever deceive me; for in all fraud and deception some imperfection is to be found, and although it may appear that the power of deception is a mark of subtlety or power, yet the desire to deceive without doubt testifies to malice or feebleness, and accordingly cannot be found in God. . . .

Whence, then, come my errors? They come from the sole fact that since the will is much wider in its range and compass than the understanding, I do not restrain it within the same bounds, but extend it also to things which I do not understand. . . .

But if I abstain from giving my judgment on anything when I do not perceive it with sufficient clearness and distinctness, it is plain that I will act rightly and will not be deceived. But if I decide to deny or affirm [what is not clear and distinct], then I no longer make use as I should of my free will. . . .

So long as I restrain my will within the limits of my knowledge so that it forms no judgment except on matters which are clearly and distinctly repre-

sented to it by the understanding, I can never be deceived. For every clear and distinct perception is without doubt something and hence cannot derive its origin from what is nothing, but must of necessity have God as its author—God, I say, who, being supremely perfect, cannot be the cause of any error; and consequently we must conclude that such a perception is true.[46]

Having found the source of truth and knowledge, Descartes turns to address the final major philosophical question that confronts him: Does the material world around him really exist, or is it merely a figment of his imagination?

Now that I have noted what must be done to arrive at a knowledge of the truth, my principal task is to endeavor to emerge from the state of doubt into which I have these last days fallen, and to see whether nothing certain can be known regarding material things. . . . Nothing further remains, then, but to inquire whether material things exist. . . . I find that . . . there is in me a certain passive faculty of perception, that is, of receiving and recognizing the ideas of material things. . . . But, since God is no deceiver, it is very manifest that He does not communicate to me these ideas directly and by Himself, nor yet by the intervention of some creature [different from the material objects I think I perceive]. For since He has given me no faculty to recognize that this is the case, but, on the other hand, a very great inclination to believe that they are conveyed to me by material objects, I do not see how He could be defended from the accusation of deceit if these ideas were produced by causes other than material objects. Hence we must allow that material things exist.[47]

Thus, the existence of a perfect God is our only guarantee that our knowledge about the world is accurate. If it were not for God, we could never be sure that any of our so-called knowledge of external reality is true. For earlier philosophers, God was primarily the foundation of reality: He is what

45. Ibid., 100–102.

46. René Descartes, *Meditations*, ch. 4, trans. Elizabeth S. Haldane and G. R. T. Ross, in *The Philosophical Works of Descartes* (Cambridge: Cambridge University Press, 1911), 172, 175–176, 178.
47. Ibid., 179, 185, 191.

accounts for the existence of the objects in the universe. But for Descartes God is primarily the foundation of our knowledge: He is what accounts for the fact that we can know the objects in our universe.

Descartes's philosophy made him famous, and within a short time at least two of the crowned heads of Europe were asking his advice. In 1649 Descartes received an invitation from Queen Christina of Sweden who requested him to instruct her in the mysteries of philosophy. Being eager to please her, Descartes traveled north to Sweden and there began tutoring the busy queen at the only hour she had free: five o'clock in the morning. The bitter cold and the early hour combined to weaken Descartes's health and within a few months he caught pneumonia. On February 11, 1650, Descartes died.

QUESTIONS

1. What is the difference between theology and philosophy? Between religion and philosophy? Evaluate this statement: "The God of the philosophers is not the God of religion." Can religion be rational?

2. Evaluate each of Aquinas's proofs for the existence of God. Why do you think a believer like Aquinas would be concerned with proving God's existence? Does it make sense to believe without proof? Why or why not?

3. Does Aquinas's theory of analogy really explain how it is possible for religious believers to speak about God? Contemporary theories of language hold that words mean whatever we, the speakers of the language, *intend* them to mean. How can we intend words to have a meaning when applied to God that we do not understand? Does Aquinas's theory imply that God must be *like* the world He creates?

4. Some people have held that Aquinas's views about right and wrong are a Christianized version of Aristotle's views on virtue. Do you agree? What aspects of Aquinas's views about morality would an atheist have to reject? Which aspects would he be able to retain?

5. Compare the interests and the approaches of Descartes and Aquinas. What accounts for these

differences? Which seem to be more "modern"? Why?

6. How useful are Descartes's "four rules" for "discovering the truth"? Could you use them, for example, as the basis for discovering the truth about God for yourself? Explain.

7. Descartes criticizes all philosophy prior to his because "no single thing is to be found in it which is not subject to dispute, and in consequence which is not dubious." Explain whether this criticism applies to Descartes's own philosophy and to his own views about God. Why would Descartes have felt that his philosophy is immune from his criticism?

8. How reasonable is Descartes's "method of doubt"? Evaluate this quote: "Descartes's method of doubt shows that we cannot know for certain that there is a world around us or that any conclusions we have reached about this external world are true. Moreover, Descartes fails miserably in his attempts to show that we can know anything for certain about the external world. After Descartes, we must resign ourselves to complete skepticism about the external world and must forever remain locked up within our minds."

9. Evaluate Descartes's proof for the existence of God. How does it compare to Anselm's "ontological proof"? Is Descartes's proof immune from the method of doubt?

10. Is Descartes correct in claiming that "if I abstain from giving my judgment on anything when I do not perceive it with sufficient clearness and distinctness, it is plain that I will act rightly and will not be deceived"? Did you decide "of your free will" whether or not to believe what you believe?

11. Can the existence of a good, all-powerful God be reconciled with the fact of human error?

LEO TOLSTOY

The Death of Ivan Ilyitch

Most people would agree that there is no greater evil that can beset an individual than to be afflicted with a terminal illness. What possible value and purpose could it have? In "The Death of Ivan Ilyitch," master storyteller Leo Tolstoy (1828–1910) provides a glimpse of the inner torment of a man who faces up to the fact that he is dying. In sketching one man's struggle to deal with his own mortality, Tolstoy portrays dying as an opportunity for profound introspection. Keep in mind as you read the story that in all his work Tolstoy aims to show the presence and influence of God in our lives.

CHAPTER VIII

It was morning.

It was morning merely because Gerasim had gone, and Piotr, the lackey, had come. He put out the candles, opened one curtain, and began noiselessly to put things to rights. Whether it were morning, whether it were evening, Friday or Sunday, all was a matter of indifference to him, all was one and the same thing. The agonizing, shooting pain, never for an instant appeased; the consciousness of a life hopelessly wasting away, but not yet departed; the same terrible, cursed death coming nearer and nearer, the one reality, and always the same lie,—what matter, then, here, of days, weeks, and hours of the day?

"Will you not have me bring the tea?"

"He must follow form, and that requires masters to take tea in the morning," he thought; and he said merely:—

"No."

"Wouldn't you like to go over to the divan?"

"He has to put the room in order, and I hinder him; I am uncleanness, disorder!" he thought to himself, and said merely:—

"No; leave me!"

SOURCE: Leo Tolstoy, "The Death of Ivan Ilyitch", *The Death of Ivan Ilyitch and Other Stories*, trans. Louise and Aylmer Maude (London: Oxford University Press, 1934). Reprinted by permission of Oxford University Press.

The lackey still bustled about a little. Ivan Ilyitch put out his hand. Piotr officiously hastened to him:—

"What do you wish?"

"My watch."

Piotr got the watch, which lay near by, and gave it to him.

"Half-past eight. They aren't up yet?"

"No one at all. Vasili Ivanovitch"—that was his son—"has gone to school, and Praskovia Feodorovna [Ivan's wife] gave orders to wake her up if you asked for her. Do you wish it?"

"No, it is not necessary.—Shall I not try the tea?" he asked himself. "Yes . . . tea . . . bring me some."

Piotr started to go out. Ivan Ilyitch felt terror-stricken at being left alone. "How can I keep him? Yes, my medicine. Piotr, give me my medicine.—Why not? perhaps the medicine may help me yet."

He took the spoon, sipped it.

"No, there is no help. All this is nonsense and delusion," he said, as he immediately felt the familiar, mawkish, hopeless taste.

"No, I cannot have any faith in it. But this pain, . . . why this pain? Would that it might cease for a minute!"

And he began to groan. Piotr came back.

"Nothing . . . go! Bring the tea."

Piotr went out. Ivan Ilyitch, left alone, began to groan, not so much from the pain, although it was horrible, as from mental anguish.

"Always the same thing, and the same thing; all these endless days and nights. Would it might come very soon! What very soon? Death, blackness? No, no! Anything rather than death!"

When Piotr came back with the tea on a tray, Ivan Ilyitch stared long at him in bewilderment, not comprehending who he was, what he was. Piotr was abashed at this gaze; and when Piotr showed his confusion, Ivan Ilyitch came to himself.

"Oh, yes," said he, "the tea; very well, set it down. Only help me to wash, and to put on a clean shirt."

And Ivan Ilyitch began to perform his toilet. With resting spells he washed his hands and face, cleaned his teeth, began to comb his hair, and looked into the mirror. It seemed frightful, perfectly frightful, to him, to see how his hair lay flat upon his pale brow.

While he was changing his shirt, he knew that it would be still more frightful if he gazed at his body; and so he did not look at himself. But now it was done. He put on his khalat, wrapped himself in his plaid, and sat down in his easy-chair to take his tea. For a single moment he felt refreshed; but as soon as he began to drink the tea, again that same taste, that same pain. He compelled himself to drink it all, and lay down, stretching out his legs. He lay down, and let Piotr go.

Always the same thing. Now a drop of hope gleaming, then a sea of despair rising up, and always pain, always melancholy, and always the same monotony. It was terribly melancholy to the lonely man; he longed to call in some one, but he knew in advance that it is still worse when others are present.

"Even morphine again . . . to get a little sleep! . . . I will tell him, tell the doctor, to find something else. It is impossible, impossible so."

One hour, two hours, would pass in this way. But there! the bell in the corridor. Perhaps it is the doctor. Exactly: it is the doctor, fresh, hearty, portly, jovial, with an expression as if he said, "You may feel apprehension of something or other, but we will immediately straighten things out for you."

The doctor knows that this expression is not appropriate here; but he has already put it on once for all, and he cannot rid himself of it—like a man who has put on his dress-coat in the morning, and gone to make calls.

The doctor rubs his hands with an air of hearty assurance.

"I am cold. A healthy frost. Let me get warm a little," says he, with just the expression that signifies that all he needs is to wait until he gets warmed a little, and, when he is warmed, then he will straighten things out.

"Well, now, how goes it?"

Ivan Ilyitch feels that the doctor wants to say, "How go your little affairs?" but that he feels that it is impossible to say so; and he says, "What sort of a night did you have?"

Ivan Ilyitch would look at the doctor with an expression which seemed to ask the question, "Are you never ashamed of lying?"

But the doctor has no desire to understand his question.

And Ivan Ilyitch *says:*—

"It was just horrible! The pain does not cease, does not disappear. If you could only give me something for it!"

"That is always the way with you sick folks! Well, now, it seems to me I am warm enough; even the most particular Praskovia Feodorovna would not find anything to take exception to in my temperature. Well, now, how are you really?"

And the doctor shakes hands with him.

And, laying aside his former jocularity, the doctor begins with serious mien to examine the sick man, his pulse and temperature, and he renews the tappings and the auscultation.

Ivan Ilyitch knew for a certainty, and beyond peradventure, that all this was nonsense and foolish deception; but when the doctor, on his knees, leaned over toward him, applying his ear, now higher up, now lower down, and with most sapient mien performed various gymnastic evolutions on him, Ivan Ilyitch succumbed to him, as once he succumbed to the discourses of the lawyers, even when he knew perfectly well that they were deceiving him, and why they were deceiving him.

The doctor, still on his knees on the divan, was still performing the auscultation, when at the door were heard the rustle of Praskovia Feodorovna's silk dress, and her words of blame to Piotr because he had not informed her of the doctor's visit.

She came in, kissed her husband, and immediately began to explain that she had been up a long time; and only through a misunderstanding she had not been there when the doctor came.

Ivan Ilyitch looked at her, observed her from head to foot, and felt a secret indignation at her fairness and her plumpness, and the cleanliness of her hands, her neck, her glossy hair, and the brilliancy of her eyes, brimming with life. He hated her with all the strength of his soul, and her touch made him suffer an actual paroxysm of hatred of her.

Her attitude toward him and his malady was the same as before. Just as the doctor had formulated his treatment of his patient and could not change it, so she had formulated her treatment of him, making him feel that he was not doing what he ought to do, and was himself to blame; and she liked to reproach him for this, and she could not change her attitude toward him.

"Now, just see! he does not heed, he does not take his medicine regularly; and, above all, he lies in a position that is surely bad for him—his feet up."

She related how he made Gerasim hold his legs.

The doctor listened with a disdainfully good-natured smile, as much as to say:—

"What is to be done about it, pray? These sick folks are always conceiving some such foolishness. But you must let it go."

When the examination was over, the doctor looked at his watch; and then Praskovia Feodorovna declared to Ivan Ilyitch that, whether he was willing or not, she was going that very day to call in the celebrated doctor to come and have an examination and consultation with Mikhaïl Danilovitch—that was the name of their ordinary doctor.

"Now, don't oppose it, please. I am doing this for my own self," she said ironically, giving him to understand that she did it all for him, and only on this account did not allow him the right to oppose her.

He said nothing, and frowned. He felt that this lie surrounding him was so complicated that it was now hard to escape from it.

She did all this for him, only in her own interest; and she said that she was doing it for him, while she was in reality doing it for herself, as some incredible thing, so that he was forced to take it in its opposite sense.

The celebrated doctor, in fact, came about half-past eleven. Once more they had auscultations; and learned discussions took place before him, or in the next room, about his kidney, about the blind intestine, and questions and answers in such a learned form that again the place of the real question of life and death, which now alone faced him, was driven away by the question of the kidney and the blind intestine, which were not acting as became them, and on which Mikhaïl Danilovitch and the celebrity were to fall instantly and compel to attend to their duties.

The famous doctor took leave with a serious but not hopeless expression. And in reply to the timid question which Ivan Ilyitch's eyes, shining with fear and hope, asked of him, whether there was a possibility of his getting well, it replied that it could not vouch for it, but there was a possibility.

The look of hope with which Ivan Ilyitch followed the doctor was so pathetic that Praskovia Feodorovna, seeing it, even wept, as she went out of the library door in order to give the celebrated doctor his honorarium.

The raising of his spirits, caused by the doctor's hopefulness, was but temporary. Again the same room, the same pictures, curtains, wallpaper, vials, and his aching, pain-broken body. And Ivan Ilyitch began to groan. They gave him a subcutaneous injection, and he fell asleep.

When he woke up it was beginning to grow dusky. They brought him his dinner. He forced himself to eat a little *bouillon*. And again the same monotony, and again the advancing night.

About seven o'clock, after dinner, Praskovia Feodorovna came into his room, dressed as for a party, with her exuberant bosom swelling in her stays, and with traces of powder on her face. She had already that morning told him that they were going to the theater. Sarah Bernhardt had come to town, and they had a box which he had insisted on their taking.

Now he had forgotten about that, and her toilet offended him. But he concealed his vexation when he recollected that he himself had insisted on their taking a box, and going, on the ground that it would be an instructive, esthetic enjoyment for the children.

Praskovia Feodorovna came in self-satisfied, but, as it were, feeling a little to blame. She sat down, asked after his health, as he saw, only for the sake of asking, and not so as to learn, knowing that there was nothing to learn, and began to say what was incumbent on her to say,—that she would not have gone for anything, but that they had taken the box; and that Elen and her daughter and Petrishchef—the examining magistrate, her daughter's betrothed—were going, and it was impossible to let them go alone, but that it would have been more agreeable to her to stay at home with him. Only he should be sure to follow the doctor's prescriptions in her absence.

"Yes—and Feodor Petrovitch"—the betrothed—"wanted to come in. May he? And Liza!"

"Let them come."

The daughter came in, in evening dress, with her fair young body,—her body that made his anguish more keen. But she paraded it before him, strong, healthy, evidently in love, and irritated against the disease, the suffering, and death which stood in the way of her happiness.

Feodor Petrovitch also entered, in his dress-coat, with curly hair à la Capoul, with long sinewy neck tightly incased in a white standing collar, with a huge white bosom, and his long, muscular legs in tight black trousers, with a white glove on one hand, and with an opera hat.

Immediately behind him, almost unnoticed, came the gymnasium scholar, in his new uniform, poor little fellow, with gloves on, and with that terrible blue circle under the eyes, the meaning of which Ivan Ilyitch understood.

He always felt a pity for his son. And terrible was his timid and compassionate glance. With the exception of Gerasim, Vasya alone, it seemed to Ivan Ilyitch, understood and pitied him.

All sat down; again they asked after his health. Silence ensued. Liza asked her mother if she had the opera-glasses. A dispute arose between mother and daughter as to who had mislaid them. It was a disagreeable episode.

Feodor Petrovitch asked Ivan Ilyitch if he had seen Sarah Bernhardt. Ivan Ilyitch did not at first understand his question, but in a moment he said:—

"No . . . why, have you seen her yet?"

"Yes, in 'Adrienne Lecouvreur.' "

Praskovia Feodorovna said that she was especially good in that. The daughter disagreed with her. A conversation arose about the grace and realism of her acting,— the same conversation, which is always and forever one and the same thing.

In the midst of the conversation, Feodor Petrovitch glanced at Ivan Ilyitch, and grew silent. The others glanced at him, and grew silent. Ivan Ilyitch was looking straight ahead with gleaming eyes, evidently indignant at them. Some one had to extricate them from their embarrassment, but there seemed to be no way out of it. No one spoke; and a panic seized them all, lest suddenly this ceremonial lie should somehow be shattered, and the absolute truth become manifest to all.

Liza was the first to speak. She broke the silence. She wished to hide what all felt, but she betrayed it.

"One thing is certain,—*if we are going*, it is time," she said, glancing at her watch, her father's gift; and giving the young man a sign, scarcely perceptible, and yet understood by him, she smiled, and arose in her rustling dress.

All arose, said good-by, and went.

When they had gone, Ivan Ilyitch thought that he felt easier: the lying was at an end; it had gone with them; but the pain remained. Always this same pain, always the same terror, made it hard as hard could be. There was no easing of it. It grew ever worse, always worse.

Again minute after minute dragged by, hour after hour, forever the same monotony, and forever endless, and forever more terrible—the inevitable end.

"Yes, send me Gerasim," was his reply to Piotr's question.

CHAPTER IX

Late at night his wife returned. She came in on her tiptoes, but he heard her; he opened is eyes, and quickly closed them again. She wanted to send Gerasim away, and sit with him herself. He opened his eyes, and said:—

"No, go away."

"You suffer very much."

"It makes no difference."

"Take some opium."

He consented, and drank it. She went.

Until three o'clock he was in a painful sleep. It seemed to him that they were forcing him cruelly into a narrow sack, black and deep; and they kept crowding him down, but could not force him in. And this performance, horrible for him, was accompanied with anguish. And he was afraid, and yet wished to get in, and struggled against it, and yet tried to help.

And here suddenly he broke through, and fell . . . and awoke.

There was Gerasim still sitting at his feet on the bed, dozing peacefully, patiently. But he was lying there with his emaciated legs in stockings resting on his shoulders, the same candle with its shade, and the same never ending pain.

"Go away, Gerasim," he whispered.

"It's nothing; I will sit here a little while."

"No, go away."

He took down his legs, lay on his side on his arm, and began to pity himself. He waited only until Gerasim had gone into the next room, and then he no longer tried to control himself, but wept like a child. He wept over his helplessness, over his terrible loneliness, over the cruelty of men, over the cruelty of God, over the absence of God.

"Why hast Thou done this? Why didst Thou place me here? Why, why dost Thou torture me so horribly?"

He expected no reply; and he wept because there was none, and could be none.

The pain seized him again; but he did not stir, did not call. He said to himself:—

"There, now again, now strike! But why? What have I done to Thee? Why is it?"

Then he became silent; ceased not only to weep, ceased to breathe, and became all attention: as it were, he heard, not a voice speaking with sounds, but the voice of his soul, the tide of his thoughts, arising in him.

"What dost thou need?" was the first clear concept possible to be expressed in words which he heard.

" 'What dost thou need? What dost thou need? " he said to himself. "What? Freedom from suffering. To live," he replied.

And again he gave his attention, with such effort that already he did not even notice his pain.

"To live? how live?" asked the voice of his soul.

"Yes, to live as I used to live—well, pleasantly."

"How didst thou live before when thou didst live well and pleasantly?" asked the voice.

And he began to call up in his imagination the best moments of his pleasant life. But, strangely enough, all these best moments of his pleasant life seemed to him absolutely different from what they had seemed then,—all, except the earliest remembrances of his childhood. There, in childhood, was something really pleasant, which would give new zest to life if it were to return. But the person who had enjoyed that pleasant existence was no more; it was as if it were the remembrance of some one else.

As soon as the period began which had produced the present *he*, Ivan Ilyitch, all the pleasures which seemed such then, now in his eyes dwindled away, and changed into something of no account, and even disgusting.

And the farther he departed from infancy, and the nearer he came to the present, so much the more unimportant and dubious were the pleasures.

This began in the law-school. There was still something even then which was truly good; then there was gayety, there was friendship, there were hopes. But in the upper classes these good moments became rarer.

Then, in the time of his first service at the governor's, again appeared good moments; these were the recollections of love for a woman. Then all this became confused, and the happy time grew less. The nearer he came to the present, the worse it grew, and still worse and worse it grew.

"My marriage . . . so unexpected, and disillusionment and my wife's breath, and sensuality, hypocrisy! And this dead service, and these labors for money; and thus one year, and two, and ten, and twenty,—and always the same thing. And the longer it went, the more dead it became.

"It is as if all the time I were going down the mountain, while thinking that I was climbing it. So it was. According to public opinion, I was climbing the mountain; and all the time my life was gliding away from under my feet. . . . And here it is already . . . die!

"What is this? Why? It cannot be! It cannot be that life has been so irrational, so disgusting. But even if it is so disgusting and irrational, still, why die, and die in such agony? There is no reason.

"Can it be that I did not live as I ought?" suddenly came into his head. "But how can that be, when I have done all that it was my duty to do?" he asked himself. And immediately he put away this sole explanation of the enigma of life and death as something absolutely impossible.

"What dost thou wish now?—To live? To live how? To live as thou livest in court when the usher proclaims, 'The court is coming! the court is coming'?

"The court is coming—the court," he repeated to himself. "Here it is, the court. Yes; but I am not guilty," he cried with indignation. "What for?"

And he ceased to weep; and, turning his face to the wall, he began to think about that one thing, and that alone. "Why, wherefore, all this horror?"

But, in spite of all his thoughts, he received no answer. And when the thought occurred to him, as it had often occurred to him, that all this came from the fact that he had not lived as he should, he instantly remembered all the correctness of his life, and he drove away this strange thought.

CHAPTER X

Thus two weeks longer passed. Ivan Ilyitch no longer got up from the divan. He did not wish to lie in bed, and he lay on the divan. And, lying almost all the time with his face to the wall, he still suffered in solitude the same inexplicable sufferings, and still thought in solitude the same inexplicable thought.

"What is this? Is it true that this is death?"

And an inward voice responded:—

"Yes, it is true."

"Why these torments?"

And the voice responded:—

"But it is so. There is no why."

Farther and beyond this, there was nothing.

From the very beginning of his malady, from the time when Ivan Ilyitch for the first time went to the doctor, his life was divided into two conflicting tendencies, alternately succeeding each other. Now it was despair, and the expectation of an incomprehensible and frightful death; now it was hope, and the observation of the functional activity of his body, so full of interest for him. Now before his eyes was the kidney, or the intestine, which, for the time being, failed to fulfill its duty. Then it was that incomprehensible, horrible death, from which it was impossible for any one to escape.

These two mental states, from the very beginning of his illness, kept alternating with one another. But the farther the illness progressed, the more dubious and fantastical became his ideas about the kidney, and the more real his consciousness of approaching death.

He had but to call to mind what he had been three months before, and what he was now, to call to mind with what regularity he had been descending the mountain; and that was sufficient for all possibility of hope to be dispelled.

During the last period of this solitude through which he was passing, as he lay with his face turned to the back of the divan,—a solitude amid a populous city, and amid his numerous circle of friends and family,—a solitude deeper than which could not be found anywhere, either in the depths of the sea, or in the earth,—during the last period of this terrible solitude, Ivan Ilyitch lived only by imagination in the past.

One after another, the pictures of his past life arose before him. They always began with the time nearest to the present, and went back to the very remotest,—to his childhood, and there they rested.

If Ivan Ilyitch remembered the stewed prunes which they had given him to eat that very day, then he remembered the raw, puckery French prunes of his childhood, their peculiar taste, and the abundant flow of saliva caused by the stone. And in connection with these recollections of taste, started a whole series of recollections of that time,—his nurse, his brother, his toys.

"I must not think about these things; it is too painful," said Ivan Ilyitch to himself. And again he transported himself to the present,—the button on the back of the divan, and the wrinkles of the morocco. "Morocco is costly, not durable. There was a quarrel about it. But there was some other morocco, and some other quarrel, when we tore father's portfolio and got punished, and mamma brought us some tarts."

And again his thoughts reverted to childhood; and again it was painful to Ivan Ilyitch, and he tried to avoid it, and think of something else.

And again, together with this current of recollections, there passed through his mind another current of recollections about the progress and rise of his disease. Here, also, according as he went back, there was more and more of life. There was more, also, of excellence in life, and more of life itself. And the two were confounded.

"Just as this agony goes from worse to worse, so also my life has gone from worse to worse," he thought. "One shining point, there back in the distance, at the beginning of life; and then all growing blacker and blacker, swifter and swifter, in inverse proportion to the square of the distance from death," thought Ivan Ilyitch.

And the comparison of a stone falling with accelerating rapidity occurred to his mind. Life, a series of increasing tortures, always speeding swifter and swifter to the end,—the most horrible torture.

"I am falling." . . .

He shuddered, he tossed, he wished to resist it. But he already knew that it was impossible to resist; and again, with eyes weary of looking, but still not able to resist looking at what was before him, he stared at the back of the divan, and waited, waited for this frightful fall, shock, and destruction.

"It is impossible to resist," he said to himself. "But can I not know the wherefore of it? Even that is impossible. It might be explained by saying that I had not lived as I ought. But it is impossible to acknowledge that," he said to himself, recollecting all the legality, the uprightness, the propriety of his life.

"It is impossible to admit that," he said to himself, with a smile on his lips, as if some one were to see that smile of his, and be deceived by it.

"No explanation! torture, death . . . why?"

CHAPTER XI

Thus passed two weeks. In these weeks, there occurred an event desired by Ivan Ilyitch and his wife. Petrishchef made a formal proposal. This took place in the evening. On the next day, Praskovia Feodorovna went to her husband, meditating in what way to explain to him Feodor Petrovitch's proposition; but that very same night, a change for the worse had taken place in Ivan Ilyitch's condition. Praskovia Feodorovna found him on the same divan, but in a new position. He was lying on his back; he was groaning, and looking straight up with a fixed stare.

She began to speak about medicines. He turned his eyes on her. She did not finish saying what she had begun, so great was the hatred against her expressed in that look.

"For Christ's sake, let me die in peace!" said he.

She was about to go out; but just at this instant the daughter came in, and came near to wish him good-morning. He looked at his daughter as he had looked at his wife, and, in reply to her questions about his health, told her dryly that he would quickly relieve them all of his presence. Neither mother nor daughter said anything more; but they sat for a few moments longer, and then went out.

"What are we to blame for?" said Liza to her mother. "As if we had made him so! I am sorry for papa, but why should he torment us?"

At the usual time the doctor came. Ivan Ilyitch answered "yes," "no," not taking his angry eyes from him; and at last he said:—

"Now see here, you know that you don't help any, so leave me!"

"We can appease your sufferings," said the doctor.

"You cannot even do that; leave me!"

The doctor went into the drawing-room, and advised Praskovia Feodorovna that it was very serious, and that there was only one means—opium—of appeasing his sufferings, which must be terrible.

The doctor said that his physical sufferings were terrible, and this was true; but more terrible than his physical sufferings were his moral sufferings, and in this was his chief torment.

His moral sufferings consisted in the fact that that very night, as he looked at Gerasim's sleepy, good-natured face, with its high cheek-bones, it had suddenly come into his head:—

"But how is it if in reality my whole life, my conscious life, has been wrong?"

It came into his head that what had shortly before presented itself to him as an absolute impossibility—that he had not lived his life as he ought—might be true. It came into his head that the scarcely recognizable desires to struggle against what men highest in position considered good,—desires scarcely recognizable, which he had immediately banished,—might be true, and all the rest might be wrong. And his service, and his course of life, and his family, and these interests of society and office—all this might be wrong.

He endeavored to defend all this before himself. And suddenly he realized all the weakness of what he was defending. And there was nothing to defend.

"But if this is so," he said to himself, "and I am departing from life with the consciousness that I have wasted all that was given me, and that it is impossible to rectify it, what then?"

He lay flat on his back, and began entirely anew to examine his whole life.

When in the morning he saw the lackey, then his wife, then his daughter, then the doctor, each one of their motions, each one of their words, confirmed for him the terrible truth which had been disclosed to him that night. He saw in them himself, all that for which he had lived; and he saw clearly that all this was wrong, all this was a terrible, monstrous lie, concealing both life and death.

This consciousness increased his physical sufferings, added tenfold to them. He groaned and tossed, and threw off the clothes. It seemed to him that they choked him, and loaded him down.

And that was why he detested them.

They gave him a great dose of opium; he became unconscious, but at dinner-time the same thing began again. He drove them from him, and threw himself from place to place.

His wife came to him, and said:—

"Jean, darling, do this for me (*for me!*). It cannot do any harm, and sometimes it helps. Why, it is a mere nothing. And often well people try it."

He opened his eyes wide.

"What? Take the sacrament? Why? It's not necessary. But, however . . ."

She burst into tears.

"Will you, my dear? I will get our priest. He is so sweet!"

"Excellent! very good," he continued.

When the priest came, and confessed him, he became calmer, felt, as it were, an alleviation of his doubts, and consequently of his sufferings; and there came a moment of hope. He again began to think about the blind intestine and the possibility of curing it. He took the sacrament with tears in his eyes.

When they put him to bed after the sacrament, he felt comfortable for the moment, and once more hope of life appeared. He began to think of the operation which they had proposed.

"I want to live, to live," he said to himself.

His wife came to congratulate him. She said the customary words, and added:—

"You feel better, don't you?"

Without looking at her, he said:—

"Yes."

Her hope, her temperament, the expression of her face, the sound of her voice, all said to him one thing:—

"Wrong! all that for which thou hast lived, and thou livest, is falsehood, deception, hiding from thee life and death."

And as soon as he expressed this thought, his exasperation returned, and, together with his exasperation, the physical, tormenting agony; and, with the agony, the consciousness of inevitable death close at hand. Something new took place: a screw seemed to turn in him, twinging pain to show through him, and his breathing was constricted.

The expression of his face, when he said "yes," was terrible. After he had said that "yes," he looked straight into her face, and then, with extraordinary quickness for one so weak, he threw himself on his face and cried:—

"Go away! go away! leave me!"

CHAPTER XII

From that moment began that shriek that did not cease for three days, and was so terrible that, when it was heard two rooms away, it was impossible to hear it without terror. At the moment that he answered his wife, he felt that he was lost, and there was no return, that the end had come, absolutely the end, and the question was not settled, but remained a question.

"U! uu! u!" he cried in varying intonations. He began to shriek, *N'ye khotchu*—I won't;" and thus he kept up the cry on the letter *u*.

Three whole days, during which for him there was no time, he struggled in that black sack into which an invisible, invincible power was thrusting him. He fought as one condemned to death fights in the hands of the hangman, knowing that he cannot save himself, and at every moment he felt that, notwithstanding all the violence of his struggle, he was nearer and nearer to that which terrified him. He felt that his suffering consisted, both in the fact that he was being thrust into that black hole, and still more that he could not make his way through into it. What hindered him from making his way through was the confession that his life had been good. This justification of his life caught him and did not let him advance, and more than all else tormented him.

Suddenly some force knocked him in the breast, in the side, still more forcibly compressed his breath; he was hurled through the hole, and there at the bottom of the hole some light seemed to shine on him. It happened to him as it sometimes does on a railway carriage when you think that you are going forward, but are really going backward, and suddenly recognize the true direction.

"Yes, all was wrong," he said to himself; "but that is nothing. I might, I might have done right. What is right?" he asked himself, and suddenly stopped.

This was at the end of the third day, two hours before his death. At this very same time the little student noiselessly stole into his father's room, and approached his bed. The moribund was continually shrieking desperately, and tossing his arms. His hand struck upon the little student's head. The little student seized it, pressed it to his lips, and burst into tears.

It was at this very same time that Ivan Ilyitch fell through, saw the light, and it was revealed to him that his life had not been as it ought, but that still it was possible to repair it. He was just asking himself, "What is right?" and stopped to listen.

Then he felt that some one was kissing his hand. He opened his eyes, and looked at his son. He felt sorry for him. His wife came to him. He looked at her. With open mouth, and with her nose and cheeks wet with tears, with an expression of despair, she was looking at him. He felt sorry for her.

"Yes, I am a torment to them," he thought. "I am sorry for them, but they will be better off when I am dead."

He wanted to express this, but he had not the strength to say it.

"However, why should I say it? I must do it."

He pointed out his son to his wife by a glance, and said:—

"Take him away . . . I am sorry . . . and for thee."

He wanted to say also, *Prosti*—Forgive," but he said, "*Propusti*—Let it pass;" and, not having the strength to correct himself, he waved his hand, knowing that he would comprehend who had the right.

And suddenly it became clear to him that what oppressed him, and was hidden from him suddenly was lighted up for him all at once, and on two sides, on ten sides, on all sides.

He felt sorry for them; he felt that he must do something to make it less painful for them. To free them, and free himself, from these torments, "How good and how simple!" he thought.

"But the pain," he asked himself, "where is it?—Here, now, where art thou, pain?"

He began to listen.

"Yes, here it is! Well, then, do your worst, pain!"

"And death? where is it?"

He tried to find his former customary fear of death, and could not.

"Where is death? What is it?"

There was no fear, because there was no death.

In place of death was light!

"Here is something like!" he suddenly said aloud. "What joy!"

For him all this passed in a single instant, and the significance of this instant did not change.

For those who stood by his side, his death-agony was prolonged two hours more. In his breast something bubbled up, his emaciated body shuddered. Then more and more rarely came the bubbling and the rattling.

"It is all over," said some one above him.

He heard these words, and repeated them in his soul.

"It is over! death!" he said to himself. "It does not exist more."

He drew in one more breath, stopped in the midst of it, stretched himself, and died.

QUESTIONS

1. How would you describe the "same inexplicable sufferings," "the same inexplicable thought" that plague Ilyitch?

2. The more he suffers, the more Ilyitch approaches the unavoidable truth about his life. What is that truth?

3. What is the realization that allows Ilyitch to die peacefully?

4. What value does Tolstoy find in suffering, isolation, and death?

5. Do you find Tolstoy's response an adequate resolution to the problem of evil?

SUGGESTIONS FOR FURTHER READING

Cahn, S. M., and D. Shatz, eds. *Contemporary Philosophy of Religion.* New York: Oxford, 1982. This collection of essays provides wide-ranging discussions of many of the philosophical issues raised by religion.

Camus, Albert. *The Plague.* New York: Vintage, 1972. The theme of evil permeates this novel by a leading existentialist. Ultimately, Camus's is a humanistic posture, based on compassion for the meaningless plight that all people suffer.

Copleston, F. C. *Aquinas.* Baltimore, Md.: Penguin Books, 1955. This frequently reprinted paperback is written by a philosopher who is sympathetic to Aquinas's thought. It is an excellent introduction.

Dostoyevski, Fyodor. *The Brothers Karamazov.* New York: Signet, 1971. Especially relevant in this classic is book 5, Chapter 4, in which Ivan's philosophical crisis over the presence of evil in the world crystallizes.

Friedman, Maurice. *The Human Way: A Dialogical Approach to Religion and Human Experience.* Chambersburg, Pa.: Anima Books, 1982. An existentialist approach to religion.

Fynn. *Mister God, This Is Anna.* New York: Ballantine, 1974. A short, captivating true story of a little girl whose presence, wit, and theology changed the author's life. Its theology seems to encapsule and cut through Christian theology in a way that no other testament does.

Hick, John. *Evil and the God of Love.* rev. ed. New York: Harper & Row, 1978. A fascinating discussion of the problem of God and evil.

Hick, John. *Philosophy of Religion*. 3d ed. Englewood Cliffs, N.J.: Prentice-Hall, 1983. An introduction to the central issues in the philosophy of religion.

Huxley, Julian. *Religion Without Revelation*. New York: New American Library (Mentor Books), 1957. Huxley argues for agnosticism and for religion as a way of life independent of revelation and theistic belief. Huxley claims to support his belief with scientific evidence.

Kenny, Anthony. *Descartes*. New York: Random House, 1968. This is an excellent paperback introduction to the thought of Descartes.

Kushner, Harold S. *When Bad Things Happen to Good People*. New York: Avon Books, 1981. A moving discussion of the problem of evil.

Lewis, C. S. *Mere Christianity*. New York: Macmillan, 1960. In this short paperback, a former atheist explains his religious philosophy.

Mackie, J. L. *The Miracle of Theism: Arguments for and Against the Existence of God*. New York: Oxford, 1983. A concise survey of the traditional arguments.

Macquarrie, J. *Twentieth Century Religious Thought*. rev. ed. New York: Scribners, 1981. A survey of developments in the philosophy of religion during the twentieth century.

Matson, Wallace I. *The Existence of God*. Ithaca, N.Y.: Cornell University Press, 1965. A detailed examination of the arguments for the existence of God by an agnostic.

Moody, Raymond. *Life After Life*. New York: Bantam, 1976. Physician Moody not only presents accounts from people of their experiences during intervals when they were pronounced clinically dead but also compares these accounts with those found in ancient writings, including Plato's. This book is as provocative as it is intriguing.

Ogden, S. M. *The Reality of God and Other Essays*. New York: Harper & Row, 1966. Ogden argues that the reality of God is the central problem for today's world.

Pike, Nelson, ed. *God and Evil*. Englewood Cliffs, N.J.: Prentice-Hall, 1964. An interesting anthology of discussions of this basic problem.

Ring, Kenneth. *Life at Death: A Scientific Investigation of the Near-Death Experience*. New York: William Morrow, 1982. An interesting discussion of near-death experiences.

Russell, Bertrand. *Religion and Science*. New York: Oxford University Press (Galaxy Books), 1961. Russell reviews the historical conflict between religion and science. He argues that the ascendancy of science has had positive intellectual and humanistic influences on religion.

Schmidt, Roger. *Exploring Religion*. Belmont, Calif.: Wadsworth, 1980. A well-written textbook covering a variety of aspects of religion, including traditional arguments for God and the problem of evil.

Smith, George H. *Atheism: The Case Against God*. Buffalo, N.Y.: Prometheus, 1979. A defense of atheism.

Smith, Huston. *The Religions of Man*. New York: Harper & Row, 1958. This paperback contains clear accounts of the major religions of the world.

Tremmel, William. *Religion: What Is It?* New York: Holt, Rinehart and Winston, 1976. A highly readable attempt to define religion. Provides an analysis of religious phenomena that does justice to the practice of religion in many cultures.

Warren, Thomas B., and Wallace I. Matson. *The Warren-Matson Debate on the Existence of God*. Jonesboro, Ark.: National Christian Press, 1978. A fascinating debate between a believer and an agnostic.

Watts, Alan. *The Way of Zen*. New York: Random House, 1957. This is a very popular and readable presentation of Zen Buddhism, including its nature, history, and value. A more simplified version of the same material is found in Watts's *The Spirit of Zen*. New York: Grove Press (Evergreen edition), 1960.

CHAPTER 4

Reality and Being

The true lover of knowledge is always striving after being. . . . He will not rest at those multitudinous phenomena whose existence is appearance only.

PLATO

Introduction

From the earliest times philosophers have wondered about the nature of reality. Is it matter? Nonmatter? A combination? Actually, an inquiry into the nature of reality is a good way to throw light on the issue of self-identity. Since we inevitably view ourselves as unique in the scheme of reality, any description of reality is bound to reflect our view of human nature and, by implication, of the self. To understand this point, consider the following hypothetical situation.

You have fallen in love with a wonderful person. For the first time in your life you are giving serious thought to marriage. You express your happiness and your plans to a very close professor friend at college. The professor couldn't be happier for you. Naturally, he asks if it is anyone he knows. You doubt it, but you mention the name. Upon hearing the name, the professor gives a remarkably accurate description of your friend, even down to a birthmark on the inner right arm. You are astonished. Because you are sure the professor has never met your friend, you ask him how he did that.

"Because I manufactured your friend," says the professor. Manufactured! The professor insists that he's not fooling, that he's been doing it for years, that a number of his creations are around, living happy, constructive lives. In fact, one of his own is a very important person. Before you catch yourself, your mind rifles through a list of important people—Ronald Reagan, Reggie Jackson, Chris Evert—could one of these be the professor's creation? Absurd!

"Sure, sure," you tell him, "but you didn't leave any loose wires dangling out anywhere, did you?"

Not only did he not, but he also assures you that you will never be able to detect the slightest difference between your beloved and what we commonly call a human.

"You mean it isn't immortal?" you ask the professor.

"Of course not," he says. "As far as we know, all humans are mortal. So this creation is, too. It will age and be subject to the same physical laws that govern all organic life."

"What about having children?" you want to know.

He assures you that it is capable of reproducing. It functions sexually like any normal human. It will satisfy all your needs—physical, emotional, and intellectual—and all your desires. His creation will be, in brief, the ideal mate.

Farfetched? Probably. A mechanical creation that is identical with a human is still the product more of fiction than of science. But unleash your imagination for a minute. What if the professor took you into his basement lab and demonstrated

---

Let us settle ourselves, and work and wedge our feet downward through the mud and slush of opinion, and prejudice and tradition, and delusion, and appearance, that alluvion which covers the globe . . . . till we come to a hard bottom of rocks in place, which we can call *reality*.

JAMES THOMSON

Reality, however, has a sliding floor.

RALPH WALDO EMERSON

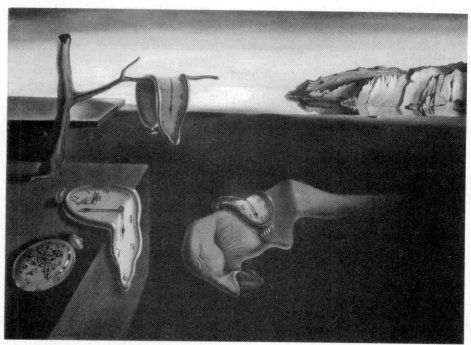

The Persistence of Memory, Salvador Dalí. 1931. "The critical study of the nature of reality is called metaphysics. But perhaps we can never say what reality ultimately is; perhaps the question and any subsequent theories are meaningless."

his craft before your disbelieving eyes? What if he showed you his creations and convinced you beyond a doubt that not only could he do what he claimed but that he was doing it, and that your intended mate was one of his products? Would you still marry that individual?

In answering this question, you will probably reveal what you see as ultimately real—as the essence of all being, including yourself. In philosophy, the critical study of the nature of reality is called **meta-physics**, one of whose subdivisions is **ontology**, which is the theory of the nature of being and existence. Here we shall use the case of the android to launch metaphysical inquiries. Perhaps we can never say what reality ultimately is; perhaps the question and any subsequent theories are meaningless. In this chapter we will investigate these issues to see what light they can throw on the question of what we are. Here are the main points we will make.

MAIN POINTS

1. Metaphysics is the branch of philosophy that studies reality and being.

2. Ontology, a subdivision of metaphysics, is the study of being and existence.

3. Materialism is the position that reality is ultimately matter.

4. Idealism is the position that reality is ultimately nonmatter: idea, mind, spirit, or law, for example.

5. Pragmatism rejects all absolutistic assumptions about reality. It seems committed to scientific method and empirical inquiry, while admitting the pluralistic nature of reality.

6. The concept of being plays an important part in existentialism and phenomenology. Both philosophies are founded on disillusionment with past philosophies and on a preoccupation with the individual.

7. Husserlian phenomenology emphasizes consciousness as the ultimate reality. Heidegger's phenomenology stresses being. What is ultimately real for the phenomenologist is pure consciousness, which itself has being.

8. Like phenomenology, Buddhism eschews the distinction between knower and known, between subject and object. We are one with our experiences. But Buddhism considers the question of personal freedom irrelevant.

9. Existentialism stresses individual freedom and the lack of an essential human nature and of behavioral guidelines.

10. Linguistic analysts believe that the question of ultimate reality is meaningless because no statement relating to ultimate reality can be proved. There are only two kinds of epistemologically meaningful statements: analytic and synthetic.

QUESTIONS

1. Suppose in the year 2020 you pick up a telephone and hear a voice at the other end. You are not sure whether the voice belongs to a real human being or to a computer that is programmed to fool you into thinking it is a real human being. Are there any questions you can ask it that would allow you to determine whether the voice is human?

2. Is it possible that nothing else exists in the universe besides yourself? Is it possible that the people and things you see around you are all products of your own mind much like a dream? How could you show that other things exist in the universe besides yourself and your ideas?

Reality as Matter

Meet Ruth. She has also met and fallen in love with someone very special, Max. Ruth also has a professor friend in whom she confides, only to hear the professor claim that he has produced Max in his basement lab. Although Ruth does not believe the professor, the conversation has made her restless. She finally decides to tell her brother Brad.

Brad couldn't care less that the creature has been so created. As far as he is concerned, if he cannot ever detect a difference between it and an ordinary human, then there is no difference. But Ruth points out that because the creature was not born as we are, there really is a difference between us and it. But Brad thinks being born is not so special. After all, cats, rattlesnakes, and chimpanzees are born. Does that mean Ruth should marry one? No, but Ruth insists that it does mean that she should marry a person, and this—this thing just isn't a person. "But what's so sacred about being a person?" Brad asks. Ruth is astonished. Brad then mentions a book about human behavior that he has been reading, which claims that much of what we do can be explained in terms of glands.

"I'll give you a for instance," Brad tells Ruth. "Let's say you're in the grocery store some night when a guy comes in and holds it up. He's got a gun and he's waving it around real crazy. Naturally, you're scared to death. Then all of a sudden, before you even know what you're doing, you spring at him."

"Me?"

"Yeah, you. Just like that! You leap through the

air and clobber him. Smash! He's down. Then the cops come. They give you a medal. You're a real hero. The storekeeper even gives you a six-pack!"

"So?"

"So, do you know why you're a hero?"

"Why?"

"Glands."

"You're kidding."

"Nope. You reacted as you did largely because your glands pumped out adrenalin. It's that simple."

Ruth is not convinced. She asks how he would explain feelings like love or guilt or uncertainty, the impulse to believe in God, and the urge to write a book or compose a song. Brad insists that those impulses, too, can be explained physiochemically. He mentions how brain surgeons have altered

---

PHILOSOPHY AND LIFE 4.1

Our Knowledge of the World

What kind of world do we live in? Physicists today generally describe it as a flux of energy that exists in different forms at different levels. Due to the limitations of our sense organs, not all of the world's energy reaches our brain. Indeed, a relatively small part of the electromagnetic spectrum, that is, of the entire range of radiation, can stimulate our eyes. In other words, while we can hear or feel parts of it, we can't see a large portion of the spectrum. Electromagnetic energy covers a wide range of wavelengths, from extremely short gamma rays, having wavelengths of about a billionth of an inch, to the extremely long radio waves, which have wavelengths that are miles long. In fact, we can see very little of the electromagnetic spectrum.

Our ears also sense a limited range of the mechanical vibrations transmitted through the air. Similarly, while we can smell and taste certain chemical substances and feel the presence of some objects in contact with our skin surface, most of what occurs in our environment cannot be perceived by these senses either. In effect, the great flux of energy that physicists say exists is largely lost to our senses. We know about it only indirectly, through specially devised instruments that can detect radio waves, X rays, infrared rays, and other energy forms that we can't directly experience.

What implications do these facts hold for our view of reality? If nothing else, they should make us wonder just how complete a picture of reality we have and how accurate our interpretation of it is. In *New Pathways in Science*, Sir Arthur Eddington addresses this issue.

As a conscious being I am involved in a story. The perceiving part of my mind tells me a story of a world around me. The story tells of familiar objects. It tells of colors, sounds, scents belonging to these objects; of boundless space in which they have their existence, and of an ever-rolling stream of time bringing change and incident. It tells of other life than mine busy about its own purposes.

As a scientist I have become mistrustful of this story. In many instances it has become clear that things are not what they seem to be. According to the storyteller I have now in front of me a substantial desk; but I have learned from physics that the desk is not at all the continuous substance that it is supposed to be in the story. It is a host of tiny electric charges darting hither and thither with inconceivable velocity. Instead of being solid substance my desk is more like a swarm of gnats.

So I have come to realize that I must not put overmuch confidence in the storyteller who lives in my mind.

QUESTIONS

1. Undoubtedly things often are not what they appear to be. But to say that is to imply another experience of things. Can we be sure that alternative experiences are any closer to how things are?

2. If a desk is indeed more like "a swarm of gnats" than a solid substance, what practical difference does that make in the way you live? Or is such a question irrelevant?

SOURCE: Sir Arthur Eddington, *New Pathways in Science* (Ann Arbor: University of Michigan Press, 1959), 11. Reprinted by permission.

not only human behavior but feelings as well; how they have erased intense spiritual feelings in people; how they have turned psychopathic killers into placid, if unproductive, citizens.

"When you come right down to it," Brad says, "everything is just matter, and all matter is subject to physiochemical explanation. It's that simple" (see *Philosophy and Life 4.1*).

Is it that simple? Is matter the ultimate constituent of reality, including you and me? In replying to Ruth's inquiry, Brad reveals a concept of reality that inclines him to say without reservation that he would marry such a creature. We can call his metaphysical view *materialism*.

THE DEVELOPMENT OF MATERIALISM

Materialism, the view that the ultimate constituent of reality is matter, is at least as old as the ancient Greeks. Democritus (460–360 B.C.) believed that reality could be explained in terms of matter. The smallest pieces of matter he called atoms; he described them as solid, indivisible, indestructible, eternal, and uncreated. Atoms were not qualitatively distinguishable from one another, and they constantly moved through space, where they combined to form the recognizable physical objects of the universe. According to Democritus, the universe consisted of atoms and empty space. He believed that even the soul, which he equated with reason, consisted of atoms. In this atomic universe "all things happen by virtue of necessity, the vortex being the cause of the creation of all things."[1]

But Democritus's theory never became popular, for by that time people had become disenchanted with the many attempts to explain the cosmos. At various times, philosopher-scientists viewed water, fire, air, or earth as the fundamental substance of reality. Others believed that reality could best be explained in terms of constant change. Eventually, interest centered on more personal concerns, such

as how one might lead a good and contented life. This interest was sparked by classical philosophy.

Although their interests reached much further than such questions, the Greek philosophers Socrates, Plato, and Aristotle did see the moral life as the road to knowledge and truth. The rise of Christianity fanned this interest in personal conduct, which predominated throughout the Middle Ages. Instrumental to this interest was the idea of a soul, which assumed a religious dimension that included personal immortality. Such an emphasis gave the view of reality a distinctly nonmaterial bias that held sway into the seventeenth century, when growing interest in the world and the rise of scientific method and scientific discovery turned minds once again to materialism.

Awakened by the discoveries of Copernicus, Kepler, Galileo, and Newton, people of the seventeenth century watched science cultivate a full-blown materialism. Committed to the belief that the world could be quantified, scientists made the materialistic claim that all was matter. In the systematic philosophy of Thomas Hobbes (1588–1679), for example, we see the Democritean belief that everything can be explained in terms of matter in motion.

> Every object is either a part of the whole world, or an aggregate of parts. The greatest of all bodies, or sensible objects, is the world itself; which we behold when we look round about us from this point of the same which we call the earth. Concerning the world, as it is one aggregate of many parts, the things that fall under inquiry are but few; and those we can determine, none. Of the whole world we may inquire what is its magnitude, what its duration, and how many there be, but nothing else.[2]

Similarly, anticipating many contemporary psychological theories, Hobbes postulated that mental states were brain states and that a "general inclination of all mankind" was "a perpetual and restless desire of power after power." (For a fuller discussion

---

1. Quoted in Diogenes Laërtius, *Lives and Opinions of Eminent Philosophers*, vol. 2, trans. R. D. Hicks (Cambridge, Mass.: Harvard University Press, 1925), 455.

2. Thomas Hobbes, "Elements of Philosophy," in *The English Works of Thomas Hobbes*, vol. 1, ed. Sir W. Molesworth (London: J. Bohn, 1839), chap. 1, sec. 8.

of Hobbes's views, see the showcase at the end of this chapter.) In 1748 Julien Offroy de La Mettrie carried Hobbesian psychology further when he published *Man a Machine*, a book which argues that humans are nothing more than complex machines. In de La Mettrie, materialism reached its only logical conclusion.

You may wonder what had happened to the religious doctrine of the soul. What remained of the creature supposedly made in the image of God and possessed of an eternal destiny? So much medieval superstition, declared the materialists. Even Newton's mechanical universe was rapidly growing obsolete, because Newton had proposed a God who regulated things. In contrast, astronomer-mathematician Pierre Laplace proposed his theory of a self-regulating universe, which gained some respectability by the early nineteenth century. In 1812 Laplace formulated his "Divine Calculator," a mathematical physicist of sorts, which knew the velocities and positions of all the particles in the world at a particular instant and could calculate all that had happened and all that would happen. Laplace's universe needed not a God but a super-computer as regulator. Bertrand Russell describes the situation nicely: "When Laplace suggested that the same forces which are now operative (according to Newton's laws) might have caused the planets to grow out of the sun, God's share in the course of nature was pushed still further back. He might remain as Creator, but even that was doubtful, since it was not clear the world has a beginning in time."[3] An interesting footnote to this historical development: It is said that when Napoleon asked Laplace why his theory omitted God, Laplace simply replied that God was an unnecessary hypothesis.

But these early materialists' optimistic faith that humans could eventually explain the universe and themselves has tarnished over the last century, as we shall see. Nevertheless, just as a culture generally lags behind its science, so today we frequently find ourselves as enthusiastically materialistic as our nineteenth-century counterparts.

---

3. Bertrand Russell, *A History of Western Philosophy* (New York: Simon & Schuster, 1945), 537.

There exists no kind of spiritual substance or entity of a different nature from that of which matter is composed.

HUGH ELLIOT

Today, philosophical materialism takes many forms, but all have at least four characteristics that survive from the past. First, materialism seeks answers through objective methodology. Specifically, it is committed to the scientific method of observation, analysis, and tentative conclusions. What cannot be found out by this method cannot be known. Second, materialism is deterministic; that is, it believes that every event has a cause. Some materialists attribute these causes to physiochemical processes. Others would add biological causes. Still others introduce psychological, sociological, and anthropological causes. We may not know the causes, they say, but they nevertheless exist. Third, materialism denies any form of supernaturalistic belief, including belief in spirit, soul, mind, or any other nonmaterial substance. Reality is composed of matter and only of matter. Finally, materialism is reductionistic; it attempts to explain the whole exclusively in terms of its parts or units.

OBJECTIONS TO MATERIALISM

We said earlier that materialism, at least in twentieth-century scientific circles, has lost considerable ground. Let us rejoin Ruth and Brad and see why.

RUTH: I don't understand how you can deny what so many people have believed for so long.

BRAD: What's that?

RUTH: The existence of a nonmaterial reality.

BRAD: You mean a soul?

RUTH: A soul, a spirit, a mind—call it what you want.

BRAD: Look, a lot of people once believed the earth was the center of the universe, but that didn't make it so, did it?

RUTH: That was different. This is a belief that defies full scientific contradiction. What you seem to forget is that the very thing you seem to be calling us—machines—*we* have created. *We* have invented them. If it weren't for people like the professor, these mechanical creations wouldn't exist to begin with. The creation isn't the creator, Brad. Machines aren't people. People love and hate, they dream, they hope, they strive. They write great books and compose beautiful music.

BRAD: So what?

RUTH: So how can you explain all this in terms of physiochemical causes?

How can Brad deny what is fundamentally real to so many people? This is what Ruth is asking. She is also asking how he can reduce to material explanations those human qualities and behaviors that are supposedly unique, such as consciousness. She does not feel that consciousness can be explained totally in terms of the physiochemical; neither can ideas or concepts be so described.

RUTH: You say that everything in existence can be explained physiochemically. Then what about human consciousness?

BRAD: What about it?

RUTH: How do you explain states of consciousness that we experience? How do you explain, for example, my experience of seeing something red, let alone the more complex experiences like being in love?

BRAD: Look, what you're calling consciousness is no more than a brain state. When you're seeing red, your brain is merely functioning in a certain way. The same is true with love or any other experience.

RUTH: All right, suppose you're having a brain operation. In the operating room are mirrors placed so that you can observe what's happening. Now, the surgeon peels back the top of your skull and you observe your own brain.

An age of science is necessarily an age of materialism. Ours is a scientific age, and it may be said with truth that we are all materialists now.

HUGH ELLIOT

BRAD: So?

RUTH: So you can observe even the nerve pathways that are stimulated when you experience a color—red, for example. You can see precisely what ganglion reacts whenever you see red. Every time the surgeon shows you red, sure enough, that thing starts wiggling.

BRAD: Okay. That's my brain state for the experience of red.

RUTH: Are you saying that the red you see and what's happening in your brain when you see it are the same thing?

BRAD: Right.

RUTH: Then why isn't the surgeon seeing red?

BRAD: What do you mean?

RUTH: Well, he's observing your brain state, too, isn't he? If your brain state equals the experience of red, why isn't the surgeon having the same experience when he observes your brain state?

BRAD: Because he has his own experience of red, that's why.

RUTH: All right, let me ask you this. Can you have the surgeon's experience of red?

BRAD: Of course not. But I could observe his brain state of red.

RUTH: So what you're saying is that the brain state and the experience are really two different things.

BRAD: Okay, maybe they are. So what?

RUTH: Plenty. What makes them different is that one is publicly observable and the other isn't. Everybody can observe the brain state. Why? Because it's physical. But only the individual can have the experience that accompanies the brain state. And that's because it's nonphysical; it's *nonmaterial.*

Brad initially insists that Ruth's example portrays the brain observing itself. Yet consciousness, understanding, and experience seem to stand outside the particular brain state observed. Brad would seem to be having two experiences: one of the brain state itself, the other of the experience that the brain state signals. The experience does not seem to be physical, although it is undoubtedly accompanied by a brain and nerve state. How can the strict materialist account for this fact? Does it suggest the presence of a nonmaterial reality? Is there at the core of all being something that cannot be measured, pinpointed, or spatialized?

Contemporary scientific materialist J. J. C. Smart (1920–) thinks not. In the view of this Australian philosopher, mental states are identical with brain states. Smart contends that future scientific discovery will demonstrate that all human experiences are identical with processes taking place in the brain. Smart justifies his claim by arguing that a nonphysical property couldn't possibly develop in the course of animal evolution. In a 1963 article, he states the issue and his view.

But what about consciousness? Can we interpret the having of an after-image or of a painful sensation as something material, namely, a brain state or brain process? We seem to be immediately aware of pains and after-images, and we seem to be immediately aware of them as something different from a neurophysiological state or process. For example, the after-image may be green speckled with red, whereas the neurophysiologist looking into our brains would be unlikely to see something green speckled with red. However, if we object to materialism in this way we are victims of a confusion which U. T. Place has called "the phenomenological fallacy." To say that an image or sense datum is green is not to say that the conscious experience of having the image or sense datum is green. It is to say that it is the sort of experience we have when in normal conditions we look at a green apple, for example. Apples and unripe bananas can be green, but not the experiences of seeing them. An image or a sense datum can be green in a derivative sense, but this need not cause any worry, because, on the view I am defending, images and sense data are not constituents of the world, though the processes of having an image or a sense datum are actual processes in the world. The experience of having a green sense datum is not itself green; it is a process occurring in grey matter. The world contains plumbers, but does not contain the average plumber: it also contains the having of a sense datum, but does not contain the sense datum. . . .

It may be asked why I should demand of a tenable philosophy of mind that it should be compatible with materialism, in the sense in which I have defined it. One reason is as follows. How could a nonphysical property or entity suddenly arise in the course of animal evolution? A change in a gene is a change in a complex molecule which causes a change in the biochemistry of the cell. This may lead to changes in the shape or organization of the developing embryo. But what sort of chemical process could lead to the springing into existence of something nonphysical? No enzyme can catalyze the production of a spook! Perhaps it will be said that the nonphysical comes into existence as a by-product: that whenever there is a certain complex physical structure, then, by an irreducible extraphysical law, there is also a nonphysical entity. Such laws would be quite outside normal scientific conceptions and quite inexplicable: they would be, in Herbert Feigl's phrase, "nomological danglers." To say the very least, we can vastly simplify our cosmological outlook if we can defend a materialistic philosophy of mind.[4]

In essence, Smart is defending the position that states of consciousness are identical with states of the brain. This identity is termed *contingent identity.* To grasp the meaning of contingent identity, consider an example originally advanced by the German mathematician and philosopher Gottlob Frege. Frege pointed out that from ancient times the very bright star visible in the heavens just before sunset has been called "the evening star." Similarly, the bright star apparent just after sunrise has been referred to as "the morning star." Of course, the

---

4. J. J. C. Smart, "Materialism," *Journal of Philosophy* (24 October 1963). Reprinted by permission.

ancients didn't know that these were one and the same "star," the planet Venus.

Think about the implications. If the Greek astronomer-mathematician Aristarchus had said that the morning star is identical with the evening star, he would have been correct. But, of course, he couldn't have proved it. Only the development of telescopes and other astronomical instruments could provide proof. So, although the object denoted by the phrase "morning star" is identical with the one denoted by "evening star," the identity is not apparent by examining the meanings of the words, as it is in statements like "3 squared equals 9" and "A triangle has three sides."[5] Rather, it must be discovered by science.

When Smart speaks of a contingent identity between mental and brain phenomena, he means that the phrase "mental phenomenon" names the same object or set of conditions as the phrase "brain phenomenon." But this identity is a contingent one; it cannot be deduced from the meanings of the words; it must be discovered by science.

Not all philosophers agree with Smart's analysis. The well-known American philosopher Norman Malcolm (1911–), for one, sees flaws in it.

> I wish to go into Smart's theory that there is a contingent identity between mental phenomena and brain phenomena. If such an identity exists, then brain phenomena must have all the properties that mental phenomena have. . . . I shall argue that this condition cannot be fulfilled.
>
> a. First, it is not meaningful to assign spatial locations to some kinds of mental phenomena, e.g., thoughts. Brain phenomena have spatial location. Thus, brain phenomena have a property that thoughts do not have. Therefore, thoughts are not identical with any brain phenomena.
>
> b. Second, any thought requires a background of circumstances ("surroundings"), e.g., practices, agreements, assumptions. If a brain event were identical with a thought, it would require the same. The circumstances necessary for a thought cannot be described in terms of the entities and laws of physics. According to Smart's scientific

materialism, everything in the world is "explicable in terms of physics." But if the identity theory were true, not even those brain events which are identical with thoughts would be "explicable in terms of physics." Therefore, the identity theory and scientific materialism are incompatible. . . .

> According to the identity theory, the identity between a thought and a brain event is contingent. If there is a contingent identity between A and B, the identity ought to be empirically verifiable. It does not appear that it would be empirically verifiable that a thought was identical with a brain event. Therefore, if a thought and a brain event are claimed to be identical, it is not plausible to hold that the identity is contingent.[6]

The debate about the nature of consciousness has arisen in the midst of some startling discoveries in atomic physics. For a long time we have known that all matter consists of molecules, of which there are a tremendous number of types. But there are only about one hundred types of atoms, which make up each molecule. Before the twentieth century, no one believed that atoms could be split. Today we know that several particles make up the atom: electron, proton, and neutron. Yet everything in existence cannot be explained in terms of these three particles.

Physicists have discovered over two hundred so-called elementary particles. Some believe that they are made up of still more elementary particles, called quarks. The point is that modern science is showing reality to be ever more complex.

But, even more important, these elementary particles do not seem to be matter. They are more likely energy forces. True, matter may depend on interactions of elementary particles, but the particles themselves seem to be composed of energy, not matter. And what is energy? Nobody knows for sure. Whatever it is, it is in motion and exerts force, but it does not appear to be matter as matter is traditionally understood.

Ever since the early 1930s, when Werner Heisenberg discovered that atomic activity is not uni-

---

5. See Robert P. Wolff, *About Philosophy* (Englewood Cliffs, N.J.: Prentice-Hall, 1976), 290–291.

6. Norman Malcolm, "Scientific Materialism and the Identity Theory," *Journal of Philosophy* (24 October 1963): 662–663. Reprinted by permission.

form, materialism has been losing credibility. Heisenberg formulated his principle of indeterminacy on a startling premise: that there is no orderly causation. Because electrons change their positions at random, rational prediction is not possible. In his article "The Dematerialization of Matter," philosopher-scientist N. R. Hanson states the full implications of Heisenberg's discovery:

> Matter has been dematerialized, not just as a concept of the philosophically real, but now as an idea of modern physics. Matter can be analyzed down to the level of fundamental particles. But at that depth the direction of the analysis changes, and this constitutes a major conceptual surprise in the history of science. The things which for Newton typified matter—e.g., an exactly determinable state, a point shape, absolute solidity—these are now the properties electrons do not, because theoretically they cannot, have. . . .
>
> The dematerialization of matter . . . has rocked mechanics at its foundations. . . . The 20th century's dematerialization of matter has made it conceptually impossible to accept a Newtonian picture of the properties of matter and still do a consistent physics.[7]

As a result, many scientists, including Heisenberg, believe that we are more likely to have an idealistic universe than a materialistic one. Their view finds some support in the unified field theories of Einstein and contemporary scientists such as Kip Thorne. When electromagnetic and gravitational phenomena are synthesized, matter disappears entirely, leaving only "field." To understand better what is meant by an idealistic universe, let us consider idealism as an explanation of ultimate reality.

QUESTIONS

1. Does being born in the way that humans are distinguish us from other forms of life? Would you agree that normal childbirth, including premature

birth and cesarean section, is a defining characteristic of being a person?

2. In his split-brain experiments, R. W. Sperry showed that either half of the brain can function alone efficiently. If your brain were so severed, would there be two of you? What if you substituted another person's half brain for half of your own? Would you be two people?

3. Look up the meaning of *materialism* as it is ordinarily used. Do you detect any connection between its ordinary and its philosophical meanings?

4. At one point, Ruth claims that the *persistence* of a belief in the soul removes this belief from the realm of superstition or ignorance. Do you agree? Can you think of any other beliefs that have so persisted? What about beliefs that lasted an extremely long time but are no longer widely held?

5. To explain things, would you introduce sciences in addition to the physical sciences that Brad advances? Which ones?

6. Do you think Ruth's example of the self-witnessing brain proves that states of consciousness are different from brain states?

7. Our discussion so far has focused almost exclusively on the problem of self. How is this question relevant to the question of what is real?

8. The eighteenth-century English poet Alexander Pope, exuding the enthusiasm of his age for scientific discovery, wrote an "Epitaph Intended for Sir Isaac Newton, in Westminster Abbey."

> Nature and Nature's laws lay hid in night;
> God said, "*Let* Newton *be!*" and all was Light.

What view of human nature does Pope suggest? Do you think Heisenberg's indeterminacy principle advances, sets back, or has no effect on the belief that all can be explained in terms of cosmic laws?

9. Does research into the causes of human thought, consciousness, and behavior indicate a growing simplicity or a growing complexity of understanding?

10. Do you see the workings of the universe as orderly? Why or why not? (You might first define *orderliness* in terms of predictability.)

7. N. R. Hanson, "The Dematerialization of Matter," in *The Concept of Matter*, ed. Ernan McMillin (Notre Dame, Ind.: University of Notre Dame Press, 1963), 556–557.

SECTION 4.3

Reality as Nonmatter

Modern atomic theory has led many people to claim that reality consists of more than matter. If we push the question of reality far enough, matter alone does not seem to account for everything; things are not only what they appear to be.

Today, many would argue that ultimate reality resembles some cosmic law, such as Einstein's relativity equation $E = mc^2$ (energy equals mass times the speed of light squared). This law, they say, not only describes how things work but also implies a principle that underlies everything, gives everything design and purpose, and orders our experiences.

The study of the theory that there is design or purpose working in the structure of the universe is termed **teleology**. One of the outstanding teleologists in the history of philosophy was Aristotle. He believed that the subject matter of metaphysics consists of certain concepts or categories fundamental to change. Substance is perhaps the most fundamental of these categories. By *substance* Aristotle meant anything that can have attributes or properties but which itself cannot serve as an attribute or property for something else. The simplest examples of substances are everyday objects: trees, houses, shoes, rocks, and so on. We can attribute certain characteristics to these substances, such as greenness to trees or hardness to rocks, but we can't attribute "treeness" or "rockness" to anything. Of particular concern to Aristotle was how substances change, for example, how the substance acorn changes to the substance oak.

As we saw in a showcase in Chapter 2, Aristotle explained change by distinguishing four kinds of "causes." By *cause* Aristotle meant anything that explains why a thing changes as it does. Aristotle's four causes are the *material, formal, efficient,* and *final* causes. The material cause refers to the material of which something is composed. Thus, in the growth of an acorn to an oak, we can talk about the organic material or stuff of which the acorn is composed as its material cause. By a thing's formal cause Aristotle meant its essence, its defining or identifying characteristics. The formal cause or essence of an acorn is the characteristics of the acorn that make it the seed of an oak tree and not, say, the seed of an elm. An efficient cause refers to the agent or agents that bring about a change. Thus, the parent oak tree, the person who plants the seed, the sun, the rain, and all other environmental causes that produce the seed and make it grow and mature constitute efficient causes. When an acorn actually becomes an oak, Aristotle viewed it as having attained its purpose or "end." The end, goal, or purpose that a substance inwardly strives to attain is its final cause.

We've simplified Aristotle's view to make a point: Aristotle's universe is basically teleological. In other words, it's a universe governed by purposes or ends. In his work *Physics*, Aristotle argues that purposeful action is present in all things that come to be.

Further, where a series has a completion, all the preceding steps are for the sake of that. Now surely as in intelligent action, so in nature; and as in nature, so it is in each action, if nothing interferes. Now intelligent action is for the sake of an end; therefore the nature of things also is so. Thus if a house, e.g., had been a thing made by nature, it would have been made in the same way as it is now by art; and if things made by nature were made also by art, they would come to be in the same way as by nature. Each step then in the series is for the sake of the next; and generally art partly completes what nature cannot bring to a finish, and partly imitates her. If, therefore, artificial products are for the sake of an end, so clearly also are natural products. The relation of the later to the earlier terms of the series is the same in both.

This is most obvious in the animals other than

man: they make things neither by art nor after inquiry or deliberation. Wherefore people discuss whether it is by intelligence or by some other faculty that these creatures work—spiders, ants, and the like. By gradual advance in this direction we come to see clearly that in plants too that is produced which is conducive to the end—leaves, e.g., grow to provide shade for the fruit. If then it is both by nature and for an end that the swallow makes its nest and the spider its web, and plants grow leaves for the sake of the fruit and send their roots down (not up) for the sake of nourishment, it is plain that this kind of cause is operative in things which come to be and are by nature. And since "nature" means two things, the matter and the form, of which the latter is the end, and since all the rest is for the sake of the end, the form

must be the cause in the sense of "that for the sake of which." . . .

It is plain then that nature is a cause, a cause that operates for a purpose.[8]

In contrast to this teleological view, materialists generally reject the idea of purpose or goals in nature, primarily because of the difficulty, if not the impossibility, of examining scientifically nature's supposed teleological characteristics. Instead, materialists focus on the laws of mechanics to explain

***

8. Aristotle, *Physics*, trans. R. P. Hardie and R. K. Gaye, in *The Oxford Translation of Aristotle*, ed. W. D. Ross (Oxford: Oxford University Press, 1930). Reprinted by permission of Oxford University Press.

PHILOSOPHY AND LIFE 4.2

The Neutrino

The neutrino is perhaps the most bewildering of all the elementary particles known to physics, and among the most philosophically provocative. It has no physical properties—no mass, no electric charge, and no magnetic field. It is neither attracted nor repelled by the electric and magnetic fields of passing particles. Thus, a neutrino originating in the Milky Way or in some other galaxy and travelling at the speed of light can pass through the earth as if it were so much empty space. Can it be stopped? Only by a direct, head-on collision with another elementary particle.

***

Sources: V. A. Firsoff, *Life, Mind and Galaxies* (New York: W. A. Benjamin, 1967).
Arthur Koestler, *The Roots of Coincidence* (New York: Random House, 1972), 63.

The chances of that are infinitesimally small. Fortunately, there are so many neutrinos that collisions do occur. Otherwise, physicists would never have detected them. Just think, even as you read this sentence, billions of neutrinos coming from the sun and other stars are passing through your skull and brain. And how would the universe appear to a neutrino? Eminent astronomer V. A. Firsoff provides a picture.

The universe as seen by a neutrino eye would wear a very unfamiliar look. Our earth and other planets simply would not be there, or might at best appear as thin patches of mist. The sun and other stars may be dimly visible, in as much as they emit some neutrinos. . . . A neutrino brain might suspect our existence from certain secondary effects, but would find

it very difficult to prove, as we would elude the neutrino instruments at his disposal.

Our universe is no truer than that of the neutrinos—they exist, but they exist in a different kind of space, governed by different laws. . . . The neutrino . . . is subject neither to gravitational nor to electromagnetic field. . . . It might be able to travel faster than light, which would make it relativistically recede in our time scale.

QUESTIONS

1. What impact does the presence of neutrinos have on your view of reality?

2. Arthur Koestler writes: "To the unprejudiced mind, neutrinos have indeed a certain affinity with ghosts—which does not prevent them from existing." What does this mean?

change—what Aristotle termed efficient princi- ples. They insist that matter alone can explain the changes that we observe in the world. Can matter alone account for the general teleological tenden- cies in the operation of things? Can sheer coinci- dence? Can an accidental combination of electrons?

Some critics argue that the survival-of-the- fittest theory does not fully explain evolution over millions and millions of years from very simple organisms to incredibly complex ones, from a mindless glob to human intelligence. Instead, non- materialists see purpose in evolution. They see direction in the operation of nature. In Chapter 3 we saw that modern followers of the design argu- ment, for example, hold that the organic world can be explained only in terms of a divine intelligence that gives nature direction. They see mind behind the way that things interrelate and function. Pur- pose, direction, and mind are concepts foreign to materialism. Yet many people say that when we push our investigation of physical phenomena far enough, we end up in just such a mental world, a world of idea, not matter. This is why nonmater- ialists are often called idealists.

Idealists, unlike materialists, see a mental or spiritual force operating that accounts for the order and purpose in nature that they perceive. Nature, they believe, is goal directed; it evolves not by chance but by design. That humankind is coming to understand more and more of the wonders of nature suggests an underlying law operating in the universe. This law or principle, they say, is not matter but idea. Like materialism, idealism has a long history.

The great majority of mankind are satisfied with appearances, as though they were realities and are often more influenced by the things that seem than by those that are.

NICCOLÒ MACHIAVELLI

THE DEVELOPMENT OF IDEALISM

Although idealists differ, let us define **idealism** as the belief that reality is essentially idea, thought, or mind rather than matter. Whether idealists believe that there is a single, absolute mind or many minds, they invariably emphasize the mental or spiritual, not the material, presenting it as the cre- ative force or active agent behind all things.

The belief that reality is ultimately idea is at least as old as the ancient Greek Pythagoras (about 600 B.C.). Plato, however, first formalized it. He held that individual entities are merely shadows of reality, that behind each entity in our experience is a perfect Form or Ideal. This Form or Ideal is what makes the entity understandable to the human mind. Individual entities come and go, but the Forms are immortal and indestructible.

Such thinking fit in well with the Christian thought developed by Saint Augustine (354–430). In his work *The City of God*, Augustine warns us to beware of the world and the flesh, because they are temporary. What is real is the spiritual world, the world without matter. Although we are citizens of the physical world, we are ultimately intended to be citizens of the spiritual world of God. This is our divine destiny. For Augustine and fellow Chris- tians, Jesus Christ is the embodiment of all perfec- tion, of all "Forms"; he is the meaning of all that is. As Saint John writes, "In the beginning was the Word and the Word was with God and the Word was God. He was in the beginning with all things." Notice that John says the *Word* was God—in Greek, the *logos*, which means "law" as well as "word." In the nineteenth century, the German romantic Goethe would express a similar idealistic notion through his immortal *Faust*: "In the beginning was the meaning."

But the founder of modern idealism is George Berkeley, who reacted against the growth of mate- rialist philosophies like Hobbes's. Berkeley claimed that the only reality that exists is the conscious mind and its ideas or perceptions. Berkeley did not deny the reality of the world. He only denied that the world is independent of mind. Berkeley claimed that all of our acquaintance with the external world consists of the sensations and perceptions of our

The Solar System, Helmut Wimmer. "According to Hobbes, 'The Universe, that is the whole mass of things that are, is corporeal, that is to say, body.' But according to Berkeley, 'All the Choir of Heaven and the furniture of the world, in a word all those bodies which compose the mighty frame of the world, have no substance without a mind; so long as they are not actually perceived, . . . they have no existence at all.' "

senses. We have no evidence for saying that there is anything else to reality other than these sensations and perceptions. So, Berkeley concluded, we have no reason to postulate the existence of any external physical reality. All that exists are the mental sensations and ideas we experience and the minds in which we experience them." For Berkeley, then, reality is nothing more than the perceptions and ideas we have and the minds in which these

perceptions exist. The external world is that collection of perceptions we mistakenly call physical reality. But where does that collection of perceptions derive its uniformity, consistency, and continuity? This can only be explained as the work of the supreme mind: the mind of God. It is God who produces in our minds the display of perceptions that we call the external world, and it is He who gives this display its order and stability. The orderly succession of events that Ruth perceives in everything Berkeley attributed to the will of God. (For a fuller explanation of Berkeley's views, see the showcase on Berkeley at the end of this chapter.)

In order to appreciate the varieties of idealism, it's helpful to distinguish between two kinds of idealism, subjective and objective. Berkeley's version of idealism is useful because it includes elements of both.[9]

Berkeley claimed that things are ultimately mental, or mind-dependent. This mind-dependency can be viewed as either "me-dependent" or "other-dependent." At least in its initial stages, Berkeley's idealism is me-dependent.

Berkeley said that we find out about the things of the world through experience. We learn of trees, rocks, houses, cats, and dogs through our experience of them. But experience is using our senses—seeing, touching, tasting, smelling, and hearing. When we use our senses, we get sightings of light or color; feelings of hard or soft, smooth or rough; smells of sweetness or decay. So, for Berkeley, all things are bundles of deliverances of the senses or some combination of such deliverances.

Berkeley viewed these deliverances of the senses as one's own perceptions. Thus, any thing that I experience is the sum of my perceptions of that thing. Since these perceptions are my own, everything I perceive is me-dependent. This me-dependency translates into mind-dependency, since Berkeley assumed that perception is a mental act and that all perceptions are located in some part of the mind. If we stop Berkeley's analysis right here, we're left with **subjective idealism,** or *subjective immaterialism*, the position that the world consists of my own mind and things that are dependent on it. But Berkeley went further and introduced an objective dimension.

Berkeley pointed out that not all the contents of my mind are the same. Ideas vary. Some are short lived, even changeable at my will. Others occur regularly and seem constant. For instance, if

you choose to, you can imagine that you are now basking in the warm sun on a South Sea island. The air is balmy, the vegetation lush, and the sounds mellow and serene. In contrast, consider your usual route to class; you experience the same landmarks repeatedly—perhaps the library, gym, and the old clock tower—and when you get to class, you experience a comparable regularity, a steadiness about your perceptions. This latter collection of perceptions is clearly different from the imaginings that transported you to the South Sea island. The difference seems to be that your perceptions of the way to class are more than me-dependent.

If your classroom is a collection of perceptions, it must be dependent on mind—if not your own mind, then some other mind. For Berkeley this other mind was ultimately the mind of God. This second stage of idealism, or immaterialism, is termed *objective* because it is independent of certain of my perceptions. The advantages of objective idealism are that it accounts for the steadiness or regularity of our experiences and it allows the world to be viewed as an ultimately intelligible system because it is the product of mind.[10]

Despite the many varieties of idealism, they all appear to share several characteristics. First, they all believe in mind, spirit, or thought as what is ultimately real. Second, they perceive purpose, order, and meaning in the workings of things. Third, they see some kind of purpose acting in our lives. As there are laws governing the operations of the physical universe, so there are laws governing the operations of our own lives: moral laws. Finally, all forms of idealism are as reductionistic as materialism. The tension between idealism and materialism is in the kind of reductions that each proposes. Both speak of trees and rocks and houses as having "parts," in the sense that a tree has bark and pulp and a house has a roof and a foundation. They have a far more subtle meaning in mind, for bark, pulp, roofs, and foundations also have parts. Both materialism and idealism agree that trees and

---

9. See Elmer Sprague, *Metaphysical Thinking* (New York: Oxford University Press, 1978), 93–103.

10. Ibid., 97.

houses are complexes of simples, but they disagree on what kind of complexes such entities are and how they are to be analyzed. Of course, if you reject the idea that things are complexes, then neither materialism nor idealism has any basis. In other words, both assume that things are analyzable into simples.[11]

---

11. Ibid., 93–94.

OBJECTIONS TO IDEALISM

As we have seen, idealists generally rely heavily on the assumption that there are order and purpose in the universe. Critics consider the terms *order* and *purpose* to be vague. They claim that in using these words idealists are evasive. They argue that experience consists in part of such seemingly chaotic and purposeless events as natural disasters (the so-called acts of God), the human catastrophes of

---

PHILOSOPHY AND LIFE 4.3

Evidence of the Soul

For several years the American Society for Psychical Research has been carefully conducting the research called for in the will of an obscure seventy-year-old Arizona miner named James Kidd who died in 1946. The old miner left a will that read:

Phoenix Arizona
  Jan 2nd 1946
*this is my first and only will
and is dated the second day in
January 1946. I have no, heir's
have not been married in my life,
an after all my funeral expenses
have been paid and $100. one hundred
dollars to some preacher of the
gospital to say farewell at my
grave sell all my property which
is all in cash and stocks with
E F Hutton Co Phoenix some in
safety box, and have this balance
money to go in a research or some
scientific proof of a soul of the
human body which leaves at death
I think in time their can be a
Photograph of soul leaving the
human at death,*
      James Kidd

The stocks held by E. F. Hutton were worth more than $200,000. Several groups came forward to claim the money, asserting that they would carry out the research stipulated in Kidd's will. Superior Court Judge Robert Myers, before whom the will was read, was faced with the task of trying to determine what group should get the money. After ten years of deliberations, the estate was awarded to the American Society for Psychical Research. A few years later the ASPR announced early results of its search for the soul.

Six out-of-body (OBE) projects have been conducted. An OBE "fly-in" and an attempt to correlate OBE's and apparitions both supported the OBE hypothesis, but other interpretations (e.g. ESP) are possible. Perceptual experiments with OBEs and psychophysiological studies of subjects gave similar results: evidence in harmony with OBE hypothesis but other explanations possible. Instrumental recordings (i.e. photos) and a test of mediums gave negative results.

Deathbed studies of apparitions, visions, hallucinations, etc. (reported by attending doctors and nurses) supported the conclusion that "some of the dying patients indeed appeared to be already experiencing glimpses of ecsomatic existence." But again, other interpretations can't be ruled out; so these results "should not be taken as a final balance of evidence for or against survival." Masses of data are still being processed.

SOURCE: *ASPR Newsletter,* 24 (July 1976).

QUESTIONS

1. What kind of evidence could *disprove* the existence of a nonmaterial soul? What kind could *prove* the existence of a soul?

2. How would you have decided who was to receive the money if you were in the position of Judge Robert Myers?

disease and war, and the personal and national tragedies of senseless deaths The French writer Voltaire perhaps best summed up this criticism in *Candide*, in which he uses ironic wit to question philosopher Leibnitz's (1646–1716) belief that everything happens for the best in this "best of all possible worlds." At one point in that philosophical tale, Candide points out to Martin the merits of a shipwreck. "You see that crime is sometimes punished; that scoundrel of a Dutch shipowner has had the fate he deserved." Martin responds, "Yes, but did the passengers who were on the ship have to perish too?"[12]

In addition, critics claim that idealists commit the fallacy of **anthropomorphism**; that is, they attribute human characteristics to the universe as a whole. It is one thing to speak of people as having minds, but another to speak of the universe as having one. Similarly unwarranted, say critics, is the leap from ideas to Idea.

Critics also wonder who has ever experienced mind, idea, or spirit independent of a matter-energy system. They point out that it is not even necessary to posit a nonmaterial reality to account for what we observe. This criticism suggests further objections, which require a closer look at subjective and objective idealism.

Subjective idealism's claim that whatever I perceive is either one of my perceptions or a collection of my perceptions is at least puzzling. If I'm looking at a tree, I want to say that there's a difference between my seeing and the tree that I see. Subjective idealism makes no such distinction. Indeed, if I persist that there is more to the tree than my perceivings, subjective idealists might ask me how this "more" is to be found out. They might add that there is no other way to find out about trees than to use our senses. Thus, if I claim that there's more to the tree than my perceiving, I am postulating the existence of something that I cannot know. I can hardly have solid grounds for claiming something that I can't know to exist.

"But," as philosopher Elmer Sprague points out,

Laws of Nature are God's thoughts thinking themselves out in the orbits and the tides.

C. H. PARKHURST

"it still seems odd to say that I perceive my perceptions, and not that I perceive something out there to be perceived. It seems odd to say that to perceive the [tree] is but to perceive my own mind. It is all very well for the Subjective Immaterialist to say 'That's just the way it is.' Less hardy mortals still wonder if we might not say something else instead."[13] Sprague concedes that what subjective idealists say cannot be disproved experimentally because their theories cannot be falsified. But we can still ask them how they know that their claim is true. Ultimately, the claim seems to hinge on the assumption that perceptible things are mere collections of perceptible qualities. But why this assumption? Why not the more commonsensical distinction between perceptions and the objects of perceptions?

Related to this assumption is subjective idealism's insistence that things are collections of perceptible qualities. This belief only follows if we don't make a sharp distinction between perceptible things and our perceptions. But can we really say how things are without making such a distinction? Subjective idealism does not really seem to answer the question of what things are—rather, it seems to dissolve it. Things are as I perceive them. But this apparently rules out the possibility of objective knowledge.

As for objective idealism, we observed two apparent strengths: It explains why perceptible things persist in the mind, and it offers an intelligible world system. Sprague, however, believes that neither of these aspects is as strong as it may appear.

Recall your classroom experience. You perceive the classroom because some other mind, call it God,

---

12. Voltaire, *Candide*, trans. Tobias George Smollet (New York: Washington Square Press, 1962), 77.

13. Sprague, *Metaphysical Thinking*, 98.

perceives it all the time, thus holding the classroom in place each time you happen to perceive it. But do we really need such an explanation? In answering why things persist in our minds, can't a materialistic explanation suffice? You can account for the composition of the classroom or of the things that you pass en route to it. And should they one day disappear, you can also account for that eventuality: They fell down, were torn down, or were blown up. Why the additional Why? that idealists ask?

Objective idealists seem to think that the usual accounts of things won't do. They seek some ultimate explanation. Thus, "God minds it." But what does that tell us? While the classroom stands, God minds it. When it lies in ruins, it does so because God minds it. We're left wondering what "God minds it" adds to a commonsensical accounting.

Objective idealists also claim that the world is intelligible because it's a product of mind. But whose mind? God's mind, some say, or some sort of cosmic intelligence. But simply because our own mind may be intelligible, does that mean God's is? How are we to know God's mind? How can we distinguish between our own perceptions, which by strict idealistic principles we can never get beyond, and God's perceptions? It seems that idealism must answer these questions before it can be considered as the most compelling explanation of ultimate reality.

Are we, in the last analysis, forced to choose between materialism or idealism? Is there some middle ground? For Voltaire's Candide, the answer is to reject both extremes: extreme materialism, which he sees as leading to nothingness, and extreme idealism, which leads to blind optimism. Yes, disorder, chaos, even evil exist. But Candide does not succumb to them. He feels that to cure evil, we must first recognize its reality and its inevitability. He decides that he can cultivate virtue and justice, although he probably will not find them in the universe. Thus, Candide attempts to avoid what he considers the false dilemma of all or nothing. His attitude uses the practical consequences of a belief. In this sense, it is pragmatic. Pragmatism offers another approach to reality.

QUESTIONS

1. Some argue for a principle that is at work in the universe. Perhaps such a universal law is at the bottom of everything, gives everything design and purpose, and orders our experiences. Do you see such a principle or law?

2. Can there be a principle or law at work without a purpose or goal? If not, must the idealist account for the purpose of things?

3. In what sense is it true that the relationships among things are the only meaningful reality? Can you think of anything that you can understand without reference to something else?

4. It has often been said that idealism encourages a withdrawal from the world, a retreat from secular problems, and an immersion in otherworldly concerns. As a result, the idealist neglects real and pressing social concerns. Explain why you think this charge is justified or not justified.

5. Read Alexander Pope's "Essay on Man." What is his metaphysical position? What would be Candide's reaction to it?

Great men are they who see that spiritual is stronger than any material force, that thoughts rule the world.

RALPH WALDO EMERSON

Reality in Pragmatism

William James: "Pragmatism is the attitude of looking away from first things, principles, 'categories,' supposed necessities; and of looking towards last things, fruits, consequences, facts."

Pragmatism is a philosophical movement that has grown up in the last hundred years through the writings of Charles S. Peirce, William James, and John Dewey. James defines pragmatism as "the attitude of looking away from first things, principles, 'categories,' supposed necessities; and of looking towards last things, fruits, consequences, facts."[14] Pragmatism is also a reaction to traditional systems of philosophy, such as materialism and idealism. These systems, claim the pragmatists, have erred in looking for absolutes. Debates like those between Ruth and Brad are pointless, for reality is hardly a single thing. Nature is many things: It is pluralistic. And we are part of it. Using intelligence and reason, we can understand and exercise some control over nature; we can help create it.

To grasp the metaphysical content of pragmatism, it is essential to understand its general approach to philosophy and the social climate out of which it arose.[15]

PRAGMATISM'S APPROACH TO PHILOSOPHY

Pragmatism is decidedly humanistic. Peirce, James, and Dewey tried to understand philosophy and reformulate its problems in the light of psychology,

sociology, scientific method, and the insights provided by the arts. They opposed the insularity of philosophy, its failure to view problems in a larger human and social context. "In a subject like philosophy," wrote James, "it is really fatal to lose connection with the open air of human nature, and to think in terms of shop-tradition only."[16] Philosophy was not just a self-contained discipline with its own cluster of problems; it was an instrument used by living individuals who were wrestling with personal and social problems and struggling to clarify their standards, directions, and goals. Such impulses were not novel to philosophy, but pragmatism took this position deliberately, systematically, and vigorously.

John Dewey, writing in *Reconstruction in Philosophy*, argued that all philosophy arises out of people's continual struggles to deal with social and

---

14. William James, *Pragmatism: A New Name for Some Old Ways of Thinking* (New York: Longmans, Green, 1907), 54–55.
15. The following discussion is indebted to Charles Frankel, *The Golden Age of American Philosophy* (New York: George Braziller, 1960), 1–17.

---

16. Quoted in Frankel, *The Golden Age*, 3.

moral problems. Two important observations follow from this fact. One, philosophy cannot be
understood without an awareness of the social forces
that have produced it. Two, and more important
here, any philosophy or doctrine has worth only
to the degree that it assists people in resolving their
problems. Notice especially this second point in
the following passage from *Reconstruction in
Philosophy.*

> This is the trait which, in my opinion, has
> affected most deeply the classic notion about the
> nature of philosophy. Philosophy has arrogated to
> itself the office of demonstrating the existence of a
> transcendent, absolute or inner reality and of
> revealing to man the nature and features of this
> ultimate and higher reality. It has therefore
> claimed that it was in possession of a higher organ
> of knowledge than is employed by positive science
> and ordinary practical experience, and that it is
> marked by a superior dignity and importance—a
> claim which is undeniable *if* philosophy leads man
> to proof and intuition of a Reality beyond that
> open to day-by-day life and the special sciences.
>
> This claim has, of course, been denied by var-
> ious philosophers from time to time. But for the
> most part these denials have been agnostic and
> skeptical. They have contented themselves with
> asserting that absolute and ultimate reality is
> beyond human ken. But they have not ventured to
> deny that such Reality would be the appropriate
> sphere for the exercise of philosophic knowledge
> provided only it were within the reach of human
> intelligence. Only comparatively recently has
> another conception of the proper office of philoso-
> phy arisen. This course of lectures will be devoted
> to setting forth this different conception of philos-
> ophy in some of its main contrasts to what this
> lecture has termed the classic conception. At this
> point, it can be referred to only by anticipation
> and in cursory fashion. It is implied in the account
> which has been given of the origin of philosophy
> out of the background of an authoritative tradi-
> tion; a tradition originally dictated by man's imagi-
> nation working under the influence of love and
> hate and in the interest of emotional excitement
> and satisfaction. Common frankness requires that
> it be stated that this account of the origin of phi-
> losophies claiming to deal with absolute Being in a
> systematic way has been given with malice pre-
> pense. It seems to me that this genetic method of

John Dewey: **"Philosophy originated not out of intellectual material, but out of social and emotional
material."**

> approach is a more effective way of undermining
> this type of philosophic theorizing than any
> attempt at logical refutation could be.
>
> If this lecture succeeds in leaving in your minds
> as a reasonable hypothesis the idea that philosophy
> originated not out of intellectual material, but out
> of social and emotional material, it will also suc-
> ceed in leaving with you a changed attitude
> toward traditional philosophies. They will be
> viewed from a new angle and placed in a new
> light. New questions about them will be aroused
> and new standards for judging them will be
> suggested.[17]

We should note that pragmatism evidences a
confidence in the ability and power of the mind to
make the world over. The universe is plastic and
unfinished; the human intellect can make its ideals
a reality. Peirce, James, and Dewey believed that
ideas can actually lead the way in human life. This

---

17. John Dewey, *Reconstruction in Philosophy* (New York: Henry
Holt, 1920), 406–407.

ideal underlay their insistence that the truth of an idea lies in its capacity to get us through life in a desirable way.

Corollary to this is the view that all thinking exists to defend personal interests and unconscious wishes that thinking cannot change. All thinking strengthens or secures some human interest. Rather than compromising human ideals, this notion shows that ideals have a natural home in the world and that new ways of thinking have been discovered to realize these ideals more effectively.

Understandably, pragmatism damns any belief that limits what the human mind and will can accomplish. "Damn the absolute," James once wrote to a fellow philosopher. And more than once he penned, "Pragmatism looks to the future."[18] The future is limited only by human aspiration, and that is limited by the human capacity to slough off inherited beliefs in eternal truths. Philosophy must recognize this.

PRAGMATISM AND SCIENCE

In implementing its approach to philosophy, pragmatism had to address several issues and movements of the day. One was Darwin's theory of evolution. Before Darwin's theory, educated people believed that there was a divine plan or purpose operating in the world. But Darwin's theory does not explain things by an appeal to divine ends. Evolution occurs by *chance variation*. While usefulness occasionally explains the survival of a new trait, it does not account for its initial appearance.

Darwin's theory was reinforced by another dominant idea of nineteenth-century science: mechanistic determinism. In essence, mechanistic determinism holds that the future is already determined, and that all human activity amounts to just so much character interplay in a drama whose conclusion is already written. If all the goals of science were achieved, they would reveal the structure of the universe. Pragmatism had to speak to this conception of a "block universe," in which everything is predestined.

> **There are people for whom even the reality of the external world constitutes a grave problem. I do not address them; I presuppose a minimum of reason in my readers.**
>
> PAUL FEYERABEND

A third nineteenth-century movement was generated by social Darwinism and Herbert Spencer's individualism. In essence, these views assert that unchecked competition between individuals is nature's way of improving the species. Poverty and suffering are natural ways of eliminating the unfit. Charity and compassion, unless controlled, are social threats. Personal responsibility, while perhaps desirable in personal relations or in public administration, is unsuited for business. As Charles Frankel points out in his *The Golden Age of American Philosophy*, this doctrine was a "strange amalgam of incompatible notions. It combined a belief in universal change with a belief in an eternally right and unalterable order of society. It confused natural facts or pseudo-facts with moral laws. It applied generalizations about biological individuals to legal constructs like corporations. It assumed the state was the only agency in society that could place barriers in the path of individual initiative."[19] Yet it was no stranger than similar amalgams of scientific misinformation that existed before and have existed since. More to the point, pragmatism developed in counterpoint to this individualism. "Underneath the most abstract philosophical discussions—discussions about the reality of the Absolute, the meaning of truth, the logic of value-judgments—one can hear the echoes of a clamorous social scene and one can sense the impatience of sensitive men with ideas that had become the cloaks of callousness and complacency."[20]

---

18. Quoted in Frankel, *The Golden Age*, 7.

19. Frankel, *The Golden Age*, 12.
20. Ibid.

For many people at this time, some form of idealism served to neutralize dyspeptic implications of evolution, mechanistic determinism, and Spencerian individualism. After all, idealism generally relegated all scientific theory to the realm of the relative. In contrast, idealism dealt with *ultimate* reality, characterized by a single, harmonious moral order. In a word, idealism provided support for traditional religious views and for moral criticism. However, idealism generally ignored the empirical methods of the sciences, and it even ignored evolution itself. Thus, for pragmatists, idealism did not deal effectively with the problems of the age.

The pragmatic alternative denies sharp distinctions between matter and mind, science and morals, and experience and reason. For pragmatists, human ideas and ideals must be examined from the biological and social points of view and treated as instruments for making sense of experience. Any idea or ideal must be judged in terms of its context. Its value depends on its problem-solving capacity. The heart of pragmatism is the pragmatic method.

THE PRAGMATIC METHOD

The pragmatic method proposes that we discover what our ideas mean by studying their consequences in actual experience. As such, the method is critical of abstractions, making them responsible and accountable in the light of observable facts. Any inferences about the world drawn from metaphysical inquiries must have premises that refer to facts in the world and not to human reasoning alone. We cannot base judgments on their connectedness to some presupposed transcendent or ultimate reality. Any judgment must be rooted in the things of experience that are meaningful to humans. Thus, any view of reality is tied to the values inherent in social traditions. In effect, there are no ultimate principles, no self-evident values, and no irreducible sense data. In fact, pragmatism allows no certainties. Ultimately the test of an idea or ideal is its capacity to solve the particular problems that it addresses. Both materialism and idealism fail this test.

Pragmatists differ in their practice—understandably, since pragmatism is not a monolithic system of thought. For example, Peirce was concerned with the logical implications of ideas, not their psychological effects. He focused on the scientific function of ideas—their role in fostering reasoned consensus. In contrast, James, a physiologist and psychologist, was interested in ideas as events in personal experience, as instruments of will and desire. Dewey was neither a student of logic and science nor a psychologist. His main interest was social criticism. He used the pragmatic method to reassess the functions of education, logic, the arts, and philosophy in human civilization. Nonetheless, the observations about pragmatism presented here underlay the thought of each of these highly influential American philosophers, and the pragmatic method guided their thoughts.

Applied to metaphysical questions, the pragmatic method indicates certain criteria for determining what's real. In general, materialists rely on sense observation and scientific method; idealists, primarily on reason. In contrast, James accepted neither of these as the final determinant of reality. In fact, he argued that people recognize a number of realities. Among them are the worlds of sense experience; of scientific knowledge; of belief and opinion; and of the transcendent, religious, or the supernatural. According to James, each of us selects the reality that is most personally meaningful. In effect, we choose our own ultimate reality. While metaphysicians speak of one world as having more reality than another, James interpreted their view as expressing a relation to our emotional and active life. Simply put, reality is what stimulates and interests us, and will ultimately determines what our reality is.

While rejecting scientific method as the exclu-

Materialists and madmen never have doubts.

G. K. CHESTERTON

sive determinant of reality, pragmatists nonetheless employ it in order to learn the secrets of reality and self. But they do not look for cosmic mind or reason; the fact that we have minds does not mean that the universe does, as some idealists would contend. Pragmatism asserts that mind is real but only as a function of behavior. We develop this function when we learn about the things around us. For pragmatists, thinking is coming to understand the connection between action and consequence.

OBJECTIONS TO PRAGMATISM

The opponents of pragmatism do not consider it an acceptable middle ground between materialism and idealism. They claim that it is muddled thinking, that it has no clear notion of what it understands to be real. Pragmatists claim to know only their experiences, which critics argue is a claim of idealism. Peirce, in fact, opted for a version of idealism. But if we know only our experiences, how can we maintain the pragmatic belief of an objective physical reality?

Critics also disagree that mind is just a function of behavior, that it is only an instrument of biological survival. They point out that people meditate, contemplate, and use the mind to compose great symphonies and to ask philosophical questions, yet these activities do not seem necessary for biological survival. Mind, say the pragmatists, exists to fulfill desires. Then why the commitment to scientific inquiry? Why such a stress on impartiality when seeking truth and not more reliance on the subjective impulses of the mind?

Finally, critics suggest that pragmatism erases the distinction between the structure of the mind and the structure of the universe, between the knowledge of facts and facts that exist whether or not they are known.[21] Because of pragmatism's emphasis on the mind's capacity to impose order on an open, unlimited world, there appears to be no antecedent order in the world, no configuration of things aside from what we may think or desire. This is especially true of the pragmatism proposed by James and Dewey. Pragmatists, of course, do not deny the existence of a world independent of the presence of human beings, but they do deny that anything in the world is settled or finished.

QUESTIONS

1. What are the assumptions of materialism and idealism that pragmatism ignores?

2. In what respects does pragmatism incorporate materialism and idealism?

3. If you were a pragmatist, how would you reconcile your belief that you can know only your experiences with your belief that an objective reality exists?

4. Compare and contrast the everyday and philosophical meanings of *pragmatist*.

---

21. Ibid., 7.

We only think when we are confronted with a problem.

JOHN DEWEY

SECTION 4.5

Reality as Being

As for Ruth, pragmatism would not seem to provide an acceptable compromise, since she believes in an idealistic concept of order and purpose. Pragmatism shares more materialistic outlooks. She would also reject the pragmatic diagnosis that there is no difference in things if none is detectable. And she would hardly accept the contention that the mind is only a function of behavior. So, let's see what happens when she takes the issue to Max, her fiancé, and is shown yet another alternative.

RUTH: You know, Max, the other day the professor said something really strange.

MAX: What's that?

RUTH: He said he'd made you in his lab.

MAX: That's funny. He told me the same thing about you.

RUTH: You're kidding.

MAX: But he said you'd be like a human in every way.

RUTH: That you wouldn't be able to detect the slightest difference?

MAX: That's what he said. And that you'd make the perfect mate . . .

RUTH: Even if I was mechanical, right?

MAX: That's about it. Tell me something, Ruth. If I were a mechanical man, would you hesitate to marry me?

RUTH: Oh, Max, the whole question's so silly. I'm really tired of talking about it.

MAX: Then give me a simple yes or no.

RUTH: Well . . . I guess yes, I would have some doubts.

MAX: Why?

RUTH: Why? Isn't that obvious? I mean, you'd be more thing than man.

MAX: More human *machine* than human *being*, is that what you mean?

RUTH: Yes, I guess so. I mean, if you came into the world the same as the rest of us, that would make you one of us, wouldn't it? You'd be fully human.

MAX: Fully human? You make it sound as if my dues would be all paid up, that I'd be a member in good standing of the human race.

RUTH: Well, you'd be in better standing than if you had come by way of the professor's cellar, that's for sure.

MAX: What would you like me to do—go back and come into the world again?

RUTH: Max, don't be so silly. You make it sound as if we're actually talking about you.

MAX: I think you are.

RUTH: You're not going to tell me that the professor actually did create you?

MAX: Look, you said you loved me, right?

RUTH: *Love*— not *loved*. I love you right now, this very minute. And I want to be with you as long as you want me to be.

MAX: Why? Why do you love me?

RUTH: What a silly question!

MAX: Then humor me. Tell me why.

RUTH: Why? Because you're you, that's why.

MAX: But what am I, Ruth—really?

RUTH: Well, who is Max, *really*? Max is kind and he's tender; he's loving and honest; he's handsome and intelligent . . . and he's going to be insufferably vain if I go on any more!

MAX: My incredible humility will prevent that.

RUTH: Oh! You're hopeless!

MAX: Seriously, is all that what you think I am? Is that your concept of me?

RUTH: I suppose that's part of it.

MAX: Then the professor comes along and blows it. He says something that changes that concept. He says I'm not what you think I am, that I'm not like you or him or anybody else because I didn't come on the scene the way everyone else has. Suddenly this information overshadows everything else you know about me. Suddenly you don't know whether you want to marry me. Suddenly you don't know whether you can love me in the way you did before.

RUTH: But do you blame me?

MAX: It's not a question of blame, Ruth. It's a question of *why* you loved me in the first place. You say it's because I am me. But I'm still me. I'm still the same being I was before the professor dropped his bomb. I haven't changed at all.

RUTH: But that's not true. Something about you has changed for me, something very important.

MAX: Some *thing*, yes. But not me. I am the same. If I lost an arm, would you still love me?

RUTH: You know I would. But you're not comparing that to being a brainchild of science, are you?

MAX: In a way I am. Because it's clear that, for you, *what* or *who* I am is more important than *that* I am.

RUTH: Listen, do you think for a minute that I'd care if you were wealthy or had a fancy sports car or anything like that?

MAX: Of course you wouldn't.

RUTH: Because if I did, I'd be treating you just like a thing.

MAX: That's right. But you can treat people like things more subtly.

RUTH: How?

MAX: Well, you can treat me like a thing when you insist that I be human. That's really no different from insisting that I be a Republican or a Democrat; that I be a Catholic, Protestant, or Jew; that I be a white or black. Why must I be some *thing*?

Why can't I just *be*? Why not be happy with my just plain old *being* and leave it at that?

RUTH: But I am.

MAX: I really don't think so. Because if you were, it wouldn't matter whether or not I was human. It would only matter that I *was*.

RUTH: You mean I'd love you just for existing.

MAX: Not *for* existing, just existing. You'd love my existing.

RUTH: I don't understand.

MAX: Well, you wouldn't, you couldn't love anything specific; you'd love the very core of me, my *being*.

RUTH: But I do love your soul.

MAX: That's not what I mean. My being is not my soul or mind or body.

RUTH: Then what is it?

MAX: It can't be described. It defies language because it's not a thing. It is my unique act of existing.

RUTH: You've got me confused with all this talk of being. I'm afraid I'm not following.

MAX: That's because English doesn't help us very much. There's only one word for *being* in English, and that usually refers to some *thing*. But take German. In German there are two words for being— *das Seinde* and *das Sein*. *Das Seinde* means being as a thing, an object. You're a being, I'm a being, Brad's a being, the professor's a being.

RUTH: I see, being in the sense of someone *being* a student or a worker or a writer.

MAX: Right. They'd be some thing; they'd be *a* being. But *das Sein* means being as an activity, not a thing. It refers to the *being* of the thing.

RUTH: You mean the student as *being* instead of the student as a being.

MAX: Yes. In the same way you can speak of the lover as a being or simply as being. When you view the lover as *a* being, it seems to me that you view the lover as a thing. But when you view the lover as *being*, you don't.

RUTH: So you're saying that I shouldn't love you so much because you're you, but because you *are*.

MAX: I think so.

RUTH: I never thought of that.

Max does not want to consider reality piecemeal. Traditional outlooks, in trying to simplify life, reduce it to an abstraction. But there is nothing abstract about existing. Existence is what is ultimately real. And existence involves individuals who exist. We find this emphasis on existence and the individual in two twentieth-century movements, phenomenology and existentialism.

Phenomenology and existentialism share a number of outlooks on the human condition. First, both phenomenologists and existentialists observe suffering and pain as the overriding human experience. They point out that we suffer all kinds of pain: physical, emotional, and psychological. We feel anxious, uncertain, and indecisive. We know what it is to dread, to feel despair, and to hurt. Daily we face the reality of death. True, we are not always conscious of death's imminence, but it is always with us.

Building on this insight into the human condition, phenomenologists and existentialists claim that we shall never understand the primacy of the individual as long as we explain life and people objectively. In reducing individuals to scientific explanations, materialism makes things of people. In explaining reality in terms of cosmic mind, idealism submerges individual self in universal ego. Truth about life and ourselves is not something to be grasped and repeated in nice, neat statements. We experience truth, like everything else, through living; the truth is within, not without.

Despite these general similarities, various points distinguish phenomenology from existentialism.

PHENOMENOLOGY

To understand phenomenology, look at the term itself. *Phenomenology* consists of the Greek root *phenomenon*, meaning "what appears," and the suffix *logy*, meaning "the study of." Without becoming enmeshed in the historical development of the term, we can say that in contemporary philosophy *phenomenology* means the study of what appears to consciousness.

In his *Phenomenology of Perception*, Maurice Merleau-Ponty (1907–1961) says, "The aim of phenomenology is described as the study of experiences with a view to bringing out their 'essences,' their underlying 'reason.' "[22] Phenomenology is the philosophical school that contends that being is the underlying reality, that what is ultimately real is our consciousness, which itself is being. For the founder of phenomenology, Edmund Husserl (1859–1938), the overriding reality is the consciousness itself. You can think away everything, but you cannot think away thought. What is ultimately real is pure consciousness, which we reach by removing attention from the specific experiences that occupy it.

To understand what Husserl is saying, it's helpful to know more about him. An entry in his diary from 1906 provides a good look at what concerned him:[23] "I have been through enough torment from lack of clarity and from doubt that covers back and forth. Only one need absorbs me: I must win clarity else I cannot live; I cannot bear life unless I can believe that I shall achieve it."[24] His intense desire for certainty was intensified by the relativism of the age, as evidenced in both pragmatism and scientism, that is, by adherence to or belief in scientific method as the only reliable way of knowing anything. In Husserl's view, relativism was self-contradictory. Anyone who denied the possibility of absolute certainty was involved in a contradiction, for to deny that possibility was to logically allow the existence of "an objectively valid science."

Of course, this argument wouldn't budge pragmatists. They would have likely viewed Husserl's insistence on an objectively valid science as indicating more his fear of uncertainty than the existence of such a science. Nonetheless, Husserl attacked relativism, not only because he viewed it as inconsistent but also because he felt that it generated undesirable social consequences. Writing in

---

22. Quoted in Edo Pivcevic *Husserl and Phenomenology* (London: Hutchinson University Library, 1970), 11.
23. See W. T. Jones, *From Kant to Wittgenstein and Sartre* (New York: Harcourt Brace Jovanovich, 1969), 385–399.
24. Quoted in H. S. Spiegelberg, *The Phenomenological Movement* (The Hague: Martinus Nijhoff, 1965), 82.

1935, when the Nazis held power, Husserl viewed the European crisis as fundamentally attributable to the gradual erosion of the belief in rational certainty.

For Husserl, rational certainty was the discovery of the Greeks. Europe inherited it from them through Western culture. Recall that the attitude of Plato and Aristotle was one of the disinterested spectator, the overseer of the world. With this attitude, they were led to a distinction between the presented and the real world, and ultimately to a universally valid truth—to truth in itself. Curiously, this analysis parallels Dewey's description of the Greek attitude. But Dewey, and pragmatism generally, condemned it because it locked people into ultimate principles, self-evident views, and a hierarchy of absolute values. Instead, Dewey wanted philosophy to adopt the methods of natural science and to turn to practical problems that beset individuals and society. In contrast, Husserl attributed the "crisis of European man" to a blind allegiance to the methods of natural science. His prescription was to revive the disinterested attitude and to return to rationality in the original Greek sense.

Specifically, Husserl objected to the application of the methods of natural science to the psychic life, to treating psychic phenomena as if they are material objects. Such thinking leads to a caricature of reality, a naive form of dualism wherein the physical world is mind-dependent. What's more, he saw psychology as compounding this error. Having distinguished between minds and bodies, psychologists treated minds as if they were like bodies. Husserl proposed a radically different investigative method to avoid these errors, a method, he believed, that would ultimately be applicable to all the sciences. The perfection of phenomenology would demonstrate that the quest for certainty was not futile or frivolous. It would accomplish this by establishing a firm foundation for the sciences.

Vital to understanding Husserl's method is understanding his phenomenological stance, as opposed to what he called "the natural standpoint."

Our first outlook upon life is that of natural human beings, imagining, judging, feeling, willing, *"from the natural standpoint."* Let us make clear to ourselves what this means in the form of simple meditations which we can best carry on in the first person.

I am aware of a world, spread out in space endlessly, and in time becoming and become, without end. I am aware of it, that means, first of all, I discover it immediately, intuitively, I experience it. Through sight, touch, hearing, etc., in the different ways of sensory perception, corporeal things somehow spatially distributed are *for me simply there,* in verbal or figurative sense "present," whether or not I pay them special attention by busying myself with them, considering, thinking, feeling, willing. . . .

[Further,] what is actually perceived, and what is more or less clearly copresent and determinate (to some extent at least), is partly pervaded, partly girt about with a *dimly apprehended depth or fringe of indeterminate reality.* I can pierce it with rays from the illuminating focus of attention with varying success. . . .

As it is with the world in its ordered being as a spatial present—the aspect I have so far been considering—so likewise is it with the world in respect to its *ordered being in the succession of time.* This world now present to me, and in every waking "now" obviously so, has its temporal horizon, infinite in both directions. . . .

[Moreover,] this world is not there for me as a mere *world of facts and affairs,* but, with the same immediacy, as a *world of values,* a *world of goods,* a *practical world.* . . . I find the things before me furnished not only with the qualities that befit their positive nature, but with value-characters such as beautiful or ugly, agreeable or disagreeable, pleasant or unpleasant, and so forth. . . .

We emphasize a most important point once again in the sentences that follow: I find continually present and standing over against me the one spatio-temporal fact-world to which I myself belong, as do all other men found in it. . . . This "fact-world," as the word already tells us, I find to *be out there,* and also *take it just as it gives itself to me as something that exists out there.* All doubting and rejecting of the data of the natural world leaves standing the *general thesis of the natural standpoint.* "The" world is as fact-world always there; at the most it is at odd points "other" than I supposed, this or that under such names as "illusion," "hallucination," and the like, must be struck *out of it,* so to speak; but the "it" remains ever . . .

a world that has its being out there. To know it more comprehensively, more trustworthily, more perfectly than the naive lore of experience is able to do . . . is the goal of the *sciences of the natural standpoint.*[25]

People usually assume the natural standpoint toward the world. This consists of being aware of a world that is "simply there," whether or not we pay any special attention to it. This "fact-world," as Husserl calls it, we find to be "out there," and we take it just as it gives itself to us. Despite all doubting and rejecting of the data of this natural world, he says that most of us would usually insist that the world as a fact-world is always present. Occasionally this fact-world differs from what we supposed: We experience illusions or hallucinations. But a world that has its being out there remains. In other words, although we may suspect or even reject parts of our experience, we most often unquestioningly accept the world as a whole. Indeed, this natural standpoint seems a most reasonable position. Yet Husserl asks us to question it—to suspend judgment about the world as a whole.

Husserl does not want us to abandon the thesis of the natural standpoint—that the fact-world has its being out there—but to set it aside. He asks us to *"set it as it were out of action"* to *"disconnect it, bracket it."* The natural standpoint still remains, but we simply make no use of it. We reserve judgments based on the natural standpoint. Although we continue to be conscious of the entire natural world, which is continually there for us, we phenomenologically bracket it, an act that "completely bars us from using any judgment that concerns spatio-temporal existence."

To illustrate Husserl's meaning, suppose you are looking at a die in the palm of your hand. What do you experience? From the natural standpoint, the die is a cube of a certain color and size. There are dots on each side, from one to six of them. What happens when we bracket this experience,

as Husserl suggests? You do not doubt the *experience* of having the die in hand, but you do not assume that you *actually* have a die in hand. After all, it may be that you are dreaming, hallucinating, or imagining, and that your hand is actually empty. What Husserl is asking you to do, then, is to not assume that the die has being in the mode of existence. This is what he means by the phenomenological stance, which he would prescribe for all our experience.

Husserl is suggesting that we suspend the truth claims of our everyday cognitive processes. Because we assume the natural standpoint, this suspension seems unnatural for most of us. Why should I not assume that I actually have a die in my hand when I can feel and see it? Husserl insists that such bracketing, far from leaving us in a state of ignorance and skepticism, will present important truths that would otherwise elude us. He believes that these truths are important because whatever remains after bracketing is absolutely certain. The obvious question is What survives bracketing? In general, Husserl believes that what survives is consciousness; ultimate reality consists of consciousness. "For what can remain over when the whole world is bracketed, including ourselves and our thinking? . . . Consciousness in itself has a being of its own which in its absolute uniqueness of nature remains unaffected by the phenomenologic disconnection."[26]

By *consciousness* Husserl means that which involves both an act of intending (the experience of *being conscious of* something) and the intended object (*that of which* one is conscious). For example, when you look at the palm of your hand, you may be conscious of a white die, on one of whose faces is a black dot. Husserl points out that from the natural standpoint we hardly ever doubt this kind of fact. But, says Husserl, we *can* doubt that there was in fact a white die on your palm. However, it is not possible to doubt the *experience* of having seen and felt the die in the palm of your hand. Moreover, within this experience, it is possible to distinguish the die (the intentional object) from your act of intending it. When you bracket,

25. Edmund Husserl, *Ideas: General Introduction to Pure Phenomenology,* trans. W. R. Boyce-Gibson (New York: Macmillan, 1931), secs. 27, 30. Reprinted by permission of Macmillan Publishing Co., Inc., and George Allen & Unwin Ltd.

26. Ibid., sec. 33.

what you experience is both your experiencing (that is, intending) of the die in the palm of your hand and the die as experienced (that is, intended) by you.

Further thought about how objects are present to consciousness persuaded Husserl to emphasize acts of intending more than the objects themselves. Bracketing revealed to him deeper and deeper levels of ego activity that are impossible to understand without profound phenomenological training. Suffice it to say that when all is bracketed, including ourselves, Husserl contends that consciousness remains. When we bracket our whole world, we tap our essence and realize that something precedes our experiences, namely being. "It therefore remains as a region of Being which is in principle unique and can become in fact the field of a new science—the science of phenomenology."[27]

For Husserl, phenomenology is a new science of being. It reveals a sphere of being that is ultimate, in the sense that it presents itself with certainty within our experience. Studying being is not, for Husserl, investigating another reality. It is delving deeper and deeper into the only reality—consciousness.

Another phenomenologist, Martin Heidegger (1889–1976), made this question of being his primary concern. The problem with traditional thinking, claims Heidegger, is that it is confused over the question of "Being." Being is the very existing of the thing. Max tells Ruth that she is more interested in what he is than in his *being*. Heidegger would make the same distinction. When we talk of being itself, we are talking about the very act of existing. Being does not consist of all the characteristics of the individual, for that is to speak of the individual as *a* being. On the other hand, to speak of the individual's Being is to acknowledge that when all qualities and properties not necessary to being as being are stripped away, Being remains as *this* being, as individual.

Being is a difficult concept to communicate, because it is not a thing, although we may identify it with things. But this identification makes it all the more elusive, for we end up identifying the thing with Being. This is what Max says Ruth is doing. You may have heard someone say, "Love me for what I am." Max is saying, "Don't love me for what I am; love my *am*! Love my being, not what you may see as an expression of it: matter, mind, or soul." If we are to understand reality, says Heidegger, we must abandon our mad commitment to the world of things. By becoming conscious of our own Being, we may better understand the Being that underlies everything. At that point we may establish a meaningful relationship with another person.

This emphasis on reality as being underlies the view of the human as an existential being. But it is also curious to note its connection with Buddhist thought, even though, as we have previously seen, Buddhism seems to share some outlooks with the scientific view of the human, especially in its denial of self and of personal freedom.

Although Heidegger is undoubtedly a Western thinker, his thought has enough Oriental flavor to lead him to remark, on reading the work of Zen scholar D. T. Suzuki, "If I understand this man correctly, this is what I have been trying to say in all my writings."[28] The Oriental thinker is generally more concerned not with an objective, empirically verifiable reality but with the inner nature of the self. The world of the senses is short-lived and illusory. As a result, Eastern thought is preoccupied not with what is real but with *being* real. It distinguishes between the idea of ourselves and the immediate concrete feeling of ourselves. As Zen scholar Alan Watts puts it: "Zen points out that our precious 'self' is just an idea. . . . When we are no longer identified with the idea of ourselves, the entire relationship between subject and object, knower and known undergoes a sudden and revolutionary change. It becomes a real relationship, a mutuality in which the subject creates the object just as much as the object creates the subject. The knower no longer feels himself to be independent of the known; the experiencer no longer feels him-

---

27. Quoted in Pivcevic, *Husserl and Phenomenology*, 11.

28. D. T. Suzuki, *Zen Buddhism*, ed. William Barrett (Garden City, N. Y.: Doubleday Anchor Books, 1956), xi–xii.

self to stand apart from the experience."[29] If we are looking for a concrete reality, we shall find it *between* the individual and the world, "as the concrete coin is 'between' the abstract, Euclidean surfaces of its two sides."[30]

Obviously, Eastern thought eschews the polarities of knower and known, experiencer and experience, and subject and object, because they are artificial and preclude true knowledge of self and being. Heidegger, too, seems to consider this Western penchant for dividing a great error that began with Plato, who located truth in the intellect. Against the intellect Plato set nature—a realm of objects to be studied, manipulated, and quantified. Today we find ourselves inheritors of this tradition, technological "masters" of the planet. Along with this dubious distinction, we have suffered, as Heidegger and Eastern thinkers have also observed, an estrangement from being and from ourselves, which the will to power and dominance only intensifies.

The emphasis that phenomenologists have given to consciousness and being takes a more concrete form in the philosophy of existentialism.

EXISTENTIALISM

We mentioned some of the intellectual currents to which the phenomenologists reacted. Of special note was the increasingly popular assumption that an objective knowledge of the human could be attained by applying the methods of empirical science to sociology and psychology. Existentialism, too, can be viewed partially as a reaction to this. Like phenomenology, existentialism is unsympathetic to science as a cognitive enterprise, suspicious of scientism, and wary of the application of scientific method to the solution of economic and political problems. What interests existentialists is the subjective flow of experience. But whereas phenomenologists might suggest that we become truly a self in the classical contemplation of a truth, existentialists find self-definition in the passionate commitment to act and deed. This fact must be

remembered to understand existentialism's metaphysical leanings.

In sketching the thought of Husserl, we began by quoting from his diary. We glimpsed the energizing force behind his philosophy: the need for certainty. It's useful to contrast this with an entry from *The Journals* of the founder of modern existentialism, Søren Kierkegaard (1813–1855):

> What I really lack is to be clear in my mind *what I am to do*, not what I am to know, except insofar as a certain understanding must precede every action. The thing is to understand myself, to see what God really wishes *me* to do; the thing is to find a truth which is true *for me*, to find *the idea for which I can live and die*. What would be the use of discovering so-called objective truth, of working through all the systems of philosophy and of being able if required, to review them all and show up the inconsistencies within each system;—what good would it do me to be able to develop a theory of the state and combine all the details into a single whole, and so construct a world in which I did not live, but only held up to the view of others;—what good would it do me to be able to explain the meaning of Christianity if it had *no* deeper significance *for me and for my life*;—what good would it do me if truth stood before me, cold and naked, not caring whether I recognized her or not, and producing in me a shudder of fear rather than a trusting devotion? I certainly do not deny that I still recognize an *imperative of understanding* and that through it one can work upon men, *but it must be taken up into my life*, and *that is* what I now recognize as the most important thing.[31]

Several themes are worth noting in this entry. First, Kierkegaard, like Husserl, is concerned with clarity—not the clarity of some absolute truth but the clarity of what he is to do. This emphasis on action and doing recurs in all existentialist thinking, and it constitutes a lens through which existentialists view all philosophical questions, including metaphysical ones. Second, notice the emphasis Kierkegaard gives to the subjective—to "I," "me," and "my life." This is also a recurring theme in

---

29. Alan Watts, *The Way of Zen* (New York: Pantheon, 1957), 120–121. Reprinted by permission.
30. Ibid., 122.

31. Søren Kierkegaard, *The Journals of Kierkegaard*, trans. A. Dru (London: Collins, 1958), 44. Reprinted by permission of Oxford University Press.

existential philosophy and literature. Third, observe Kierkegaard's religiosity. He wants to know what God expects of him. Kierkegaard, a Lutheran, was a deeply religious thinker, and the central issue of his life and thought was what it means to be a Christian. How is an individual to bridge the gap between himself and his Maker, between creation and Creator?

For Kierkegaard, reality cannot be separated from existence. To exist is to struggle, to face opposition, and to experience passion; to exist is to make decisions, not to flounder. What's more, existence and selfhood are identical. To exist is *to become* a self, not just to be a self. It follows, then, that things that are not selves do not have an independent status. They exist only insomuch as they are "for" selves, for things that truly exist.

Even this crude sketch of Kierkegaard's thought shows the self as the focus of reality. But it is not an emphasis on the self as thinker, but as doer and actor, as decision maker. Kierkegaard's metaphysical concerns focus on the inner reality of what it is to be human; consequently he was preoccupied with the predicament of decision making: What is *really* real? Kierkegaard wants people to take decisions seriously. More important, he wants people to relate the decision predicament to religion, specifically to Christianity, which he sees as the only cure for the agony of decision making.

※ Friedrich Nietzsche (1844–1900) disagrees. True, the individual is what matters; existence must be stressed above everything else; traditional thought is ultimately irrelevant to the human condition. But Christianity, holds Nietzsche, is not different from traditional thinking. Its conventional values and morality inhibit rather than encourage individual freedom and growth, which can occur only in the absence of a traditional God. Thus, Nietzsche's problem is how to live in a world in which "God is dead." To say that God is dead is to say that there is no cosmic order. What looks like a cosmic, objective order is a mere projection of the human's desperate need to believe in a universe with reason and purpose. In contrast, Nietzsche's universe is characterized by "Eternal Recurrence"; that is, everything eternally recurs, everything that has ever

happened happens again and again into infinity. Is Nietzsche, in fact, implying an order? Isn't perpetual recurrence a kind of order? Not really, because in his view nothing in the universe could provide a rationale for the recurrence. Whatever happens, whatever we do, is in the last analysis inconsequential, because events eternally recur. This, according to Nietzsche, is the truth that we must all face eventually. If we can live without hope of any kind, even knowing that what we do will be endlessly repeated, then we have achieved salvation as human beings. How do we do this? Obviously, any prescription that Nietzsche gives cannot resemble Kierkegaard's leap of faith to God and Christianity. And it doesn't. Instead he prescribes a cosmological principle, the will to power.

Nietzsche assumes that nothing is real except the individual world of desires and passions. "We cannot step down or step up to any kind of 'reality' except the reality of our drives,"[32] he writes in *The Genealogy of Morals*. All the various drives that appear to motivate people's acts are, for Nietzsche, variants of one basic drive, the will to power. Although on the cosmological level Nietzsche never works out this principle, he does detail it on the psychological level. He holds that at the preconscious level the will to power expresses itself in every organism's attempt to use and overcome organisms less powerful than itself. "Life itself," he writes, "is essential assimilation, injury, violation of the foreign and the weaker, suppression, hardness, the forcing of one's own forms upon something else, ingestion and—at least in its mildest form—exploitation."[33] In the last analysis, Nietzsche's answer to how people are to live in a world in which God is dead is to unleash the individual's will to power. (For more on Nietzsche, see the showcase in Chapter 7.)

Although Nietzsche might have first announced atheistic existentialism, its chief exponent has been Jean-Paul Sartre (1905–1980).

---

32. Friedrich Nietzsche, *The Genealogy of Morals*, trans. F. Golffing (New York: Doubleday, 1956), 42.
33. Ibid., 201.

SARTRE

While Nietzsche seemed to welcome the news of the death of God, Sartre is deeply disturbed by it. In his essay "Existentialism and Human Decision," he writes, "The existentialist thinks it very distressing that God does not exist." In Sartre's view, since there is no God, there can be no one to conceive of a human nature. Without a human nature, we are free to be what we choose. There is nothing we ought to do, since there is nothing we ought to be. There are no absolutes, no norms of right behavior; we are on our own. We exist; whatever is uniquely ours, whatever makes each of us an individual—our **essence**—is ours for the making. We do not *discover* who we are so much as we *make* it.

Consider the implications of a godless universe. What kind of world has no God? What kind of creatures are we who were not made by any God? What are we to do who find ourselves living in a world without a God? These are some of Sartre's central concerns that cannot be answered by Kierkegaard's leap of faith. Indeed, for Sartre such an act is cowardly because it pushes people further into a world of illusion and false hope.

In contrast, Sartre's prescription for some of these dilemmas is related to his view of reality. Like phenomenologists, Sartre believes that reality exists in phenomena, that is, in "consciousness of." Furthermore, he accepts the phenomenological claim that "consciousness of" consists not only of intentions but also of intentional objects. Under intentional objects Sartre would include everything short of pure consciousness. What remains, then, is intention, that is, the pure, impersonal nothingness of consciousness. This, then, is the departure point for both phenomenology and Sartre's existentialism.

Whereas both phenomenology and existentialism reject the distinction between appearance and reality, Sartre introduces a dichotomy between appearance and consciousness. For Sartre, reality consists of two kinds of being: the being of consciousness and the being of what appears to consciousness, phenomena. He terms the former

Jean-Paul Sartre: "Thus human reality does not exist first in order to act later; but for human reality, to be is to act, and to cease to act is to cease to be."

(consciousness) "being-for-itself" and the latter (phenomena) "being-in-itself."

To grasp this distinction, consider a table that stands across the room from you. Clearly there are innumerable ways in which you can "intend" the table, that is, in which you can think about, remember, and imagine it. The table, of course, cannot perform any of these operations. It has no consciousness. Sartre calls such an intentional object being-in-itself. On the other hand, consciousness, that is, being-for-itself, can conceive of things as they are not. Consciousness involves such unique human activities as imagining, lying, negating, and questioning. Most importantly, being-for-itself makes meaning. In other words, being-for-itself exists in a world of its own making; it is its own God. It is also responsible for the world that it makes.

This distinction between being-in-itself and being-for-itself leads Sartre to conclude that humans *are* only insofar as they act. Our action may be trivial or momentous. We may move to a new town, or we may risk our lives for a cause. This is of no matter to Sartre. What counts is that we act, that is, that we freely adopt a project. When we do, we are truly human beings because we are in the mode of being-for-itself. Failing to act, we are in the mode of being-in-itself. Sartre expresses this point in *Being and Nothingness*, a definitive statement of his philosophy.

> A first glance at human reality informs us that for it being is reduced to doing. . . . Thus we find no *given* in human reality in the sense that temperament, character, passions, principles of reason would be acquired or innate *data* existing in the manner of things. . . . Thus human reality does not exist first in order to act later; but for human reality, to be is to act, and to cease to act is to cease to be. . . .
>
> Furthermore, . . . the act . . . must be defined by an *intention*. No matter how this intention is considered, it can be only a surpassing of the given toward a result to be obtained. This given . . . can not provide the reason for a phenomenon which derives all its meaning from a result to be attained; that is, from a non-existent.
>
> Since the intention is a choice of the end and since the world reveals itself across our conduct, it is the intentional choice of the end which reveals the world, and the world is revealed as this or that (in this or that order) according to the end chosen. The end, illuminating the world, is a state *of* the world to be obtained and not yet existing. . . . Thus my *end* can be a good meal if I am hungry. . . . This meal which [is] beyond the dusty road on which I am travelling is projected as the *meaning* of this road. . . .
>
> Thus the intention by a single unitary upsurge posits the end, chooses itself, and appreciates the given in terms of something which does not yet exist; it is in the light of non-being that being-in-itself is illuminated. . . .
>
> This characteristic of the for-itself implies that it is the being which finds *no help, no pillar of support* in what it *was*. But on the other hand, the for-itself is free and can cause there to be a world because the for-itself is *the being which has to be*

> *what it was in the light of what it will be.* Therefore the freedom of the for-itself appears as its *being.* . . . We shall never apprehend ourselves except as a choice in the making. But freedom is simply the fact that this choice is always unconditioned.
>
> Such a choice made without base of support and dictating its own causes to itself . . . is absurd.[34]

Sartre suggests a rather unconventional view of human behavior here. Because of the influence of social science, specifically psychological behaviorism, many people assume, let's say, that a man cheats and robs because he's a thief, and he's a thief because of the conditions to which he was exposed as he grew up. In brief, many of us assume that we are who we are because of our experiences. Sartre rejects this notion. He would argue that if a man is a thief, he chooses to be one and he chooses all that this decision entails. He could choose to be otherwise, for instance, to be an honest man. He could choose, in effect, a new project rather than the one he has adopted. Furthermore, he may do this whenever he chooses. In other words, nothing about a thief's past makes his future inevitable. In fact, there's no telling how many different projects he could undertake in defining who he will be.

For Sartre, then, first we exist. Our uniqueness, our essence, is not God-given or predetermined. Rather, it depends on whether we act. Sartre succinctly expresses this seminal insight of his philosophy in his statement "Existence precedes essence."

In contrasting phenomenology and existentialism, therefore, it seems safe to say that phenomenologists like Husserl found truth and certainty in the nothingness of consciousness, while Sartre finds the hope that he needs to live in a godless universe. In the nothingness of consciousness, Sartre finds *something*: the capacity to annihilate a given world and thus to become a self. In a word, he finds the possibility of action and with it freedom and self-identity.

Finally, even this brief exposition should indicate that existentialists are extremely diverse. They

---

34. Jean-Paul Sartre, *Being and Nothingness*, trans. H. E. Barnes (New York: Philosophical Library, 1956), 476–479. Copyright © 1956 by Philosophical Library. Reprinted by permission.

include theists and atheists, philosophers, theologians, and artists. Specifically, existentialists include Kierkegaard, the Jewish scholar Martin Buber (1878–1965), the Protestant theologian Paul Tillich (1886–1965), the atheistic Nietzsche and Sartre, the novelist Albert Camus (1913–1960), and many other thinkers, writers, and artists. Although their views often differ radically, they share the common concerns for the individual, for subjective experience, for the importance of self, for the need for personal freedom, and for the reality of personal responsibility. In our treatment of phenomenology and existentialism, we have attempted to touch only on those areas of metaphysical importance. Even here we have had to be sketchy. These important thinkers have many ideas of merit that the serious student of philosophy will want to explore.

OBJECTIONS TO PHENOMENOLOGY AND EXISTENTIALISM

Since there are so many nuances in phenomenological and existential thought, let's confine our remarks to Husserl and Sartre. As Husserl became more skilled in bracketing, he uncovered more and more activities of the ego at increasingly deeper levels. For Husserl these activities do not underlie experience but are within it, waiting to be disclosed by bracketing. But, critics have asked, what of those less adept at bracketing than Husserl? What about people who are unable to uncover these activities? It seems that if such people are not to doubt the entire method, they must view these activities as lying entirely outside of the phenomenal field.

Critics have also asked, "Are things 'self-given' when we bracket or are they not?" To illustrate, suppose you had bracketed and reported that you did not find anything that was self-given, anything that presented itself with absolute certainty within experience. Husserl might accuse you of having bracketed unsuccessfully, but you could reply that bracketing itself is a frame within which Husserl insists on viewing things. In other words, you could argue that all seeing is relative to the frame through which one chooses to view things, that is, assump-

tions, presuppositions, and values. If you were of a different philosophical bent from Husserl, you could go on and associate these frames with language. Husserl would counter that his is a special kind of seeing that's free of language when we bracket correctly. Thus, we see what is the case, and then we hunt round for the right words to describe it. But is this so? As we'll shortly see, much of twentieth-century philosophy argues that all philosophy including phenomenology, is linguistic. In other words, all thinking and seeing is related to certain preconceptions that are inherent in language. Thus, bracketing is another kind of frame, though admittedly subtler than most. Thus, what for Husserl seems certain might be better described as his own projection of the quest for certainty.

Turning to Sartre, recall that he insists that to be human is to make a world by adopting a project. Suppose, for example, that you find yourself a Christian. You didn't *choose* to become one; you simply followed a script or line or direction that, for a number of reasons, was laid out for you. For Sartre, you'd be caught up in a logical contradiction, because you would be a person who was not a person, a for-itself whose being was in the mode of an in-itself. For Sartre this evaluation is not just a bias or even a value judgment. It's an assertion of an ontological truth. But is it?

Even if you were a Christian who did not *choose* Christianity, you wouldn't be a Christian in the way that a desk is a desk or a rock is a rock. You wouldn't have being in the mode of the in-itself in the way those things do. In fact, Sartre would agree that as humans, we can't have being simply in the mode of the in-itself. Like it or not, we're condemned to be free.

If we can't *be* simply in the mode of the in-itself, then we're always in the mode of the for-itself. But is it any more possible to be in the mode of the for-itself? Suppose that you don't drift or slip into being a Christian, but you *choose* it. This fact doesn't seem to make any real difference, because once you become a Christian, you accept a set of values, ways of looking at things, and a course of conduct. Christianity becomes your "taken-for-granted," and, evidently, you now have being in the mode of the for-itself. Obviously, this problem doesn't exist only for Christians or only for those who accept some sort of authoritarian code. People who adopt nihilism as their project just as easily slip from freedom to playing the role of nihilist. Even those who adopt existential freedom as their project can slide from freedom while playing the role of the existentialist. True, some projects likely invite slippage into bad faith more than others. But is any project immune? Professor of philosophy W. T. Jones captures this paradox. "One of the difficulties for a man who is committed to 'commitment' is that in order to get things done in this world he must combine forces with other men— not only join a movement but institutionalize (even bureaucratize) it. And this, it would seem, means surrendering one's freedom and hence becoming a thing. This is the paradox Sartre encountered in his own life; it helps to explain his on-again, off-again relationship with the Communist Party."[35]

Sartre's account of the for-itself, then, seems to commit him to holding freedom as an all-or-nothing proposition. But many people see it as one of degree. The same is true of responsibility. For example, who was responsible for the Holocaust, the attempt by the German Nazi regime to exterminate the Jewish race by murdering them in prison camps during the Second World War? Some people might reply that the individual Nazi soldiers who committed the murders were responsible. But those individuals all claimed that they were merely "following orders." Were the military officers who ordered the murders responsible? What about the Nazi politicians who designed the plans that the military followed? Or those German citizens who supported the Nazi regime, or those who knew about the camps and did nothing to stop them? What about those citizens of England and the United States who were aware of the camps and also did nothing? Are these parties each responsible but to different degrees?

But responsibility in terms of degree seems to be a different view of morality from Sartre's. In his view, humans are totally responsible because they are totally free. Since all of us could have made a

---

35. Jones, *From Kant*, 444.

Man is the being through whom nothingness comes to the world. This *nothing* is human reality itself as the radical negation by means of which the world is revealed.

JEAN-PAUL SARTRE

---

world that excluded the Nazi massacre, we are all equally responsible. It's true that in *Being and Nothingness* Sartre relaxes his view by speaking of the social restraints on individual freedom, but then one wonders whether this modification is consistent, or even needs to be, with his existential phenomenology.

Despite differences, existentialist, phenomenologists, and many of their critics agree at least on one point: Statements about ultimate reality and being are meaningful. In fact, this element is shared by all the views that we have discussed so far. Whether reality is matter, idea, a combination, being, or consciousness, all of these views agree that we can sensibly talk about metaphysical issues. Yet one school of twentieth-century philosophy— the analytic school—does not concede this belief.

QUESTIONS

1. What precisely does Max mean when he says "It's clear that, for you, *what* or *who* I am is more important than *that* I am"?

2. What is the difference between being and being human?

3. In what sense are you both being and a being?

4. Show how a failure to distinguish between being as a thing and the being of a thing leads to "thingifying" everything, including people.

5. Do existentialism, phenomenology, and pragmatism share any beliefs?

6. In what sense would you call Kierkegaard a rationalist?

7. Sartre claims that Kierkegaard's leap of faith to God is cowardly and not in the true existential spirit. Why would he say this? Do you agree?

8. What does Sartre mean when he says "existence precedes essence"?

9. How would you describe what Heidegger calls your being?

10. Would Ruth's supposed objections to Max's "being" argument bring her closer to materialism than she might think? Why?

11. If Ruth objected, "If everything is being, then everything is nothing," what would she mean?

12. Is it possible to maintain a concept of individual difference if everything has being in common?

13. Sartre claims that in making a choice for self, we are really making a choice for other. Is this statement consistent with a denial of any kind of universal human nature? If it is, why did Sartre make such a claim?

SECTION 4.6

The Analytic School

We saw that phenomenology focuses on phenomena as they appear to consciousness. Twentieth-century philosophy, however, is characterized by another outlook, which, rather than focusing on the phenomena and on consciousness, concentrates on the language with which people talk about these phenomena. Such an emphasis is a vital part of what has been termed *analytical philosophy*.

Language is relevant to the questions of reality and being that we've raised in this chapter. To understand this emphasis and how some philosophers use it to throw new light on some enduring metaphysical questions, keep in mind certain basic attitudes or implied assumptions about the nature of the world and about the nature of philosophical inquiry that characterize analytical philosophy. Of course, the broad assumptions we'll mention don't necessarily characterize the thinking of every analytical philosopher. But these general characteristics do seem to catch the spirit of most of them.[36]

Analysts frequently conceive of the world as made up of numerous independent entities. It's impossible, however, to generalize about how analysts conceive of these entities. For some they're material particles; for others they're sense data; for still others they're impressions, or what they term "facts."

From this first fundamental assumption follows a second, which concerns the precise task of phi-

---

36. For a treatment of analytical philosophers, see Jones, *From Kant*, 331–335.

losophy. If the universe consists of complex entities, then philosophers should clarify our understanding of these complexes by analyzing the complex entities and identifying the simple entities of which they are composed. This is the origin of the term *analytical*, used to characterize the nature of this philosophical enterprise. Analytical philosophers hold that when the process of analysis is done thoroughly and correctly, complex realities can be clearly explained, and this clarification ought to be the function of philosophy.

Given these two basic assumptions, you can better understand the emphasis that analytical thinkers give to "clarity," which they evidently view as a very sharply focused kind of experience. This concern has led analytical philosophers, in varying degrees, to an interest in language. In their view, most of our language is ambiguous and misleading, suggesting that the universe consists of rather amorphous, internally related complex entities, when it actually consists of single atomistic entities. Consequently, they insist that before any serious philosophical inquiry can occur, everyday language must be refined and clarified. As Russell puts it: "The most important part [of philosophy] . . . consists in criticizing and clarifying notions which are apt to be regarded as fundamental and accepted uncritically. As instances I might mention: mind, matter, consciousness, knowledge, experience, causality, will, time. I believe all these notions to be inexact and approximate, essentially infected with vagueness, incapable of forming part of any exact science."[37]

For Russell the methodology of analysis led to the metaphysical doctrine of atomicity. Other philosophers, such as Ludwig Wittgenstein, used a rigorous and unflinching linguistic analysis to dissolve metaphysical problems. To these philosophers, philosophical problems were based on linguistic confusion; once a correct and thorough analysis of language was conducted, the problems dissolved. So while both types of analytical philosophers agree

that most philosophical problems are rooted in sloppy language, they differ in emphasis and ultimately in their conclusions. Some, like Russell, concentrate on the language and methods of sciences; others, like Wittgenstein, focus on ordinary language usage. The former group are variously called logical positivists, logical empiricists, or scientific empiricists; the latter are known as ordinary-language philosophers. Thus, the analytical school embraces a varied host of thinkers—Russell, Wittgenstein, Alfred J. Ayer, Rudolf Carnap, John Wisdom, and Gilbert Ryle—all of whom agree on at least one point: that the clarification of symbols, especially linguistic symbols, is of primary importance.

Ruth's professor friend is a logical positivist, although Ruth does not know it until she confronts him with her frustration. Then she learns why he thinks that the debates she has had with Brad and Max are really futile. Ruth and the professor agree on this point, but for different reasons.

RUTH: Max and I just had a fight. And do you know what it was over?

PROFESSOR: What?

RUTH: That stupid thing you said about our being your creations.

PROFESSOR: Uh-oh. I'm sorry.

RUTH: A lot of good that'll do.

PROFESSOR: So you don't think it's possible to produce a mechanical mate, is that it?

RUTH: That's not what we were arguing over. It was a lot heavier than that. It was about what's really real and things like that.

PROFESSOR: Really real?

RUTH: You know, whether everything is just matter or not matter. Or maybe being, as Max says.

PROFESSOR: You really did get into it, didn't you?

RUTH: And it's all because of you!

PROFESSOR: Well, if it's any comfort, I agree with you that debating what is really real is a futile exercise.

RUTH: You mean you think it's dumb, too?

PROFESSOR: Yes, I do.

---

37. Bertrand Russell, "Logical Atomism," in *Contemporary British Philosophy*, ed. J. H. Muirhead (New York: Macmillan, 1924), 380.

RUTH: Well, I never expected to hear that from you.

PROFESSOR: Why? Because you expect professors to serve as instigators and referees of intellectual games?

RUTH: Something like that, I guess.

PROFESSOR: Well, let me assure you I've thought considerably about those questions, Ruth. And do you know what I've decided?

RUTH: What?

PROFESSOR: That they defy verification.

RUTH: What do you mean?

PROFESSOR: Well, let me show you. Take the question that you were so hotly debating: What is reality? Now each of you had a different notion, I presume.

RUTH: That's right. Personally, I think reality is nonmaterial, some kind of spirit or mind.

PROFESSOR: Fine. Let's examine your belief: "Reality is nonmatter." Now, presumably, if you were arguing about this statement, you thought it was either true or false.

RUTH: I think it's true, but Brad and Max don't.

PROFESSOR: Let me ask you something, Ruth. How do you know when a statement, any statement, is true?

RUTH: Well, you can tell some statements are true just by looking at them.

PROFESSOR: Such as?

RUTH: "My brother Brad is a male."

PROFESSOR: How do you know that's true?

RUTH: It's self-evident. If you're talking about a brother, you must be talking about a male.

PROFESSOR: I see what you mean. Certainly, the truth of that statement is contained within the meaning of the words themselves. If you denied such a statement, the result would be an absurd self-contradiction: "My brother Brad is not a male."

RUTH: That's silly.

PROFESSOR: Right. But what about a statement like "The sun is between 90 and 95 million miles from the earth"? Is that statement self-evident?

RUTH: No. You'd have to prove that.

PROFESSOR: I agree. Somehow you'd have to measure the distance and determine if, in fact, the sun was between 90 and 95 million miles from earth.

RUTH: Of course.

PROFESSOR: What if you couldn't measure it? If you couldn't determine the precise distance? Would you call the statement false?

RUTH: No, you just wouldn't know for sure, that's all. It could still be true. You'd just have to wait and see.

PROFESSOR: So you'd say the statement is still either true or false.

RUTH: Sure.

PROFESSOR: What about a statement like "Unicorns like to eat fresh eggs"? Is that true or false?

RUTH: That's just silly.

PROFESSOR: But is it true or false?

RUTH: It's neither.

PROFESSOR: Neither?

RUTH: Because unicorns don't exist.

PROFESSOR: What difference does that make?

RUTH: Well, if unicorns don't exist, how can you say anything about them that makes sense? How would you ever go about proving it? It's just ridiculous. Say whatever you want about unicorns; it

---

Consider this table in front of us. It is not what it seems. Leibniz tells us it is a community of souls. Bishop Berkeley tells us it is an idea in the mind of God. Sober science, scarcely less wonderful, tells us it is a vast collection of electric charges in violent motion.

BERTRAND RUSSELL

doesn't make any difference, because you can't ever really find out.

PROFESSOR: All right, then, what about this statement: "There's a Coke machine on the southern polar cap of Mars"? Is that true or false?

RUTH: It's either one or the other.

PROFESSOR: How come?

RUTH: Because you can prove that. You can at least imagine what you'd have to do to prove it.

PROFESSOR: So that's not like the unicorn statement?

RUTH: No way. Coke machines, southern polar caps, Mars, all those things exist. So you know what you'd have to do to prove whether there really is a Coke machine up there. Go and see.

PROFESSOR: You seem to be saying that, except for self-evident statements, a statement is true or false only if it lends itself to being proved. And that it lends itself to being proved only if the things that make it up really exist.

RUTH: Yes, I guess I am.

PROFESSOR: All right, then, let's see where that leaves us. What about your statement "Reality is nonmatter"? Is that statement self-evident?

RUTH: If it were, Max and I wouldn't have fought.

PROFESSOR: I agree. You could certainly deny that statement and still have something that makes sense.

RUTH: Sure. Brad said reality was matter.

PROFESSOR: It seems that leaves us with having to prove the statement true.

RUTH: I suppose it does.

PROFESSOR: Well, how do you propose to do that?

For the linguistic analyst who is a logical positivist, there are two kinds of meaningful statements: analytic propositions and synthetic propositions. Defining a **proposition** as a statement that is true or false, the analyst sees *analytic* propositions as true or false by definition, by their appearance alone. In an analytic statement, the predicate—the part that follows the verb *to be*—always repeats the subject in whole or in part. Thus, "The *red* bird is *red*." Sometimes the predicate is not the same

term as the subject but carries part of the subject's meaning, as in "His *sister* is a *female*." *Female* is included in the meaning of *sister*. Ruth calls such statements self-evident; that is, their negation always results in a self-contradiction: "The red bird is not red" or "His sister is not a female."

A nonanalytic proposition is said to be *synthetic*. Synthetic propositions are those that can, at least in theory, be proved true or false by observation. This is possible only if their terms refer to observable objects or events. Those analysts who are logical positivists say that one should apply scientific methods to determine if the relationship between these objects or events is fact. "It's raining," "California is about three thousand miles from New York," and "A spirochete causes syphilis" are synthetic statements.

If a statement is neither analytic nor synthetic, logical positivists say it is epistemologically meaningless; it is nonsensical. Metaphysical statements appear to be neither analytic nor synthetic. Alfred J. Ayer puts it this way: "We may accordingly define a metaphysical sentence as a sentence which purports to express a genuine proposition but does, in fact, express neither a tautology (analytic statement) . . . nor an empirical hypothesis (synthetic statement). And as tautologies and empirical hypotheses form the entire class of significant propositions, we are justified in concluding that all metaphysical assertions are nonsensical."[38]

These analysts would view not only metaphysical statements as meaningless but most ethical, aesthetic, and theological ones as well, because most of them are neither analytic nor synthetic. Thus they would consider the following statements nonsensical: "God exists," "God doesn't exist," "Lying is wrong," "Lying is right," "A moral law operates in the universe," and "The best form of government is the one that governs least." The fact that very few people can consider such statements meaningless has led to a major objection to the analytical school.

---

38. Alfred J. Ayer, *Language, Truth and Logic*, 2d ed. (New York: Dover, 1936), 41.

OBJECTIONS TO LINGUISTIC ANALYSIS

RUTH: But you're saying that if something can't be verified it's not worth talking about.

PROFESSOR: Can't be verified at least *in principle*.

RUTH: As the Coke machine can, at least in principle?

PROFESSOR: Exactly.

RUTH: But that would make silly many of the things that people have always taken seriously.

PROFESSOR: Like what?

RUTH: Like "Democracy is the best form of government," for example. Or "Honesty is the best policy" or "It's better to give than to receive."

PROFESSOR: As well as "Man is the noblest work of God," "Admission of ignorance is the beginning of wisdom," "The unexamined life is not worth living," and all the rest. Yes, I couldn't agree more; they're meaningless statements in the sense that they're neither true nor false.

RUTH: But people still make those statements.

PROFESSOR: Of course they do.

RUTH: Then how can you deny their validity?

PROFESSOR: Because there's no way they can be verified empirically, and they're certainly not linguistically self-evident.

RUTH: But are those the only ways of measuring truth and knowledge?

PROFESSOR: The only ones we have now.

RUTH: But that doesn't mean they're necessarily the only ones.

PROFESSOR: No, not necessarily.

RUTH: Then isn't your belief based on an assumption? And isn't the assumption something that itself defies the empirical method? How would you ever verify the statement "True statements must be either linguistically self-evident or empirically verifiable"?

Ruth has not only questioned the analytical definition of a meaningful utterance but she has also accused the professor of assuming the very thing he must prove: that with respect to knowledge and truth, only analytic and synthetic statements are meaningful. Critics claim that analysts are more deductive than they themselves think, that they argue this way:

All knowledge is either analytic or synthetic.

Religious, ethical, and aesthetic statements are neither analytic nor synthetic.

Therefore, religious, ethical, and aesthetic statements are not knowledge.

But, say critics, the first statement is an assumption; it can never be proved. Perhaps utterances other than analytic and synthetic ones may transmit knowledge and truth. In effect, they charge the logical positivists with assuming that the first statement is analytic.

PROFESSOR: You're saying that my assumption is as meaningless as your statement that reality is nonmatter?

RUTH: That's right, because there's no way you can prove your assumption.

PROFESSOR: But it's necessary to start somewhere.

RUTH: Why? Can you prove it's necessary to start somewhere? How would you verify that claim? It seems to me, professor, that you're a victim of your own classification.

PROFESSOR: You mean that by reducing knowledge to what's linguistically self-evident or empirically verifiable, I haven't allowed for other possibilities?

RUTH: Not only that. You've defined other possibilities right out of existence. . . . But you have convinced me of one thing.

PROFESSOR: What's that?

RUTH: That arguing about what's real isn't so silly after all. It's not as silly as pretending the problem doesn't even exist. True, believing the way you do, you have a lot less frustration. By simply eliminating the problems, you don't have to deal with them. But isn't that really playing ostrich? Aren't the problems still there? Don't people still think about them? Even *you* devise an answer to them. If the questions don't exist, then what are your answers answering? And in answering them, haven't you yourself taken a position on a question that you say can only lead to meaningless answers?

Ruth's criticism implies what is for many one of the most disappointing aspects of some analysts: their attempt to reduce the idea of a person to sense data or to behavior. This seems to oversimplify and distort human experience by disregarding whatever lies beyond the language of science, mathematics, or formal logic. Many contemporary analysts are noticing this inadequacy, recognizing as legitimate not just one or two but many modes of meaning. Ultimately they may agree with their critics, who defend the philosopher's right and need to discuss questions not only of language, but of metaphysics, morality, religion, politics, and education as well. Certainly any description of human nature and of self that ignores these aspects of human experience seems incomplete.

QUESTIONS

1. In what sense do the logical positivists apply the adjective *meaningless* to nonsensical statements? Can something be intellectually meaningless but emotionally meaningful? Can you give an example?

2. What is your reaction to the following evaluation by analyst Alfred J. Ayer?

> It is impossible to find a criterion for determining the validity of ethical judgment . . . because they [ethical judgments] have no objective validity whatsoever. If a sentence makes no statement at all, there is obviously no sense in asking whether what it says is true or false. . . . They are pure expressions of feeling . . . unverifiable for the same reason as a cry of pain or a word of command is unverifiable—because they do not express genuine propositions.[39]

3. Which of the following statements would a logical positivist consider meaningful? Meaningless?
a. She wore a blue dress.

b. Her blue dress was green.
c. At the bottom of the ocean there's a shiny new penny lying in the belly of a dead carp.
d. The zite dwart oilated twarily near an ach grul.
e. The action in the preceding sentence takes place near an ach grul.
f. Tooth fairies never appear to bad children.
g. The good go to heaven, the bad to hell.
h. Killing orphans without reason is an evil thing to do.
i. Oxygen is necessary for combustion.
j. Love makes the world go 'round.

4. How valid do you consider Ruth's criticism that the professor's definition of what is meaningful makes a sham of the things that we take seriously?

5. Why is the professor's defense that "it's necessary to start somewhere" less convincing coming from an analyst than it would be coming from an idealist?

6. Ruth charges that the professor's position is inconsistent and self-contradictory. Why does she say this? Do you agree?

7. What would you say is the primary contribution of linguistic analysis to philosophy?

CHAPTER SUMMARY AND CONCLUSIONS

We opened this chapter by noting that what we ultimately consider real reflects and influences how we see ourselves. Questions of reality have been an abiding concern of philosophers. Such questions fall in the realm of metaphysics. We discussed a number of metaphysical views, including materialism, idealism, pragmatism, phenomenology, existentialism, and linguistic analysis. We suggested that different thinkers sometimes share certain views. However, fundamental differences separate the views sketched.

Despite the diversity of metaphysical views, many metaphysicians agree on some important issues. These points of agreement suggest insights into the self.

First, some metaphysicians agree that something exists outside the individual self. Even the subjective idealism of Berkeley does not deny the

---

39. Ibid., 107–109.

physical world, only its independence from mind. Despite Sartre's stress on self and Husserl's emphasis on consciousness, these thinkers recognize the distinction between things that lack consciousness, such as chairs, trees, and books, and those that do not, such as humans. We should quickly add, however, that many phenomenologists deplore such a dichotomy. Nonetheless, although the self may be insular, in that it is bound by the sea of its experiences, there are other human "islands," all joined by the similarity of their conditions and circumstances.

Second, some metaphysicians accept the senses and reason as primary sources of knowledge, as the tools by which the self comes to know things. True, some metaphysicians give reason a primacy that others do not; others emphasize the importance of experience. But these are differences of degree, not of substance. Many agree that by using both reason and senses, we are most likely to know ourselves and our world. At the same time, some pragmatists, existentialists, phenomenologists, and even analysts would not agree, arguing that senses and reason are products of particular conceptual frames, such as empiricism or rationalism.

Finally, various metaphysicians agree that there is an order or meaning in things that the senses and reason can discover. True, materialism may hold that the order is strictly mechanistic; idealism, that it is spiritual or even supernatural; existentialism and phenomenology, that it is being or the purpose that each of us imposes on experience; and analytical philosophy, that it is the symbolic form in which we express things. But some members within each school hold that there is some order. Most important, each of us is part of that order, whatever its nature. To know the self is at least partially to know that order and how we fit into it.

At the same time, there are fundamental differences among these metaphysical outlooks that reflect and reinforce different views of human nature and of self. For the materialist, we are part of the matter that composes the universe and are subject to the same laws. As a result, the self is the product of its experiences, the sum total of everything that has ever happened to it. There is little point in

speaking of individual responsibility or personal will, for we cannot help doing what we do. When we speak of mind, we really mean brain; when we refer to mental states, we are really talking about brain states. The purpose of any life is to understand how the parts of the universe, including the self, fit together and work. With such knowledge we can control our environment to some degree and perhaps improve the human condition.

Many linguistic analysts would add that the individual who tries to find personal meaning in religion, art, or politics or in seeking what is morally good wastes time on basically meaningless pursuits. We are most likely to understand ourselves and the world by clarifying the linguistic symbols we use to speak about these things.

For many idealists, in contrast, the individual is part of cosmic mind, spirit, idea, or perhaps life force. In this sense, individuals are alike. But each finds a self-identity in personal understanding. Only the individual can be aware of his or her own experiences. In the last analysis, it is this personal awareness, these ideas, that make each of us unique. The purpose of each life is to understand the order at work in the universe. This order is not matter but pure idea; for some it is a divine dimension, God. In understanding this cosmic order or plan, we understand our position in it and thus the self.

The pragmatist views the self as neither primarily matter nor primarily idea. Since pragmatists avoid absolutes, they choose to see the self as consisting of many dimensions, including material and ideal. The self is a complex entity consisting of experiences, which include thoughts, feelings, sensations, concepts, attitudes, and goals. Although we are tremendously influenced by environment, we can and do play a formative role in determining the nature of our experiences. Using intelligence and reason, the individual can exercise control over nature. But we shall not find personal meaning and purpose in the cosmos, because it possesses none. For personal meaning we must turn to the consequences of our actions, judging them according to the results they produce.

Existentialism shares pragmatism's skepticism of absolutistic doctrines. But more than any of the other outlooks, it stresses personal freedom. The self is essentially something in the making that is not finished until the individual dies. The self is whatever we choose to make it. We are ultimately free to think, choose, and act however we wish. Such freedom without guidelines is frightening, often leading to uncertainty, anxiety, and despair. But this, say the existentialists, is the human condition. For many phenomenologists, what we are is *that* we are. The fundamental self is not its characteristics, properties, or the other objective qualities, but being. The self is not our idea of what we are but the immediate concrete feeling of ourselves. We move furthest from a knowledge of the self when we separate self from the rest of reality, as we do when we view it as some object to be studied, quantified, and known. We are closest to the self when we strip from consciousness the experiences that occupy it. Then we realize that the self is what precedes its experiences—that is, pure being. Buddhist thinking generally agrees.

So, although members of different metaphysical schools share some beliefs, they vary in their approach to the issue of self. This variation may leave us affirming or denying the self, and viewing it as essentially rational, divine, mechanical, existential, or nonexistent. These views have dramatically different impacts on the self and its place in the world.

Hobbes and Berkeley

We have suggested throughout this chapter that people's metaphysical views influence their views on human nature. Two seventeenth-century philosophers—Thomas Hobbes and George Berkeley—illustrate the profound impact a metaphysical view can have on one's view of human nature.

Hobbes, as we briefly mentioned earlier, proposed the metaphysical view that everything in the universe is material. This metaphysical view then led him to propose a materialistic view of human nature. Hobbes believed that humans are, in effect, complicated machines. Berkeley, on the other hand, advanced the metaphysical claim that everything in the universe is spiritual or nonmaterial. This claim then led him to hold a thoroughly spiritualistic view of human nature: To be human is to be a kind of spirit.

Examining the views of Hobbes and Berkeley will help us see in some detail how metaphysics is related to the positions we take on other philosophical issues, in particular on the issue of human nature. It will become clear, also, how metaphysics can influence our view of God and of society.

HOBBES

Thomas Hobbes was a thoroughgoing materialist: He held that only material objects exist. In this respect he differed considerably from a contemporary of his, René Descartes (whom we showcased in the last chapter). Descartes carried over from medieval philosophers like Aquinas the view that reality consists of both material and immaterial (or "spiritual") entities. Hobbes rejected this dualistic view. The recent scientific discoveries in astronomy of Copernicus, Kepler, and Galileo, he reasoned, had all been based on the observation of moving bodies. Influenced by their approach to reality, Hobbes came to think that perhaps all reality could be explained in terms of the motions of bodies in space.

Born prematurely in 1588 when his mother, overcome with fear at the approach of the invading Spanish navy, went into early labor, Hobbes throughout his youth had a melancholy personality that earned him the nickname of "the Crow." The son of a clergyman, Hobbes was sent to study at Oxford at the age of fourteen, where, he tells us, he learned to hate philosophy. He apparently learned enough, however, so that when he graduated in 1608, he was hired by the wealthy and aristocratic Cavendish family as a tutor for their sons. He later remarked that the job left him more than enough time to read and study while his young charges were "making visits" in town. Traveling with the Cavendish family gave Hobbes the opportunity to see much of Europe and to become acquainted with the great thinkers of the period, especially the Italian astronomer Galileo, who at this time was busily tracing the motions of the heavenly bodies with the aid of geometry. At about the age of forty, probably under Galileo's influence, Hobbes came to the conclusion that everything in the universe could be explained in terms of the motions of material bodies and that geometry could provide the basic laws of their motions. He attempted to work out the details of this philosophy in a remarkable series of writings that included his masterpiece, *Leviathan*, and a trilogy bearing the titles *De Corpore (On Material Bodies)*, *De Homine (On Man)*, and *De Cive (On the Citizen)*. Hobbes's final years were relatively happy. He died in 1679, famous for his materialistic philosophy and the political theories that grew out of it.

Hobbes was unequivocal in stating his pivotal claim that matter is all there is in the universe. As he put it: "The Universe, that is the whole mass of things that are, is corporeal, that is to say body; and has the dimensions of magnitude, namely,

Thomas Hobbes: "The Universe is corporeal, that is to say, body, . . . and that which is not body is no part of the Universe. And because the Universe is all, that which is no part of it is nothing, and, consequently, nowhere."

length, breadth, and depth. Also every part of body is likewise body, and has the like dimensions. And, consequently, every part of the Universe is body, and that which is not body is no part of the Universe. And because the Universe is all, that which is no part of it is nothing, and, consequently, nowhere."[40] (Hobbes's old English spelling has been modernized in this and following quotes.)

In Hobbes's view the characteristics and activities of all objects, including human beings, can be explained in purely mechanical terms similar to the moving parts of a machine. "For seeing life is but a motion of limbs, the beginning whereof is in some principal part within; why may we not say, that all *automata* (engines that move themselves by springs and wheels as does a watch) have an

---

40. Thomas Hobbes, *Hobbes's Leviathan* (Oxford: The Clarendon Press, 1909), pt. 4, ch. 46, p. 524.

artificial life? For what is the *heart*, but a *spring*; and the *nerves*, but so many *strings*; and the *joints*, but so many *wheels*, giving motion to the whole body, such as was intended by the artificer?"[41]

Hobbes attempted to apply this mechanism to explain the mental activities of human beings. Many philosophers, Descartes in particular, believed the mental activities of perceiving, thinking, and willing to be evidence that human minds are spiritual or nonmaterial. Mental activities (thinking) and mental contents (thoughts) seem to have no physical characteristics (that is, they have no color, size, or position and seem to be nonbodily). Hobbes was particularly concerned with showing that even the activities of the mind could be entirely explained in terms of the motions of material bodies. He begins this task by first arguing that all of our thoughts originate in our sensations (or, as he writes, in "sense"). And sensations, he claims, are nothing more than motions in us that are caused by external objects. These motions in us travel through our nerves to our brains.

> Concerning the thoughts of man, I will consider them first singly, and afterwards in train or dependence upon one another. . . .
>
> The origin of them all, is that which we call SENSE [sensation], for there is no conception in a man's mind, which has not at first, totally, or by parts, been begotten upon the organs of sense. . . .
>
> The cause of sense is the external body, or object, which presses the organ proper to each sense . . . , which pressure, by the mediation of the nerves, and other strings and membranes of the body, continues inwards to the brain and heart, causes there a resistance, or counter-pressure, or endeavor [movement] of the heart . . . , which endeavor [movement], because [it is] *out-ward*, seems [to us] to be some matter without. And this *seeming* or *fancy*, is that which men call *sense*. [Sense] consists, as to the eye in *light*, or *color* . . . ; to the ear, in a *sound*; to the nostril, in an *odor*; to the tongue . . . , in a *savor*; and to the rest of the body, in *heat, cold, hardness, softness*, and such other qualities as we discern by *feeling*.

> All [these] qualities, . . . are, in the object that causes them, but so many . . . motions of the matter, by which it presses our organs. Neither in us, that are pressed, are they anything else, but . . . motions; for motion produces nothing but motion. . . . [Just] as pressing, rubbing, or striking the eye makes us fancy a light, and pressing the ear produces a din, so do the bodies we see, or hear, produce the same [sensations] by their . . .action.[42]

Once the motion created in our senses has traveled to the brain, the brain retains this motion, much like water continues moving after the wind stops. This "decaying" motion in our brain is the residual image that we retain in our memory. Thus, a memory of an object we perceive is nothing more than the residual motion the object leaves impressed on our brain.

> When a body is once in motion, it moves, unless something else hinders it, eternally; and whatever hinders it, cannot in an instant, but [only] in time, and by degrees, quite extinguish it. And as we see in the water, though the wind cease, the waves [continue] . . . rolling for a long time after, so also it happens in that motion which is made in the internal parts of man. . . .
>
> This decaying sense, when we would express the thing itself, . . . we call *imagination*. . . . But when we would express the decay, and signify that the sense is fading, old, and past, it is called *memory*. So that imagination and memory are but one thing.[43]

But what does all of this have to do with thinking? Hobbes held that when we are thinking, we are merely linking together the decaying images (or motions) that we have retained in our memory. Our thinking activities are thus nothing more than a sequence of motions linked together, usually as they were linked together when we first experienced them as sensations. Sometimes our thinking is "unguided," as when we daydream, and sometimes it is "regulated," as when we are trying to solve some problem.

> By *consequence* or TRAIN of thoughts, I under-

---

41. Thomas Hobbes, "Introduction," in *Leviathan*, 8.

42. Hobbes, *Leviathan*, pt. 1, ch. 1, p. 12.
43. Ibid., pt. 1, ch. 2, pp. 13–14.

stand that succession of one thought to another, which is called, to distinguish it from discourse in words, *mental discourse*.

When a man thinks on anything whatsoever, his next thought after is not altogether . . . casual. . . . The reason . . . is this. All fancies [images] are motions within us, relics of those made in the sense. And those motions that immediately succeeded one another in the sense, continue also together after sense. . . .

This train of thoughts, or mental discourse, is of two sorts. The first is *unguided, without design*, and inconstant, wherein there is not passionate thought, to govern and direct those that follow to itself, [such] as the end and scope of some desire, or other passion, in which case the thoughts are said to wander and seem impertinent one to another, as in a dream. . . .

The second is more constant, as being *regulated* by some desire and design. . . . From desire arises the thought of some means we have seen produce the like of that which we aim at; and from the thought of that, the thought of means to that mean; and so continually, till we come to some beginning within our own power. . . . The train of regulated thoughts is of two kinds: one, when of an effect imagined we seek the causes, or means that produce it. . . . The other is, when imagining anything whatsoever, we seek all the possible effects that can by it be produced.[44]

But "trains of thoughts" are not the only things produced by the motions that begin in our senses and that end in the imaginations of our brains. The motions of our imaginations also produce motions in our organs of appetite (which Hobbes thought were located mainly in the heart), and these are called "desires." The motions called desires, in turn, are what lead us to engage in "voluntary actions."

There be in animals, two sorts of *motions* peculiar to them. One [is] called *vital* . . . such as the *course* of the *blood*, the *pulse*, the *breathing*, the *concoction, nutrition, excretion, etc.* . . . . The other is . . . *voluntary motion*, as to *go*, to *speak*, to *move* any of our limbs, in such manner as is first fancied in our minds. . . . And because *going, speaking*, and the like voluntary motions, depend always

upon a precedent thought . . . , it is evident that the imagination is the first internal beginning of all voluntary motion. . . . These small beginnings of motion, within the body of man, before they appear in walking, speaking, striking, and other visible actions, are commonly called ENDEAVOR.

This endeavor, when it is toward something which causes it, is called APPETITE, or DESIRE. . . . And when the endeavor is from something, it is generally called AVERSION. . . . That which men desire, they are also said to LOVE, and to HATE those things for which they have aversion. . . . But whatsoever is the object of any man's appetite or desire, that . . . he . . . calls *good*, and the object of his hate and aversion, *evil*. . . .

As, in sense, that which is really within us is, as I have said before, only motion, caused by the action of external objects. . . . So, when the action of the same object is continued from the eyes, ears, and other organs to the heart, the real effect there is nothing but motion or endeavor, which consists in appetite or aversion, to or from the object moving [us].

When in the mind of man, appetites, and aversions, hopes, and fears, concerning one and the same thing, arise alternately; and divers good and evil consequences of the doing, or omitting the thing propounded come successively into our thoughts; so that sometimes we have an appetite to it; sometimes an aversion from it; sometimes hope to be able to do it; sometimes despair, or fear to attempt it; the whole sum of desires, aversions, hopes and fears continued till the thing be either done, or thought impossible, is that we call DELIBERATION. . . .

In *deliberation*, the last appetite, or aversion, immediately adhering to the action, or to the omission thereof, is what we call the WILL. . . . *Will*, therefore, is *the last appetite in deliberating*.[45]

Thus, Hobbes concluded, not only can a materialist philosophy fully account for all our obviously physical characteristics but it can also account for all of those inner "mental" activities that other philosophers take as evidence of a "spiritual" or nonmaterial mind: sensing, remembering, thinking, desiring, loving, hating, and willing. These mental activities do not require us to say that in

44. Ibid., pt. 1, ch. 3, pp. 18–20.

45. Ibid., pt. 1, ch. 6, pp. 39, 41, 46, 47.

addition to the material objects in the world, there also exists some kind of nonmaterial reality. There is no such thing as a nonmaterial reality: Everything consists of matter and its motions.

Hobbes felt that his materialistic philosophy also provided the foundations for a social philosophy. By examining the basic material characteristics of human individuals, he felt, he could explain why our societies are structured as they are. Hobbes began by maintaining that the central desires that affect the relations between individuals inevitably lead them to quarrel with each other.

> So that in the nature of man, we find three principal causes of quarrel. First, competition; secondly, diffidence; thirdly, glory.
>
> The first makes men invade for gain; the second, for safety; and the third, for reputation. The first use violence, to make themselves masters of other men's persons, wives, children, and cattle; the second, to defend them; the third, for trifles, as a word, a smile, a different opinion, and any other sign of undervalue, either direct in their persons, or by reflection in their kindred, their friends, their nation, their profession, or their name.[46]

Because of these antagonistic drives, individuals would inevitably strive "to destroy or subdue one another" if it were not for the restraints that the "common power" of government is able to impose on them. If men were in a "state of nature," that is, if they were in the situation they were in before there was any government to restrain them from harming each other, they would be constantly at war with each other and life would be miserable.

> Hereby it is manifest, that during the time men live without a common power to keep them all in awe, they are in that condition which is called war, and such a war as is of every man against every man. . . . In such condition, there is no place for industry, because the fruit thereof is uncertain: and consequently no culture of the earth; no navigation, nor use of the commodities that may be imported by sea; no commodious building; no instruments of moving, and remov-

ing, such things as require much force; no knowledge of the face of the earth; no account of time; no arts; no letters; no society; and which is worst of all, continual fear, and danger of violent death; and the life of man, solitary, poor, nasty, brutish, and short.[47]

In order to escape the brutal conditions of the state of nature in which their passions continually push them, men at last decide to form a government (or, as Hobbes calls it, a "Leviathan"). The reason why men form governments, then, is to set up a "common power" that possesses sufficient force to establish law and order among men and thereby put an end to their fighting. Men set up a government by entering into a "social contract" with each other. That is, they make an agreement (or "covenant") with each other to hand over all their power to a person or a group. That person or group then becomes their "sovereign" ruler and has the authority to use the power or force of the citizens themselves to enforce the law (which the sovereign makes) and to establish peace and order. Men thus emerge from the dreadful state of nature by becoming "subjects" and taking on the constraints of life in a civil society.

> The final cause, end, or design of men, who naturally love liberty and dominion over others, in the introduction of that restraint upon themselves, in which we see them live in commonwealths, is the foresight of their own preservation, and of a more contented life thereby; that is to say, of getting themselves out from that miserable condition of war, which is necessarily consequent, as has been shown, to the natural passions of men, when there is no visible power to keep them in awe, and tie them by fear of punishment to the performance of their covenants. . . .
>
> The only way to erect such a common power, as may be able to defend them from the invasion of foreigners, and the injuries of one another, and thereby to secure them in such sort, as that by their own industry, and by the fruits of the earth, they may nourish themselves and live contentedly; is, to confer all their power and strength upon one man, or upon one assembly of men, that may

---

46. Ibid., pt. 1, ch. 13, p. 96.

47. Ibid., pt. 1, ch. 13, p. 96.

reduce all their wills, by plurality of voices, unto one will: which is as much as to say, to appoint one man, or assembly of men, to bear their person; and every one to own, and acknowledge himself to be author of whatsoever he that so bears their person, shall act, or cause to be acted, in those things which concern the common peace and safety; and therein to submit their wills, every one to his will, and their judgments, to his judgment. This is more than consent or concord; it is real unity of them all, in one and the same person, made by covenant of every man with every man, in such manner, as if every man should say to every man, *I authorize and give up my right of governing myself, to this man, or to this assembly of men, on this condition, that you give up your right to him, and authorize all his actions in like manner.* . . . This is the generation of the great LEVIATHAN. . . . And he that carries this person, is called SOVEREIGN, and said to have *sovereign power*; and everyone besides, his SUBJECT.[48]

Thus, the materialist philosophy that Hobbes created also gave him, he felt, the basic concepts that allowed him to explain the formation of governments. Governments were simply the outcome of the motions we call "desires." Desires lead men to fight with each other (for their material possessions), and this results in a continual "war of all against all." A further desire or motion, the desire for peace, then leads men to form governments.

BERKELEY

George Berkeley is perhaps the most famous of all those idealist philosophers who hold that reality is primarily spiritual and not material. To some extent Berkeley was reacting to the philosophy of materialists like Hobbes whose views were becoming popular in the wake of the growing influence of the new sciences. Such materialist philosophies, Berkeley felt, left no room for God and thus were inimical to religion. What better way to combat atheism than to prove that materialism was false and that all reality is spiritual!

Berkeley was born in 1685 in Kilkenney, Ire-

George Berkeley: "All the choir of heaven and furniture of the earth, in a word all those bodies which compose the mighty frames of the world, have no substance without a mind; their being is to be perceived; consequently so long as they are not actually perceived by me or other created spirits, they must either have no existence at all or else exist in the mind of some eternal spirit."

land. As a teenager he was sent to Trinity College in Dublin where, in 1707, he graduated with a master's degree. Berkeley stayed on at Trinity College as a young teacher for six years. It was there, at the age of twenty-four, that he finished writing what was to become the classic exposition of an idealist philosophy, *A Treatise Concerning the Principles of Human Knowledge.* In 1713 Berkeley left Trinity College. He was by now an ordained Protestant minister, and in 1729 he and his recent bride traveled as missionaries to Newport, Rhode Island, where he planned to organize a college that would eventually be established in Bermuda. But funding for the college never materialized, and in 1731 he returned to England. In 1734 Berkeley became a bishop in the Church of England and was assigned to the diocese of Cloyne in Ireland. Sixteen years

48. Ibid., pt. 2, ch. 17, pp. 128, 131–132.

later, at the age of sixty-five, he retired to Oxford with his wife and family. There he died in 1753.

Berkeley held the view that all we know or perceive of the world around us are the sensations we have: the colors, sights, sounds, and tastes we experience. We commonly attribute these sensations to material objects outside us and say that in addition to the sensations we experience, there also exist material objects or "material substances" that cause these sensations in us. When our eyes see a small round patch of red, for example, we might infer that outside us there exists a material object that we call an apple and that light coming from this material object causes our eyes to have the sensation of red color. Berkeley, however, questioned this inference. He pointed out that we really have no reason to say that in addition to the sensations we experience within our minds, there *also* exists outside us (or, in his words, "without us") some kind of material objects. We do not even have any idea what these so-called material objects would be like since all we perceive are our sensations and these sensations are clearly not material objects since our sensations exist entirely in our minds (or, in Berkeley's words, "our spirits"). All that exists besides our minds or "spirits," Berkeley concluded, are the sensations we perceive in our minds and the mental images we voluntarily form in them. Berkeley used the term *ideas* to refer to the contents of our minds, including both the sensations we have and the mental images we form. Thus, for Berkeley, the world consists entirely of minds ("spirits") and ideas.

Berkeley summarized his view in the Latin slogan *esse est percipi*, which means "to exist is to be perceived": The only things that exist, besides minds, are the ideas perceived within minds. As he flamboyantly asserted, "All the Choir of Heaven and the furniture of earth, in a word all those bodies which compose the mighty frame of the world, have no substance without a mind."[49] Thus Berkeley was a complete idealist: He held the view that reality consists of nothing more than the ideas in our minds.

Berkeley's views are most clearly expounded in the short work he entitled A *Treatise Concerning the Principles of Human Knowledge*. He opens the treatise with a remark expressing what many newcomers to philosophy feel: that philosophy seems to create more "doubts and difficulties" than it seems to resolve.

> Philosophy being nothing else but the study of wisdom and truth, it may with reason be expected that those who have spent most time and pains in it should enjoy a greater calm and serenity of mind, a greater clearness and evidence of knowledge, and be less disturbed with doubts and difficulties than other men. Yet so it is, we see the illiterate bulk of mankind that walk the high road of plain common sense, and are governed by the dictates of nature, for the most part easy and undisturbed. To them nothing that is familiar appears unaccountable or difficult to comprehend. They complain not of any want of evidence in their sense, and are out of all danger of becoming skeptics. But no sooner do we depart from sense and instinct to follow the light of a superior principle, to reason, meditate, and reflect on the nature of things, but a thousand scruples spring up in our minds concerning those things which before we seemed fully to comprehend. Prejudices and errors of sense do from all parts discover themselves to our view; and, endeavoring to correct these by reason, we are insensibly drawn into uncouth paradoxes, difficulties, and inconsistencies, which multiply and grow upon us as we advance in speculation, till at length, having wandered through many intricate mazes, we find ourselves just where we were, or, which is worse, sit down in a forlorn skepticism.[50]

In order to resolve the "uncouth paradoxes, difficulties, and inconsistencies" that give philosophy a bad name, Berkeley undertakes to examine "the first principles of human knowledge," that is, the primary sources from which we draw all our knowledge. He begins by pointing out that if we look into our minds, we will see that everything we

49. George Berkeley, A *Treatise Concerning the Principles of Human Knowledge*, vol. 1 of *The Works of George Berkeley*, 3 vols., ed. George Sampson (London: George Bell and Sons, 1897), pt. 1, sec. 6, pp. 153–252.

50. Ibid., "Introduction," para. 1, p. 161.

know consists either of sensations ("ideas imprinted on the senses or perceived by attending to the passions") or mental images ("ideas formed by help of memory and imagination"). Consequently, each object we know in the world around us (such as an "apple, a stone, a tree, a book and the like") is really nothing more than a collection of ideas (sensations of color, touch, smell, taste, or hearing). In addition to ideas, he notes, there are also "active beings" or "minds." In fact, ideas can exist only in minds. Since all objects consist of ideas and since ideas can exist only in the mind, it follows that the objects in the world exist only in the mind! Berkeley argues for this startling conclusion in the following passages:

It is evident to anyone who takes a survey of the *objects* of human knowledge that they are either ideas actually imprinted on the senses, or else such as are perceived by attending to the passions and operations of the mind, or lastly, ideas formed by help of memory and imagination—either compounding, dividing, or barely representing those originally perceived in the aforesaid ways. By sight I have the ideas of light and colors, with their several degrees and variations. By touch I perceive, for example, hard and soft, heat and cold, motion and resistance, and of all these more and less either as to quantity or degree. Smelling furnishes me with odors, the palate with tastes, and hearing conveys sounds to the mind in all their variety of tone and composition. As several of these are observed to accompany each other, they come to be marked by one name, and so to be reputed as one thing. Thus, for example, a certain color, taste, smell, figure, and consistency having been observed to go together are accounted one distinct thing signified by the name "apple"; other collections of ideas constitute a stone, a tree, a book, and the like sensible things—which as they are pleasing or disagreeable excite the passions of love, hatred, joy, grief, and so forth.

But, besides all that endless variety of ideas or objects of knowledge, there is likewise something which knows or perceives them and exercises divers operations, as willing, imagining, remembering, about them. This perceiving, active being is what I call "mind," "spirit," "soul," or "myself." By which words I do not denote any one of my ideas, but a thing entirely distinct from them,

wherein they exist or, which is the same thing, whereby they are perceived—for the existence of an idea consists in being perceived.

That neither our thoughts, nor passions, nor ideas formed by the imagination exist without the mind is what everybody will allow. And it seems no less evident that the various sensations or ideas imprinted on the sense, however blended or combined together (that is, whatever objects they compose), cannot exist otherwise than in a mind perceiving them.—I think an intuitive knowledge may be obtained of this by anyone that shall attend to what is meant by the term "exist" when applied to sensible things. The table I write on I say exists, that is, I see and feel it; and if I were out of my study I should say it existed—meaning thereby that if I was in my study I might perceive it, or that some other spirit actually does perceive it. There was an odor, that is, it was smelled; there was a sound, that is to say, it was heard; a color or figure, and it was perceived by sight or touch. This is all that I can understand by these and the like expressions. For as to what is said of the absolute existence of unthinking things without any relation to their being perceived, that seems perfectly unintelligible. Their *esse* is *percipi*, nor is it possible they should have any existence out of the minds or thinking things which perceive them.

It is indeed an opinion strangely prevailing amongst men that houses, mountains, rivers, and, in a word, all sensible objects have an existence, natural or real, distinct from their being perceived by the understanding. But with how great an assurance and acquiescence soever this principle may be entertained in the world, yet whoever shall find in his heart to call it in question may, if I mistake not, perceive it to involve a manifest contradiction. For what are the forementioned objects but the things we perceive by sense? And what do we perceive besides our own ideas or sensations? And is it not plainly repugnant that any one of these, or any combination of them, should exist unperceived? . . .

But, say you, though the ideas themselves do not exist without the mind, yet there may be things like them, whereof they are copies or resemblances, which things exist without the mind in an unthinking [material] substance. I answer, an idea can be like nothing but an idea; a color or figure can be like nothing but another color or figure. If we look ever so little into our thoughts, we shall find it impossible for us to conceive a likeness except only between our ideas. Again, I ask whether those supposed originals or external things, of which our ideas are the pictures or representations, be themselves perceivable or not? If they are, then they are ideas and we have gained our point; but if you say they are not, I appeal to anyone whether it be sense to assert a color is like something which is invisible; hard or soft, like something which is intangible; and so of the rest. . . .

But, [suppose] it were possible that solid, figured, movable substances may exist without the mind, corresponding to the ideas we have of bodies, yet how is it possible for us to know this? Either we must know it by sense or by reason. As for our senses, by them we have the knowledge only of our sensations, ideas, or those things that are immediately perceived by sense, call them what you will; but they do not inform us that things exist without the mind, or unperceived, like to those which are perceived. This the materialists themselves acknowledge. It remains, therefore, that if we have any knowledge at all of external things, it must be by reason, inferring their existence from what is immediately perceived by sense. But what reason can induce us to believe the existence of bodies without the mind, from what we perceive, since the very patrons of matter themselves do not pretend there is any necessary connection betwixt them and our ideas? I say it is granted on all hands (and what happens in dreams, frenzies, and the like, puts it beyond dispute) that it is possible we might be affected with all the ideas we have now, though no bodies existed without resembling them. Hence it is evident the supposition of external bodies is not necessary for the producing of our ideas; since it is granted they are produced sometimes, and might possibly be produced always in the same order we see them in at present, without their concurrence. . . .

But, say you, surely there is nothing easier than to imagine trees, for instance, in a park, or books existing in a closet, and nobody by to perceive them. I answer you may so, there is no difficulty in it; but what is all this, I beseech you, more than framing in your mind certain ideas which you call books and trees, and at the same time omitting to frame the idea of anyone that may perceive them?

But do not you yourself perceive or think of them all the while? This therefore is nothing to the purpose; it only shows you have the power of imagining or forming ideas in your mind; but it does not show that you can conceive it possible the objects of your thought may exist without the mind. To make out this, it is necessary that you conceive them existing unconceived or unthought of, which is a manifest repugnancy. When we do our utmost to conceive the existence of external bodies, we are all the while only contemplating our own ideas. But the mind, taking no notice of itself, is deluded to think it can and does conceive bodies existing unthought of or without the mind, though at the same time they are apprehended by or exist in itself. A little attention will discover to anyone the truth and evidence of what is here said, and make it unnecessary to insist on any other proofs against the existence of *material substance*. [51]

Berkeley's views were naturally accused of leading to skepticism, the view that we cannot know anything about reality. For Berkeley's views are but a short step away from the view that since the ideas in our minds might be false and since all we know are the ideas in our minds, we can never know anything for sure about the real world. Berkeley, however, did not intend his "idealist" philosophy to encourage skepticism. On the contrary, he felt that "the grounds of Skepticism, Atheism and Irreligion" lay in *materialism*, the view that the only things that exist are material objects. Those who hold that only matter exists, he felt, were inevitably led to the view that God does not exist since God is a nonmaterial Spirit. The best way to combat atheism, then, was by proving that matter did not exist and that, on the contrary, the only existents are spirits and their ideas. Since spirits and ideas are the only reality, it is clear that in knowing these we know all the reality there is. Thus, skepticism, like atheism, is false.

Berkeley, in fact, took great pains to show that God exists. In fact, God is a crucial part of Berkeley's universe and plays an essential role as the source of the world we see displayed before our senses. If

51. Ibid., pt. 1, paras. 1–4, 8, 18, 23; pp. 179, 180–182, 186–187, 189.

we examine the ideas in our minds, he argues, we will see that some of them require the existence of another "spirit" to produce them, and this is God. It is God who produces in us the sensations we have of what we perceive as reality and who ensures that we perceive an orderly reality in which we can plan our lives and look easily toward the future. Berkeley concludes that the "surprising magnificence, beauty, and perfection" of the orderly display that God creates in our minds and that we call the world should fill us with admiration.

> I find I can excite [some] ideas in my mind at pleasure, and vary and shift the scene as oft as I think fit. It is no more than willing, and straightway this or that idea arises in my fancy [imagination]; and by the same power it is obliterated and makes way for another. . . .
>
> But whatever power I may have over my own thoughts, I find the ideas actually perceived by sense have not a like dependence on my will. When in broad daylight I open my eyes, it is not in my power to choose whether I shall see or no, or to determine what particular objects shall present themselves to my view; and so likewise as to the hearing and other senses; the ideas imprinted on them are not creatures of my will. There is therefore some *other* will or spirit that produces them.
>
> The ideas of sense are more strong, lively, and distinct than those of the imagination; they have likewise a steadiness, order, and coherence, and are not excited at random, as those which are the effects of human wills often are, but in a regular train or series, the admirable connection whereof sufficiently testifies to the wisdom and benevolence of its Author. Now the set rules or established methods wherein the mind we depend on excites in us the ideas of sense are called "the laws of nature"; and these we learn by experience which teaches us that such and such ideas are attended with such and such other ideas in the ordinary course of things.
>
> This gives us a sort of foresight which enables us to regulate our actions for the benefit of life. And without this we should be eternally at a loss; we could not know how to act on anything that might procure us the least pleasure or remove the least pain of sense. That food nourishes, sleep refreshes, and fire warms us; that to sow in the seedtime is

the way to reap in the harvest; and in general that to obtain such or such ends, such or such means are conducive—all this we know, not by discovering any necessary connection between our ideas, but only by the observation of the settled laws of nature, without which we should be all in uncertainty and confusion, and a grown man no more know how to manage himself in the affairs of life than an infant just born. . . .

> But if we attentively consider the constant regularity, order, and concatenation of natural things, the surprising magnificence, beauty, and perfection of the larger, and the exquisite contrivance of the smaller parts of the creation, together with the exact harmony and correspondence of the whole, but above all the never-enough-admired laws of pain and pleasure, and the instincts or natural inclinations, appetites, and passions of animals; I say if we consider all these things, and at the same time attend to the meaning and import of the attributes: one, eternal, infinitely wise, good, and perfect, we shall clearly perceive that they belong to the aforesaid spirit, "who works all in all," and "by whom all things consist." . . .
>
> It is therefore plain that nothing can be more evident to anyone that is capable of the least reflection than the existence of God, or a spirit who is intimately present to our minds, producing in them all that variety of ideas or sensations which continually affect us, on whom we have an absolute and entire dependence, in short "in whom we live, and move, and have our being." That the discovery of this great truth, which lies so near and obvious to the mind, should be attained to by the reason of so very few, is a sad instance of the stupidity and inattention of men who, though they are surrounded with such clear manifestations of the Deity, are yet so little affected by them that they seem, as it were, blinded with excess of light.[52]

Berkeley's idealist philosophy, then, provided him with what he thought was an irrefutable proof of the existence of spiritual reality, including God, and of the nonexistence of the material world on which Hobbes and other materialists insisted.

---

52. Ibid., paras. 28, 29–31, 146, 149, pp. 191–192, 247–248.

QUESTIONS

1. Carl Sagan has said that "Each human being is a superbly constructed astonishingly compact, self-ambulatory computer." In what respects is this similar to Hobbes's view? In what respects does it differ?

2. The contemporary philosopher J. J. C. Smart writes, "By 'materialism' I mean the theory that there is nothing in the world over and above those entities which are postulated by physics. Thus I do not hold materialism to be wedded to the billiard-ball physics of the nineteenth century. The less visualizable particles of modern physics count as matter [for me]." In what respects is Smart's materialism similar to Hobbes's? In what respects does it differ? Does Smart's materialism have any philosophical implications that are radically different from Hobbes's?

3. Hobbes claims that you are nothing more than your physical body (or your brain). If this is true, then *you* are exactly the same as *your body* (or your brain), so whatever is true of *you* must be true of *your body*. But consider the following objection to Hobbes: "Although *you* can be morally blameworthy or praiseworthy, can we say that *your body* or *your brain* is morally blameworthy or praiseworthy? Although *you* can have wishes (for example, to do math) or thoughts (for example, about philosophy), does it make sense to say that *your body* or *your brain* has these wishes or thoughts? Although *you* can love God, isn't it absurd to say *your body* or *your brain* loves God? Although it makes sense to say that *you* have a body, does it make sense to say that *your body* has a body?" Evaluate these criticisms.

4. Do you think Hobbes's description of the quarrelsomeness of human nature is an accurate description of your own self? Of others? Is Hobbes correct in claiming that without the restraints of government, you would involve yourself in a continual "war against every man" and that your life would be "solitary, poor, nasty, brutish and short"?

5. Must a materialist philosophy like Hobbes's take a pessimistic view of human beings? Contrast Hobbes's views with those of B. F. Skinner.

6. Do you agree with Berkeley's criticism that philosophy inevitably draws us "into uncouth paradoxes, difficulties, and inconsistencies, which multiply and grow as we advance, till, at length, . . . we find ourselves just as we were, or, which is worse, sit down in a forlorn skepticism"? What assumptions about the purpose and nature of philosophy does Berkeley make? How does this compare to Plato's conception of philosophy?

7. Do you think this is an adequate summary of Berkeley's main argument: "All the objects we perceive are only ideas; ideas exist only in minds; therefore all the objects we perceive exist only in minds"? Do you think any parts of this argument are false? Explain.

8. A critic once said something like the following as he kicked a rock: "There! I thus refute Berkeley!" Would this show that Berkeley's idealism is false? Why?

9. To what extent do the following two verses (of unknown authorship) correctly express the role God plays in Berkeley's philosophy:

> I have always thought that God
> Must find it exceedingly odd
> To think that his tree
> Won't continue to be
> When there's no one about in the quad.

> Dear Sir:
> Your astonishment's odd.
> For I am always about in the quad.
> And so my tree will continue to be,
> Since observed by
>   Yours faithfully,
>   God.

10. Berkeley's idealism is very different from the way we usually think of the world, but does it make any *practical* difference? Would anything be different for you if Berkeley is correct? Should you do anything differently?

HERMANN HESSE

Siddhartha

There is perhaps no more readable a work that contains the general worldview of Indian religion than Siddhartha, *the story of Siddhartha Gautama, penned by the German poet and novelist Hermann Hesse (1877–1962). While strictly speaking not a Buddhist novel or a retelling of the Buddha's life,* Siddhartha *contains elements of both. In a style befitting the sublime simplicity of the outlook, Hesse portrays the young Siddhartha as a troubled, restless spirit, who abandons home, family, and caste for wealth, power, and pleasure. But as it turns out, such pursuits are part of Siddhartha's spiritual evolution, which ultimately finds him taken with the simple life of a ferryman, wherein he's able to learn the lessons of eternality that the river teaches to those who know how to listen.*

In the selection that follows, the old and wise Siddhartha is reunited with his boyhood friend, the monk Govinda. What transpires is not only a stirring portrayal of loving reunion, but a graphic account of an Eastern view of reality, with its emphasis on the interconnectedness, the oneness, of all things.

GOVINDA

Govinda once spent a rest period with some other monks in the pleasure grove which Kamala, the courtesan, had once presented to the followers of Gotama. He heard talk of an old ferryman who lived by the river, a day's journey away, and whom many considered to be a sage. When Govinda moved on, he chose the path to the ferry, eager to see this ferryman, for although he had lived his life according to the rule and was also regarded with respect by the younger monks for his age and modesty, there was still restlessness in his heart and his seeking was unsatisfied.

He arrived at the river and asked the old man to take him across. When they climbed out of the boat on the other side, he said to the old man: "You show much kindness to the monks and pilgrims; you have taken many of us across. Are you not also a seeker of the right path?"

There was a smile in Siddhartha's old eyes as he said: "Do you call yourself a seeker,

SOURCE: Herman Hesse, *Siddhartha*, trans. Hilda Rosner. Copyright 1951 by New Directions Publishing Corporation. Reprinted by permission.

O venerable one, you who are already advanced in years and wear the robe of Gotama's monks?"

"I am indeed old," said Govinda, "but I have never ceased seeking. I will never cease seeking. That seems to be my destiny. It seems to me that you also have sought. Will you talk to me a little about it, my friend?"

Siddhartha said: "What could I say to you that would be of value, except that perhaps you seek too much, that as a result of your seeking you cannot find."

"How is that?" asked Govinda.

"When someone is seeking," said Siddhartha, "it happens quite easily that he only sees the thing that he is seeking; that he is unable to find anything, unable to absorb anything, because he is only thinking of the thing he is seeking, because he has a goal, because he is obsessed with his goal. Seeking means: to have a goal; but finding means: to be free, to be receptive, to have no goal. You, O worthy one, are perhaps indeed a seeker, for in striving towards your goal, you do not see many things that are under your nose."

"I do not yet quite understand," said Govinda. "How do you mean?"

Siddhartha said: "Once, O worthy one, many years ago, you came to this river and found a man sleeping there. You sat beside him to guard him while he slept, but you did not recognize the sleeping man, Govinda."

Astonished and like one bewitched the monk gazed at the ferryman.

"Are you Siddhartha?" he asked in a timid voice. "I did not recognize you this time, too. I am very pleased to see you again, Siddhartha, very pleased. You have changed very much, my friend. And have you become a ferryman now?"

Siddhartha laughed warmly. "Yes, I have become a ferryman. Many people have to change a great deal and wear all sorts of clothes. I am one of those, my friend. You are very welcome, Govinda, and I invite you to stay the night in my hut."

Govinda stayed the night in the hut and slept in the bed that had once been Vasudeva's. He asked the friend of his youth many questions and Siddhartha had a great deal to tell him about his life.

When it was time for Govinda to depart the following morning, he said with some hesitation: "Before I go on my way, Siddhartha, I should like to ask you one more question. Have you a doctrine, belief or knowledge which you uphold, which helps you to live and do right?"

Siddhartha said: "You know, my friend, that even as a young man, when we lived with the ascetics in the forest, I came to distrust doctrines and teachers and to turn my back on them. I am still of the same turn of mind, although I have, since that time, had many teachers. A beautiful courtesan was my teacher for a long time, and a rich merchant and a dice player. On one occasion, one of the Buddha's wandering monks was my teacher. He halted in his pilgrimage to sit beside me when I fell asleep in the forest. I also learned something from him and I am grateful to him, very grateful. But most of all, I have learned from this river and from my predecessor, Vasudeva. He was a simple man; he was not a thinker, but he realized the essential as well as Gotama. He was a holy man, a saint."

Govinda said: "It seems to me, Siddhartha, that you still like to jest a little. I believe you and know that you have not followed any teacher, but have you not yourself, if not a doctrine, certain thoughts? Have you not discovered certain knowledge yourself that has helped you to live? It would give me great pleasure if you would tell me something about this."

Siddhartha said: "Yes, I have had thoughts and knowledge here and there. Sometimes, for an hour or for a day, I have become aware of knowledge, just as one feels life in one's heart. I have had many thoughts, but it would be difficult for me to tell you about them. But this is one thought that has impressed me, Govinda. Wisdom is not communicable. The wisdom which a wise man tries to communicate always sounds foolish."

"Are you jesting?" asked Govinda.

"No, I am telling you what I have discovered. Knowledge can be communicated, but not wisdom. One can find it, live it, be fortified by it, do wonders through it, but one cannot communicate and teach it. I suspected this when I was still a youth and it was this that drove me away from teachers. There is one thought I have had, Govinda, which you will again think is a jest or folly: that is, in every truth the opposite is equally true. For example, a truth can only be expressed and enveloped in words if it is one-sided. Everything that is thought and expressed in words is one-sided, only half the truth; it all lacks totality, completeness, unity. When the Illustrious Buddha taught about the world, he had to divide it into Sansara and Nirvana, into illusion and truth, into suffering and salvation. One cannot do otherwise, there is no other method for those who teach. But the world itself, being in and round us, is never one-sided. Never is a man or a deed wholly Sansara or wholly Nirvana; never is a man wholly a saint or a sinner. This only seems so because we suffer the illusion that time is something real. Time is not real, Govinda. I have realized this repeatedly. And if time is not real, then the dividing line that seems to lie between this world and eternity, between suffering and bliss, between good and evil, is also an illusion."

"How is that?" asked Govinda, puzzled.

"Listen, my friend! I am a sinner and you are a sinner, but someday the sinner will be Brahma again, will someday attain Nirvana, will someday become a Buddha. Now this 'someday' is illusion; it is only a comparison. The sinner is not on the way to a Buddha-like state; he is not evolving, although our thinking cannot conceive things otherwise. No, the potential Buddha already exists in the sinner; his future is already there. The potential hidden Buddha must be recognized in him, in you, in everybody. The world, Govinda, is not imperfect or slowly evolving along a long path to perfection. No, it is perfect at every moment; every sin already carries grace within it, all small children are potential old men, all sucklings have death within them, all dying people—eternal life. It is not possible for one person to see how far another is on the way; the Buddha exists in the robber and dice player; the robber exists in the Brahmin. During deep meditation it is possible to dispel time, to see simultaneously all the past, present and future, and then everything is good, everything is perfect, everything is Brahman. Therefore, it seems to me that everything that exists is good—death as well as life, sin as well as holiness, wisdom as well as folly. Everything is necessary, everything needs only my agreement, my assent, my loving understanding; then all is well with me and nothing can harm me. I learned through my body and soul that it was necessary for me to sin, that I needed lust, that I had to strive for property and experience nausea and the depths of despair in order to learn not to resist them, in order to learn to love the world, and no longer compare it with some kind of desired imaginary world, some imaginary vision of perfection, but to leave it as it is, to love it and be glad to belong to it. These, Govinda, are some of the thoughts that are in my mind."

Siddhartha bent down, lifted a stone from the ground and held it in his hand.

"This," he said, handling it, "is a stone, and within a certain length of time it will perhaps be soil and from the soil it will become plant, animal or man. Previously I should have said: This stone is just a stone; it has no value, it belongs to the world of Maya, but perhaps because within the cycle of change it can also become man and spirit, it is also of importance. That is what I should have thought. But now I think: This stone is stone; it is also animal, God and Buddha. I do not respect and love it because it was one thing and will become something else, but because it has already long been everything and always is everything. I love it just because it is a stone, because today and now it appears to me a stone. I see value and meaning in each one of its fine markings and cavities, in the yellow, in the grey, in the hardness and the sound of it when I knock it, in the dryness or dampness of its surface. There are stones that feel like oil or soap, that look like leaves or sand, and each one is different and worships Om in its own way; each one is Brahman. At the same time it is very much stone, oily or soapy, and that is just what pleases me and seems wonderful and worthy of worship. But I will say no more about it. Words do not express thoughts very well. They always become a little different immediately they are expressed, a little distorted, a little foolish. And yet it also pleases me and seems right that what is of value and wisdom to one man seems nonsense to another."

Govinda had listened in silence.

"Why did you tell me about the stone?" he asked hesitatingly after a pause.

"I did so unintentionally. But perhaps it illustrates that I just love the stone and the river and all these things that we see and from which we can learn. I can love a stone, Govinda, and a tree or a piece of bark. These are things and one can love things. But one cannot love words. Therefore teachings are of no use to me; they have no hardness, no softness, no colors, no corners, no smell, no taste—they have nothing but words. Perhaps that is what prevents you from finding peace, perhaps there are too many words, for even salvation and virtue. Sansara and Nirvana are only words, Govinda. Nirvana is not a thing; there is only the word Nirvana."

Govinda said: "Nirvana is not only a word, my friend; it is a thought."

Siddhartha continued: "It may be a thought, but I must confess, my friend, that I do not differentiate very much between thoughts and words. Quite frankly, I do not attach great importance to thoughts either. I attach more importance to things. For example, there was a man at this ferry who was my predecessor and teacher. He was a holy man who for many years believed only in the river and nothing else. He noticed that the river's voice spoke to him. He learned from it; it educated and taught him. The river seemed like a god to him and for many years he did not know that every wind, every cloud, every bird, every beetle is equally divine and knows and can teach just as well as the esteemed river. But when this holy man went off into the woods, he knew everything; he knew more than you and I, without teachers, without books, just because he believed in the river."

Govinda said: "But what you call thing, is it something real, something intrinsic? Is it not only the illusion of Maya, only image and appearance? Your stone, your tree, are they real?"

"This also does not trouble me much," said Siddhartha. "If they are illusion, then I also am illusion, and so they are always of the same nature as myself. It is that which makes them so lovable and venerable. That is why I can love them. And here is a doctrine at which you will laugh. It seems to me, Govinda, that love is the most important thing in the world. It may be important to great thinkers to examine the world, to explain and despise it. But I think it is only important to love the world, not to despise it, not for us to hate each other, but to be able to regard the world and ourselves and all beings with love, admiration and respect."

"I understand that," said Govinda, "but that is just what the Illustrious One called illusion. He preached benevolence, forbearance, sympathy, patience—but not love. He forbade us to bind ourselves to earthly love."

"I know that," said Siddhartha smiling radiantly, "I know that, Govinda, and here we find ourselves within the maze of meanings, within the conflict of words, for I will not deny that my words about love are in apparent contradiction to the teachings of Gotama. That is just why I distrust words so much, for I know that this contradiction is an illusion. I know that I am at one with Gotama. How, indeed, could he not know love, he who has recognized all humanity's vanity and transitoriness, yet loves humanity so much that he has devoted a long life solely to help and teach people? Also with this great teacher, the thing to me is of greater importance than the words; his deeds and life are more important to me than his talk, the gesture of his hand is more important to me than his opinions. Not in speech or thought do I regard him as a great man, but in his deeds and life."

The two old men were silent for a long time. Then as Govinda was preparing to go, he said: "I thank you, Siddhartha, for telling me something of your thoughts. Some of them are strange thoughts. I cannot grasp them all immediately. However, I thank you, and I wish you many peaceful days."

Inwardly, however, he thought: Siddhartha is a strange man and he expresses strange thoughts. His ideas seem crazy. How different do the Illustrious One's doctrines sound! They are clear, straightforward, comprehensible; they contain nothing strange, wild or laughable. But Siddhartha's hands and feet, his eyes, his brow, his breathing, his smile, his greeting, his gait affect me differently from his thoughts. Never, since the time our Illustrious Gotama passed into Nirvana, have I ever met a man with the exception of Siddhartha about whom I felt: This is a holy man! His ideas may be strange, his words may sound foolish, but his glance and his hand, his skin and his hair, all radiate a purity, peace, serenity, gentleness and saintliness which I have never seen in any man since the recent death of our illustrious teacher.

While Govinda was thinking these thoughts and there was conflict in his heart, he again bowed to Siddhartha, full of affection towards him. He bowed low before the quietly seated man.

"Siddhartha," he said, "we are now old men. We may never see each other again in this life. I can see, my dear friend, that you have found peace. I realize that I have not found it. Tell me one more word, esteemed friend, tell me something that I can conceive, something I can understand! Give me something to help me on my way, Siddhartha. My path is often hard and dark."

Siddhartha was silent and looked at him with his calm, peaceful smile. Govinda looked steadily in his face, with anxiety, with longing. Suffering, continual seeking and continual failure were written in his look.

Siddhartha saw it and smiled.

"Bend near to me!" he whispered in Govinda's ear. "Come, still nearer, quite close! Kiss me on the forehead, Govinda."

Although surprised, Govinda was compelled by a great love and presentiment to obey him; he leaned close to him and touched his forehead with his lips. As he did this, something wonderful happened to him. While he was still dwelling on Siddhartha's strange words, while he strove in vain to dispell the conception of time, to imagine Nirvana and Sansara as one, while even a certain contempt for his friend's words conflicted with a tremendous love and esteem for him, this happened to him.

He no longer saw the face of his friend Siddhartha. Instead he saw other faces, many faces, a long series, a continuous stream of faces—hundreds, thousands, which all came and disappeared and yet all seemed to be there at the same time, which all continually changed and renewed themselves and which were yet all Siddhartha. He saw the face of a fish, of a carp, with tremendous painfully opened mouth, a dying fish with dimmed eyes. He saw the face of a newly born child, red and full of wrinkles, ready to cry. He saw the face of a murderer, saw him plunge a knife into the body of a man; at the same moment he saw this criminal kneeling down, bound, and his head cut off by an executioner. He saw the naked bodies of men and women in the postures and transports of passionate love. He saw corpses stretched out, still, cold, empty. He saw the heads of animals, boars, crocodiles, elephants, oxen, birds. He saw Krishna and Agni. He saw all these forms and faces in a thousand relationships to each other, all helping each other, loving, hating and destroying each other and become newly born. Each one was mortal, a passionate, painful example of all that is transitory. Yet none of them died, they only changed, were always reborn, continually had a new face: only time stood between one face and another. And all these forms and faces rested, flowed, reproduced, swam past and merged into each other, and over them all there was continually something thin, unreal and yet existing, stretched across like thin glass or ice, like a transparent skin, shell, form or mask of water—and this mask was Siddhartha's smiling face which Govinda touched with his lips at that moment. And Govinda saw that this mask-like smile, this smile of unity over the flowing forms, this smile of simultaneousness over the thousands of births and deaths—this smile of Siddhartha—was exactly the same as the calm, delicate, impenetrable, perhaps gracious, perhaps mocking, wise, thousand-fold smile of Gotama, the Buddha, as he had perceived it with awe a hundred times. It was in such a manner, Govinda knew, that the Perfect One smiled.

No longer knowing whether time existed, whether this display had lasted a second or a hundred years, whether there was a Siddhartha, or a Gotama, a Self and others, wounded deeply by a divine arrow which gave him pleasure, deeply enchanted and exalted, Govinda stood yet a while bending over Siddhartha's peaceful face which he had just kissed, which had just been the stage of all present and future forms. His countenance was unchanged after the mirror of the thousand-fold forms had disappeared from the surface. He smiled peacefully and gently, perhaps very graciously, perhaps very mockingly, exactly as the Illustrious One had smiled.

Govinda bowed low. Incontrollable tears trickled down his old face. He was overwhelmed by a feeling of great love, of the most humble veneration. He bowed low, right down to the ground, in front of the man sitting there motionless, whose smile reminded him of everything that he had ever loved in his life, of everything that had ever been of value and holy in his life.

QUESTIONS

1. How would you characterize Siddhartha's theory of reality?

2. What, in Siddhartha's view, is the essential difference between knowledge and wisdom?

3. Contrast Siddhartha's view of reality with a materialistic outlook.

4. With which Western metaphysical outlook does Siddhartha's view have the most in common? Where do they differ?

5. Siddhartha insists that wisdom is not communicable. Yet he seems to transmit his wisdom to Govinda when Govinda kisses him on the forehead. Is this contradictory? Did Siddhartha have a specific mode of communication in mind when he said wisdom was not communicable?

SUGGESTIONS FOR FURTHER READING

Aune, Bruce. *Metaphysics: The Elements.* Minneapolis: University of Minnesota Press, 1985. A difficult but excellent discussion of the major issues in contemporary metaphysics.

Ayer, A. J. *Language, Truth and Logic.* 2d rev. ed. New York: Dover, 1946. In this challenging book, Ayer sets out the basic arguments of the logical positivists.

Coover, Robert. *The Universal Baseball Association, Inc., J. Henry Waugh, Prop.* New York: New American Library, 1968. In this highly metaphysical novel, the main character, with the help of a deck of playing cards, creates a world of baseball players who ultimately dismiss their creator.

Ewing, A. C. *Idealism: A Critical Survey.* 3d ed. New York: Humanities Press, 1961. A critical discussion of several idealist philosophies.

Husserl, Edmund. *Phenomenology and the Crisis of Philosophy.* Translated by Quentin Lauer. New York: Harper & Row, 1965. These two essays by the "father of phenomenology" present the framework and method of Husserlian phenomenology.

Krutch, Joseph Wood. *The Measure of Man: On Freedom, Human Values, Survival and the Modern Temper.* New York: Grosset & Dunlap, 1953. Krutch argues that the materialistic view of reality and humankind is fraudulent.

Ornstein, Robert E. *The Psychology of Consciousness.* San Francisco: W. H. Freeman, 1972. Psychologist Ornstein differentiates between the two spheres of the brain and demonstrates the left hemisphere's importance as a seat of knowing that is different from and complementary to the senses and reason.

Pears, D. *Ludwig Wittgenstein.* New York: Viking Press, 1970. This readable paperback explains the life and thought of Wittgenstein in a lively fashion.

Reck, A. *Speculative Philosophy.* Albuquerque: University of New Mexico Press, 1972. Reck discusses four kinds of metaphysical theories: realism, materialism, idealism, and process philosophy.

Smith, John E. *Purpose and Thought: The Meaning of Pragmatism.* London and New Haven: Hutchinson and Yale University Presses, 1978. Smith explains the basic ideas behind pragmatism.

Urban, W. M. *Beyond Realism and Idealism*. New York: Humanities Press, 1949. In this somewhat difficult book, Urban argues that idealism and realism are complementary approaches to reality and that elements of both must be accepted.

Urmson, J. O. *Berkeley*. Oxford: Oxford University Press, 1982. This is an easily readable introduction to the life and thought of Berkeley.

Warnock, Mary. *Existentialism*. Oxford: Oxford University Press, 1970. One of the foremost writers on the subject, Warnock presents a succinct and trenchant analysis of the main concepts of existentialism.

PART III Epistemology

One of the fundamental branches of philosophy deals with knowledge. It is termed *epistemology*, from the Greek *episteme*, meaning "knowledge." *Epistemology* literally means the study of knowledge.

Specifically, **epistemology** deals with the nature, basis, and extent of knowledge. Epistemological questions are basic to all other philosophical inquiries. Everything we claim to know, whether in science, history, or everyday life, would amount to little if we were unable to support our claims. Thus, neither a concept of human nature and self, a theory of the universe, nor an assertion of an ordinary event ("This lemon tastes sour" or "It is raining") escapes the need for justification. Epistemology presents us with the task of explaining how we know what we claim to know, how we can find out what we wish to know, and how we can judge someone else's claim to knowledge.

Epistemology usually addresses a variety of problems: the structure, reliability, extent and kinds of knowledge; truth; logic and language; and science and scientific knowledge. The next two chapters deal with two major epistemological areas: knowledge and truth.

CHAPTER 5

The Nature
of Knowledge

A man is but what he knows.

FRANCIS BACON

All I know is what I read in the papers.

WILL ROGERS

Introduction

Suppose a friend asked you for an example of something you think you know. You might reply, "I know that Washington was at Valley Forge."

"How do you know that?" the person then asks. Because you read it, you say. "Do you believe everything you read?" the person asks. Of course not. But you believe this because everybody who's written about the subject says it's so. "How do they know?" the person persists. "Were they there?" No, you admit they weren't there, but they've studied the subject and are therefore in a position to know. That still doesn't satisfy your friend. "Where did they study it?" the person asks. "In books mostly," you reply."

"Now, let me see if I've got this straight," your friend says. "You claim to know from what you've read, right?" Right. "And the people you've read claim to know from what they've read. Presumably, the sources they've researched have studied the matter, too. Is that right?" Sure. "Then where does all this stop? I mean is there no one who knows this without having to read it somewhere?" Of course there is, you explain: the people who were there, the ones who were actually with Washington at Valley Forge; they witnessed it, they *know*.

Your friend then seems to digress. "Have you ever been in a car accident?" Sure, but what does that have to do with Washington? "Were there any witnesses?" There were. "What about their accounts of the accident—did they agree?" No, you admit, they didn't; but what has that to do with Washington at Valley Forge? "I'm just asking you how

reliable eyewitness testimony is to begin with," your friend explains. You concede that eyewitness testimony often isn't very reliable, but that doesn't mean it wasn't reliable at Valley Forge. "Of course not," your friend agrees, "but it does mean that the testimony might not have been reliable. In other words, what you claim to know might not be the case."

Apparently, a claim to knowledge is no simple affair. Indeed, philosophers have given considerable attention to questions concerning the nature, basis, and extent of knowledge (see Philosophy and Life, 5.1). One popular way of approaching these subjects, though by no means the only way, has been to determine whether there are different kinds of knowledge. If there are, how can they be obtained? What are their sources and what are their limits? Possibly the most common view on this issue is that there are two types of knowledge, rational knowledge and empirical knowledge. Although philosophers disagree on the exact distinction between them, rational knowledge generally means knowledge attained through reason without the aid of the senses—knowledge that is necessarily true;

When you know a thing, to hold that you know it; and when you do not know a thing, to allow that you do not know it: this is knowledge.

CONFUCIUS

As for me, all I know is that I know nothing.

SOCRATES

---

empirical knowledge is knowledge achieved through sense experience and is only probably true; that is, it can be proven false. The history of philosophical thought is replete with great conflicts about the priority given to reason and sense experience as epistemological tools. Rationalists endorse reason, arguing that only rational knowledge is certain. Empiricists generally contend that knowledge of the external world can be attained only through sense experience, since reason can only relate the facts that are presented by the senses.

In this chapter we'll look more closely at these two seminal epistemological theories. We'll also consider a third, an alternative termed *transcendental idealism*. In so doing, we hope to throw light on that aspect of the self that knows or claims to know about itself and the world outside it. Here are the chapter's main points.

PHILOSOPHY AND LIFE 5.1

Kekulé's Dream

How do we attain knowledge? By what means? Such questions address one aspect of epistemological inquiry: the sources of knowledge.

The most obvious source is sense experience. How do you know that a book is in front of you? Because you can see and feel it. But sense experience is not our only source of knowledge. If someone asked you, "How do you know that if *x* is greater than *y* and *y* is greater than *z*, that *x* is greater than *z*?" what would you say? You don't see or feel anything, but your reasoning tells you that the relation is true. Reasoning is another source of knowledge.

But sometimes we clearly get knowledge by experiences not easily defined. "I had a flash of intuition," we say, or "My intuition tells me it is so" or "All of a sudden, in a flash of intuition, I saw things

clearly." It's very difficult to define *intuition*, perhaps impossible. Nevertheless, the term does label certain kinds of experience characterized by a conviction of certainty that comes upon us quite suddenly.

Take, for example, a most famous scientific discovery. Friedrich Kekulé, professor of chemistry in Ghent, Belgium, discovered that carbon compounds can form rings. Kekulé's discovery did not come easily. For some time he'd been pondering the structure of benzene, but he couldn't explain it. Then, one afternoon in 1865, he turned his mind away from his work.

I turned my chair to the fire and dozed. Again the atoms were gamboling before my eyes. This time the smaller groups kept modestly in the background. My mental eye, rendered more acute by repeated visions of this kind, could now distinguish larger structures, of manifold conformations; long rows, sometimes more closely fitted together; all twining and twisting in a snakelike motion. But look! What was that? One of the snakes had

seized hold of its own tail, and the form whirled mockingly before my eyes. As if by a flash of lightning I awoke and this time also I spent the rest of the night working out the consequences of the hypothesis..

Kekulé had found his clue to the structure of benzene in his dream of the snake gripping its own tail.

QUESTIONS

1. What preceded Kekulé's discovery via the creative subconscious?

2. Does this tell you anything about how intuition can lead to knowledge?

3. Before Kekulé accepted the validity of his intuitive insight, he subjected it to rigorous testing. Does this suggest anything about how intuitive claims should be handled?

4. How would you distinguish between intuitive claims such as Kekulé's and others such as "My intuition tells me it'll rain tomorrow"?

SOURCE: Quoted in Gardner Lindzey, Calvin Hall, and Richard F. Thompson, *Psychology* (New York: Worth, 1975), 320.

The False Mirror, René Magritte. 1928. "Are there different kinds of knowledge? If there are, how can each be obtained? What are their source? What are their limits? Rationalists endorse reason, arguing that only rational knowledge is certain. Empiricists contend that reason can only relate the facts that are presented by the senses."

MAIN POINTS

1. There are two common views regarding the sources of knowledge: rationalism and empiricism.

2. Rationalism is a doctrine that states that knowledge is based on reason rather than on sense perception; true knowledge is not a product of experience but depends largely on the mental process of analyzing ideas.

3. René Descartes was a rationalist concerned with discovering something that he could hold as true beyond any doubt. He concluded that no one could doubt that a human is a thinking being, that a thinking thing exists, that God exists, and that the world exists. All of this, he claimed, could be established by reason alone.

4. Empiricism is a doctrine that states that all knowledge comes from or is based on sense perception and is a posteriori.

5. John Locke, one of the three most famous British empiricists (together with Berkeley and Hume), held that objects have primary qualities, which are distinct from our perception of them, such as size, shape, and weight. He also believed that they have secondary qualities, which we impose on them, such as color, smell, and texture. We know the objective world through sense experience, which is a copy of reality, and which gives us the ideas we have of reality.

6. According to Berkeley's subjectivism, we only know our own ideas. Carried to an extreme, this position can become solipsism, the position that only I exist and everything else is a creation of my subjective consciousness.

7. Hume pushed Locke and Berkeley's empiricism to its logical conclusion. Arguing that all knowledge originates in sense impressions, Hume distinguished between two forms of perceptions, impressions and ideas. Impressions are lively perceptions, as when we hear, see, feel, love, or hate. Ideas are less lively perceptions; they are reflections on sensations. Hume denied that there was any logical basis for concluding that things have a continued and independent existence outside us. He denied the possibility of any certain knowledge, arguing that both rationalism and empiricism are inadequate to lead to truth and knowledge. He is thus termed a *skeptic*.

8. Kant's transcendental idealism, an alternative to empiricism and rationalism, distinguishes between our experience of things (phenomena) and the things as they are (noumena). The mind, claimed Kant, possesses the ability to sort sense experiences and posit relationships among them. Through an awareness of these relationships, we come to knowledge.

QUESTIONS

1. What do you mean when you say you "know" something is true? If you are unsure something is true, can you *know* it is true? Does knowledge require certainty?

2. How much of your knowledge depends on trusting that others have told you the truth? Make a list of crucial facts about yourself that you learned from others or that depend on what you learned from others (for example, who your parents are, how old you are, and so on). If you learned something from others, can you really be said to *know* it? How much of our scientific knowledge depends on trusting that others have told us the truth?

3. Can you think of some things you came to know completely on your own? How did you come to know those things?

SECTION 5.2

Rationalism

By **rationalism** we mean the belief that knowledge is based on reason, not sense perception. **Perception** refers to the process by which we become aware of or apprehend ordinary objects, such as chairs, tables, rocks, and trees, through the stimulation of our senses. For most of us, seeing, hearing, smelling, touching, and tasting are such familiar processes that we accept them uncritically and rarely examine the dynamics involved. In philosophy, however, perception may have several meanings, for expressing the precise relationship between the knower and the known is crucial. As a result, there is no general agreement on the exact character of this relationship. When rationalists claim that knowledge is based on reason rather than perception, they mean that we need not and do not rely on sense experience for knowledge. They don't reject empirical knowledge; they simply deny its theoretical or scientific importance and in some cases refuse to call it knowledge at all.

In effect, rationalists contend that true knowl-

No fact can be real and no statement true unless it has a sufficient reason why it should be thus and not otherwise.

GOTTFRIED WILHELM VON LEIBNITZ

edge is not a product of experience but depends largely on our mental processes. Mathematics, for example, often serves as an ideal model of human understanding. Mathematical ideas, like the most important truths we can know, cannot be discovered by scouring the world; they can only be known by a mental process. Because true knowledge does not depend on experience, rationalists term it **a priori**, what is known independently of sense perception and thus claimed to be indubitable.

The history of philosophy records the thinking of many outstanding rationalists, including Plato (ca. 428–348 B.C.), Saint Augustine (354–430), Benedict Spinoza (1632–1677), Gottfried Wilhelm Leibnitz (1646–1716), and Georg Hegel (1770–1831). Certainly among the most noteworthy is René Descartes, a seventeenth-century scientific giant who not only invented analytic geometry but also advanced a theory of knowledge that has greatly influenced philosophy.

DESCARTES

Although rationalism appears as far back as in ancient Greece, Descartes presented the first modern statement of it. Curiously, many of us today can identify with Descartes's methodological point of departure—an attitude of doubt and skepticism. Today we might call his frame of mind disillusionment. Some would say that Descartes was smitten by a "credibility gap," not of a political sort but of an epistemological sort, for Descartes seriously wondered about what he could believe, what he could be certain of. He came to this point after years of reading, studying, and confronting the finest minds on the Continent. In effect, he asked, "What can I hold as true beyond any doubt?"

Before seeing how Descartes answered this question, let's update the issue by joining two people aboard a jet thirty-five thousand feet above some point in the United States. The man, Rob Dalton, is reading an article entitled "The West That Never Was," authored by a person who has devoted over thirty years to the study of the Old West. The article purports to separate fact from fancy, to explode some of the fictions about nineteenth-century western America. The article especially focuses on the myths fostered by western movies. The contents of the article surprise Rob Dalton, who is slowly dropping his most time-honored beliefs about the Old West. By the time he's finished reading it, he feels as if a cherished companion has just been bushwhacked. Sadly, he returns the magazine to its holder and mutters, "So goes another illusion." His seat companion, Ellen Borstin, can't help but overhear.

ELLEN: Were you speaking to me?

ROB: Oh, I'm sorry. I guess I was talking to myself. It's nothing.

ELLEN: I bet you were reading the article on the West that never was.

ROB: How did you know?

ELLEN: I had the same reaction.

ROB: Did you?

ELLEN: Just like when I learned there was no Santa Claus.

ROB: Exactly! Except that was the *first* of my *many* disillusionments.

ELLEN: I'm sorry.

ROB: There's no telling how many there's been now. I've lost track. I had one just before we left the ground, though.

ELLEN: I'm not sure I want to hear. . . . Oh, well, I'll risk it. What happened?

ROB: Well, it was odd how it happened. I was leafing through the *Times* when I decided to have something to eat before flight time. You know, something to tide me over? I decided on a hot dog and a diet Pepsi, even though I hate its aftertaste.

ELLEN: Funny, you don't look like you have to worry about your weight.

ROB: I don't. But what with all the stuff about how harmful sugar is, I'm off it. Or at least I was. That's the point. You see, as I'm waiting for my order, I read about this Harvard nutritionist who says there's nothing wrong with sugar. Well, I immediately cancel the diet and order a regular Pepsi, giant size! You'll never know how good it felt—like having a whole life-style confirmed! Naturally, I realized it was just one guy's opinion. But it was a start. At least I could drink the Pepsi without feeling I was committing slow suicide, you know what I mean? So there I am biting into my frank with the works and sipping my giant Pepsi with sugar, when I see it.

ELLEN: What?

ROB: The headline, "Hot Dogs Cause Cancer."

ELLEN: Really?

ROB: You didn't know?

ELLEN: No.

ROB: No wonder. It was with the obits.

ELLEN: How ghoulish!

ROB: That's what I thought—after I stopped gagging. It turned out that it wasn't hot dogs as much as what was in them: sodium nitrite. Did you know that sodium nitrite causes cancer in rats?

ELLEN: How horrible!

ROB: You said it . . . But at least I can eat sugar.

ELLEN: Then *you* don't know.

ROB: Know what?

ELLEN: *He* never touches the stuff himself.

ROB: Who?

ELLEN: That Harvard nutritionist.

ROB: You're kidding!

ELLEN: No, there was a big article on him in the *Saturday Review* last month.

ROB: Well, why doesn't he?

ELLEN: The article didn't say. But I thought it was curious, I mean in the light of his position and all.

ROB: Curious! I'll say it's curious. . . . You see what I'm talking about now? You just don't know what to believe anymore. It's like every day you learn something else. In every field: science, nutrition, medicine—not to mention politics and international affairs. And a lot of the time what you learn contradicts what you thought you knew. It's getting so that just as you think you know something, it's overturned. Like the Old West. I thought I had a pretty good idea of what it was like. Turns out it's about as reliable as a rubber crutch. . . . You know, this may sound crazy, but I'd really like to know what I could know for sure.

Rob Dalton seems a living testimony to the observation that many people have made about our times. We live in an age of rapid change, constant sensory input, and exploding information. Rather than making life more predictable, a fast-paced, continuous flow of data can leave us torn between existing assumptions and new information. Modern psychologists have a term for this gap: *cognitive dissonance*.

But cognitive dissonance isn't a new phenomenon. We can see variations of it in ancient Greece, when burgeoning scientific theory somehow had to fit in with mythological assumptions. Similarly, medievalists had to reconcile Copernican thought with accepted religious, philosophical, and scientific beliefs. In the seventeenth century, scientists, mathematicians, and philosophers, Descartes foremost among them, had to accommodate the growing emphasis on individual conscience and rational-scientific truths with the traditional authority and dogma of the church. This was not an easy task for those like Descartes with distinctly medieval and Aristotelian roots. Indeed, the Cartesian age was marked by a profound questioning of established religious authority, traditional doctrine, and time-honored opinion. Viewed from a twentieth-century perspective, we might portray one of the crucial problems of that era as how to accept the scientific present without severing ties with the historical, cultural, and intellectual past and thereby inviting serious personal and collective disorientation.

Descartes also seems to have felt the anxiety and doubt that Rob Dalton is experiencing. Descartes, too, became vitally concerned with discovering something that he could hold as true beyond any doubt. Descartes wrote:

> All that up to the present time I have accepted as most true and certain I have learned either from the senses or through the senses; but it is sometimes proved to me that these senses are deceptive, and it is wiser not to trust entirely to any thing by which we have once been deceived. . . .
> At the same time I must remember that I am a man, and that consequently I am in the habit of sleeping, and in my dreams representing to myself the same things or sometimes even less probable things, than do those who are insane in their waking moments. How often has it happened to me that in

René Descartes: "How do I know but that there is no earth, no heaven, no place, and that nevertheless these seem to me to exist just exactly as I now see them? How do I know that I am not deceived every time that I add two and three, or count the sides of a square?"

the night I dreamt that I found myself in this particular place, that I was dressed and seated near the fire, whilst in reality I was lying undressed in bed! At this moment it does indeed seem to me that it is with eyes awake that I am looking at this paper; that this head which I move is not asleep, that it is deliberately and of set purpose that I extend my hand and perceive it; what happens in sleep does not appear so clear nor so distinct as does all this. But in thinking over this I remind myself that on many occasions I have in sleep been deceived by similar illusions, and in dwelling carefully on this reflection I see so manifestly that there are no certain indications by which

we may clearly distinguish wakefulness from sleep that I am lost in astonishment. And my astonishment is such that it is almost capable of persuading me that I now dream. . . .

I have long had fixed in my mind the belief that an all-powerful God existed by whom I have been created such as I am. But how do I know that He has not brought it to pass that there is no earth, no heaven, no extended body, no magnitude, no place, and that nevertheless [I possess the perceptions of all these things and that] they seem to me to exist just exactly as I now see them? And, besides, as I sometimes imagine that others deceive themselves in the things which they think they know best, how do I know that I am not deceived every time that I add two and three, or count the sides of a square, or judge of things yet simpler, if anything simpler can be imagined? But possibly God has not desired that I should be thus deceived, for He is said to be supremely good. If, however, it is contrary to His goodness to have made me such that I constantly deceive myself, it would also appear to be contrary to His goodness to permit me to be sometimes deceived, and nevertheless I cannot doubt that He does permit this.

I shall then suppose, not that God who is supremely good and the fountain of truth, but some evil genius not less powerful than deceitful, has employed his whole energies in deceiving me; I shall consider that the heavens, the earth, colors, figures, sound, and all other external things are nought but the illusions and dreams of which this genius has availed himself in order to lay traps for my credulity; I shall consider myself as having no hands, no eyes, no flesh, no blood, nor any senses, yet falsely believing myself to possess all these things; I shall remain obstinately attached to this idea, and if by this means it is not in my power to arrive at the knowledge of any truth, I may at least do what is in my power [i.e., suspend my judgment], and with firm purpose avoid giving credence to any false thing, or being imposed upon by this arch deceiver, however powerful and deceptive he may be.[1]

Thus Descartes took doubt to its outer limits. Our sense perceptions, he held, may be illusions or

---

1. René Descartes, *Meditations on First Philosophy,* in *The Philosophical Works of Descartes,* trans. and ed. Elizabeth S. Haldane and G. R. T. Ross (Cambridge: Cambridge University Press, 1911), 85.

the products of our own dreams or hallucinations, and the ideas in our minds might be nothing more than the products of an evil all-powerful being that causes these sensations or ideas to form in our brains. Descartes thus came to doubt everything of which he could not be certain. He then asked: Is there anything that survives this attempt to cast doubt on absolutely everything? Is there any truth that is so certain that it cannot be doubted? Ultimately he discovered what he felt was an indubitable truth: He could not doubt that he existed. Descartes reasoned that he could not doubt that he is a thinking thing. Thus, the self whose existence I cannot doubt is the self that doubts as well as affirms, wills, and imagines. In a word, the self that thinks.

But what is a thinking being? What does it mean to say that "I am a thinking thing"? This is an important question, for in answering it, Descartes lays a rationalistic basis for knowledge. In one of the most epistemologically important of all his writings, his second meditation, Descartes attempts to describe the nature of a thinking thing. In the selection that follows, note how he abstracts from the sensuous qualities of a piece of wax, identified by perception and imagination, to demonstrate why sense experience is not the ultimate criterion of knowledge. In this way he establishes a rationalistic foundation for knowledge.

✳ Let us begin by considering the commonest matters, those which we believe to be the most distinctly comprehended, to wit, the bodies which we

---

No man knows anything distinctly, and no man ever will.

XENOPHANES

If a man will begin with certainties, he shall end in doubts. But if he will be content to begin with doubts, he shall end in certainties.

FRANCIS BACON

---

touch and see; not indeed bodies in general, for these general ideas are usually a little more confused, but let us consider one body in particular. Let us take, for example, this piece of wax: it has been taken quite freshly from the hive, and it has not yet lost the sweetness of the honey which it contains; it still retains somewhat of the odor of the flowers from which it has been culled; its color, its figure, its size are apparent; it is hard, cold, easily handled, and if you strike it with the finger, it will emit a sound. Finally all the things which are requisite to cause us distinctly to recognize a body, are met with in it. But notice that while I speak and approach the fire what remained of the taste is exhaled, the smell evaporated, the color alters, the figure is destroyed, the size increases, it becomes liquid, it heats, scarcely can one handle it, and when one strikes it, no sound is emitted. Does the same wax remain after this change? We must confess that it remains; none would judge otherwise. What then did I know so distinctly in this piece of wax? It could certainly be nothing of all that the senses brought to my notice, since all these things which fall under taste, smell, sight, touch, and hearing, are found to be changed, and yet the same wax remains.

Perhaps it was what I now think, viz. that this wax was not that sweetness of honey, nor that agreeable scent of flowers, nor that particular whiteness, nor that figure, nor that sound, but simply a body which a little while before appeared to me as perceptible under these forms, and which is not perceptible under others. But what, precisely, is it that I imagine when I form such conceptions? Let us attentively consider this, and, abstracting from all that does not belong to the wax, let us see what remains. Certainly nothing remains excepting a certain extended thing which is flexible and movable. But what is the meaning of flexible and movable? Is it not that I imagine this piece of wax being round is capable of becoming square and of passing from a square to a triangular figure? No, certainly it is not that, since I imagine it admits of an infinitude of similar changes, and I nevertheless do not know how to compass the infinitude by my imagination, and consequently this conception which I have of the wax is not brought about by the faculty of imagination. What now is this extension? Is it not also unknown? For it becomes greater when the wax is melted, greater when it is boiled, and greater still when the heat increases; and I should not conceive (clearly) according to the truth what wax is, if I did not think that even this piece that we are considering is capable of receiving more variations in extension than I have ever imagined. We must then grant that I could not even understand through the imagination what this piece of wax is, and that it is in my mind alone which perceives it. I say this piece of wax in particular, for as to wax in general it is yet clearer. But what is this piece of wax which cannot be understood excepting by the (understanding or) mind? It is certainly the same that I see, touch, imagine, and finally it is the same which I have always believed it to be from the beginning. But what must particularly be observed is that its perception is neither an act of vision, nor of touch, nor of imagination, and has never been such although it may have appeared formerly to be so, but only an intuition of the mind, which may be imperfect and confused as it was formerly, or clear and distinct as it is at present, according as my attention is more or less directed to the elements which are found in it, and of which it is composed.[2]

Descartes here is pointing out that our minds *know* that the wax remains the same piece of wax when it melts, although to our senses all of its qualities have changed. Thus our knowledge of what the wax is does not derive from the senses or the imagination but from the mind. If our knowledge of what the wax is were derived from the senses, then we would have to say that when the wax melted it was no longer the same wax since to our senses the wax completely changed when it melted. Consequently, our knowledge that the melted wax is the same wax as the unmelted wax is something that we know with the mind and not through the senses. Thus, Descartes concludes, knowledge is grasped by the mind, not by the senses. It is by an "intuition" or perception of the mind that we know what things are. But the perceptions or intuitions of our minds can be confused or they can be clear and distinct. It is only the clear and distinct ideas in our minds that provide genuine knowledge. We have a "clear" idea of something when we know its nature or essence so well that we can identify it. We have a "distinct" idea of something when we

2. René Descartes, *Second Meditation*, from *Meditations on First Philosophy*, in *The Philosophical Works of Descartes*, 190–191. Reprinted by permission.

In trying to distinguish appearance from reality and lay bare the fundamental structure of the universe, science has had to transcend the "rabble of the senses."

LINCOLN BARNETT

can distinguish it from other things. Thus for Descartes, the mind or reason is the ultimate basis of knowledge.

Descartes's view that reason is the ultimate basis of knowledge is an example of extreme rationalism. Not all rationalists are as thoroughgoing as Descartes. Some rationalists hold that although some of our knowledge derives completely from reason, nevertheless some of our knowledge also depends on the senses. The extreme rationalist, like Descartes, holds that all of our genuine knowledge derives solely from reason. Less extreme rationalists may hold that although some of our knowledge derives from the senses, nevertheless there is also some knowledge of reality that we derive solely from reason without the aid of the senses.

The extreme nature of Descartes's rationalism is especially evident in the way he approaches our knowledge of God and the world. As we saw in an earlier showcase, Descartes uses his rationalistic basis of knowledge to establish that he knows that God and the world exist. Having ascertained his own existence, he reasons that the decidedly finite and imperfect nature of his own being logically necessitates the existence of a God; for unless a perfect being exists, he, Descartes, has no basis for knowing his own imperfection. He further wonders how such an imperfect creature as a human can have an idea of perfection at all. Descartes concludes that the source of such an idea must be something perfect—God. He then infers the existence of this perfect being, for to his mind it makes little sense to attribute perfection to a nonexistent being.

Notice that in all of these reasonings, Descartes does not appeal to the testimony of his senses. His claims appeal to the mind alone; they pass, he believes, the test of a clear and distinct idea. Similarly, he postulates the existence of the world and other selves. Could a perfect God, he asks, deceive me into perceiving my own body, the outer world, and other individuals, as I obviously do? Remember that Descartes knew that he himself existed only as a thinking thing. True, he did perceive his own body and the outer world, but consistent with his method of doubt, he reasoned that these might be illusions, the devilish tricks of some mad genius. But could they be? He has, after all, proved that a perfect being exists. Is such trickery and deception in the nature of perfection? He concludes that it is not. Therefore, he reasons, the world and other selves do indeed exist. We know they exist not because our senses tell us they exist, but because the mind has reasoned to their existence on the basis of its clear and distinct ideas.

QUESTIONS

1. What does Descartes mean by a "clear and distinct idea"?

2. In your own words, explain how Descartes concluded that a human is a thinking thing.

3. Why does Descartes believe that God exists?

4. How does Descartes use the existence of God to demonstrate that a world and other selves exist?

5. Do you agree with Descartes's view that knowledge requires certainty? If you are not certain something is true, can you really *know* it is true? How much of what you believe are you certain is true?

SECTION 5.3

Empiricism

Beginning in the sixteenth century, a school of epistemology emerged that contrasted sharply with that of rationalism—empiricism. **Empiricism** is the belief that all knowledge about the world comes from or is based on the senses. Reacting sharply to rationalistic claims, empiricists claimed that the human mind contained nothing except what experience had put there. Thus, all ideas originate in sense experience. Consequently, empiricism taught that true knowledge was **a posteriori,** that is, it depends on experience; it is knowledge stated in empirically verifiable statements.

Like rationalism, empiricism has had a long and illustrious history. Elements of empiricism can be found in the writings of Aristotle (384–322 B.C.), Saint Thomas Aquinas (1224–1274), Sir Francis Bacon (1561–1626), and Thomas Hobbes (1588–1679). In modern times the first noteworthy attack on rationalism was waged by three philosophers termed the *British empiricists,* namely, John

What can give us more sure knowledge than our senses? How else can we distinguish between the true and the false?

LUCRETIUS

Locke (1632–1704), George Berkeley (1685–1753), and David Hume (1711–1776).

LOCKE

The English philosopher John Locke was the first to launch a systematic attack on the belief that reason alone could provide us with knowledge. Locke compared the mind to a blank slate, *tabula rasa,* on which experience makes and leaves its mark. In his *An Essay Concerning Human Understanding,* he stated the nature of his proposed doctrine clearly: "Let us then suppose the mind to be, as we say, white paper, void of all characters, without any ideas:—How comes it to be furnished? Whence comes it by that vast store which the busy and boundless fancy of man has painted on it with almost endless variety? Whence has it all the *materials* of reason and knowledge? To this I answer, in one word, from *experience.* In that all our knowledge is founded."[3]

It's tempting to be lulled by the apparent simplicity and common sense of Locke's assertion. But automatic acceptance misses important philosophical implications. Consider the fact that we humans make all sorts of claims, from apparently ordinary ones such as "The lemon is bitter" and "Three plus three is six" to more complex ones such as "$E = mc^2$." And yet even for the simplest claims, as Descartes demonstrated, few people could provide a sound epistemological basis. In fact, if you ask people how they know it's raining, they might tell you to go outside and see for yourself. If you ask them how they know that today is the hottest day of the year, they again might tell you to go out and *feel* it and then *listen* to the weather report. If asked how they know that a lemon is bitter and sugar is sweet, they might tell you to *taste* them. The question of knowledge, it seems, is bound up with what we perceive. Through perception we feel confident that we *know* how things are.

Do you think there's any difference between

things as they "really" are and our perception of things? Are things what they appear to be? To help place this question in the context of empiricism, let's rejoin Rob and Ellen.

ELLEN: You're serious about this, aren't you? I mean about knowing something for certain.

ROB: You bet I am.

ELLEN: Do you mean some heavy scientific truth, something like that?

ROB: *Anything.* I'll settle for the simplest, most ordinary thing for a start. . . . Go ahead, tell me something you know for sure.

ELLEN: All right. I know that the object in the rack before me is a magazine.

ROB: How?

ELLEN: Because I know a magazine when I see one. I also know that the liquid in the cup on the tray before me is coffee, because I know coffee when I see, smell, and taste it.

ROB: What if I said it was tea?

ELLEN: I wouldn't believe you.

ROB: But let's say it looks, smells, and tastes like tea to me.

ELLEN: I don't care if it looks, smells, and tastes like tea—it *isn't* tea.

ROB: You mean this thing might not be what I think it is?

ELLEN: Precisely.

ROB: So a person could not only see something, but smell, taste, hear, and feel it as well, and it might not actually be what the person's sensing.

ELLEN: Right.

ROB: Then how can you say that you know a magazine when you see one?

This is a fundamental epistemological problem that arises with all sense knowledge claims. Invariably implied in such claims is one of two beliefs: Either no qualitative distinction exists between the experience and the object of the experience (for

---

3. John Locke, *An Essay Concerning Human Understanding,* vol. 2, ed. A. C. Fraser (Oxford: Clarendon Press, 1894), 2.

John Locke: "For since the mind, in all its thoughts
and reasonings, hath no other immediate objects but
its own ideas, it is evident that our knowledge is only
conversant about them."

example, between my experience of coffee and the
coffee itself), or experience must be distinguished
from the thing itself (for example, my experience
of the coffee must be distinguished from the coffee
itself). In the first instance we face serious, perhaps
insurmountable difficulties in claiming that any
objective reality exists, since it remains indistinguishable from our own experience. In other words,
there's no difference between Ellen's experience of
the coffee and magazine and the coffee and magazine themselves. In the second instance we must
establish precisely how our sense perceptions square
with reality. This is what Rob is asking. If, as Ellen
suggests, we must distinguish our experiences of
things from the things themselves, then how does
she *know* that her experience of the magazine or
the coffee does in fact correspond with the objective reality of those things?

In proposing his theory of knowledge, empiricist Locke was asserting not only that knowledge
originates in sense experience but also that physical objects exist outside us, that they are independent of our perceptions of them. In effect, he distinguished between entities and their appearances
to us. "For since the mind, in all its thoughts and
reasonings, hath no other immediate objects but
its own ideas, it is evident that our knowledge is
only conversant about them."[4] Thus, for Locke our
knowledge of things is more accurately termed our
knowledge of our *ideas* of things. This is Rob's point
and why he inquires about the connection, if any,
between those ideas and the objective world.

✳   Locke claimed that our ideas were representative of things themselves. But the crucial question
is How? According to Locke, an object has certain
qualities distinct from our perception of it, qualities that it would have even if it were not perceived. These he called **primary qualities**. Generally, primary qualities can be measured, for
example, size, shape, and weight. These qualities,
said Locke, are in things "whether we perceive them
or not; and when they are of that size that we can
discover them, we have by these an idea of the
thing as it is in itself."[5] Thus, even if an object is
not perceived, it still has a certain size, shape, and
weight. For Locke, our ideas represent these primary qualities.

But Locke also believed that there are qualities
that are not within an object itself. A tree, for
example, has color, smell, texture, and maybe even
a certain taste. In the fall the tree may be one
color, in the spring another—as it may be one
color at dawn and another at noon. Without its
leaves, the tree may be odorless; with them, it may
be fragrant. What is the actual color of the tree?
Its actual smell? What we term *color* and *smell* are
merely powers of the tree to produce sensation in
us. The color and smell are not qualities in the tree
itself, but our own ideas. As Locke puts it, "First
our Senses, conversant about particular sensible

4. Locke, *An Essay*, vol. 4, p. 2.
5. Ibid.

PHILOSOPHY AND LIFE 5.2

Science and the Attempt to Observe Reality

Can we ever observe the world as it is, independently of ourselves? Or do our very attempts to observe the world always *change* the world? Psychologists and sociologists often face this problem, since the very fact that people are being observed leads them to behave differently than they would if they were not being observed. The more accurately you try to determine how angry you feel, for example, the less you experience the anger you are trying to observe.

Or consider the results of a famous series of experiments called the "Hawthorne" studies, which tried to discover what kinds of job conditions would improve the productivity of workers. Workers were observed under various different working conditions (including noise, darkness, bright light, music, silence, and so on). Much to their surprise, the Hawthorne researchers discovered that the productivity of the workers they studied always improved no matter what the conditions. It was only much later that the researchers realized that it was the fact that the workers were being *observed* and were being rewarded with so much *attention* that led them to be more productive. Making objective observations—that is, observations

that are not contaminated by the observer's activities and choices—is very difficult when observing the psychological or social world.

But surely the *physical* world can be observed objectively, that is, without it being changed by our observations. Or can it? Consider the problem of trying to measure precisely the temperature of a volume of warm water: If we insert a thermometer into the water, the temperature of the thermometer will change the original temperature of the water.

But it is when we reach the basic constituents of all matter—subatomic particles—that our attempts to observe the physical world most radically alter that world. For in order to observe that world, we must shoot some kind of radiation (light rays or gamma rays) at it and observe the reflected radiation. But the energy of the radiation will always disturb the subatomic particles, leaving us uncertain about what was there before the observation. In fact, modern physics explicitly holds that on principle it is impossible to observe subatomic particles without disturbing them so much that we cannot be sure where they are or how fast they are moving. Here is how a physics textbook explains the impossibility of observing the subatomic world in a way that would eliminate our uncertainty about that world.

In Newtonian mechanics, still applicable to the macroscopic world of matter, both the position and velocity of a body are easily calculable; e.g., both the position and the velocity of the earth in its orbit can be known precisely at any instant. Inside the atom this is not possible. We have already learned that electrons orbiting within atoms can absorb light energy in units proportional to the frequency of the light and that in doing so they shift energy levels. Now suppose that we could "see" an electron. You need light to see it, but when you turn on the light to see it, the electron absorbs some of the light energy and instantly moves to another energy level with a different velocity. This is implied in Heisenberg's uncertainty principle: It is impossible to obtain accurate values for the position and momentum of an electron simultaneously. In other words, observation causes a reaction on the thing observed. . . . This principle of uncertainty . . . sets fundamental limits upon our ability to describe nature.

QUESTIONS

1. What implications do the Hawthorne experiments and the uncertainty principle have for epistemology?

2. Do the Hawthorne experiments and the uncertainty principle demonstrate that we can never hope to know the world as it really is?

SOURCE: Verne H. Booth, *Elements of Physical Science: The Nature of Matter and Energy* (London: Macmillan, 1970), 327–328.

objects, do convey into the mind several distinct perceptions of things, according to those various ways wherein those objects do affect them. And thus we come by those *ideas* we have of *yellow, white, heat, cold, soft, hard, bitter, sweet,* and all those which we call sensible qualities: which when I say the senses convey into the mind what produces there those perceptions; this great source of most of the ideas we have, depending wholly upon our senses and derived by them to the understanding, I call SENSATION."[6]

According to Locke, therefore, the tree has in itself no green color; it has only the power to produce in us a sense experience or "sensation" that we call green. Such powers Locke calls **secondary qualities.**

We know how things are, therefore, because of our ideas, which represent the primary qualities of the external world. For example, if we experience the tree as being a certain height, we can trust that idea to resemble how the tree really is; if we experience it to have a certain circumference, we can trust that idea to resemble how the tree really is. Thus, we come to know the things around us by having sense experiences of their primary qualities; these experiences resemble the entities themselves.

During the early part of this century, a group of men composed a book entitled *Essays in Critical Realism.* Their view shows a marked Lockean flavor. Like Locke, the critical realists do not believe that the perception of entities is so direct as to be indistinguishable from things themselves. It is not the outer object that is present in the consciousness, they argue, but **sense data.** Sense data are the images or sense impressions—the immediate contents of sense experience—which, according to the critical realists, indicate the presence and nature of perceived objects. Only by inference can we go beyond sense data to the object itself. Critical realists believe that sense data provide accurate contact with entities, that they reveal what objects are and thus what the external world is like. They believe that three factors are involved: (1) a per-

ceiver, knower, or conscious mind; (2) the entity or object, consisting of primary qualities; and (3) the sense data, which serve as a bridge between the perceiver and the object.

Still, a question nags: How can we be sure that our perceptions are truly representative of the objects perceived? Locke tried to answer this question with his so-called copy theory. Consider the operation of the senses as so many cameras snapping pictures. The senses are "photographing" everything that comes into contact with them. The resulting photographs of our experiences are obviously not the things themselves but copies of them. These copies, claimed Locke, are so much like the actual things that through knowing and understanding them we come to comprehend the world around us. As Locke puts it, "When our senses do actually convey into our understandings any idea, we cannot but be satisfied that there doth something *at that time* really exist without us, which doth affect our senses, and by them give notice of itself to our apprehensive faculties, and actually produce that idea which we then perceive; and we cannot so far distrust their testimony, as to doubt that such *collections* of simple ideas as we have observed by our senses to be united together, do really exist together."[7] He is insisting that the senses can do two things: certify that things outside the self actually exist and provide an accurate picture of those things.

But no matter how representative, a photograph is not the thing itself. A difference remains between copy and thing, between our idea of something and the thing itself. If we are in touch with only our ideas of things, how do we know that they are really like the things themselves?

Furthermore, pictures are frequently distortions of reality. Perhaps the camera is malfunctioning. Are our senses perfect receivers of information? Even if they are, it is not likely that your sense experiences are identical with mine. Whose, then, are more representative? Such unanswered questions led philosophers to propose alternative views to Locke's.

---

6. Ibid., 4.

7. Ibid., 1–2.

Thus, in Locke's own time other empiricists objected that he had not fully accounted for the representative nature of our ideas. They seriously questioned whether he had fully explained how we can be sure that our sense experiences accurately represent how things actually are. Remember that Descartes could rely on a perfect God whose existence he had derived from the clear and distinct idea of his own existence. Locke's theory, in contrast, originating in sense experience, did not include such an epistemologically influential being. As a result, it was left open to challenge from within the empirical camp. The foremost challenge was presented by the Irish bishop George Berkeley.

BERKELEY ✳

Berkeley agreed with Locke that ideas originate in sense experience. Although he also accepted Locke's argument that secondary qualities are subjective, Berkeley insisted that the same could be said of primary qualities. In A *Treatise Concerning the Principles of Human Knowledge*, Berkeley says,

> They who assert that figure, motion, and the rest of the primary or original qualities do exist without mind in unthinking substances do at the same time acknowledge that colors, sounds, heat, cold and such like secondary qualities, do not; which they tell us are sensations, existing in the mind alone, that depend on and are occasioned by the different size, texture, and motion of the minute particles of matter. . . . Now if it be certain that those original qualities are inseparably united with other sensible qualities, and not, even in thought, capable of being abstracted from them, it plainly follows they exist only in the mind. But I

desire anyone to reflect, and try whether he can, by any abstraction of thought conceive the extension and motion of a body without all other sensible qualities. For my own part, I see evidently that it is not in my power to frame an idea of a body extended and moving but I must . . . give it some color or sensible quality, which is acknowledged to exist only in the mind. In short, extension, figure and motion, abstracted from all other qualities, are inconceivable. Where therefore the other sensible qualities are, there must these be also, to wit, in the mind and nowhere else.[8]

In other words, if heat or cold is a secondary quality—a quality only of the mind, as Locke insists—then why aren't figure and extension secondary qualities as well? For example, a coin appears round from one angle and linear from another, just as a tree appears taller from the bottom of a hill than from the top. Why? Because, says Berkeley, all qualities are mind-dependent. Indeed, to think of sensible qualities as existing in outward objects is ridiculous.

For Berkeley, only minds and their ideas exist. In saying that an idea exists, Berkeley means that it is perceived by some mind. In other words, for ideas *esse est percipi*: "to be is to be perceived." On the other hand, minds are not dependent for their existence on being perceived, because they are perceivers. For Berkeley, therefore, what exists is the conscious mind or some idea or perception held by that mind. Objects do not exist independent of consciousness.

What we know then are our ideas or perceptions. Ellen knows only her idea of that magazine; that is all she can possibly know. Because Berkeley claims that we know only our own ideas, he is sometimes termed a *subjectivist*. The subjectivist contends that there can be no entity without a perceiver and that everything that is real is a conscious mind or a perception by a conscious mind. When we say that an entity exists, we mean that

---

When we do our utmost to conceive the existence of external bodies we are all the while only contemplating our own ideas.

GEORGE BERKELEY

---

8. George Berkeley, *A Treatise Concerning the Principles of Human Knowledge,* in *The Works of George Berkeley,* vol. 1, ed. A. C. Fraser (Oxford: Clarendon Press, 1901), 87.

it is perceived or at least that it could be perceived if we were to do thus and so.

Carried to an extreme, Berkeley's thinking can become **solipsism**, the position that only I exist and that everything else is just a creation of my subjective consciousness. This position contends that the only perceiver is myself. Other persons and objects have no independent existence but exist solely to the degree that I am conscious of them.

But it is unfair to push Berkeley's position that far; he never did. To avoid such excesses, Berkeley relied on an outside source for his ideas: God. Things continue to exist even when no human mind is perceiving them, because God is forever perceiving them. God always has them "in mind." But now other problems arise, the chief one being: If all that exists is a conscious mind and some perception by that mind, how do we know that God exists? If we

PHILOSOPHY AND LIFE 5.3

The Egocentric Predicament

In 1910 American philosopher Ralph Barton Perry published an article entitled "The Ego-Centric Predicament." In it he makes a point about "objects/events" outside us, that is, real objects. Perry addresses a question that Western philosophers have long debated: What's the metaphysical status of objects/events? What are things like outside our perception of them?

Perry reasoned that we can never observe things apart from our perception of them. This was obvious enough to Perry, because we must perceive any real object/event in order to know it. If we can't know things apart from our perception of them, then we can never know whether our perception of things changes them—thus, the egocentric predicament.

Professor of philosophy James Christian has extended Perry's point by suggesting that the ego-

centric predicament entails an *illusion*. This egocentric illusion lies in the fact that all our mortal lives we must occupy a physical organism: that is, we must occupy a point in space and time. As a result, it appears to each of us that we are the center of creation. Conversely, it appears to each of us that the whole cosmos revolves around that point in the space-time that we occupy. What's more, wherever we go in space-time, this egocentric illusion pursues us, since we move our center. In a word, every living, conscious creature experiences itself as the true center of the cosmos, when in fact the cosmos has no true center.

Christian observes that when all humans take themselves as the center of things, we make *aristocentric* claims, that is, inordinate claims to superiority for oneself or one's group. Aristocentric claims arise because we fail to correct for the egocentric illusion. Taking ourselves as cosmic centers, we may claim that our existence has special meaning, that we have a special knowledge or message, or that we have special powers. Rarely, how-

ever, do we make these claims in the singular. This is not surprising, for our arrogant pride would invite scorn and ridicule. But we do make aristocentric claims in the plural: "*We* are something special," "*We* are favored people," or "*We* have a unique destiny." The beauty of such claims is that they're so easily reinforced by group members. Sociologists have a word for any form of aristocentrism—*ethnocentricity*, the preoccupation with and belief in the superiority of one's own culture.

When Ralph Barton Perry spoke of the egocentric predicament, he had in mind a timeless metaphysical concern. But, as so often happens, purely philosophical musings have a way of slipping into our everyday lives.

QUESTION

1. The great historian Arnold Toynbee once observed that a human self cannot be brought into harmony with absolute reality unless it rids itself of self-centeredness. Why is this so?

SOURCE: James Christian, *Philosophy: An Introduction to the Art of Wondering* (New York: Holt, Rinehart and Winston, 1973), 50–58.

cannot say that something material exists, how can we insist that something nonmaterial, like God, does? In one of his dialogues between Hylas (substitute "Locke") and Philonus (substitute "Berkeley"), Berkeley anticipates just such an objection.

HYLAS: Answer me, Philonus. Are all our ideas perfectly inert beings? Or have they any agency included in them?

PHILONUS: They are altogether passive and inert.

HYLAS: And is not God an agent, a being purely active?

PHILONUS: I acknowledge it.

HYLAS: No idea therefore can be like unto, or represent, the nature of God.

PHILONUS: It cannot.

HYLAS: Since therefore you have no idea of the mind of God, how can you conceive it possible that things should exist in His mind? Or, if you can conceive the existence of Matter, notwithstanding I have no idea of it? . . . You admit . . . that there is a spiritual Substance, although you have no idea of it; while you deny there can be such a thing as material Substance, because you have no notion or idea of it. Is this fair dealing? To act consistently, you must either admit Matter or reject Spirit.[9]

"Admit Matter or reject Spirit"—this was something Berkeley seemed unwilling to do. Some claim it was because Berkeley never intended to make such a rigorous criticism of Locke, that from the outset he disbelieved the existence of matter and tried to use the empirical method to prove this belief. When the empirical method seemed to disprove what he wanted to believe, Berkeley forsook it. In fairness to Berkeley, however, we should note the difficulty of defending the sense of the contention that there are objects that are *not* objects— objects that are unknown to subjects and that are unthought and unexperienced. Surely Berkeley at least anticipated this problem, with which another

idealist, Immanuel Kant, would subsequently deal. And, of course, Berkeley felt he had good reasons for not applying empirical method completely. Specifically, we have direct experience of our own conscious selves, which are not hypothetical or inferred entities on the order of God.

Finally, let us be certain about Berkeley's claims. He does not deny that there are houses, books, trees, cats, and people. But he does deny that these or any other physical objects exist independently of our minds. For Berkeley, there are not beds and then sense experiences of beds that copy or resemble beds, as Locke believed. There is only the sense experience of beds. A bed, or any other physical object, is composed of a collection of ideas.

But if we talk of our experience of a bed, we seem to be suggesting that there is a bed to be experienced. This is because our language is misleading. There simply is no appropriate way to speak of the contents of our sense experiences without mentioning the name of the physical object that we believe is experienced. But Berkeley would not accept the existence of the physical object. Yes, for Berkeley there are beds, but *not* experiences of beds caused by beds—that is, by physical objects existing outside and independently of us. Berkeley held that *bed* and all other words for physical objects are names of "recurring patterns" of sense experiences, and no more. Physical objects are groups of sense experiences that we are constantly aware of, bundles of sense data.

Although an empiricist, Berkeley was ultimately unwilling to deny the spiritual substances whose existences he wished to prove. In short, he seems to have used empiricism to disprove what he disbelieved to begin with but to have recoiled from it when it threatened to disprove his deepest convictions. Nevertheless, he remains a critical link in understanding the dialectical development of empiricism, which Scottish philosopher David Hume extended to its logical limits.

HUME AND SKEPTICISM

It's fair to say that David Hume pushed Locke's empiricism to a thorough skepticism, that is, to a denial of the possibility of certain knowledge about

---

9. George Berkeley, *Three Dialogues Between Hylas and Philonus,* in *The Works of George Berkeley,* 447–479.

matters of fact. In other words, empirical knowledge is only probable. How Hume came to this conclusion is a long and complex affair, which we can only sketch here. (For a fuller discussion of Hume, see the showcase at the end of this chapter.)

To begin, Hume asserts that the contents of the mind can be reduced to those given by the senses and experience. He calls these *perceptions*. In Hume's view, perceptions take two forms, what he terms *impressions* and *ideas*. The distinction between them and how they relate to knowing are vital to understanding Humean thought. In his *An Enquiry Concerning Human Understanding*, Hume clearly explains what he means by ideas and impressions.

> Here, therefore, we may divide all the perceptions of the mind into two classes or species, which are distinguished by their different degrees of force and vivacity. The less forcible and lively are commonly denominated *Thoughts* or *Ideas*. The other species want a name in our language, and in most others; I suppose, because it was not requisite for any, but philosophical purposes, to rank them under a general term or appellation. Let us therefore use a little freedom, and call them *Impressions*; employing that word in a sense somewhat different from the usual. By the term *impression*, then, I mean all our more lively perceptions, when we hear, or see, or feel, or love, or hate, or desire, or will. And impressions are distinguished from ideas, which are the less lively perceptions of which we are conscious, when we reflect on any of those sensations or movements above mentioned.[10]

Clearly, then, in distinguishing impressions from ideas, Hume employs an empirically observable criterion: a difference in degree of "liveliness." Thus, original perceptions are quite vivid, as are those of color or emotion. Their vividness declines, however, when we subsequently reflect upon them or have ideas about them. The pain you feel when you hammer your thumb is an impression; the memory of what you feel is an idea.

Consistent with this insight is the Humean belief that there can be no ideas without sense impressions. This follows from his contention that every idea is a faint impression. Thus, if there are no impressions, there are no ideas. However, not every idea reflects an impression. We can, after all, conceive of a golden mountain or a virtuous horse, even if we've never had an impression of either. How is this possible? Hume answers that in such cases our imagination combines ideas that were acquired through impressions. As Hume puts it:

> But though our thought seems to possess this unbounded liberty, we shall find, upon a nearer examination, that it is really confined within very narrow limits, and that all this creative power of the mind amounts to no more than the faculty of compounding, transposing, augmenting, or diminishing the materials afforded us by the senses and experience. When we think of a golden mountain, we only join two consistent ideas, *gold* and *mountain*, with which we were formerly acquainted. A virtuous horse we can conceive; because, from our own feeling, we can conceive virtue; and this we may unite to the figure and shape of a horse, which is an animal familiar to us. In short, all the materials of thinking are derived either from our outward or our inward sentiments: the mixture and composition of these belong alone to the mind and will. Or, to express myself in philosophical language, all our ideas or more feeble perceptions are copies of our impressions or more lively ones.[11]

Building on this thesis, Hume then turns to the issue that concerned Locke and Berkeley as well as Descartes: the existence of an external reality. Since there can be no ideas without prior sense impressions, Hume concludes that there is no rational justification for the belief that anything has continued an independent existence outside us. After all, impressions are internal subjective states and thus are not proof of a continued external reality. In other words, the subjectivity of all perceptions, including ideas, plus the illegitimacy of pseudo ideas for which there are no corresponding impressions (for example, matter, cause, and self), casts doubt on the external world.

To grasp this point, let's rejoin Ellen and Rob.

---

10. David Hume, *An Enquiry Concerning Human Understanding*, ed. L. A. Selby-Bigge (Oxford: Clarendon Press, 1894), sec. 2, p. 18.

11. Ibid., 19.

We can never arrive at the real nature of things from the outside. However much we investigate, we can never reach anything but images and names. We are like a man who goes round a castle seeking in vain for an entrance and sometimes sketching the facades.

ARTHUR SCHOPENHAUER

Ellen has thought a while about Rob's claim that we're only in touch with our experiences of things. While conceding this, she's not entirely clear about its epistemological implications.

ELLEN: Okay, but even if all I'm in touch with is my experience of the magazine, that's something anyway. After all, I'm having a particular kind of experience which, say, is different from my experience of coffee. And as far as I can determine, the experience is consistent, since each time I look at the magazine I see the same thing. To me that's a lot, because it allows me to deal with things. It provides a sort of predictiveness that lets me order my life.

ROB: Granted. But if you think about it, that predictive quality you talk about may be an illusion.

ELLEN: What do you mean?

ROB: Close your eyes for a second. Now, tell me, does the magazine exist?

ELLEN: I presume it does.

ROB: But do you *know* it does?

ELLEN: Well, no, because I'm not having an experience of it. But that doesn't mean the magazine ceases to exist.

ROB: No, it doesn't. But it suggests that you can't claim to know that something continues to exist when your experience of it is interrupted.

ELLEN: You mean, I don't know for sure that there's anything outside or below the cloud bank we're flying through.

ROB: As far as I'm concerned, we don't even know that there's a pilot up front.

ELLEN: But we're acting as if we did. I mean everybody's sitting here, calm in the thought that somebody's flying this thing.

ROB: Agreed. But we can't be any more certain of that than you can be sure that that magazine continues to exist when you're not experiencing it.

Like Rob Dalton, Hume concedes that we always act *as if* a real external world of things exists, but he asks how we can be sure of the continued existence of things when we interrupt our sensation of them. For example, before you lies this book. You're sustaining an impression of it, perhaps a tactual and visual sensation. Then you interrupt that sensation by removing your hands and closing your eyes. You may now have an idea of the book, but that idea is not enough to confirm its continued existence. Then why do we commonly believe the book continues to exist? Because when we open our eyes the book sits before us. If we persisted in this exercise, the result would be the same.

There is an apparent constancy in things that leads us to believe that they continue to have an independent existence external to us. But for Hume this belief is just that, a belief, and not a rational proof. The assumption that our impressions are connected with things lacks any foundation in reasoning. What's more, even when we have an impression of the thing itself, such as this book, we have only that impression, which we can't distinguish from the book. In short, Hume believes that there is no way for the mind to reach beyond impressions and the subsequent ideas. In other words, Hume goes philosophically further than the exchange between Rob and Ellen. Not only does Ellen not know whether the magazine exists when her eyes are closed, but she doesn't know it when they're open. In short, Hume seriously doubts that there is a world external to consciousness.

This discussion may resemble Berkeley's doctrine that to be is to be perceived. But recall that

The Dream, **Henri Rousseau. 1910. "All the sensory experiences we are having are compatible with our merely dreaming of a world around us while that world is in fact very different from the way we take it to be."**

Berkeley has a God who sustains things in a continued existence when no person is perceiving them. Hume, in contrast, does not rely on any such theological prop. He applies the doctrine of empiricism as rigorously as he can, regardless of its implications. As a result, he extends this skeptical line of reasoning beyond the existence of objects and things to questions concerning the existence of God and even of the self.

Hume's theory, then, ends in skepticism; that is, Hume ends with the view that we can never know whether or not our ideas about reality are accurate. Perhaps this was inevitable. Descartes had earlier pointed out that the sensations of our senses or the ideas in our minds may or may not correspond to the world outside the mind. The sensa-

tions or ideas in our minds, he held, may be generated by illusions, by our own dreams or hallucinations, or even by an evil all-powerful being that causes these sensations or ideas to form in our minds. This possibility—that the sensations or ideas within us might not represent the real world outside—led Descartes to doubt everything. But Descartes was able to get rid of his doubts by reasoning that God would not lead us to think a world outside existed unless such a world really did exist.

Hume also accepted Descartes's basic premise: It is possible that the ideas in our minds may not correspond to a reality outside the mind. But unlike Descartes, Locke, or Berkeley, Hume did not rely on God to save him from skepticism. With cold logic, Hume argues that even our ideas about God may not correspond to reality. Indeed, Hume claimed, we are acquainted only with the "impressions" and "ideas" in our minds and have no access to any other "reality." We have no way of knowing that the impressions and ideas in our minds represent any reality outside the mind.

Many contemporary philosophers are inclined to agree with Hume. The contemporary philosopher Barry Stroud, for example, argues that we have to accept Descartes's claim that since we might be dreaming, the sensations and thoughts in our minds might not correspond to any reality outside the mind. But once we accept the possibility that the sensations and thoughts within us might not represent a real world outside or independent of the mind, Humean skepticism is inevitable. We have no way of checking to see what the real world might be like except by using the sensations and thoughts within us. Real knowledge of the world is forever lost to us. As Stroud puts it:

> If we are in the predicament Descartes finds himself in at the end of his *First Meditation* we cannot tell by means of the senses whether we are dreaming or not; all the sensory experiences we are having are compatible with our merely dreaming of a world around us while that world is in fact very different from the way we take it to be. Our knowledge is in that way confined to our sensory experiences. There seems to be no way of going beyond them to know that the world around us really is this way rather than that. . . .
>
> What *can* we know in such a predicament? We can perhaps know what sensory experiences we are having, or how things seem to us to be. At least that much of our knowledge will not be threatened by the kind of attack Descartes makes on our knowledge of the world beyond our experiences. What we can know turns out to be a great deal less than we thought we knew before engaging in that assessment of our knowledge. Our position is much more restricted, much poorer, than we had originally supposed. We are confined at best to what Descartes calls "ideas" of things around us, representations of things or states of affairs which, for all we can know, might or might not have something corresponding to them in reality. We are in a sense imprisoned within those representations, at least with respect to our knowledge. Any

Knowledge is the knowing that we cannot know.

RALPH WALDO EMERSON

attempt to go beyond them to try and tell whether the world really is as they represent it to be can yield only more representations, more deliverances of sense experience which themselves are compatible with reality's being very different from the way we take it to be on the basis of our sensory experiences. . . .

We would be in the position of someone waking up to find himself locked in a room full of television sets and trying to find out what is going on in the world outside. For all he can know, whatever is producing the patterns he can see on the screens in front of him might be something other than well-functioning cameras directed on to the passing show outside the room. The victim might switch on more of the sets in the room to try to get more information, and he might find that some of the sets show events exactly similar or coherently related to those already visible on the screens he can see. But all those pictures will be no help to him without some independent information, some knowledge which does not come to him from the pictures themselves, about how the pictures he does see before him are connected with what is going on outside the room. The problem of the external world is the problem of finding out, or knowing how we could find out, about the world around us if we were in that sort of predicament. It is perhaps enough simply to put the problem this way to convince us that it can never be given a satisfactory solution.[12]

But not all philosophers have accepted Hume's skepticism. In fact, it was precisely to resolve this skepticism that in the eighteenth century Immanuel Kant turned his attention to questions about the nature of knowledge. His investigations even-

---

12. Barry Stroud, *The Significance of Philosophical Skepticism* (Oxford: Clarendon Press, 1984), 31–33. Reprinted by permission of Oxford University Press.

tually resulted in a unique blend of empiricism and rationalism called *transcendental idealism.* This new approach to knowledge, Kant claimed, is the only way of solving the skeptical problems raised by the rationalists and empiricists.

QUESTIONS

1. For Locke, shape is a primary quality and color a secondary quality. Do you agree or disagree with the following statements? Why? Consequently, would you agree or disagree with Locke's distinction?
a. When something is not being perceived, it has shape but not color.
b. You can experience shape with more than one sense, but not color.
c. The shape of a thing never changes, but its color does so frequently.
d. A thing without color can have shape.

2. Locke believed that we come into the world as a "blank slate." Ideas come after sense experiences. Would you agree that we can have no ideas without first having sense experiences? Or would you hold that at least some ideas (for example, "Everything must have a cause," "There is a God," "Murdering a two-year-old baby for your own pleasure is evil") do not depend on sense experience?

3. Does Berkeley's idealism deny an objective reality?

4. According to Berkeley, in what sense can we not know anything?

5. Explain this statement: "Berkeley's subjectivism originates in a physical world and ends in denying knowledge of it."

6. What evidence would you give to prove that while you were sleeping, a physical reality outside you persisted?

7. What does Hume mean by asserting that there can be no ideas without sense impressions?

8. Explain why Hume concludes that there's no rational justification for saying that anything has a continued and independent existence outside us.

9. Describe what you consider to be the fundamental epistemological difference between Hume and Berkeley.

10. Justify the assertion that Hume pushed Locke's empiricism to its logical conclusion.

11. How does Hume push Descartes's method of doubt to its logical conclusion?

12. Do you see any way of showing that Barry Stroud is wrong when he says that we are like "someone waking up to find himself locked in a room full of television sets and trying to find out what is going on in the world outside"? Do you think there is any way of finding out what is "going on in the world outside" your mind? Do you agree with Stroud's view that we must end up as Humean skeptics?

SECTION 5.4

Transcendental Idealism and Kant

The fundamental epistemological question that concerned the German philosopher Immanuel Kant (1724–1804) was how to deal with Hume's wholesale skepticism. Sensing the pivotal point that philosophy had reached, Kant tried to determine whether one could validly argue that reason can attain knowledge of reality that is certain. He attempted to find out whether any a priori knowledge of reality was possible or whether humans could aspire only to limited and uncertain knowledge through experience.

In his most influential work, *Critique of Pure Reason*, Kant attacks the problem by addressing the rationalistic claim to a priori knowledge—that we can know reality independently of sense perception. Living in the midst of the revolution of empiricism, Kant is highly skeptical of such Cartesian claims as that the existence of God is implied in our concept of a perfect being. Kant insists that such assertions are not the certainties that rationalists often make them out to be. Indeed, he accepts Hume's proposition that experience is the only basis of true knowledge of reality. Unwilling to end the debate there, Kant further asks whether there is anything we can know from experience through a source or sources other than our senses. In other words, does anything that we humans bring to experience allow us to know reality? Thus, while accepting experience as the only basis for sure knowledge of reality, Kant doesn't accept that empiricism accounts for *all* knowledge. Thus, he seeks to establish something essential to human nature that enables humans to know reality from sense perceptions. In his *Critique of Pure Reason* Kant states his concern. "But though all our knowledge begins with experience, it does not follow that it all arises out of experience. For it may well be that even our empirical knowledge is made up of what we receive through impressions and of what our own faculty of knowledge . . . supplies from itself."[13]

To understand Kant's resolution of this problem, it's necessary to grasp his distinction between the *content* and *form* of knowledge. For Kant, content comes from sense experience, form from reason. Our senses provide content such as tastes, smells, sounds, and shapes, but they don't reveal relationships, laws, or causes—this is done by the mind.

This point is illustrated when Rob, Ellen, and everyone else aboard the aircraft are jolted when it suddenly drops. Coffee spills, lunches threaten to come up, and passengers are sent reeling. Just as abruptly, however, the plane stabilizes and tranquility returns. In the aftermath, the cabin is abuzz with speculation about what caused the event. "Air pockets," most seem to suspect. But the precise cause is of less concern to Ellen than that everyone intuitively seeks a causal explanation for the disruption.

ELLEN: Did you notice how we all *knew* that something caused us to drop?

ROB: That's normal enough.

13. Immanuel Kant, *Critique of Pure Reason*, 2d ed., trans. N. Kemp Smith (London: Macmillan, 1929), 1–2.

Empiricists and rationalists alike are dupes of the same illusion. Both take partial notions for real parts.

HENRI BERGSON

247

Nude Descending a Staircase, No. 2, **Marcel Duchamp. "Kant holds that the mind possesses mental 'categories.' These categories organize our perceptions into the orderly world we experience. The world as we experience it results in part from the sensations provided by our senses, and in part from the workings of the mind. The senses provide the content or stuff of experience; the mind provides its form or orderly structure."**

ELLEN: I think there's more in it than normalcy.

ROB: What?

ELLEN: Well, let's suppose that we *are* just in touch with our experiences. Then we can't know how things actually are outside our experiences of them.

ROB: Sure, that's my whole point.

ELLEN: But let's say we've got some inborn capacity to make sense of those experiences.

ROB: You mean some inner ability that allows us to know things?

ELLEN: That's right. That would make knowledge possible.

The search for a cause of what happened to the plane might have impressed Kant epistemologically as it did Ellen. He would have likely observed that the mind leads us to look for causes. True, no one may ever discover the cause of the plane's descent—or of anything else, for that matter. But we know that causation is involved, that an event we experience in the world does not occur without prior causes. In fact we rely on this prior knowledge of cause and effect to make sense out of our experiences of events in the world around us. We cannot make sense of things simply happening for no reason at all: The mind must force events to fit into the mold of cause-effect if it is to know and understand them.

Similarly, Kant holds that the mind possesses other ideas or mental "categories" by which it orders sense perceptions so that knowing is possible. These categories organize our perceptions into the orderly world we experience. The world as we experience it results in part from the sensations provided by our senses and in part from the workings of the mind. The senses provide the content or stuff of experience; the mind provides its form or orderly structure. So, as we noted, the senses provide things like colors, tastes, feelings, and smells, for "all our knowledge begins with experience." But the mind imposes order and structure upon these sense perceptions "from what our own faculty of knowledge supplies from itself." For example, for every event our senses perceive, the mind knows there is a prior cause: Events as we experience them must occur in orderly relationships of cause and effect. The mind knows these relationships are there because it has the ability to organize sense perceptions by imposing these relationships on them *before we even become aware of them.* We need not elaborate here except to emphasize that for Kant, these abilities allow us to make sense of our experience. (For a fuller explanation of Kant's views, see the showcase at the end of the next chapter.)

According to Kant's theory, we cannot perceive things as they might actually exist before the mind organizes our sensations of them. We never perceive *things as they are in themselves,* which he calls the *noumena.* All we can ever know are *things as they appear to us,* which he calls the *phenomena.* The noumena stimulate the senses; the sensations that follow are organized by our mental categories so that we perceive them as the phenomenal things of the ordered and causally connected everyday world of experience. Thus, the orderly world as we experience it is created entirely by the mind out of the sensations provided by the senses and contains causal relationships.

Notice that Kant ultimately tries to resolve the same problem with which Descartes, Locke, Berkeley, and Hume struggled: How can we know that our perceptions and thoughts accurately represent the world outside of us? Once Descartes raised doubts about whether our ideas about the world were accurate, Hume's skepticism seemed inevitable. Kant responded to Hume's skepticism with an answer that was simple but revolutionary. All these earlier philosophers had assumed that the world around us is independent of our minds and that if we are to know this world, the ideas in our minds must conform to what that independent world is like. Kant rejected this fundamental assumption. Instead, he held, the world around us is a world that our own mind constructs, so that world must conform to our minds. How do we know that the ideas in our minds more or less correspond to what the world is like? We know they correspond, because the mind constructs the world in accordance with its own ideas and categories. Because the world is constructed in accordance with our ideas, our ideas have to be accurate representations of the world. Thus skepticism is banished.

Kant's revolutionary claim that the world must conform to our own ideas is often referred to as the "Copernican revolution" in knowledge. Copernicus revolutionized astronomy by rejecting the view that the sun revolves around the earth and replacing it with the view that the earth revolves around the sun. In a similar way, Kant revolutionized our views of knowledge by rejecting the assumption that the mind should conform to the world and replacing it with the view that the world must con-

PHILOSOPHY AND LIFE 5.4

Society and Truth

J. Samuel Bois in *The Art of Awareness* reports the following experiment:

A *psychologist employed seven assistants and one genuine subject in an experiment where they were asked to judge how long was a straight line that they were shown on a screen.*

SOURCE: J. Samuel Bois, *The Art of Awareness* (Dubuque, Iowa: William C. Brown, 1973).

The seven assistants, who were the first to speak and report what they saw, had been instructed to report unanimously an evidently incorrect length. The eighth member of the group, the only naive subject in the lot, did not know that his companions had received such an instruction, and he was under the impression that what they reported was really what they saw. In one-third of the experiments, he reported the same incorrect length as they did. The pressure of the environment had influenced his own semantic *reaction and had distorted his vision. When one of the assistants, under the secret direction of the experimenter, started reporting the correct length, it relieved that pressure of the environment, and the perception of the uninformed subject improved accordingly.*

QUESTION

1. To what extent does our sense knowledge depend on what we *think* we *should* be seeing?

form to the mind. Only this revolutionary view, Kant held, has the power to free us from skepticism.

But not everyone has agreed with Kant. Some people continue to insist that our sense experience must conform to an independent world of things in themselves if they are to give us true knowledge. Others claim that Kant's theory is itself a kind of skepticism.

ROB: But aren't you forgetting something?

ELLEN: What?

ROB: Well, suppose that you'd slept through this whole thing.

ELLEN: You mean, I didn't feel my stomach drop or see people falling into the aisle?

ROB: Right.

ELLEN: So?

ROB: So that tells me that even if your mind does

PHILOSOPHY AND LIFE 5.5

Knowledge and Gestalt Psychology

Some patterns of visual stimulation are more meaningful to us than others. Consider the following pattern. How would you describe it?

—————————
—————————

—————————
—————————

—————————

Probably you'd say that you see three sets of two horizontal lines each rather than six separate lines. This is so because you perceive items close to each other as a whole. Again, consider this pattern:

o   x   o
o   x   o
o   x   o

Because we perceive items that resemble each other as units, you'd probably describe what you see as two vertical rows of circles and one of X's rather than three horizontal rows of circles and X's.

Why is one pattern of visual stimulation meaningful while another is not? One answer lies in past experience: Patterns that outline shapes are meaningful if they match shapes that have been experienced and remembered. But meaningfulness also seems to be imposed by the organization of the visual system.

Some years ago a group of German psychologists, Kurt Koffka and Wolfgang Köhler among them, studied the basic principles of organization in perception. They insisted that a perception of form is an innate property of the visual system. This group of psychologists became known as Gestaltists, from the German word *Gestalt*, meaning "form."

Gestaltists focus on subjective experience and the exploration of consciousness. They see the most significant aspect of experience as being its wholeness, or interrelatedness. Thus, Gestaltists believe that any attempt to analyze behavior by studying its parts is futile because such an approach loses the

basic characteristic of experiences: their organization, pattern, and wholeness. For Gestaltists no stimulus has constant significance or meaning. It all depends on the patterns surrounding events. For example, a 5′10″ basketball player looks small when seen as part of a professional basketball team but of normal size as part of a random group of individuals.

As part of their focus on subjective experience and the exploration of consciousness, Gestalt psychologists have formulated a number of descriptive principles of perceptual organization. Two are illustrated above in our two simple patterns: the principles of similarity and proximity.

QUESTIONS

1. Do Gestaltists owe anything to the theories of knowledge that preceded their investigations?

2. What connections do you see between Gestalt psychology and Kantianism?

sort out all these sense experiences as you say, it can't do anything without first having them.

ELLEN: Of course not. In order to make sense out of something, you must have something to begin with.

ROB: That's my point. We're back where we started. Everything's hanging on the senses. And, as far as I'm concerned, our experiences of things are different from the things themselves. So, we never know that our experiences correspond with the way things actually are.

ELLEN: And so we can't know anything for sure?

ROB: I think not.

ELLEN: And that leaves you as depressed as ever.

ROB: Not quite. Just think, if we can't know anything for sure, then I can't be sure that I don't know anything for sure!

ELLEN: You mean there's hope?

ROB: For sure!

Rob has suggested a number of questions that raise an important objection to Kant's position. First, if experience is the only true basis of knowledge, then it is reasonable to question the reliability of the senses as sources of that knowledge. After all, the mind can't order the stuff of sense experience until it receives that stuff. Of course, Kant claims that what the senses give us does not correspond to how things are to begin with—it is already informed by the categories. Thus, we never perceive things as they actually are. If things as such are unknowable, then we appear to be faced with thorough skepticism. We could also wonder about the mental categories themselves—whether Kant has provided a complete list and description and whether they're the same for everyone.

Despite these apparent drawbacks, Kant's thought does constitute a serious attempt to analyze the nature of knowledge. Kant not only shows the limitations of knowledge but also validates knowledge within its proper field. More specifically, Kant is noteworthy for his portrayal of the questioning, inquisitive nature of the mind. This conception of the mind's role as a questioner of

A desire of knowledge is the natural feeling of mankind.

SAMUEL JOHNSON

nature constitutes a new way of considering the nature of the self and its objects, and, most important, it suggests a new approach to the study of perception (see Philosophy and Life 5.5).[14]

QUESTIONS

1. Kant claims that true knowledge has its basis in experience. At the same time, he states that a priori knowledge is possible. Is this a contradiction?

2. Kant concludes that we can only obtain knowledge of appearances (phenomena) and never of the way things actually are (noumena). Does this make him a skeptic? If not, what distinguishes his view from skepticism?

3. Many authors have noted that Kant's theory of the unity of consciousness changed the dispute between rationalists and empiricists. What do you think they mean by this?

CHAPTER SUMMARY AND CONCLUSIONS

We began by noting that the issues of who we are and how we are to live are tied to the question of knowledge. Historically, philosophers have asked, "If there are different kinds of knowledge of reality, how can they be obtained?" The most common view is that there are two types of such knowledge: rational and empirical. Among the outstanding rationalists is René Descartes, who attempted to demonstrate the validity of a priori knowledge, that is, knowledge independent of sense perception.

In vigorous reaction to Descartes and ration-

---

14. See W. T. Jones, *Kant to Wittgenstein and Sartre* (New York: Harcourt Brace Jovanovich, 1969), 98.

alists are the British empiricists: Locke, Berkeley, and Hume. They insist that all knowledge of reality is a posteriori; that is, it follows from experience. One crucial problem that empiricists face arises from their distinction between an objective reality and our experience of it. If these are differentiated, how do we know that our experiences correspond with how things are? Locke's answer is that our experiences represent the outside world. Berkeley says that all we ever know are our own ideas; only conscious minds and their perceptions exist. For Hume reality is not truly knowable.

Immanuel Kant proposed his theory to demonstrate that knowledge of reality is possible. While Kant argues that true knowledge of reality has its basis in sense experience, he also claims that the mind has innate capacities to order that sense experience and thus arrive at knowledge.

Knowledge, then, is not as simple as we may have thought. And neither, therefore, are our claims to know who and what we are. But the views about knowledge briefly traced in this chapter show us several important options. We may agree with the empiricists that all our knowledge ultimately derives from the senses. If so, then we must agree that the only human reality we can know is what can be sensed: what can be seen, heard, smelled, or touched. To be human is to be nothing more than something that can be seen, heard, smelled, or touched. On the other hand, we may agree with the rationalists that at least some of our knowledge derives from what our reason can perceive without the aid of the senses. If we agree with this rationalist view, then human reality need not be limited to what our senses reveal. If we agree with the rationalists, then it is possible to hold that our minds can perceive a reality that cannot be perceived by the senses, and it is possible to hold that to be human is at least in part to be a creature that transcends the senses. That, presumably, was what Descartes was getting at when he claimed that with the mind he could "clearly and distinctly perceive" that he was a nonextended or nonphysical thinking being. He was claiming that to be human is to be something that transcends the senses.

The history we have reviewed also presents us with another kind of option: the option between seeing ourselves as having an essentially passive mind that must conform to the world it knows or seeing ourselves as having an active mind that shapes the world it knows. From Descartes to Hume, the assumption that prevailed was the view that the world we perceive exists independently of us and that we know that world only when our ideas conform to that world. In this view, our minds are passive: They are like soft lumps of clay on which the world makes its representative imprints or like mirrors that passively reflect images of the passing world. In this view, the knowing human self is essentially a passive receptacle. On the other hand, we might agree with Kant that the world we know is wholly or partly created by ourselves as knowers. Kant viewed the knowing self as active: It molds and shapes the materials provided by experience, it introduces all or some of the order and structure we see in the world we experience. The knowing self is not passive; instead, it provides the basic categories in terms of which I see the world. As a knower I create to a lesser or greater degree the world I know, and my own ideas shape and determine the world I experience.

Yet a third option that the theories of knowledge present is the terrifying option between skepticism and knowledge. If we accept the skeptical view that we can never be sure whether our ideas about reality are accurate, then we must acknowledge that we cannot really know who or what we are. For each of us is part of reality, and if we have no access to reality, then we have no access to ourselves. We may agree that although we *seem* to be made of flesh and blood, yet we cannot be sure; we may agree that although we *seem* to be social creatures who live in a world of other selves whom we love and care for, yet we can never know whether this is true. Skepticism implies that we can never discover who or what we really are. On the other hand, if we conclude that skepticism is wrong and that our minds can acquire genuine knowledge about the world, then it is open to us to inquire into how much we can know about what it is to be human. It is possible for us to discover who we are. The very possibility of embarking on a voyage of self-discovery requires that we reject skepticism.

Hume

David Hume: "Here, therefore, is a proposition which might banish all metaphysical reasonings: When we entertain any suspicion that a philosophical term is employed without any meaning, we inquire, *from what impression is that supposed idea derived?* And if it be impossible to assign any, this will confirm our suspicion."

The man who exerted the deepest influence on our modern perspectives on knowledge is the eighteenth-century philosopher David Hume. To a large extent, the philosophers who followed Hume either enthusiastically embraced his empiricist views or desperately sought to find ways of refuting his claims. In either case, they were reacting to the radical empiricism he formulated. Everyone who follows Hume must take his arguments into account.

We showcase Hume in this chapter because of his pervasive influence on our views on knowledge. But, in addition, we hope that by considering Hume's work, the reader will appreciate how our views on knowledge can affect our views on human nature, God, and the sciences. Hume's empiricist views on knowledge led him to raise crucial questions in all of these areas.

HUME

David Hume, the "ultimate skeptic," was born in 1711 into a comfortable family who lived on a small country estate called "Ninewells" in Edinburgh, Scotland. Hume's father died when David was two. His mother, who took over the task of rearing him, said of the boy: "Davey is a well-meanin' critter, but uncommon weakminded." Nevertheless, a few weeks before his twelfth birthday, in 1723 Hume entered Edinburgh University, where his family hoped he would be able to earn a degree in law. But university life was unpleasant for Hume, and two years later he dropped out without finish-

ing his degree, having convinced his family that he could as easily study law at home. Hume later wrote, "My studious disposition, my sobriety, and my industry gave my family a notion that the law was a proper profession for me. But I found an insurmountable aversion to everything but the pursuits of philosophy and general learning, and while they fancied I was poring over [the legal texts of] Voet and Vinnius, Cicero and Vergil were the authors which I was secretly devouring."[15] As a teenager Hume sat around the house reading and complaining that he was being forced to struggle with various physical and mental ailments. In his late teens Hume convinced himself that he had found

15. David Hume, *The Essays Moral, Political and Literary* (1741) (Oxford: Oxford University Press, 1963), p. 608.

a truly new philosophy. As he put it: "There seemed to be opened up to me a new Scene of Thought, which transported me beyond measure and made me, with an ardour natural to young men, throw up every other pleasure or business to apply entirely to it." David now spent much of his day trying to think out and express to others the "new" thoughts he felt he had discovered.

Although living at home, Hume apparently managed to get around. At the age of twenty-two David was accused by a young woman named Anne Galbraith of fathering her child who had been conceived out of wedlock. Hume was sent away to work in the office of a Bristol merchant, but his efforts there were half-hearted, and before the year was out he had quit the job he so detested and was sent to live in France on a tiny allowance. There, he spent the next three years living in "rigid frugality" while devoting himself to writing a book, *A Treatise of Human Nature*, in which he tried to express his new philosophy. The book was finished and published in 1737, and by 1739 David was once again living at home in Ninewells, confident that he would soon be famous. To his bitter disappointment, when the book appeared no one cared: "It fell dead-born from the press, without reaching such distinction as even to excite a murmur from the zealots."[16]

In 1745 Hume tried to get a position teaching ethics at Edinburgh University but was turned down. Instead he took the job of tutor to a young marquise who, unfortunately, turned out to be insane. The next several years Hume spent alternately working as a secretary for a general and living at home. He wrote continuously during this period, writing, among other things, a much shorter and simplified version of his *Treatise* entitled *An Enquiry Concerning Human Understanding* and numerous essays on politics, literature, history, and economics. In 1752 Hume secured a position as librarian at Edinburgh University but was fired when the curators objected that his selection of books, such as *The History of Love-Making Among the French*, was "obscene."

But by 1763 Hume's writings had made him famous, and that year, when he traveled to France as secretary for the British ambassador, he was regaled on all sides and found himself at the center of the intellectual life of Parisian high society. There he met and had an intense love affair with the Countess de Boufflers. But three years later, in 1766, having grown homesick, Hume left the countess and returned to England. After working for three years as undersecretary of state, Hume retired in 1769 to Edinburgh, where he lived "very opulent" and, finally, very famous, until his death in 1776.

Like Berkeley before him, Hume based his philosophy on the observation that all of our genuine knowledge (or "thoughts") about the world around us derives from the sensations provided by our senses. To explain this, Hume divided the contents of our minds into two groups: our sensations (which he called "impressions") and our thoughts. All of our thoughts, he held, are "copies" of our sensations and are derived from our sensations. Even our complex thoughts, such as the thought of a golden mountain, are formed by putting together memories of simple sensations we once experienced: the sensation of gold and the sensation of mountain. Hume concluded that since genuine knowledge depends on prior sense experience, assertions that were not based on sense experience could not be genuine knowledge.

Everyone will readily allow that there is a considerable difference between the perceptions of the mind when a man feels the pain of excessive heat or the pleasure of moderate warmth, and when he afterwards recalls to his memory this sensation or anticipates it by his imagination. . . .

Here, therefore, we may divide all the perceptions of the mind into two classes or species, which are distinguished by their different degrees of force and vivacity. The less forcible and lively are commonly denominated *Thoughts* or *Ideas*. . . . Let us . . . use a little freedom and call [the other class] *Impressions*. . . . By the term *impression*, then, I mean all our more lively perceptions, when we hear, or see, or feel, or love, or hate, or desire, or will. . . .

Nothing, at first view, may seem more unbounded than the thought of man. . . . What

---

16. Ibid.

never was seen or heard of, may yet be conceived. . . .

But though our thought seems to possess this unbounded liberty, . . . all this creative power of the mind amounts to no more than the faculty of compounding, transposing, augmenting, or diminishing the materials afforded us by the senses and experience. When we think of a golden mountain, we only join two consistent ideas, *gold* and *mountain*, with which we were formerly acquainted. . . . In short, all the materials of thinking are derived either from our outward or our inward sentiments. . . . Or, to express myself in philosophical language, all our ideas or more feeble perceptions are copies of our impressions or more lively ones.

To prove this, the two following arguments will, I hope, be sufficient. First: When we analyze our thoughts or ideas, however compounded or sublime, we always find that they resolve themselves into such simple ideas as were copied from a precedent feeling or sentiment. Even . . . the idea of GOD as meaning an infinitely intelligent, wise, and good Being, arises from reflecting on the operations of our own mind, and augmenting, without limit, those qualities. . . .

Second: If it happens, from a defect of the organ, that a man is not susceptible of [some] sensation, we always find that he is as little susceptible of the correspondent ideas. A blind man can form no notion of colors, [nor] a deaf man of sounds.

Here, therefore, is a proposition which . . . might . . . banish all that jargon which had so long taken possession of metaphysical reasonings. . . . When we entertain any suspicion that a philosophical term is employed without any meaning or idea (as is but too frequent), we need but inquire, *from what impression is that supposed idea derived?* And if it be impossible to assign any, this will serve to confirm our suspicion.[17]

Hume's "proposition"—that meaningful concepts must be "derived" from "impressions"—was a crucial step in his attempt to undermine the claims to knowledge that we make. If a concept is not based on the sensations or "impressions" of our sense experience, he held, then it must be meaningless. Hume applied this idea ruthlessly. He argued that claims about the existence of an "external world" were meaningless. All we are acquainted with are the sensations we have. We have no grounds, then, for saying that in addition to our sensations there also exists an external world that somehow causes us to have those sensations.

By what argument can it be proved, that the perceptions of the mind must be caused by external objects, . . . and could not arise either from the energy of the mind itself, . . . or from some other cause still more unknown to us?

It is a question of fact, whether the perceptions of the senses be produced by external objects resembling them: how shall this question be determined? By experience surely, as all other questions of a like nature. But here experience is, and must be entirely silent. The mind has never anything present to it but the perceptions, and cannot possibly reach any experience of their connection with objects. The supposition of such a connection is, therefore, without any foundation in reasoning.[18]

Not only are we unable to know whether there is an outer world, we are also unable to claim that there is any *inner self*. The very idea of a personal *me*, of the inner person called "I," has no foundation, Hume claims.

There are some philosophers who imagine we are every moment intimately conscious of what we call our SELF; that we feel its existence and its continuance in existence; and are certain, beyond the evidence of a demonstration, both of its perfect identity and simplicity. . . .

Unluckily all these positive assertions are contrary to that very experience which is pleaded for them, nor have we any idea of *self.* . . . For from what impression could this idea be derived? . . . If any impression gives rise to the idea of self, that impression must continue invariably the same, through the whole course of our lives; since self is supposed to exist after that manner. But there is no impression constant and invariable. Pain and pleasure, grief and joy, passions and sensations suc-

---

17. David Hume, *An Enquiry Concerning Human Understanding,* sec. 2, pp. 17–20.

18. Hume, *An Enquiry,* sec. 12, pt. 1, pp. 152–153.

ceed each other, and never all exist at the same time. It cannot, therefore, be from any of these impressions, or from any other, that the idea of self is derived; and consequently there is no such idea. . . .

For my part, when I enter most intimately into what I call *myself*, I always stumble on some particular perception or other, of heat or cold, light or shade, love or hatred, pain or pleasure. I never can catch *myself* at any time without a perception, and never can observe anything but the perception. . . .

[S]etting aside some metaphysicians . . . , I may venture to affirm of the rest of mankind, that they are nothing but a bundle or collection of different perceptions, which succeed each other with an inconceivable rapidity, and are in a perpetual flux and movement. . . . The mind is a kind of theater, where several perceptions successively make their appearance, pass, re-pass, glide away, and mingle in an infinite variety of postures and situations.[19]

We cannot know whether there is any outer world beyond our sensations because all we are acquainted with are our sensations. Neither can we know whether there is an inner self because, again, all we experience is a constant flow of sensations, and we never perceive, among these sensations, an object called an inner self. All we can say, Hume claims, is that we are "a bundle or collection of different perceptions." Beyond the existence of these perceptions, we can know nothing.

What, then, is left for us to know? Perhaps a great deal. For we are at least acquainted with the perceptions our senses display before us. And from these perceptions we can reason to others. For example, if I perceive a flame, then I know that there will be heat; if I hear a voice, then I know that a person must be present. This kind of knowledge is based on our knowledge of cause and effect. I have learned that flames *cause* heat, so I reason from the flame to the heat; I have found that voices are the *effects* of people, so I reason from the voice to the person. In fact, all the natural sciences con-

sist of laws based on our knowledge of cause and effect. On the basis of a few experiments, for example, the science of physics asserts that if an object is dropped, gravity will cause it to fall at 32 ft/sec^2. Clearly, then, from the present things we perceive, our knowledge of causes allows us to know what the future will be like. And all the natural sciences—physics, chemistry, biology—are based on this kind of causal knowledge.

But Hume, in what is perhaps the most devastating attack on knowledge, argues that none of our knowledge of cause and effect has a rational basis. And if our causal knowledge is not rationally justified, then all the natural sciences are similarly unjustified. Hume began by pointing out that all our knowledge of causal laws rests on our experience of the world.

All reasoning concerning matter of fact seems to be founded on the relation of *Cause and Effect*. . . . A man, finding a watch or any other machine in a desert island, would conclude that there had once been men in that island. All our reasonings concerning fact are of the same nature. . . . The hearing of an articulate voice and rational discourse in the dark assures us of the presence of some person. Why? Because these are the effects of the human [being]. . . .

If we would satisfy ourselves, therefore, concerning the nature of that evidence which assures us of matters of fact, we must inquire how we arrive at the knowledge of cause and effect.

I shall venture to affirm, as a general proposition which admits of no exception, that the knowledge of this relation . . . arises entirely from experience, when we find that any particular objects are constantly conjoined with each other.[20]

All causal knowledge, Hume is saying, is based on our experience that in the past, events of one kind have been "constantly conjoined" with events of another kind. In the past, for example, I may have seen that when one billiard ball hits another, the second ball always rolls away. Thus the event of one billiard ball striking another has been "constantly conjoined" in my past experience with the event of the second ball rolling away. All the causal

19. David Hume, *A Treatise of Human Nature*, ed. L. A. Selby-Bigge (Oxford: Clarendon Press, 1896), bk. 1, pt. 4, sec. 6, pp. 251–253.

20. Hume, *An Enquiry*, sec. 4, pt. 1, pp. 26–27.

laws of the natural sciences and all the causal knowledge of our everyday lives, then, are based on our past experience of such "constant conjunctions." But this scientific and everyday reliance on past experience, Hume points out, raises a problem. How do we know that past experience is a reliable guide for the future?

> [W]e always presume when we see like sensible qualities, . . . that effects similar to those which we have experienced will follow from them. . . . The bread which I formerly ate nourished me. . . . But does it follow that other bread must also nourish me at another time? The consequence seems nowise necessary. . . . These two propositions are far from being the same: *I have found that such an object has always been attended with such an effect,* and *I foresee, that other objects which are, in appearance similar, will be attended with similar effects.* The connection between these two propositions is not intuitive.[21]

In the passage above, Hume is suggesting that all causal reasoning is based on the *assumption* that the future will be like the past. When I see a flame and reason that it will be hot, it is because *in the past* when I perceived flame I also perceived heat. But, Hume asks, how do we know that the future will be like the past? Clearly, there is no way of *proving* that the future will be like the past.

> That there are no demonstrative arguments in the case seems evident, since it implies no contradiction that the course of nature may change, and that an object, seemingly like those which we have experienced, may be attended with different or contrary effects. May I not clearly and distinctly conceive that a body falling from the clouds, and which in all other respects resembles snow, has yet the taste of salt or feeling of fire? Is there any more intelligible proposition than to affirm that all the trees will flourish in December and January and decay in May and June? Now whatever is intelligible and can be distinctly conceived, implies no contradiction and can never be proved false by any demonstrative argument.[22]

So we cannot *prove* with "demonstrative arguments" that the future will be like the past. Perhaps, then, we know that the future will be like the past because of *past experience?* No, Hume replies, we cannot use past experience to show that the future will be like the past. For if we don't know that the future will be like the past, then we don't know that *past* experience is a reliable guide. To argue that past experience proves we can rely on past experience is to argue in a circle.

> For all inferences from experience suppose, as their foundation, that the future will resemble the past, and that similar powers will be conjoined with similar sensible qualities. If there be any suspicion that the course of nature may change, and that the past may be no rule for the future, all experience becomes useless, and can give rise to no inference or conclusion. It is impossible, therefore, that any arguments from experience can prove this resemblance of the past to the future, since all these arguments are founded on the supposition of that resemblance. Let the course of things be allowed hitherto ever so regular, that alone, without some new argument or inference proves not that for the future it will continue so. Their secret nature and consequently all their effects and influence, may change, without any change in their sensible qualities. This happens sometimes, and with regard to some objects: why may it not happen always, and with regard to all objects? What logic, what process of argument, secures you against this supposition?[23]

Hume's conclusion is devastating: We have no way of *knowing* that causal claims are justified. All the causal laws of the sciences and our everyday causal reasonings are based on an assumption that we cannot prove nor rationally justify: the assumption that the future will be like the past. But if we cannot rationally show that the future will be like the past, then why do we continually move past our experience to conclusions about the future? Because, Hume claims, we are creatures of nonrational habit.

> Suppose [a person] has lived so long in the world as to have observed similar objects or events

21. Ibid., sec. 4, pt. 2, pp. 33–34.
22. Ibid., 35.

23. Ibid., 37–38.

to be constantly conjoined together. What is the consequence of this experience? He immediately infers the existence of one object from the appearance of the other. . . . There is some . . . principle which determines him to form such a conclusion.

This principle is CUSTOM or HABIT. For wherever the repetition of any particular act or operation produces a propensity to renew the same act or operation, without being impelled by any reasoning or process of the understanding, we always say that this propensity is the effect of *custom.* . . .

Custom, then, is the great guide of human life. It is that principle alone which renders our experience useful to us, and makes us expect, for the future, a similar train of events with those which have appeared in the past.[24]

All claims about causal connections, then, are based on our experience that, in the past, events of a certain kind have been "constantly conjoined" with events of another kind. And habit moves us from this past experience to the conclusion that in the future, all similar events will be similarly conjoined. That is, from our past experience of the "constant conjunction" of events, we conclude by habit that one kind of event "causes" a second kind. But we cannot provide any rational justification for this habit of moving from the past to the future. All the causal laws of the sciences and all the causal "knowledge" of everyday life is based on nonrational "habit."

We cannot know whether an external world exists; we cannot say that the self exists; we cannot rationally justify the causal laws of any of the natural sciences nor the causal reasonings of our everyday life. Can skepticism extend further? Yes. Hume went on to attack the foundations of religious belief: the claim that God exists.

Hume felt that the best arguments for God's existence were causal arguments: those which hold that God must exist because the design of the universe requires an all-powerful intelligent creator. But all causal reasonings depend on past experience, Hume points out, and we have no past experience of other gods creating universes. Although our past experience of human beings and their products leads us to say that things like watches require intelligent human creators, we have no past experience of other universes and gods that could lead us to say that universes require intelligent gods to create them.

In works of *human* art and contrivance, it is allowable to advance from the effect to the cause, and returning back from the cause, to form new inferences concerning the effect. . . . But what is the foundation of this method of reasoning? Plainly this: that man is a being whom we know by experience. . . . When, therefore, we find that any work has proceeded from the skill and industry of man, as we are otherwise acquainted with the nature of the animal, we can draw a hundred inferences concerning what may be expected from him; and these inferences will all be founded in experience and observation.

The case is not the same with our reasonings from the works of nature. The Deity is known to us only by his productions, and is a single being in the universe, not comprehended under any species or genus, from whose experienced attributes or qualities we can, by analogy, infer any attribute or quality in him. . . .

I much doubt whether it be possible for a cause to be known only by its effect . . . [when it has] no parallel and no similarity with any other cause or object that has ever fallen under our observation. It is only when two *species* of objects are found to be constantly conjoined, that we can infer the one from the other; and were an effect presented, which was entirely singular, and could not be comprehended under any known *species*, I do not see that we could form any conjecture or inference at all concerning its cause. If experience and observation and analogy be, indeed, the only guides which we can reasonably follow in inferences of this nature, both the effect and cause must bear a similarity and resemblance to other effects and causes which we know, and which we have found in many instances to be conjoined with each other. I leave to your own reflection to pursue the consequences of this principle.[25]

----

24. Hume, *An Enquiry*, sec. 5, pt. 1, pp. 42–44.

25. Hume, *An Enquiry*, sec. 11, pp. 143–144, 148.

The "consequence of this principle," of course, is that we cannot argue from the existence of an orderly universe to the existence of an intelligent God. Hume's skepticism, then, left our edifice of knowledge in shambles. The external world, the self, the causal laws of the natural sciences, our everyday causal reasoning, and our religious claims are all called into question. Can knowledge be saved? Many people think that Hume's arguments definitively destroyed all hope that it might be. But in Germany a very ordinary man, Immanuel Kant, was spurred by Hume's skepticism into constructing what many people look on as the most breathtakingly creative response that could be made to Hume. Whether that response succeeded, you must decide after reading the showcase on Kant in the next chapter.

QUESTIONS

1. How would you explain Hume's distinction between "impressions" and "ideas"? How can Hume say that all ideas are "copies" of impressions? Does Hume himself bring up any ideas that he thinks are *not* copies of impressions?

2. Hume says that philosophical terms must be tested by asking "From what impression is that supposed idea derived?" Do you think this is a good test? Are there any terms or "supposed ideas" that you would have to reject if you applied this test to your own ideas? If you applied this "test" to Hume's own philosophical terms, do you think they would all pass his test? Why?

3. How are Hume's ideas about the self similar to the Buddhist view of the self referred to in Chapter 2? Do you think Hume's view of the self is a correct analysis of *your self*? Why?

4. How would you summarize Hume's criticism of the assumption that the future will resemble the past? Can you detect any weaknesses in his criticism? Explain in your own words what Hume means when he writes, "It is impossible, therefore, that any arguments from experience can prove this resemblance of the past to the future, since all these arguments are founded on the supposition of that resemblance."

5. Hume asserts that all ideas are copies of impressions. Is this a generalization from his own past experience? If so, then how do you think Hume would respond to this criticism: "Since Hume has shown that past experience cannot provide real knowledge of the future, he cannot claim to know that all ideas must be, now and in the future, copies of impressions."

6. Do you see any way of showing that Hume must be mistaken in his claim that the causal laws of the sciences rest on nothing more than "habit"?

CARLOS CASTANEDA

The Teachings of Don Juan

In 1960, while studying the medicinal plants used by Indians in Arizona, UCLA anthropology graduate student Carlos Castaneda met an elderly Yaqui Indian named don Juan. As Castaneda soon learned, don Juan was a "sorcerer, medicine man, curer." By the Indian's own account, however, don Juan was a "man of knowledge." Castaneda subsequently spent five years studying with don Juan, after which he published The Teachings of Don Juan, *from which the excerpt below is taken. He subsequently rejoined don Juan for further study, which he described in later books.*

In the selection that follows, don Juan describes the enemies of knowledge and what a person must do to overcome them. In one sense the reading has little to do with the theories of knowledge just discussed. In another, it relates directly to all of them, for the obstacles to knowledge obstruct any kind of knowledge, whatever its nature, whatever its limitations. In other words, in the view of don Juan, whatever one's view of knowledge—whether rational, empirical, or phenomenal—one cannot be said to be a person of knowledge until the enemies of knowledge have been defeated.

SATURDAY, APRIL 8, 1962

In our conversations, don Juan consistently used or referred to the phrase "man of knowledge," but never explained what he meant by it. I asked him about it.

"A man of knowledge is one who has followed truthfully the hardships of learning," he said. "A man who has, without rushing or without faltering, gone as far as he can in unraveling the secrets of power and knowledge."

"Can anyone be a man of knowledge?"

"No, not anyone."

"Then what must a man do to become a man of knowledge?"

"He must challenge and defeat his four natural enemies."

"Will he be a man of knowledge after defeating these four enemies?"

"Yes. A man can call himself a man of knowledge only if he is capable of defeating all four of them."

SOURCE: Carlos Castaneda, *The Teachings of Don Juan* (Berkeley: University of California Press, 1968), 56–60. Reprinted by permission.

"Then, can *anybody* who defeats these enemies be a man of knowledge?"

"Anybody who defeats them becomes a man of knowledge."

"But are there any special requirements a man must fulfill before fighting with these enemies?"

"No. Anyone can try to become a man of knowledge; very few men actually succeed, but that is only natural. The enemies a man encounters on the path of learning to become a man of knowledge are truly formidable; most men succumb to them."

"What kind of enemies are they, don Juan?"

He refused to talk about the enemies. He said it would be a long time before the subject would make any sense to me. I tried to keep the topic alive and asked him if he thought *I* could become a man of knowledge. He said no man could possibly tell that for sure. But I insisted on knowing if there were any clues he could use to determine whether or not I had a chance of becoming a man of knowledge. He said it would depend on my battle against the four enemies—whether I could defeat them or would be defeated by them—but it was impossible to foretell the outcome of that fight.

I asked him if he could use witchcraft or divination to see the outcome of the battle. He flatly stated that the results of the struggle could not be foreseen by any means, because becoming a man of knowledge was a temporary thing. When I asked him to explain this point, he replied:

"To be a man of knowledge has no permanence. One is never a man of knowledge, not really. Rather, one becomes a man of knowledge for a very brief instant, after defeating the four natural enemies."

"You must tell me, don Juan, what kind of enemies they are."

He did not answer. I insisted again, but he dropped the subject and started to talk about something else.

SATURDAY, APRIL 15, 1962

As I was getting ready to leave, I decided to ask him once more about the enemies of a man of knowledge. I argued that I could not return for some time, and it would be a good idea to write down what he had to say and then think about it while I was away.

He hesitated for a while, but then began to talk.

"When a man starts to learn, he is never clear about his objectives. His purpose is faulty; his intent is vague. He hopes for rewards that will never materialize, for he knows nothing of the hardships of learning.

"He slowly begins to learn—bit by bit at first, then in big chunks. And his thoughts soon clash. What he learns is never what he pictured, or imagined, and so he begins to be afraid. Learning is never what one expects. Every step of learning is a new task, and the fear the man is experiencing begins to mount mercilessly, unyielding. His purpose becomes a battlefield.

"And thus he has stumbled upon the first of his natural enemies: Fear! A terrible enemy—treacherous, and difficult to overcome. It remains concealed at every turn of the way, prowling, waiting. And if the man, terrified in its presence, runs away, his enemy will have put an end to his quest."

"What will happen to the man if he runs away in fear?"

"Nothing happens to him except that he will never learn. He will never become a man of knowledge. He will perhaps be a bully, or a harmless, scared man; at any rate, he will be a defeated man. His first enemy will have put an end to his cravings."

"And what can he do to overcome fear?"

"The answer is very simple. He must not run away. He must defy his fear, and in spite of it he must take the next step in learning, and the next, and the next. He must be fully afraid, and yet he must not stop. That is the rule! And a moment will come when his first enemy retreats. The man begins to feel sure of himself. His intent becomes stronger. Learning is no longer a terrifying task.

"When this joyful moment comes, the man can say without hesitation that he has defeated his first natural enemy."

"Does it happen at once, don Juan, or little by little?"

"It happens little by little, and yet the fear is vanquished suddenly and fast."

"But won't the man be afraid again if something new happens to him?"

"No. Once a man has vanquished fear, he is free from it for the rest of his life because, instead of fear, he has acquired clarity—a clarity of mind which erases fear. By then a man knows his desires; he knows how to satisfy those desires. He can anticipate the new steps of learning, and a sharp clarity surrounds everything. The man feels that nothing is concealed.

"And thus he has encountered his second enemy: Clarity! That clarity of mind, which is so hard to obtain, dispels fear, but also blinds.

"It forces the man never to doubt himself. It gives him the assurance he can do anything he pleases, for he sees clearly into everything. And he is courageous because he is clear, and he stops at nothing because he is clear. But all that is a mistake; it is like something incomplete. If the man yields to this make-believe power, he has succumbed to his second enemy and will fumble with learning. He will rush when he should be patient, or he will be patient when he should rush. And he will fumble with learning until he winds up incapable of learning anything more."

"What becomes of a man who is defeated in that way, don Juan? Does he die as a result?"

"No, he doesn't die. His second enemy has just stopped him cold from trying to become a man of knowledge; instead, the man may turn into a buoyant warrior, or a clown. Yet the clarity for which he has paid so dearly will never change to darkness and fear again. He will be clear as long as he lives, but he will no longer learn, or yearn for, anything."

"But what does he have to do to avoid being defeated?"

"He must do what he did with fear: he must defy his clarity and use it only to see, and wait patiently and measure carefully before taking new steps; he must think, above all, that his clarity is almost a mistake. And a moment will come when he will understand that his clarity was only a point before his eyes. And thus he will have overcome his second enemy, and will arrive at a position where nothing can harm him anymore. This will not be a mistake. It will not be only a point before his eyes. It will be true power.

"He will know at this point that the power he has been pursuing for so long is finally his. He can do with it whatever he pleases. His ally is at his command. His wish is the rule. He sees all that is around him. But he has also come across his third enemy: Power!

"Power is the strongest of all enemies. And naturally the easiest thing to do is to give in; after all, the man is truly invincible. He commands; he begins by taking calculated risks, and ends in making rules, because he is a master.

"A man at this stage hardly notices his third enemy closing in on him. And suddenly, without knowing, he will certainly have lost the battle. His enemy will have turned him into a cruel, capricious man."

"Will he lose his power?"

"No, he will never lose his clarity or his power."

"What then will distinguish him from a man of knowledge?"

"A man who is defeated by power dies without really knowing how to handle it. Power is only a burden upon his fate. Such a man has no command over himself, and cannot tell when or how to use his power."

"Is the defeat by any of these enemies a final defeat?"

"Of course it is final. Once one of these enemies overpowers a man there is nothing he can do."

"Is it possible, for instance, that the man who is defeated by power may see his error and mend his ways?"

"No. Once a man gives in he is through."

"But what if he is temporarily blinded by power, and then refuses it?"

"That means his battle is still on. That means he is still trying to become a man of knowledge. A man is defeated only when he no longer tries, and abandons himself."

"But then, don Juan, it is possible that a man may abandon himself to fear for years, but finally conquer it."

"No, that is not true. If he gives in to fear he will never conquer it, because he will shy away from learning and never try again. But if he tries to learn for years in the midst of his fear, he will eventually conquer it because he will never have really abandoned himself to it."

"How can he defeat his third enemy, don Juan?"

"He has to defy it, deliberately. He has to come to realize the power he has seemingly conquered is in reality never his. He must keep himself in line at all times, handling carefully and faithfully all that he has learned. If he can see that clarity and power, without his control over himself, are worse than mistakes, he will reach a point where everything is held in check. He will know then when and how to use his power. And thus he will have defeated his third enemy.

"The man will be, by then, at the end of his journey of learning, and almost without warning he will come upon the last of his enemies: Old age! This enemy is the cruelest of all, the one he won't be able to defeat completely, but only fight away.

"This is the time when a man has no more fears, no more impatient clarity of mind—a time when all his power is in check, but also the time when he has an unyielding desire to rest. If he gives in totally to his desire to lie down and forget, if he soothes himself in tiredness, he will have lost his last round, and his enemy will cut him down into a feeble old creature. His desire to retreat will overrule all his clarity, his power, and his knowledge.

"But if the man sloughs off his tiredness, and lives his fate through, he can then be called a man of knowledge, if only for the brief moment when he succeeds in fighting off his last, invincible enemy. That moment of clarity, power, and knowledge is enough."

QUESTIONS

1. In what sense is one never a "man of knowledge"?

2. Describe how fear is an enemy of knowledge. How would such an observation apply directly to the study of philosophy?

3. Can don Juan's concept of "clarity" in any way be related to epistemological skepticism?

4. In what sense could the empirical movement be considered an attack on the enemy "fear"?

5. In what sense was Descartes fighting "clarity" and in another sense succumbing to it?

SUGGESTIONS FOR FURTHER READING

Ayer, A. J. *Hume.* New York: Hill and Wang, 1980. This paperback contains an accessible treatment of Hume by a philosopher sympathetic to his thought.

Berrill, N. J. *Man's Emerging Mind.* New York: Dodd, Mead, 1955. A British zoologist argues that through the senses, science, and our "inward nature," we have come to know the world around us. Love and hope, claims Berrill, are natural outgrowths of our evolution, and at our best we "represent the spirit of the universe."

Delbruck, Max. *Mind from Matter? An Essay on Evolutionary Epistemology.* Palo Alto, Calif.: Blackwell Scientific Publications, 1986. This brilliant and all-encompassing book tries to bring together the knowledge of the sciences and the epistemological problems of philosophy.

Doney, Willis, ed. *Descartes.* New York: Doubleday Anchor, 1967. A nice study of various problems in Descartes's theory of knowledge.

Dunn, John. *Locke.* Oxford: Oxford University Press, 1984. This short and easily readable book provides a good introduction to the life and thought of John Locke.

Kemp, John. *The Philosophy of Kant.* New York: Oxford University Press, 1968. A challenging but accessible summary of Kant's central ideas.

Lehrer, Keith. *Knowledge.* Oxford: Oxford University Press, 1974. In this short paperback, Lehrer discusses what knowledge is.

Morton, A. *A Guide Through the Theory of Knowledge.* Encino, Calif.: Dickenson, 1977. This is a nice introductory treatment of the major topics in epistemology.

Polanyi, Michael. *Personal Knowledge: Towards a Post-Critical Philosophy.* New York: Harper & Row, 1958. Scientist-turned-philosopher Polanyi rejects scientific detachment as an ideal of knowledge. A vital component of knowledge is the passionate contribution of the person knowing what is being known. A most important alternative ideal of knowledge.

Urmson, J. C. *Berkeley.* Oxford: Oxford University Press, 1982. This short work presents a readable introduction to Berkeley's life and thought.

Wooldridge, Dean E. *Mechanical Man: The Physical Basis of Intelligent Life.* New York: McGraw-Hill, 1968. Wooldridge, a research engineer, argues that human intelligence, consciousness, and behavior are explained solely through physical laws.

CHAPTER 6　　　　Truth

No one is so wrong as the man who knows all the answers.

THOMAS MERTON

Introduction

We remarked in the last chapter that our view about who and what we are is closely connected to our views about knowledge. Our views about ourselves are affected by what we think the ultimate sources of our knowledge are, by our views about the activity or passivity involved in knowing, and by our views about skepticism and the very possibility of discovering who we are. In this chapter we will examine another aspect of the important topic of knowledge: its relation to truth. To see how closely truth and knowledge are related, let us begin by getting a clear idea about what knowledge itself is.

What exactly do we mean when we say we know something? For instance, "I know that my car is in the parking lot." Just what do you mean when you say that? Stating the question more formally, if we let *p* represent any proposition, what requirements must we meet to claim that we know *p*?

For one thing, we *believe* that *p* is the case. If you claim to know that your car is in the parking lot, you believe it. You don't just have a hunch, an inkling, or a suspicion. You have a positive belief. Think about that. Imagine what your audience would think if you said, "I know that my car is in the parking lot, but I don't believe it." They'd think it very peculiar and rightly so. After all, if you're claiming to know something, how can you not believe it? Of course, we sometimes seem to dissociate belief from knowledge, as in "I know the president has been assassinated, but I don't believe it." But this is a rhetorical utterance. We actually do believe it; otherwise we wouldn't be shocked. Intellectually we believe it, but emotionally we're incredulous. To assert that you know *p*, then, is to have a certain attitude toward *p*, that is, to believe that it is so. Thus, "I know *p*" implies "I believe *p*."

Of course, "I believe *p*" does not imply "I know *p*." We can and do believe all sorts of things: that there's life in outer space, that we are in excellent health, that God exists, that Denver is the capital of the United States. But that doesn't mean we know all of these things. In a word, knowledge implies belief, but belief does not imply knowledge.

Knowledge also implies evidence or justification. When you say, "I know that my car is in the parking lot," you imply not only that you believe it but that you have evidence for it. So, "I know *p*" implies "I have evidence or justification for *p*." Suppose someone claims to know that the stock market will plunge next week. You'd likely ask, "How do you know that?" If the person responded, "Because I believe it," you'd not take the claim seriously. Belief merely indicates an attitude toward something; it does not justify it. Only evidence does that. Another word for evidence or justification is *warrantability*. If someone claims to know that the stock market will plunge next week, they are implying a warranted belief. They have evidence or justification for what they believe.

Can we then correctly speak of knowledge as warranted belief? No. Suppose the stock market does not plunge next week. Clearly the person didn't know, although this doesn't mean that the belief was not warranted. It simply suggests that knowledge implies more than warranted belief. It also implies *truth*. For you to know that your car is in the parking lot, your car must actually be there. You may believe it, and your belief may be warranted. But to know it, you need more: the truth.

Truth is the object of philosophy, but not always of philosophers.

CHURTON COLLINS

In brief, you may not say that you know *p* unless *p* is true.

We have now reached a useful definition of knowledge. Knowledge is warranted, true belief. To understand knowledge fully, then, we must understand warrantability and truth, the subjects of this chapter.

Warrantability and truth are important epistemological issues. They also affect our lives deeply, because they relate to our beliefs. Which of my beliefs are warranted? How can I determine what I'm justified in believing and what I'm not? What can I accept as true? How can I determine the truth? When you realize that your self-image and social interactions are tremendously affected by your beliefs and working assumptions, the issues of warrantability and truth become more than philosophical abstractions. In science, religion, moral-

---

PHILOSOPHY AND LIFE 6.1

Beliefs, Values, and Attitudes

Have you ever been told you have a rotten attitude or maybe a good one? "You'll never get anywhere with that attitude," someone says, or "Now, that's the right attitude." At some time we've all been told, "You better change your attitude." Well, how do you do that? Just what is an attitude, and how does it arise?

There are many definitions of *attitude*. They all share the idea of a hypothetical construct that we invent to make better sense of things. We infer the operation of attitude from observing that people generally behave consistently toward the objects in their experience. That is, we associate attitude with the fact that people's future behavior is pretty much like their past behavior. For simplicity, then, let's define an attitude as a predisposition to respond to an object with a positive or negative affect.

An attitude is different from a belief. A belief is what we consider to be true. It's a probability statement about reality. For example, suppose you believed that reducing the money supply will lead to a healthy economy. That is, you think that a healthy economy will be a likely result of reducing the amount of money in circulation. Is there any connection between belief and attitude?

Your attitude toward reducing the money supply would depend on the value you place on a healthy economy. If you valued it, you'd have a positive attitude toward reducing the money supply.

Some psychologists have argued that an attitude is the conclusion of a syllogism having a belief and a value as premises. For example:

Reducing the money supply will lead to a healthy economy (belief).
A healthy economy is a highly desirable state (value).
Therefore, I support reducing the money supply (attitude).

In short, it takes a belief and a value to produce an attitude.

Most of our attitudes probably stem from a handful of values. Values are very important to us. They help define us, give us identity. Not surprisingly, we don't abandon them easily. If you want to change an attitude, therefore, you won't have much luck trying to change the value in the syllogism producing the attitude. Instead, change the belief. Since a belief is simply a truth expectation based on argument and fact, it can be changed by additional argument and fact.

QUESTIONS

1. Devise an attitude-producing syllogism of your own. What facts would make you alter your belief?

2. Examine your value premise. It obviously functions as a truth in producing your attitude. But is it true? On what basis?

3. What assumptions support your value premise?

4. How would you establish their truth? After completing this chapter, reconsider your responses.

SOURCES: Ladd Wheeler et al., *General Psychology* (Boston: Allyn & Bacon, 1975), 501.
E. E. Jones and H. B. Gerard, *Foundations of Social Psychology* (New York: Wiley, 1967).

ity, the arts, and politics, we hold beliefs that influence how we relate and respond to the world, how we live our lives, and what we do. Just how sound are our beliefs? To answer this question, we must consider warrantability and truth. If our beliefs are not sound, we should abandon them and seek alternatives. If they are sound, then we can feel secure and confident in pursuing them. The issue of knowledge as warranted, true belief, then, is crucial both philosophically and practically (see Philosophy and Life 6.1). Here are the main points of this chapter.

MAIN POINTS

1. Knowledge is warranted, true belief.

2. Warrantability is another name for justification or evidence.

3. Warrantability depends on whether the statement to be analyzed is logical, semantic, or empirical.

4. A true proposition describes an actual state-of-affairs.

5. There are three traditional theories of truth: correspondence, coherence, and pragmatic.

6. The correspondence theory of truth claims that the truth of a statement depends on its relation to the world of facts: A statement is true if and only if it corresponds to the facts. Objection: If we know only our sense experiences, how can we ever get outside them to verify how reality actually is? What does *correspondence* mean? Precisely what is a fact?

7. The coherence theory of truth claims that the truth of a statement depends on its relation to other statements: A statement is true if and only if it coheres or fits in with that system of statements that we already accept. Objection: Coherence is no guarantee of truth. If the first statements are false, they can produce a coherent system of consistent error. There is much disagreement even among idealists over first judgments.

8. The pragmatic theory claims that truth depends on what works. A statement is true if and only if it effectively solves a practical problem and thereby experientially satisfies us. This theory is the cornerstone of pragmatism, an essentially American philosophy that rose in the nineteenth century through the writings of Charles Peirce, William James, and John Dewey. The pragmatist sees the human as needing to use the practical consequences of beliefs to determine their truth and validity. Objection: There's no necessary connection between truth and workability. Truth is rendered a psychological, not an epistemological, concern, and it can become relative.

> # What everybody echoes as true today, may turn out to be falsehood tomorrow, mere smoke of opinion.
>
> HENRY DAVID THOREAU

> # The greatest friend of truth is Time, her greatest enemy is Prejudice, and her constant companion is Humility.
>
> C. C. COLTON

WARRANTED BELIEF

When is a belief warranted? When do I have justification for a belief? Any answer depends on the kind of statement I'm uttering. Let's look at a variety of propositions (true or false statements) to illustrate the point.

1. X is not non-X.

2. X is either Y or non-Y.

3. All humans are vertebrates.

4. No circle is square.

5. The sum of the interior angles in a triangle is equal to two right angles.

6. The sum of the squares of the sides of a right triangle is equal to the square of the hypotenuse.

7. This is a robin.

8. Sacramento is the capital of California.

9. I am in pain.

10. It seems to me to be green.

Each of these propositions is warranted in suitable circumstances. We'd be on solid ground if we believed them. Why?

Propositions 1 and 2 are warranted in any circumstances because a denial of them paralyzes all thought. If they are not warranted, then we can forget about ever thinking intelligently. Put another way, their denial is self-contradictory.

But what about 3 and 4? Their warrantability cannot be established in the same way. It lies in the meaning of the terms themselves. Proposition 3 is true because the meaning of vertebrates is included in the meaning of humans, and the proposition asserts this inclusion. Similarly, in 4, the meaning of circle excludes the meaning of square, and the proposition asserts this exclusion.

The warrantability of proposition 5, in contrast with the previous propositions, lies in its being a theorem that we can deduce from the postulates and definitions of Euclidean geometry. The same reasoning holds for 6 in its geometrical sense. In its algebraic sense, its warrantability follows from a comparable set of assumptions. The warrantability of 5 and 6, then, is furnished by the systems of which they are parts.

The remaining propositions suggest still other conditions of warrantability. Propositions 7 and 8 are hypotheses. Like all hypotheses, they must be confirmed. In other words, when you say, "This is a robin," your statement entails numerous other statements. Some pertain to birds and animals generally, others to flight, color, and plumage. If the original statement is consistent with all the entailed statements, and they themselves are warrantable propositions, then your original statement is true. "This is a robin" is confirmed. The same applies to "Sacramento is the capital of California."

On the other hand, 9 and 10 are basic statements, which don't require that kind of confirmation. Basic statements pertain to sense data; consequently, they can only be false if the speaker is lying. So their warrantability is found in the immediately experienced qualities of first-person experience. [1]

When I say that I am warranted in believing the preceding propositions, I mean that I have sufficient reason for believing them. Of course, sufficiency raises a problem. Just how much support, evidence, or justification do I need for a warranted belief? Useful here is an awareness of the modes of warranty. Take, for example, propositions 1 and 2. These are said to have logical warrantability; that is, they appeal to laws of thought or logic that we consider necessarily true. Thus, proposition 1 accords with the law of identity: A is A. Everything we say presupposes that A is A. If you speak of a tree, you presuppose that the tree is a tree. If the tree were not a tree, what could you even be speaking of? Proposition 2 accords with the law of excluded middle: Everything is either A or non-A. Thus, something is either a tree or not a tree, a piece of chalk or not a piece of chalk, a desk or not a desk. Logically there can be no middle ground.

Propositions 3 and 4 represent semantic warrantability; that is, their warrantability can be determined merely by analyzing the meaning of the terms used and their connections. Propositions 5 and 6 have systemic warrantability. This means that they derive their warranty from the logical interdependence of all propositions in a deductive system. Propositions 7 through 10 are cases of empirical warrantability. Their warranty stems from a confirmatory relation to specific qualities of first-person experience. Sometimes, as with 7 and 8, confirmation must be sought outside the self in the real world. Other times, as in 9 and 10, personal experience, if honestly reported, is enough.

In addition to the warranted, true belief implied by knowledge, we can also have warranted, false beliefs and unwarranted, true beliefs. In neither case do we have knowledge. These beliefs particularly arise in matters of fact, in empirical statements about the world, such as propositions 7 and

---

1. For a discussion of warrantability, see W. H. Werkmeister, *The Basis and Structure of Knowledge* (New York: Greenwood Press, 1968), especially 125–161.

8. For example, it's arguable that in the past people were warranted in believing that the earth was flat and unwarranted in believing that it was spherical. So, warrantability and truth do not logically imply each other; that is, they are logically independent. *Warranty* is another word for justification or evidence. It comes in degrees, as does belief, but truth does not.

We come, then, to the next concern of this chapter: truth. What is truth? More to the point, what does it mean for a belief to be true?

QUESTIONS

Which of the following can be warranted beliefs? Why?

1. This dog before me is an English shepherd.

2. I have a heart.

3. All things have qualities.

4. Hubert Humphrey once lived.

5. 3 times 2 is 6.

6. The sun will rise tomorrow.

7. A robin is a bird.

8. There's intelligent life in outer space.

9. If the battery in my car is dead, the car won't start.

10. If I release this pen and it's unsupported, it will fall.

Theories of Truth

In our everyday lives we usually get along nicely without pondering the question of truth. Since we make and affirm all sorts of statements, we seem to have little trouble dealing with truth. Thus, if someone says, "Washington is the nation's capital" or "Snow is white," we say, "That's true." But even though we may make the distinction between truth and falsity hundreds of times a day, we may have difficulty in expressing that distinction. What do we mean, then, when we say that a proposition is true?

Professor of philosophy John Hospers gives a lucid presentation of truth worth outlining here.[2] He begins by introducing the concept of states-of-affairs. A state-of-affairs is a condition, circumstance, or event. Obviously, there are numerous states-of-affairs in the world. The awesome amount of snow that crippled the midwestern and eastern United States in 1979 is a state-of-affairs; if your dog is brown and white, that's another state-of-affairs. States-of-affairs exist even if no one ever reports them, and they exist independently of language. But, of course, we can and do describe them, specifically in propositions.

This suggests a useful definition of truth. "A true proposition describes a state-of-affairs that occurs; or, in the cases of a proposition about the

2. John Hospers, *Introduction to Philosophical Analysis* (Englewood Cliffs, N.J.: Prentice-Hall, 1967).

"Even though we make the distinction between truth and falsity hundreds of times a day, we may have difficulty in expressing that distinction. What is truth?"

past, a state-of-affairs that did occur; or in the case of the future, that will occur."[3] Thus, if "There is a piece of chalk in the classroom" describes an actual state-of-affairs, then the proposition is true. In contrast, a false proposition describes a state-of-affairs that does not exist (or didn't or won't). "Denver is the capital of the United States" is a false proposition.

Hospers acknowledges that there may be different kinds of truth and that we may discover the truths of different propositions in different ways. But in his view, regardless of the means that we use to discover the truth of propositions, the propositions are true if they describe actual states-of-affairs.

Even if we assume that this is an adequate definition of truth, we're still left wondering how we determine if a proposition is true, how we discover truth. Like warrantability, the answer very much depends on the kind of statements we're dealing with. The history of philosophy records several ways of looking at and determining truth. We'll consider three important ones: correspondence, coherence, and pragmatic. Each makes a unique contribution to discovering the truth of statements.

CORRESPONDENCE THEORY

Undoubtedly the most popular theory of truth is that truth is a correspondence. According to **correspondence theory,** if a proposition is true, it corresponds with a fact. Thus, "Water boils at 212 degrees Fahrenheit at sea level" is a true proposition, because it corresponds with a fact: Water does boil at 212 degrees Fahrenheit at sea level. A good example of a correspondence theorist is British empiricist John Locke.

But the correspondence theory doesn't find support only in the philosophical past. Bertrand Russell's stand is a good recent example. For Russell, what we say is true if it corresponds to reality. In other words, there is a realm of facts independent of us ("Paris is in France," "My father is dead," and "The Yankees won the World Series in 1978"). Russell maintains that while truth and falsehood

are properties of beliefs, they depend on the relations of the beliefs to other things. Thus, the truth of the belief that Paris is in France depends on whether that belief corresponds to the fact that Paris is indeed in France. In his *The Problems of Philosophy*, Russell expresses his position.

> There are three points to observe in the attempts to discover the nature of truth, three requisites which any theorist must fulfill.
> (1) Our theory of truth must be such as to admit of its opposite, falsehood. A good many philosophers have failed adequately to satisfy this condition: they have constructed theories according to which all our thinking ought to have been true, and have then had the greatest difficulty in finding a place for falsehood. In this respect our theory of belief must differ from our theory of acquaintance, since in the case of acquaintance it was not necessary to take account of any opposite.
> (2) It seems fairly evident that if there were no beliefs there could be no falsehood, and no truth either, in the sense in which truth is correlative to falsehood. If we imagine a world of mere matter, there would be no room for falsehood in such a world, and although it would contain what may be called "facts," it would not contain any truths, in the sense in which truths are things of the same kind as falsehoods. In fact, truth and falsehood are properties of beliefs and statements: hence a world of mere matter, since it would contain no beliefs or statements, would also contain no truth or falsehood.
> (3) But, as against what we have just said, it is to be observed that the truth or falsehood of a belief always depends upon something which lies outside the belief itself. If I believe that Charles I died on

---

The contemplation of truth and beauty is the proper object for which we were created, which calls forth the most intense desires of the soul, and of which it never tires.

WILLIAM HAZLITT

---

3. Ibid., 114–115.

the scaffold, I believe truly, not because of any intrinsic quality of my belief, which can be discovered by merely examining the belief, but because of an historical event which happened two and a half centuries go. If I believe that Charles I died in his bed, I believe falsely: no degree of vividness in my belief, or of care in arriving at it, prevents it from being false, again because of what happened long ago, and not because of any intrinsic property of my belief. Hence, although truth and falsehood are properties of beliefs, they are properties dependent upon the relations of the beliefs to other things, not upon any internal quality of the beliefs.

The third of the above requisites leads us to adopt the view—which has on the whole been commonest among philosophers—that truth consists in some form of correspondence between belief and fact.[4]

Bertrand Russell: "Hence, although truth and falsehood are properties of beliefs, they are properties dependent upon the relations of the beliefs to other things, not upon any internal quality of the beliefs. This leads us to the view that truth consists in some form of correspondence between belief and fact."

To understand Russell's version of the correspondence theory, it's necessary to see how he distinguishes a true judgment from a false one. To understand this requires familiarity with some of his language.

First, in any act of judgment, there is a mind that judges and terms about which the mind judges. Russell calls the mind the *subject* in the judgment, and the remaining terms the *objects*. Thus, when a student judges that Booth shot Lincoln, the student is the subject, while the objects are *Booth*, *shot*, and *Lincoln*. Russell calls the subject and objects together *constituents*.

Whenever we judge, we relate things; that is, we order them. This is indicated by word arrangement. The student's judgment "Booth shot Lincoln" is different from his judgment "Lincoln shot Booth," even though the constituents are identical. What makes one true, the other false? Correspondence with a fact. If the relationship between the terms in the judgment corresponds with the relationship between Booth, shot, and Lincoln, then the judgment is true.

Thus a belief is *true* when it corresponds with a certain associated complex, and *false* when it does

not. Assuming, for the sake of definiteness, that the object of the belief are two terms and a relation, the terms being put in a certain order by the "sense" of the believing, then if the two terms in that order are united by the relation into a complex, the belief is true; if not, it is false. This constitutes the definition of truth and falsehood that we were in search of. Judging or believing is a certain complex unity of which a mind is a constituent; if the remaining constituents, taken in the order which they have in the belief form a complex unity, then the belief is true; if not, it is false.[5]

For Russell, only when a sentence expresses relations between words that mirror or correspond to the relations of a complex fact can the sentence be considered meaningful or true. Thus, if the sentence "The Golden Gate Bridge spans a strait in west central California connecting the Pacific Ocean and San Francisco Bay" is meaningful and true, it is because it mirrors the relation between the bridge and the strait as described. The correspondence

---

4. Bertrand Russell, *The Problems of Philosophy* (London: Oxford University Press, 1912), 283–284.

5. Ibid., 285.

theory seems altogether reasonable. But it does have some weaknesses.

To draw out some of the objections to this theory and to stimulate more thinking about truth, let's have some fun by concocting an outrageous courtroom situation. The prosecution has just called Wilbur Scaife, a witness whose testimony is sure to destroy the case of nationally famous defense attorney and talk show celebrity Lamont P. Eveready. Never has Eveready had a greater challenge than to discredit witness Scaife, and he must do so fast!

BAILIFF: Do you swear to tell the truth, the whole truth, and nothing but the truth, so help you God?

SCAIFE: I do.

EVEREADY: Objection, Your Honor.

JUDGE: But the witness has not even taken his seat.

EVEREADY: Defense objects, Your Honor, on grounds that the witness has perjured himself.

JUDGE: Perjured himself? Why, he hasn't even answered a question yet.

EVEREADY: Defense humbly begs to differ, Your Honor. The witness has sworn to tell the truth, the whole truth, and nothing but the truth. Defense contends that the witness Wilbur Scaife is in no position to meet that oath, since he knows nothing of the truth of which he speaks.

JUDGE: Knows nothing of . . .

EVEREADY: To put it simply, Your Honor, Scaife doesn't know the truth from a hole in the ground.

SCAIFE: Oh, yeah? You want to step outside and say that?

JUDGE: The witness will contain himself. Can Defense prove this contention?

EVEREADY: Defense can and will, Your Honor.

JUDGE: Then proceed.

EVEREADY: Thank you, Your Honor. Now, Mr. Scaife, you have just sworn a holy oath before God Almighty to tell the truth, the whole truth, and nothing but the truth. Is that correct?

SCAIFE: Yes.

EVEREADY: Presumably, you have sworn this oath knowing full well what it means.

SCAIFE: Yes, I have. It means I'm going to tell the truth.

EVEREADY: The whole truth and nothing but the truth.

SCAIFE: You said it.

EVEREADY: Now, Scaife, what in your opinion is the truth?

SCAIFE: The truth? The truth is the way things are.

EVEREADY: The way things are. All right, *American flag*—is that the truth?

SCAIFE: What about the American flag?

EVEREADY: Oh, I must say something *about* it?

SCAIFE: Well, sure. How else would you know if you got the truth or not?

EVEREADY: I see. So what you're really saying is that the truth refers not so much to the ways things are as it does to a *statement* about the ways things are. In other words, it would be silly to say "American flag" is true. But it would make perfect sense to say "There's a red, white, and blue American flag in this courtroom."

SCAIFE: Now you've got the truth, mister.

EVEREADY: You mean that statement is true?

SCAIFE: You bet your life it is.

EVEREADY: And tell the court, Scaife, how you know the statement "There is a red, white, and blue American flag in this courtroom" is true.

SCAIFE: Because I see that flag right over there.

EVEREADY: Because you see it. Tell me, Scaife, does everything you see lead you to make a true statement?

SCAIFE: I don't get you.

EVEREADY: Let me illustrate. You've no doubt seen a pencil resting in a glass of water.

SCAIFE: Sure.

EVEREADY: How would you describe such a pencil?

SCAIFE: You mean that it looks bent?

La Trahison des Images, René Magritte. "Just how does a true proposition correspond to a fact or a state-of-affairs? There's no resemblance between a proposition and a state-of-affairs. Does a statement correspond to fact in the way that titles of books on library cards correspond to the books themselves? That is, is there some sort of one-to-one correspondence? If so, what is gained?"

EVEREADY: It looks bent. Your eyes report it as bent.

SCAIFE: But it's not.

EVEREADY: No, it's not. Consequently, the statement "That pencil is bent" is not true, is it?

SCAIFE: No way.

EVEREADY: And yet your eyes report it as true, don't they?

SCAIFE: But it's different here with the flag. The flag is actually here, the way you said it was. The pencil isn't. That's the difference.

EVEREADY: The flag is actually here, the way I said it was. . . . Your Honor, the Defense wishes to call from the gallery for one question only Ms. Bertha Moynier.

PROSECUTION: I object, Your Honor. Counsel's line of questioning has no purpose except to rattle, confuse, and intimidate the witness.

JUDGE: The irregularity of his request forces me to warn Defense that for his and his client's sake, the Bench hopes all this has some constructive end.

EVEREADY: I assure the Bench it has.

JUDGE: Will Ms. Moynier please rise?

EVEREADY: Ms. Moynier, will you please tell the court whether the following statement is true: "There is a red, white, and blue American flag in this room."

MOYNIER: I don't know.

SCAIFE: What! She must be blind!

EVEREADY: I compliment you on your powers of deduction, Scaife. Ms. Moynier is, in fact, blind.

JUDGE: What's the meaning of this demonstration, Eveready?

EVEREADY: Your Honor, the purpose of this exercise is to show the court that what the witness, Wilbur Scaife, *thinks* is truth is in fact nothing but hearsay. Indeed, what the witness *thinks* is truth consigns truth to the very dubious area of sense data interpretation. Such interpretation must be purely subjective and need not have anything to do with the way things actually are.

PROSECUTION: Your Honor, I have sat here patiently while the Defense has made a mockery of this court. I submit that he has gone beyond the role of court jester and is now showing open contempt for the Bench itself!

EVEREADY: If the court will allow, the Defense would like to call from the gallery Mr. Bartholomew Peabody in order to prove the sincerity of Defense's cause.

JUDGE: With great reluctance, the Bench asks Mr. Bartholomew Peabody to rise.

EVEREADY: Thank you, Your Honor. Mr. Peabody, will you tell the court whether the following statement is true: "There is a red, white, and blue American flag in this courtroom."

PEABODY: Well, if you want to know the truth, what you say is so and it isn't.

EVEREADY: Would you explain to the court why my statement is true and not true?

PEABODY: First, you do have a flag, all right. Any fool can see that.

Truth is the highest thing that man may keep.

CHAUCER

What is truth?

PONTIUS PILATE

SCAIFE: There! What did I tell you?

JUDGE: The witness will restrain himself.

PEABODY: But it's not a red, white, and blue flag. It's red, white, and green.

SCAIFE: Green! He must be color-blind!

EVEREADY: Must he? Why? Because he disagrees with you?

PROSECUTION: Your Honor, how long will the Bench allow this travesty to continue?

EVEREADY: On the contrary, Your Honor, the court is hardly witnessing a travesty. Rather, in a matter of minutes, the court has heard three persons report different "truths" while supposedly observing the same object at the same time. Yet the witness Wilbur Scaife would have us believe that the truth characterizes that statement which reports an actual fact. I respectfully submit, Your Honor, that we can never know how things really are, because the only way we can come to such knowledge is through sense experience, which I have just demonstrated to be unreliable.

JUDGE: Is Defense suggesting that in this case the testimonies of a blind and a color-blind person are equal to that of a normally sighted one?

EVEREADY: Your Honor, may I respectfully answer with another question? Just what constitutes normal sight? Is it not a convention, a standard that the majority sets? Would the court submit the question of truth to a head count?

JUDGE: On the question of whether there is in fact a red, white, and blue American flag in this courtroom, the court might seriously entertain such a proposal.

EVEREADY: So be it, Your Honor. I submit the question to the gallery. Let a show of hands determine the truth of the statement "There is a red, white, and blue American flag in this courtroom."

JUDGE: Nobody? Not a single hand?

PROSECUTION: I object, Your Honor! The Defense has obviously stacked the gallery as a card shark would a deck of playing cards.

EVEREADY: The Prosecution's powers of deduction are as astonishing as Wilbur Scaife's, Your Honor.

True, the defense has stacked the gallery, but only to demonstrate that, when we insist that truth is an agreement between a statement of fact and the fact itself, we play the game of life with a stacked deck.

In effect, Eveready is asking, "Since we know only our experiences, how can we ever get outside them to verify what reality actually is?" The correspondence theory of truth seems to assume that we know not only our experiences of things but also *facts* about the world, that is, how the world actually is. Otherwise, how could truth be described as a correspondence between statement and fact? Of course, correspondence theorists might reply that the correspondence is between statements and

reality *as interpreted by us.* But just who is "us"? Everyone, each individual, a consensus? And how do we ever know our interpretation is correct to begin with? Furthermore, if truth is a correspondence between statement and fact as interpreted by us, then we say nothing at all about the world outside ourselves; we only address whether we are correctly or incorrectly representing what we believe.

Then there's the question of just what is a fact, a philosophical concern having profound implications outside the study of philosophy (see Philosophy and Life 6.2). Sometimes *fact* means "true proposition," as in, "It's a fact that I'm six feet tall." In other words, "The sentence 'I am six feet tall' is a true proposition." But using *fact* in this way results in circularity: A proposition is true if it cor-

---

PHILOSOPHY AND LIFE 6.2

Historical Facts

What is a historical fact? Take, for example, what passes for a simple historical fact: "In the year 49 B.C. Caesar crossed the Rubicon." This is a familiar fact, and one of some importance. Yet, as the most distinguished American historian Carl L. Becker pointed out over a half century ago, this simple fact has strings tied to it. It depends on numerous other facts, so that it has no meaning apart from the web of circumstances that produced it. This web of circumstances, of course, was the chain of events arising out of the relation of Caesar to Pompey, the Roman senate, and the Roman republic. Becker states:

SOURCE: Carl L. Becker, "What Are Historical Facts?" Quoted in *Coming Age of Philosophy*, ed. Roger Eastman (San Francisco: Canfield Press, 1973), 451–452.

Caesar had been ordered by the Roman Senate to resign his command of the army in Gaul. He decided to disobey the Roman Senate. Instead of resigning his command, he marched on Rome, gained the mastery of the Republic, and, at last, we are told, bestrode the narrow world like a colossus. Well, the Rubicon happened to be the boundary between Gaul and Italy, so that by the act of crossing the Rubicon with his army Caesar's treason became an accomplished fact and the subsequent great events followed in due course. Apart from these great events and complicated relations, the crossing of the Rubicon means nothing, is not an historical fact properly speaking at all. . . . [It is] a symbol standing for a long series of events which have to do with the most intangible and immaterial realities, viz.: the relation between Caesar and the millions of people of the Roman world.

Clearly, for Becker "the simple historical fact" is only a symbol, an affirmation about an event. And since it's hardly worthwhile to term a symbol cold or hard, indeed dangerous to call it true or false, one might best speak of historical facts as being more or less appropriate.

QUESTIONS

1. Could Becker's analysis be applied to this statement: "The Japanese bombed Pearl Harbor on 7 December 1941"?

2. Would it be accurate to say that historians deal not with an event but with statements that affirm the fact that the event occurred? If so, what's the difference?

responds with a true proposition. Or *fact* may mean the same as "actual state-of-affairs." In this case the correspondence theory is identical with Hospers's definition of a true proposition—one that describes a state-of-affairs that is actual, that is, a fact. Nonetheless, the correspondence theory uses the word *corresponds* and not *describes*, and *corresponds* is the word that can cause confusion.

Just how does a true proposition correspond to a fact or a state-of-affairs? It certainly doesn't correspond in the way that a color sample on a color chart corresponds with a color of paint on a wall. In that case there's a *resemblance* between the sample and the wall paint. But there's no resemblance between a proposition and a state-of-affairs, or even between a sentence and a state-of-affairs. Does a statement correspond to fact in the way that titles of books on library cards correspond to the books themselves? That is, is there some sort of one-to-one correspondence—for each card, a book; for each book, a card? If so, what is gained? It seems

at least as clear to say that a true proposition describes an actual state-of-affairs and dispose of the inherently misleading "correspondence."[6]

COHERENCE THEORY

Exasperated by Eveready's protests, the judge has summoned him and the prosecution to the bench.

JUDGE: Now see here, Eveready, this line of interrogation can't continue. It's making a shambles of my court.

PROSECUTION: Amen!

JUDGE: Eveready, aren't you at all interested in the law?

EVEREADY: Of course I am, Your Honor. But I'm also interested in truth. Does Your Honor think the law and the truth are mutually exclusive?

_____

6. See Hospers, *Introduction to Philosophical Analysis*, 116.

PHILOSOPHY AND LIFE 6.3

Truth and Paradox

The concept of truth has been intensively studied by logicians during the twentieth century. In fact, the vigorous attempts logicians and mathematicians have made to clarify the notion of truth have led to some of the greatest and most far-reaching mathematical discoveries of this century. Much of this work has been inspired by the realization that the very notion of truth seems to give rise to troublesome paradoxes and contradictions.

One of the earliest examples of the troublesome contradictions that the notion of truth can create is attributed to the ancient Greek philosopher Eubulides, who wrote,

"A man says that he is not telling the truth. Is what he says true or false?" If what the man says is true, then the man is not telling the truth, so what he says must be false! But if what the man says is false, then it is false that he is not telling the truth, so what he says must be true! Thus, assuming what the man says is true leads us to a contradiction, and assuming what the man says is not true also leads us to a contradiction. In either case, the very notion of truth here seems to generate a contradiction.

The same kinds of contradictions are generated by much simpler statements, such as "This statement is not true" or

> The sentence in the box on this page is false.

But why should it matter that the very concept of truth generates contradictions? Because, unfortunately, once a single contradiction is allowed, it is easy to prove with rigorous logic that *any statement whatsoever* is true. That is, anything can be proved once you accept a contradiction. This is fairly easy to show.

Let the letter Q stand for any statement you want, such as "Unicorns exist." Now suppose that you accept as true the statement "God

JUDGE: Stop putting words in my mouth! You think I'm Scaife?

EVEREADY: I beg your pardon, Your Honor.

JUDGE: Pardon not granted. Didn't they teach you in law school the kind of truth on which much of the judicial process is based?

EVEREADY: *Kind* of truth? Are there *kinds* of truth, Your Honor?

PROSECUTION: Stop sassing the judge.

JUDGE: I'll be the judge of who's sassing me. Let me ask you something, Eveready.

EVEREADY: Proceed.

JUDGE: How are innocence and guilt determined?

EVEREADY: By a trial.

JUDGE: And what happens at a trial? I mean a normal trial, not this circus.

EVEREADY: Well, at a normal trial, lawyers present cases.

JUDGE: Exactly. And isn't it true that in theory the better case wins?

EVEREADY: In theory.

JUDGE: And what makes for the better case, Eveready?

EVEREADY: Obviously, persuading the jury.

JUDGE: Obviously. And which case, in theory, should persuade the jury?

EVEREADY: The one that hangs together better.

JUDGE: Precisely. Your job is to present the jury with pieces of a puzzle, isn't it? The jury's job is to take each piece and evaluate it. How? Well, let's see. They can't go back to the scene of the crime or to the circumstances that you describe, can they? No, they can't. So how do they figure out if a particular piece is true? I'll tell you how: usually by seeing how it fits in with all the other pieces. If it fits in, if it's consistent, if it doesn't contradict any of the other pieces, then it's true. At the very end,

---

is good." Call this statement *P*. And suppose you also accept as true the contradictory statement "God is not good." Call this statement *not-P*. Now consider the following statement:

(1) *Either* P *is true or* Q *is true.*

You must accept that statement (1) is true, since you previously accepted that *P* is true. However, since you also accepted *not-P*, this means that *P* is not true. That is, you must also accept statement 2.

(2) P *is not true.*

Now you have accepted statements 1 and 2. But from statements 1 and 2, of course, it logically follows that

(3) Q *is true.*

And so you must accept that *Q* is true, that is, that unicorns exist! So by accepting the contradiction that *P* is true and that *not-P* is also true, we can logically prove that unicorns exist. In fact, anything at all can be proved with rigorous logic once a contradiction is accepted.

The terrible consequences that would follow should the concept of truth we accept involve contradictions were what led twentieth-

century logicians and mathematicians to invest considerable energy in trying to come up with ways to avoid contradictions. Unfortunately, this work has not yet come to any firm conclusions. The possibility that our notion of truth may be contradictory still lurks.

QUESTIONS

1. Can you conceive of some ways of avoiding the contradictions that truth seems to involve?

2. Can you conceive of some ways of avoiding the argument that once a contradiction is accepted, anything can be proved?

if you've presented a good case, all the pieces fit. The truth is right in front of their noses. "This person," they declare, "is guilty" or "not guilty."

Notice how the judge's theory of truth differs from the correspondence theory. According to him, a statement is true if it is consistent with other statements that are regarded as true. The essential test is not correspondence between statement and actual fact but coherence between statement and other relevant statements. Notice that the judge wants to know if the case hangs together, if all the pieces fit together. This **coherence theory** of truth, as it is called, insists that truth is a property of a related group of consistent statements. A particular statement is true if it is integrated within the framework of all the other statements already accepted as true.

Mathematics is a good example of the coherence theory in operation. Building on a certain number of basic statements, mathematics constructs an entire system of "truths." In science, likewise, theories generally gain respectability when they are coherent with the body of accepted judgments. Brand Blanshard (1892–), a contemporary coherence theorist, illustrates the meaning of coherence in *The Nature of Thought* when he arranges a number of familiar systems in a series according to the degree of coherence.

> At the bottom would be a junk heap, where we could know every item but one and still be without any clue as to what that remaining item was. Above this would come a stone-pile, for here you could at least infer that what you would find next would be a stone. A machine would be higher again, since from the remaining parts one could deduce not only the general character of a missing part, but also its special form and function. This is a high degree of coherence, but it is very far short of the highest. You could remove the engine from a motorcar while leaving the other parts intact, and replace it with any one of thousands of other engines, but the thought of such an interchange among human heads or hearts shows at once that the interdependence in a machine is far below that of the body. Do we find then in organic bodies the highest conceivable coherence? Clearly not. Though a human hand, as Aristotle said, would

Any judgment is true if it is both self-consistent and coherently connected with our system of judgments as a whole.

EDGAR S. BRIGHTMAN

hardly be a hand when detached from the body, still it would be something definite enough; and we can conceive systems in which even this something would be gone. Abstract a number from the number series and it would be a mere unrecognizable x; similarly, the very thought of a straight line involves the thought of the Euclidean space in which it falls. It is perhaps in such systems as Euclidean geometry that we get the most perfect examples of coherence that have been constructed. If any proposition were lacking, it could be supplied from the rest; if any were altered, the repercussions would be felt through the length and breadth of the system. Yet even such a system as this falls short of the ideal system. Its postulates are unproved; they are independent of each other, in the sense that none of them could be derived from any other or even from all the others together; its clear necessity is bought by an abstractness so extreme as to have left out nearly everything that belongs to the character of actual things. A completely satisfactory system would have none of these defects. No proposition would be arbitrary, every proposition would be entailed by the others jointly and even singly, no proposition would stand outside the system. The integration would be so complete that no part could be seen for what it was without seeing its relation to the whole, and the whole itself could be understood only through the contribution of every part.[7]

Blanshard is describing an ideal of coherence. Still, is the systemic coherence of propositions with each other alone a guarantee of truth? Recall that

---

7. Brand Blanshard, *The Nature of Thought* (New York: Macmillan, 1941), 464–465. Reprinted by permission of George Allen & Unwin Ltd.

almost everyone once believed that the earth was the center of the solar system. This belief stemmed from the ancient Greek astronomer Ptolemy (of the second century A.D.). Why did everyone believe this? Because it made sense and accorded with commonsensical observation. It fit in with the widespread and naive experience of things. Also, it was part of Ptolemy's system of judgments, which, as a result of their extreme consistency, held sway for fifteen hundred years. In fact, the major difference between the theory of Ptolemy and the theory of Copernicus, which replaced it, was that the latter was simpler. Yet both theories were consistent. The point is that coherence dose not seem to distinguish between consistent truth and consistent error. A judgment may be true if it is consistent with other judgments, but what if the other judgments are false? If first judgments are not true, they can produce a system of consistent error.

Another objection is that a coherence theory in the last analysis seems to rely on correspondence. After all, if a judgment is coherent, it must cohere with another judgment. But what of first judgments? With what do they cohere? If they are first, they cannot cohere with anything. Their truth, then, can only be verified by determining whether they report an actual fact. But this is the correspondence theory. Proponents of the coherence theory, however, insist that a judgment of fact itself can be verified only by the coherence theory. Blanshard illustrates this point.

> Suppose we say, "the table in the next room is round"; how should we test this judgment? In the case in question, what verifies the statement of fact is the perceptual judgment that I make when I open the door and look. But then what verifies the perceptual judgment itself? . . . To which the reply is, as before, that a judgment of fact can be verified only by the sort of apprehension that can present us with a fact, and that this must be a further judgment. And an agreement between judgments is best described not as a correspondence, but as coherence.[8]

8. Brand Blanshard, "The Nature of Thought," in *Philosophical Interrogation*, eds. Sidney and Beatrice Rome (New York: Holt, Rinehart and Winston, 1964), 210.

Brand Blanshard: "A judgment of fact can be verified only by the sort of apprehension that can present us with a fact, and this must be a further judgment. And an agreement between judgments is best described not as a correspondence, but as coherence."

PRAGMATIC THEORY

Because of the evident weaknesses in the correspondence and coherence theories, philosophers of recent times have suggested another possibility, the pragmatic theory of truth. Let us see how it works by returning to the judge's chambers.

PROSECUTION: Well, if you want my opinion, I think the whole discussion is silly. I mean, if you want to know what's true, find out what works.

EVEREADY: What?

JUDGE: Are you saying that if something works, it's true?

PROSECUTION: What else can it be? How else can you judge what's true, except by its results? Take the theory of the sun-centered solar system, for example. What makes it true is that it works. It is true because it accurately describes a situation in such a way that people can use that description to produce desired results. That theory's allowed us to plot the position of the heavenly bodies, estimate the distance between them, send satellites into space, and put men on the moon. Previous theories couldn't have produced these results. They just wouldn't have worked. That's why they were untrue, while this one is true.

EVEREADY: But if what works is true, what's stopping it from not working?

PROSECUTION: Nothing. Then it wouldn't be true any longer. The trouble with you, Eveready, is that you're hung up on the idea that truth is something absolute, something unchanging and unchangeable. Well, it's not! And you'd better get used to that. Where do you think truth comes from, anyway? It comes from you and me and the judge. And every man, woman, and child who's ever lived or will live. It doesn't grow on trees for the picking. People make it! They change it and they make it again. We make our own truth!

EVEREADY: So, according to you, if something works, it's true.

PROSECUTION: Exactly.

EVEREADY: Well, it sounds to me like you're saying that if I believe I'm Napoleon, I *am* Napoleon.

PROSECUTION: Your belief that you're Napoleon must face the test of truth: How does the belief work out in practice? Does it lead to satisfactory results? In your case, it wouldn't. People would be frightened by you, they'd avoid you, they'd probably lock you up and throw away the key. Your belief doesn't work. So, it's not true.

EVEREADY: Well, what about the theory that the earth was once visited by astronaut gods? Presumably the belief worked for its author. It produced satisfactory results for him, just as you say the truth must. Now, does that make his theory true?

PROSECUTION: You make it sound as if the author were merely claiming to be happy or to have a toothache, Eveready. His claim isn't just a private one, you know. He's not just reporting his own internal state. He's making a public claim. So, as with all public claims, satisfactory results depend

Science seeks only the *most generally useful* systems of classification; these it regards for the time being, until more useful classifications are invented, as "true."

S. I. HAYAKAWA

on more than just the results produced for a single person.

EVEREADY: But how do you know if his claim works or not?

PROSECUTION: Test it. Try it and see if it works. What else does it explain? What else does it account for? What use can we make of it? That's how to find out if it works.

The prosecution's idea of truth is different from both the correspondence and the coherence theories. He would admit that we can know only our experiences; as a result, truth cannot be what corresponds with reality. But he would also view the coherence theory as far too abstract and impractical to use to measure truth. Instead, he wishes to introduce usefulness as the measure of truth. Truth, he insists, can be defined only in relation to consequences. A statement is true if people can use that statement to achieve results that they desire. There is no absolute truth, or truth that is unchanging. To verify a belief as truth, we should see if the belief satisfies the whole of human nature over a long period of time, if it can be proved scientifically, or if it aids us individually or collectively in the biological struggle for survival. In short, the prosecution argues for a pragmatic theory of truth. This position essentially states: If something works, it is true.

The pragmatic theory of truth is the cornerstone of **pragmatism,** an essentially American philosophy that has developed during the nineteenth and twentieth centuries, especially through the writings of Charles S. Peirce (1839–1914), William James (1842–1910), and John Dewey (1859–1952). Having tired of older European outlooks, especially those that viewed humans primarily in rational or scientific terms, the pragmatists see humans as needing to use the practical consequences of beliefs to determine their truth and validity. Especially objectionable to pragmatists is the traditional concept of truth as being fixed and inert. In contrast, pragmatists conceive of truth as being dynamic and changing, as subjective and relative. Like the correspondence and coherence theories, the pragmatic theory of truth has many forms. But the classic version was put forth by William James in *Pragmatism: A New Name for Some Old Ways of Thinking*. In it he clearly distinguishes the pragmatic theory from other theories of truth.

> Truth, as any dictionary will tell you, is a property of certain of our ideas. It means their "agreement," as falsity means their disagreement, with "reality." Pragmatists and intellectualists both accept this definition as a matter of course. They begin to quarrel only after the question is raised as to what may precisely be meant by the term "agreement," and what by the term "reality," when reality is taken as something for our ideas to agree with.
>
> In answering these questions the pragmatists are more analytic and painstaking, the intellectualists more offhand and irreflective. The popular notion is that a true idea must copy its reality. Like other popular views, this one follows the analogy of the most usual experience. Our true ideas of sensible

Begin by believing with all your heart that your belief is true, so that it will work for you; but then face the possibility that it is really false, so that you can accept the consequences of the belief.

JOHN RESECK

The falseness of an opinion is not for us any objection to it . . . . The question is how far it is life-furthering, life-preserving, species-preserving, perhaps species-creating.

FRIEDRICH NIETZSCHE

> things do indeed copy them. Shut your eyes and think of yonder clock on the wall, and you get just such a true picture or copy of its dial. But your idea of its "works" (unless you are a clock-maker) is much less of a copy, yet it passes muster, for it in no way clashes with the reality. Even though it should shrink to the mere word "works," that word still serves you truly; and when you speak of the "time-keeping function" of the clock, or of its spring's "elasticity," it is hard to see exactly what your ideas can copy.
>
> You perceive that there is a problem here. Where our ideas cannot copy definitely their object, what does agreement with that object mean? Some idealists seem to say that they are true whenever they are what God means that we ought to think about that object. Others hold the copy-view all through, and speak as if our ideas possessed truth just in proportion as they approach to being copies of the Absolute's eternal way of thinking.
>
> These views, you see, invite pragmatistic discussion. But the great assumption of the intellectualists is that truth means essentially an inert static relation. When you've got your true idea of anything, there's an end of the matter. You're in possession; you *know*; you have fulfilled your thinking destiny. You are where you ought to be mentally; you have obeyed your categorical imperative; and nothing more need follow on that climax of your rational destiny. Epistemologically you are in stable equilibrium.
>
> Pragmatism, on the other hand, asks its usual question. "Grant an idea or belief to be true," it says, "what concrete difference will its being true make in any one's actual life? How will the truth

be realized? What experiences will be different from those which would obtain if the belief were false? What, in short, is the truth's cash-value in experiential terms?"

The moment pragmatism asks this question, it sees the answer: *True ideas are those that we can assimilate, validate, corroborate and verify. False ideas are those that we can not.* That is the practical difference it makes to us to have true ideas; that, therefore, is the meaning of truth, for it is all that truth is known as.

This thesis is what I have to defend. The truth of an idea is not a stagnant property inherent in it. Truth *happens* to an idea. It *becomes* true, is *made* true by events. Its verity *is* in fact an event, a process: the process namely of its verifying itself, its veri-*fication*. Its validity is the process of its valid-*ation*.

But what do the words verification and validation themselves pragmatically mean? They again signify certain practical consequences of the veri-

fied and validated idea. It is hard to find any one phrase that characterizes these consequences better than the ordinary agreement-formula—just such consequences being what we have in mind whenever we say that our ideas "agree" with reality. They lead us, namely, through the acts and other ideas which they instigate, into or up to, or towards, other parts of experience with which we feel all the while—such feeling being among our potentialities—that the original ideas remain in agreement. The connections and transitions come to us from point to point as being progressive, harmonious, satisfactory. This function of agreeable leading is what we mean by an idea's verification.[9]

According to James, then, truth is not based on a comparison of statement and some objective,

9. William James, *Pragmatism: A New Name for Some Old Ways of Thinking* (New York: Longmans, Green, 1907), 198–199.

PHILOSOPHY AND LIFE 6.4

Science and Truth

Are scientific theories true in the same sense that, say, the sentence "The sky looks blue" is true? Not all scientists are convinced they are, including Stanislav Grof, who holds that scientific theories are nothing more than conceptual models that scientists use to organize whatever data about reality is available to them at any given time. According to Grof, scientific theories are merely useful approximations to reality and they should not be mistaken for true descriptions of what reality itself is. Continued scientific research inev-

SOURCE: Stanislav Grof, *Ancient Wisdom and Modern Science* (New York: SUNY Press, 1984).

itably produces data that does not fit the leading theories the scientific community holds at any point in time, forcing scientists to replace those theories with new ones. But the new theories are themselves only useful approximations eventually destined to be revised.

To illustrate his view, Dr. Grof points to the way in which modern scientific research has forced us to abandon the theories of Isaac Newton that provided the foundations of Western science for the past three hundred years. Newton's scientific theories view the universe like a machine made up of solid matter in the form of indestructible particles called atoms. These solid

material particles

. . . influence each other by forces of gravitation and interact according to fixed and unchangeable laws. Their interaction occurs in absolute space, which is three-dimensional, homogeneous, and independent of the presence of matter. Time in the Newtonian universe is unidimensional, flowing evenly from the past . . . to the future. Newton's universe . . . is strictly deterministic: If we knew all the factors operating at present, we [could] . . . predict any event in the future. . . .

This mechanistic model of the universe, however, was gradually undermined by research that led external state-of-affairs, or on the inclusion of a statement in a coherent system of beliefs. In James's view, the essential problem with those views is that their adherents have failed to ask the right questions. They shouldn't ask how judgments correspond or relate to reality, but precisely what makes them true. For James, the truth of an idea or judgment lies in what he terms the *practical difference* that it makes in our lives, that is, whether its predictions pan out. Although pragmatism was a new, vigorous approach to the problem of truth that matched the youth and energy of nineteenth-century America, it is not without flaws.

Is there any necessary connection between what is true, on the one hand, and what happens to work or be useful, on the other? Critics of pragmatism often raise this question. They object that James reduces epistemological and logical matters to the psychological and pragmatic. Truth cannot be based on the fallible judgments of humankind. What's true may indeed work, but what works isn't necessarily true. Furthermore, what works for you may not work for me or even anybody else. This at least raises questions about the meaning of *works*.

In what sense is the pragmatic theory better than the more traditional philosophies? Pragmatism maintains that it is more useful. But any judgment about usefulness seems to involve a large dose of subjectivity. Couldn't traditional philosophers claim that their views of truth are better in terms of their own preferences? It seems that they can. In fact, can we ask whether it is true that one view is more useful than another in a sense in which *true* does not mean useful?[10]

---

10. W. T. Jones, *Kant to Wittgenstein and Sartre* (New York: Harcourt Brace Jovanovich, 1969), 300.

---

scientists to formulate a new theory of the universe that was utterly different from the seventeenth century theory. Newton's theory that the universe was made up of solid and indestructible material atoms disintegrated as new experimental evidence indicated that atoms were mostly empty, containing strange subatomic packets of force. Then, surprisingly, further research indicated that these subatomic particles seemed to change their nature depending on how they were observed, while Einstein's theories demolished Newton's views on space and time.

Subatomic particles showed the same paradoxical nature as light, *manifesting either particle properties or wave properties depending on the arrangement of the experiment. . . . Newton's three-dimensional space and unidimensional time were replaced by Einstein's four-dimensional continuum of space-time. In the new physics, the objective world cannot be separated from the observer, and linear causality is not the only and mandatory connecting principle in the cosmos. The universe of modern physics is not the gigantic mechanical clockwork of Newton, but a unified network of events and relations.*

This new theory of the universe, however, like Newton's theory, is nothing more than a useful construct accepted by a particular community of scientists at a particular point in the evolution of science, claims Grof.

QUESTIONS

1. Are scientific theories true or are they mere mental constructs that are useful for dealing with reality? What is truth as it applies to science?

2. What, if anything, distinguishes the truth of scientific theories from the truth of our everyday knowledge of the world? What distinguishes the truth of scientific theories from the truth of your answers to these questions?

Such subjectivity implies that there can be one truth for you, another for me. This relativism can easily warp judgment, disincline us to view evidence impartially and objectively, and ultimately lead us all astray.

QUESTIONS

1. Do you think it is ever possible to "tell the whole truth"? Explain.

2. Is describing truth as a correspondence between a statement and how things actually are begging the question? In what sense does such a definition not answer the question "What is truth?" but endorse a version of that question?

3. Eveready claims, "Indeed, what the witness *thinks* is truth consigns truth to the very dubious area of sense data interpretation. Such interpretation must be purely subjective and need not have anything to do with the way things actually are." Cite instances or cases that illustrate Eveready's charge.

4. Do you think that there are two kinds of truth, subjective and objective—truth as an individual perceives it and truth as it actually is? Or is there just one objective truth, and everything else merely belief and opinion?

5. Show how the following statements pass the test of coherence: (a) I am a rational being; (b) I am a divine being; (c) I am a mechanical being; (d) I am an existential being; (e) I am no self.

6. Take some theory, perhaps in psychology, anthropology, economics, or history, and put it to the coherence test. Does it pass? Can you find an opposing theory that passes as well? What might you conclude about the coherence theory of truth?

7. In what sense do claims of extrasensory perception not fit in with what we claim to know? In what sense do they?

8. Demonstrate how the coherence theory of truth ultimately seems to rely on the correspondence theory. How would proponents of the coherence theory object to this claim?

9. Do you believe in God? If you do, describe how this belief, working through the coherence theory of truth, influences how you see yourself, other people, the world around you, and the future of humankind.

10. Consider the fact that you are studying to enter some profession. Demonstrate how this intention is working as a truth in your life and serving as the cornerstone for a structure of other truths.

11. Take some event from the recent past, such as the Vietnam war. Show how the coherence theory of truth operated to formulate policy and direct activity. Do you think our apparent failure in Vietnam is a vindication of the coherence theory of truth? An indictment? Both? Neither?

12. Cite a belief that you consider true primarily on pragmatic grounds.

13. Give an example of people creating their own truth.

14. In a sense, truth for the pragmatist is an extension of belief. Illustrate how belief can make truth. Do you detect dangers in this position? How would this position affect how you view yourself? In what sense will you be tomorrow what you decide to be today?

15. In opposition to the pragmatists and their theory of truth, critics charge, "But don't you see that you're encouraging us to see things as we would have them and not as they are?" Do you agree with this criticism?

16. Can you think of anything that, although true, does not work? Something that, although it works, is not true?

Observations and Conclusions

If we look closer at the various positions that Eveready assumes, we shall notice that, rather than being contradictory, the three theories of truth are compatible with one another.

First, Eveready believes that truth is not something that changes or is relative. Yet, at the outset of Scaife's testimony, he went to great lengths to prove the opposite: that truth is relative. Eveready could object that what he was actually demonstrating was the relativity of belief, not of truth—that the statement "There is a red, white, and blue American flag in this courtroom" is in fact either true or false, but we just don't know which it is. But how does he know that the proposition must be true or false? Eveready seems to have no recourse but to declare that there are true statements. Of course, he might insist that we can never know the truth even though there are true propositions.

Some philosophers have been that skeptical. The ancient Greek Gorgias (483–376 B.C.) claimed that we could never know if there even was such a thing as truth. Consequently, he believed that seeking truth was futile. But most skeptics stop short of this conclusion. The best known is David Hume, who for all his skepticism nevertheless admitted, in his *A Treatise of Human Nature*, "Whether I be really one of those skeptics who hold that all is uncertain . . . I should reply that this question is entirely superfluous, and that neither I, nor any person was ever sincerely and constantly of that opinion."[11] The fact is that extreme skepticism founders on self-contradiction, for to know you cannot know is to know something. Eveready must at least believe that true propositions exist; otherwise he could not claim to know that he does not know. Ultimately, Eveready, like most of us, must operate as if there are true propositions if for no other reason than to dispose of patent falsehoods.

Thus, despite his railing to the contrary, Eveready holds as true a belief that gives his life meaning, produces satisfactory results, and, in short, works. In other words, his belief that truth exists is founded in pragmatic theory. Furthermore, Eveready takes this belief as self-evident, as a first judgment with which he compares additional judgments and on which he organizes his whole life. So he must subscribe to the idea that the truth is what hangs together—that is, to the coherence theory of truth. Such an assumption provides grounds for his claiming that the statement "There is a red, white, and blue American flag in this courtroom" is either true or false. Finally, on what basis is this statement to be judged true? It seems that Eveready must admit that there can be no other basis than whether there is *in fact* a red, white, and blue American flag in the courtroom. But here he calls on the correspondence theory.

But to synthesize these theories requires analysis, not just a fabricated example. One way to do

---

11. David Hume, *A Treatise of Human Nature*, vol. 1, ed. L. A. Selby-Bigge (Oxford: Clarendon Press, 1896), 7.

I love truth. I believe humanity has need of it. But assuredly it has much greater need still of the untruth which flatters it, consoles it, gives it infine hopes.

ANATOLE FRANCE

this is to view the unique contribution that each theory makes in the realm of truth. Unquestionably, the correspondence theory fits the empirical realm. If I want to know whether it's true that New York is approximately three thousand miles from Los Angeles, that oxygen is necessary for fire, or that it's raining, I can effectively use the correspondence test. If the statements correspond to the facts, then I can accept them as true.

On the other hand, coherence provides a nice test for logical, semantic, or systemic truth. Thus, if I want to know whether it's true that a chair cannot be a nonchair, that 56 divided by 7 is 8, or that all bachelors are unmarried, then I need only see if these statements fit in with other statements that I accept as true.

Finally, the pragmatic test seems very helpful to the many value judgments that we make. Thus, "Lying is wrong," "God exists," "Pleasure is the only intrinsic good," and such statements form a very important part of our lives. So do value judgments in the arts, politics, education, and other walks of life. Frequently, the best—and sometimes the only—way to verify such judgments is by applying the tests of workability. Do these beliefs pan out? The pragmatic theory is in a unique position to help answer this question.

Ultimately the theories of truth are complementary. Rather than viewing them as incompatible, we'd best use them to help determine the truth of the various kinds of statements that we utter. We may accept Hospers's definition that a true proposition is one that describes an actual state-of-affairs, but how we discover the truth of any proposition depends largely on what kind of statement it is.

Every man seeks for truth, but God only knows who has found it.

LORD CHESTERFIELD

QUESTIONS

1. Make three lists of statements: (1) statements you feel you accept mostly on pragmatic grounds, (2) statements you feel you accept mostly because they cohere with other beliefs you have, and (3) statements you accept because you feel they correspond to reality. What general claims can you make about the areas or fields where you tend to rely on a pragmatic theory of truth? Where you tend to rely on a coherence theory? Where you tend to rely on a correspondence theory?

2. What statements about *yourself* do you accept on pragmatic grounds? On the grounds of coherence? On the grounds of correspondence with reality?

CHAPTER SUMMARY AND CONCLUSIONS

We opened this chapter by noting that knowledge is warranted, true belief. We discussed the different modes of warrantability as they apply to various kinds of statements. We then defined a true proposition as describing an actual state-of-affairs and discussed three theories of truth: correspondence, coherence, and pragmatic.

In the last analysis, no one theory—correspondence, coherence, or pragmatic—is a complete and ever-reliable solution to the problem of truth. Each has its shortcomings and strengths. Equally important, each theory plays a part in the search for and discovery of self.

In everyday life we frequently use the test of correspondence to arrive at truth. From our earliest days in school, we are rewarded for reporting things "as they are"—Paris is the capital of France, two hydrogen atoms combine with one oxygen atom to form water. This is the primary way of gleaning information about the world. The correspondence theory also allows us to know about the quantifiable aspects of the self—height, weight, blood pressure, body temperature, and so on. This information, in turn, helps us to stay well: to know when to diet, when to relax, and when to exercise.

When we ignore these quantifiable aspects of self, we risk injury or illness.

But not all aspects of self are so easily quantified. In the complex area of personal experience, for example, the correspondence theory is not so useful. How would you verify the statement "That person loves me"? You cannot verify it as you can verify "I have a temperature." You would probably evaluate it on the basis of the person's behavior toward you: "If that person loves me, would that person have said that?" In other words, you would test through coherence, asking if the person's actions were consistent with loving somebody. Of course, you would be making an assumption about what loving is.

Our assumptions frequently distort our views of self and the world. For example, a man who is ashamed to cry publicly because it isn't manly may be acting consistently with an assumption that is warping his personality. Likewise, a woman who refuses to call a man for a date because women shouldn't be aggressive is acting consistently with an assumption that may be inhibiting her. The sources of the assumptions that we live by are less relevant here than the fact that we unconsciously measure our concepts, feelings, attitudes, and actions against them as if they were self-evident truths. Thus, we do use the coherence theory of truth, but it is valuable only if our first judgments are accurate. This caution is especially applicable to those judgments concerning self or human nature.

If you were wondering whether a particular individual loved you, you would frequently test pragmatically by asking, in effect, what practical difference the person's loving or not loving you makes in the person's life. Does it affect how the person feels or thinks, what the person desires and how the person behaves? You might also ask the same questions of yourself. Suppose that even after you answered these questions you were still undecided. The pragmatic theory recognizes the non-mental aspect of the self, which can and should influence decisions in cases like these. We often listen to the reasons of the heart that reason knows little about, to paraphrase the seventeenth-century French philosopher Blaise Pascal.

Thus, the correspondence, coherence, and pragmatic theories of truth can work together. They can be seen as supplementing one another instead of as mutually contradictory. Truth, for example, might be conceived as that characteristic of a statement that corresponds to a fact (correspondence); but whenever we cannot determine the fact, we must rely on how consistent that statement or judgment is with established truth (coherence) or how useful its consequences are (pragmatism). On the other hand, truth might be conceived as a property that statements have when they have useful consequences (pragmatism), but the most useful consequence of a statement is having it turn out to correspond to the facts (correspondence) or to be consistent with other accepted truths. Perhaps the reader may be able to see even better ways of bringing these three theories together into a satisfactory whole. Or, perhaps, he or she may simply conclude that only one of the theories is satisfactory and that the others must be rejected. Whatever one decides, it is clear that the theories embody helpful and useful ways of understanding the self and its relationship to the world of knowledge.

There are four sorts of men:
He who knows not and knows not he knows not: he is a fool—shun him;
He who knows not and knows he knows not: he is simple—teach him;
He who knows and knows not he knows: he is asleep—wake him.
He who knows and knows he knows: he is wise—follow him.

LADY BURTON

Kant

In the last chapter we saw how Hume's empiricism led philosophy into the dead end of skepticism. If Hume's radical empiricism is accepted, then we can never hope to learn the truth about ourselves, God, or the universe.

In this chapter we will showcase a philosopher who claimed to have found a way around Hume's skepticism and who, in doing so, revolutionized our views about knowledge and truth. This is the eighteenth-century philosopher Immanuel Kant.

Immanuel Kant is regarded by many as the greatest of all philosophers, especially in the field of epistemology. His unique contribution was to argue that the world of our experience is a world that our own mind constructs. Our mind can indeed know the truth about the world around us, he argued, because that world is constructed by the mind itself.

We showcase Kant in this chapter because of the radical and profound contributions he made to our conceptions of knowledge and truth. But reading Kant will also allow us to see how his revolutionary views about knowledge influenced his views on morality and God. Kant, too, exemplifies how our epistemological views affect our positions on other philosophical issues.

KANT

Although he revolutionized philosophy, Kant lived a very ordinary life. He spent all of his eighty years (1724–1804) in the small town in which he was born: Königsberg (now Kaliningrad, USSR). There he grew up and there he went to college, supporting himself in part by his winnings from playing pool with other students. And it was in Königsberg that Kant remained after graduating, eventually attaining a position as a teacher in the local university. As a teacher, Kant came to schedule his activities so precisely that neighbors used to set their clocks when he passed their houses on his daily afternoon walk. Although Kant remained a bachelor all of his life, he had a number of close women friends and had a reputation for being a funny, witty, and entertaining host at the dinner parties he frequently had.

But although Kant never left the place of his birth, his books put him in touch with all the intellectual currents of the eighteenth century. He was well acquainted, therefore, with the tremendous new discoveries in the natural sciences and was especially impressed with Newton's discoveries in physics. But when Kant came across the writings of Hume, these discoveries seemed threatened. For Hume argued that our so-called scientific knowledge is not rationally justified. In particular, he pointed out that the cause-and-effect laws of science go beyond the evidence scientists have for them. Scientists observe *a few times* that certain events have been conjoined *in the past*, and they conclude that those kinds of events *must always* cause each other *in the future*. But how do scientists know that events must always be causally connected in the future as in the past?

Kant realized that Hume's objection was devastating. If Hume was correct, then all our scientific knowledge was unjustified. Moreover, Kant soon discovered that there were other areas of knowledge that contained judgments that went beyond the evidence of our senses.

> I openly confess that my recollection of David Hume was the very thing which many years ago first interrupted my dogmatic slumber and gave my investigations in the field of speculative philosophy a quite new direction. I was far from following him in the conclusions at which he arrived. . . .
>
> I therefore first tried to see whether Hume's objection could not be put into a general form. I soon found that the concept of the connection of

cause and effect was by no means the only concept by which the understanding thinks the connection of things *a priori* [that is, independently of experience].[12]

Kant found three areas of knowledge where we make statements about the world that go beyond the evidence provided by our sense experience. Examples of these kinds of statements are the following:

1. In the sciences of geometry and arithmetic:

   "The shortest distance between two points must always be a straight line."

   "The square of the hypotenuse of a right angle triangle must always equal the sum of the squares of the two sides."

   "The sum of 798 and 857 must always equal 1655."

2. In the natural sciences:

   "All events must always have a cause."

3. In philosophical metaphysics:

   "There must exist a God that causes the universe."

Kant termed these *synthetic* statements to indicate that each gives us genuine information about the world around us. Geometry, for example, tells us that the world will always obey the law that the square of the hypotenuse of right angle triangles equals the sum of the squares of the two sides, while the natural sciences tell us that all events must have a cause. By contrast, Kant used the term *analytic* to refer to statements that merely give us information about the meanings of words, such as "Bachelors are unmarried males."

Kant also called the statements in the above list *a priori*, pointing out two features of such statements: First, as Hume said, these statements go beyond what we can establish through our sense experience. For example, we could never check *all* right angle triangles, yet geometry says the square of their hypotenuses *always* equals the sum of the squares of their sides. Second, we establish that

these statements *must* be true by relying on thought processes within the mind. The laws of geometry, for example, are established in the mind. A priori statements, then, are necessary and universal: They state something that we know by mental processes *must* be true and that *always* holds. By contrast, Kant used the term *a posteriori* to refer to statements that can be established by sense observations, such as "This room is empty" and "The sky above is blue." A posteriori statements are neither necessary nor universal.

But how can we know a priori propositions about the world without going outside of our minds? How do we know, for example, that the outer world must always obey the laws of geometry when we can establish these laws completely within the mind? How do we know that every event must always have a cause when we have not examined every event? Is Hume correct in saying that such synthetic a priori statements are unjustified?

> Now the proper problem of pure reason is contained in the question: How are *a priori* synthetic judgments possible? . . .
>
> Among philosophers, David Hume came nearest to envisaging this problem, but still he was very far from conceiving it with sufficient definiteness and universality. He occupied himself exclusively with the synthetic proposition regarding the connection of an effect with its cause, and he believed himself to have shown that such an *a priori* proposition is entirely impossible. . . . If he had envisaged our problem in all its universality, . . . he would then have recognized that, according to his own argument, pure mathematics, which certainly contains *a priori* synthetic propositions, would also not be possible. . . .
>
> In the solution of our above problem, then, we are at the same time deciding as to the possibility of the employment of pure reason in establishing and developing all those sciences which contain *a priori* knowledge of objects, and have therefore to answer the questions: How is pure mathematics possible? How is pure science of nature possible? . . . How is metaphysics . . . possible?[13]

---

12. Immanuel Kant, *Prolegomena to Any Future Metaphysics*, trans. Lewis White Beck (New York: Bobbs-Merrill, 1950), 8.

13. Immanuel Kant, *Critique of Pure Reason* (1781), trans. Norman Kemp Smith (New York: St. Martin's Press, 1929), B19–B22.

To save our knowledge from Hume's skepticism, Kant had to show that we are justified in making statements that give us real information about the world but are established completely within the mind. To solve that problem, Kant embarked on what he called "a critique of pure reason"—an investigation of what our minds can know apart from the senses.

Kant began his investigation by granting Hume's view of our senses. Hume pointed out that all our knowledge of the world begins with sensations within us: colors, shapes, sounds, tastes, feels, smells. The senses, Hume said, provide us with a continual stream of endlessly changing "perceptions which succeed each other with an inconceivable rapidity and are in a perpetual flux and movement. . . . The mind is a kind of theater, where several perceptions successively make their appearance, pass, re-pass, glide away, and mingle in an infinite variety of postures and situations."[14]

But Kant noticed something Hume missed. It is true that all we receive from the senses are the sensations within us. Yet we do not *experience* a mere display of sensations within us. When I open my eyes, I do not experience changing sensations of light and colors playing in my own vision. Instead, I see *objects* that appear to be *outside* of me. For example, when I look down, I am not aware of a squarish blob of whiteness within my vision. Instead I see it as the white page of a book a few inches away. Somehow, the sensations (colors and shapes) that continually play in my vision appear to me as objects outside of me.

The same is true of my other senses. They, too, only provide a stream of sensations within me. But I experience them as belonging to particular objects outside of me. For example, I do not merely sense ringing, booming, rustling sound sensations in my hearing. Instead, I seem to hear noises coming from some particular place in the room; perhaps a rustling noise from the pages of my book or a voice from a particular person in front of me. Each sensation of sound, feel, and smell appears to be the sound, feel, and smell of objects outside me.

Kant argued that somehow our mind takes the many separate sensations within our senses and *organizes* them into objects that appear to be "outside" ourselves. That is, our mind takes the sensations that appear in our senses and organizes them into objects that appear to us to be in space. It is as if my mind carries within itself a three-dimensional representation of space, and every sensation is given a position within this mental image of space. This three-dimensional representation of space is like a mental box within which my mind systematically places its sensations so that they appear to me as objects in space.

In fact, Kant argues, we could not experience objects as being outside of us without this three-dimensional representation of space in our minds. Kant argues that even to perceive objects as outside of ourselves, we *already* have to know what outside is, that is, we have to know what space is. Moreover, although we can imagine an empty space without objects, we cannot imagine an object that is not in space. This also proves, according to Kant, that our mental representation of space has to be in our minds prior to our experience of objects.

> Space is not an empirical concept which has been derived from outer experiences. For in order that certain sensations be referred to something outside me (that is, to something in another region of space from that in which I find myself), and, similarly, in order that I may be able to represent them as outside and alongside one another, and . . . as in different places, the representation of space also must be presupposed. The representation of space cannot, therefore, be . . . obtained from the relations of outer . . . [experience]. On the contrary, this outer experience is itself possible at all only through that representation.
>
> Space is a necessary *a priori* representation which underlies all outer perceptions. We can never represent to ourselves the absence of space, though we can quite well think of it as empty of objects. It must therefore be regarded as the condi-

---

14. David Hume, *A Treatise of Human Nature*, ed. L. A. Selby-Bigge (Oxford: Clarendon Press, 1894), bk. I, pt. 4, sec. 6, pp. 252–253.

tion of the possibility of . . . [sense experiences], and not as . . . [something] dependent on them.[15]

Space, then, is merely a mental representation in our minds that helps us organize our sensations so that they appear to us to be objects outside of us. There is nothing more to space than this mental image. Space does not exist independently of us outside our mind. As Kant puts it:

> Space does not represent any property of things in themselves, nor does it represent them in their relation to one another. That is to say, space does not represent any determination that attaches to objects themselves and which remains even when abstraction has been made of all the subjective conditions of perception.
>
> It is therefore solely from the human standpoint that we can speak of space, of extended objects, etc. . . . This predicate can be ascribed to things only insofar as they appear to us, that is, only to objects of sensibility [of the senses].[16]

Kant's view—that space does not exist outside the mind—may seem strange. But his view provides the key to one of his major questions: How do we know that the laws of geometry must hold true for all objects in the world even though these laws are established within the mind? Kant's solution is simple and brilliant.

First, he argues, the laws of geometry are nothing more than the laws of the mental image of space that is in our minds. That is why we can establish the laws of geometry by simply examining our inner image of space without having to examine the outer world.

Second, Kant points out, the mind puts every object we experience into this mental representation of space. All our sensations are organized by the mind into objects within its representation of space so that they appear to us as if they exist in space outside. Every object we experience will have

to appear within this mental image and therefore must obey its laws. Since the laws of geometry are the laws of our mental representation, every object we experience will have to obey the laws of geometry.

Thus, Kant provided a solution to the problem that puzzled philosophers for centuries: How do we know without going outside our minds that all objects will obey the laws of geometry? The only solution, Kant held, is that we establish the laws of geometry completely a priori by simply looking within our own minds at its own three-dimensional image of space. We know all the objects we perceive will obey these laws because the mind places all objects within this mental image so that for us they are in space.

Using similar arguments, Kant showed that all our experience must obey the laws of arithmetic. The laws of arithmetic, he said, are the laws of time: They are laws about how units follow one after another, just like numbers follow one after another.

But where do we get our image of time? Just as we organize sensations by inserting them in space, we also organize them by inserting them in time. So time is also one of the structures of the mind. Time is like a long filing system we use to organize our sensations by placing each one at a certain point in the system. Since the image of time is within us, we can know its laws by just examining it. And since the mind makes everything we experience appear to be in time, everything must obey the laws of time. And these laws are the laws of arithmetic.

So the synthetic a priori statements of geometry and arithmetic are justified. Although these

---

15. Kant, *Critique*, trans. N. K. Smith, B38–B39. (Note: The word *intuition* has been replaced here and elsewhere in the translations below with the much more familiar term *perception*.)
16. Ibid., B42–B43.

We have to live today by what truth we can get today, and be ready tomorrow to call it falsehood.

WILLIAM JAMES

statements give us information about the structure of the world, we do not have to examine every object in the world to know these statements hold true of everything we will ever perceive. The synthetic a priori statements of geometry and arithmetic can be established by simply examining our inner images of time and space. Space and time are merely structures within the mind in which we position the objects our mind makes out of the sensations it receives, so that to our minds these objects exist in space and time.

But Kant also had to show that the synthetic a priori statements of the natural sciences were justified. In particular, he had to show that the causal laws of science were justified. How did he do this? Kant's solution to this problem is remarkably similar to his solution to the problem of geometry and mathematics. Kant points out that the mind organizes its sensations so that they appear to us as objects that change through time. How does the mind do this? The mind organizes its sensations into such independent objects by using twelve rules or "categories." The most important of these rules or categories turns out to be the basic law underlying the natural sciences: that all perceived events must have a cause. So just as we know that every object we experience will be organized in space and time, we can also be sure that every event we experience will be causally related to other events. How exactly did Kant prove this? Kant's argument is difficult, but with a bit of work it can be understood.

Kant first points out that our sensations appear to us to be of independent objects that last through time and that change. For example, during the time I look at this book, I feel that I am seeing the same book. My sensations appear to me to be of an object that lasts through time. And as I turn its pages, the same book appears to me to be changing.

In order to make my sensations appear to be changing objects, Kant says, the mind has to bring its sensations together in three ways. First, the mind has to receive or "apprehend" the many separate sensations provided by the senses. For example, each separate moment I look at the changing white book, my senses produce new and different sensations of white color. To keep perceiving the book,

then, I have to keep receiving all of these separate sensations. Second, the mind has to remember the past sensations. For example, in perceiving the book, I have to keep in mind the past sensations of white, as I receive new sensations. If I continually forgot the past sensations, it would be as though a new book were continually appearing before me each moment. Third, the mind has to connect or relate the later sensations to the earlier ones. That is, the mind has to recognize that the earlier sensations and the later ones are sensations of the same object. For example, I must recognize that my later slightly different sensations of the book are sensations of the same book I saw earlier. Otherwise, the earlier and later sensations would appear to me as many separate images of different books floating in my memory. This recognition or connection of earlier and later sensations is what finally makes me feel that I am seeing the same book but that it is changing through time.

> Each perception [of an object] is made up of a multiplicity [of sensations] . . . In order to change this multiplicity [of separate sensations] into a single thing [an object], it is necessary first to run through and collect the multiplicity [of sensations]. This act I call the "synthesis of apprehension." . . .
>
> But if I were always to drop out of thought the earlier sensations . . . , and did not reproduce them [in my memory] while advancing to the next ones, then a complete perception [of an object] would never form. . . . The synthesis of apprehension is therefore inseparably connected with [what I will call] the "synthesis of reproduction."
>
> [Moreover,] if we were not conscious that what we are thinking of now is the same as what we thought a moment before, all reproduction in the series of perceptions would be in vain. Each perception would . . . be a new one. . . . The multiplicity could never form a whole, because it would not have that unity that [my] consciousness alone can give it [by recognizing that what I perceive now is the same as what I perceived earlier].[17]

---

17. Immanuel Kant, *Kritik Reinen Vernunft* [Critique of Pure Reason], trans. Manuel Velasquez (Germany: Johann Friedrich Hartknoch, 1981), A99–A103.

But the mind's ability to collect sensations into unified objects that change through time would not be possible unless the mind itself also lasted through time. Suppose, for example, that I am looking at a book and receiving new sensations of white color each passing moment. If the later sensations are to be connected to the earlier ones, the *same* mind has to receive the earlier and the later ones. This means my mind has to last through time: It has to last through the earlier and later sensations. Thus, the process of receiving, remembering, and connecting sensations into objects that last through time requires a mind that also lasts through time. The unification of sensations into objects requires a "unified" mind that connects sensations. "[But] there can be in us no kind of knowledge, no connection or unifying of one bit of knowledge with another, unless there is a unified consciousness which precedes all the data of perception. . . . This pure original unchanging consciousness I call 'transcendental apperception.' "[18]

The mind, then, is a single consciousness that remains the same through time contrary to Hume's claim that the mind is only a bundle of disconnected sensations. In fact, Kant argues, the mind *must* connect its sensations because it must bring all these separate sensations into itself.

If we want to discover the internal foundation of this unifying of perceptions . . . , we must begin with pure [transcendental] apperception. Sensations would be nothing to us, and would not concern us in the least, if they were not received into our [unified] consciousness. . . . Knowledge is impossible in any other way. We are conscious *a priori* of our own enduring identity with regard to all perceptions we know. Our enduring identity is a necessary condition for us to have these perceptions. For perceptions could not be perceptions of anything for me unless they . . . could at least be connected together into [my] one consciousness. This principle stands firm *a priori*, and may be called the "transcendental principle of the unity"

of all the multiplicity of our perceptions (and therefore also of sensation).[19]

What Kant is saying here is that our mind connects and unifies its sensations because it *has to*. It has to connect them together because the many sensations my senses produce must all enter one mind: my own single mind. But in order to enter into my one mind, they have to be brought together into one.

As Kant says, this point—that the mind *has to* unify its sensations—is crucial. It is crucial because if the mind has to unify its sensations into objects, then we know that the connections the mind imposes on objects are necessary.

What kinds of connections does the mind make between objects? Kant argues that there are twelve kinds of connections or "categories" that the mind must impose on its sensations. Only the most important of these, the relation of cause and effect, will concern us here.

Kant tries to show that the mind *must* impose causal relationships on its sensations if they are to appear as objects that change independently of us. Kant begins his argument by pointing out that changes we perceive can follow each other in an order that I can determine or in an order that is fixed. But changes whose order I determine are not changes in independent objects outside of me; they are merely changes in me. For example, if I look first at the top of a house, and then down to the basement, the order of my perceptions is one I determine by my own will. I can change the order by simply looking first at the basement and then at the roof. So these changes in my perceptions are merely changes in *me*. They are not independent changes in the *objects* outside of me. On the other hand, changes whose order is fixed or "necessary" are changes that I see as changes in independent objects outside of me. For example, if I see a boat being carried down a river by the current, I will first perceive the boat upriver, and then I will perceive the boat downstream. The order of these per-

18. Ibid., A107.

19. Ibid., A116.

ceptions is not one I determine by my own will: I cannot change the order. So I know that the changes in my perceptions of the boat are changes in the *objects* outside of me (in the boat being carried by the current); they are not merely changes in *me*. And I know this only because the order of these changes is fixed by necessary causal laws and not by me. So if our sensations are to appear as objects that change independently of ourselves, they must be related by causal laws.

> The Principle of the succession of time, according to the Law of Causality: All changes take place according to the law of connection between cause and effect.
> Proof: The apprehension of the multiplicity of phenomena is always successive. The perceptions of the parts [of objects] follow one upon another. . . . Thus, for instance, the apprehension of the multiplicity in the phenomenal appearance of a house that stands before me is successive. . . . Every apprehension of an event is [similarly] . . . a perception following on another perception. But as this applies to all synthesis of apprehension, as in the phenomenal appearance of a house, that apprehension would not be different from any other.
> But I observe that if in a phenomenon which contains an event I call the antecedent state of perception A, and the subsequent B, B can only follow A in my apprehension, while the perception A can never follow B, but can only precede it. I see, for instance, a ship gliding down a stream. My perception of its place below follows my perception of its place higher up in the course of the stream, and it is impossible in the apprehension of this phenomenon that the ship should be perceived first below and then higher up. We see, therefore, that the order in the succession of perceptions in our apprehension is here determined, and our apprehension regulated by that order. In the former example of a house my perceptions could begin with the apprehension of the roof and end in the basement, or begin below and end above; they could apprehend the manifold of the empirical intuition from right to left or from left to right. There was therefore no determined order in the succession of these perceptions. . . . [But] in the apprehension of an event there is always a rule which makes the order of the succes-

sive perceptions necessary. . . . Thus only can I be justified in saying, not only of my apprehension, but of the phenomenon itself, that there exists in it a succession, which is the same as to say that I cannot arrange the apprehension otherwise than in that very order. . . .
> If therefore experience teaches us that something happens, we must always presuppose that something precedes on which it follows by rule. Otherwise I could not say of the object that it followed, because its following in my apprehension only, without being determined by rule in reference to what precedes, would not justify us in admitting an objective following. It is therefore always with reference to a rule by which phenomena as they follow, that is as they happen, are determined by an antecedent state, that I can give an objective character to my subjective synthesis (of apprehension); nay, it is under this supposition only that an experience of anything that happens becomes possible.[20]

Thus, Kant proved that all events in the world we experience have to be causally connected. Let us review the steps of his argument. First, Kant showed that the mind connects ("synthesizes") its sensations into objects that last through time. It does this through apprehension, reproduction, and recognition. Second, this connecting of sensations into objects shows that our mind is unified. Third, since the mind is unified, it *must* connect its sensations together. Fourth, one of the connections the mind must impose on its sensations is the connection of cause and effect, for our sensations would not seem to us to be sensations of independently changing objects unless they were causally connected to each other.

Hume, then, was wrong. Hume had said that the laws of the sciences are not well founded, in particular the laws of causality: We have no evidence that events must always be causally connected to each other. Kant, however, proved that all events we experience in the world outside of us *must* be connected by causal laws. For that world is a world that the mind puts together out of its sensations by bringing these sensations together into

---

20. Immanuel Kant, *Critique of Pure Reason*, trans. Friedrich Max Müller (New York: Macmillan, 1896), 774, 155–160.

a single mind. In order to bring sensations together so that they seem to be sensations of independently changing objects, the mind must connect them by causal relations. The mind, that is, *must* use the category of cause and effect to connect our sensations so that they appear to us as the independently changing world of trees, oceans, mountains, and stars that we see around us. Only by recognizing that we construct the world in our mind in this way, Kant says, can we escape Hume's skepticism about the causal laws of science.

Kant called the world as it appears in our minds the "phenomenal" world and distinguished it from the "noumenal" world. The "noumenal" world is the collection of things as they exist in themselves apart from our perception of them in our mind. Clearly, we can never know what the noumenal world is like: All we can know is the phenomenal world of things as they appear to us after they have been organized by the mind.

What about Hume's skepticism about God? Reluctantly, Kant agreed that we cannot *prove* that there is a God. The "cosmological" proofs for God, Kant pointed out, say that God must exist because He had to "cause" the universe. But the only causality there is in the universe is the causality our own minds put there: The concept of a cause is merely a category of the mind, nothing more. So we cannot appeal to causality to prove that God exists. Other metaphysical arguments for the existence of God, Kant held, make similar illegitimate use of concepts that are merely categories of the mind. None of these metaphysical arguments are valid proofs of the existence of God.

But Kant's views on God do not end here. Kant went on to attempt to show that the existence of God should be accepted on the basis of our moral commitments. To understand this aspect of Kant, we must examine his views on morality.

Kant argued that a person is moral to the extent that he or she follows a principle he called "the categorical imperative": "I ought never to act unless I can will my maxim to serve as a universal law." A "maxim" for Kant is the reason a person has for doing something. And a maxim "serves as a universal law" if every person consistently acts on that reason. So the categorical imperative is the moral

principle that whenever I do something, my reasons for doing it must be reasons that I would (and could) be willing to have everyone act on. For example, suppose I wonder whether I should help the needy, and my reason for being reluctant to help them is simply that I do not want to take the trouble. According to Kant, I must ask myself: Would I be willing to have everyone refrain from helping others when they did not want to take the trouble? Clearly, I would *not* be willing to have everyone do this, since I myself might need the help of others in some situations. Therefore, it would be wrong for me to refrain from helping those in need. Kant claims that sometimes it is absolutely *impossible* for everyone to act on the immoral reasons we are tempted to act on. In such cases it is absolutely immoral to act on those reasons.

> The ordinary reason of humanity in its practical judgments agrees perfectly with this, and always has in view the principle here suggested. For example, suppose that I ask myself: Would it be morally permissible for me to make a promise I do not intend to keep when I am in trouble? . . . The shortest and most unerring way for me to discover whether a lying promise is consistent with duty is to ask myself: Could I will to have my maxim (that is, the principle, "I will get out of my difficulties with false promises") serve as a universal law, for myself as well as for others; and would I be able to say to myself, "Everyone may make a false promise when he finds himself in a difficulty that he cannot escape in any other way"? As soon as I ask myself these questions, I become aware that although I might desire to lie, I could not will to have lying become a universal law. For if lying promises became the rule, there would soon be no promises at all. There would be no promises because people would stop believing each other when they said that they intended to keep their promises; and if one person overhastily accepted the lying promise of another, that person would soon learn to do the same thing to others. So as soon as my maxim became a universal law, it would destroy itself.
>
> I do not, therefore, need any great genius to see what I have to do so that my will can be morally good. Even if I have very little experience of the world, even if I cannot prepare for all contingencies ahead of time, all I have to ask myself is this:

Could you will to have your maxim serve as a universal law? If not, then you should not act on that maxim.[21]

How does Kant argue for the categorical imperative? For Kant, moral right and wrong depend on the interior motives on which the person acts. Kant argues that to the degree that a person is interiorly motivated merely by self-interest or merely by the pleasure he gets from an action, the action "has no moral worth." A person's behavior has "moral worth" only to the extent that the person is motivated by "duty," that is, by the belief that all human beings ought to act this way. Consequently, an action has moral worth only to the extent that the person is motivated by reasons that he feels everyone else can and ought to act on.

Kant claimed that the categorical imperative could be expressed in a second way: "Act in such a way that you always treat humanity, whether in your own person or in the person of any other, never simply as a means, but always at the same time as an end." Or, never treat people *only* as means but always also as ends. By this Kant meant that we should never treat people only as tools to be manipulated or forced into serving our interests. Instead, we should always treat people as ends, that is, as free rational persons who must be given the opportunity to decide for themselves whether or not they will go along with our plans.

> A man who is thinking of making a lying promise will realize that he would be using others merely as means because he would not be letting them participate in the goal of the actions in which he involves them. For the people I would thus be using for my own purposes would not have consented to be treated in this way and to that extent they would not have participated in the goals to be attained by the action. Such violations of the principle that our humanity must be respected as an end in itself are even clearer if we take examples of attacks on the freedom and prop-

erty of others. It is obvious that the person who violates such rights is using people merely as means without considering that as rational beings they should be esteemed also as ends; that is, as beings who must be able to participate in the goals of the actions in which they are involved with him.[22]

According to Kant, this second way of expressing the categorical imperative is really equivalent to the first. The first version says that what is morally right for me must be morally right for others, or that everyone must be treated the same. The second version says that just as I give myself the opportunity to decide what I will do, I must also give others the same opportunity, or, again, that everyone must be treated the same. The second version, however, unlike the first, emphasizes that morality requires us to respect the freedom of all rational persons.

Kant points out that if the categorical imperative defines morality, then morality and happiness do not necessarily coincide. For the morally good person is the one who follows the categorical imperative even when this is not in his self-interest and even when he takes no pleasure in doing so. Consequently, morally good people often suffer and fail to get what is in their self-interest in this world. On the other hand, evil people who consistently pursue their self-interest and pleasure, even by taking advantage of others, often prosper in this world. In this world, good people who deserve happiness often do not get it, while evil people who do not deserve it do.

This mismatch between morality and happiness, Kant holds, is wrong, and all of us feel it ought not to be this way. In fact, we feel an obligation to seek a world where the good prosper and the evil do not, and our sense of obligation requires us to believe that such a world is possible. Such a perfect world, Kant calls a "summum bonum," the supremely good state of affairs. But, he says, only a good God could bring such a perfect world into existence (perhaps in another life). So, if we believe such a world is possible (and we have an obligation

21. Immanuel Kant, *Grundlegung zur Metaphysik der Sitten* [Groundwork of the Metaphysics of Morals], in *Immanuel Kant Werkausgabe*, vol. 7, ed. Wilhelm Weischedel (Frankfurt, Germany: Insel Verlag Wiesbaden, 1956), trans. Manuel Velasquez (Copyright © 1987 by Manuel Velasquez), 28–30.

22. Ibid., 62.

Immanuel Kant: "There can be no doubt that all our knowledge begins with experience. But though all our knowledge begins with experience, it does not follow that it all arises out of experience. For it may well be that even our empirical knowledge is made up of what we receive through impressions and of what our own faculty of knowledge supplies from itself."

to believe it is), we must assume that God exists. Thus, although we cannot *prove* that God exists, morality forces us to assume that He does.

> We ought to endeavor to promote the *summum bonum*, which, therefore, must be possible. Accordingly, the existence of a cause of all nature, distinct from nature itself, and containing the principle of this connection, namely the exact harmony of happiness with morality, is also *postulated.* . . . The *summum bonum* is possible in the world only on the supposition of a Supreme Being having a causality corresponding to moral character. Now a being that is capable of acting on the conception of laws is an *intelligence* (a rational being), and the causality of such a being according to this conception of laws is his *will*; therefore the supreme cause of nature, which must be presupposed as a condition of the *summum bonum*, is a

being which is the cause of nature by *intelligence* and *will*, consequently its author, that is God. . . . Now it was seen to be a duty for us to promote the *summum bonum*. Consequently it is not merely allowable, but it is a necessity connected with duty as a requisite, that we should presuppose the possibility of this *summum bonum*. And as this is possible only on condition of the existence of God, it inseparably connects the supposition of this with duty; that is, it is morally necessary to assume the existence of God.[23]

Thus, Kant shifted the argument for God's existence away from metaphysics, where every other philosopher had placed it. Other philosophers had assumed that God's existence had to be proved by relying on metaphysical concepts such as the concept of causality, and such arguments had been ruthlessly demolished by the skepticism of Hume. Kant tried to show that these arguments had to fail because metaphysical concepts are merely categories in our minds; they can tell us nothing about things as they are in themselves. Instead, Kant claimed, we must believe in God on the basis of our moral commitments: Morality forces us to hold that God exists. For morality tells us that the good people must be rewarded and evil ones punished, and only a God could bring about such a "summum bonum." By thus placing belief in God in the realm of morality, Kant hoped, belief would be secure from the attacks of Humean skepticism.

In spite of his very ordinary life, then, Kant's philosophy was truly revolutionary. Kant taught us to believe that the world conforms to the categories of the mind, whereas we had always assumed that the mind must conform its categories to the world. He taught us that morality requires us to respect the freedom of others whether or not this pleases us, and consequently, that being moral and being happy may not coincide in this life. And he taught us to believe in God on the basis of morality instead of on the basis of metaphysical arguments. These were truly new ways of looking at the universe, new ways of thinking about ourselves and

---

23. Immanuel Kant, *Critique of Practical Reason*, trans. T. K. Abbott (London: Longmans Green, 1927), pt. 1, bk. 2, ch. 2, para. 5, pp. 220–222.

the world in which we live. It is hard to imagine a more revolutionary view of our situation.

QUESTIONS

1. In your own words, explain Kant's problem: "How are a priori synthetic judgments possible?"

2. Summarize in your own words how Kant tries to show that a priori synthetic judgments in geometry and arithmetic are "possible."

3. In your own words, why does Kant say that our mind *must* connect its sensations together into objects? Why does Kant say that the mind must connect its sensations into objects that are causally connected? In your view, does Kant really answer Hume?

4. Some people have said that Kant cannot be called a rationalist or an empiricist. Why do you think they say this? Do you see any rationalist elements in Kant? Do you see any empiricist elements?

5. Is Kant's first version of the categorical imperative the same as the "Golden Rule": Do unto others as you would have them do unto you?

6. In your view, what would Kant's categorical imperative imply about the morality of suicide? About the morality of the death penalty? Explain.

7. Do you feel that Kant's own argument for accepting the existence of God is correct? Why?

RYŪNOSUKE AKUTAGAWA

In a Grove

What is truth? How are knowledge claims to be verified? Is it possible to know anything with certainty? Few short stories so dramatically raise these questions as "In a Grove," by Japanese writer Ryūnosuke Akutagawa (1892–1927). A lonely cedar grove is the backdrop for this tale of rape and violent death, in which objective truth stands like a figure at high noon, casting no shadow. Ask yourself what actually did happen in the cedar grove. And be careful that your own view isn't as colored as the views of the witnesses themselves.

THE TESTIMONY OF A WOODCUTTER QUESTIONED BY A HIGH POLICE COMMISSIONER

Yes, sir. Certainly, it was I who found the body. This morning, as usual, I went to cut my daily quota of cedars, when I found the body in a grove in a hollow in the mountains. The exact location? About 150 meters off the Yamashina stage road. It's an out-of-the-way grove of bamboo and cedars.

The body was lying flat on its back dressed in a bluish silk kimono and a wrinkled head-dress of the Kyoto style. A single sword-stroke had pierced the breast. The fallen bamboo-blades round it were stained with bloody blossoms. No, the blood was no longer running. The wound had dried up, I believe. And also, a gadfly was stuck fast there, hardly noticing my footsteps.

You ask me if I saw a sword or any such thing?

No, nothing, sir. I found only a rope at the root of a cedar near by. And . . . well, in addition to a rope, I found a comb. That was all. Apparently he must have made a battle of it before he was murdered, because the grass and fallen bamboo-blades had been trampled down all around.

"A horse was near by?"

No, sir. It's hard enough for a man to enter, let alone a horse.

SOURCE: Ryūnosuke Akutagawa, *Rashomon and Other Stories*, trans. Takashi Kojima (Copyright 1952 by Liveright Publishing Corporation). Reprinted by permission.

THE TESTIMONY OF A TRAVELING BUDDHIST PRIEST
QUESTIONED BY A HIGH POLICE COMMISSIONER

The time? Certainly, it was about noon yesterday, sir. The unfortunate man was on the road from Sekiyama to Yamashina. He was walking toward Sekiyama with a woman accompanying him on horseback, who I have since learned was his wife. A scarf hanging from her head hid her face from view. All I saw was the color of her clothes, a lilac-colored suit. Her horse was a sorrel with a fine mane. The lady's height? Oh, about four feet five inches. Since I am a Buddhist priest, I took little notice about her details. Well, the man was armed with a sword as well as a bow and arrows. And I remember that he carried some twenty odd arrows in his quiver.

Little did I expect that he would meet such a fate. Truly human life is as evanescent as the morning dew or a flash of lightning. My words are inadequate to express my sympathy for him.

THE TESTIMONY OF A POLICEMAN QUESTIONED
BY A HIGH POLICE COMMISSIONER

The man that I arrested? He is a notorious brigand called Tajomaru. When I arrested him, he had fallen off his horse. He was groaning on the bridge at Awataguchi. The time? It was in the early hours of last night. For the record, I might say that the other day I tried to arrest him, but unfortunately he escaped. He was wearing a dark blue silk kimono and a large plain sword. And, as you see, he got a bow and arrows somewhere. You say that this bow and these arrows look like the ones owned by the dead man? Then Tajomaru must be the murderer. The bow wound with leather strips, the black lacquered quiver, the seventeen arrows with hawk feathers—these were all in his possession I believe. Yes, sir, the horse is, as you say, a sorrel with a fine mane. A little beyond the stone bridge I found the horse grazing by the roadside, with his long rein dangling. Surely there is some providence in his having been thrown by the horse.

Of all the robbers prowling around Kyoto, this Tajomaru has given the most grief to the women in town. Last autumn a wife who came to the mountain back of the Pindora of the Toribe Temple, presumably to pay a visit, was murdered, along with a girl. It has been suspected that it was his doing. If this criminal murdered the man, you cannot tell what he may have done with the man's wife. May it please your honor to look into this problem as well.

THE TESTIMONY OF AN OLD WOMAN QUESTIONED
BY A HIGH POLICE COMMISSIONER

Yes, sir, that corpse is the man who married my daughter. He does not come from Kyoto. He was a samurai in the town of Kokufu in the province of Wakasa. His name was Kanazawa no Takehiko, and his age was twenty-six. He was of a gentle disposition, so I am sure he did nothing to provoke the anger of others.

My daughter? Her name is Masago, and her age is nineteen. She is a spirited, fun-loving girl, but I am sure she has never known any man except Takehiko. She has a small, oval, dark-complected face with a mole at the corner of her left eye.

Yesterday Takehiko left for Wakasa with my daughter. What bad luck it is that things should have come to such a sad end! What has become of my daughter? I am resigned to giving up my son-in-law as lost, but the fate of my daughter worries me sick. For heaven's sake leave no stone unturned to find her. I hate that robber Tajomaru, or whatever his name is. Not only my son-in-law, but my daughter . . . (Her later words were drowned in tears.)

TAJOMARU'S CONFESSION

I killed him, but not her. Where's she gone? I can't tell. Oh, wait a minute. No torture can make me confess what I don't know. Now things have come to such a head, I won't keep anything from you.

Yesterday a little past noon I met that couple. Just then a puff of wind blew, and raised her hanging scarf, so that I caught a glimpse of her face. Instantly it was again covered from my view. That may have been one reason; she looked like a Bodhisattva. At that moment I made up my mind to capture her even if I had to kill her man.

Why? To me killing isn't a matter of such great consequence as you might think. When a woman is captured, her man has to be killed anyway. In killing, I use the sword I wear at my side. Am I the only one who kills people? You, you don't use your swords. You kill people with your power, with your money. Sometimes you kill them on the pretext of working for their good. It's true they don't bleed. They are in the best of health, but all the same you've killed them. It's hard to say who is a greater sinner, you or me. (An ironical smile.)

But it would be good if I could capture a woman without killing her man. So, I made up my mind to capture her, and do my best not to kill him. But it's out of the question on the Yamashina stage road. So I managed to lure the couple into the mountains.

It was quite easy. I became their traveling companion, and I told them there was an old mound in the mountain over there, and that I had dug it open and found many mirrors and swords. I went on to tell them I'd buried the things in a grove behind the mountain, and that I'd like to sell them at a low price to anyone who would care to have them. Then . . . you see, isn't greed terrible? He was beginning to be moved by my talk before he knew it. In less than half an hour they were driving their horse toward the mountain with me.

When he came in front of the grove, I told them that the treasures were buried in it, and I asked them to come and see. The man had no objection—he was blinded by greed. The woman said she would wait on horseback. It was natural for her to say so, at the sight of a thick grove. To tell you the truth, my plan worked just as I wished, so I went into the grove with him, leaving her behind alone.

The grove is only bamboo for some distance. About fifty yards ahead there's a rather open clump of cedars. It was a convenient spot for my purpose. Pushing my way through the grove, I told him a plausible lie that the treasures were buried under the cedars. When I told him this, he pushed his laborious way toward the slender cedar visible through the grove. After a while the bamboo thinned out, and we came to where a number of cedars grew in a row. As soon as we got there, I seized him from behind. Because he was a trained, sword-bearing warrior, he was quite strong, but he was taken by surprise, so there was no help for him. I soon tied him up to the root of a cedar. Where did I get a rope? Thank heaven, being a robber, I had a rope with me, since I might have to scale a wall at any moment. Of course it was easy to stop him from calling out by gagging his mouth with fallen bamboo leaves.

When I disposed of him, I went to his woman and asked her to come and see him, because he seemed to have been suddenly taken sick. It's needless to say that this plan also worked well. The woman, her sedge hat off, came into the depths of the grove, where I led her by the hand. The instant she caught sight of her husband, she drew a small sword. I've never seen a woman of such violent temper. If I'd been off guard, I'd have got a thrust in my side. I dodged, but she kept on slashing at me. She might have wounded me deeply or killed me. But I'm Tajomaru. I managed to strike down her small sword without drawing my own. The most spirited woman is defenseless without a weapon. At least I could satisfy my desire for her without taking her husband's life.

Yes, . . . without taking his life. I had no wish to kill him. I was about to run away from the grove, leaving the woman behind in tears, when she frantically clung to my arm. In broken fragments of words, she asked that either her husband or I die. She said it was more trying than death to have her shame known to two men. She gasped out that she wanted to be the wife of whichever survived. Then a furious desire to kill him seized me. (Gloomy excitement.)

Telling you in this way, no doubt I seem a crueler man than you. But that's because you didn't see her face. Especially her burning eyes at that moment. As I saw her eye to eye, I wanted to make her my wife even if I were to be struck by lightning. I wanted to make her my wife . . . this single desire filled my mind. This was not only lust, as you might think. At that time if I'd had no other desire than lust, I'd surely not have minded knocking her down and running away. Then I wouldn't have stained my sword with his blood. But the moment I gazed at her face in the dark grove, I decided not to leave there without killing him.

But I didn't like to resort to unfair means to kill him. I untied him and told him to cross swords with me. (The rope that was found at the root of the cedar is the rope I dropped at the time.) Furious with anger, he drew his thick sword. And quick as thought, he sprang at me ferociously, without speaking a word. I needn't tell you how our fight turned out. The twenty-third stroke . . . please remember this. I'm impressed with this fact still. Nobody under the sun has ever clashed swords with me twenty strokes. (A cheerful smile.)

When he fell, I turned toward her, lowering my blood-stained sword. But to my great astonishment she was gone. I wondered to where she had run away. I looked for her in the clump of cedars. I listened, but heard only a groaning sound from the throat of the dying man.

As soon as we started to cross swords, she may have run away through the grove to call for help. When I thought of that, I decided it was a matter of life and death to me. So, robbing him of his sword, and bow and arrows, I ran out to the mountain road. There I found her horse still grazing quietly. It would be a mere waste of words to tell you the later details, but before I entered town I had already parted with the sword. That's all my confession. I know that my head will be hung in chains anyway, so put me down for the maximum penalty. (A defiant attitude.)

THE CONFESSION OF A WOMAN WHO HAS COME TO THE *SHIMIZU* TEMPLE

That man in the blue silk kimono, after forcing me to yield to him, laughed mockingly as he looked at my bound husband. How horrified my husband must have been! But no matter how hard he struggled in agony, the rope cut into him all the more tightly. In spite of myself I ran stumblingly toward his side. Or rather I tried to run toward him, but the man instantly knocked me down. Just at the moment I saw an indescribable light in my husband's eyes. Something beyond expression . . . his eyes make me shudder even now. That instantaneous look of my husband, who couldn't speak a word, told me all his heart. The flash in his eyes was neither anger nor sorrow . . . only a cold light, a look of loathing. More struck by the look in his eyes than by the blow of the thief, I called out in spite of myself and fell unconscious.

In the course of time I came to, and found that the man in blue silk was gone. I saw only my husband still bound to the root of the cedar. I raised myself from the bamboo-blades with difficulty, and looked into his face; but the expression in his eyes was just the same as before.

Beneath the cold contempt in his eyes, there was hatred. Shame, grief, and anger . . . I don't know how to express my heart at that time. Reeling to my feet, I went up to my husband.

"Takehiko," I said to him, "since things have come to this pass, I cannot live with you. I'm determined to die, . . . but you must die, too. You saw my shame. I can't leave you alive as you are."

This was all I could say. Still he went on gazing at me with loathing and contempt. My heart breaking, I looked for his sword. It must have been taken by the robber. Neither his sword nor his bow and arrows were to be seen in the grove. But fortunately my small sword was lying at my feet. Raising it over head, once more I said, "Now give me your life, I'll follow you right away."

When he heard these words, he moved his lips with difficulty. Since his mouth was stuffed with leaves, of course his voice could not be heard at all. But at a glance I understood his words. Despising me, his look said only, "Kill me." Neither conscious nor unconscious, I stabbed the small sword through the lilac-colored kimono into his breast.

Again at this time I must have fainted. By the time I managed to look up, he had already breathed his last—still in bonds. A streak of sinking sunlight streamed through the clump of cedars and bamboos, and shone on his pale face. Gulping down my sobs, I untied the rope from his dead body. And . . . and what has become of me since I have no more strength to tell you. Anyway I hadn't the strength to die. I stabbed my own throat with the small sword, I threw myself into a pond at the foot of the mountain, and I tried to kill myself in many ways. Unable to end my life, I am still living in dishonor. (A lonely smile.) Worthless as I am, I must have been forsaken even by the most merciful Kwannon. I killed my own husband. I was violated by the robber. Whatever can I do? Whatever can I . . . I . . . (Gradually, violent sobbing.)

THE STORY OF THE MURDERED MAN, AS TOLD THROUGH A MEDIUM

After violating my wife, the robber, sitting there, began to speak comforting words to her. Of course I couldn't speak. My whole body was tied fast to the root of a cedar. But meanwhile I winked at her many times, as much as to say "Don't believe the robber." I wanted to convey some such meaning to her. But my wife, sitting dejectedly on the bamboo leaves, was looking hard at her lap. To all appearances, she was listening to his words. I was agonized by jealousy. In the meantime the robber went on with his clever talk, from one subject to another. The robber finally made his bold, brazen proposal. "Once your virtue is stained, you won't get along well with your husband, so won't you be my wife instead? It's my love for you that made me be violent toward you."

While the criminal talked, my wife raised her face as if in a trance. She had never looked so beautiful as at that moment. What did my beautiful wife say in answer to him while I was sitting bound there? I am lost in space, but I have never thought of her answer without burning with anger and jealousy. Truly she said, . . . "Then take me away with you wherever you go."

This is not the whole of her sin. If that were all, I would not be tormented so much in the dark. When she was going out of the grove as if in a dream, her hand in the robber's, she suddenly turned pale, and pointed at me tied to the root of the cedar, and said "Kill him! I cannot marry you as long as he lives." "Kill him!" she cried many times, as if she had gone crazy. Even now these words threaten to blow me headlong into the bottomless abyss of darkness. Has such a hateful thing come out of a human mouth ever before? Have such cursed words ever struck a human ear, even once? Even once such a . . . (A sudden cry of scorn.) At these words the robber himself turned pale. "Kill him," she cried, clinging to his arms. Looking hard at her, he answered neither yes nor no . . . but hardly had I thought about his answer before she had been knocked down into the bamboo leaves. (Again a cry of scorn.) Quietly folding his arms, he looked at me and said, "What will you do with her? Kill her or save her? You have only to nod. Kill her?" For these words alone I would like to pardon his crime.

While I hesitated, she shrieked and ran into the depths of the grove. The robber instantly snatched at her, but he failed even to grasp her sleeve.

After she ran away, he took up my sword, and my bow and arrows. With a single stroke he cut one of my bonds. I remember his mumbling, "My fate is next." Then he disappeared from the grove. All was silent after that. No, I heard someone crying. Untying the rest of my bonds, I listened carefully, and I noticed that it was my own crying. (Long silence.)

I raised my exhausted body from the root of the cedar. In front of me there was shining the small sword which my wife had dropped. I took it up and stabbed it into my breast. A bloody lump rose to my mouth, but I didn't feel any pain. When my breast grew cold, everything was as silent as the dead in their graves. What profound silence! Not a single bird-note was heard in the sky over this grave in the hollow of the mountains. Only a lonely light lingered on the cedars and mountains. By and by the light gradually grew fainter, till the cedars and bamboo were lost to view. Lying there, I was enveloped in deep silence.

Then someone crept up to me. I tried to see who it was. But darkness had already been gathering round me. Someone . . . that someone drew the small sword softly out of my breast in its invisible hand. At the same time once more blood flowed into my mouth. And once and for all I sank down into the darkness of space.

QUESTIONS

1. On what fact, if any, do the robber, wife, and husband agree?

2. If you were reporting what had occurred in the grove to a friend who knew nothing of the event, what would you feel safe in saying—what would you report as fact? On what basis—correspondence, coherence, or pragmatism?

3. Assume that the testimonies of the woodcutter, priest, policeman, and old woman are accurate. Which, if any, of the principal accounts fits in with these testimonies best?

4. What we perceive is frequently influenced by our beliefs and biases—even how we see ourselves. Show this in the testimonies of the robber, wife, and husband.

5. Do you think it's accurate to say that, regardless of how anyone perceived it, a given set of objective events occurred that day in the grove? If you say yes, how would you prove it?

SUGGESTIONS FOR FURTHER READING

Castaneda, Carlos. *A Separate Reality*. New York: Simon & Schuster, 1972. The author covers the first five years of his relationship with the Yaqui Indian don Juan, whose truth and sources of knowledge defy conventional epistemological attitudes. A book sure to leave the reader asking just what truth is.

Huxley, Aldous. *The Doors of Perception*. New York: Harper & Row, 1970. Huxley records his experiences with the drug mescaline. His account raises questions about the senses and the mind but especially about knowledge and truth.

Pirandello, Luigi. "It Is So If You Think So." In *Naked Masks: Five Plays*, edited by Eric Bentley. New York: Dutton, 1952. Italian novelist and playwright Pirandello concerns himself in this play with the mental state of a character called Ponza. Is Ponza insane and keeping his wife and her mother from seeing one another? Or is he sane, and the mother not really the mother at all but a madwoman who has never accepted the death of her daughter? The play raises pertinent questions about the subjective/objective nature of truth.

Russell, Bertrand. *Human Knowledge: Its Scope and Limits*. New York: Simon & Schuster, 1948. This is a clear, readable review of many philosophical topics, including science, language, and probability, as well as knowledge and perception.

Stoppard, Tom. *Jumpers*. New York: Grove Press, 1974. Stoppard, one of today's foremost dramatists, explores the difficulty of sustaining philosophical truth in the midst of the absurd, the comic, and the pathetic. In this play a philosopher delivers a lecture while bedlam reigns around him.

White, Alan R. *Truth*. Garden City, N. Y.: Doubleday, 1970. This book offers a thoughtful treatment of the different meanings of truth, including three traditional and three modern concepts.

PART IV   Values

Traditionally, ethics has investigated the problem of values in human conduct. Ethics investigates questions involving right conduct, good character, and life fulfillment. It examines the meanings of value terms in order to clarify our moral discourse and to justify ethical judgments. Social and political philosophy concerns questions about social structures and political systems. Social and political philosophy examines values as they relate to the state and the roots of social obligations.

The next two chapters deal with two important value matters: ethics and social philosophy.

CHAPTER 7   Ethics

Man is the only animal that blushes, or needs to.
MARK TWAIN

Introduction

No people in history have had so much of the world's bounty and so much time in which to use it as we have. It is no wonder that we keep hearing the phrase "quality of life." After all, many of us are now in a position to seek, if not share, the "good life." But just what is this good life? Various interests will gladly tell us, from the latest brand of beer to transcendental meditation. All pretend to offer a value worth our time and money, if not our devotion. The number of interests vying for our loyalties boggles the mind. To which drummer should we march? What values should we pursue?

Much of how we see ourselves is determined by what we value, for our values shape our thoughts, feelings, actions, and perceptions. Our values also express who and what we are. In the past, perhaps because of strong family ties, values were served up at the dinner table. We frequently attended a particular church, voted for a certain party, read select magazines, and behaved in a prescribed way because our parents did. But for many today family bonds, once strong and far-reaching, often extend no farther than the nearest freeway; loyalty stretches no farther than the next meal. The affinity that many once felt for family is now often felt for a friend or a cause. In most instances, however, these experiences with family substitutes are not long-lived or profound enough to instill lasting values. The results are frequently short, although often intense, romances with various values that can leave us intellectually dizzy.

Just what values should we hold and pursue?

What values should we nourish in our own lives, in the running of our country, in our artistic tastes? So important are these questions in expressing and shaping us that we shall devote the next two chapters to them. We do this not to provide easy, simple-minded answers but to provide a framework in which to develop our own value systems. In this chapter we explore the nature of values and then focus on ethics. The main points of this chapter are the following:

MAIN POINTS

1. Ethics is the study of those values that relate to our moral conduct, including questions of good and evil, right and wrong, and moral responsibility.

2. Normative ethics is the reasoned search for principles of moral behavior. Metaethics examines normative judgments, paying special attention to the meaning of the language used.

3. Consequentialist theories claim that the morality of an action depends only on its consequences.

4. Egoism is the consequentialist position that states: Always act in such a way that your actions promote your own best long-term interests.

5. Act utilitarianism is the consequentialist position that states: Always act in such a way that your actions produce the greatest happiness for the most people.

6. Rule utilitarianism is the consequentialist position that states: Always act in such a way that the rule of your actions produces the greatest happiness for the most people.

7. Situationism is the normative position that is based on the belief that the moral action produces the greatest amount of Christian love of all the possible actions.

8. Divine command enjoins us to follow the law of God.

9. Kant's categorical imperative is the normative position that states: Always act in such a way that your reasons for acting are reasons you could will to have everyone act on in similar circumstances.

10. Ross's theory of prima facie duties obliges us to perform the action with the greatest amount of prima facie rightness over wrongness.

11. Buddhism emphasizes volition and ties morality to wisdom. Its moral code has a negative and positive component.

12. The concept of moral responsibility is associated with the concept of excusability, which holds that there are circumstances under which we should excuse people for their decisions and conduct.

13. In response to the claim that moral responsibility is not possible in a strictly deterministic universe, four main positions can be identified: hard determinism, indeterminism, soft determinism, and self-determinism.

THE NATURE OF VALUES

Individually and collectively, people express many different values. In clothes, some prefer sportswear, others more formal attire. In food, some like the spicy, others the bland. In books, some people read mysteries, others devour science fiction. On it goes, from religion to art, politics to education—values in every area of human affairs.

How do values arise? Where do they come from? Why does one person see beauty in an ocean, while another is unmoved? Why does one person risk life and limb to ensure justice, while another stands

A cynic is a man who knows the price of everything and the value of nothing.

OSCAR WILDE

There is nothing either good or bad,
But thinking makes it so.

WILLIAM SHAKESPEARE

detached and indifferent? Our values are largely shaped and formed by experience. Thus, the sea holds out little beauty for one who has watched a loved one die in it. The person who has felt the sting of racial or sexual discrimination can understandably develop a hearty appetite for fair and just treatment, even at great personal risk. In a word, the values we hold, as individuals and as groups, are inseparable from the endlessly changing experiences of our lives.

History reveals that no society has ever been without some value system, and every individual has some code of values. The issue, therefore, is not whether we are to have values but what those values will be—whether they will advance or retard life, whether they will be consistent or not. Before we examine one field of values—ethics—it will be helpful to introduce some general ideas concerning values.

First, philosophers distinguish between a fact and a value. A *factual judgment* describes an empirical relationship or quality. For example, "Washington, D.C., is the nation's capital" and "Water boils at 212 degrees Fahrenheit at sea level" are factual statements. A *value judgment,* on the other hand, assesses the worth of objects, acts, feelings, attitudes, even people. For example, "Beethoven was a good composer," "I should visit my sick brother," and "You were wrong in lying" are value judgments.

Throughout our discussion of value issues, one question will recur: Do value judgments express knowledge or feelings? When I say "Beethoven was a good composer" or "You were wrong in lying," am I expressing a truth or a personal preference? The answer is uncertain, underscoring the fact that there is little agreement on how the term *value* should be defined. Perhaps the best definition we can give is that a **value** is an assessment of worth. This is how we'll use the term.

Another concern is whether values are subjective or objective. When I say, for example, that the *Mona Lisa* is beautiful, does the value I express originate in me or in the painting? Some say that a value is the subjective satisfaction of a human want, desire, or need. Others claim that a value is a quality within an object that satisfies the individual and is therefore objective. Still others contend that a value has both subjective and objective elements.

According to our Greek and Judeo-Christian traditions, there are certain absolute, unchanging values that are rooted in the nature of the universe or given by God. Because these traditions posit a moral order, we believe that we can call things good or evil regardless of what anyone thinks.

In modern times another view of the nature of values has arisen. In this view, values undergo change. The human person is a growing entity in a changing, dynamic universe, and values reflect this changing process. Consequently, there are no fixed or immutable values. Rather, as human conditions change, values also change.

Finally, the *selection* of values is important. Just what should we value? There is general agreement that certain groups of values exist, such as the moral, political, aesthetic, religious, and intellectual, and that genetic, biological, and cultural influences produce many of these values. But there is little agreement about the nature of these values, their relative importance, or their relationship to one another. Nevertheless, most philosophers use the following principles in discussing value issues:

1. We should prefer what is of intrinsic value to what is of extrinsic value. *A thing has intrinsic value when it is valued for its own sake.* For example, some believe that pleasure has intrinsic value; that is, it is worthwhile in itself, not because it can yield something else. *On the other hand, a thing has extrinsic value when it is a means to something else.* A film could be said to have extrinsic value; that is, it is not a value in itself but can yield a value, perhaps pleasure. But intrinsic and extrinsic values are not necessarily mutually exclusive. What is valued in

"Are values objective or subjective? When I say, for example, that the *Mona Lisa* is beautiful, does the value I express originate in me or in the painting?"

itself may also be a means to something else, as in the case of knowledge. Knowledge is worthwhile in itself, but also because it may lead to a job, affluence, or prestige.

2. We should prefer values that are productive and lasting to ones that are not. Physical and material values are generally less productive and long-lived than social, artistic, intellectual, and religious values. Long after a new car has worn out or a fortune has been spent, a genuine friendship or one's personal integrity persists.

3. We should choose our own values according to our own goals and ideals. When we allow values to be thrust upon us, we live others' lives, not our own. Our values should be consistent with one another and responsive to our own circumstances and experiences.

4. Finally, in choosing between two values, we should prefer the greater. What constitutes the greater will be determined largely by the previous three criteria. When we must choose between two evils, we should choose the lesser, again allowing these criteria to influence our choice.

These principles are themselves expressions of fundamental values. In what are they grounded? The rich legacy of Western culture. Again, we are reminded of the experiential basis of all assessments of worth, of all values.

One aspect of our values applies to the realm of human conduct, that is, moral values. For example, some value pleasure, because for them pleasure has intrinsic worth. They believe that they should seek pleasure and avoid pain at all times. Others, in contrast, place a premium on virtue, such as integrity or honesty. They believe that virtue is worthwhile in itself and should be pursued, even at great personal inconvenience. Still others might opt for other moral values, such as self-realization or love. As in all cases involving assessments of worth, people cherish any number of moral values. But how do we know which moral values to choose? Should we, for example, chiefly value pleasure, virtue, some other value, or a combination of values? While admittedly a most difficult problem to solve, this question is one concern of the study of ethics, and it has profound implications not only for individuals but for nations as well.

QUESTIONS

1. Consider the following overarching values (developed by Dr. Milton Rokeach, a psychologist) and rank them in order of their importance to you: freedom, security, equality, beauty, peace, love, pleasure, salvation, excitement, comfort, self-respect, friendship, knowledge, contentment, inner harmony, wisdom, sense of accomplishment. Now consider the following personal qualities and rank them in order of their importance to you: being

logical, forgiving, clean, loving, obedient, honest, polite, responsible, ambitious, self-disciplined, open-minded, cheerful, competent. Now look over both lists and ask yourself whether there are any conflicts between the personal qualities you value and the overarching values you have. What conclusions can you draw about yourself?

2. Are there other values or personal qualities that are valuable to you but that are not mentioned in the lists above?

3. Categorize the values listed in question 1 as *intrinsic* or *extrinsic*.

4. Do you feel that you yourself have chosen the values you have, or have your values been imposed on you by your parents, school, peers, and society?

Inability to tell good from evil is the greatest worry of man's life.

CICERO

The Divisions of Ethics

Let's define **ethics** as the branch of philosophy that studies what constitutes good and bad human conduct, including related actions and values. In understanding this definition, it's helpful to view all ethical questions as involving a choice. Suppose, for example, that after not answering your telephone for several hours, you finally take a call. The caller, a friend, expresses frustration at having failed to reach you earlier and asks whether you were home. You were home, of course, but simply didn't feel like answering the phone. Naturally you could tell the person the unvarnished truth. But since such behavior is uncharacteristic of you, the person will likely expect an explanation or feel slighted. In short, saying that you weren't home seems less complicated than telling the truth. What should you do?

Invariably all ethical questions involve a decision about what one should do in a specific instance. Notice the word *should*. Ethical questions are not concerned with what one *would* do (an essentially psychological concern) but what one *ought to* do. Judgments about such decisions are generally expressed with words like *right* and *wrong, should* and *ought,* or *obligation* and *duty.* For instance, "I *ought* to tell the caller I was home" or "Telling the caller I wasn't home is the *right* thing to do." A good portion of ethics is devoted to the philosophical problems concerning the right thing to do or what we should do, that is, to questions of obligation.

But, at the same time, implied in any choice is a value or value judgment. If you decide to tell the caller you were home, your action betrays a commitment to some value, perhaps to truth. If you choose to lie, again your action reflects a value, perhaps your own pleasure. In effect, every choice involves an assessment of worth. We feel obliged to behave a certain way because we seek a specific value or good. These values, just as the actions themselves, can be described with words such as *good, bad, evil, desirable, undesirable, beneficial, harmful,* and so on. In addition to dealing with questions of obligation, therefore, ethics deals with questions of value. Taken together, questions of obligation and value form the heart of ethics.

Occasionally the term *ethics* is used interchangeably with *morals.* Business or medical ethics, for example, is generally synonymous with morals. Although this is acceptable, a precise usage would apply the terms *morals* and *moral* to the conduct itself, while the terms *ethics* and *ethical* would refer to the study of moral conduct or to the code that one follows. Thus, the specific act of telling the caller you were home could be described as moral or immoral. But what makes any act moral or immoral, right or wrong, would fall within the province of ethics. When we speak of moral problems, then, we generally refer to specific problems, such as "Is lying ever right?" or "Is stealing always wrong?" In contrast, we can look at ethical problems as being more general and theoretical. Thus, "What makes any act, such as lying or stealing, right or wrong?" and "What makes any entity good?" are ethical problems. In short, morality refers to the degree to which an action conforms to a standard or norm of human conduct. Ethics refers to the philosophical study of values and of what constitutes good and bad human conduct.

Sometimes the term *nonmoral* arises in the study of ethics. This term refers to what lies outside the

---

He cannot long be good that knows not why he is good.

RICHARD CAREW

---

sphere of moral concern. Thus, whether I choose to answer my telephone and whether a manufacturer packages a product in a vertical or horizontal container are essentially nonmoral questions. However, nonmoral questions can quickly take on moral overtones. For example, telling a friend to call me at a certain hour and then refusing to answer the call could raise a moral question. Likewise, if the shape of a container could mislead the consumer about the quantity of its contents, then it could constitute a moral question.

In dealing with human conduct from the perspective of obligation and value, ethics investigates a variety of related concerns. Among them are whether a standard of morality exists that applies to all people at all times everywhere, the precise nature of moral responsibility, the conditions under which one is morally accountable or responsible, and the proper end of law. When ethicists use words like "good" or "right" to describe a person or action, they generally mean that the person or action conforms to some standard. A good person or action has certain desirable qualities. Ethicists often disagree about the nature of those standards and desirable qualities and follow different paths in establishing standards and discovering which qualities are desirable. For purposes of understanding, though, we can view ethics as divided into two fields—normative ethics and nonnormative ethics.

NORMATIVE ETHICS

Normative ethics involves an attempt to determine precisely what moral standards to follow so that our actions may be morally right or good. There are two areas of normative ethics: applied and general. Applied normative ethics is the attempt to explain and justify positions on specific moral problems, such as sex outside marriage, capital punishment, euthanasia, and reverse discrimination. This area of normative ethics is termed *applied* because the ethicist applies or uses general ethical principles in an attempt to resolve specific moral problems. For example, in defending an act of civil disobedience, a person might appeal to principles of justice and equality. When such general principles are arranged into an ethical theory, the second field of normative ethics emerges: general normative ethics.

General normative ethics is the reasoned search for principles of human conduct, including a critical study of the major theories about which things are good, which acts are right, and which acts are blameworthy. It attempts to determine precisely what moral standards to follow so that our actions may be morally right or good. For most of us, ethical actions spring from some standard: "Do unto others as you would have them do unto you"; "Act in such a way that you bring about the greatest good for the greatest number"; "Always act in your own best interests." Which principle should we adopt? General normative ethics, in part, tries to answer this question by attempting to formulate and defend a system of basic ethical principles which presumably is valid for everyone.

Two broad categories of general normative theories can be distinguished: teleological and deontological. *Teleological* derives from the word *teleology,* which literally means "the theory of ends or purposes." Teleological theories maintain that the morality of an action depends on the nonmoral consequences that the action brings about. For simplicity, we shall refer to teleological theories as *consequentialist.* Two important consequentialist theories that we will consider are egoism and utilitarianism. Egoism is concerned with the best consequences for self, utilitarianism with the best consequences for everyone.

Deontological derives from the word *deontology,* which refers to the theory or study of moral commitment. Deontological theories maintain that the morality of an action depends on factors other than consequences. Again, for simplicity, we will refer to deontological theories as *nonconsequentialist.* Three important nonconsequentialist theories we will consider are divine command, categorical imperative, and prima facie duties. Divine command is concerned with acting in such a way that one's actions conform to the laws of God. The categorical imperative is concerned with acting in such a way that one could wish the maxim of one's action to become a universal law. Prima facie duties are concerned with acting in accordance with an

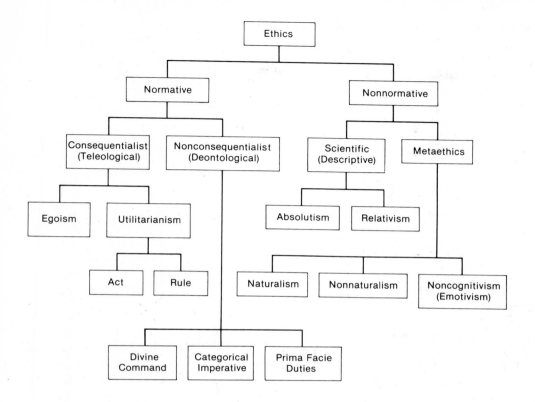

overriding obligation as indicated by the circumstances involved.

Since the terms *consequentialist* and *nonconsequentialist* actually pinpoint the difference between teleological and deontological theories, we'll use these simpler terms in the pages ahead, where we will consider the major theories in each group and indicate the theory of value that generally accompanies each theory.[1]

NONNORMATIVE ETHICS

Nonnormative ethics consists of either (1) a factual investigation of moral behavior or (2) an analysis of the meaning of the terms used in moral discourse and an examination of the moral reasoning by which moral beliefs can be shown to be true or false. Like

normative ethics, nonnormative ethics consists of two fields: scientific or descriptive study, and metaethics.

Scientific or Descriptive Study

The scientific or descriptive study of morality involves factual investigation of moral behavior. It is concerned with how people do in fact behave. This approach is used widely in the social sciences. For example, anthropologists and sociologists investigate and describe moral attitudes. They report on how moral attitudes and codes differ from society to society, investigating and describing the values and behaviors of different societies. Thus, anthropologists tell us that Eskimos used to abandon their elderly on the ice and allow them to die of starvation and exposure, and that some African tribes kill infant twins and require that a man marry his brother's widow. That societies often differ markedly in their values and conceptions of right and

1. See Jacques Thiroux, *Ethics* (Encino, Calif.: Glencoe Press, 1980), 34.

wrong has led many to advance a doctrine called *ethical relativism.*

In order to understand ethical relativism, one must first be familiar with ethical absolutism. *Ethical absolutism* is the doctrine that there exists one and only one correct moral code. Absolutists maintain that this same code applies to everyone, everywhere, and at all times, even though not everyone actually follows it. What is a moral duty for me must also be a duty for you. What is a moral duty for an American must also be a moral duty for an Asian, African, European, and aborigine. If euthanasia is wrong, it is wrong for everyone, at all times, everywhere. That a society may see nothing wrong with euthanasia or lying or cannibalism in no way affects the rightness or wrongness of such actions. Ethical absolutists do not necessarily claim that their code is the true and valid one. But they do insist that there is a true moral code and that this code is the same for all people in all ages.

Ethical relativism is the doctrine that denies that there is a single moral standard that is universally applicable to all people at all times. Relativists deny that there exists only one correct moral code, law, principle, or standard. They insist that there are many correct moral codes. As the name implies, ethical relativists insist that morality is relative to one's society: Each society has a moral code, and an action is morally right if it is approved of by the moral code of one's society.

Ethical relativism is not the same as cultural relativism. Cultural relativism is a sociological fact: Research proves the existence of many obviously different and often contradictory moral codes. Ethical relativists are not merely saying that what is thought right in one part of the world is frequently thought wrong in another. Scientific or descriptive

---

Modern morality consists in accepting the standard of one's age.

OSCAR WILDE

Right and wrong exist in the nature of things. Things are not right because they are commanded, nor wrong because they are prohibited.

R. G. INGERSOLL

---

ethics has established this fact that even absolutists accept. Rather, ethical relativists assert that precisely the same action that is right in one society at one time can be wrong in another. Thus, putting to death anyone over eighty years old can be right in the jungles of New Guinea and wrong in the United States. Such a claim is quite different from saying that putting octogenarians to death is *thought* to be right in one place and *thought* to be wrong in another. In brief, ethical relativists believe that whatever a society *thinks* is right is *in fact* right.

Although many people unthinkingly adopt the view that something is morally right if and only if their society thinks it is morally right, this doctrine is very difficult to defend when it is critically examined. Critics point out that in modern societies, it is almost impossible to determine what "the ethical beliefs of my society" are supposed to be. For example, are Americans supposed to think that abortion is right or that it is wrong? Are we supposed to think that euthanasia is right or that it is wrong? Since our society is so strongly divided on these issues, it is almost impossible to say what our society believes on these matters. Moreover, even if we could determine that, say, 40 percent of Americans believe that abortion is wrong while 60 percent think it is right, does this fact mean that I myself *have* to hold that abortion is right? Does this mean that the 40 percent minority *must* be wrong and that everyone has to believe whatever the majority believes? Suppose everyone in society believes that slavery is right except me. Does this mean that I must be wrong? Indeed, if society's beliefs determine what the "correct" morality is for me, then I can never criticize my own society.

But we shall not take the time here to explore ethical relativism. Whether we agree with absolutism or relativism, we still must decide what we ought to do individually and collectively. Presumably this requires some standard on the basis of which to make decisions. So, whether I am an absolutist or a relativist, the question remains: How ought I to behave and how ought my society to behave?

Metaethics

The second field of nonnormative ethics is called *metaethics*. **Metaethics** is the highly technical discipline investigating the meaning of ethical terms, including a critical study of how ethical statements can be verified. Largely the province of philosophers, metaethics is concerned with the meanings of such important ethical terms as *right*, *obligation*, and *responsibility*. Accordingly, metaethicists would be more concerned with the meanings of such words as *good* or *bad* than with what things are good or bad. If you maintained, for instance, that an act of euthanasia was right, the metaethicist might ask: Just what do you mean by *right*? Metaethical positions often are classified as representative of naturalism, nonnaturalism, and emotivism (or noncognitivism).

Naturalism maintains that ethical statements can be translated into nonethical statements. One naturalistic position—autobiographical naturalism—contends that an ethical statement simply

---

PHILOSOPHY AND LIFE 7.1

Ethics and Animals

The continual production of new chemical substances has led to the widespread use of animals to test these new products. These tests often involve extreme suffering and can lead to slow and excruciatingly painful deaths for their animal victims. In the Draize test, for example, concentrated solutions of cosmetics are dripped into the open eyes of rabbits; the toxicity of the cosmetics is then determined by measuring the level of painful injuries and blindness inflicted on the rabbits' eyes. Other procedures inflict worse suffering on test animals. Here, for example, is a report describing the testing of a nasal decongestant.

J. Weikel, Jr., and K. Harper of the Mead Johnson Research Center at Evansville, Indiana, and the Huntingdon Research Center, Huntingdon, England, studied the acute toxicity of amidephrine mesylate [a nasal decongestant] in 96 rabbits, 16 rhesus monkeys, 8 squirrel monkeys, 5 cats, 376 rats, and an unstated number of dogs and mice. The substance was administered to the animals by mouth, by injetion, into the nostrils, and tested for irritancy on the eyes and penises of rabbits. Rats and mice, regardless of the mode of administration, lost the power of muscular coordination, their eyes watered and their eyeballs protruded. Lethal doses caused, in addition, salivation, convulsions, and hemorrhage about the nose and mouth. Rabbits showed similar symptoms. Cats had a profuse watery discharge from the nose, diarrhea, and vomiting. Dogs lost muscular coordination, salivated, and had diarrhea.

QUESTIONS

1. Does morality extend to animals? Do animals have moral rights?

2. All beef products (hamburgers, steaks, and so on) currently sold in the United States are produced through painful slaughtering processes, and purchasing beef provides financial support for these processes. If animals have moral rights, is it wrong for you to consume beef when you can instead eat vegetable protein?

3. How should the pain and harm inflicted on animals be balanced against the benefits animal tests provide for humans?

SOURCE: Peter Singer, *Animal Liberation* (New York: Random House, 1975), 49.

expresses the approval or disapproval of the speaker. For example, when you say, "That act of euthanasia was right," you mean "I approve of that act of euthanasia." Another naturalistic position—sociological naturalism—holds that an ethical statement simply expresses the approval or disapproval of the majority. Thus, "That act of euthanasia was right" means "The majority approves of that act of euthanasia." Still another naturalistic position—theological naturalism—claims that an ethical statement expresses divine approval or disapproval. Accordingly, "That act of euthanasia was right," in effect, means "God (or some equivalent reference) approves of that act of euthanasia."

Nonnaturalism, in contrast to naturalism, is the position which holds that an ethical statement defies translation into a nonethical form. Nonnaturalists insist that at least some ethical words can be defined only in terms of other ethical words. Thus, nonnaturalists might argue that the statement "That act of euthanasia was right" can only be translated into other ethical statements, such as "That act of euthanasia was proper" or "That act of euthanasia should have been performed," or "That act of euthanasia was good." Nonnaturalists hold that naturalistic translations would be like trying to define *hour* in other than temporal terms, or *inch* in other than spatial terms. It just cannot be done. The motto "You can't get an is out of an ought" nicely captures the nonnaturalistic position. In other words, words like *good*, *right*, and *should* are so basic in ethics that there are no other words by means of which to define them.[2]

English philosopher and nonnaturalist G. E. Moore (1873–1958) attempted to refute naturalistic theories by use of the so-called open-question technique. Moore argued that no matter what property of a thing you assert, someone can always meaningfully grant that the thing has the property but then ask: Is that property good? Thus, "I grant that Fred Jones is very happy (property), but is happiness always and everywhere good?" "I acknowledge that Jeannine Cox is an honest woman,

but is honesty good?" Perhaps happiness and honesty are good. But, in Moore's view, one cannot claim that they are simply on the basis of a definition of *good* which others might reject.

Moore went so far as to assert that *good* is verbally indefinable, just as some other words are, for example, *red* and *pleasure*. He claimed that to identify *good* with any natural object was to commit the naturalistic fallacy. Writing in his most important work, *Principia Ethica*, Moore explains what he means.

> Suppose a man says, "I am pleased"; and suppose that it is not a lie or a mistake but the truth. Well, if it is true, what does that mean? It means his mind, a certain definite mind, distinguished by certain definite marks from all others, has at this moment a certain definite feeling called pleasure. "Pleased" *means* nothing but having pleasure, and though we may be more pleased or less pleased, and even, we may admit for the present, have one or another kind of pleasure; yet insofar as it is pleasure we have, whether there be more or less of it, and whether it be of one kind or another, what we have is one definite thing, absolutely indefinable, some one thing that is the same in all the various degrees and in all the various kinds of it that there may be. We may be able to say how it is related to other things: that, for example, it is in the mind, that it causes desire, that we are conscious of it, etc., etc. We can, I say, describe its relations to other things, but define it we can *not*. And if anybody tried to define pleasure for us as being any other natural object; if anybody were to say, for instance, that pleasure *means* the sensation of red, and were to proceed to deduce from that that pleasure is a color, we should be entitled to

---

2. John Hospers, *Introduction to Philosophical Analysis* (Englewood Cliffs, N.J.: Prentice-Hall, 1967), 573.

The foundations of morality are like all other foundations: if you dig too much about them the superstructure will come tumbling down.

SAMUEL BUTLER

G. E. Moore: "If anybody tried to define pleasure for us as being any other natural object, if anybody were to say, for instance, that pleasure *means* the sensation of red, and were to proceed to deduce from that that pleasure is a color, we should be entitled to laugh at him and to distrust his future statements about pleasure. Well, that would be the same fallacy which I have called the naturalistic fallacy."

laugh at him and to distrust his future statements about pleasure. Well, that would be the same fallacy which I have called the naturalistic fallacy. That "pleased" does not mean "having the sensation of red," or anything else whatever, does not prevent us from understanding what it does mean. It is enough for us to know that "pleased" does mean "having the sensation of pleasure," and though pleasure is absolutely indefinable, though pleasure is pleasure and nothing else whatever, yet we feel no difficulty in saying that we are pleased.[3]

Given their position, nonnaturalists clearly come close to asserting that ethical statements cannot be verified, that they cannot be determined true

or false. How then does the nonnaturalist handle ethical statements? Moore advises that we reflect on them and determine as well as we can, whether we believe the statements are true. There are no empirical observations, no mathematical or logical calculations, which would enable us to discover the truth of ethical statements. All we can do is distinguish them carefully from other statements, particularly those with which they might easily be confused, and then reflect on them and see whether, after this reflection, we believe that they are true.

Emotivism (or noncognitivism) can be broadly defined as a metaethical position which claims that ethical statements are used to evoke a predetermined response or to encourage a predetermined behavior. According to emotivists, ethical statements can be used, indeed are used, to make someone feel or behave in a certain way. For example, if a teacher says to a student, "Cheating is wrong," the teacher may not be expressing a moral position on cheating but rather trying to instill in the student a certain attitude toward cheating. The teacher may also be trying to elicit a noncheating behavior. Ethical statements, therefore, amount to commands such as "Don't cheat" or "Don't lie" or "Don't break promises." The essential difference between autobiographical naturalism and emotivism is that the former holds that ethical statements are subjective and verifiable, while the latter believes that they are subjective but *not* verifiable.

The flowchart on page 317 organizes the different fields of normative and nonnormative ethics that we have just sketched. In the remainder of this chapter we shall flesh out the predominant normative theories. The coverage stresses normative theories because this is the approach that most of us take. In our personal and social lives, we want to determine for ourselves some principles or standards of moral behavior. Also, in recent years ethicists have renewed their interest in normative ethics in an attempt to deal with today's urgent moral issues.

QUESTIONS

1. Explain the difference between ethics and morals.

2. Which of the following claims would belong to

3. G. E. Moore, *Principia Ethica* (London: Cambridge University Press, 1903), 12–13.

the field of normative ethics? To nonnormative ethics? To metaethics?

a. Abortion is wrong.

b. Many Americans believe that abortion is immoral.

c. Murder means a wrongful killing.

d. Rights are nonsense walking on stilts.

e. The distribution of wealth in the United States is unjust.

f. The majority of college students have engaged in sexual behavior they feel is wrong.

Consequentialist (Teleological) Theories

Let us join two city policemen, Obie and The Kid, on their tour of duty. Obie is the veteran, the "hair-bag" in police slang. The Kid is fresh out of the police academy, with ideas gathered more from school than from the street.

OBIE: I see where B. B. McGeester was sprung this morning.

KID: McGeester?

OBIE: Maybe you don't know him. I busted him three times. Fourth last month. The third time he served a total of eighteen months for pushing snow. Then he was out—"rehabilitation," they call it. Last month I nailed him for murder two.

KID: I take it you don't think they should have released him.

OBIE: Ask the storekeeper he killed if B. B. should have been released. Civil rights. They said this morning his civil rights had been violated. Well, I say if you're not civil, you don't deserve civil rights.

KID: You don't think a criminal has any civil rights?

OBIE: He loses them the day he breaks the law, that's what I think. But the minute we bust him, some judge who's never been in the street says, "Mister McGeester, sir, we apologize for violating your civil rights. We hope we haven't inconvenienced you." "Oh no, Your Honor, not in the least. But don't let it happen again. Because if you do, I'm going to sue the pants off you. How's a guy supposed to make a dishonest living if you keep violating his civil rights?"

KID: But what if his civil rights *were* violated, Obie? What if he was being held illegally?

OBIE: What if, what if, what if . . . what if an hour after he's released he breaks some storekeeper's head; what if tomorrow he rapes some woman in the park; what if next week he swipes a car and runs over a child? Believe me, Kid, it's not right. It's downright immoral! And it won't be long before you see what I mean.

What Obie means is that an action is wrong if its consequences are undesirable. And since releasing criminals on the basis of a civil rights violation often leads to additional crime, it is immoral. What would you rather have, Obie would ask, a civil right violated or a known felon walking the street? Just consider the consequences and that should tell you.

Traditionally many ethicists have contended that moral rightness must be determined by appeal to the consequences of an action. If the consequences are good, the act is right. If the consequences are bad, the act is wrong. Thus, a **consequentialist theory** measures the morality of action on the basis of the nonmoral consequences. Consequentialists consider the ratio of good to evil that an action produces. The right action is the one that produces, will probably produce, or is intended to produce at least as great a ratio of good to evil as any other action. The wrong action is the one that does not.

For example, suppose that while driving down an almost deserted street one night, you momentarily take your eyes off the road and then strike a parked car. You stop and cautiously look around. There's no one in sight, and no house lights are on. Using a flashlight, you estimate the damage to the parked car at about $200. You'd like to leave a note on the windshield, but you don't have insurance or the money to pay for the damage. Besides, the parked car is a new Corvette, and you assume that the owner must have insurance.

If you were a consequentialist, in determining what you should do, you'd evaluate the nonmoral consequences of the two choices. If you left a note, you would probably have to pay for the damage. That would greatly complicate your life: You'd have to work to pay off the debt, let other expenses slide, greatly reduce your luxuries, and possibly need to quit school. In contrast, if you don't leave a note, you might go unpenalized while the owner foots the bill. Of course, the owner is likely to be hopping mad, perhaps even deciding to treat other motorists spitefully. Furthermore, you may be found out; that could mean considerable trouble. This is a consequentialist analysis.

An obvious question arises here: In evaluating the nonmoral consequences of an action, whom do consequentialists have in mind? Clearly, if you evaluate the consequences just for yourself in the preceding illustration, you would likely make a different judgment than if you evaluate the consequences for the Corvette's owner. In deciding what to do, then, should we evaluate the consequences only for ourselves, or should we consider the effects on all people involved? The answers to these questions form the bases for two consequential theories: egoism and utilitarianism.

EGOISM

Some ethicists believe that in deciding the morality of an action, we should consider only the consequences for ourselves. These ethicists are called egoists. **Egoism** contends that we should always act in a way that promotes our own best long-term interests. Although egoists argue about what actions will do this, they agree that once such actions are determined, we should take them. This notion does not imply, however, that we should do whatever we want; often our best immediate interests are not our best long-term ones.

Just what do egoists mean by "self-interests"? It's tempting to think that they must mean pleasure; that is, I act in my best interests when I do what is calculated to bring me the most pleasure. Holding this belief makes me a hedonist. **Hedonism** is the ethical philosophy which holds that only pleasure is worth having for its own sake. In a word, hedonists view pleasure and only pleasure as having intrinsic value. It is true that many egoists are hedonistic, as was the ancient Greek philosopher Epicurus (341–270 B.C.), who argued that people should live so as to bring about as much pleasure for themselves as possible. But two points need stressing. First, where egoists (or any normative theorists, for that matter) are hedonistic, it's important to determine what they mean by *pleasure*. Second, not all egoists are strict hedonists.

With respect to the first point, few popular definitions of pleasure would correspond with Epicurus's definition. Rather than with sensual gratification, Epicurus associated pleasure with what he termed *sober thinking*:

> When I say that pleasure is the goal of living I do not mean the pleasures of libertines and the pleasures inherent in positive enjoyment. . . . I mean, on the contrary, the pleasure that consists in freedom from bodily pain and mental agitation. The pleasant life is not the product of one drinking party after another or of sexual intercourse. . . . On the contrary, it is the result of sober thinking—namely, investigation of the reasons for every act of choice and aversion, and elimination of those false ideas about the gods and death which are the chief source of mental disturbances.[4]

While preaching the pursuit of pleasure, Epicurus nonetheless discouraged excess and recommended simplicity and moderation. He even considered the limitation of appetite to be a major good because "becoming habituated to a simple rather than a lavish way of life provides us with the full complement of health; it makes a person ready for the necessary business of life; it puts us in a position of advantage when we happen upon sumptuous fare at intervals and prepares us to be fearless in facing fortune."[5]

As for the second point above, many egoists identify the good not with pleasure but with knowledge, power, or rational self-interest. Some, in fact,

associate it with self-realization, which is the promotion of all one's capacities. While popularized through the thought and writings of contemporary psychologists such as Abraham Maslow, the self-realization doctrine is also evident in the works of classical philosophers. In *The Republic*, for example, Plato discusses the three active principles within each person: Reason, Appetite, and Spirit (see Chapter 2). For Plato, each part has a role to play. When these elements work together, they result in personal harmony, order, and peace—self-realization. Similarly, in the first systematic presentation of morality, *Nicomachean Ethics*, Aristotle stresses the life of reason, which entails the harmonious development of all functions of the human organism.

Today self-realization as a goal of the good life continues to find philosophical expression. For example, British philosopher Francis Herbert Bradley argues that satisfaction is only possible when one achieves self-realization, that is, a harmonious integration of all one's desires. Only then can a person become a self, an individual.

The point is that an egoist is not necessarily a hedonist. On the contrary, ethical egoists may hold any theory of value. They all agree, however, that individuals should pursue courses of action that will advance their own best long-term interests.

Ethical egoism does pose a number of problems. First is the issue of conflicting interests, which Kurt Baier (1917–) has expressed quite graphically. He asks us to imagine two presidential candidates, whom we will call Brown and Kory. It's in the interests of both to be elected, but only one can succeed. It follows, then, that it would be in Brown's interest but not in Kory's if Brown were elected, and vice versa. Similarly, it would be in Brown's interest but not in Kory's if Kory were liquidated, and vice versa. More important, Brown ought to do everything possible to get rid of Kory; in fact, it would be wrong for Brown not to do so. Likewise Kory, knowing that his own liquidation is in Brown's interests, ought to take steps to foil Brown's endeavors. Indeed, it would be wrong for Kory not to do so. "It follows," writes Baier, "that if [Kory] prevents [Brown] from liquidating him, his act must be said to be both wrong and not wrong—wrong

---

4. Epicurus, "Letter to Menoeceus," in *The Philosophy of Epicurus*, ed. George K. Strodach (Evanston, Ill.: Northwestern University Press, 1963), 175.

5. Ibid., 176.

Morals are a personal affair; in the war of righteousness every man fights for his own hand.

ROBERT LOUIS STEVENSON

because it is the prevention of what [Brown] ought to do, his duty, and wrong for [Brown] not to do it; not wrong because it is what [Kory] ought to do, his duty, and wrong for [Kory] not to do it."[6] Baier's point is that egoism seems unable to resolve conflicts of interest, which he assumes a moral theory should do. Without that assumption, however, there are no conflicts, just a fully relativized situation in which each individual believes in his own best interests.

Related to this objection is a second: the inconsistency that ethical egoism introduces into moral counsel. To illustrate, let's suppose that Brown and Kory seek out the advice of Parnell. Parnell tells Brown to do whatever's necessary to prevent Kory from getting the job and to ensure that he, Brown, secures it. However, Parnell tells Kory to do whatever's necessary to prevent Brown from getting the job and to ensure that he, Kory, secures it. In her counsel, Parnell recommends two conflicting courses of action as being right. Critics of ethical egoism fault a moral theory that allows such flagrant inconsistency in moral counsel. However, in fairness to egoism, they are again assuming a collective value. Egoism by definition holds no such value, so why measure it by one?

Some critics think that the most serious weakness of ethical egoism is that it undermines the moral point of view, which many ethicists accept as a necessary part of moral decision making. By the "moral point of view," they mean the attitude of one who attempts to see all sides of an issue without being committed to the interests of a particular individual or group. In short, the moral point of view is one of impartiality and disinterest. The

moral point of view can be thought of as the perspective taken by an ideal observer or judge. An ideal observer, or ideal judge, has three key characteristics. First, the ideal observer is impartial or unbiased, that is, he does not treat himself as a special case. The ideal observer is as impartial in considering what he should do as he would be in deciding what someone unknown to him, someone in whom he has no special interest, should be. Second, the ideal observer has full knowledge of the facts of the situation to be judged. Third, the ideal observer can imaginatively identify with any person involved in the situation. If an individual possessed these characteristics, he or she would be a perfect moral judge of any situation; the person would be able to say what was right and wrong. Additionally, the ideal observer's view would tell the meaning of right and wrong.[7]

If we accept the legitimacy of this perspective, we must look for it in any proposed ethical standard. But ethical egoists cannot take the moral point of view as described because, by definition, they are always influenced by what is in their own best interest, regardless of the issues, principles, circumstances, or individuals involved. Thus, Brown and Kory cannot be impartial or disinterested in determining the right courses for them to follow. What's more, if Parnell is an egoist, she can't maintain the moral point of view as described, for she must counsel each candidate with her own interest in mind.

But is the moral point of view realistic? How can anyone be completely impartial or disinterested? We can't. Some would even argue that approximating the perspective of the ideal observer is a surefire way to moral indecision, inaction, and passivity, because, rather than engaging the issues of the day, we likely will withdraw from them. All moral decision making and action may involve a passional element, an essentially nonrational commitment of will that makes disinterest impossible. If this is so—and one could mount a powerful argument for it—then the most serious objection to egoism dissolves.

---

6. Kurt Baier, *The Moral Point of View* (Ithaca, N.Y.: Cornell University Press, 1958), 189.

7. See Hospers, *Introduction to Philosophical Analysis*, 570.

Obviously, the objections to egoism arise from holding a collective rather than a strictly subjective value. In fact, many consequentialists focus not on self-interest but on the interests of all involved. Such is the emphasis of the normative theory termed *utilitarianism*.

UTILITARIANISM

In contrast to egoism, utilitarianism asserts that the promotion of *everyone's* best interest is the standard of morality. In brief, **utilitarianism** claims that we should always act so as to produce the greatest possible ratio of good to evil for all concerned. Again, as with all consequentialist positions, good and evil are taken to mean nonmoral good and evil.

As formulated and developed by Jeremy Bentham (1748–1832) and John Stuart Mill (1806–1873), utilitarianism maintains that what is of intrinsic value or what is good in itself is pleasure, or happiness; this was unequivocally stated in the opening chapter of Bentham's *Introduction to the Principles of Morals and Legislation*. Notice in the excerpt from that chapter cited below how Bentham moves from the pleasure and pain experienced by an individual to that experienced by the group. In so doing, he lays the basis for the utilitarian moral principle that actions are right to the extent that they promote happiness and pleasure for all, wrong to the extent that they tend to produce pain and the absence of pleasure.

> I. Nature has placed mankind under the governance of two sovereign masters, *pain* and *pleasure*. It is for them alone to point out what we ought to do, as well as to determine what we shall do. On the one hand the standard of right and wrong, on the other the chain of causes and effects, are fastened to their throne. They govern us in all we do, in all we say, in all we think: every effort we can make to throw off our subjection, will serve but to demonstrate and confirm it. In words a man may pretend to abjure their empire: but in reality he will remain subject to it all the while. The *principle of utility* rec-

ognizes this subjection, and assumes it for the foundation of that system, the object of which is to rear the fabric of felicity by the hands of reason and of law. Systems which attempt to question it, deal in sounds instead of sense, in caprice instead of reason, in darkness instead of light.

> But enough of metaphor and declamation: it is not by such means that moral science is to be improved.

> II. The principle of utility is the foundation of the present work: it will be proper therefore at the outset to give an explicit and determinate account of what is meant by it. By the principle of utility is meant that principle which approves or disapproves of every action whatsoever, according to the tendency which it appears to have to augment or diminish the happiness of the party whose interest is in question: or, what is the same thing in other words, to promote or to oppose that happiness; I say of every action whatsoever; and therefore not only of every action of a private individual, but of every measure of government.

> III. By utility is meant the property in any object, whereby it tends to produce the benefit, advantage, pleasure, good, or happiness (all this in the present comes to the same thing) to prevent the happening of mischief, pain, evil, or unhappiness to the party whose interest is considered; if that party be the community in general, then the happiness of the community: if a particular individual, then the happiness of that individual.

> IV. The interest of the community is one of the most general expressions that can occur in the phraseology of morals: no wonder that the meaning of it is often lost. When it has a meaning, it is this. The community is a fictitious *body*, composed of the individual persons who are considered as constituting as it were its *members*. The interest of the community then is, what?—the sum of the interests of the several members who compose it.

> V. It is in vain to talk of the interest of the community, without understanding what is the interest of the individual. A thing is said

to promote the interest, or to be *for* the interest, of an individual, when it tends to add to the sum total of his pleasures: or, what comes to the same thing, to diminish the sum total of his pains.

VI. An action then may be said to be conformable to the principle of utility, or, for shortness sake, to utility, (meaning with respect to the community at large) when the tendency it has to augment the happiness of the community is greater than any it has to diminish it.

VII. A measure of government (which is but a particular kind of action, performed by a particular person or persons), may be said to be conformable to or dictated by the principle of utility, when in like manner the tendency which it has to augment the happiness of the community is greater than any which it has to diminish it.[8]

In contrast with Bentham's original formulation, many modern utilitarians would view things other than happiness or pleasure as having intrinsic worth. Such things include power, knowledge, beauty, or moral qualities. These views are often termed *ideal utilitarianism*, and they have attracted philosophers such as G. E. Moore[9] and Hastings Rashdall.[10] Since we'll be considering primarily classical utilitarianism, we'll use *good* to mean "pleasure." What we'll say about classical utilitarianism, however, applies equally to pluralistic positions, if for "pleasure" the phrase "intrinsic good" is substituted.

At the outset one may wonder whether pleasure can be calculated, as the utilitarian doctrine seems to require. Bentham thought it could. In attempting to determine how much pleasure and pain would result from a person's action, he for-

Jeremy Bentham: **"Nature has placed mankind under the governance of two sovereign masters, *pain* and *pleasure*. They govern us in all we do, in all we say, in all we think. The principle of utility recognizes this subjection."**

mulated a hedonistic calculus, that is, a calculation of pleasure based on a number of criteria, such as the intensity of the pleasure, how long it lasted, how certain it was to occur, and how likely it was to produce additional pleasure. Later Mill added quality to Bentham's calculus, by which he meant the moral superiority that one pleasure holds over another. Although Bentham's calculus doesn't allow an exact calculation of pleasure and pain, it presents valuable criteria for evaluating actions other than on the basis of immediate gratification.

In developing his calculus, Bentham seemed to have in mind a particular utilitarian theory of obligation, termed *act utilitarianism*, as distinguished from *rule utilitarianism*.

---

8. Jeremy Bentham, *Introduction to the Principles of Morals and Legislation* (1798) (Oxford: Oxford University Press, 1823), chap. 1, pp. 1–5.

9. Moore, *Principia Ethica*.

10. Hastings Rashdall, *A Theory of Good and Evil: A Treatise on Moral Philosophy*, 2 vols. (New York: Oxford University Press, 1924).

Act and Rule Utilitarianism

Act utilitarianism is the normative position that contends we should act so as to produce the greatest happiness for the most people. In other words, before acting, ask yourself: What will be the consequences of my action not only for myself but also for everyone else involved? If the consequences are good (that is, they are calculated to produce more happiness or pleasure than any other action will produce), the action is right; if they are bad (that is, they are not so calculated), then the action is wrong. In effect, for the act utilitarian, the end justifies the means. This can raise problems.

KID: Obie, you remember that big drug bust on the East Side last month?

OBIE: Sure, I remember it. That's another example of what I'm talking about. "Entrapment" they called it, and threw it right out of court.

KID: But it *was* entrapment.

OBIE: Look, Kid, when you're trying to catch a criminal, you're interested in what works. Am I right?

KID: Do you really believe it doesn't matter how you accomplish something just so long as you accomplish it?

OBIE: When it comes to incorrigibles, that's exactly what I believe.

KID: But how can you break the law to keep it?

OBIE: Hey, just because something's the law doesn't make it right. A lot of laws are bad. That's the whole point. Take capital punishment, for instance. I say if a man murders in cold blood, he loses his right to live.

KID: What if he's innocent?

OBIE: What're you talking about, *innocent*? Didn't I just say he murdered in cold blood?

KID: But suppose he's innocent this particular time. Suppose he's guilty of a lot of other things, maybe even murders, but on this particular occasion he's innocent.

OBIE: How can he be innocent if he's guilty of so much to begin with?

KID: He's innocent in this one instance. That's what I'm saying.

OBIE: And guilty all the rest of the time?

KID: Right.

OBIE: And he's gotten away with it all?

KID: Suppose he has.

OBIE: Then I say, when you get the chance, nail him.

KID: You know what you're saying? You're saying it's okay to railroad somebody, to send him up for something he didn't do.

OBIE: He did plenty. You said so yourself.

KID: But not this particular thing.

OBIE: A technicality.

KID: A technicality!

OBIE: Look, you got a choice: You either get this guy off the streets or you don't. Now, are you going to tell me we should leave him out there on some technicality? Use your head, Kid, this is a public menace we're talking about, not some Boy Scout. You're removing a public menace from the streets! Who cares how you do it?

KID: Then why not just shoot him and save us all a lot of time and money?

OBIE: Because we're a law-abiding country.

What if an action that promises the greatest good for the greatest number, such as imprisoning an innocent person, appears to be patently wrong? The consequences of removing a chronic public threat, although never certain, appear to provide greater safety and happiness for the vast majority of people. Yet suppose that in this particular case the individual is innocent.

A number of ethicists point out that we get into such dilemmas when we apply the "greatest happiness" principle to a *particular act* and not to the rule that the act implements. What we should be concerned with is the consequences of keeping or breaking the operative rule under which a particular act falls. This is a *rule utilitarian* position. For example, in this case the ethical rule that the Kid is defending seems to be "People should never be imprisoned for something they didn't do." To determine whether to railroad the person in question, we must determine whether this is a good rule. Evaluate the consequences of breaking it. How much fear and anxiety would arise if we all knew that we could be imprisoned for something we did not do? Would these feelings make us happy or not? Would breaking such a rule leave us feeling secure? Would it perhaps encourage us to break the law when we could, since abiding by it would be as perilous as breaking it? The consequences of breaking the rule may not constitute as much collective happiness as abiding by it. If not, say the rule utilitarians, acting in a way that violates this rule would be bad, whereas acting in a way that promotes the rule would be good. In short, **rule utilitarianism** maintains that we should act in such a way that the rule governing our actions produces the greatest happiness for the most people.

But is it that simple? What about this rule: "When people are chronic and deliberate violators of the law, and they are found by reasonable criteria to be public menaces, it is good and desirable to imprison them, even for something they did not do"? The consequences of violating this rule appear to be similar to the consequences of violating the preceding rule. It would seem bad, then, not to promote this rule, and good to promote it. In brief, it is not easy to say what a good rule is. It is especially difficult to assess the rule on the basis of its consequences, since they are generally problematic. But is any other basis possible? Some think that we must consider criteria other than consequences in evaluating morality. Before consider-

ing these nonconsequentialist views, however, it's important for us to complete our overview of utilitarianism by mentioning that it has received a novel twist in recent years. Specifically, act utilitarianism has been reformulated within the context of what is generally termed *situation ethics*, a movement having a broad impact on contemporary morality.

SITUATION ETHICS

For simplicity, we'll confine our observations to the situation ethics proposed by Christian moralist Joseph Fletcher. Fletcher views situation ethics as one of three primary avenues for making moral decisions. The other two are the legalistic, which contends that moral rules are absolute laws that must always be obeyed, and the antinomian or existential (for example, act utilitarianism), which contends that no guidelines exist, that each situation is unique and so requires a new decision. According to Fletcher, legalism is overly directive, antinomianism unacceptably nondirective. Both, he feels, are unworkable. Situation ethics falls between these two extremes but apparently closer to antinomianism.

Like utilitarians, Fletcher is very much concerned with the consequences of our actions. But rather than acting so as to produce the greatest happiness for the greatest number, Fletcher advocates that we produce the most Christian love, that is, the greatest amount of love fulfillment and benevolence. **Situation ethics** is the doctrine that contends that the moral action produces the greatest amount of Christian love of all the possible actions.

For Fletcher, rules and principles are valid only if they serve love in a specific situation. Therefore, when making a moral decision, it's crucial to be fully acquainted with all the facts surrounding the case as well as with the probable consequences of each possible action. In this Fletcher is decidedly consequentialist; in fact, he is utilitarian. But he also argues that after all the calculations are completed, one must choose the act that will best serve

---

To be happy here is man's chief end,
For to be happy he must needs be good.

KIRKE WHITE

love, that is, what Christian tradition has called *agape* (ah-GAH-pay).

Christianity teaches that agape is unselfish love, epitomized by Jesus, who made the ultimate sacrifice for love of humankind. Agape is a principle describing the type of actions that Christians are to regard as good. In a word, agape is loving concern, characterized by a love of God and neighbor.

Fletcher contends that agape is the one unexceptionable principle. In this he differentiates himself from consequentialists generally and utilitarians particularly. For Fletcher, something is valid only if it serves love in any situation; even the proscriptions of the Ten Commandments and the injunctions of the Sermon on the Mount should be viewed as cautious generalizations, not as absolutely binding moral principles. In this respect, Fletcher agrees with Martin Luther's statement that "when the law impels one against love, it ceases and should no longer be a law. But where no obstacle is in the way, the keeping of the law is a proof of love, which lies hidden in the heart. Therefore you have need of the law, that love may be manifested; but if it cannot be kept without injury to the neighbor, God wants us to suspend and ignore the law."[11] In effect, Fletcher's position is that traditional Christian moral laws are fine and even obligatory, but only if they serve love. When they don't, we can, even must, break them.

It's easy, however, to misconstrue Fletcher. His agape principle is not a limp standard that can be used to justify anything. On the contrary, the hallmarks of agape are prudence and careful evaluation, characterized by a willing of the neighbor's good. As such, justice is an integral part of Fletcher's doctrine. But Fletcher doesn't seem to associate justice with the efficiency espoused by utilitarians. For utilitarians, justice is tantamount to producing the most happiness. This is why Obie can prosecute a man for something he did not do. In contrast, Fletcher sees justice as giving people their due. When we truly love, we must practice justice. Justice is inseparable from love. "*Agape* is what is due to all others," he writes, "justice is nothing other than love working out its problems."[12]

Fletcher believes that in formulating social policies, the Christian should join with the utilitarian in trying to produce the greatest good for the greatest number, or, as he calls it, "the greatest amount of neighbor welfare for the largest number of neighbors possible." Thus, the hedonistic calculus of utilitarianism becomes for Fletcher the "agape calculus."[13]

In summary, for Fletcher nothing is good in itself except love, that is, Christian love, or *agape*. Love becomes the standard of moral decision making. It is identical with justice, which is love distributed. When do we love? When we will the good of our neighbor. Finally, love's decisions are determined by particular situations; nothing but the end ever justifies the means.[14]

A number of features of Fletcher's situationism are appealing to many people. First, by focusing on loving concern, Fletcher brings to human relationships a much-needed emphasis on the primacy of individuals and on their welfare. Too often, especially under strictly utilitarian doctrines, the centrality of human beings can be lost within or diminished by the group ideal. Fletcher's situationism decisively restores the human dimension with its emphasis on "willing of the neighbor's good."

Second, in rejecting the moral legalism, Fletcher in effect eliminates what is often a person's chief way of avoiding personal moral responsibility. By following a legalistic line, individuals needn't grapple with moral decisions. At the same time, legalism leaves individuals with the impression that the law represents the limit of their moral obligations, whether the law is of a civil or moral nature. As a result, legalism can easily undercut moral accountability by removing moral decision making from individual control. In rejecting legalism, then, situationism seems to energize the whole concept of moral accountability.

---

11. Martin Luther, *Works*, vol. 5, ed. J. N. Linker (Luther House, 1905), 175.

12. Joseph Fletcher, *Situation Ethics: The New Morality* (Philadelphia: Westminster Press, 1966), 95.

13. Luther Binkley, *Conflict of Ideals* (New York: D. Van Nostrand, 1969), 265.

14. Ibid., 254.

Be sure you are right, then go ahead.

DAVID CROCKETT

Despite these strengths, situationism is not without flaws. First, it is not a definite decision-making procedure. In illustrating how love's decisions are determined by particular situations, Fletcher cites the example of a young woman who is asked by an American intelligence agency to use sex to blackmail an enemy spy. Should she value her chastity more than patriotism and service to her country? Fletcher's answer is no.

But why not? Why couldn't she appeal to the same patriotic motives to preserve her chastity? She might reason that her country should not exploit a person sexually, whatever the reason. She might feel that information gathering does not give government agencies a blanket justification for demanding any kind of behavior. In other words, she might as easily interpret her refusal to be sexual bait as more patriotic and rendering a greater service to her country than her consent. In short, she might see her refusal as the most loving thing to do. Thus, in situation ethics, the same motives could result in different actions.

Second, critics argue that Fletcher actually espouses the antinomianism that he rejects. To understand this objection fully, we must distinguish between two kinds of rules: summary and general. A *summary rule* contends that following the practice advocated or avoiding the practice prohibited is *generally* the best way of acting. Thus, the following are summary rules: "Telling the truth is generally love fulfilling" or "Paying your debts is generally love fulfilling." Summary rules clearly allow exceptions. General rules, on the other hand, do not. A *general rule* contends that you must *always* follow the practice advocated and avoid the one prohibited. Thus: "Telling the truth is always love fulfilling" and "Paying your debts is always love fulfilling."

It seems that Fletcher must deny the existence of general rules, lest he fall into the legalism that he condemns. If, on the other hand, he espouses summary rules, then individuals would determine for themselves when the interests of loving concern transcend summary rules. Of course, should he deny summary as well as general rules, then he would be advocating the antinomian or existentialist position. In fact, Fletcher does express rules: "No unwanted and unintended baby should ever be born." "Exploiting persons is always wrong," "Sex which does not have love as its partner, its senior partner, is wrong." If these are summary rules, under what conditions does loving concern allow one to transcend them?

Due to the problems associated with consequentialist ethics, many ethicists feel that some criteria other than consequences must be used as moral measuring rods. The theories of these ethicists are placed under the heading of *nonconsequentialist* ethics.

QUESTIONS

1. Some people argue that everyone is ultimately an ethical egoist. What do they mean by this? Do you agree? Would this prove that egoism is the basis for all ethics?

2. What are the connotations of the word *egoism*? Are these connotations compatible with what you know about ethical egoism?

3. With which concepts of knowledge and reality do you think ethical egoism is compatible?

4. How prevalent do you think ethical egoism is in contemporary society?

5. Below are four ethical problems. How would an act utilitarian solution differ from a rule utilitarian solution in each case?

a. An aide is conferring with the president of the United States:

Mr. President, it's imperative that you win the upcoming election. If you don't, subversives will take over the government. This could spell the end of our government as we know it. We could present the public with all the facts and let them decide, but that would only alarm and panic them. There's another way, and that is to use the enormous financial connections of this administration to manipulate and mold public opinion. This, it's true, will necessitate illegal election contributions, misrepresentation of facts, and considerable fancy footwork in the campaign. But it's an immediate, practical, and judicious solution in the best interests of the nation.

b. The daughter of a very rich and important public figure has been kidnapped. The kidnappers threaten to murder the young woman unless her father delivers $250,000 in ransom money. Authorities have told him that if he does so he'll only be encouraging future terrorist activities that will invariably involve more people, more suffering, and more deaths.

c. Taxpayer Smith decides that there are plenty of things he dislikes about the way the U.S. government is run: exorbitant defense spending, collusion between business and government, mismanaged funds, and so on. As a result, he is contemplating not paying his income taxes.

d. Jones and Brown are debating whether a person has a moral obligation to obey all laws. Jones claims that deliberately breaking a law is immoral. Brown denies this.

6. What would situationists say in the preceding cases? How would they resolve the dilemmas?

Nonconsequentialist (Deontological) Theories

The most influential nonconsequentialist theories can best be categorized as either proposing a single rule that governs human conduct or proposing multiple rules. Two significant single-rule nonconsequentialist theories are the divine command theory and Immanuel Kant's categorical imperative theory.

DIVINE COMMAND THEORY

The **divine command theory** is a single-rule nonconsequentialist normative theory that says we should always do the will of God. In other words, whatever the situation, if we do what God wills, then we do the right thing; if we do not do what God wills, then no matter what the consequences, we do wrong.

Notice that this theory does not state that we should obey God's law because we will therefore promote our own or the general good or be faithful to some virtuous principles. Perhaps we will accomplish these ends, but the sole justification for obeying God's law is that God wills it. The theory also does not defend the morality of an action by promising some supernatural reward to the faithful. True, perhaps the faithful will be rewarded, and perhaps behaving righteously is in their best long-term interests, but divine command theorists wouldn't justify moral actions on such egoistic grounds.

What is valuable, for divine command theorists, is independent of what any individual thinks or likes and what any society happens to sanction. Moral laws are established by God; they are universally binding for all people and are eternally true, regardless of whether they are universally obeyed. Such God-established laws are generally interpreted in a religious tradition. The Ten Commandments are a good example. These laws, claim their adherents, apply to everybody everywhere and their value does not depend on what produces human satisfaction, either individually or collectively.

The justification of such moral laws is usually divine authority and its supposed expression through humans and their institutions. Thus the Bible or the Koran may be appealed to as an authority, as may a religious institution or leader.

Even a cursory look at the divine command theory reveals a couple of inherent weaknesses. First, how do we know what God has commanded? True, divine command theorists frequently point to sacred books or scriptures as guidelines. Yet, how do we know that these writings represent the inspired word of God? Some would assert that the scriptures say so. But such circular reasoning won't do. After all, how do we know that there is a God at all? And if there is, can we be sure that He or She expressed Himself or Herself in one source and not in another?

In addition, the divine command theory can't satisfactorily explain why God commands something. In other words, does God command something because it is right, or is something right because God commands it? If the former, then the theory appears to collapse because it contends that something is right *because* God commands it. If the latter, then anything that God commands must be right. Should God command cruelty, then cruelty would be right—a most difficult proposition to defend.

Goodness does not more certainly make men happy than happiness makes them good.

W. S. LANDOR

Philosophers have not been indifferent to these objections. In the eighteenth century Immanuel Kant attempted to present single-rule nonconsequentialist theory based, not on religious teaching, but on reason alone.

KANT'S CATEGORICAL IMPERATIVE

To understand Kant's thought, note the emphasis he places on the idea of good intentions. Kant believed that nothing was good in itself except a "good will." Intelligence, judgment, and all other facets of the human personality are perhaps good and desirable, but only if the will that makes use of them is good. To quote Kant:

> It is impossible to think of anything in the universe—or even beyond it—that is good without qualification, except a good will. Intellectual talents such as intelligence, cleverness, and good judgment are undoubtedly good and desirable in many respects; so also are character traits such as courage, determination, and perseverance. But these gifts of nature can become quite evil and harmful when they are at the service of a will that is not good. It is the same with gifts of fortune such as power, wealth, honor, and even health and that general well-being and contentment we call happiness. These will produce pride and conceit unless the person has a good will, which can correct the influence these have on the mind and ensure that it is adapted to its proper end. Moreover, an impartial rational spectator would not feel any pleasure at seeing a person without a good will enjoying continuous happiness. Thus it seems that having a good will is a necessary condition for even deserving happiness.[15]

By "will" Kant meant the uniquely human capacity to be motivated by reasons or "maxims." A "good will" is a will that is motivated to perform an act because it is a *moral duty* and not merely because the act is in one's self-interest or gives one pleasure. And to be motivated by duty, according

---

15. Immanuel Kant, *Grundlegung zur Metaphysik der Sitten* [Groundwork of the Metaphysics of Morals] in *Immanuel Kant Werkausgabe,* vol. 7, ed. Wilhelm Weischedel (Frankfurt, Germany: Insel Verlag Wiesbaden, 1956), trans. Manuel Velasquez (Copyright © 1987 by Manuel Velasquez), 18.

Immanuel Kant: *"I am never to act unless I am acting on a maxim that I can will to become a universal law.* Only this principle can prevent duty from becoming a vain delusion."

to Kant, is to be motivated to do something because one believes it is the way all human beings ought to behave. Acting morally, then, is acting only on those maxims or reasons that you believe everyone—universally—ought to live up to. For Kant, therefore, my will is "good without qualification" only if it always has in view one principle: Can I will that my maxim be followed by everyone as a universal law? Kant expresses this same idea by asking us to imagine that the laws of nature force everyone to follow the maxims that I act on. Would I still perform the actions I plan to perform if I knew that my maxims would become laws of nature that everyone would have to follow? If not, then I should not perform the action. These crucial aspects of Kant's theory of ethics are presented in the following passage from Kant's masterpiece, *Foundations of the Metaphysics of Morals.* Notice that Kant does not rely on a consideration of consequences.

But what sort of law can this be that mere awareness of it is enough to make the absolutely good will choose to follow it regardless of the results? Since I have ruled out every motive based on the desirable results of obeying any particular law, no other motive is left for the good will to act

on except the motive of obeying the [moral] law simply because it is a universal law. That is, *I am never to act unless I am acting on a maxim that I can will to become a universal law.*

Thus, the basic principle that the will must follow is the principle of conforming to universal law (as distinct from a law that would require a particular action). Only this principle can prevent duty from becoming a vain delusion and a mythical notion. . . .

We can express the basic principle of the categorical imperative in different words if we first note that the universal laws of cause and effect that govern the world are what we properly mean by "nature" in the most general sense of the word (these laws give nature its form). For nature is the existence of things insofar as they are structured by general laws. Consequently, the basic principle of the categorical imperative can also be expressed in the following version: *Act as if the maxims you choose to follow always became universal laws of nature.*

We will now enumerate a few of the duties that follow from this version of the categorical imperative. We will adopt the usual practice of classifying duties into perfect and imperfect duties and subclassifying each of these into duties to ourselves and duties to others.

1. Perfect duty to oneself. Imagine a man who has been reduced to despair by a series of misfortunes. Suppose he feels tired of living, but is still able to ask himself whether it would be contrary to duty to take his own life. So he asks whether the maxim of his action could become a universal law of nature. His maxim is this: "Out of self-love I will adopt the principle that I will end my life once it contains more evils than satisfactions." Our man can then ask himself whether this principle, which is based on the feeling of self-love, can become a universal law of nature. He will see at once that a system of nature that contained a law that destroyed life by means of the very feeling whose function it is to sustain life would contradict itself. Therefore, such a law could not be part of a system of nature. Consequently, his maxim cannot become a universal law of nature so it violates the basic principle of morality.

2. Perfect duty to others. Imagine another person who finds himself forced to borrow some money. He knows that he will not be able to repay it, but he also knows that nobody will lend him anything unless he promises to repay it. So he is tempted to make such a promise. But he asks himself: Would such a promise be consistent with duty? If he were to make such a promise the maxim of his action would be this: "When I need money, I will borrow it and promise to repay it even if I know that I will never do so." Now I personally might be able to live according to this principle of self-interest. But the question is: Is it right? So I ask myself: What if my maxim were to become a universal law? Then I see at once that it could never even become a universal law of nature since it would contradict itself. For suppose it became a general rule that everyone started making promises he never intended to keep. Then promises themselves would become impossible as well as the purposes one might want to achieve by promising. For no one would ever believe that anything was promised to him, but would mock all "promises" as empty deceptions.

3. *Imperfect duty to oneself.* Imagine a third man who has a useful natural ability that he could develop through practice and exercise. However, he is comfortably situated and would rather indulge in pleasure than make the effort needed to develop and improve himself. But he asks himself whether his maxim of neglecting his natural gifts as he is tempted to do is consistent with his duty. He sees then that a system of nature could conceivably exist with such a universal law, even if everyone (like the South Sea islanders) were to let his talents rust and devoted his life to idleness, amusement, and sex—in a word, to pleasure. But although his maxim *could* be conceived as a universal law of nature, he could not *will* it to be a universal law of nature; that is, he could not will such a law to be implanted in us like a natural instinct. For our natural abilities enable us to achieve whatever goals we might have, so every rational person who has any goals whatever necessarily wills to have his abilities develop.

4. *Imperfect duty to others.* Imagine a fourth man who is prosperous, while he sees that others have to put up with great wretchedness. Suppose he could help them, but he asks himself: What concern is it of mine? Let everyone have whatever happiness God or his own efforts can give him. For my part I will not steal from people or envy their fortune. But I do not want to add to their well-being or help them when they are in need! Undoubtedly, if such a way of thinking became

universal, the human race could continue to exist; it might even be better off than if everyone were to talk about sympathy and good will and occasionally practiced it, but generally continued to cheat whenever they could and betrayed and violated the rights of others. However, although that maxim *could* be a universal law of nature, one could not *will* it to be a universal law of nature without having one's will come into conflict with itself. For we know that many situations will arise in which one will need the love and concern of others. So if one were to will such a law of nature, one would be depriving himself of that aid he knows he will need.

These are a few of the duties that can be derived from the principle we have laid down. They fall into two classes. The basic rule for evaluating the morality of our actions is this: We must be *able to will* that the maxim of our action should be a universal law. One class of duties (the perfect duties) consists of actions whose maxim cannot even be consistently *conceived* as a universal law of nature, much less could we *will* such maxims to be universal laws of nature. The second class of duties (the imperfect duties) consists of actions whose maxims *could* become universal laws of nature, but it is impossible for us to *will* that their maxims should be universal laws since such a will would be in conflict with itself. It is easy enough to see that the first class of actions violates our strict duties, while the second class violates only what it would be meritorious for us to do. Thus these four examples cover the main kinds of duties and show that

---

To do as you would be done by, is the plain, sure, and undisputed rule of morality and justice.

LORD CHESTERFIELD

Do not do unto others as you would they should do unto you. Their tastes may not be the same.

BERNARD SHAW

---

even the strictness of the obligation can be determined by this one principle and not by reference to the purpose of the action.[16]

Kant believed, then, that there was just one command or imperative that was categorical—that is, one that presented an action as necessary of itself, without regard to any other end. He believed that from this one categorical imperative, this universal command, all commands of duty could be derived. Kant's **categorical imperative** states that we should act in such a way that the maxim, or general rule, governing our action could be willed to become a universal law.

Consider his example of making a promise that you are willing to break if it suits your purposes. Your maxim can be expressed thus: When it suits my purposes, I'll break promises that I have made. This maxim could not be universally acted upon, because it involves a contradiction of will. On the one hand, you are willing to make promises and honor them; on the other, you are willing to break those promises. Notice that Kant is not a utilitarian: He is not arguing that the consequences of a universal law condoning promise breaking would be bad and therefore the rule is bad. Instead, he is claiming that the rule is self-contradictory; the institution of promise making would dissolve if such a maxim were universalized. His appeal is to logical consistency, not to consequences.

Although there is only one categorical imperative, Kant felt it could be stated in different ways. One very important formulation of it is: Act so that you always treat people as ends in themselves and never merely use them as means. This insight may be at the root of the disagreement between our two police officers.

OBIE: What gets me, Kid, is that people like you make it sound like I'm doing society a disservice by keeping these thugs off the street. When, in fact, the opposite is true.

KID: But that's not the point, Obie. Even if society's interests are served, you don't put someone in jail for something he didn't do.

---

16. Ibid., 28, 51–55.

Veracity is the heart of morality.

THOMAS HUXLEY

OBIE: Even if he did a lot of other stuff, and will probably do more?

KID: That's right.

OBIE: Well, I guess I'm dense, because I don't see that at all.

KID: That's because you don't see anything wrong with using people to accomplish social goals.

The Kid's charge surely couldn't be applied to Kant. On the contrary, Kant emphasized that every rational creature has inherent worth, which results solely from the possession of rationality. Rational creatures possess what Kant termed an "autonomous, self-legislating will." In other words, they can evaluate their actions, make rules for themselves, and direct their conduct according to these self-imposed rules.

But Kant's theory is not airtight. First, duties frequently conflict, and Kant's theory does not seem to give us an obvious way of resolving such conflicts. If, as Kant argues, it is always wrong to tell a lie and always wrong to break a promise, then which do I choose when these duties conflict? Second, the acts the categorical imperative condemns as being *always* wrong seem not always to be wrong. For example, Kant says it is absolutely wrong ever to lie, no matter what good might come of telling the lie. But is lying always wrong? Is it wrong to lie to save your life? To save someone from serious pain or injury? There is no compelling reason why certain actions should be prohibited without exception. Apparently Kant failed to distinguish between persons' making no exceptions to rules and rules' having no exceptions. If a person should make no exceptions to rules, then one should never except oneself from being bound by a rule. But it does not therefore follow that the rule has no exceptions and can never be qualified. In fairness to Kant, however, it should be noted that the limitations of his examples do not necessarily discredit his ethical theory.

In the twentieth century a nonconsequentialist British ethicist named William David Ross turned his attention to the conflicting-duties problem that Kant's theory seems incapable of resolving. The result is a multiple-rule nonconsequentialist theory generally referred to as Ross's *prima facie duties*.

ROSS'S PRIMA FACIE DUTIES

OBIE: You're not telling me you'd turn a guy like that loose, are you?

KID: That's exactly what I'm telling you.

OBIE: But you said yourself he was one of those incorrigibles.

KID: But he's innocent in this particular case.

OBIE: What's that got to do with it?

KID: Everything.

OBIE: You realize that he's going to go out and do the same thing again?

KID: Maybe so.

OBIE: And that you've got a duty to protect society?

KID: I know that.

OBIE: And despite that you'd release him?

KID: I would.

OBIE: How come?

KID: Because I don't believe it's right to imprison somebody for something he didn't do. It's just not fair.

Considering only consequences often seems inadequate for resolving moral decisions. The choice is frequently between duties. Thus, a person may have a duty to protect society. At the same time, the person has a duty to uphold justice. When those duties conflict, as here, which takes precedence? For Obie, it's the duty to protect society; for the Kid, it's justice. Who's right? William David Ross turned his attention to such questions in his work *The Right and the Good* (1930).

At the outset of his book, Ross makes it clear that he rejects the consequentialist belief that what

makes an act right is whether it produces the most good. As he notes, consequences of conflicting courses of action frequently counterbalance each other. So, instead of a consequentialism, Ross argues that in deciding among ethical alternatives, we must determine which duties we fulfill by performing or not performing each alternative.

Consistent with this insight is Ross's rejection of the claim that there is but one thing of intrinsic value. For Ross there are four things that are intrinsically worthwhile: pleasure, virtue, knowledge, and the distribution of pleasure and pain according to virtue. Because these things don't share any single value-making property, they can't be reduced to any single intrinsic good. A theory of value that holds several things as being intrinsically valuable is termed *axiological pluralism*. Ross's pluralism, evident in his theory of value, also appears in his theory of obligation.

As Ross explains, an act may fall under a number of rules at once, not just a single rule. For example, the rule to keep a promise may in a given circumstance conflict with the rule not to do anyone harm. For example, suppose that political candidate Ida Simpson promises a wealthy builder that if he funds her campaign and she gets elected, she'll deliver him an attractive government contract. Simpson is subsequently elected and makes good her promise. As it happens, the contractor does good work and offers competitive prices. But, of course, Ida Simpson doesn't even consider any other bids.

On the one hand, Simpson has fulfilled her promise, which she may have viewed as binding. On the other hand, she's violated her duty to society, which trusts that she will not collude with private interests to advance her own or their own welfare but will always act strictly in the interest of the public good. As a result, we'd probably believe that Simpson acted immorally, but not because the consequences of her action were unfavorable. She acted wrongly because the reasons against what she did count more than the reason for what she did. Such an analysis evaluates the conflicting duties to determine the most compelling.

In such cases, the possible acts are motivated by a number of reasons. Each reason in turn appeals to a moral duty—to keep a promise, to be faithful to the people who trust you, to be fair, to be honest. Each of these moral duties provides grounds for a particular action, and yet no single one provides sufficient grounds. The task is to choose the most obligatory duty, but first we must have a knowledge of prima facie duties.

The term *prima facie* means "at first sight" or "on the surface." By **prima facie duties**, Ross means duties that dictate what we should do when other moral factors aren't considered. Stated another way, prima facie duties are duties that generally obligate us; that is, they ordinarily impose a moral obligation but may not in a particular case because of circumstances. An **actual duty** is the action that one ought to perform after considering and weighing all the prima facie duties involved.

In *The Right and the Good*, Ross lists six categories of prima facie duties, although he concedes that this breakdown may be incomplete. First are duties that rest on previous acts of our own, such as promises. Ross calls these *duties of fidelity*. Under duties of fidelity, Ross would place not only the honoring of promises but also the obligation not to lie, "which seems to be implied in the act of entering into conversation," and to fulfill contracts that we've entered into, including oaths we've sworn. Under duties of fidelity Ross also lists duties of reparation (repairing wrongful acts). If, for example, I damage something that belongs to someone else, I've an obligation to make restitution.

A second category is duties that rest on acts of other people toward us. Ross terms these *duties of gratitude*. In effect, Ross argues that we're bound by obligations arising from relationships that exist between people, such as those between friends or relatives. Suppose, for example, an especially good friend is suddenly in need of assistance. I'm duty bound to do all I can to help this individual, who in the past has acted so selflessly toward me.

A third category is *duties of justice*, by which he means those duties that rest on the fact or possibility of a distribution of pleasure or happiness that is not in accordance with the merits of the people concerned. Imagine the case of imprisoning a man for a crime he never committed. No matter how much good might result from his imprisonment, such a punishment violates justice.

Ross lists as a fourth category *duties of beneficence*, duties toward people whose virtue, intelligence, or happiness we can improve. For example, I've an obligation to help out a corner beggar in genuine need if I can afford it; if I can help someone correct a costly mistake that they chronically make, I'm duty bound to do it.

Ross's fifth category is *duties of self-improvement*, that is, duties to improve our own condition with respect to virtue, intelligence, or happiness. Thus, just as we've obligations to help others, we are also duty bound to help improve ourselves. An exceptionally talented person who fritters away time, energy, and potential violates this duty. In contrast, a person who seizes opportunities for self-improvement honors it.

The last, and most important, of Ross's six categories is *duties of nonmaleficence*, which are duties of not injuring others. We're obliged to avoid hurting others physically, emotionally, and psychologically. In fact, Ross inevitably allows this duty to override any other duty with which it conflicts.

In summary, Ross presents six categories of prima facie duties, although there may be more categories. However, he does insist that we acknowledge and willingly accept the six categories without argument. His appeal for their acceptance does not rely primarily on reason and argument but on intuition. In other words, Ross invites us to reflect on certain situations, such as telling the truth. If we do, he's convinced that we'll accept his claim that these are true duties.

When faced with a situation that presents conflicting prima facie duties, Ross tells us, we must follow the more obligatory, our actual duty. The actual duty has the greatest amount of prima facie rightness over wrongness.

Although Ross addresses the most important question of conflicting duties, his theory is not without weaknesses. First, how do we know what our prima facie duties are? Ross claims that these are self-evident truths to anyone of sufficient mental maturity who has given them enough attention. But here he seems to presuppose traditional, collective values. What if people disagree with his categories? Ross would say that they lack "sufficient mental maturity" or that they didn't give the proposition "sufficient attention." But then we must decide on the precise nature of "sufficient mental maturity" and what it means to give something "sufficient attention."

More serious, however, is the fact that it's difficult, if not impossible, to determine the relative weight and merit of conflicting duties. When faced with a situation that presents conflicting duties, how do we determine our actual duty? In the case of two conflicting duties, Ross counsels, "The act is one's duty which is in accord with the more strin-

PHILOSOPHY AND LIFE 7.2

Getting to Know You: The Corporate Probe

Beth Broheimer was annoyed. "Over and over again, the same question," she thought. "What do they think I am—a thief?"

Do you think most companies take advantage of people who work for them when they can? Did you ever think about stealing money from places where you have worked? Do you believe you are too honest to steal?

At the very least, Beth decided, these were odd questions to ask someone who was applying for a job at The Gap, a chain of several hundred modern clothing outlets specializing in shirts, jackets, and Levi's jeans. But the questions went on.

If you knew that a member of your family was stealing from a place where he works, do you think you would report it to the owner of the company? Were you ever tempted to take company money without actually taking

SOURCE: Peter Schrag, "Confess to Your Corporate Father: Does Your Boss Know What You Do When You're Alone?" *Mother Jones* (August 1978): 56–60.

any? Do you keep out of trouble at all costs? Do you think it okay to get around the law if you don't actually break it?

Why such questions? The answer's simple: The Gap, like numerous discount and drug stores, banks, brokerage houses, and fast-food restaurants, was subjecting Beth to a preemployment screen to determine whether she'd be likely to steal from the firm as an employee. Is such a determination possible? Yes, claim the sponsors of one such test, the Reid Report, devised by Reid and Associates, a polygraph firm based in Chicago. But the Reid Report asks other questions of the job candidate, which at best seem to relate only indirectly to the inventory's purpose.

How much money do you pay each month as a result of divorce or separate maintenance for the support of your wife and children? In the past five years about how much money, if any, have you gambled?

Before completing the Reid Report, Beth Broheimer will have answered questions about loans and

debts, outside income, and personal habits (including drug and drinking habits). Indeed, by the time she's finished, she will have revealed to her prospective employer many important details of her financial status; her criminal record, if any; her physical and mental health; and her personal life.

What will become of this information? Reid will keep the inventory dealing directly with theft. The rest of the information will be returned to her employer. And, oh yes, Reid and Associates will or will not recommend Beth Broheimer for employment at The Gap.

QUESTIONS

1. Does an employer have a right to subject a potential employee to such tests?

2. Is it proper for employers to know the details of their employees' personal lives?

3. What considerations do consequential and nonconsequential theories raise for deciding whether or not to use these tests?

gent prima facie obligation." In cases of more than two conflicting duties, he says, "That act is one's duty that has the greatest balance of prima facie rightness over wrongness." But without assigning weights to duties, how can we determine the "most stringent" obligation or "the greatest balance of prima facie rightness over wrongness"?

This completes our overview of the main currents in Western ethical theory. In keeping with our intention of providing an intercultural perspective, we should at least mention the rich moral legacy of Eastern religion and philosophy. Although we can't explore all Eastern moral thought, we can look more closely at one we've already met, Buddhism.

BUDDHIST ETHICS

For centuries in the Western world, moral, religious, and philosophical scholars have exhorted people to practice "the good, the true, and the beautiful" to attain happiness. In recent years scholars have rediscovered the Buddhist method of incorporating this advice into a system that leads to wisdom or ultimate reality.

Buddhism's emphasis on ethical behavior can be generalized in two ways. First, volitional actions are regarded of supreme importance because according to the moral law of causation (karma), they determine our destiny. We will be what we have been; what we do will determine what we become. Second, ethics is considered the parent of wisdom, in that reflection on the wholesomeness or unwholesomeness of volitional actions leads to discipline of the mind, which eventually results in insight and enlightenment. Thus, we are always brought to the following dictum: "Morality is washed all round with wisdom, and wisdom is washed all round with morality. Wherever there is morality, there is wisdom, and wherever there is wisdom there is morality. From the observing of the moralities comes wisdom and from observing of wisdom comes morality. Morality and wisdom together reveal the height of the world. It is just as if one should wash one hand with the other or one foot with the other;

exactly so is morality washed round with wisdom and wisdom with morality."[17] The Buddhist standards of morality, then, must always be conducive to the attainment of nirvana (enlightened wisdom) and the realization of the Four Noble Truths. The Buddhist ethical ideal is that of the self-reliant person, the individual who has attained personal enlightenment. Of course, as we've indicated elsewhere, enlightenment is not derived from logical deduction. But this does not mean that the individual should therefore wait for a supernatural revelation. Recall that the Fourth Noble Truth is that of the way to the cessation of suffering, which, Buddhism teaches, we must follow continuously and diligently throughout the present life. We do this essentially by following three short axioms.

> Cease to do evil;
>
> Learn to do good;
>
> Purify your own mind.[18]

In his marvelous treatment of this subject, Buddhist scholar H. Saddhatissa says that the first line, "Cease to do evil," sums up the code of Buddhist morality contained in five precepts, which constitute the negative aspects of Buddhist morality.[19] These precepts can be viewed as a "clearing away of the weeds from the soil,"[20] an ordering of the outer life before turning to the inner life, to the development and liberation of the mind, which are the goals of Buddhist teaching. These precepts represent the first steps that one can take after reading, hearing, and pondering Buddhist teaching and establishing some confidence in it. But it's important not to view these precepts as a set of rules, for Buddhism stresses the cultivation of wisdom and discernment. In other words, blind obedience to the following precepts is not encouraged:

---

17. *Dighanikaya*, vol. 1, eds. T. W. Rhys Davies and J. E. Carpenter (Pali Text Society, 1947), 124.

18. *Dhammapada*, ed. Suriyagoda Sumangala (Pali Text Society, 1914), 124.

19. See H. Saddhatissa, *The Buddha's Way* (New York: George Braziller, 1971).

20. Ibid., 32.

1. Refrain from harming living things.

2. Refrain from taking what is not given.

3. Refrain from a misuse of the senses.

4. Refrain from wrong speech.

5. Refrain from taking drugs or drinks which tend to cloud the mind.[21]

These precepts are worthy of close inspection.

The first precept implies an increasing awareness of the sanctity of life. This can easily—and mistakenly—be read as "Thou shalt not kill." Remember that there are no "thou shalts" in Buddhist morality. More important, this is not just an injunction against murder or wanton killing; it suggests an abstinence from injuring or in any way harming living things. If you savor the full implications of this, intriguing questions arise. For example, "The question arises whether my gastronomical pleasure should be satisfied at the expense of 'living things,' whether animals should be slaughtered so that I may disport myself in their borrowed plumes. And then the questions begin to go deeper. What of my murderous impulses when I am thwarted or humiliated? What of the secret joy I feel when someone I dislike is 'put down'?"[22] Just imagine the ever-increasing questions and doubts that a Westerner might have on trying to implement this first precept. So much the better; for while initially disturbing us, such unrest, Buddhism teaches, ultimately results in a life having a new significance and perspective. We develop a new sense of respect for self and others that permeates all our thinking.

The second precept asks us to refrain from taking what is not given. Again, the easy translation is "Thou shalt not steal." But this is grossly inadequate, for this precept invites us to develop toward the owners of inanimate objects the same respect that the first precept enjoins toward living things. Rather than merely an injunction against stealing, this second precept necessitates waiting until things

Buddha: **"Morality is washed all round with wisdom, and wisdom is washed all round with morality. It is just as if one should wash one hand with the other or one foot with the other; exactly so is morality washed round with wisdom and wisdom with morality."**

are offered us. Thus, a quiet, serene patience replaces the frenzied, rapacious attitude of those living by an "I want" dictum.

The third precept, which asks us to refrain from a misuse of the senses, again is often erroneously translated as a commandment against sexual misconduct, "Thou shalt not covet thy neighbor's wife" or "Don't fornicate." But this is an incomplete understanding. We're advised to refrain from the misuse of the body and bodily sensations. Thus, artificially stimulating the appetite for food is as

---

21. Ibid., 28.
22. Ibid.

much to be eschewed as adultery or incest. By this precept, personal habits that lead to obesity, muscular deterioration, or any pollution of the body and its organs are to be avoided. However, Buddhism does not ask its adherents to become ascetics. It simply invites them to be ceaselessly aware of the quality and degree of one's sensual activity. The sense should be enjoyed, not jaded; used, not abused.

As for the fourth precept, Buddhist literature is replete with varieties of "wrong speech." Lying, slander, gossip, malicious talk generally, violation of secrets—the list goes on. The key thing is a call for self-honesty. By avoiding wrong speech, we establish a link between "right thought" and "right action." We practice right speech when we use conversation for knowing people, for understanding others and ourselves. Using a contemporary buzz word, we can translate right speech to right *communication*, whether it involves conversation, advertising, or political speeches.

The fifth precept takes us into the heart of Buddhist morality. Recall that the cardinal concept of Buddhist human ethics is enlightenment and illumination. The central teaching is a system of meditation designed to clarify the mind so that knowledge and insight may arise in it and be reflected freely. It follows that anyone seriously interested in attaining the state of enlightened wisdom would refrain from indulgences that impair the clarity of mental vision, shroud doubts and uncertainties in a kind of euphoria, and encourage seeing things other than as they are.

As said earlier, these five precepts are summed up in the first axiom of Buddhist moral teaching, "Cease to do evil." These precepts, however, are only the ground breaking and the weeding. The constructive work begins with the second axiom, "Learn to do good." This leads us to the positive aspects of Buddhist morality.

Buddhist literature sparkles with various lists of "wholesome" states or "things to be encouraged," which are contrasted with "unwholesome" states or "things to be discouraged." Among the most prominent of the wholesome: *dāna*, which means "giving."

Again, there's a tendency to equate this with the *caritas* (charity) principle of the New Testament. But the earliest descriptions of *dāna* belie this equation. *Dāna* is not encouraging philanthropic gifts, tithing, or making charitable contributions to worthy causes. Rather *dāna* implies the gradual developing of the *will* to give whenever the need arises.

This suggests another prominent Buddhist virtue: *mettā*, often translated as "loving kindness." Whereas *dāna* is one outward manifestation of concern for the welfare of others, *mettā* embraces the whole sphere of that concern. "To develop *mettā* is to develop the state of mind wherein the joys and sorrows, the well-being and the problems of others are as important to me as my own.[23] In other words, *mettā* requires that we break down the barriers between self and others. "It has often been said that the follower of the Buddha should endeavor to feel towards all men—relations, friends, acquaintances and enemies—just as a mother feels towards her child."[24] Undoubtedly, this is a tough task. Nonetheless, according to the Buddhist code, we must do this if we're to make any spiritual progress.

But perhaps the Buddhist virtue most difficult for the Western mind to grasp is the "transference of merit." We can perhaps best appreciate this by pondering the fact that a time comes when, having avoided evil and done good, we realize our inherent selfishness: We are doing good to reap for ourselves the harvest of enlightened wisdom. At this point Buddhism invites us to practice "transference of merit," that is, to learn to will that the benefits of our good actions return not to us alone but to all humanity. "Each act of generosity, each movement of love, is no longer to be toted up in my personal account book but is to rebound to the benefit of all. Rather like a stream which feeds the ocean and which is replenished, not by means of the same water flowing back to it, but in the course of time with the falling of the rains."[25]

---

23. Ibid., 33.
24. Ibid.
25. Ibid., 34.

In summary, while there are similarities between traditional Western ethics and Buddhist ethics, there are also fundamental differences. One is the Eastern nonreliance on rules and commandments. Remember that both the negative and positive aspects of Buddhist morality should be looked on as invitations, not proscriptions. Second is the emphasis on the individual. In the last analysis, the individual avoids evil and cultivates good to facilitate personal enlightenment. Third, Buddhist morality takes root in a metaphysical outlook. Conducting our lives morally is an expeditious way to experience reality. Fourth is Buddhism's encouraging practitioners to dig into their own experiences, to be open to the universe. If the path of the heart is followed, consideration of the consequences of action is irrelevant. If we are open to the disclosure of the world, then congruence of being and cosmos will follow.

QUESTIONS

1. Reconsider the four situations on pages 331–332 from the viewpoint of a divine command theorist. What decisions and actions do you think are called for? Would the judgments differ from the act utilitarian's? The rule utilitarian's?

2. Can the categorical imperative be applied toward resolving the four situations described previously? Illustrate.

3. Would it be possible or desirable to universalize the following maxims?

a. "Never work unless you absolutely must."

b. "Always do your own thing unless it hurts somebody else."

c. "Give nothing and expect nothing in return."

d. "Sell all you have and give to the poor."

e. "Let your conscience be your guide."

f. "Always stick by your friends."

g. "Never discriminate against someone on the basis of race, religion, color, or sex."

h. "Never punish a child physically."

i. "Without prior approval, you should never take something that doesn't belong to you."

4. Reexamine the four situations on pages 331–332. What duties may be involved? Would the duty ethicist's perspective prescribe obligations that differ from the act utilitarian's? The rule utilitarian's?

5. In the play *The Victors*, Jean-Paul Sartre portrays six French Resistance fighters captured and tortured by the Nazis, who wish to extract vital troop movement information from them. Just before his painful interrogation, one of the prisoners, fifteen-year-old François, informs his fellow cellmates that he'll reveal all rather than be tortured as they have been. His cellmates have a choice: Silence him, or let him speak and thus imperil the lives of sixty French soldiers. Lucy, the boy's sister, is among the prisoners. Seeing herself bound by fidelity to the other troops, she votes to kill François. From the viewpoint of a prima facie duty theorist, would you say she acted wrongly? Does she have a conflicting duty because she's the boy's sister? One of the other prisoners ultimately strangles François. Did he act wrongly?

6. Apply each of Buddhism's five precepts to appropriate aspects of your life. What changes would they necessitate?

7. What weaknesses, if any, do you detect in Buddhist ethics?

8. What social changes can you think of that an implementation of Buddhist ethics might bring about? (For example, how would it alter advertising or marketing generally? What impact would it have on television, if any?)

Judging and Applying Moral Theories

Having completed our overview of major consequentialist and nonconsequentialist ethical theories of value and obligation, we should now ask: Which, if any, of these theories ought we to adopt as a personal code of ethics? Unfortunately, we can apply no one principle in choosing, no absolute standard for simplifying the choice. As a result, we're ultimately left to our own devices—to our own experience, reasoning, and intuition. Perhaps the whole enterprise of trying to formulate and justify moral principles is futile and should be abandoned. While such a reaction is understandable, it is, in the last analysis, unfounded.

That an ethical theory lacks perfection doesn't mean that it's useless or that the pursuit of a satisfactory theory is hopeless. Human relationships inevitably present a tangled web of subtle, ill-defined problems. What's more, since relationships are constantly changing, so are the problems and our perspectives of them. The ethical theories we've discussed are just that, theories. They're conceptual frameworks by which we can intelligently conduct moral investigation. What's more, ethical theories are in as constant need of reexamination and refinement as is, say, the democratic theory of government. Their imperfect state, then, is less a flaw than a testimony to the ability of humankind to constantly improve on what it possesses.

Each of these theories has an impressive range of applications. In criticizing them, philosophers invariably focus on their weaknesses. Although some people might call such activity "nit-picking," it is consistent with the philosophical enterprise of pursuing truth and certainty. Philosophers raise cases that tend to break the theory down and to test its strength. Failing to grasp this aspect of the philosophical enterprise, one can easily conclude that ethical theories and moral philosophizing offer little if anything of worth. But this would be a gross overstatement that even the harshest critics would not accept. Such a view would be as indefensible as scrapping the theory of biological evolution or of quantum mechanics because they are incomplete or unsatisfactory in important ways. As in the world of science, we face complex realities in the realm of human relationships that by nature seem to preclude total success. And this requires cooperative attempts to test the range of theoretical applications.

Granting that these theories, though imperfect, are extremely useful, isn't the selection of one theory ultimately arbitrary? If none of them can be proved correct, doesn't it matter little which one, if any, we choose? Although this is an understandable reaction, we should reflect on the meaning of the word *arbitrary*.

It's true that it would probably be arbitrary if a person decided that, since ethical theories generally agree on basic ideals, it doesn't matter which code is followed. But such a position would be unsound because different codes commit us to different principles. The thoughtful person recognizes these differences and chooses. Such a choice, rooted in a consideration of alternatives, cannot be arbitrary. Indeed, it's based on the best available evidence. In the words of British philosopher R. M. Hare: "To describe such ultimate decisions as arbitrary . . . would be like saying that a complete description of the universe was utterly unfounded, because no further fact could be called upon in corroboration of it. This is not how we use the words 'arbitrary' and 'unfounded.' Far from being arbitrary, such a decision would be the most well-founded of decisions, because it would be based upon a consideration of everything upon which it could possibly be founded."[26]

---

26. R. M. Hare, *The Language of Morals* (Oxford: Clarendon Press, 1952), 69.

Finally, we should note that the fundamental worth of studying and understanding ethical thought is not to obtain definitive guides to moral conduct. Rather, the value lies in becoming aware of the moral options available to us for dealing with complex moral decisions on a personal and collective level. Let's try to tie together all that we've said by reflecting on this complexity.

THE COMPLEXITY OF MORAL DECISIONS

To understand the complexity of moral decisions and how an understanding of normative positions can help to elucidate them, imagine a convalescent home. Janet, a twenty-two-year-old nurse, works at Sunnyview. Janet likes her work very much and hopes some day to be a physician. She particularly enjoys the elderly people she attends and considers herself more a friend than a nurse. For the most part, they feel the same about her.

Janet is particularly fond of one old gentleman, Mr. Pitman; he reminds her of her grandfather, who died only a year before after a long and painful illness. In his prime, Mr. Pitman was vigorous, but now his eighty years have hobbled and enfeebled him. He has no family and depends on welfare to pay his bills. He despises Sunnyview so much that he has tried to take his life twice. Although alert and rational, he sees no point in living. Sunnyview officials have told him that if he persists in his suicide attempts, he will be transferred to a state psychiatric hospital for the remainder of his life.

The long shadows of a winter's afternoon have just fallen across Mr. Pitman's room when we join him and Janet.

MR. PITMAN: Janet, you once said you'd do anything for me.

JANET: I would, Mr. Pitman, you know that.

MR. PITMAN: Anything?

JANET: Anything in the world.

MR. PITMAN: You wouldn't fool an old man, would you?

JANET: You know better than that.

MR. PITMAN: Yes, I suppose I do. . . . Tomorrow when you come in, would you bring me a bottle of . . . sleeping pills?

PHILOSOPHY AND LIFE 7.3

Sex in Class

A newspaper reported on a college instructor and the course he offered at a local campus.

The glib former professor of the psychology of sex [Dr. Singer] . . . was suspended with pay . . . after he said in a published interview that he had been "romantically involved" with some of his students, attended student parties where there was nudity and

SOURCE: *San Jose Mercury News* 25 January 1983.

sex, and openly discussed giving homework credit for sexual experimentation. . . . Singer insisted that he gave students credit for optional sexual experimentation only when he believed the experience would be safe for them. But he conceded that there may be "some legitimate controversy" over what is safe. Those who elected to use the option included a woman who was living with a man and wanted to have a bisexual student join them in bed, and several heterosexual women who decided to try lesbian experiences,

Singer said. "I happen to think that a straight woman having a lesbian experience is just fine," he said, "that there is virtually no risk involved."

QUESTIONS

1. Do you agree that sexual experimentation is "just fine" as long as all parties are safe from risk? What is the meaning of *safe* here? Of *risk*?

2. What is the function and purpose of education?

JANET: Sleeping pills? You know you don't have to send out for those, Mr. Pitman. The doctor will prescribe them if you can't sleep.

MR. PITMAN: You don't understand. I have no trouble sleeping. It's waking up that's the bother.

JANET: You mean . . .

MR. PITMAN: I mean I wish a quick and painless death. But at the same time, I don't want you to get into any trouble on my account. So here, take this money.

JANET: I'm sorry, Mr. Pitman, I can't do that.

MR. PITMAN: You can't do it? But, Janet, I thought you were my friend.

JANET: But you can't ask me to help you . . .

MR. PITMAN: Die? Janet, I'm old and I'm sick. And tomorrow I'll be even older and sicker. It will never be different. Only worse. You don't wish that for me, do you?

JANET: No, of course I don't. But it'd be wrong for me to do what you ask.

MR. PITMAN: Why would it be wrong?

JANET: Because it goes against everything people believe is right and good. You know that, Mr. Pitman.

MR. PITMAN: No, I don't. I don't know that. All I know is there's no one in this bed suffering but me. Where are all those right and decent people? Out there, out in the streets and in the film shows and in front of television sets. They're not feeling all the pain and hurt, Janet. I am—Robert Pitman—I'm feeling it all. And the loneliness—the agony of having nobody, no family, no friends, just people like you who come to work here and poke me and prop me up. Those good and decent people you speak of—what right do they have to tell me what to do? Let them lie here awhile and then tell me that. In the meantime I say it's right, Janet, and I want you to help me.

Janet has been asked to help someone kill himself. On what basis should she decide whether to help? Her reaction that "it goes against everything people believe is right and good" doesn't satisfy Mr. Pitman; nor from the view of morality should it,

because it begs the question. Left unexplored is the reason for social disapproval. Janet's appeal is strictly to popular opinion. Popular opinion is not necessarily erroneous, but on the other hand, it isn't a foolproof way to select values in ethics or in any other value area. Recall the third principle of value issues: We should choose our own values based on our own goals and ideals. Just as important, when we allow values to be thrust upon us, we live others' lives, not our own. This is the philosophical point of Mr. Pitman's impassioned reaction.

Ultimately society may have compelling reasons for condemning what Mr. Pitman has asked Janet to do, and thus she may be wise to abide by its standard. But without evaluating those reasons within the general paradigm of ethical theory, who can say? As an egoist, act utilitarian, or situationist would advise, Mr. Pitman implores Janet to focus on the specific circumstances of his case. Should she?

Notice that the issue here is not whether suicide is moral, although that issue no doubt enters the question. The main issue is whether a person under these circumstances should help another person to end his life. Thus, it would be entirely consistent for Janet to see nothing wrong with suicide but still insist that it's wrong for her to help someone take his life. Why shouldn't she comply with Mr. Pitman's request? What's her moral justification? If she should, then again, why? By following the rest of the conversation, we can observe the subtle interplay of ethical theories that's often evident when people agonize over the right thing to do. Just as important, we can see how the abstract can quickly become disquietingly concrete, how theoretical weaknesses lead to tangible problems, and what moral options are available to those who face tough decisions.

"Tut, tut, child!" said the Duchess. "Everything's got a moral, if you only can find it."

LEWIS CARROLL

JANET: But I can't help you, Mr. Pitman.

MR. PITMAN: Do you think it's wrong for me to take my life?

JANET: I'm not sure. But I think almost everybody would say it's wrong for me to help you.

MR. PITMAN: Now listen. If I had a family, if people were depending on me, if there were loved ones who would be deeply hurt by my action . . .

JANET: But I will be, Mr. Pitman.

MR. PITMAN: That's kind of you, my dear. But can you honestly say that your hurt will be greater than what I'm going through? What I *will* go through?

JANET: No, probably not.

The element of utilitarianism is clear in this exchange. True, suicide is not the moral issue here,

---

PHILOSOPHY AND LIFE 7.4

IVF Research

Of all the futuristic applications of science, one of the most challenging to our ethics is our ability to tinker with human life outside the womb. While fascinated by experiments that hold out the promise of new life, as in the case of Louise Brown, the first test-tube baby, we recoil at the thought of a brave new world in which babies are not born but decanted.

Precipitating this concern today is *in vitro fertilization* (IVF), the process by which a human ovum or egg is removed from a woman's body and fertilized in a laboratory petri dish. Thus, life begins outside the womb, as Louise Brown began her life.

While the principles of IVF have been known for some time, federal funds for IVF research have, in effect, been forbidden since 1973. And yet, in September 1978, the government's Ethics Advisory Board, established to monitor experiments on human subjects, convened in Bethesda, Maryland. Its purpose was to consider the tough moral issues involved in IVF research and whether federal funds should be provided to support it.

The two tasks are separate but related, for whether one counsels federal sponsorship depends at least in part on one's moral view of the nature of such research.

To illustrate, consider an experiment that proposes to perfect ways to repair defective genes inside human ova and sperm and to identify immunization processes that might be activated to help the body reject cancer cells. Few would question the potential good of such research. However, moral questions arise and sides are taken over the question of how scientists will conduct this research.

One researcher, Dr. Pierre Soupart of Vanderbilt University, has applied for a federal grant to conduct experiments in which human ova would be fertilized in the lab and allowed to develop for six days, after which the embryos will die and their cells will be examined for chromosomal or other defects attributable to artificial conception. Some authorities argue that embryos are "biologically alive" from the instant of fertilization. Thus, it would be intrinsically wrong to create, use, and then

deliberately discard them. Others, in contrast, do not consider the early embryo a human subject. Consequently, they see nothing intrinsically objectionable in such an experiment.

Whether such experiments are right or wrong, and consequently whether the government should fund them, largely depends on whether the early embryo is human in the moral sense and therefore to be protected. In advising the National Institutes of Health on what government policy should be, the board must answer this question.

QUESTIONS

1. If you were a board member, what would your position be?

2. On what moral grounds should the board make its recommendations?

3. Suppose the government did ultimately subsidize experiments that you thought were immoral; would you feel morally obliged to take action in opposition?

but Mr. Pitman believes that the consequences of his suicide are relevant to whether it is right or wrong for Janet to help him. He is not, however, egoistic, as one might expect from his previous statements. He does not assume that only consequences to himself are at stake. In effect, he asks Janet to compare the consequences of his proposal for all concerned.

MR. PITMAN: Then why not help me?

JANET: But what if I helped everyone who asked me to do that?

MR. PITMAN: But not everyone is asking you.

JANET: Would you believe that Mrs. Kandinsky asked me the same thing last month?

MR. PITMAN: Mrs. Kandinsky. The poor soul. . . . But Mrs. Kandinsky has a family to consider.

JANET: You think that makes her suffering any less? Am I supposed to just help people without families, Mr. Pitman? Or those with families that don't love or visit them? Or maybe those with families who only visit them on Christmas and Thanksgiving?

MR. PITMAN: Why not just help those who are desperate and who beg you, like me? Is that so hard, Janet? Wouldn't that be the right thing to do?

JANET: I don't know. Do you know what Mrs. Kandinsky said to me yesterday? That she's looking forward to the spring and the birth of her grandchild. So you tell me, Mr. Pitman, what's desperation? How do you measure it?

How do you make up a rule to cover situations like these? This is what Janet is asking Mr. Pitman. She does not wish to consider the consequences of his isolated act. She wants to look at the rule that the act is following. Assuming the role of the rule utilitarian, Mr. Pitman says simply that she should aid anyone who asks and who is desperate. But precisely what does *desperate* mean? How many of us have not felt at some time desperate enough to die, only to have that feeling pass like a nightmare?

MR. PITMAN: Janet, I thought you were my friend.

JANET: But I am, Mr. Pitman. And I'll continue to be.

MR. PITMAN: Well, don't friends generally do things for each other?

JANET: Yes, but . . .

MR. PITMAN: Didn't you tell me just a minute ago that there wasn't anything you'd not do for me?

JANET: But that didn't include helping you hurt yourself.

MR. PITMAN: *Anything,* Janet; you said you'd do *anything* for me.

The conversation has turned; the consequences of the action are no longer the issue. Now the issue is duties that have accrued in the past, especially the duty to fidelity. Janet has made a promise to Mr. Pitman, and he is trying to hold her to it. In his eyes she is duty bound. But, she says, the promise didn't include helping him commit suicide. This raises the question of just how far promises go. Are all promises contingent on mental reservations, conscious or otherwise? When people promise to love and honor "from this day forward till death do us part," does that promise exclude "incompatibility," "irreconcilable differences," and the like, which excuse from their marriage vows more than half the people who take them? It is one thing to argue normatively that we are bound to be faithful to the promises we make; it is another to specify the nature, conditions, and limitations of a promise.

JANET: But I've made another promise, Mr. Pitman.

MR. PITMAN: What other promise?

JANET: To help you stay well and healthy. I've sworn to help you stay alive, not to help you die.

As we have previously seen, duties often conflict. Perhaps Janet does have a personal obligation to Mr. Pitman stemming from promises she has made to him. But she also has a professional obligation to him that stems from an oath that she took when becoming a nurse.

MR. PITMAN: All right, Janet. Let me ask you one thing and I'll not bother you anymore. If you don't respect my wishes, can you truly say that you acted out of love?

JANET: I don't think I understand.

MR. PITMAN: If you don't help me die with dignity, can you honestly say that you chose not to out of a genuine desire to do what's best for me?

JANET: What you're saying is that if I loved you, I'd help you commit suicide.

MR. PITMAN: I suppose I am.

JANET: I don't know, Mr. Pitman, I really don't. But let me ask you something. Can you say you truly act out of love when you ask me to help you end your life?

MR. PITMAN: I would like to think I can. . . . But I guess I don't know either.

As a last resort to enlist her aid, Mr. Pitman endorses a form of situationism. But loving concern, it seems, is much easier dealt with in the abstract that in the concrete. Who is to say that a denial of his request would not be an act of greater loving concern than an honoring of it? Indeed, if Janet thought it to be, intended it to be, by definition it apparently would be. If nothing else, however, Mr. Pitman's inquiry presses Janet to assess further the nature of her decision. It also forces Mr. Pitman to examine the moral nature of his request.

In the end we all must decide, perhaps not whether it's right to help an old man end his life or to imprison a known felon for a crime that the person didn't commit, but other issues that are pressing for us. On what basis do we make these decisions, which shape who and what we are and will be? Failing to engage and resolve these questions, we run a grave risk of leaving undeveloped a significant facet of human nature and self, the moral aspect.

Suppose that you have accepted one of the normative theories, according to which certain acts are right and others are wrong. Suppose further that Janet helps Mr. Pitman end his life. On the basis of your theoretical preference, you judge that Janet's action was wrong. But having made this judgment, you can always ask further: Should or should not Janet be held responsible for her act? In other words, you can ask whether Janet is at

fault, and, therefore, should be blamed for what she did. These questions cut to a basic issue in the study of ethics: moral responsibility. The issue of moral responsibility is one with far-reaching ethical implications. So, in concluding our overview of ethics, we will briefly consider this issue.

QUESTIONS

1. Describe some situations that have confronted you that posed a moral dilemma for you. What do you feel you *should* have done in each of those situations? What moral theories do you feel come closest to explaining why you should have done that?

2. Consider a situation that confronted you with a moral dilemma. Discuss what each of these theories of obligation would have required you to do: utilitarianism, situation ethics, Kant's categorical imperative, Ross's prima facie duties, Buddhist ethics. Does each of these theories provide clear guidance about what you should do? Explain.

3. Try living a day according to the utilitarian principle. What problems do you find yourself facing as you go through your day attempting to apply utilitarianism?

4. Some philosophers hold that utilitarianism imposes extremely heavy obligations on us, while others hold that Kant's categorical imperative imposes even heavier obligations. Which of these two theories of obligation do you think would be easier to follow? Why?

Moral Responsibility

EXCUSABILITY

A good way to enlighten the issue of moral responsibility is to connect it to the concept of excusability, that is, the circumstances under which we excuse people for their decisions and conduct. Ethicists generally speak of four kinds of conditions under which we ordinarily excuse people, that is, hold them blameless or not morally responsible: (1) excusable ignorance of the consequences or circumstances of an act; (2) the presence of a constraint that forced the person to do the act and that was so strong that no ordinary amount of will power could overcome it; (3) the presence of circumstances beyond the person's control; and (4) the absence of either the ability or the opportunity, or both, to do the right thing in the given situation.[27]

Excusable Ignorance of Consequences

We excuse people when we don't believe they were aware of the unfavorable consequences their actions would produce or because they couldn't reasonably have been expected to know how to prevent the consequences. For example, today health professionals are cautious, or should be, about subjecting patients to x-rays because of the potential dangers of radiation exposure. Years ago, however, medical personnel were not aware of this serious potential threat. Therefore, barring cases of egregiously

excessive and unnecessary x-ray exposure, we generally would not hold health professionals morally responsible for damage from x-rays administered during that time. But today we would.

Not knowing how to prevent bad consequences which are foreseen by someone may also warrant excusability. Thus, we wouldn't hold a Sunnyview patient at fault for not knowing what to do if Mr. Pitman suddenly experienced cardiac arrest. But we might blame Janet or the other health professionals at Sunnyview if they were present during the incident because, presumably, they are in a position to take corrective action, although, of course, not to guarantee the results.

Constraints

We usually excuse people when we think that they could not help what they did, that they had little or no choice in a matter. The constraint may be either external or internal. External constraint refers to outside factors or forces. When situations involve external constraints, we typically speak of people acting against their wills. A bank teller who at gunpoint turns over the bank's money to a robber is acting against his or her will. As a result, we would not condemn such behavior or blame the teller, for the act was done under coercion. In contrast, we would certainly find fault with the teller who, of his or her own free will, helped the robber, perhaps by telling the person beforehand the best time to rob the bank.

In the second form of constraint, internal, the compelling element comes from inside rather than from someone else. We speak of people who act in certain ways because they feel an overwhelming inner urge, desire, craving, or impulse to do so. Accordingly, we normally would not hold a kleptomaniac morally accountable for shoplifting a watch from a jewelry shop, or patients responsible for damage they cause during periods of postoperative psychosis. In contrast, we would surely blame the robber who carefully and coolly orchestrated the robbery of the jewelry shop, while feeling no inner drive to carry out the plan. By the same token, we would blame patients who, fully aware of what they

---

27. Paul Taylor, *Problems of Moral Philosophy*, 2d ed. (Belmont, Calif.: Dickenson, 1972), 277.

The Raft of the Medusa, Théodore Géricault. Géricault's painting portrays survivors of an 1817 shipwreck who floated for weeks on a makeshift raft desperately cannibalizing each other to stay alive. Ordinarily we excuse actions when we think that people lacked the ability to do the right act. Were the survivors of the *Medusa* morally responsible for what they did?

were doing, that is, acting of their own free will, throw destructive and disruptive temper tantrums.

Uncontrollable Circumstances

When, in our estimation, the circumstances of an act were beyond the person's control, we generally excuse the behavior. There are many circumstantial excuses that we readily accept as legitimate. Illnesses, accidents, unexpected duties are typical cases. Thus, we would not hold Janet responsible for arriving late for her hospital shift if, through no fault of her own, she was involved in an automobile accident. Were we to learn, however, that the accident was caused by Janet's reckless driving, we likely would hold her accountable for her tardiness.

Lack of Alternatives

Ordinarily we excuse actions when we think that people lacked either the ability or the opportunity to do the right act. If a man can't swim, we wouldn't blame him for not jumping into a pool and trying to save a drowning child (although we would hold him responsible for not summoning aid or not throwing the child a life preserver). Similarly, if the man could swim, but failed to save the child because he saw him only when it was too late, he lacked the opportunity to save the child. Therefore, we would not consider him morally responsible.

In sketching these four conditions, philosophy professor Paul Taylor indicates that there are two important points to realize. First, insofar as any actual situation satisfies one or more of these conditions, it can be sharply contrasted with a situation of the opposite kind in which these conditions are not met. Second, situations of both kinds do occur in everyday life.

Thus, just as there are cases where a person could not have foreseen the harmful consequences of his act, there are other cases where a person does foresee such consequences and still chooses to do the act. (A man who intends to murder someone not only foresees that his victim will die but wants this to happen.) Just as there are acts done under the coercion of another person, so there are acts done when no such external constraint is present. A man who fires a shotgun at the house of a civil-rights worker in the South may have decided to do it entirely by himself and may have acted under no external compulsion. It is possible, indeed, to act in opposition to a considerable amount of external constraint. Whenever a person commits a crime he does so in spite of, rather than because of, such external constraints as threat of punishment, fear of the police, and general social disapproval. Again, consider the case in which an internal urge or drive compels a person to act against his own will. This kind of case is to be contrasted with that of a person freely choosing to do something after carefully deliberating about it. A man might be in full control of himself as he works out a plan to embezzle funds, and feel under no compulsion as he calmly carries out his plan. In connection with the third kind of situation, just as we are sometimes prevented from doing what we ought to do by circumstances beyond our control, there are other cases where we don't do what we ought simply because we don't want to. We sometimes try to avoid our obligations when we find them onerous. Finally, although in a given situation we may lack the ability or the opportunity to do what would be right, just as often we have the capacity and the opportunity to do any number of alternatives open to our choice and yet we knowingly choose to do what is wrong. For example, the man who does not report accurately his income in order to avoid paying a tax certainly has the ability and opportunity to make out an accurate report, and knows that this would be the right thing for him to do.[28]

Thus, in everyday life there are occasions when we excuse people and occasions when we hold them responsible for their acts.

The preceding observations about moral responsibility probably seem commonsensical enough. And they remain so, until the theory of determinism, or universal causation, is applied to human choice and conduct. Then things tend to grow murky.

DETERMINISM

As we saw in Chapter 2, determinism is the theory that everything in the universe is totally ruled by causal laws. Accordingly, every event has a prior condition, and all events are at least theoretically predictable if all the prior conditions are known. The principle of determinism is widely used by the sciences of psychology, sociology, and anthropology in accounting for human behavior. Without doubt, these sciences have gone far in helping us understand why we act, feel, and choose as we do. And doubtless as these sciences continue to develop, our knowledge about human feelings, motives, and beliefs will be further enriched. Along with such knowledge probably will develop an ability to give causal explanations about human decisions and conduct. As a result, many people are beginning to think of humans as they think about animals or machines: They take the same scientific view toward all of them. In so doing, they view behavior not as chance events occurring haphazardly or in unpredictable ways, but rather as events that happen in an orderly way. This order, they say, is discovered when scientists are able to explain the events in terms of causal laws.

What has determinism to do with the condi-

One may go wrong in many different ways, but right only in one, which is why it is easy to fail and difficult to succeed—easy to miss the target and difficult to hit it.

ARISTOTLE

---

28. Ibid., 279–280.

tions for excusability and moral responsibility? Many believe that moral responsibility is incompatible with determinism. They claim that in cases where the four types of conditions of excusability do not hold, people may *appear* to be under no constraints; and they may *appear* to have the ability and opportunity to choose any number of alternatives and to act on them. But, the argument goes, these appearances are mere illusions. If choices and actions are causally determined, then, given the causal laws operating in the situation of choice, only one course of action can possibly occur: the one which will be the effect of the previous causes that are occurring in the situation. In other words, the act that a person ultimately chooses to do is inevitable, since there was a set of events which, of itself, was sufficient for producing the choice; and, because that sufficient condition was present, the choice of that act had to occur. In brief, the person could not have acted other than he or she did. If this explanation is so, if determinism operates in the realm of human decision and conduct, then determinism appears to be incompatible with freedom and responsibility in an ethical sense.

How, then, is the so-called moral self to be understood? In response to the assertion that moral responsibility is not possible in a strictly deterministic universe, four main positions emerge: hard determinism, indeterminism, soft determinism, and self-determinism.

Hard Determinism

Hard determinism is based on the rigid causality apparent in the physical universe. Freedom is incompatible with this view, for to admit freedom is to admit an element of unpredictableness in the universe. What, then, is "free choice"? According to hard determinists, free choice amounts to little more than human ignorance. We think we are free merely because we cannot predict our own or others' future behavior. While we cannot help engaging in the process of deliberation, the choice we make is forced on us by whichever set of motives is strongest. To insist that we are free and that we could have acted otherwise is to speak so much gibberish. After all, say hard determinists, there

could never be any possible proof that we could have acted otherwise since the proof is precisely what never did occur, and never will occur. Does this mean, then, that criminals, say, are not morally responsible for what they do? Precisely. According to hard determinists, a life of crime is predetermined by genetic inheritance and environment. Neither a criminal, nor Janet, nor Mr. Pitman, nor any of us is responsible in an ethical sense for what we do: Factors other than the self cause us to act as we do. By this account it is not so much false as meaningless to say that individuals are responsible for their own characters, decisions, and actions.

Indeterminism

The opposite of hard determinism is **indeterminism**, the view that humans are exceptions to the rigid causation that occurs in nature. Like determinists, indeterminists agree that the laws of causality may apply to everything else in nature. But indeterminists make of humans an exception to these causal laws. Causal laws do not apply to our free choices. How are our choices, then, to be explained? According to indeterminists, there are no causes for our free choices; our free acts are uncaused events that are not brought about by anything. Thus, human beings are not merely personalities entirely explainable in empirical terms, as hard determinism holds. Rather, humans are also moral agents. When humans are confronted by a choice between right and wrong, they consider themselves to be free agents with a moral self. It is the person's moral self that makes the choice and can accordingly be held accountable.

Soft Determinism

Hard determinism and indeterminism share an assumption: Determinism is incompatible with moral responsibility. Confronted with a choice between determinism and no responsibility, or responsibility but no determinism, hard determinists choose determinism; indeterminists choose responsibility. In contrast, advocates of **soft determinism** attempt to reconcile freedom and responsibility with determinism. They do this by limiting both concepts to the point where their evident incompatibility vanishes.

Soft determinists concede that in the sense that humans cannot choose to act against their individual characters, they are determined. But in the sense that humans are often free from outside compulsion and can thus conduct themselves unhampered in doing what they choose, they are free agents. Thus, while Janet's character in part is the product of outside forces, she is not wholly shaped by them. On the contrary, she has helped shape her own character by her previous personal choices. She has helped make herself what she is.

Given that Janet is responsible for her individual character, she is responsible for the choices she makes according to her character. Yes, every act is caused, but not by something outside her. It is caused by the kind of being she has become by reason of her previous personal choices. In this way, soft determinists claim that they have avoided the mistake of indeterminists, who admit of causeless acts; and that of hard determinists, who consider responsibility a fiction.

While soft determinism appears to wed freedom and moral responsibility with determinism, it leaves some key questions unanswered. First, if Janet, or any of us, is not free to act against her individual character, doesn't this mean that she is always subject to inner constraints? If she is, then the freedom

of soft determinism seems pointless. Second, if her character, which determines whether or not she will help Mr. Pitman end his life, has been molded by her own previous free choices, doesn't it follow that each of her free choices, in turn, was determined by that state of her own character at that previous moment, and so on back to childhood when deliberate free choice was impossible? Given this analysis, what kind of freedom does Janet or any of us have? In short, critics say that in trying to reconcile moral freedom and responsibility with determinism, soft determinists have blurred what is worthwhile in each.

Self-Determinism

Self-determinism accepts the doctrine of determinism that nothing can happen without a cause. It follows that our free acts are caused acts. In the case of human decisions and conduct, humans themselves are the cause of the act. When individuals choose, their choices are not made by something else outside or inside the person, but are the acts of the very person. Indeed, the very meaning of *person*, say self-determinists, implies someone who makes his or her own choices. Thus, individuals cause their own acts. While it is true that we are strongly influenced by motives and must deliberate between them, in the final analysis we are not necessitated by them either way. In the end we choose for ourselves.

Critics like hard determinists charge that self-determinists have evaded the issue. As we saw, hard determinists say that no acts are free acts. They insist that it would be impossible to prove that a person could have acted otherwise than he or she did (that is, freely), because the very proof is an act which did not occur and cannot occur. Self-determinists, they say, do nothing to meet this objection.

In reply, the self-determinist might say that this objection only holds if one assumes that all causes necessarily produce only one determined effect. But in the realm of human decisions and conduct, say self-determinists, individuals function as free agents: They can produce any one of several alternative effects on the basis of a choice. Critics object that

---

Morality, said Jesus, is kindness to the weak; morality, said Nietzsche, is the bravery of the strong; morality, said Plato, is the effective harmony of the whole. Probably all three doctrines must be combined to find a perfect ethic; but can we doubt which of the elements is fundamental?

WILL DURANT

this is having it both ways: endorsing the doctrine of determinism, while at the same time rejecting, or at least warping, it.

It's apparent that none of these viewpoints presents an airtight case. Because it denies freedom and moral responsibility, hard determinism does not accord with how we generally experience our own actions. Indeterminism, in proposing the notion of uncaused acts, seemingly preserves freedom and responsibility at the expense of scientific respectability. Soft determinism, which tries to reconcile freedom and responsibility with determinism, apparently does away with something worthwhile in each. And self-determinism may end up warping the doctrine of determinism in an attempt to preserve freedom and responsibility.

The controversy about freedom and determinism ultimately is a metaphysical one: It cuts to fundamental assumptions about reality and being. At the same time, it has profound implications for ethics, because the position one chooses in the controversy affects one's idea of moral responsibility, among other things.

QUESTIONS

1. Describe some situations when you were wrongly blamed for something for which you were not morally responsible. Which of the four kinds of excusing conditions were present?

2. Is there any kind of experience you could have that would prove that hard determinism is false? Explain.

3. Write down the fundamental moral principles you feel you should live up to. Why are these the appropriate moral principles to live up to? How would you show someone that you are not mistaken in adopting these moral principles?

CHAPTER SUMMARY AND CONCLUSIONS

We opened this chapter by observing that values, like so many other things today, are changing. The study of values includes debates about whether value judgments express knowledge or feeling, whether values are subjective or objective, and what is of value. One important value area is ethics. Normative ethics is the search for principles of good conduct. Broadly speaking, normative ethics can be divided into the consequentialist and nonconsequentialist schools. The consequentialist school, in turn, can be subdivided into egoism, act utilitarianism and rule utilitarianism, and situationism; the nonconsequentialist school into single- and multiple-rule nonconsequentialism: divine command, Kant's categorical imperative, and Ross's prima facie duties. In addition, Buddhism offers a rich moral legacy that Westerners find increasingly appealing.

Whether or not we choose to acknowledge them as such, the moral values we hold and the obligations we feel constitute expressions of who we are, how we see things, and how we wish to be seen by others. In choosing a moral life-style, we're really defining a large part of our selves. Yet, the complexity of moral decision making persists; the choices remain murky. The question that continues to nag us is: What moral life-style should I adopt to live the fullest, most rewarding life I can?

As stated throughout this chapter, there is no certain answer. The nature of moral decision making disallows scientific assurance. Nevertheless, we can garner factors from our discussion that seem appropriate to a personal morality. First, any moral code you follow must be your own, not in the sense that you alone follow it, but in the sense that you have arrived at it through your powers of reason and reflection on your experience. Granted, we cannot fully escape our social, cultural, and religious backgrounds; nor would we want to. Nevertheless, if our morality is to be an expression of self, we must carefully reflect on the values we have inherited, weighing their merits and liabilities in the light of our own lives, times, and circumstances. Such reflection places heavy emphasis on self-growth, especially on increasing our knowledge and awareness of self and the world and on being willing to adjust our moral views as relevant new discoveries arise. It also recognizes the dynamic, experimental value of morality.

The second factor appropriate to a personal morality is related to the first. It stems from

Immanuel Kant's concept of a good will. As just suggested, to make moral decisions primarily on the basis of social or institutional influence is to surrender what most people consider a uniquely human quality: the individual capacity to make moral decisions. These outside forces should not be our primary reasons for acting morally. For the mature and thoughtful person, right intention or good will is a necessary ingredient of the true moral act. This ingredient introduces the elements of motive, sincerity, and love. It is true that these are hazy concepts, but they frequently clear up in context. For example, the motives of the person who gives to charity primarily for the sake of a tax write-off are different from those of the person who gives to improve the conditions of the less fortunate; the intention of the person who flatters to ingratiate is different from that of the person who speaks the truth for its own sake. The teachings of ethicists and great moral leaders have stated or implied the importance of right intention, good will, or love in the moral act.

But these two subjective elements of a personal moral code, moral self-determination and right intention, are insufficient to ensure right action. After all, we may be morally self-determining and well intentioned but do something heinous. The third element, therefore, is an objective one, involving a consideration of the results or consequences of our actions. It seems that consequences must be a factor in any moral stance, for to be indifferent to the consequences of our actions is to act irresponsibly—that is, without moral regard. As we have seen, however, determining the consequences of an action is often difficult. It requires much evidence, analysis, and reflection. Even then we cannot be certain. But without such an examination, our action will not be in the highest sense moral.

No doubt there are other factors that you might wish to introduce. But these three—self-determination, right intention, and consideration of consequences—are the building blocks of a personal moral code.

Mill and Nietzsche

In this chapter we examined utilitarianism as one moral theory among many. But in fact utilitarianism is today not merely one among many: It is probably the dominant moral theory of our culture. Most people hold, for example, that when deciding how tax monies should be spent, the government should invest in those projects that will provide the greatest good for the greatest number. And when individuals try to explain why a certain course of action is immoral, they will often proceed by pointing to the overall benefits or harm the action will impose on human beings. In these and many other ways we show that utilitarian ways of thinking have a deep hold on us, since these are all ways of focusing on the idea of maximizing utility. It is appropriate, therefore, that we should showcase here a thinker who was largely responsible for popularizing utilitarian morality: the nineteenth-century philosopher John Stuart Mill.

But while many of us today hold a utilitarian morality, others reject morality altogether. Many people are skeptical about the claims of morality, holding that morality is a sham of some kind. In this showcase, therefore, we will also discuss the

An eye for an eye only ends up making the whole world blind.

GANDHI

views of another nineteenth-century philosopher, but one who was completely skeptical about morality: Friedrich Nietzsche. By considering and contrasting the views of these two great philosophers, you may find it easier to make up your own mind about the nature and reality of moral principles.

MILL

Born in England in 1806, John Stuart Mill was early subjected to an intense, rigorous, and unrelenting regime of study under the stern tutelage of his father, James Mill. At the age of three Mill's father started him on Greek, and by eight Mill was learning Latin. By the time he was fourteen, Mill had read most of the major Greek and Latin classics, surveyed all of world history, intensively studied logic and mathematics, and received a good deal of training in philosophy. But in spite of the terrific concern shown for his education, his feelings were starved. Predictably, shortly after his nineteenth birthday, Mill suffered a nervous breakdown. As he later put it in his *Autobiography*: "The habit of analysis has a tendency to wear away the feelings . . . I was thus, as I said to myself, left stranded at the commencement of my voyage, with a well-equipped ship and a rudder, but no sail."[29] Mill turned, then, to cultivating his feelings by reading poetry, and a few years later found himself involved in a romance with Harriet Taylor, the wife of a merchant. The two remained deeply but discreetly devoted to each other for twenty long years, until the death of her husband left the two finally free to marry in 1851. A great genius, Harriet had a terrific influence on Mill's thought virtually from the moment they met, and many of Mill's most important works were influenced by her. In 1858, however, only seven years after they were married, Harriet died while the two were on vacation in France. Mill lived on until 1873, when he died after a brief illness.

Mill was introduced at the age of fifteen to the writings of Jeremy Bentham, a close friend of his

29. John Stuart Mill, *Autobiography*, in *John Stuart Mill, Autobiography and Other Writings*, ed. Jack Stillinger (Boston: Houghton Mifflin, 1969), 84.

John Stuart Mill: "Actions are right in proportion as they tend to promote happiness, wrong as they tend to produce the reverse of happiness. By happiness is intended pleasure and the absence of pain, by unhappiness, pain and the privation of pleasure."

father and a radical utilitarian philosopher. The British utilitarians held that morality depends on the "utility"—that is, the pleasure or happiness—actions produce. Bentham held that the morality of an action depends on "its tendency to produce pains and pleasures." An action is morally right to the extent that it produces pleasure or happiness for those affected by the action, and it is wrong to the extent that it produces pain or unhappiness. The morally best action, Bentham held, is the one that, all things considered, will produce the greatest balance of pleasure over pain. Moreover, Bentham wrote, we can measure the quantity of any pleasure or pain by looking mainly at "(1) its Intensity; (2) its Duration; (3) its Certainty; and (4) its Proximity." But we should also examine: "(5) its Fecundity [Productiveness of other pleasures or pains]; (6) its Purity [or connection to other pleasures or pains]; . . . (7) its Extent, that is, the number of persons . . . who are [likely to be] affected by it."[30] By thus measuring the quantity of pleasures and pains produced by an action and comparing them to those produced by the other actions we could perform in its place, we can determine which action is the morally proper action for us on any occasion.

Mill later wrote that after reading this utilitarian philosophy of Bentham, "the feeling rushed upon me, that all previouis moralists were superseded, and that here indeed was the commencement of a new era of thought. . . . The 'principle of utility' understood as Bentham understood it . . . gave unity to my conceptions of things. I now had opinions, a creed, a doctrine, a philosophy; in one among the best senses of the word, a religion; the inculcation and diffusion of which could be made the principal outward purpose of a life."[31] Throughout his life Mill adhered to this conviction that all of our activities should aim at increasing the amount of pleasure or happiness in the world.

But Mill did not accept Bentham's views uncritically. In a short book entitled *Utilitarianism*, one of the most influential works on ethics ever published, Mill attempted to improve on Bentham's views by correcting what he thought was Bentham's major mistake: Bentham's assumption that only the *quantity* of pleasure and pain matters. On the contrary, Mill argued, the *kind* or *quality* of pleasure and pain that an action produces must be taken into consideration when judging the morality of the action. Moreover, judgments about which kinds of pleasures are the best can only be made by competent judges: those who have experienced all the pleasures in question. The judgments of competent judges, Mill says, show that the "higher" human pleasures are more valuable than the "lower" pleasures of animals. Consequently, when determining the morality of an action, we must not only weigh the quantity of pleasures and pains the action will produce but also take into account the *kinds* of pleasures and pains it produces. Mill wrote:

The creed which accepts as the foundation of

morals "utility" or the "greatest happiness principle" holds that actions are right in proportion as they tend to promote happiness; wrong as they tend to produce the reverse of happiness. By happiness is intended pleasure and the absence of pain; by unhappiness, pain and the privation of pleasure. . . .

Now such a theory of life excites in many minds, and among them in some of the most estimable in feeling and purpose, inveterate dislike. To suppose that life has (as they express it) no higher end than pleasure—no better and nobler object of desire and pursuit—they designate as utterly mean and groveling, as a doctrine worthy only of swine, to whom the followers of Epicurus were, at a very early period, contemptuously likened; and modern holders of the doctrine are occasionally made the subject of equally polite comparisons by its German, French, and English assailants.

When thus attacked, the Epicureans have always answered that it is not they, but their accusers, who represent human nature in a degrading light, since the accusation supposes human beings to be capable of no pleasures except those of which swine are capable. . . . Human beings have faculties more elevated than the animal appetites and, when once made conscious of them, do not regard anything as happiness which does not include their gratification. . . . [T]here is no known Epicurean theory of life which does not assign to the pleasures of the intellect, of the feelings and imagination, and of the moral sentiments a much higher value as pleasures than to those of mere sensation. It must be admitted, however, that utilitarian writers in general have placed the superiority of mental over bodily pleasures chiefly in the greater permanency, safety, uncostliness, etc., of the former—that is, in their circumstantial advantages rather than in their intrinsic nature. And on all these points utilitarians have fully proved their case; but they might have taken the other and, as it may be called, higher ground with entire consistency. It is quite compatible with the principle of utility to recognize the fact that some kinds of pleasure are more desirable and more valuable than others. It would be absurd that, while in estimating all other things, quality is considered as well as quantity, the estimation of pleasure should be supposed to depend on quantity alone.

---

30. Jeremy Bentham, *An Introduction to the Principles of Morals and Legislation* (Oxford: Oxford University Press, 1823), 51.

31. Mill, *Autobiography*, 41–42.

If I am asked what I mean by difference of quality in pleasures, or what makes one pleasure more valuable than another, merely as a pleasure, except its being greater in amount, there is but one possible answer. Of two pleasures, if there be one to which all or almost all who have experience of both give a decided preference, irrespective of any feeling of moral obligation to prefer it, that is the more desirable pleasure. If one of the two is, by those who are competently acquainted with both, placed so far above the other that they prefer it, even though knowing it to be attended with a greater amount of discontent, and would not resign it for any quantity of the other pleasure which their nature is capable of, we are justified in ascribing to the preferred enjoyment a superiority in quality so far outweighing quantity as to render it, in comparison, of small account.

Now it is an unquestionable fact that those who are equally acquainted with and equally capable of appreciating and enjoying both do give a most marked preference to the manner of existence which employs their higher faculties. Few human creatures would consent to be changed into any of the lower animals for a promise of the fullest allowance of a beast's pleasures; no intelligent human being would consent to be a fool, no instructed person would be an ignoramus, no person of feeling and conscience would be selfish and base, even though they should be persuaded that the fool, the dunce, or the rascal is better satisfied with his lot than they are with theirs. They would not resign what they possess more than he for the most complete satisfacton of all the desires which they have in common with him. If they ever fancy they would, it is only in cases of unhappiness so extreme that to escape from it they would exchange their lot for almost any other, however undesirable in their own eyes. A being of higher faculties requires more to make him happy, is capable probably of more acute suffering, and certainly accessible to it at more points, than one of an inferior type; but in spite of these liabilities, he can never really wish to sink into what he feels to be a lower grade of existence. . . . It is better to be a human being dissatisfied than a pig satisfied; better to be Socrates dissatisfied than a fool satisfied. And if the fool, or the pig, are of a different opinion, it is because they only know their own side of the question. The other party to the comparison knows both sides. . . .

From this verdict of the only competent judges, I apprehend there can be no appeal. On a question which is the best worth having of two pleasures, or which of two modes of existence is the most grateful to the feelings, apart from its moral attributes and from its consequences, the judgment of those who are qualified by knowledge of both, or, if they differ, that of the majority among them, must be admitted as final. . . .

I must again repeat what the assailants of utilitarianism seldom have the justice to acknowledge, that the happiness which forms the utilitarian standard of what is right in conduct is not the agent's own happiness but that of all concerned. As between his own happiness and that of others, utilitarianism requires him to be as strictly impartial as a disinterested and benevolent spectator. In the golden rule of Jesus of Nazareth, we read the complete spirit of the ethics of utility. "To do as you would be done by," and "to love your neighbor as yourself," constitute the ideal perfection of utilitarian morality.[32]

But what proof can be given that utilitarianism is true? Mill tries to show, first, that the pleasure or happiness of everyone is *one* of the things that humans find "desirable as an end." It is clear, he argues, that each person desires his own pleasure or happiness, so it is clear, he concludes, that the happiness or pleasure of everyone is generally "desirable."

No reason can be given why the general happiness is desirable, except that each person, so far as he believes it to be attainable, desires his own happiness. This, however, being a fact, we have not only all the proof which the case admits of, but all which it is possible to require, that happiness is a good, that each person's happiness is a good to that person, and the general happiness, therefore, a good to the aggregate of all persons.[33]

Second, Mill argues, the *only* thing that humans find desirable is happiness or pleasure. Mill claims that if people desire other things—such as virtue, money, power, or fame—it is because these are

32. John Stuart Mill, *Utilitarianism* (1861) (New York: Bobbs-Merrill, 1957), 10–22.
33. Ibid., 44–45.

means to happiness and consequently they have become a "part" of our happiness. So desire for these things, according to Mill, "is not a different thing from the desire of happiness."

> What, for example, shall we say of money? . . . From being a means to happiness, it has come to be itself a principal ingredient of [some] individuals' conception of happiness. The same may be said of the majority of the great objects of human life: power, for example, or fame. . . . In these cases the means have become a part of the end. . . . What was once desired as an instrument for the attainment of happiness has come to be desired for its own sake. In being desired for its own sake it is, however, desired as *part* of happiness. The person is made, or thinks he would be made, happy by its mere possession; and is made unhappy by failure to obtain it. The desire of it is not a different thing from the desire of happiness any more than the love of music or the desire of health. They are included in happiness.[34]

Happiness, then, is an end we seek in our actions, and it is the only end we ever seek. Mill concludes, therefore, that happiness or pleasure is the proper aim of all of our actions.

Mill's most important application of utilitarianism occurred in a short work entitled "Essay on Liberty." In this essay Mill argues that every human being has a right to liberty. Unlike earlier philosophers, however, he does not defend this right on the grounds that it is "self-evident." Instead, Mill argues that everyone is entitled to liberty because respecting the right to liberty will promote the "utility" or happiness of everyone in society.

Mill maintains that one of the greatest problems in modern democracies is the "tyranny of the majority." In a democracy, the majority rules, and this majority may oppress minorities whose views they dislike.

> The will of the people . . . practically means the will of the most numerous or the most active *part* of the people—the majority, or those who succeed in making themselves accepted as the majority; the people, consequently, *may* desire to oppress a part of their number, and precautions are as much needed against this as against any other abuse of power. . . . [I]n political speculations "the tyranny of the majority" is now generally included among the evils against which society requires to be on its guard. . . .
>
> Like other tyrannies, the tyranny of the majority was at first, and is still vulgarly, held in dread, chiefly as operating through the acts of the public authorities. But . . . when society is itself the tyrant . . . its means of tyrannizing are not restricted to the acts which it may do by the hands of its political functionaries. Society can and does execute its own mandates. . . . Protection, therefore, against the tyranny of the magistrate is not enough; there needs protection also against the tyranny of the prevailing opinion and feeling, against the tendency of society to impose, by other means than civil penalties, its own ideas and practices as rules of conduct on thoe who dissent from them; to fetter the development and, if possible, prevent the formation of any individuality not in harmony with its ways, and compel all characters to fashion themselves upon the model of its own.[35]

Mill therefore argues for a principle that aims at protecting the individual against the tyranny of the majority. This principle is that society may use force on individual consenting adults only for the purpose of preventing harm to others. Individuals must be left free to think or live as they please as long as they do not harm others.

> The object of this essay is to assert one very simple principle, as entitled to govern absolutely the dealings of society with the individual in the way of compulsion and control, whether the means used be physical force in the form of legal penalties or the moral coercion of public opinion. That principle is that the sole end for which mankind are warranted, individually or collectively, in interfering with the liberty of action of any of their number is self-protection. That the only purpose for which power can be rightfully exercised over any member of a civilized community, against his will, is to prevent harm to others. . . . The only part of the conduct of anyone for which he is

---

34. Ibid., 46–47.

35. John Stuart Mill, *On Liberty* (1859) (New York: Bobbs-Merrill, 1956), 6–7.

amenable to society is that which concerns others. In the part which merely concerns himself, his independence is, of right, absolute. Over himself, over his own body and mind, the individual is sovereign.

It is perhaps hardly necessary to say that this doctrine is meant to apply only to human beings in the maturity of their faculties. We are not speaking of children or of young persons below the age which the law may fix as that of manhood or womanhood. . . .

But there is a sphere of action in which society, as distinguished from the individual, has, if any, only an indirect interest. . . . This, then, is the appropriate region of human liberty. It comprises, first, the inward domain of consciousness, demanding liberty of conscience in its most comprehensive sense, liberty of thought and feeling, absolute freedom of opinion and sentiment on all subjects . . . Secondly, the principle requires liberty of tastes and pursuits, of framing the plan of our life to suit our own character; of doing what we like . . . without impediment from our fellow-creatures, so long as what we do does not harm them, even though they should think our conduct foolish, perverse, or wrong. Thirdly, . . . the liberty, within the same limits, of combination among individuals; freedom to unite for any purpose not involving harm to others: the persons combining being supposed to be of full age and not forced or deceived.[36]

The reason why this principle should be adopted, Mill maintains, is because it is consistent with utilitarianism. That is, the greatest utility or happiness will result if this principle is followed.

It is proper to state that I forego any advantage which could be derived to my argument from the idea of abstract right as a thing independent of utility. I regard utility as the ultimate appeal on all ethical questions; but it must be utility in the largest sense, grounded on the permanent interests of man as a progressive being. Those interests, I contend, authorize the subjection of individual spontaneity to external control only in respect to those actions of each which concern the interest of other people.[37]

To show that utilitarianism requires liberty, Mill first argues that society will be better off if everyone has the liberty to think and say what they wish than if individuals are forced to adopt certain beliefs. If society forces individuals to drop certain beliefs and these beliefs are true or partly true, then clearly, Mill maintains, society will be worse off. Only free debate can bring out the truth. But even if society wants to force individuals to adopt certain *true* beliefs, it will be better if it does not force them to do so. For the meaning and forcefulness of our true beliefs will be lost, Mill contends, if we suppress all free discussion and do not let all citizens freely debate their ideas with each other. Even true ideas become fossilized and lifeless if they are not vigorously and passionately argued in open debate.

We have now recognized the necessity to the mental well-being of mankind (on which all their other well-being depends) of freedom of opinion, and freedom of the expression of opinion, on four distinct grounds, which we will now briefly recapitulate:

First, if any opinion is compelled to silence, that opinion may, for aught we can certainly know, be true. To deny this is to assume our own infallibility.

Secondly, though the silenced opinion be an error, it may, and very commonly does, contain a portion of truth; and since the general or prevailing opinion on any subject is rarely or never the whole truth, it is only by the collision of adverse opinions that the remainder of the truth has any chance of being supplied.

Thirdly, even if the received opinion be not only true, but the whole truth; unless it is suffered to be, and actually is, vigorously and earnestly contested, it will, by most of those who receive it, be held in the manner of a prejudice, with little comprehension or feeling of its rational grounds. And not only this, but, fourthly, the meaning of the doctrine itself will be in danger of being lost or enfeebled, and deprived of its vital effect on the character and conduct: the dogma becoming a mere formal profession, inefficacious for good, but cumbering the ground and preventing the growth of any real and heartfelt conviction from reason or personal experience.[38]

---

36. Ibid., 13, 15–16.
37. Ibid., 14.

38. Ibid., 64.

Society, then, will be better off if it does not suppress even false beliefs but allows all opinions to be freely debated. Freedom of conscience and expression thus produces more utility than suppression. Moreover, Mill argues, freedom to live as one chooses also benefits society. It benefits society, first, because such freedom will allow each individual to develop his or her particular powers, and thus individuals will be happier in society. Second, society can learn from the "experiments" people make of their own lives when they are allowed to live as they choose. Mill concludes, therefore, that, on utilitarian grounds, freedom of the individual must be protected against the "tyranny of the majority."

NIETZSCHE

The most powerful attack ever launched against morality was the attack made by Friedrich Nietzsche. Nietzsche was born in 1844 in Roeken, Germany. His father having died when Nietzsche was four, he was raised by a household of women consisting of his mother, sister, grandmother, and two aunts. In 1864 Nietzsche went off to college, studying first at the University of Bonn and then transferring to the University of Leipzig. There, perhaps experiencing the first effects of his freedom, Nietzsche soon found himself suffering from a case of syphilis, which at that time was incurable. The disease had little immediate effect on his scholarly skills, however, and he soon managed to impress his professors, particularly the widely respected Friedrich Ritschel. When Nietzsche graduated from Leipzig, Ritschel gave him an enthusiastic recommendation, and Nietzsche quickly secured a position as a professor at the University of Basel in 1869. Unfortunately, his health by now was succumbing to his disease, and in 1878 Nietzsche was forced to resign his position due to poor health. Most of the rest of his life was spent in terrible loneliness. Several times he proposed marriage to different women but was firmly rejected by each. In 1889 Nietzsche abruptly went mad. Much of the next eleven years Nietzsche spent in a madhouse or under the care of his doting sister. He died on 25 August 1900.

In the major writings he produced before he went mad, Nietzsche proposed the insightful view that the traditional values and ethical systems of the West were collapsing even as he wrote. The major source of their collapse, he felt, was the loss of belief in God. "God is dead," he declared, having been killed by our own modern philosophies and beliefs. Since we no longer believe in God, it will be difficult for us to believe in the traditional values and ethical views that Christians and others had defended by appealing to God. The death of God has left us floating directionless in a cold empty space. Nietzsche announced the death of God by using the highly poetic image of a madman.

The Madman.—Have you ever heard of the madman who on a bright morning lighted a lantern and ran to the market-place calling out unceasingly: "I seek God! I seek God!"—As there were many people standing about who did not believe in God, he caused a great deal of amusement. Why! is he lost? said one. Has he strayed away like a child? said another. Or does he keep himself hidden? Is he afraid of us? Has he taken a sea-voyage? Has he emigrated?—the people cried out laughingly, all in a hubbub. The insane man jumped into their midst and transfixed them with his glances. "Where is God gone?" he called out. "I mean to tell you! *We have killed him,*—you and I! We are all his murderers! But how have we done it? How were we able to drink up the sea? Who gave us the sponge to wipe away the whole horizon? What did we do when we loosened this earth from its sun? Whither does it now move? Whither do we move? Away from all suns? Do we not dash on unceasingly? Backwards, sideways, forwards, in all directions? Is there still an above and below? Do we not stray, as through infinite nothingness? Does not empty space breathe upon us? Has it not become colder? Does not night come on continually, darker and darker? Shall we not have to light lanterns in the morning? Do we not hear the noise of the grave-diggers who are burying God? Do we not smell the divine putrefaction?—for even Gods putrefy! God is dead! God remains dead! And we have killed him! How shall we console ourselves, the most murderous of all murderers? The holiest and the mightiest that the world has hitherto possessed, has bled to death under our knife,—who will wipe the blood from us? With what water could we cleanse ourselves? What lustrums, what sacred games shall we have to devise? Is not the magnitude of this deed too great for us? Shall we not ourselves have to become Gods, merely to seem worthy of it? There never was a greater event,—and on account of it, all who are born after us belong to a higher history than any history hitherto!"—Here the madman was silent and looked again at his hearers; they also were silent and looked at him in surprise. At last he threw his lantern on the ground, so that it broke in pieces and was extinguished. "I come too early," he then said, "I am not yet at the right time. This prodigious event is still on its way, and is traveling,—it has not yet reached men's ears. Lightning and thunder need time, the light of the stars needs time, deeds need time, even after they are done, to be seen and heard. This deed is as yet further from them than the furthest star,—*and yet they have done it!*"—It is further stated that the madman made his way into different churches on the same day, and there intoned his *Requiem aeternam deo.*[39]

But the death of God, for Nietzsche, was not necessarily a bad thing. For belief in God had encouraged the illusion that there are universal and absolute truths that everyone must accept. But in fact, Nietzsche maintained, there is no absolute truth. Instead, all our beliefs are nothing more than so many interpretations or "perspectives," ways we have of looking at the world. There is an indefinite number of possible interpretations of the world, all of them equally true and equally false. But some of these are more useful than others because some have the advantage of enabling us to live and gain power over the world. Such "useful" beliefs, although as false as any others, are the ones we count as part of the "truth." As Nietzsche put it: "*Truth is that sort of error* without which a particular type of living being could not live. The value for *life* is ultimately decisive."[40]

Although Nietzsche did not believe that there is one "true" interpretation of the universe, he did think that some interpretations or ways of under

Friedrich Nietzsche: "God is dead! God remains dead! And we have killed him! How shall be console ourselves, the most murderous of all murderers? Shall we not ourselves have to become Gods?"

standing the universe were better than others. In particular, he argued that the best way of interpreting the universe was in terms of what he called the "will to power." Every event in the universe, Nietzsche maintained, could be interpreted as being produced by a force he called the "will to power." It was a useful hypothesis, he felt, to interpret events in the universe in terms of something with which we are familiar: the activity of our own wills.

We must risk the hypothesis that everywhere we recognize "effects" there is an effect of will upon will; that all mechanical happenings, insofar as they are activated by some energy, are will-power, will-effects.—Assuming, finally, that we succeeded in explaining our entire instinctual life as the development and ramification of one basic form of will (of the will to power, as I hold); assuming that one could trace back all the organic functions to this will to power, including the solution of the problems of generation and nutrition (they are one problem)—if this were done, we should be justi

39. Friedrich Nietzsche, *The Joyful Wisdom,* trans. Thomas Common, in *The Complete Works of Friedrich Nietzsche,* vol. 10, ed. Oscar Levy (New York: Macmillan, 1944), 167–169.

40. Quoted in Frederick Copleston, *A History of Philosophy,* vol. 7 (Garden City, N.Y.: Doubleday, 1963), 183.

fied in defining *all* effective energy unequivocally as *will to power*.[41]

If everything in the universe is interpreted as a result of a will to power, then all human actions must also be seen as outcomes of the will to power. The primary drives of human beings are not the pursuit of pleasure and the avoidance of pain (as Mill had argued). Instead, human beings are primarily motivated by the desire to increase their power over things and over people. As Nietzsche put it: "Life itself is essential assimilation, injury, violation of the foreign and the weaker, suppression, hardness, the forcing of one's own forms upon something else, ingestion and—at least in its mildest form—exploitation."[42] In fact, Nietzsche felt, our theories and beliefs about the world should also be seen as instruments of the will to power. Interpretations of the world are instruments we use to extend our power over the world and over each other.

Just as there are no absolute truths about the world, so also there are no absolute truths about morality. Any morality, Nietzsche claimed, is also merely an interpretation of the world: "There are no moral phenomena, only moralistic interpretations of phenomena," and "There are no moral facts." Like any other kind of interpretation, a morality cannot be said to be absolutely true or false; it can only be a more-or-less useful instrument for the will to power. Moralities, then, are interpretations that are used as instruments to exert power over others or over the natural world. Nietzsche argues, for example, that Kant, like every other moralist, proposed his moral theory in order to impose his own values.

> Apart from the value of such assertions as "there is a categorical imperative in us," one can always ask: What does such an assertion indicate about him who makes it? There are systems of morals which are meant to justify their author in the eyes of other people; other systems of morals are meant to tranquilize him, and make him self-satisfied;

with other systems he wants to crucify and humble himself; with others he wishes to take revenge; with others to conceal himself; with others to glorify himself and gain superiority and distinction;—this system of morals helps its author to forget, that system makes him, or something of him, forgotten; many a moralist would like to exercise power and creative arbitrariness over mankind; many another, perhaps, Kant especially, gives us to understand by his morals that "what is estimable in me, is that I know how to obey—and with you it *shall* not be otherwise than with me![43]

Mill's argument for utilitarianism, Nietzsche argues, was also an attempt to impose on others his personal preferences. In Mill's case these were preferences he shared with his fellow British citizens. Utilitarian arguments are merely an attempt to impose on the world the values of the English.

> Observe, for example, the indefatigable, inevitable English utilitarians. . . . In the end, they all want *English* morality to be recognized as authoritative, inasmuch as mankind, or the "general utility," or "the happiness of the greatest number,"—no! the happiness of *England* will be best served thereby. They would like, by all means, to convince themselves that the striving after *English* happiness, I mean after *comfort* and *fashion* (and in the highest instance, a seat in Parliament), is at the same time the true path of virtue; in fact, that insofar as there has been virtue in the world hitherto, it has just consisted in such striving.[44]

The ethical systems proposed by the major moral philosophers, then, are nothing more than manifestations of the will to power. The same is true of the popular moralities the masses folow. In his survey of the history of moralities, Nietzsche wrote, he had discovered two basic kinds of popular moralities. One kind was the "slave moralities" that weak people—especially the Christians—had devised as instruments to acquire power over the strong. The other kind was the "master moralities"

---

41. Friedrich Nietzsche, *Beyond Good and Evil*, trans. M. Cowan (Chicago: Henry Regnery, 1955), 43.

42. Ibid., 201.

43. Friedrich Nietzsche, *Beyond Good and Evil*, trans. Helen Zimmern, in *The Complete Works of Friedrich Nietzsche*, vol. 2, ed. Oscar Levy, 106.

44. Ibid., 174.

that had been devised by the strong to assert their power over the weak.

A master morality is the kind of morality that would normally develop in those individuals who are the strongest, those who are born with the power to dominate others. This type of morality values strength, intelligence, courage, revenge, and power seeking. In this morality a person is "good" to the extent that he has the strength to overpower others. This type of morality extols the individual.

On the other hand, a slave morality is the type of morality that is fashioned by weak groups of people. A slave morality values whatever is useful or beneficial to the weak, such as sympathy, kindness, pity, patience, humility, and helping those in need. In a slave morality the "good" person is the one who helps the weak, while the dominating individual is seen as "evil." Slave moralities are the moralities of the "herd," since they extol the group and not the individual.

In a tour through the many finer and coarser moralities which have hitherto prevailed or still prevail on the earth, I found certain traits recurring regularly together and connected with one another, until finally two primary types revealed themselves to me, and a radical distinction was brought to light. There is *master*-morality and *slave*-morality;—I would at once add, however, that in all higher and mixed civilizations, there are also attempts at the reconciliation of the two moralities; but one finds still oftener the confusion and mutual misunderstanding of them, indeed, sometimes their close juxtaposition—even in the same man, within one soul. The distinctions of moral values have either originated in a ruling caste, pleasantly conscious of being different from the ruled—or among the ruled class, the slaves and dependents of all sorts. In the first case, when it is the rulers who determine the conception "good," it is the exalted, proud disposition which is regarded as the distinguishing feature, and that which determines the order of rank. The noble type of man separates from himself the beings in whom the opposite of this exalted, proud disposition displays itself: he despises them. Let it at once be noted that in this first kind of morality the antithesis "good" and "bad" means practically the same as "noble" and "despicable";—the antithesis

"good" and "evil" is of a different origin. The cowardly, the timid, the insignificant, and those thinking merely of narrow utility are despised; moreover, also, the distrustful, with their constrained glances, the self-abasing, the dog-like kind of men who let themselves be abused, the mendicant flatterers, and above all the liars;—it is a fundamental belief of all aristocrats that the common people are untruthful. "We truthful ones"—the nobility in ancient Greece called themselves. It is obvious that everywhere the designations of moral value were at first applied to *men*, and were only derivatively and at a later period applied to *actions*; it is a gross mistake, therefore, when historians of morals start with questions like, "Why have sympathetic actions been praised?" The noble type of man regards himself as a determiner of values; he does not require to be approved of; he passes the judgment: "What is injurious to me is injurious in itself"; he knows that it is he himself only who confers honor on things; he is a creator of values. He honors whatever he recognizes in himself; such morality is self-glorification. In the foreground there is the feeling of plenitude, of power, which seeks to overflow, the happiness of high tension, the consciousness of a wealth which would fain give and bestow:—the noble man also helps the unfortunate, but not—or scarcely—out of pity, but rather from an impulse generated by the super-abundance of power. The noble man honors in himself the powerful one, him also who has power over himself, who knows how to speak and how to keep silence, who takes pleasure in subjecting himself to severity and hardness, and has reverence for all that is severe and hard. "Wotan placed a hard heart in my breast," says an old Scandinavian Saga: it is thus rightly expressed from the soul of a proud Viking. Such a type of man is even proud of *not* being made for sympathy; the hero of the Saga therefore adds warningly: "He who has not a hard heart when young, will never have one." The noble and brave who think thus are the furthest removed from the morality which sees precisely in sympathy, or in acting for the good of others, or in *désintéressement*, the characteristic of the moral; faith in oneself, pride in oneself, a radical enmity and irony towards "selflessness," belong as definitely to the noble morality, as do a careless scorn and precaution in presence of sympathy and the "warm heart."—It is the powerful who *know* how to honor, it is their art, their domain for invention. The profound reverence for age and for tradition—all law rests on this double reverence,—the belief and prejudice in favor of ancestors and unfavorable to newcomers, is typical in the morality of the powerful; and if, reversely, men of "modern ideas" believe almost instinctively in "progress" and the "future," and are more and more lacking in respect for old age, the ignoble origin of these "ideas" has complacently betrayed itself thereby. A morality of the ruling class, however, is more especially foreign and irritating to present-day taste in the sternness of its principle that one has duties only to one's equals; that one may act towards beings of a lower rank, toward all that is foreign, just as seems good to one, or "as the heart desires," and in any case "beyond good and evil": it is here that sympathy and similar sentiments can have a place. The ability and obligation to exercise prolonged gratitude and prolonged revenge—both only within the circle of equals,—artfulness in retaliation, *raffinement* of the idea in friendship, a certain necessity to have enemies (as outlets for the emotions of envy, quarrelsomeness, arrogance—in fact, in order to be a good *friend*): all these are typical characteristics of the noble morality, which, as has been pointed out, is not the morality of "modern ideas," and is therefore at present difficult to realize, and also to unearth and disclose.—It is otherwise with the second type of morality, *slave-morality*. Supposing that the abused, the oppressed, the suffering, the unemancipated, the weary, and those uncertain of themselves, should moralize, what will be the common element in their moral estimates? Probably a pessimistic suspicion with regard to the entire situation of man will find expression, perhaps a condemnation of man, together with his situation. The slave has an unfavorable eye for the virtues of the powerful; he has a skepticism and distrust, a *refinement* of distrust of everything "good" that is there honored—he would fain persuade himself that the very happiness there is not genuine. On the other hand, *those* qualities which serve to alleviate the existence of sufferers are brought into prominence and flooded with light; it is here that sympathy, the kind, helping hand, the warm heart, patience, diligence, humility, and friendliness attain to honor; for here these are the most useful qualities, and almost the only means of supporting the burden of existence. Slave-morality is essentially the morality of utility. Here is the seat of the origin of the famous antithesis "good" and "evil":—power and dangerousness are assumed to reside in the evil, a certain dreadfulness, subtlety, and strength, which do not admit of being despised. According to slave-morality, therefore, the "evil" man arouses fear: according to master-morality, it is precisely the "good" man who arouses fear and seeks to arouse it, while the bad man is regarded as the despicable being. The contrast attains its maximum when, in accordance with the logical consequences of slave-morality, a shade of depreciation—it may be slight and well-intentioned—at last attaches itself even to the "good" man of this morality; because, according to the servile mode of thought, the good man must in any case be the *safe* man: he is good-natured, easily deceived, perhaps a little stupid, *un bonhomme*. Everywhere that slave-morality gains the ascendancy, language shows a tendency to approximate the significations of the words "good" and "stupid."—A last fundamental difference: the desire for *freedom*, the instinct for happiness and the refinements of the feeling of liberty belong as necessarily to slave-morals and morality, as artifice and enthusiasm in reverence and devotion are the regular symptoms of an aristocratic mode of thinking and estimating.—Hence we can understand without further detail why love as *a passion*—it is our European speciality—must absolutely be of noble origin; as is well known, its invention is due to the Provençal poet-cavaliers, those brilliant ingenious men of the "gai saber," to whom Europe owes so much, and almost owes itself.[45]

Although Nietzsche clearly favored the "master moralities" and argued that we should rid ourselves of our "slave moralities," he did not feel that one morality was more "true" than another. As there is no longer any God, there are no longer any objective moralities. Moralities are our own inventions.

What then, alone, can our teaching be?—That no one gives man his qualities, either God, society, his parents, his ancestors, nor himself (this nonsensical idea, which is at last refuted here, was taught as "intelligible freedom" by Kant, and per-

---

45. Ibid., 227–232.

haps even as early as Plato himself). No one is responsible for the fact that he exists at all, that he is constituted as he is, and that he happens to be in certain circumstances and in a particular environment. The fatality of his being cannot be divorced from the fatality of all that which has been and will be. This is not the result of an individual attention, of a will, of an aim, there is no attempt at attaining to any "ideal man," or "ideal happiness" or "ideal morality" with him—it is absurd to wish him to be careering towards some sort of purpose. *We* invented the concept "purpose"; in reality purpose is altogether lacking. One is necessary, one is a piece of fate, one belongs to the whole, one is in the whole—there is nothing that could judge, measure, compare, and condemn our existence, for that would mean judging, measuring, comparing and condemning the whole. *But there is nothing outside the whole!* The fact that no one shall any longer be made responsible, that the nature of existence may not be traced to a *causa prima*, that the world is an entity neither as a sensorium nor as a spirit—*this alone is the great deliverance*—thus alone is the innocence of becoming restored . . . The concept "God" has been the greatest objection to existence hitherto. . . . We deny God, we deny responsibility in God: thus alone do we save the world.[46]

The significance of Nietzsche's attack on morality cannot be underestimated. If Nietzsche is correct, then moral principles are nothing more than subtle or not-so-subtle tools that the weak use to secure their power over the strong. Morality is a sham. The moral principles proposed by Christians, utilitarians, or Kantians are nothing more than their attempt to impose their will on others. When I say, for example, that everyone should be charitable or that everyone should seek to maximize the happiness of everyone else, I am really trying to get you to be charitable to me or trying to get you to maximize my happiness. Moral principles are thus nothing more than an expression of the will to power.

Thus, just as Hume's views had threatened epis-

temology, so now Nietzsche's views threatened to destroy morality.

QUESTIONS

1. Do you think Mill's version of utilitarianism really improves on Bentham's version? Is Mill saying that the views of the majority determine what is morally right or wrong?

2. Can you think of any circumstances in which the action that would maximize happiness would be an immoral action? Would Mill agree that this proves that utilitarianism is mistaken? Why?

3. What position would Mill take on the question whether pornography should be legal? On the question of whether drugs should be legal? On the question of whether motorcycle riders should be required legally to wear safety helmets?

4. Can you explain in your own words what Nietzsche means when he says that "all mechanical happenings . . . are will-power, will-effects"?

5. How does Mill's view of human nature differ from Nietzsche's? Which of these views, in your judgment, is closest to the truth? Why?

6. Explain the differences between "slave moralities" and "master moralities." Explain how slave moralities are supposed to be expressions of the "will to power." Explain how *all* moralities are supposed to be expressions of the will to power. Do you agree? Why?

---

46. Friedrich Nietzsche, *The Twilight of the Idols*, trans. A. M. Ludovici, in *The Complete Works of Friedrich Nietzsche*, vol. 16, ed. Oscar Levy, 43.

JEAN ANOUILH

Antigone

What must one do when faced with a decision between advancing the maximum good and doing what one believes is right? Undoubtedly among the toughest moral choices are those that pit desirable consequences against personal principles. Such is the theme of French playwright Jean Anouilh's Antigone.

The play, adapted from the original by the great Greek tragedian Sophocles, involves a clash of wills between Creon, king of Thebes, and his niece Antigone concerning the burial of her brother and his nephew, Polynices. Because Polynices led a revolt against his own brother Eteocles, thus igniting a civil war in which the two brothers killed each other, Creon has decreed Polynices an enemy of the state and a traitor. Specifically, he has ordered that Polynices not be given a proper burial as the ultimate censure and a warning to all would-be revolutionaries. Antigone, however, has other ideas. She insists that her brother be given a proper burial, as Eteocles has received.

In the selection below, Antigone has been brought before Creon by guards who have caught her throwing dirt on Polynices' body. Notice that in the confrontation between uncle and niece, both operate from essentially unselfish positions. Creon, on the one hand, is committed to advancing the greatest social good. Antigone, on the other hand, is basically moved by principles of love, decency, justice, and other aspects of duty. In the end, Creon and Antigone, while moved by nonegoistic impulses, nevertheless stand unreconciled, testimony to the apparently unbridgeable gap between two points on a moral continuum: the one motivated by social consequences, the other by nonconsequentialist duties.

CREON: Why did you try to bury your brother?

ANTIGONE: I owed it to him.

CREON: I had forbidden it.

ANTIGONE: I owed it to him. Those who are not buried wander eternally and find no rest. If my brother were alive, and he came home weary after a long day's hunting, I should kneel down and unlace his boots, I should fetch him food and drink, I should see that his bed was ready for him. Polynices is home from the hunt. I owe it to him to unlock the house of the dead in which my father and my mother are waiting to welcome him. Polynices has earned his rest.

SOURCE: Jean Anouilh, *Antigone*, adapt. and trans. Lewis Galantiere (Copyright 1946 by Random House, Inc., and renewed 1974 by Lewis Galantiere). Reprinted by permission of Random House, Inc.

CREON: Polynices was a rebel and a traitor, and you know it.

ANTIGONE: He was my brother.

CREON: You heard my edict. It was proclaimed throughout Thebes. You read my edict. It was posted up on the city walls.

ANTIGONE: Of course I did.

CREON: You knew the punishment I decreed for any person who attempted to give him burial.

ANTIGONE: Yes, I knew the punishment.

CREON: Did you by any chance act on the assumption that a daughter of Oedipus, a daughter of Oedipus's stubborn pride, was above the law?

ANTIGONE: No, I did not act on that assumption.

CREON: Because if you had acted on that assumption, Antigone, you would have been deeply wrong. Nobody has a more sacred obligation to obey the law than those who make the law. You are a daughter of lawmakers, a daughter of kings, Antigone. You must observe the law.

ANTIGONE: Had I been a scullery maid washing my dishes when that law was read aloud to me, I should have scrubbed the greasy water from my arms and gone out in my apron to bury my brother.

CREON: What nonsense! If you had been a scullery maid, there would have been no doubt in your mind about the seriousness of that edict. You would have known that it meant death; and you would have been satisfied to weep for your brother in your kitchen. But you! You thought that because you come of the royal line, because you were my niece and were going to marry my son, I shouldn't dare have you killed.

ANTIGONE: You are mistaken. Quite the contrary. I never doubted for an instant that you would have me put to death.

(A pause, as Creon *stares fixedly at her)*

CREON: The pride of Oedipus! Oedipus and his headstrong pride all over again. I can see your father in you—and I believe you. Of course you thought that I should have you killed! Proud as you are, it seemed to you a natural climax in your existence. Your father was like that. For him as for you human happiness was meaningless; and mere human misery was not enough to satisfy his passion for torment. *(He sits on a stool behind the table)* You come of people for whom the human vestment is a kind of straitjacket: it cracks at the seams. You spend your lives wriggling to get out of it. Nothing less than a cozy tea party with death and destiny will quench your thirst. The happiest hour of your father's life came when he listened greedily to the story of how, unknown to himself, he had killed his own father and dishonored the bed of his own mother. Drop by drop, word by word, he drank in the dark story that the gods had destined him, first to live and then to hear. How avidly men and women drink the brew of such a tale when their names are Oedipus—and Antigone! And it is so simple, afterward, to do what your father did, to put out one's eyes and take one's daughter begging on the highways.

Let me tell you, Antigone: those days are over for Thebes. Thebes has a right to a king without a past. My name, thank God, is only Creon. I stand here with both feet firm on the ground; with both hands in my pockets; and I have decided that so long as I am king—being less ambitious than your father was—I shall merely devote myself to introducing a little order into this absurd kingdom; if that is possible.

Don't think that being a king seems to me romantic. It is my trade; a trade a man has to work at every day; and like every other trade, it isn't all beer and skittles. But since it is my trade, I take it seriously. And if, tomorrow, some wild and bearded messenger walks in from some wild and distant valley—which is what happened to your dad—and tells me that he's not quite sure who my parents were, but thinks that my wife Eurydice is actually my mother, I shall ask him to do me the kindness to go back where he came from; and I shan't let a little matter like that persuade me to order my wife to take a blood test and the police to let me know whether or not my birth certificate was forged. Kings, my girl, have other things to do than to surrender themselves to their private feelings. *(He looks at her and smiles)* Hand *you* over to be killed! *(He rises, moves to end of table and sits on the top of table)* I have other plans for you. You're going to marry Haemon; and I want you to fatten up a bit so that you give him a sturdy boy. Let me assure you that Thebes needs that boy a good deal more than it needs your death. You will go to your room, now, and do as you have been told; and you won't say a word about this to anybody. Don't fret about the guards: I'll see that their mouths are shut. And don't annihilate me with those eyes. I know that you think I am a brute, and I'm sure you must consider me very prosaic. But the fact is, I have always been fond of you, stubborn though you always were. Don't forget that the first doll you ever had came from me *(A pause. Antigone says nothing, rises and crosses slowly below the table toward the arch. Creon turns and watches her; then)* Where are you going?

ANTIGONE *(Stops downstage. Without any show of rebellion)*: You know very well where I am going.

CREON *(After a pause)*: What sort of game are you playing?

ANTIGONE: I am not playing games.

CREON: Antigone, do you realize that if, apart from those three guards, a single soul finds out what you have tried to do, it will be impossible for me to avoid putting you to death? There is still a chance that I can save you; but only if you keep this to yourself and give up your crazy purpose. Five minutes more, and it will be too late. You understand that?

ANTIGONE: I must go and bury my brother. Those men uncovered him.

CREON: What good will it do? You know that there are other men standing guard over Polynices. And even if you did cover him over with earth again, the earth would again be removed.

ANTIGONE: I know all that. I know it. But that much, at least, I can do. And what a person can do, a person ought to do.

(Pause)

CREON: Tell me, Antigone, do you believe all that flummery about religious burial? Do you really believe that a so-called shade of your brother is condemned to wander forever homeless if a little earth is not flung on his corpse to the accompaniment of some priestly abracadabra? Have you ever listened to the priests of Thebes when they were mumbling their formula? Have you ever watched those dreary bureaucrats while they were preparing the dead for burial—skipping half the gestures required by the ritual, swallowing half their words, hustling the dead into their graves out of fear that they might be late for lunch?

ANTIGONE: Yes, I have seen all that.

CREON: And did you never say to yourself as you watched them, that if someone you really loved lay dead under the shuffling, mumbling ministrations of the priests, you would scream aloud and beg the priests to leave the dead in peace?

ANTIGONE: Yes, I've thought all that.

CREON: And you still insist upon being put to death—merely because I refuse to let your brother go out with that grotesque passport; because I refuse his body the wretched consolation of that mass-production jibber-jabber, which you would have been the first to be embarrassed by if I had allowed it. The whole thing is absurd!

ANTIGONE: Yes, it's absurd.

CREON: Then why, Antigone, why? For whose sake? For the sake of them that believe in it? To raise them against me?

ANTIGONE: No.

CREON: For whom then if not for them and not for Polynices either?

ANTIGONE: For nobody. For myself.

(A pause as they stand looking at one another)

CREON: You must want very much to die. You look like a trapped animal.

ANTIGONE: Stop feeling sorry for me. Do as I do. Do your job. But if you are a human being, do it quickly. That is all I ask of you. I'm not going to be able to hold out forever.

CREON (Takes a step toward her): I want to save you, Antigone.

ANTIGONE: You are the king, and you are all-powerful. But that you cannot do.

CREON: You think not?

ANTIGONE: Neither save me nor stop me.

CREON: Prideful Antigone! Little Oedipus!

ANTIGONE: Only this can you do: have me put to death.

CREON: Have you tortured, perhaps?

ANTIGONE: Why would you do that? To see me cry? To hear me beg for mercy? Or swear whatever you wish, and then begin over again?

(A pause)

CREON: You listen to me. You have cast me for the villain in this little play of yours, and yourself for the heroine. And you know it, you damned little mischiefmaker! But don't you drive me too far! If I were one of your preposterous little tyrants that Greece is full of, you would be lying in a ditch this minute with your tongue pulled out and your body drawn and quartered. But you can see something in my face that makes me hesitate to send for the guards and turn you over to them. Instead, I let you go on arguing; and you taunt me, you take the offensive. (He grasps her left wrist) What are you driving at, you she-devil?

ANTIGONE: Let me go. You are hurting my arm.

CREON (*Gripping her tighter*): I will not let you go.

ANTIGONE (*Moans*): Oh!

CREON: I was a fool to waste words. I should have done this from the beginning. (*He looks at her*) I may be your uncle—but we are not a particularly affectionate family. Are we, eh? (*Through his teeth, as he twists*) Are we? (Creon *propels* Antigone *round below him to his side*) What fun for you, eh? To be able to spit in the face of a king who has all the power in the world; a man who has done his own killing in his day; who has killed people just as pitiable as you are—and who is still soft enough to go to all this trouble in order to keep you from being killed.

(*A pause*)

ANTIGONE: Now you are squeezing my arm too tightly. It doesn't hurt any more.

(Creon *stares at her, then drops her arm*)

CREON: I shall save you yet. (*He goes below the table to the chair at end of table, takes off his coat and places it on the chair*) God knows, I have things enough to do today without wasting my time on an insect like you. There's plenty to do, I assure you, when you've just put down a revolution. But urgent things can wait. I am not going to let politics be the cause of your death. For it is a fact that this whole business is nothing but politics; the mournful shade of Polynices, the decomposing corpse, the sentimental weeping and the hysteria that you mistake for heroism—nothing but politics.

Look here. I may not be soft, but I'm fastidious. I like things clean, ship-shape, well scrubbed. Don't think that I am not just as offended as you are by the thought of that meat rotting in the sun. In the evening, when the breeze comes in off the sea, you can smell it in the palace, and it nauseates me. But I refuse even to shut my window. It's vile; and I can tell you what I wouldn't tell anybody else: it's stupid, monstrously stupid. But the people of Thebes have got to have their noses rubbed into it a little longer. My God! If it was up to me, I should have had them bury your brother long ago as a mere matter of public hygiene. I admit that what I am doing is childish. But if the featherheaded rabble I govern are to understand what's what, that stench has got to fill the town for a month!

ANTIGONE (*Turns to him*): You are a loathsome man!

CREON: I agree. My trade forces me to be. We could argue whether I ought or ought not to follow my trade; but once I take on the job, I must do it properly.

ANTIGONE: Why do you do it at all?

CREON: My dear, I woke up one morning and found myself King of Thebes. God knows, there were other things I loved in life more than power.

ANTIGONE: Then you should have said no.

CREON: Yes, I could have done that. Only, I felt that it would have been cowardly. I should have been like a workman who turns down a job that has to be done. So I said yes.

ANTIGONE: So much the worse for you, then. I didn't say yes. I can say no to anything I think vile, and I don't have to count the cost. But because you said yes, all that you can do, for all your crown and your trappings, and your guards—all that you can do is to have me killed.

CREON: Listen to me.

ANTIGONE: If I want to. I don't have to listen to you if I don't want to. You've said your yes. There is nothing more you can tell me that I don't know. You stand there, drinking in my words. *(She moves behind chair)* Why is it that you don't call your guards? I'll tell you why. You want to hear me out to the end; that's why.

CREON: You amuse me.

ANTIGONE: Oh, no, I don't. I frighten you. That is why you talk about saving me. Everything would be so much easier if you had a docile, tongue-tied little Antigone living in the palace. I'll tell you something, Uncle Creon: I'll give you back one of your own words. You are too fastidious to make a good tyrant. But you are going to have to put me to death today, and you know it. And that's what frightens you. God! Is there anything uglier than a frightened man!

CREON: Very well. I am afraid, then. Does that satisfy you? I am afraid that if you insist upon it, I shall have to have you killed. And I don't want to.

ANTIGONE: I don't have to do things that I think are wrong. If it comes to that, you didn't really want to leave my brother's body unburied, did you? Say it! Admit that you didn't.

CREON: I have said it already.

ANTIGONE: But you did it just the same. And now, though you don't want to do it, you are going to have me killed. And you call that being a king!

CREON: Yes, I call that being a king.

ANTIGONE: Poor Creon! My nails are broken, my fingers are bleeding, my arms are covered with the welts left by the paws of your guards—but I am a queen!

CREON: Then why not have pity on me, and live? Isn't your brother's corpse, rotting there under my windows, payment enough for peace and order in Thebes? My son loves you. Don't make me add your life to the payment. I've paid enough.

ANTIGONE: No, Creon! You said yes, and made yourself king. Now you will never stop paying.

CREON: But God in Heaven! Won't you try to understand me! I'm trying hard enough to understand you! There had to be one man who said yes. Somebody had to agree to captain the ship. She had sprung a hundred leaks; she was loaded to the water-line with crime, ignorance, poverty. The wheel was swinging with the wind. The crew refused to work and were looting the cargo. The officers were building a raft, ready to slip overboard and desert the ship. The mast was splitting, the wind was howling, the sails were beginning to rip. Every man jack on board was about to drown—and only because the only thing they thought of was their own skins and their cheap little day-to-day traffic. Was that a time, do you think, for playing with words like yes and no? Was that a time for a man to be weighing the pros and cons, wondering if he wasn't going to pay too dearly later on; if he wasn't going to lose his life, or his family, or his touch with other men? You grab the wheel, you right the ship in the face of a mountain of water. You shout an order, and if one man refuses to obey, you shoot straight into the mob. Into the mob, I say! The beast as nameless as the wave that crashes down upon your deck; as nameless as the whipping wind. The thing that drops when you shoot may be someone who poured you a drink the night before; but it has no name. And you, braced at the wheel, you have no name, either. Nothing has a name—except the ship, and the storm. (*A pause as he looks at her*) Now do you understand?

ANTIGONE: I am not here to understand. That's all very well for you. I am here to say no to you, and die.

CREON: It is easy to say no.

ANTIGONE: Not always.

CREON: It is easy to say no. To say yes, you have to sweat and roll up your sleeves and plunge both hands into life up to the elbows. It is easy to say no, even if saying no means death. All you have to do is to sit still and wait. Wait to go on living, wait to be killed. That is the coward's part. *No* is one of your man-made words. Can you imagine a world in which trees say no to the sap? In which beasts say no to hunger or to propagation? Animals are good, simple, tough. They move in droves, nudging one another onward, all traveling the same road. Some of them keel over; but the rest go on; and no matter how many may fall by the wayside, there are always those few left which go on bringing their young into the world, traveling the same road with the same obstinate will, unchanged from those who went before.

ANTIGONE: Animals, eh, Creon! What a king you could be if only men were animals!

(*A pause. Creon turns and looks at her*)

CREON: You despise me, don't you? (Antigone *is silent. Creon goes on, as if to himself*) Strange. Again and again, I have imagined myself holding this conversation with a pale young man I have never seen in the flesh. He would have come to assassinate me, and would have failed. I would be trying to find out from him why he wanted to kill me. But with all my logic and all my powers of debate, the only thing I could get out of him would be that he despised me. Who would have thought that the white-faced boy would turn out to be you? And that the debate would arise out of something so meaningless as the burial of your brother?

ANTIGONE (*Repeats contemptuously*): Meaningless!

CREON (*Earnestly, almost desperately*): And yet, you must hear me out. My part is not an heroic one, but I shall play my part. I shall have you put to death. Only, before I do, I want to make one last appeal. I want to be sure that you know what you are doing as well as I know what I am doing. Antigone, do you know what you are dying for? Do you know the sordid story to which you are going to sign your name in blood, for all time to come?

ANTIGONE: What story?

CREON: The story of Eteocles and Polynices, the story of your brothers. You think you know it, but you don't. Nobody in Thebes knows that story but me. And it seems to me, this afternoon, that you have a right to know it too. (*A pause as Antigone moves to chair and sits*) It's not a pretty story. (*He turns, gets a stool from behind the table and places it between the table and the chair*) You'll see. (*He looks at her for a moment*) Tell me, first. What do you remember about your brothers? They were older than you, so they must have looked down on you. And I imagine that they tormented you—pulled your pigtails, broke your dolls, whispered secrets to each other to put you in a rage.

ANTIGONE: They were big and I was little.

CREON: And later on, when they came home wearing evening clothes, smoking cigarettes, they would have nothing to do with you; and you thought they were wonderful.

ANTIGONE: They were boys and I was a girl.

CREON: You didn't know why, exactly, but you knew that they were making your mother unhappy. You saw her in tears over them; and your father would fly into a rage because of them. You heard them come in, slamming doors, laughing noisily in the corridors—insolent, spineless, unruly, smelling of drink.

ANTIGONE (*Staring outward*): Once, it was very early and we had just got up. I saw them coming home, and hid behind a door. Polynices was very pale and his eyes were shining. He was so handsome in his evening clothes. He saw me, and said: "Here, this is for you"; and he gave me a big paper flower that he had brought home from his night out.

CREON: And of course you still have that flower. Last night, before you crept out, you opened a drawer and looked at it for a time, to give yourself courage.

ANTIGONE: Who told you so?

CREON: Poor Antigone! With her nightclub flower. Do you know what your brother was?

ANTIGONE: Whatever he was, I know that you will say vile things about him.

CREON: A cheap, idiotic bounder, that is what he was. A cruel, vicious little voluptuary. A little beast with just wit enough to drive a car faster and throw more money away than any of his pals. I was with your father one day when Polynices, having lost a lot of money gambling, asked him to settle the debt; and when your father refused, the boy raised his hand against him and called him a vile name.

ANTIGONE: That's a lie!

CREON: He struck your father in the face with his fist. It was pitiful. Your father sat at his desk with his head in his hands. His nose was bleeding. He was weeping with anguish. And in a corner of your father's study, Polynices stood sneering and lighting a cigarette.

ANTIGONE: That's a lie.

(*A pause*)

CREON: When did you last see Polynices alive? When you were twelve years old. *That's* true, isn't it?

ANTIGONE: Yes, that's true.

CREON: Now you know why. Oedipus was too chicken-hearted to have the boy locked up. Polynices was allowed to go off and join the Argive army. And as soon as he reached Argos, the attempts upon your father's life began—upon the life of an old man who couldn't make up his mind to die, couldn't bear to be parted from his kingship. One after another, men slipped into Thebes from Argos for the purpose of assassinating him, and every killer we caught always ended by confessing who had put him up to it, who had paid him to try it. And it wasn't only Polynices. That is really what I am trying to tell you. I want you to know what went on in the back room, in the kitchen of politics; I want you to know what took place in the wings of this drama in which you are burning to play a part.

Yesterday, I gave Eteocles a State funeral, with pomp and honors. Today, Eteocles is a saint and a hero in the eyes of all Thebes. The whole city turned out to bury him. The schoolchildren emptied their savings boxes to buy wreaths for him. Old men, orating in quavering, hypocritical voices, glorified the virtues of the great-hearted brother, the devoted son, the loyal prince. I made a speech myself; and every temple priest was present with an appropriate show of sorrow and solemnity in his stupid face. And military honors were accorded the dead hero.

Well, what else could I have done? People had taken sides in the civil war. Both sides couldn't be wrong; that would be too much. I couldn't have made them swallow the truth. Two gangsters was more of a luxury than I could afford. *(He pauses for a moment)* And this is the whole point of my story. Eteocles, that virtuous brother, was just as rotten as Polynices. That great-hearted son had done his best, too, to procure the assassination of his father. That loyal prince had also offered to sell out Thebes to the highest bidder. Funny, isn't it? Polynices lies rotting in the sun while Eteocles is given a hero's funeral and will be housed in a marble vault. Yet I have absolute proof that everything that Polynices did, Eteocles had plotted to do. They were a pair of blackguards—both engaged in selling out Thebes, and both engaged in selling out each other; and they died like the cheap gangsters they were, over a division of the spoils.

But, as I told you a moment ago, I had to make a martyr of one of them. I sent out to the holocaust for their bodies; they were found clasped in one another's arms—for the first time in their lives, I imagine. Each had been spitted on the other's sword, and the Argive cavalry had trampled them down. They were mashed to a pulp, Antigone. I had the prettier of the two carcasses brought in, and gave it a State funeral; and I left the other to rot. I don't know which was which. And I assure you, I don't care. *(Long silence, neither looking at the other)*

ANTIGONE *(In a mild voice)*: Why do you tell me all this?

CREON: Would it have been better to let you die a victim to that obscene story?

ANTIGONE: It might have been. I had my faith.

CREON: What are you going to do now?

ANTIGONE *(Rises to her feet in a daze)*: I shall go up to my room.

CREON: Don't stay alone. Go and find Haemon. And get married quickly.

ANTIGONE *(In a whisper)*: Yes.

CREON: All this is really beside the point. You have your whole life ahead of you— and life is a treasure.

ANTIGONE: Yes.

CREON: And you were about to throw it away. Don't think me fatuous if I say that I understand you; and that at your age I should have done the same thing. A moment ago, when we were quarreling, you said I was drinking in your words. I was. But it wasn't you I was listening to; it was a lad named Creon who lived here in Thebes many years ago. He was thin and pale, as you are. His mind, too, was filled with thoughts of self-sacrifice. Go and find Haemon. And get married quickly, Antigone. Be happy. Life flows like water, and you young people let it run away through your fingers. Shut your hands; hold on to it, Antigone. Life is not what you think it is. Life is a child playing round your feet, a tool you hold firmly in your grip, a bench you sit down upon in the evening, in your garden. People will tell you that that's not life, that life is something else. They will tell you that because they need your strength and your fire, and they will want to make use of you. Don't listen to them. Believe me, the only poor consolation that we have in our old age is to discover that what I have said to you is true. Life is nothing more than the happiness that you get out of it.

ANTIGONE *(Murmurs, lost in thought)*: Happiness . . .

CREON *(Suddenly a little self-conscious)*: Not much of a word, is it?

ANTIGONE *(Quietly)*: What kind of happiness do you foresee for me? Paint me the picture of your happy Antigone. What are the unimportant little sins that I shall have to commit before I am allowed to sink my teeth into life and tear happiness from it? Tell me: to whom shall I have to lie? Upon whom shall I have to fawn? To whom must I sell myself? Whom do you want me to leave dying, while I turn away my eyes?

CREON: Antigone, be quiet.

ANTIGONE: Why do you tell me to be quiet when all I want to know is what I have to do to be happy? This minute; since it is this very minute that I must make my choice. You tell me that life is so wonderful. I want to know what I have to do in order to be able to say that myself.

CREON: Do you love Haemon?

ANTIGONE: Yes, I love Haemon. The Haemon I love is hard and young, faithful and difficult to satisfy, just as I am. But if what I love in Haemon is to be worn away like a stone step by the tread of the thing you call life, the thing you call happiness; if Haemon reaches the point where he stops growing pale with fear when I grow pale, stops thinking that I must have been killed in an accident when I am five minutes late, stops feeling that he is alone on earth when I laugh and he doesn't know why— if he too has to learn to say yes to everything—why, no, then, no! I do not love Haemon!

CREON: You don't know what you are talking about!

ANTIGONE: I do know what I am talking about! Now it is you who have stopped understanding. I am too far away from you now, talking to you from a kingdom you can't get into, with your quick tongue and your hollow heart. *(Laughs)* I laugh, Creon, because I see you suddenly as you must have been at fifteen: the same look of impotence in your face and the same inner conviction that there was nothing you couldn't do. What has life added to you, except those lines in your face, and that fat on your stomach?

CREON: Be quiet, I tell you!

ANTIGONE: Why do you want me to be quiet? Because you know that I am right? Do you think I can't see in your face that what I am saying is true? You can't admit it, of course; you have to go on growling and defending the bone you call happiness.

CREON: It is your happiness, too, you little fool!

ANTIGONE: I spit on your happiness! I spit on your idea of life—that life that must go on, come what may. You are all like dogs that lick everything they smell. You with your promise of a humdrum happiness—provided a person doesn't ask too much of life. I want everything of life, I do; and I want it now! I want it total, complete: otherwise I reject it! I will *not* be moderate. I will *not* be satisfied with the bite of cake you offer me if I promise to be a good little girl. I want to be sure of everything this very day; sure that everything will be as beautiful as when I was a little girl. If not, I want to die!

QUESTIONS

1. Point to the utilitarian aspects of Creon's position.

2. With which ethical theory (or theories) do you think Antigone's position is compatible?

3. What do you think Kant would say of the relative merit of each position?

4. Eventually Creon has Antigone killed. Could his action be defended on a utilitarian basis? On any other?

SUGGESTIONS FOR FURTHER READING

Adler, Mortimer. *Six Great Ideas.* New York: Macmillan, 1981. In this interesting paperback Adler discusses truth, goodness, beauty, liberty, equality, and justice. With the exception of the chapters on truth and beauty, most of Adler's discussion relates to normative concerns.

Bok, Sissela. *Lying: Moral Choice in Public and Private Life.* New York: Random House, 1978. This excellent paperback provides an interesting and readable account of the ethics of deception.

Bok, Sissela. *Secrets: The Ethics of Concealment.* New York: Random House, 1983. Bok here provides an outstanding treatment of the ethical issues raised by attempts to conceal information from others.

Burgess, Anthony. *A Clockwork Orange.* New York: Norton, 1963. The central question in this disturbing novel is: Who is less moral, an individual with no moral sense or the society that attempts to "rehabilitate" him?

Fried, Charles. *An Anatomy of Values: Problems of Personal and Social Choice.* Cambridge, Mass.: Harvard University Press, 1970. This book nicely demonstrates the connection between values and choices, both on an individual and collective level. It is of particular help in sorting out values.

Mackie, John. *Ethics: Inventing Right and Wrong.* Middlesex, England: Penguin Books, 1977. Mackie argues in this challenging paperback that ethical principles are not *discovered* but *invented* by human beings.

May, Bernard. *The Philosophy of Right and Wrong.* London: Routledge & Kegan Paul, 1986. This is a difficult but interesting approach to ethics written by an "analytic" philosopher.

May, Rollo. *Love and Will.* New York: Norton, 1969. Existential psychotherapist May stresses the freedom of individuals to make the choices that maximize self-realization, but he balances this value against social responsibility.

Meilaender, D. *The Theory and Practice of Virtue.* Notre Dame, Ind.: University of Notre Dame Press, 1984. In this paperback Meilaender discusses an often-overlooked aspect of ethics: virtue.

Mill, John Stuart. *Utilitarianism: With Critical Essays.* Edited by Samuel Gorovity. Indianapolis, Ind.: Bobbs-Merrill, 1971. This book contains a collection of twenty-eight crucial essays on Mill's philosophy, as well as the text of Mill's *Utilitarianism* and a chapter from *A System of Logic.*

Muller, Herbert J. *The Children of Frankenstein.* Bloomington: Indiana University Press, 1970. This is an interesting and informative analysis of the decline of values in the face of increasing technology.

Nietzsche, Friedrich. *On the Genealogy of Morals.* Edited by Walter Kaufman. New York: Vintage, 1967. While attacking the ethics of humility and self-denial in this classic, Nietzsche provides deep insight into the subsurface motives for adhering to such ethics.

Norman, Richard. *The Moral Philosophers.* Oxford: Oxford University Press, 1983. In this introductory paperback Norman gives a brief overview of the moral philosophies of the major ethical thinkers.

Rachels, James. *The Elements of Moral Philosophy.* New York: Random House, 1986. This short introduction to ethics is simple and easy to read.

Singer, Peter. *Practical Ethics.* New York: Cambridge University Press, 1979. An avowed utilitarian discusses several contemporary moral dilemmas including euthanasia, discrimination, and aid to the needy.

Thomas, William. *Mill.* Oxford: Oxford University Press, 1985. In this short book Thomas provides an overview of Mill's ideas and life.

CHAPTER 8

Social Philosophy

Freedom and bread enough for all are inconceivable together.

FYODOR DOSTOYEVSKI

Introduction

In his first State of the Union address, President Reagan said that "the taxing powers of government must be used to provide revenues for legitimate government purposes. It must not be used to regulate the economy or bring about social change." Reagan argued passionately for the long-range objective of getting government off our backs. Critics, however, would argue that government has not gone far enough, that taxes should be used more aggressively to right social and economic inequities. It is not our purpose to debate the merit of those positions, but to key on an issue that is embedded in them. The issue concerns the role of government in society. How big a part should government play in regulating our lives?

How active a role the state (the highest authority in society) and its primary instrument, government, ought to take in the lives of its citizens invites an inquiry into the proper relation between individual and society. Aristotle observed that the human is a social animal. We work with, depend on, and relate to one another for our survival and prosperity. The totality of the relationships among people is known as society. A specific society consists of a group of human beings broadly distinguished from other groups by its interests, institutions, and culture. Because society so strongly influences our attitudes, values, loyalties, and outlooks, it is useful to examine the relationship between the individual and society in order to shed more light on the unifying theme of this text: self-identity.

In approaching this topic, we will focus on four related issues. First, since a determination of the proper relationship between individual and society inevitably raises questions of fairness and equity, we will begin with the problem of justice. Second, after laying out some influential theories of justice, we will consider the basis on which the power and authority of the state may be justified. This will require a close look at contract theory, which forms the theoretical foundations for the legitimacy of our state and government. But even if the power of the state can be justified, there is the question of the extent of its authority and power over the individual. So, third, we will talk about government control over its citizens. The subject of government control seems naturally to invite examination of the primary way that government exercises its control: law. So, fourth and finally, we will consider the meaning of law and its relation to freedom. Thus, (1) justice, (2) the justification of the state, (3) government control, and (4) law are the main subjects of this chapter.

These concepts and issues have one thing in common: They arise out of the social milieu. Although they have ethical and political implications, they do not directly involve either ethics or politics. They are not ethics, because they are not primarily concerned with establishing a norm of good conduct; they are not political, because they are not concerned with evaluating political power and the institutions that exercise it. Rather these concerns fall into the category of **social philosophy**, which is the application of moral principles

Freedom is nothing else but the right to live as we wish.

EPICTETUS

to the problems of society, including the problems of freedom and justice. In our overview of social philosophy, then, here are the points we will stress.

MAIN POINTS

1. Distributive justice refers to the fairness with which a community distributes benefits and burdens among its members.

2. The classical Greek view of justice, as expressed by Plato and Aristotle, associates justice with merit or desert.

3. Several British philosophers of the eighteenth and nineteenth centuries, among them John Stuart Mill, associate justice with social utility.

4. Associating justice with social utility raises the problem of balancing individual rights and interests with the common good.

5. A modern formulation of social justice, expressed by John Rawls, associates justice with equality.

6. Most of us today accept a contractual justification for the power and authority of the state, that is, that the state acquires its legitimacy through consent of the governed.

7. Contract theory has its roots in the thought of Thomas Hobbes, John Locke, and Jean-Jacques Rousseau.

8. Regarding government control, modern con-

PHILOSOPHY AND LIFE 8.1

Society and the Bomb

The decision to drop the nuclear bomb that killed tens of thousands of the civilian inhabitants of the city of Hiroshima on 6 August 1945 was made while the United States was at war with Japan. Henry L. Stimson, the American Secretary of War at the time, later explained that he advised President Truman to drop the bomb on the basis of utilitarian reasoning.

I felt that to extract a genuine surrender from the [Japanese] Emperor and his military advisers, they must be administered a tremendous shock which would carry convincing proof of our power to destroy the Empire. Such an effective shock would save

Sources: Henry L. Stimson, "The Decision to Use the Atomic Bomb," *Harper's Magazine* 194 (February 1947): 101–102, 106, 107. John C. Ford, "The Hydrogen Bombing of Cities," *Theology Digest* (Winter 1957).

many times the number of lives, both American and Japanese, that it would cost. . . . Our enemy, Japan, . . . had the strength to cost us a million more [lives]. . . . Additional large losses might be expected among our allies and . . . enemy casualties would be much larger than our own. . . . My chief purpose was to end the war in victory with the least possible cost in lives. . . . The face of war is the face of death; death is an inevitable part of every order that a wartime leader gives. The decision to use the atomic bomb was a decision that brought death to over a hundred thousand Japanese. . . . But this deliberate, premeditated destruction was our least abhorrent choice.

Objecting to this kind of utilitarian justification for killing the inhabitants of cities with nuclear weapons, philosopher-theologian John C. Ford wrote:

[Is] it permissible, in order to win a just war, to wipe out such an area with death or grave injury, resulting indiscriminately, to the majority of its ten million inhabitants? In my opinion the answer must be in the negative. . . . [It] is never permitted to kill directly noncombatants in wartime. Why? Because they are innocent. That is, they are innocent of the violent and destructive action of war, or of any close participation in the violent and destructive action of war.

QUESTIONS

1. Is killing the innocent always wrong, no matter what the consequences?

2. Would you side with Stimson or Ford about the morality of dropping the bomb?

3. Do you agree that in some circumstances the use of nuclear weapons is morally permissible?

tract theorists stake out a position somewhere between anarchism and totalitarianism, leaning toward willing individual cooperation or a strong authoritarian state; these leanings are reflected in the contemporary meanings of *conservative* and *liberal*, terms whose meanings differ significantly from their classical formulations.

9. Contractual theorists believe that the state has the right and duty to pass laws.

10. Thomas Aquinas distinguished among divine (eternal), natural, and human law. He believed that you could break a human law if it was not consistent with a divine law or a natural law.

11. We enjoy "freedoms-from"—that is, guarantees against state interference, such as the Bill of Rights.

QUESTIONS

1. What is a society? Draw up a list of groups that are not societies and a list of groups that you would say are societies. What are the major differences between the members of both groups?

2. Should small groups of experts make any of the major decisions for society, or should all major decisions be made by majority rule? Explain.

3. Which of the following issues would you classify as personal moral issues and which would you classify as social issues: pornography, war, nuclear weapons, abortion, premarital sex, racial discrimination, civil disobedience, labor unions.

Justice

In thinking about the proper relationship between individual and society, one inevitably confronts the issue and problem of justice. It's common to think of justice in terms of crime and punishment. Sometimes, we read of a criminal being sent to prison, and we infer that justice was meted out. Other times, we hear of someone's not being punished for apparent wrongdoing, and we bemoan the miscarriage of justice. In short, we commonly think of justice in terms of retribution, that is, punishment given for some wrongdoing.

But we can think of justice in terms other than retribution. In fact, in a larger sense, justice deals with distribution, not merely retribution. Questions and issues arise daily about how things should be allocated. The issues may involve the distribution of wealth and goods. Thus, given the relative scarcity of a society's resources, how should they be distributed? Should everyone receive the same amount? Ought those most in need receive the lion's share? Or should the resources be distributed according to the individual's potential contributions to society? If individuals belong to groups who have been unfairly discriminated against, should these persons receive special consideration and treatment? Who should have access to medical care: only those who can afford it? Everyone who needs it? Those who likely will be most benefited?

The issues of distribution needn't be confined to wealth and goods. Equally important is the distribution of privilege and power. Education raises such issues. Who should be educated? Everyone?

Only those who can afford an education? Only those who promise to benefit society? Other questions of privilege and power can also be asked. Who shall be permitted to vote? To drive? To drink? Should everyone be treated the same under the law? Or should certain individuals—for example, juveniles—receive special consideration?

All of these issues raise questions of justice, as much as do issues of crime and punishment. But the justice involved is distributive, not retributive. *Distributive justice* refers to the relation between a community and its members. As implied in the name, distributive justice is concerned with the fair and proper distribution of public benefits and burdens among the members of a community. While distributive justice operates in all organizations, it applies chiefly to the state's relationship with its members.

Clearly, the subject of distributive justice touches many areas, from jobs to income, from taxes to medical services. Embedded in any answer to the question of how jobs should be assigned, income and taxes determined, and medical resources allocated, will be a principle of distributive justice; that is, some assumption about what is the proper way of distributing what is available when there isn't enough for all. For example, it's commonly argued that jobs should be distributed on the basis of talent and ability. Again, in the tax code of 1980, large corporations were given tax breaks because it was felt that they would reinvest their savings, thus increasing jobs and productivity, which in turn would benefit the whole of society. And some today claim that medical services should be provided on the basis of need. Each of these assertions implies some standard that should be considered in the distribution of certain resources: desert, social benefit, need. Whether or not these or other principles should be taken into account is one basic concern of distributive justice.

But no matter the principle which serves as the standard for distribution, it ordinarily can be traced, and ideally should be, to a fully developed theory of justice. Thus, the person who invokes talent and ability as the principle of job distribution probably views justice itself in terms of merit. Likewise, the person who argues for special tax advantages for large corporations is viewing justice in terms of social utility. And those who think that medical resources should be equally available to all likely view justice chiefly in terms of equality: Everyone should be treated equally in the sense that all should get the same medical care. In fact, merit, social utility, and equality have served as focal points for various theories of justice down through the years and continue to exert profound influence on our current views of justice and the proper relationship between individual and society.

MERIT

Plato proposed the first significant theory of justice, one associated with giving to individuals what is their due. In Plato's view, justice in the state is exactly what it is in the individual: a harmony between the various parts for the good of the whole. Social justice, then, requires cooperation among all members of a society. As a result, the interests of the individual must be subordinated to those of society.

Such a notion had a decided impact on the overwhelming majority of the Greek population, who were poor and powerless. The submissive role these people played, especially the slaves, was considered vital to the overall success of the society. Consequently, their interests and rights were kept to a minimum. Indeed, they themselves expected reward only insofar as their actions benefited their superiors. Such an attitude could only be fostered in a rigidly structured society, whose sharply drawn class divisions left no confusion about one's place, role, or expectations in life. This is precisely the kind of society that Plato erects in *The Republic*: a

---

You have no more right to consume happiness without producing it than to consume wealth without producing it.

BERNARD SHAW

Plato: **"When one who is by nature a worker attempts to enter the warrior class, or one of the soldiers tries to enter the class of guardians, this meddling brings the city to ruin. That then is injustice. But the doing of one's own job by each class is justice and makes the city just."**

system in which every individual has his or her place, and justice means that each acts and is treated accordingly. Justice, in Plato's view, then, becomes associated with merit, in the sense that individuals are treated and expected to act according to the kinds of persons they are, according to the roles that nature has best fitted them to perform. In the following passage from *The Republic*, Plato states his position quite clearly.

I think that justice is the very thing, or some form of the thing which, when we were beginning to found our city, we said had to be established throughout. We stated, and often repeated, if you remember, that everyone must pursue one occupation of those in the city, that for which his nature best fitted him.

Yes, we kept saying that.

Further, we have heard many people say, and have often said ourselves, that justice is to perform one's own task and not to meddle with that of others.

We have said that.

This then, my friend, I said, when it happens, is in some way justice, to do one's own job. And do you know what I take to be proof of this?

No, tell me.

I think what is left over of those things we have been investigating, after moderation and courage and wisdom have been found, was that which made it possible for those three qualities to appear in the city and to continue as long as it was present. We also said that what remained after we found the other three was justice.

It had to be.

And surely, I said, if we had to decide which of the four will make the city good by its presence, it would be hard to judge whether it is a common belief among the rulers and the ruled, or the preservation among the soldiers of a law-inspired belief as to the nature of what is, and what is not, to be feared, or the knowledge and guardianship of the rulers, or whether it is, above all, the presence of this fourth in child and woman, slave and free, artisan, ruler and subject, namely that each man, a unity in himself, performed his own task and was not meddling with that of others.

How could this not be hard to judge?

It seems then that the capacity for each in the city to perform his own task rivals wisdom, moderation, and courage as a source of excellence for the city.

It certainly does.

You would then describe justice as a rival to them for excellence in the city?

Most certainly.

Look at it this way and see whether you agree: you will order your rulers to act as judges in the courts of the city?

Surely.

And will their exclusive aim in delivering judgment not be that no citizen should have what belongs to another or be deprived of what is his own?

That would be their aim.

That being just?

Yes.

In some way then possession of one's own and the performance of one's own task could be agreed to be justice.

That is so.

Consider then whether you agree with me in this: if a carpenter attempts to do the work of a cobbler, or a cobbler that of a carpenter, and they exchange their tools and the esteem that goes with the job, or the same man tries to do both, and all the other exchanges are made, do you think that this does any great harm to the city?

No.

But I think that when one who is by nature a worker or some other kind of moneymaker is puffed up by wealth, or by the mob, or by his own strength, or some other such thing, and attempts to enter the warrior class, or one of the soldiers tries to enter the group of counselors and guardians, though he is unworthy of it, and these exchange their tools and the public esteem, or when the same man tries to perform all these jobs together, then I think you will agree that these exchanges and this meddling bring the city to ruin.

They certainly do.

The meddling and exchange between the three established orders does very great harm to the city and would most correctly be called wickedness.

Very definitely.

And you would call the greatest wickedness worked against one's own city injustice?

Of course.

That then is injustice. And let us repeat that the doing of one's own job by the moneymaking, auxiliary, and guardian groups, when each group is performing its own task in the city, is the opposite, it is justice and makes the city just.

I agree with you that this is so.[1]

Apparent in this selection and throughout *The Republic* is Plato's insistence not only on severe class distinctions but on the natural *inequality* of individuals. Aristotle too shared the assumption that individuals are unequal, and thus justice is giving to unequal individuals their unequal due. Indeed, in his *Politics*, Aristotle defended slavery, because he believed that those who were slaves were naturally suited for that role and would be wretched and ineffectual were they made free. Both he and Plato believed that different people should have different roles in society and that justice means that each should act and be treated according to his or her role.

It is interesting to speculate how Plato and Aristotle might react to some contemporary concerns that raise questions of justice. For example, it seems safe to say that both would object to heterogeneous grouping in public schools (that is, the practice of placing students of diverse abilities in the same class, as opposed to homogeneous grouping, in which only students of like ability are placed in a class). Also, they likely would object to giving all aliens the same privileges as citizens (for example, education and medical care) and to treating men and women as equals. As for the draft, they wouldn't object to discriminating between males and females, but they might to subjecting every male of a certain age to the draft. The just thing would be to conscript only those suited to be soldiers.

Many of us today would find Plato's and Aristotle's theory of justice objectionable because of its assumption that individuals are unequal. But it should be remembered that the presupposition of equality is as much an assumption as the presupposition of inequality and as such requires a defense. Even though we may not share the Greek view of inequality, our own conceptions of justice are in other important ways deeply indebted to both Plato and Aristotle. For example, like these two philo-

Our object in the construction of the state is the greatest happiness of the whole, and not that of any one class.

PLATO

It is better that some should be unhappy, than that none should be happy, which would be the case in a general state of equality.

SAMUEL JOHNSON

---

1. Plato, *The Republic*, trans. G. M. A. Grube (Indianapolis, Ind.: Hackett, 1974). Reprinted by permission.

Society never advances.

RALPH WALDO EMERSON

sophical luminaries, we today hold that equals should be treated equally. The difference, of course, is that we espouse *egalitarianism,* which is the view that all are equal by virtue of their being human beings; whereas Plato and Aristotle did not endorse universal equality. Also, in his concern with the distribution of a society's resources, Aristotle anticipated an issue of social justice that is of vital national and international concern today. In addition, and perhaps most importantly, Aristotle clearly recognized the importance of justice for the poorest and least powerful members of society. In his view, justice was most important for these members of the community inasmuch as they, unlike the rich and powerful, could not fend for themselves. Finally, much of the theorizing since the time of the Greeks, in effect, has been a response to Plato's claim that justice is giving everyone what is his or her due. Specifically, much of the writing since Plato has attempted to explain what an individual is due and why. Inevitably, this has called for an inspection of the relation between justice and equality, which we will see as we turn to the theory of justice associated with social utility.

SOCIAL UTILITY

The theory that views justice in terms of social utility has its roots in the social and political thought of a number of British philosophers of the eighteenth and nineteenth centuries. This position is foundationally different from the Greeks in that it starts from the assumption that everyone is equal; in contrast, the Greeks, as we saw, assumed inequality.

The assumption of equality is one that we can readily identify with, having been reared in a society erected on the premise that "all men are created equal." Accordingly, in the United States it is widely believed that everyone is entitled to a period of roughly the same kind of education; that the sexes should be treated equally; that individuals should be treated equally before the law; that everyone should have equal job opportunities and equal access to medical care; that everyone should be allowed to practice religion, speak freely, travel, and so on. Similarly, we reject slavery in principle because it violates our belief that everyone is equal. We even object to snobbery, presumably because we believe that one person is not necessarily better than another because of wealth, family, intelligence, or some other criterion. The point is that we needn't look far to see evidence that, at least in theory, our society is erected on a commitment to egalitarianism. But this commitment leads to theoretical and operational problems that you must be aware of to understand the thrust of the social utility theory.

To get an idea of these problems, consider the practice of heterogeneous grouping in the classroom. Consistent with the belief that everyone is equal, we try to ensure that everyone has roughly the same educational opportunities, at least in the formative years. Accordingly, thirty students of widely differing abilities and capacities may be placed in the same class at the same time with the same instructor. Faced with such essential diversity, teachers often end up teaching at the nonexistent "average" class member. As likely as not, the instructional level will be too high for the slowest class members and too low for the swiftest. As a result, the slowest don't learn, the swiftest get bored; both "turn off." Is this just?

Again, medical technology today has made the wondrous dream of organ transplants an astonishing reality. Corneas, hearts, kidneys, even livers— all can be transplanted with more or less success. But there's a rub: Demand exceeds supply. Who should get available organs when there aren't enough to go around? By a strict egalitarian calculation, presumably everyone who needs a heart, say, should have an equal chance of getting it. But suppose that two people are in need of the only available heart. One of them is an internationally renowned neurosurgeon in her forties whose survival promises to benefit countless persons. The other is a sixty-five-year-old derelict, who for three decades has wantonly abused his body and whose survival promises little if any benefit for anyone, except possibly himself. Is it just to treat these individuals as equals in determining who will receive the heart? Or is it more just that they be treated as unequals?

Here's one final example to point up the problem of justice inherent in a commitment to universal equality. With rare exceptions (for example, in the case of prisoners), every adult in our society is entitled to vote. But certainly not all are informed. Yet, the votes of the uninformed count as much as those of the informed. Is this just? Or is it an example of systematic injustice?

Doubtless, the examples could be multiplied. But the point should already be clear: There are cases in which the public interest clashes with the requirements of equal treatment. For Greek theorists like Plato and Aristotle, this is no great problem, because they are associating justice with merit, not equality. But for modern theorists, who largely take equality as a natural fact, the tension between public interest and demand for equal treatment poses an urgent problem. Indeed, it is one that British philosophers have engaged for several centuries, and that has given rise to the theory of justice associated with social utility.

We already indicated that certain British philosophers started from the premise that everyone is equal. But while philosophers such as Thomas Hobbes, John Locke, and David Hume endorsed equality, they did not take this to mean that unequal treatment is never permissible. On the contrary, they associated justice with what assures peace and security for all. In other words, justice means the public interest or social utility. What advances the good of society, or at least most of its citizens, is just. Notice that, in contrast to the Greek view, there is no acknowledgment here of giving individuals what befits them according to their station or role in life, or according to what they are by nature designed to be. Yes, individuals should get what is their due, but their due must be determined by appeal to the common good. The ultimate criterion of justice, then, is utility; that is, public interest or the satisfaction of the interests of at least the majority of people in society.

The most explicit statement of the utility view

Equality in society beats inequality, whether the latter be of the British-aristocratic sort or of the domestic-slavery sort.

ABRAHAM LINCOLN

is expressed by John Stuart Mill (whom we showcased in Chapter 7). Writing in *Utilitarianism*, Mill concedes that the notion of equality often is part of both our conception and practice of justice. But he does not believe that equality constitutes the essence of justice. While the notion of justice varies in different persons, says Mill, it always conforms to the individual's idea of utility. Thus, all people believe that equality is the dictate of justice *except* when they feel that expediency requires inequality. Then they are likely to say, for example, that the famous surgeon and the skid-row bum should not be treated as equals in determining who will get the available heart. Since preserving the life of the surgeon promises more social benefit, expediency requires inequality of treatment: The surgeon should get the organ.

In Mill's view, then, expediency is the ever-present criterion in determining what is just and unjust. Whatever the institution, policy, or program, its justness depends ultimately on one's opinion about expediency respecting the phenomenon. Is reverse discrimination just? It all depends on whether it serves the public interest better than any other alternative posed to ensure comparability of opportunity. Does a fee-for-service medical system best serve society's interests? Does a selective service system that conscripts males but not females most effectively advance the common good? While individual answers may vary, each of them, according to Mill, will be based on an opinion about the expediency of the practice. What is considered expedient will be considered just; what is not considered expedient will not be considered just.

But what about the various interpretations that

expediency lends itself to? You might regard a policy of reverse discrimination expedient; I might not. Similar interpretive differences can arise on any issue. Does this make utility a hopelessly uncertain standard for determining what is just? Mill thinks not. In fact, he thinks that all notions of justice are susceptible to the same objection. In the following passage from *Utilitarianism* he makes this point and an additional critical one: In the last analysis all cases of justice are also cases of expediency.

John Stuart Mill: **"Justice remains the appropriate name for certain social utilities which are vastly more important and therefore more absolute and imperative, than any others are as a class."**

We are continually informed that utility is an uncertain standard, which every different person interprets differently, and that there is no safety but in the immutable, ineffaceable, and unmistakable dictates of justice, which carry their evidence in themselves and are independent of the fluctuations of opinion. One would suppose from this that on questions of justice there could be no controversy; that, if we take that for our rule, its application to any given case could leave us in as little doubt as a mathematical demonstration. So far is this from being the fact that there is as much difference of opinion, and as much discussion, about what is just as about what is useful to society. Not only have different nations and individuals different notions of justice, but in the mind of one and the same individual, justice is not some one rule, principle, or maxim, but many which do not always coincide in their dictates, and, in choosing between which, he is guided either by some extraneous standard or by his own personal predilections.

For instance, there are some who say that it is unjust to punish anyone for the sake of example to others, that punishment is just only when intended for the good of the sufferer himself. Others maintain the extreme reverse, contending that to punish persons who have attained years of discretion, for their own benefit, is despotism and injustice, since, if the matter at issue is solely their own good, no one has a right to control their own judgment of it; but that they may justly be punished to prevent evil to others, this being the exercise of the legitimate right of self-defense. Mr. Owen, again, affirms that it is unjust to punish at all, for the criminal did not make his own character; his education and the circumstances which surrounded him have made him a criminal, and

for these he is not responsible. All these opinions are extremely plausible; and so long as the question is argued as one of justice simply, without going down to the principles which lie under justice and are the source of its authority, I am unable to see how any of these reasoners can be refuted. For in truth every one of the three builds upon rules of justice confessedly true. The first appeals to the acknowledged injustice of singling out an individual and making him a sacrifice, without his consent, for other people's benefit. The second relies on the acknowledged justice of self-defense and the admitted injustice of forcing one person to conform to another's notions of what constitutes his good. The Owenite invokes the admitted principle that it is unjust to punish anyone for what he cannot help. Each is triumphant so long as he is not compelled to take into consideration any other maxims of justice than the one he has selected; but as soon as their several maxims are brought face to face, each disputant seems to have exactly as much to say for himself as the others. No one of them can carry out his own notion of justice without trampling upon another equally binding. These are difficulties; they have always been felt to be such; and many devices have been invented to turn rather than to overcome them. As a refuge from the last of the three, men imagined what they called the freedom of the will—fancying that they could not justify punishing a man whose will is in a thoroughly hateful state unless it be supposed to have come into that state through no influence of anterior circumstances. To escape from the other difficulties, a favorite contrivance has been the fiction of a contract whereby at some unknown period all the members of society engaged to obey the laws and consented to be punished for any disobedience to them, thereby giving to their legislators the right, which it is assumed they would not otherwise have had, of punishing them, either for their own good or for that of society. This happy thought was considered to get rid of the whole difficulty and to legitimate the infliction of punishment, in virtue of another received maxim of justice, *volenti non fit injuria*— that is not unjust which is done with the consent of the person who is supposed to be hurt by it. I need hardly remark that, even if the consent were not a mere fiction, this maxim is not superior in authority to the others which it is brought in to supersede. It is, on the contrary, an instructive specimen of the loose and irregular manner in which supposed principles of justice grow up. This particular one evidently came into use as a help to the coarse exigencies of courts of law, which are sometimes obliged to be content with very uncertain presumptions, on account of the greater evils which would often arise from any attempt on their part to cut finer. But even courts of law are not able to adhere consistently to the maxim, for they allow voluntary engagements to be set aside on the ground of fraud, and sometimes on that of mere mistake of misinformation.

To take another example from a subject already once referred to. In co-operative industrial association, is it just or not that talent or skill should give a title to superior remuneration? On the negative side of the question it is argued that whoever does the best he can deserves equally well, and ought not in justice to be put in a position of inferiority for no fault of his own; that superior abilities have already advantages more than enough, in the admiration they excite, the personal influence they command, and the internal sources of satis-

faction attending them, without adding to these a superior share of the world's goods; and that society is bound in justice rather to make compensation to the less favored for this unmerited inequality of advantages than to aggravate it. On the contrary side it is contended that society receives more from the more efficient laborer; that, his services being more useful, society owes him a larger return for them; that a greater share of the joint result is actually his work, and not to allow his claim to it is a kind of robbery; that, if he is only to receive as much as others, he can only be justly required to produce as much, and to give a smaller amount of time and exertion, proportioned to his superior efficiency. Who shall decide between these appeals to conflicting principles of justice? Justice has in this case two sides to it, which it is impossible to bring into harmony, and the two disputants have chosen opposite sides; the one looks to what it is just that the individual should receive, the other to what it is just that the community should give. Each, from his own point of view, is unanswerable; and any choice between them, on grounds of justice, must be perfectly arbitrary. Social utility alone can decide the preference.

The considerations which have now been adduced resolve, I conceive, the only real difficulty in the utilitarian theory of morals. It has always been evident that all cases of justice are also cases of expediency; the difference is in the peculiar sentiment which attaches to the former, as contradistinguished from the latter. If this characteristic sentiment has been sufficiently accounted for; if there is no necessity to assume for it any peculiarity of origin; if it is simply the natural feeling of resentment, moralized by being made coextensive with the demands of social good; and if this feeling not only does but ought to exist in all the classes of cases to which the idea of justice corresponds—that idea no longer presents itself as a stumbling block to the utilitarian ethics. Justice remains the appropriate name for certain social utilities which are vastly more important, and therefore more absolute and imperative, than any others are as a class (though not more so than others may be in particular cases); and which, therefore, ought to be, as well as naturally are, guarded by a sentiment, not only different in degree, but also in kind; distinguished from the milder feeling which attaches to the mere idea of promoting human pleasure or convenience at once by the more definite nature of its commands and by the sterner character of its sanctions.[2]

Since Mill's utilitarian theory of justice is a logical extension of his ethical theories, it is understandable that it should invite some of the same objections. First, even if what we consider expedient we also consider just, ought we? For example, there are laws against possessing amounts of marijuana that exceed specified limits. Whether or not there ought to be such laws, or whether or not such laws are just, is another issue. To assume that merely because the laws exist that they ought to exist, or that they are necessarily just, is to commit a fallacy. Again, there are laws prohibiting active euthanasia, that is, taking direct measures to end the life, say, of someone hopelessly ill and in excruciating pain. But ought there to be such laws? That is another issue. In respect to Mill's view, merely because we may think of justice in terms of expediency does not necessarily mean that we ought to. Perhaps we should think of it in other terms—as, for example, the Greeks did or as strict egalitarians do.

A second, and operationally more troublesome, problem with social utility arises from the inevitable clash of individual and public interests. Surely, there are cases when the general utility can be served only at the expense of a single individual, or perhaps a group of them. Take, for example, the currently volatile issue of installing commercial nuclear power plants. Even assuming (1) that the plants are the most efficient source of energy available (which, of course, is debatable) and (2) that they pose only remote and minimal hazards to individuals living near them, is it just for the state to insist that these individuals must bear even a negligible risk or undergo dislocations for the good of society? Again, in recent years considerable money and domestic resources have been diverted from human services to national defense. Some individuals and groups (for example, the poor, the young, the elderly, the infirm) seem to be directly injured

2. John Stuart Mill, *Utilitarianism* (1861) (New York: Bobbs-Merrill, 1957), 68–69. Reprinted by permission.

Society exists for the benefit of its members; not the members for the benefit of society.

HERBERT SPENCER

as a result. The justification for the realignment of priorities largely takes the form of an appeal to the national interest. Does this appeal to social utility of itself make a program intended to shore up national defense at the expense of the most vulnerable members of society just? Of course, one could respond that the utility of a specific act by itself cannot give an adequate concept of justice, that what is needed is a theory of general practice along the lines of rule utilitarianism. But as we have seen elsewhere (see Chapter 7), rule utilitarianism still allows the possibility of a practice that systematically increases the general utility at the expense of some individual or group. Is this just? Utility theorists would say it is just, simply because justice ultimately has no concrete meaning apart from expediency.

But not all agree. In fact, what is perhaps the most powerful contemporary theory of justice attempts to reassert the primacy of individual rights by placing the emphasis on the advantages of a practice to the least advantaged members of society. In so doing, it clearly ties together the concepts of justice and equality. Such a theory has been proposed by the American philosopher John Rawls.

JUSTICE AS FAIRNESS

John Rawls presents his theory as a modern alternative to utilitarianism. Rawls argues that the principles that govern a society must be "acceptable" to everyone, otherwise society will not be "stable" but subject to unrest. But principles that are perceived as "unfair," Rawls claims, will not be acceptable to everyone. Why should people accept principles that unfairly favor others at their expense? Clearly, the principles on which a stable society is based must be principles that are fair to everyone. Utilitarianism, Rawls argues, is not fair to everyone, since it may allow practices that increase the general utility at the expense of minority groups. Therefore, a stable society cannot be based on utilitarian principles.

As an alternative to utilitarianism, Rawls proposes two principles: the principle of *equal liberty* and the *difference principle.* The principle of equal liberty is meant to govern primarily society's political institutions (its constitution, government, courts, legislative system, and laws). The principle of equal liberty states that "each person participating in a [political] practice or affected by it has an equal right to the most extensive liberty compatible with a like liberty for all."[3] Basically, the principle of equal liberty means that everyone must have as *many* political rights and freedoms as possible, as long as everyone has the *same* ("equal") political rights and freedoms. Everyone, for example, must have at least the same voting rights, the same legal rights, the same right to trial by jury, the same freedom of speech, the same freedom of conscience, the same freedom of the press, and so on. In the political sphere, then, everyone must be equal and everyone must be granted the maximum degree of freedom that is compatible with everyone else having the same degree of freedom. Because the principle of equal liberty requires equality, Rawls argues, it is fair to everyone. Consequently, society's political institutions will be stable as long as they are based on this fair principle.

Rawls's second principle, the difference principle, is intended to govern primarily a society's social and economic institutions. Unlike the *political* arena where everyone must be equal, the social and economic arenas, according to Rawls, must allow for some inequalities. Rawls holds that inequalities are necessary in the social and economic arenas to serve as incentives for greater productivity. If greater economic rewards (income and wealth) are given to those who work harder and who have greater abilities, they will be motivated to be more productive, and all society will benefit.

But inequalities obviously raise the possibility of unfairness and therefore of instability. Those who are disadvantaged (those who cannot work or who have few talents and abilities) can be disfavored by principles that allow inequalities. Consequently, Rawls proposes that inequalities should be allowed only if the plight of the disadvantaged is relieved (through welfare programs, for example). The second principle he proposes, then, which is to govern the inequalities in our social and economic institutions, states: "Social and economic inequalities are to be arranged so that they are . . . to the greatest benefit of the least advantaged."[4] Rawls calls this the "difference principle" because it focuses on the differences among people. The difference principle is fair, Rawls argues, because it is based on *reciprocity*, on "tit-for-tat." The principle benefits those who are able and talented because they are allowed to compete for the more favored jobs and positions. Their efforts thus add to the productivity of society. But the disadvantaged also benefit because some of the goods produced by the efforts of the talented are transferred to the disadvantaged through welfare programs. Thus the advantaged "repay" the disadvantaged for the inequalities from which they benefit. This reciprocity, Rawls claims, is what makes the difference principle fair to everyone. A society's economic and social institutions will therefore be stable if they are governed by the difference principle.

Although many people support the ideals of fairness that Rawls's principles embody, not everyone does so. One of Rawls's strongest critics is his Harvard colleague, Robert Nozick. In his book *Anarchy, State, and Utopia,* Nozick points out that Rawls advocates a "patterned" theory of justice. A patterned theory is one that says that goods should be distributed among the members of a society according to a certain pattern or formula. If goods are not yet distributed according to this formula, then goods must be taken from some citizens and

---

3. John Rawls, "Justice as Fairness," in *Philosophy, Politics, and Society,* eds. Peter Laslett and W. G. Runciman (New York: Barnes & Noble, 1962), 133.

---

4. John Rawls, *A Theory of Justice* (Cambridge, Mass.: Harvard University Press, 1972), 255.

given to others until the required distribution is achieved. Rawls's theory is patterned because it requires that goods be distributed according to his two principles.

Nozick objects that any patterned theory that advocates a certain distribution of goods always leads to the unjust use of force and coercion. People's free choices, he says, will always upset any pattern society tries to establish. Some individuals unjustly will be forced to give up their goods to others until the required distribution is achieved again. Nozick provides an ingenious example to illustrate his claim.

Nozick asks us to imagine a society in which goods are already distributed in accordance with some patterned concept of justice like Rawls's. Each person then holds the goods each should hold, no more and no less. Suppose, for instance, that a basketball star freely agrees to play several exhibition games for which he receives one dollar per ticket each game. Millions of fans freely agree to give him one dollar to watch him play. As a result of these many free choices, at the end of the season, the player holds several million dollars: He now holds more goods than he should hold. The patterned principles therefore will require that some of the star's goods be taken away from him and redistributed to others until the proper distribution is once again reestablished. Thus, patterned principles continually require that goods be taken from some and given to others in order to reestablish the distribution that people's free choices continually change.

Nozick argues, however, that if a distribution is changed by people's *free* choices, then there can be nothing wrong with it. For example, the fans knew their money was going to the basketball star, so they can have no complaint. As for those who did not see the game, their goods are unaffected. Thus, there was nothing wrong with the distribution that resulted from these free choices.

Nozick is raising several objections to Rawls's principles. One is that Rawls is using the better-off people in society to ensure the welfare of the worst off. Nozick regards this ethic as fundamentally unjust. As a corollary, he claims Rawls is not impartial, for he is seeing things only through the eyes of the worst off. Finally, he objects to Rawls's apparent contention that under certain circumstances individuals are not entitled to what they create. A person's entitlement is very much a part of Nozick's thinking, and his work is largely devoted to spelling out this concept.

But perhaps in applying Rawls's difference principle to a specific transaction, Nozick has warped it, or at least overburdened it. After all, Rawls's principle is addressing the backdrop against which public policies and decisions about redressing inequalities are to be made. It is not speaking directly to specific, small scale instances of the sort Nozick cites. More important, Rawls is not making the socialistic argument that all property should be shared. He says only that society must help the most disadvantaged members. This does not at all mean that everyone has a right to an equal share. In other words, Rawls's concept of justice does not equate fair distribution with equal distribution. Yes, individuals have a just claim to whatever they have acquired, as long as the acquisition occurred within the context of a fair social policy. In the following paragraph, taken from his "A Kantian Conception of Equality," Rawls makes these very points concerning his difference principle:

> In explaining this principle, several matters should be kept in mind. First of all, it applies in the first instance to the main public principles and policies that regulate social and economic equalities. It is used to adjust the system of entitlements and rewards, and the standards and precepts that this system employs. Thus the difference principle holds, for example, for income and property taxation, for fiscal and economic policy; it does not apply to particular transactions or distributions, nor, in general, to small scale and local decisions, but rather to the background against which these take place. No observable pattern is required of actual distributions, nor even any measure of the degree of equality. . . . What is enjoined is that the inequalities make a functional contribution to those least favored. Finally, the aim is not to eliminate the various contingencies, for some such contingencies [that is, social primary goods such as (1) rights, liberties and opportunities; (2) income and wealth; (3) the social bases of self-respect] seem inevitable. Thus even if an equal distribution

of natural assets seemed more in keeping with the equality of free persons, the question of redistributing these assets (were this conceivable) does not arise, since it is incompatible with the integrity of the person. Nor need we make any specific assumptions about how great these variations are: we only suppose that, as realized in later life, they are influenced by all three contingencies. The question, then, is by what criterion a democratic society is to organize cooperation and arrange the system of entitlements that encourages and rewards productive efforts. We have a right to our natural abilities and a right to whatever we become entitled to by taking part in a fair social process. The problem is to characterize this process.[5]

In the last analysis, Rawls's thought is most significant and controversial because it has connected justice with aiding the least advantaged. While most, if not all, of us today would agree that government should secure equal political rights,

many would not have government secure material goals and social services for the disadvantaged. Indeed, in the 1980s there has been a concerted effort at the federal executive level to roll back welfare programs in these areas. Rawls is claiming that justice requires not only political equality but a social order that respects the rights of individuals to material goods and social services. On this point he puts considerable distance between himself and the mainstream of what in the 1980s is termed conservative fiscal thinking.

The preceding discussion gives witness to the claim that justice poses a profound problem to social and political philosophers. While we mentioned only a handful of philosophers, we spanned more than two millennia, from classical Greeks such as Plato and Aristotle to contemporary theoreticians such as John Rawls. There is no single theory of justice that receives universal endorsement. Indeed our own society seems ambivalent, giving at various times priority to merit, social utility, or equality. The challenge continues to be what it has always been: to effect a proper balance—whatever and

5. John Rawls, "A Kantian Conception of Equality," *Cambridge Review* (February 1974), 97.

PHILOSOPHY AND LIFE 8.2

Welfare

About 14 percent of our population, or 33 million Americans, lived in poverty in 1986, 8 million more than in 1977, and one out of four children was poor. Also in 1986 unemployment continued to hover at 7 percent for the sixth straight year, the longest stretch since the Great Depression. According to a congressional subcommittee, there were perhaps 2.5 million homeless Americans in 1986, and this trend continues. A

SOURCE: *Los Angeles Times*, 26 December 1982.

news report describes the plight of the growing number of impoverished citizens.

When the last in a series of fast-food jobs expired for him, Michael Anthony Reed, 21, started living in his Toyota [parked on Denver's streets] with his 21-year-old wife and infant daughter [Holly Reed]. Holly Reed died of hypothermia while bundled in blankets in the family car. . . .

Joe Wilkerson, 25, and his wife, Shiela, 22, are from Chicago. They are typical of the "new homeless."

. . . Joe lost his $25,000-a-year job as a forklift operator. . . . So they sold all they had, left the house they rented in Chicago, and headed west with their two sons. In a month, their money—about $500—was gone. . . . "My husband, myself, and my two sons," [said Shiela] "were walking in the cold and the kids asked, 'Where are we going?' and we said, 'We don't know.' "

QUESTION

1. Should the government provide welfare for families like the Reeds and the Wilkersons?

wherever that may be—between public and private interests. In fact, the state is empowered to do this; for by definition it is the authority with the power to define the public interest and to enforce its definition. This means that it is the state that draws the line of demarcation between individual and society. All would agree that this is an awesome power.

For as long as philosophers have pondered the meaning of justice, they have also grappled with the question of the legitimacy of the state and its primary instrument, government. On what basis is the power of the state justified? While any answer to this question inevitably will reflect one's concept of justice, the question of the legitimacy of the state, of the justification of its power, is distinct from the problem of justice. It is to this question that we now turn.

QUESTIONS

1. Is it just to be taxed to fund something that you do not morally subscribe to?

2. Can you think of a situation in which it is more just to treat people differently than to treat them equally?

3. Is the law requiring young people to remain in school to a certain age just? Is the one that requires parents or guardians to enroll their children or charges in a school just?

4. Rawls argues for a view of justice from the position of the worst off in society. Would it be unrealistic to argue a case for a view from the position of the best off in the society? How might you do this?

5. Applying Rawls's difference principle view to your society, which groups do you think would receive preferential economic treatment? Why?

6. What evidence indicates that Rawls's theory is already operating in your society?

SECTION 8.3

The Justification of the State

The state is the highest authority in a society with the legal power to define the public interest and enforce its definition. One clear example of the state's doing this can be seen in the graduated income tax system. The state sets priorities, that is, defines the public interest; then it taxes citizens in order to implement these priorities. In theory, Americans pay taxes proportional to their incomes: The more they make, the greater the proportion of income tax they pay. Many feel this is fair. But with demands for and costs of goods and services rising, a sizable number of people think that this system is unfair, especially people who disagree with the programs for which taxes are spent. Take, for example, the case of a childless couple, the Millers.

Bruce Miller, a chemical engineer, and his wife Marge, a dental hygienist, have no dependents and can claim very few deductions. As a result, they pay a hefty income tax every year. Although they like to consider themselves loyal Americans who

Government is emphatically a machine: to the discontented a "taxing machine," to the contented a "machine for securing property."

THOMAS CARLYLE

are willing to bear their share of the nation's expenses, in recent years they have grown resentful of the tax system and are seriously thinking about voting for an initiative that will limit not only property tax but income tax as well.

BRUCE: You know, I really think it's unfair that the government takes such a big bite of our income.

MARGE: What bothers me even more than the amount is the way it's spent.

BRUCE: Well, there's a lot of waste. There's no question about that.

MARGE: I don't even mean the waste. Do you realize that our money is being used to support things we don't directly benefit from? Take that swimming pool they put in the high school last year. We're never going to use that. And we don't have any children who ever will. But our property tax has gone up this year to help pay for it, so we wind up paying for it whether we like it or not.

BRUCE: I see what you mean. But I'll tell you what really galls me even more than being forced to pay for something we're not going to use.

MARGE: What's that?

BRUCE: Being forced to pay for something I think is wrong.

MARGE: Like what?

BRUCE: Well, I know that you disagree with me on this, but I don't think abortion is right. And yet I'm helping to finance the abortion clinics that the state's set up.

MARGE: You know, I never thought of that. Even though I do support abortion, I think you're right. You shouldn't be forced to violate your conscience. That's what you're saying, isn't it?

BRUCE: You bet it is.

Notice that the Millers are resentful not of paying taxes but of how their tax money is spent. They are questioning the fairness of a system that compels them under penalty of law to pay for some programs that they cannot in good conscience support.

But there is an even broader question that this case raises which does not relate directly to the graduated income tax system or to any other specific program, policy, or measure that the state implements in enforcing its definition of the public interest. That question is: What justifies the power of the state in the first place? What gives the state the right to tax, conscript, arm, educate, or do any of the myriad things it does? It is true that the Millers are not asking this question. To be sure, very few of us ever do. We criticize various state intrusions into our lives and liberties, but never plumb the deeper theoretical issue that underlies any specific utilization of governmental power. That issue concerns the legitimacy of the state per se. Understanding that issue gives us some basis for intelligently evaluating specific uses of that power. Stated another way, it is impossible to determine whether a government has misused its power until we determine what are the rightful limits of that power. And determining the rightful limits of authority, in turn, ultimately calls for an inquiry into the legitimacy of the state's authority and power to begin with.

At different times in various societies, theories have been advanced to define the legitimacy of the state and justify its power. At times the power of the state has been justified by appeal to divine authority. Thus some rulers have claimed the power to rule as a divine right, as a kind of mandate from some deity. Other times, the state has been justified by appeal to the public interest. Accordingly, insofar as the state furthers the public interest, it is justified. But the theory that most of us today accept is that the state is justified by the consent of the governed; that is, the legitimacy of the state stems from an agreement of the governed to be ruled by the state. The most influential modern versions of this viewpoint are captured in the term *social contract*, which refers to a complex theory of state legitimacy that has extraordinary importance for us today.

CONTRACT THEORY

The so-called **contract theory** is both an explanation of the origin of the state and a defense of its authority that philosophers have frequently used.

Thomas Hobbes: "Hereby it is manifest that during the time men live without a common power to keep them all in awe, they are in that condition which is called war, and such a war, as is of every man against every man, and the life of man is solitary, nasty, brutish, and short."

We see versions of contract theory as far back as Plato, but its most noteworthy proponents were Thomas Hobbes (whom we showcased in Chapter 4) and John Locke. More than any other person, Hobbes was the founder of modern political philosophy. Political theorists before him, such as Plato, Aristotle, Saint Augustine, and Thomas Aquinas, had emphasized that the state was subject to human control. In contrast, Hobbes based his political philosophy on the principles of seventeenth-century scientific materialism. According to this doctrine, the world is a mechanical system that can be explained in terms of the laws of motion. Even the behavior of humans or complex societies, it was argued, are reducible to geometric and physical explanations. From this view of reality Hobbes deduced how things must of necessity occur.

In his most famous work, *Leviathan*, Hobbes portrays humans as selfish, unsocial creatures driven by two needs: survival and personal pleasure. Therefore, human life is characterized by constant struggle, strife, and war, with individual pitted against individual in a battle for self-preservation and gain. In Hobbes's words:

> Hereby it is manifest, that during the time men live without a common power to keep them all in awe, they are in that condition which is called war; and such a war, as is of every man, against every man. . . .
>
> Whatsoever therefore is consequent to a time of war, where every man is enemy to every man; the same is consequent to the time, wherein men live without other security, than what their own strength, and their own invention shall furnish them withal. In such condition, there is no place for industry; because the fruit thereof is uncertain: and consequently no culture of the earth; no navigation, nor use of the commodities that may be imported by sea; no commodious building; no instruments of moving, and removing, such things as require much force; no knowledge of the face of the earth; no account of time; no arts; no letters; no society; and which is worst of all, continual fear, and danger of violent death; and the life of man, solitary, poor, nasty, brutish, and short.
>
> The passions that incline men to peace, are fear of death; desire of such things as are necessary to commodious living; and a hope by their industry to obtain them. And reason suggesteth convenient articles of peace, upon which men may be drawn to agreement. These articles, are they, which otherwise are called the Laws of Nature.[6]

Notice in the final paragraph that Hobbes, while asserting that the instinct for self-preservation is the basic drive behind human behavior, states that humans have the capacity to reason.

Although Hobbes never viewed reason as moving us to act, he did hold that reason could regulate human actions and anticipate their results. This rationality enabled people to evaluate the long-term results of behavior originally motivated by self-interest.

Rational concern for their own survival and for their best long-term interests impels humans to enter

---

6. Thomas Hobbes, *Leviathan* (London: J. Bohn, 1839), pt. 1, ch. 15.

into a contract with one another that forms the basis for society. Because they recognize that otherwise their lives are destined to be "solitary, poor, nasty, brutish, and short," humans accept an authority outside themselves that has the power to force all to act in the best interests of the majority. For Hobbes the agreement that establishes this authority is irrevocable. Once set up, the political body wielding this power exercises complete authority over its subjects and remains in power as long as it is able to compel them to do what they otherwise would not do.

The society that individuals contract for thus becomes superior to the individuals. For Hobbes, the state cannot bear any resistance to its rule. If such resistance becomes effective, the state has proven itself unable to govern—in which case the established officials no longer rule and the people are no longer their subjects. At that point the people revert to their natural state of struggle for self-preservation and gain until they form another contract.

In contrast with Plato's and Hobbes's rather pessimistic views, John Locke viewed humans as essentially moral beings who ought to obey natural moral rules. Whereas Hobbes saw warfare as the human's natural state, Locke saw it at least partly as a system of natural moral laws. As a result, Locke viewed humans as being by nature free and equal, regardless of the existence of any government. Government, he argued, doesn't decree mutual respect for the freedom and liberties of all—nature does. Humans are by nature free, rational, and social creatures. They establish governments because three things are missing in the state of nature: (1) a firm, clearly understood interpretation of natural law, (2) unbiased judges to resolve disputes, and (3) personal recourse in the face of injustices. So, in order to maintain their natural rights, individuals enter into a social contract. In one portion of his brilliant and most influential political writing, *Essay Concerning the True and Original Extent and End of Civil Government* (1690), Locke explains the end of political society and government.

123. If man in the state of Nature be so free as has been said, if he be absolute lord of his own

John Locke: "It is not without reason that man seeks out and is willing to join in society with others for the mutual preservation of their lives, liberties and estates, which I call by the general name—property."

person and possessions, equal to the greatest and subject to nobody, why will he part with his freedom, this empire, and subject himself to the dominion and control of any other power? To which it is obvious to answer, that though in the state of Nature he hath a right, yet the enjoyment of it is very uncertain and constantly exposed to the invasion of others; for all being kings as much as he, every man his equal, and the greater part no strict observers of equity and justice, the enjoyment of the property he has in this state is very unsafe, very insecure. This makes him willing to quit this condition which, however free, is full of fears and continual dangers; and it is not without reason that he seeks out and is willing to join in society with others who are already united, or have a mind to unite for the mutual preservation of their lives, liberties and estates, which I call by the general name—property.

124. The great and chief end, therefore, of men uniting into commonwealths, and putting themselves under government, is the preservation of

their property; to which in the state of Nature there are many things wanting.

Firstly, there wants an established, settled, known law, received and allowed by common consent to be the standard of right and wrong, and the common measure to decide all controversies between them. For though the law of Nature be plain and intelligible to all rational creatures, yet men, being biased by their interest, as well as ignorant for want of study of it, are not apt to allow of it as a law binding to them in the application of it to their particular cases.

125. Secondly, in the state of Nature there wants a known and indifferent judge, with authority to determine all differences according to the established law. For every one in that state being both judge and executioner of the law of Nature, men being partial to themselves, passion and revenge is very apt to carry them too far, and with too much heat in their own cases, as well as negligence and unconcernedness, make them too remiss in other men's.

126. Thirdly, in the state of Nature there often wants power to back and support the sentence when right, and to give it due execution. They who by any injustice offended will seldom fail where they are able by force to make good their injustice. Such resistance many times makes the punishment dangerous, and frequently destructive to those who attempt it.

127. Thus mankind, notwithstanding all the privileges of the state of Nature, being but in an ill condition while they remain in it are quickly driven into society. Hence it comes to pass, that we seldom find any number of men live any time together in this state. The inconveniencies that they are therein exposed to by the irregular and uncertain exercise of the power every man has of punishing the transgressions of others, make them take sanctuary under the established laws of government, and therein seek the preservation of their property. It is this makes them so willingly give up every one his single power of punishing to be exercised by such alone as shall be appointed to it amongst them, and by such rules as the community, or those authorized by them to that purpose, shall agree on. And in this we have the original right and rise of both the legislative and executive power as well as of the governments and societies themselves.[7]

In short, individuals create a political entity capable of preserving the inherent rights of "life, liberty, and estate." This contract is based on the consent of the majority, and all agree to obey the decisions of the majority. The state's authority is limited by the terms of the contract, which is continually reviewed by the citizenry. So, unlike Hobbes's absolutistic state, Locke's state is specific and limited. Most important, one of the fundamental moral rights in Locke's political state is the right to resist and to challenge authority. Whereas Hobbes believed that resistance to authority was never justified, Locke regarded such a right as essential. Although the contrast between Hobbes and Locke is sharp, they do agree that rationality enables humans to perceive the necessity of forming a social contract.

This contract theory, especially as enunciated by Locke, led directly to the social philosophy of Jean-Jacques Rousseau (1712–1778), who some consider the foremost articulator of the social contract theory. However, Rousseau did not appeal to a self-evident natural law as Locke had. He argued that if people are to act morally, then they must live under laws that they freely accept. Rousseau's emphasis, then, was on personal moral autonomy, the capacity and right of individuals to live under laws that they prescribe for themselves. Thus, for Rousseau the fundamental requirement of a morally acceptable government is that the governed have freely subscribed to a common body of law.

The very idea of the power and the right of the People to establish Government, presupposes the duty of every individual to obey the established Government

GEORGE WASHINGTON

7. John Locke, *Essay Concerning the True and Original Extent and End of Civil Government* (1690), vol. 4 (Oxford: Clarendon Press, 1894), 4.

Jean-Jacques Rousseau: "Each of us places in common his person and all his power under the supreme direction of the general will; and as one body we all receive each member as an indivisible part of the whole."

In his most important work, *Of the Social Contract*, Rousseau describes his contract theory.

The clauses of this contract are so determined by the nature of the act that the slightest modification would render them vain and ineffectual; so that, although they have never perhaps been formally enunciated, they are everywhere the same, everywhere tacitly admitted and recognized, until, the social pact being violated, each man regains his original rights and recovers his natural liberty while losing the conventional liberty for which he renounced it.

These clauses, rightly understood, are reducible to one only, viz, the total alienation to the whole community of each associate with all his rights; for, in the first place, since each gives himself up entirely, the conditions are equal for all; and, the conditions being equal for all, no one has any interest in making them burdensome to others.

Further, the alienation being made without

reserve, the union is as perfect as it can be, and an individual associate can no longer claim anything; for, if any rights were left to individuals, since there would be no common superior who could judge between them and the public, each, being on some point his own judge, would soon claim to be so on all; the state of nature would still subsist, and the association would necessarily become tyrannical or useless.

In short, each giving himself to all, gives himself to nobody; and as there is not one associate over whom we do not acquire the same rights which we concede to him over ourselves, we gain the equivalent of all that we lose, and more power to preserve what we have.

If, then, we set aside what is not of the essence of the social contract, we shall find that it is reducible to the following terms: "Each of us puts in common his person and his whole power under the supreme direction of the general will; and in return we receive every member as an indivisible part of the whole."

Forthwith, instead of the individual personalities of all the contracting parties, this act of association produces a moral and collective body, which is composed of as many members as the assembly has voices, and which receives from this same act its unity, its common self (*moi*), its life, and its will. This public person, which is thus formed by the union of the individual members, formerly took the name of CITY, and now takes that of REPUBLIC or BODY POLITIC, which is called by its members STATE when it is passive, SOVEREIGN when it is active, POWER when it is compared to similar bodies. With regard to the associates, they take collectively the name of PEOPLE, and are called individually CITIZENS. . . .[8]

Rousseau's reference to the "general will" deserves some elaboration, since general will is a cornerstone in his social contract. The general will should be contrasted with the "will of all," or unanimity of feeling. A group of wills is *general* when each member of the group aims at the common good, which is what Rousseau has in mind. True, the general will and the will of all might result in

---

8. Jean-Jacques Rousseau, *The Social Contract*, in *Ideal Empires and Republics*, ed. Oliver H. G. Leigh (London: M. Walter Dunne, Publisher, 1901), 13–14.

The Declaration of Independence, John Trumbull. "Both the declaration and Locke's contract agree that when a government infringes on the individual rights of life, liberty, and the pursuit of happiness (or property, for Locke), the people have a right to dismiss it."

the same course, for each group member may see his or her own best interests being served. But Rousseau felt that agreement is more likely when everyone tries to determine whether a proposed action is best for the good of all, for the general good, rather than just for self.

Rousseau argues further that the general will, unlike the will of all, represents a true consensus— it's what everyone wants. Even when the minority must conform to majority will, there is no coercion or violation of personal freedom because everyone, even the minority members, seeks the general good. In other words, everyone is agreed on the end; they differ only in what they believe the means should be. Ultimately, they all get what they want: promotion of the common good. One glaring flaw in the whole arrangement, of course, is the assumption that the majority view accords with the general good. Such a bald appeal to head counting is, to say the least, highly questionable.

Nonetheless, Rousseau's version of the social contract has a decided Lockean flavor. A decade later Thomas Jefferson would also sound a Lockean chord in these lines from the Declaration of Independence: "To secure these rights [life, liberty and the pursuit of happiness], governments are instituted among Men, deriving their just powers from the consent of the governed. That whenever any Form of Government becomes destructive of these ends, it is the Right of the People to alter or to abolish it, and to institute a new Government, laying its foundation on such principles and organizing its powers in such form, as to them shall seem most likely to effect their safety and Happiness." Both the Declaration and Locke's contract agree that when a government infringes on the individual rights of life, liberty, and the pursuit of happiness (or property, for Locke), the people have the right to dismiss it.

But precisely when does a government destroy

those rights? Perhaps it would be easy to determine when a government is depriving us of our right to life, but what about liberty and the pursuit of happiness? It could be argued that these liberties are political and civil in nature and can thus be spelled out constitutionally. Still, it is one thing for a constitution to guarantee the right of assembly, but quite another for a mayor to interpret an assembly as a mob and for a court to uphold this interpretation. In other words, the U.S. Constitution, like the contract theory on which it is based, provides a general framework to ensure liberties but leaves great latitude for the interpretation and possible restriction of those liberties.

Determining when a government is infringing on the pursuit of happiness is even more difficult. Some might argue that a graduated income tax inhibits the pursuit of happiness. When a wealthy person's earnings and holdings are taxed considerably more than an average-income person's, is the government infringing on the wealthy person's pursuit of happiness? This is really the basis for the Millers' discontent.

MARGE: You know, when you actually sit down and start adding up all the things you don't morally support and subtract from your taxes how much is going to each, you come up with quite a sum.

BRUCE: You can say that again. I'd like to have every penny of my tax money that went to that Vietnam war.

MARGE: We both thought that was wrong.

BRUCE: But we helped finance it.

MARGE: And the maddening thing about it is that we end up depriving ourselves of things that will make us happy in order to support many things we don't think are right.

BRUCE: That sure is a switch, isn't it? I thought the job of government was to help in our pursuit of happiness, not to hinder it.

Under the social contract, then, we give up certain rights to gain others. Specifically, under our political system we are guaranteed the rights to life, liberty, and the pursuit of happiness. The problem for today is: Is the government acting in such a way as to secure these rights? Or is the government acting in such a way that it is actually depriving us of these rights?

There are no simple answers to these questions about the proper limits of government control. Complicating matters is the fact that evaluating the justice of the social contract requires a high degree of moral development. Evidence suggests that most people lack such a degree of moral awareness (see Philosophy and Life 8.3). Nevertheless, even if the authority and power of the state are justified, we can and should inquire about their proper limits. We can ask, for example, whether a tax code should be used as a mechanism for social change. Just how far the state or government ought to go in the exercise of its authority and power in controlling the lives of its citizens provokes analysis about the nature of government control.

QUESTIONS

1. What is the fundamental difference between Hobbes's and Locke's contract theory concepts?

2. The contract theory contends that we should obey the state because we have contractually promised to do so. How, if at all, have you contracted to obey the state?

3. The Declaration of Independence contends that "whenever any Form of Government becomes destructive" of individual life, liberty, and the pursuit of happiness, "it is the Right of the People to alter or to abolish it." Under what circumstances, if any, would you personally exercise this right? Specifically, what conditions must prevail for you to act to alter or abolish your form of government?

SECTION 8.4

Government Control

Regarding the extent to which the state or its primary instrument, government, should enter into the lives of its citizens, two extreme positions are immediately apparent: **anarchism** and **totalitarianism**. Anarchists express unswerving faith in individual ability and show little, if any, confidence in the state. Accordingly, anarchists argue that the state should be abolished as unnecessary. At the other extreme, totalitarians place such strong emphasis on the efficient workings of the state that they are willing to sacrifice most individual rights and interests. Thus, totalitarians believe that government should absorb the whole of human life.

Between these polar opposites are more moderate positions represented by most contractual theories and by our own society. Typifying these positions is a confidence in both individual ability and the reasonably just state that falls short of a total endorsement of either. These moderate views try to maintain a proper balance between claims of the individual and state, between private and public interests.

Clearly no government has ever succeeded in perfectly effecting this moderate theory of government control, but many, including our own, continue to hold it as an ideal. One factor that challenges the realization of this ideal is that individuals and groups who on the one hand espouse it, on the other have leanings to one side or the other: toward confidence in individual ability or in state authority. These leanings are not so pronounced as to warrant the labels *anarchism* or *totalitarianism*. A more accurate classification might term them *individualism* and *paternalism*. In any event, one must understand these leanings in order to understand why it is so difficult in our own society to effect the ideal of a proper balance between the public interest on the one hand and individual interests on the other. So, it would be quite profitable for us to consider individualism and paternalism and show how these interplay with moderate approaches to government control.

INDIVIDUALISM

Some historical background is necessary to understand the philosophy of **individualism**. This can be provided with reference to the contract theory we've just sketched. The earliest formulations of modern contract theory were made against the backdrop of two significant trends. One was the desire to break away from established patterns of thinking. The second was the belief in universal law. (See Chapter 4 for more about the philosophy of materialism.) Here it's enough to emphasize that these two intellectual main currents carried the silt of social, political, and economic developments in the eighteenth and nineteenth centuries, as well as the philosophy of individualism.

For example, the tendency toward freedom and independence was fostered by an economic theory known as **laissez-faire**, which accompanied the industrial revolution. According to this theory, business and commerce should be free from governmental control so that the entrepreneur can pursue free enterprise. Adam Smith (1723–1790), the leading spokesperson for laissez-faire economics, insisted that governmental interference in private enterprise must be reduced, free competition encouraged, and enlightened self-interest made the rule of the day. If commercial interests are left free to pursue self-interest, then the market forces of supply and demand will discipline them into producing efficiently those goods that society most needs and wants. Egoistic pursuits will produce the greatest happiness for the greatest number. The essence of Smith's position can be seen in the following passage from his most influential *The Wealth of Nations*. Notice that Smith, while discussing the need to restrict imports, actually underscores the broad enabling assumption that underlies his economics.

> But the annual revenue of every society is always precisely equal to the exchangeable value of the whole annual produce of its industry, or rather is precisely the same with that exchangeable value. As every individual, therefore, endeavors as much as he can both to employ his capital in the support of domestic industry, and so to direct that industry that its produce may be of the greatest value; every individual necessarily labors to render the annual revenue of the society as great as he can. He generally, indeed, neither intends to promote the public interest, nor knows how much he

PHILOSOPHY AND LIFE 8.3

Stages of Moral Development

Any discussion of social justice that refers to reciprocity, equality, and human dignity is bound to lose a great many people. The reason is that most of us simply don't grasp the abstract principles involved. Why not?

Psychologist Lawrence Kohlberg has thrown as much light on this question as anybody. In his view, individuals pass through three levels of moral development, the pre-conventional, the conventional, and the postconventional. Each of these levels is subdivided into two stages for a total of six stages. Stages 1 and 2 comprise what Kohlberg calls the preconventional level, characterized by unquestioning obedience and the satisfaction of one's own needs. At Stage 1, one's moral views derive almost entirely from cultural labels of good and bad and from the physical power of those who define good and bad. At Stage 2 one generally regards as right whatever satisfies one's own needs. At both of these stages, concepts of fairness, justice, and loyalty are totally absent. Any reciprocity evident operates strictly in an instrumental sense: "You scratch my back, and I'll scratch yours."

At the next, or conventional, level, Kohlberg says that individuals attempt to please others and satisfy social conventions, customs, and laws. Thus, at Stage 3 good conduct is viewed as what pleases and helps others and what is approved by society. Behavior is judged by intention rather than exclusively in terms of consequences. Kohlberg's example of Stage 3 morality: Charlie Brown of *Peanuts* fame. At Stage 4 individuals are still authority oriented but recognize a personal stake in the maintenance of law and order. Thus, Stage 4 morality is characterized by duty to society and respect for the law, which is not yet perceived as a social contract open to change but as being fixed and immutable. Thus, racism may be wrong, but one shouldn't break the law to protest against it, for that invites social chaos.

The last, or postconventional, level represents higher values and the questioning of the existing legal system in the light of social utility and such abstract principles as justice and human dignity. Thus, in Stage 5 a social contract orientation develops, characterized by a recognition of the value of consti-

tutional rights and legal procedures. Here is evident an emphasis on possible change of the social contract, based on social utility. In Kohlberg's view, Stage 5 reasoning represents the "official morality" of the U.S. government and is expressed in the U.S. Constitution. Thus, breaking a law to protest racial inequality would be right if it helped change an unjust law. In Kohlberg's view, some people, but hardly a majority, reach this stage. The final stage, Stage 6, is characterized by an individual's formulating abstract moral principles that are not so much prescriptions for behavior as universal principles of justice, reciprocity, equality, and respect for all people. Few people reach this stage.

QUESTIONS

1. At what stage are you?

2. At what stage are most people whom you know?

3. Research indicates that people cannot comprehend moral reasoning two stages above their own. What are the implications of this for creating a just society?

Adam Smith: "By preferring the support of domestic to that of foreign industry, he intends only his own security; and by directing that industry in such a manner as its produce may be of the greatest value, he intends only his own gain, and he is in this, as in many other cases, led by an invisible hand to promote an end which was no part of his intention."

is promoting it. By preferring the support of domestic to that of foreign industry, he intends only his own security; and by directing that industry in such a manner as its produce may be of the greatest value, he intends only his own gain, and he is in this, as in many other cases, led by an invisible hand to promote an end which was no part of his intention. Nor is it always the worse for the society that it was no part of it. By pursuing his own interest he frequently promotes that of the society more effectually than when he really intends to promote it. I have never known much good done by those who affected to trade for the public good. It is an affection, indeed, not very common among merchants, and very few words need be employed in dissuading them from it.[9]

9. Adam Smith, *The Wealth of Nations* (1776), ed. C. J. Bullock (New York: Colliers, 1909), 379.

Thinkers like Thomas Malthus (1766–1834) and David Ricardo (1772–1823) argued that a natural law or order operated in social affairs as surely as Newton's laws of gravitation and motion operated in nature. Therefore, natural law would regulate prices and wages. Such thinking was bolstered by the nineteenth-century utilitarianism of John Stuart Mill.

Like Smith, Mill feared government interference in the economy. A government should interfere, said Mill, only in those matters for which society itself cannot find solutions. Such matters should be resolved according to the principle of utility, which holds that what is good is that which produces the greatest happiness for the greatest number of people. Under no circumstances should the government unnecessarily restrict individual freedom, including the individual's right to realize as much pleasure and progress for himself as possible.

At least three beliefs characterize the philosophy of individualism as it appeared in the eighteenth and nineteenth centuries: (1) Individuals should be free to pursue their own interests without interference, providing they do not impinge on the rights and interests of others; (2) individuals should be allowed to earn as much money as they can and to spend it however they choose; and (3) individuals should not expect the government to aid or inhibit their economic growth, for such interference only destroys individual incentive and creates indolence. So, in order to combat the antiquated laws and regulations that fettered humans, to keep pace with the scientific discoveries of natural law, and to bury the last vestiges of feudalism, eighteenth- and nineteenth-century thinkers elevated the importance of individualism. These thinkers were termed *liberals* and their political philosophy *liberalism.*

Classical liberalism placed great importance on individual rights, especially those concerning economic matters. The government, these liberals felt, should interfere only as a last resort. John Locke, for example, believed that since we are by nature free, any form of government is an encroachment on that freedom. For Locke, state power was inherently at odds with individual liberty: They govern best who govern least.

Much as happened since that time. Basically, the individual has lost control of the means of production (the means by which a society produces its goods). For one thing—as Karl Marx (1818–1883), whom we will later showcase, observed as early as the middle of the nineteenth century—exorbitant costs, complex machinery, increasing demands, and intense competition have worked against individual productiveness. Specialization in the textile and steel industries has tended to depersonalize the worker. Whereas the economy of the industrial revolution was characterized by relatively free and open competition, the economy of the twentieth century is made up of a relatively few enormous holding companies, which can secretly fix prices, eliminate smaller competitors, and monopolize an industry. Occasionally the government regulates industry, as the Justice Department did in 1974 when it attempted to sever Western Electric from I.T.&T. But most efforts are token and ineffective. Today's corporation apparently wishes government to stay out of its business only when things are going well. Frequently, however, when a company is about to fail, it expects to be subsidized as a "vital industry," as did Penn Central, Pan American Airlines, and Chrysler Corporation. And businesses openly solicit governmental favors in return for political support. Many politicians offer the plums of favorable tariffs, franchises, and laws in return for whopping sums of money. It is little wonder that today we find ourselves largely trying to undo the solutions of the nineteenth century. In so doing, yesterday's liberals often become today's conservatives.

Although generalizations can be dangerously misleading, we might risk saying that today's liberals frequently feel that in many areas the best government is the one that governs *most*. Although they would agree with Locke that individuals are perhaps by nature free, they would add that individuals are *in fact* unfree. Therefore, government should free individuals by vigorously—some would say intrusively—directing social change. People's only hope of gaining freedom and equality, they claim, is through governmental action. Furthermore, they probably would not agree with Locke that state power is inherently at odds with individual liberty. Without governmental interference, they would point out, we'd still have sweatshops, rampant segregation, subminimal wages, inadequate roads and transportation, and substandard schools, colleges, hospitals, and waterworks; and we would be without many services that government now provides. Whereas Locke viewed the adequately structured government as promoting individual liberties and rights and leaving individuals free to earn their own livings as they see fit, contemporary liberals view that kind of government as the reason we have monopolies, ruthless competition, slums, unemployment, and social inequalities. It is that very "rugged individualism" preached by classical liberals that contemporary liberals like Philip Slater[10] say underlies many of our social ills. In brief, today's liberals generally believe that the human condition can be improved by government.

Clearly liberalism today is significantly different from the classical liberalism espoused by John Locke and later by Jeremy Bentham and John Stuart Mill. True, there are similarities: Both types believe that humans are social animals greatly influenced by environment; both claim that the job of government is to promote the general welfare; both uphold the sacredness of life, liberty, and the pursuit of happiness. But the differences are major. Whereas classical liberals tried to limit government, contemporary liberals often expand it. Whereas classical liberals paid only token attention to the state's role in promoting individualism, today's liberals think that strong communal bonds are necessary to preserve individual life, liberty, and the pursuit of happiness, and that government must play a vital role in strengthening these bonds. Finally, whereas classical liberals held individuals ultimately responsible for their own liberty and prosperity, contemporary liberals generally hold political authority responsible for these things. In short, in trying to strike a proper balance between private and public interests, today's liberal generally emphasizes the need for a strong government presence to ensure individual cooperation and opportunity.

---

10. See Philip Slater, *The Pursuit of Loneliness* (Boston: Beacon Press, 1971).

PATERNALISM

Paternalism, sometimes termed *statism*, leans toward a strong state presence and has little confidence in individual ability without the guiding hand of government. Its corresponding economic theory would be socialism, although paternalism can exist without socialism (for example, in pre–French Revolution mercantilist monarchies). When not socialistic, paternalism allows private property but limits the scope of private enterprise in its use. Additionally, paternalism tends to impose regulations on business and charges the state with the duty of undertaking all public works. Although in theory paternalism does not dismiss the value of individual and family, in practice it gives government an active role in directing the affairs of each, as a parent might a child.[11] If we were looking for a political ideology that corresponds with paternalism as classical liberalism does with individualism, then classical *conservatism* would be a likely choice, specifically the conservatism of the English political philosopher Edmund Burke (1729–1797).

Central to Burke's political ideology is a distrust of the individual. Emphasis on individualism, he felt, led to the anarchy of the French Revolution. Certainly, individualism was incompatible with social and political stability, Burke's primary concern. For Burke, society represented an organic and mystic link binding the past, present, and future. The state, therefore, was not an artificial but an organic structure, nourished by religious fervor, patriotism, and faith. This concept of the state as an organism persuaded Burke to preserve tradition, to nurture respect for established institutions such as religion and private property, and to honor whatever had survived for generations. As a result, Burke considered radical changes signs of disaster, contending that all change must evolve naturally and never represent a rupture with the past. Social progress requires reform, not revolution.

Obviously, Burke's political ideas emphasize institutions over individuals. The survival of the state is by far more important than individual

11. See Milton A. Gonsalves, *Fagothey's Right and Reason*, 7th ed. (St. Louis: C. V. Mosby, 1981), 360.

> # Nothing is so galling to a people, not broken in from the birth, as a paternal, or, in other words, a meddling government, a government which tells them what to read and say and eat and drink and wear.
>
> THOMAS B. MACAULAY

interests, which always must be consistent with tradition. Individual rights exist side by side with duties, which, along with faith and loyalty, provide the mortar of a solid society. Unlike liberals, Burke believed that individuals are not by nature equal. This belief, along with his observations of political unrest in Europe, led him to distrust the masses, democracy, and popular rule. As a result, Burke's ideal state is ruled by a landed aristocracy whose circumstances of birth, breeding, and education mark them as natural rulers. Only such aristocrats are capable of enforcing the law and inspiring respect for traditions and institutions.

As is true of classical and contemporary liberals, classical and contemporary conservatives differ in their conceptions of individualism. Whereas Burke showed little if any faith in the individual, today's conservatives seem ambivalent. They often support political proposals that promise to restore traditional moral values and many, though not all, expect the government to initiate programs and pass laws that advance these values (for example, anti-abortion and anti-pornography legislation, the inclusion of creationism theory in public school biology curricula). This desire for government intervention in individual matters appears at odds with conservatives' optimism about the individual's capacity to manage his own economic affairs. Many conservatives resist and oppose government interference in the economic sphere as vigorously as did the classical liberals of the nineteenth century.

Contemporary conservatives frequently argue

that governmental interference is strangling society. If the government would only allow individual states, communities, and people more power of self-determination, problems would straighten out. Instead, they say, the federal government regulates commerce, education, transportation, and utilities more and more. Rather than liberating individuals, government watches over them from cradle to grave, thereby destroying initiative and self-respect. As a result, many conservatives today agree with David Riesman's judgment that "no ideology . . . can justify the sacrifice of an individual to the needs of the group."[12]

Thus, conservatism has maintained its emphasis on order, continuity, traditional institutions, and personal discipline. But, with economic problems increasing, the disparity between the haves and the have-nots more evident than ever, and growing pressure on government to redress these and other inequalities, contemporary conservatives like Nozick seem inclined to define individualism in terms of economic rather than political freedom. Since contemporary liberals like Rawls argue for more governmental involvement to redress economic and social inequities, ideological tension is bound to arise. This tension results from a fundamental difference between liberals, who espouse the greatest possible equality among individuals, and conservatives, who espouse the greatest possible respect for individual rights. At the core of this difference is the aforementioned problem of justice and what constitutes the just society.

The preceding observations should be viewed as cautious generalizations, which are subject to some glaring exceptions because of the various nuances within contemporary liberal and conservative thinking. But there is little question that the differences usually can be accounted for in terms of one's leaning toward individual ability or a strong state. And there is no question that the terms *liberal* and *conservative* are indeed slippery ones whose meanings today sometimes border on diametric opposition to their classical formulations.

But whatever the stripe of today's liberal or conservative, whether the leaning is toward individual initiative or a strong authoritarian state, both believe in varying solutions to the same key problem. That problem concerns striking a proper balance between private and public interests. In other words, both espouse the middle way between anarchism and totalitarianism. What's more, they believe that government should positively assist private initiative for the common good.

One very important power implied in the belief that government has a definite role in helping individuals advance the general welfare is that the government has the right and duty to pass laws. Indeed, when we think of "law," what comes first to mind is the law of the state. This is what the great Christian philosopher and theologian Saint Thomas Aquinas seemingly had in mind when he gave his classical definition of law as "nothing else than an ordinance of reason for the common good promulgated by him who has care of the community."[13] So, although there are various moderate views on government control, all these views share the belief that, whatever the proper balance between individual and state, the state and government have the right and duty to exercise control through law. So important is law in distinguishing between private and public rights and interests, in articulating the basic tenets of contract theory, that it warrants our attention.

QUESTIONS

1. In *The Pursuit of Loneliness*, Philip Slater contends that our cultural emphasis on individualism is frustrating the spirit of community that is needed to solve many of our social problems. This love for individualism is warring against "the wish to live in trust and fraternal cooperation with one's fellows in a total and visible collective entity."[14] Do you agree that the United States is experiencing this

12. David Riesman, *Individualism Reconsidered* (Garden City, N.Y.: Doubleday, 1954), 27.

13. Saint Thomas Aquinas, *Summa Theologica*, in *Basic Writings of Saint Thomas*, vol. 2, ed. Anton Pegis (New York: Random House, 1968), 4.

14. Slater, *Pursuit of Loneliness*, 27.

cultural emphasis and that it is having the consequences that Slater sees?

2. Slater also argues that "our approach to social
problems is to decrease their visibility: out of sight,
out of mind. This is the real foundation of racial
segregation, especially its most extreme case, the
Indian 'reservation.' The result of our social effort
has been to remove the underlying problems of our
society farther and farther from daily experience
and daily consciousness, and hence to decrease, in
the mass of the population, the knowledge, skill,
resources and motivation necessary to deal with
them."[15] Do you agree?

3. Do you agree with Riesman's statement "No
ideology, however noble, can justify the sacrifice
of an individual to the needs of the group"?

4. In what ways can excessive concern with individualism actually undermine individualism?

5. How true to the laissez-faire ideal is our present
economy?

6. Is Mill's political philosophy consistent with his
ethical philosophy, which argues that the moral
action is one that produces the greatest happiness
for the most people?

7. How realizable today is Mill's belief that "the
only freedom which deserves the name, is that of
pursuing our own good in our own way, so long as
we do not attempt to deprive others of theirs, or
impede their efforts to obtain it"?

8. Burke believed that the state has the right to
compel the individual to conform to its ideas of
social and personal excellence. Do you agree that
in certain areas the state has this right? In what
areas? Are there areas today in which the state is
exercising a right you believe it does not have?

9. "Democrats are generally liberal and Republi-
cans are generally conservative." Do you agree with
this generalization? Would you prefer to qualify the
statement by specifying an area (economics, for
example)? What are the connotations of *liberal* and
conservative? Cite particular politicians you would
misrepresent by putting them into either of these
categories.

---

15. Ibid., 15.

SECTION 8.5

Law

Traditionally, the line of demarcation between
the individual and society has been the *law*, by
which we mean a rule or body of rules that tell
individuals what they may and may not do.

Our Western legal system, which we have
inherited from the Judeo-Christian tradition, is a
hierarchy of laws. For example, when a town law
and a state law conflict, the state law takes precedence. Likewise, federal laws take precedence
over state laws. Does anything take precedence over
federal law, over the so-called law of the land? Both
the Jewish and the Christian traditions maintain
allegiance to a law that transcends any state, which
they have historically referred to as the "law of
God." We find a similar concept in ancient Greek
philosophy.

The Stoics, members of the school of thought
founded by Zeno around 300 B.C., believed that
the world does not operate by blind chance but by
reason. The universe, they believed, is rational, in
the sense that it operates according to laws that
the human mind can discover. This orderliness or
world reason the Stoics termed *nature* and *logos*
("word"). Since people are happy when they act
in accordance with nature—with the order of the
universe—the purpose of institutions, according to
the Stoics, is to enact laws that reflect this single
universal law. Thus, what we today call *civic laws*
have their basis in natural law. Natural law generally refers to (1) a pattern of necessary and universal regularity holding in physical nature or (2)
a moral imperative, a description of what ought to

Saint Thomas Aquinas: "Law is nothing else than an ordinance of reason for the common good promulgated by him who has care of the community."

happen in human relationships. It's the second definition that concerns us here.

The Christian philosopher and theologian Saint Augustine presented a well-thought-out scheme of law in his *City of God*. In fact, Augustine's thought influenced Saint Thomas Aquinas, who in the Middle Ages distinguished among several kinds of law. First is divine or eternal law—that is, God's decrees for the governance of the universe. According to Thomas, all things obey eternal law, and how they behave simply reflects this law. Thus, a flame rises and a stone falls. God, then, is the lawmaker of the universe; things behave as they do because He so decrees it.

The eternal law also applies to humans, but in humans this law is merely a moral imperative that humans are free to disobey. Morality, as Thomas conceived it, is not an arbitrary set of rules for behavior; rather, the basis of moral obligation is built into the very nature of the human in the form of various inclinations, such as the preservation of life, the propagation of the species, and the search

for truth. The moral law, then, is founded on these natural inclinations and the ability of reason to discern the right course of conduct. The rules of conduct corresponding to these inherent human features are called natural law.

A good part of Thomas's theory of natural law had already been worked through by Aristotle. In *Ethics*, Aristotle distinguished between natural and conventional justice. According to Aristotle, some forms of behavior are wrong because they violate a local law that has been passed to regulate that behavior in that particular jurisdiction. To use a contemporary example, consider the laws many localities pass against jaywalking. Since the law is local and depends completely on the decisions of the local inhabitants, such a law is *conventional*, not *natural*. In contrast, Aristotle argued that some laws are based on human nature and on the nature of our societies. The behavior they prohibit is wrong under any circumstances. Murder and theft are two examples. These are wrong not because a particular group has passed laws against them but because they run counter to the social nature of human beings: Humans must live in societies, and societies cannot survive without such laws. Both Aristotle and Thomas believed that humans can discover the natural basis for human conduct through reason. But Thomas went further, contending that the human's existence and nature can only be understood in relation to God.

For Thomas, then, law deals primarily with reason. Our reason uncovers the rules and standards to which human behavior should conform. Law consists of these rules and standards for human acts and is therefore based on reason. What's more, the natural law is dictated by reason. Since God created everything, human nature and natural law are best comprehended as the product of God's wisdom or reason.

In summary, for Thomas, natural law consists of that portion of the eternal law that pertains directly to humans. The basic precepts of the natural law are preservation of life, propagation and education of offspring, and the pursuit of truth and a peaceful society. These precepts reflect God's intentions for the human in creation and can be discovered and understood by reason.

Martin Luther King, Jr.: "Any law that uplifts human personality is just. Any law that degrades human personality is unjust. All segregation statutes are unjust because segregation distorts the soul and damages the personality."

Although these precepts do not vary, their enforcement does. Since different societies are influenced by different topographies, climates, cultures, and social customs, Thomas believed that different codes of justice are needed. He called these specific codes of justice *human law*. The function of rulers is to formulate human law by informing themselves of the specific needs of their communities and then passing appropriate decrees. So, whereas natural law is general enough to govern the community of all humans, human law is specific enough to meet the requirements of a particular society.

For Thomas, then, there are two points of difference between human law and natural or divine law. First, human law applies to a specific group,

society, or community; second, it is the expressed decrees of a human agent and not the laws operating in the universe at large. Nevertheless, a human law is a law because it articulates divine law. That is, human law is not law because it emanates from a legislator or ruler but because it implements divine law.

From Thomas's theory of law we can draw one conclusion that is particularly relevant to our discussion: Subjects have the right to rebel. This conclusion follows from his idea that human law must be obeyed only when it expresses natural law. Since humans are capable of poor judgment, rulers can pass unjust laws that are not in accord with natural law.

In his famous "Letter from Birmingham Jail," civil rights leader Martin Luther King, Jr., relied in part on this point to defend his civil disobedience of segregation laws.

> A just law is a man-made code that squares with the moral law or the Law of God. An unjust law is a code that is out of harmony with the moral law. To put it in the terms of Saint Thomas Aquinas: An unjust law is a human law that is not rooted in eternal law and natural law. Any law that uplifts human personality is just. Any law that degrades human personality is unjust. All segregation statutes are unjust because segregation distorts the soul and damages the personality. It gives the segregator a false sense of superiority and the segregated a false sense of inferiority.[16]

But when people refer to a higher law, they do not always mean a religious or God-given law. Many men who refused to fight in the Vietnam war, for example, were no doubt atheists, but they felt that to fight would violate their personal code of behavior. By higher law, then, we mean any law that an individual considers to take precedence over the body of rules that governs the activities within the state. When people appeal to a higher law, presumably they feel that the state has exceeded its rightful authority over them. But precisely when is this?

---

16. Martin Luther King, Jr., "Letter from Birmingham Jail," in *The Norton Reader*, 3d ed., ed. Arthur M. Eastman (New York: Norton, 1973), 665.

When does the state exceed its authority over the individual? To what extent do the government and the public interest have authority over individuals and individual action? This question assumes special importance in the light of psychological studies that show how reluctant people are to question authority (see Philosophy and Life 8.4). The answer to this question, in part, calls for an examination of freedom and its relation to the law.

FREEDOM

Were we concerned with and should we value only efficiency in government, then any evaluation of the rightful limits of governmental authority would be relatively simple. Only required would be a determination of whether or not government intrusions as exercised through law best serve public interest. By this strictly social utility account, it is entirely possible that the most authoritarian government might prove the most efficient. Indeed, a popular explanation for the relative ease with which the Soviet Union, compared with the United States, can marshall its citizens behind a policy or program is that by nature a totalitarian regime does not require a consensus of national opinion as a democracy does.

But clearly in our society we are concerned with more than efficiency, more than a well-oiled governmental machine. We are also concerned with justice and individual rights. To be sure, efficiency is not always compatible with the dictates of justice and individual rights, both of which contract theory regards as of paramount importance. The trouble is that contract theory is not clear about the status of individual rights. One of those rights, which concerns us here, is freedom.

The kind of freedom we have in mind can be called political and social freedom, which includes the freedoms of speech, religion, and governance. History records many heroic battles fought to secure these freedoms as well as to win equality, that is, the same treatment for all citizens in a state. Freedom finds what may be its classic description in John Stuart Mill's essay On Liberty, in which the British social and political philosopher presents a powerful case for political individualism.

One of Mill's concerns is the freedom of the individual. He is specifically concerned with what actions individuals in society may perform. In essence, Mil claims that society may interfere with the individual in matters involving other people but not in matters involving only the individual. In effect, he distinguishes between two spheres of interest, the outer and the inner. A matter belongs to the outer sphere if it involves more than just a few individuals and to the inner if it involves only the self or a few others. The following excerpt from On Liberty captures the spirit of Mill's position:

> What, then, is the rightful limit to the sovereignty of the individual over himself? Where does the authority of society begin? How much of human life should be assigned to individuality, and how much to society?
>
> Each will receive its proper share, if each has that which more particularly concerns it. To individuality should belong the part of life in which it is chiefly the individual that is interested; to society, the part which chiefly interests society.
>
> Though society is not founded on a contract, and though no good purpose is answered by inventing a contract in order to deduce social obligations from it, everyone who receives the protection of society owes return for the benefit, and the fact of living in society renders it indispensable that each should be bound to observe a certain line of conduct towards the rest. This conduct consists, first, in not injuring the interests of one another; or rather certain interests, which, either by express legal provision or by tacit understanding, ought to be considered as rights; and secondly, in each person's bearing his share (to be fixed on some equitable principle) of the labors and sacrifices incurred for defending the society or its members from injury and molestation. These conditions society is justified in enforcing, at all costs to those who endeavor to withhold fulfillment. Nor is that all that society may do. The acts of an individual may be hurtful to others, or wanting in due consideration for their welfare, without going to the length of violating any of their constituted rights. The offender may then be justly punished by opinion, though not by law. As soon as any part of a person's conduct affects prejudicially the interests of others, society has jurisdiction over it, and the question whether the general welfare will

or will not be promoted by interfering with it, becomes open to discussion. But there is no room for entertaining any such question when a person's conduct affects the interests of no persons besides himself, or need not affect them unless they like (all the persons concerned being of full age, and the ordinary amount of understanding). In all such cases, there should be perfect freedom, legal and social, to do the action and stand the consequences.[17]

Although Mill appears to have drawn some line of demarcation between society and individual, the distinction seems fuzzy. Just how many constitute "a few others"? Furthermore, Mill argues that since the individual and not society is the best judge of what advances self-interest, the individual should be free from interference in such pursuits. But it seems that we do not always know our best interests. Suppose a man who enjoys heroin "shoots up" every day. This matter might fall within the inner sphere, in which case he should be free from interference. Yet his behavior is probably not in his best interests. Therefore, it could easily be argued that his behavior should be interfered with.

The problem is that Mill's concept of freedom guarantees noninterference but not much else. What kind of freedom allows a drug addict to shoot himself into oblivion? This kind of freedom is a negative freedom, a "freedom-from." These are the kinds of freedom guaranteed us by the Bill of Rights—freedoms from outside influence. But perhaps something more positive is needed, a "freedom-to."

Freedoms-to are positive freedoms that guarantee people certain goods: the right to an education; the right to medical care; the right to a decent neighborhood; the right to equal opportunity regardless of race, national origin, or sex; and the right to equal pay for work of equal worth. When the freedoms-to are combined with the freedoms-from, we seem to have a better description of political and social freedom and of a climate favorable to personal security and growth. Just as important, we have a basis for viewing law as an essential part of freedom rather than just a limit on it.

Without understanding the distinction between negative and positive freedoms, we are hard pressed to understand intense social unrest. For example, seeing freedom only as freedoms-from, we would probably say that all Americans are equally free. But the concept of freedom-to clearly shows that some of us are freer than others. Without certain freedoms-to, some people will have very little freedom.

A currently divisive issue in the United States, as we have seen, is how much the government should interfere to guarantee freedoms-to. Some contend that there is already too much interference, that the executive, legislative, and particularly the judicial branches of government are poking their collective noses into areas where they do not belong. In short, there are too many bad laws. Others claim that governmental interference is needed, that society has grown too unwieldy for individuals to fight their own battles for freedom. In short, there are too few good laws. Although these positions differ in their solutions, they are concerned with the same central problem that has occupied us throughout this chapter: how to best strike a balance between public and private interest. In other words, they are concerned with the problem of justice.

QUESTIONS

1. What laws, if any, do you regard as unjust? Why?

2. Does the state have the right to make laws concerning homosexuality, pornography, and marijuana?

3. To what extent do you feel that your own ability to live as you believe is limited by laws?

4. Do you think that every American has a right to a college education?

5. Do you think that every American has a right to medical care?

6. Do you believe that all people have the right to determine the political system under which they live? If you do, does one state have a moral obli-

---

17. John Stuart Mill, *On Liberty* (1859) (London: J. M. Dent, 1910), 77–78.

gation to assist another that is fighting to exercise that right? Is there any point at which that obligation ends?

CHAPTER SUMMARY AND CONCLUSIONS

We opened this chapter by keying on a recurring issue in any determination of the proper relation between individual and society: the problem of justice. One influential theory, developed by Plato and Aristotle, associates justice with merit. Another, developed primarily by English philosophers such as Hobbes, Locke, Hume, and especially Mill, associates justice with social utility. Still another, most recently articulated by John Rawls, identifies

justice with equality and aid to the disadvantaged. The problem of justice is related to but distinct from a second issue: the basis on which the power and authority of the state may be justified. While there are a number of theories of the legitimacy of the state, contract theory is the view on which our own society's conception of power and governance is based. Even if the power of the state can be justified by contract theory, we can always ask about the extent of government control: To what extent ought the state and its primary instrument, government, exercise its authority and power over the individual? In response, two extreme views are identifiable. Anarchism has unflinching confidence in the individual and none in the state; by contrast, totalitarianism shows confidence in a strong

---

PHILOSOPHY AND LIFE 8.4

The Milgram Studies

To what extent will people in our society follow the orders of those thought to be in authority? Apparently to a considerable extent. At least that's what a series of experiments conducted by Stanley Milgram indicates.

Milgram's experiments consisted of asking subjects to administer strong electric shocks to people whom the subjects couldn't see. The subjects could supposedly control the shock's intensity by means of a shock generator with thirty clearly marked voltages, ranging from 15 to 450 volts and labeled from "Slight Shock (15)" to "XXX—Danger! Severe Shock (450)."

The entire experiment, of course, was contrived: No one was actually administering or receiving a shock. The subjects were led to believe that the "victims" were

being shocked as part of an experiment to determine the effect of punishment on memory. The victims, who were in fact confederates of the experimenters, were strapped in their seats with electrodes attached to their wrists "to avoid blistering and burning." They were told to make no noise until a "300-volt shock" was administered, at which point they were to make noise loud enough for the subjects to hear (for example, pounding on the walls as if in pain). The subjects were reassured that the shocks, though extremely painful, would cause no permanent tissue injury.

When asked, a number of psychologists said that no more than 10 percent would honor the request to administer a 450-volt shock. In fact, well over half did—twenty-six out of forty. Even after hearing the

victims' pounding, 87.5 percent of the subjects (thirty-five out of forty) applied more voltage. The conclusions seem unmistakable: A significant number of people in society, when urged by legitimate authority and when being paid, will hurt others.

QUESTIONS

1. Under what conditions, if any, does society have the right to expect its members to kill or injure other human beings?

2. Under what conditions, if any, may individuals refuse?

3. In order to conduct this experiment, experimenters had to lie to subjects and expose them to considerable stress. Do you think that was moral? If so, on what grounds?

The Third of May, Francisco Goya. "To what extent ought the state and its primary instrument, government, exercise its authority and power over the individual?"

state and government, and little if any in the individual. The consensus view in our own society falls somewhere between these extremes, with leanings toward individualism, that is, willing individual cooperation; or paternalism, confidence in a strong authoritarian state. These leanings show up, respectively, in what we term political conservatism and liberalism, both of which differ significantly from their classical formulations. Whatever their leaning, contract theorists believe that the state and government have the right and duty to exercise control through law, which traditionally has demarcated individual and society. Laws guarantee freedoms-from, but in a broader sense they also guarantee freedoms-to.

From time immemorial men and women have valued individualism as experienced through freedom and liberties. Indeed, individualism has been the most influential philosophy of freedom in modern Western society. Whether we talk of economic, religious, or political freedom, the emphasis is on the individual. The philosophy of individualism is rooted in the valuing of the human personality and the conviction that human progress relies on the free exercise of individual energy.

The purposes of individualism seem commendable enough. As sociologist Robert Nisbet points out in *The Quest for Community*: "No fault is to be found with the declared purposes of individualism. As a philosophy it has correctly emphasized the fact that the ultimate criteria of freedom lie in the greater or lesser degrees of autonomy possessed by *persons*. A conception of freedom that does not center upon the ethical primacy of the person is either naive or malevolent."[18]

---

18. This and other Nisbet quotes are from: Robert Nisbet, *The Quest for Community* (New York: Oxford University Press, 1953).

But, as Nisbet observes, the unquestioned ethical centrality of the individual does not make an inherited eighteenth- or nineteenth-century philosophy of individualism equally valid. The reason is that, historically, individualism is more than an ethic. It is also a psychology and an implied theory of the relation between people and their institutions. In Nisbet's view, many of the difficulties with the philosophy of individualism that we presently face stem from an unconscious effort to keep the ethical aspect of individualism alive when we have overlooked and even tried to suppress the psychological and sociological premises of this philosophy. To fully appreciate Nisbet's valuable remarks, we must first separate the assumptions of classical individualism from those of contemporary individualism.

When the fundamental principles of individualism were being formulated in the doctrine of classical liberalism, the human was viewed as a self-sufficient, rational, stable, and secure being who moved inexorably toward freedom and order. In short, the human was idealized as being equipped with both the instincts and the reason that could make it autonomous. In retrospect, we can now see how thinkers actually abstracted certain moral and psychological characteristics from a social organization and attributed them to individuals, rendering those characteristics the "timeless, natural qualities of the *individual*, who was regarded as independent of the influences of any historically developed social organization." In other words, the qualities given to persons actually were qualities of a set of institutions or groups, all of which were aspects of historical tradition.

Recall Hobbes. With the laws of mechanics and motions before him, Hobbes reduced everything to human atoms in motion. Just as the physical scientists of the day dealt with physical atoms in space, so did Hobbes try to build theoretical systems on human atoms alone. Like others, he strived to develop his social and political thought from the purest resources of reason, from the rigorous development of potentialities that reason taught lay everywhere in human nature.

As Nisbet sees it, institutions and groups were rendered secondary, "as shadows, so to speak, of the solid reality of men," to the inherent rationality and self-sufficiency of humans. Inevitably the strategy of freedom became one of releasing individuals from institutional shackles. In short, while the philosophy of individualism began with an emphasis on the ethical primacy of the individual, it evolved into a rationalist psychology bent on freeing individuals from traditional associations and cultures. Only in this way, it was argued, could the truly free individual unfold.

What emerged in the eighteenth century and developed in the nineteenth, then, were systems of economic, religious, and intellectual freedom founded on the assumption that the essence of human behavior lies within the individual and not in the relation between the individual and institutions. Hence rose the dichotomy between persons and society. The free society was ideally conceptualized as one in which individuals were free from groups, institutions, and classes. It would consist of socially and morally separated individuals. Social order would result from a natural equilibrium of economic and political forces. As Nisbet puts it: "Freedom would arise from the individual's release from all the inherited personal interdependencies of traditional community; and from his existence in an impersonal, natural, economic order."

This self-discovery and self-consciousness swelled as society assumed more and more of an impersonal, mechanical structure. Ultimately, the price of individual freedom was viewed as detachment from the world, a defining of society in strictly objective, impersonal terms. What we have, then, is something quite remarkable—in Nisbet's words, "the conception of society as an aggregate of morally autonomous, psychologically free individuals, rather than as a collection of groups." Politically, this roughly translated into a society that abstracts all legitimate influence and authority from primary communities (for example, family, religion, professional organizations, and so on) and invests them in the state. This setup is what contract theorists seem to have in mind. Thus, Hobbes had no affection for associations based on locality, interest, faith, kinship, or household. He brooked no system of authority other than the state, which he believed best allows individuals to pursue rational self-interest. Similarly, Rousseau believed the state would effectuate the independence of the individual from society by realizing the individual's dependence on self. For Rousseau, the state, the "General Will," was the instrument for freeing individuals from tyrannical societal restrictions.

"What is significant here," writes Nisbet, "is that when the philosophical individualists were dealing with the assumed nature of man, they were dealing in large part with a hypothetical being created by their political imagination." The truth of this observation is apparent in the thinking of nineteenth-century English liberals, nearly all of whom conceived of freedom as emancipation from custom, tradition, and every kind of local group. In short, freedom lay outside association, not within. Mill is a perfect example of this thinking. In *On Liberty* he clearly implies that community or association membership is an unfortunate restriction on the individual's creative powers. Today we don't quarrel with Mill's concept of individuality, but we do puzzle over his necessary conditions for the full development of individualism.

Even a cursory look at the studies in modern social psychology reveals increasing numbers of people seeking communal refuge. A large and growing area of psychology and social science emphasizes the contemporary preoccupation with disintegration and disorganization, as evidenced by numerous studies of community and family disor-ganization, personality disorientation, industrial alienation, and dissolution of ethnic subcultures. Numerous studies have detailed the rise of the nuclear family (parents and children living in a household) and the decline of the extended family (parents, children, and other blood relatives living in a household). "However empirical his studies of social relationships," Nisbet writes, "however bravely he rearranges the semantic elements of his terminology to support the belief in his own moral detachment, and however confidently he may sometimes look to the salvational possibilities of political legislation for moral relief, it is plain that the contemporary student of human relations is haunted by perceptions of disorganization and the possibility of endemic collapse." Thirty years ago, Kingsley Davis, one of America's foremost sociologists, made the same point when he asked, "Can the anonymity, mobility, impersonality, specialization, and sophistication of the city become the attributes of a stable society, or will society fall apart?"[19] Questions and observations like these point up that the eighteenth- and nineteenth-century rationalist image of the human is inadequate in theory and unacceptable in practice. We realize today that we are not self-sufficient in social isolation, that human nature cannot be deduced simply from the constituents of our germ plasma, and that an individual is vitally connected to social groups. We realize that these affiliations must be acknowledged.

As a theoretical construct, individualism was tolerable when the primary elements of social organization were still vital and psychologically meaningful. Indeed, it was extremely useful when these elements were overbearing and oppressive. But today classical individualism lacks this pragmatic justification. Now the main psychological problem is not release but reintegration.

An essential tenet of contemporary psychology and sociology is that individuality cannot be studied or understood except as the product of value-oriented human interactions. In other words, we

---

Those who cannot remember the past are condemned to repeat it.

GEORGE SANTAYANA

What experience and history teach us is this—that people and governments never have learned anything from history, or acted on principles deduced from it.

G. W. F. HEGEL

---

19. Kingsley Davis, *Human Society* (New York: Macmillan, 1949), 342.

cannot comprehend human nature without considering the vast array of social norms and cultural incentives. Furthermore, because culture is always the product of social relationships, the influence of these social relationships must be recognized to understand human nature. Nisbet expresses this point well: "The greatest single lesson to be drawn from the social transformations of the twentieth century, from the phenomena of individual insecurity and the mass quest for community, is that the intensity of men's motivations toward freedom and cultures is unalterably connected with the relationships of a social organization that has structural coherence and functional significance. From innumerable observations and controlled studies we have learned that the discipline of values *within* a person has a close and continuing relationship with the discipline of values supported by human inter-relationships." In other words, only by fixing their own conduct in a group's culture can individuals keep their own beliefs and values secure in the face of the ceaseless fluctuations of moods, influences, and stimuli that assault them today.

In the late 1960s and 1970s, a communitarian consciousness emerged that showed a strong tendency to transcend the narrow bounds of individualism enunciated by classical liberalism. One result of this trend was experimental living ventures that attracted millions of people. Some of these communal living arrangements were highly organized and philosophically grounded; others consisted of a handful of persons who lived in the same house and shared resources. Communal living arrangements continue to exist, although their popularity has declined since the sixties, and they are organized on a variety of bases. They may be democratic, anarchistic, or headed by a single charismatic leader. The organizing principles may be religious-spiritual and political, solely political, or psychological, or there may be no established values at all. Whatever the setup, the most important ingredient to the success of such communities is almost always the closeness among the individuals. Communes that don't offer their members some intimate contact seem to dissolve within a short time.[20]

It would be grossly inaccurate to characterize such experimental living alternatives as being anti-individual. On the contrary, they all seem to recognize the need to define self within an associative context. Unable to satisfy this need within the framework of a "superstate," organizers have attempted to satisfy it by re-creating basic historical, social, and interpersonal relations. They seem determined to end the bifurcation between individual and society that emerged in the eighteenth and nineteenth centuries. At the same time, history records the horrific evolution of group experiments into totalitarian states when they reduce a complex world to cant formulas and accept belief systems that respond to dogma or a megalomaniac's discipline, as at Jonestown.[21] Ironically, such groups often end up re-creating what they try to escape.

There are many lessons to be learned from such failures. An important one in this discussion's context is that we cannot live outside history. Groups that try to do so become infected with nostalgia for some lost Eden and thus become spiritually enslaved; such communities become breeding grounds for intolerance, passivity, and paranoia. Our challenge is to create a society that both allows people to live within history and gives expression to their spiritual longings, that is, to strike a proper balance between individual and society.

In the new age, the dominant note in the corporate consciousness of communities is a sense of being parts of some larger universe, whereas, in the age which is now over the dominant note in their consciousness was an aspiration to be universes in themselves.

ARNOLD TOYNBEE

---

20. See R. M. Kanter, "Communes," *Psychology Today* 4:2.
21. See "Nightmare in Jonestown," *Time*, 4(December 1978): 27.

Marx and Rawls

Two philosophies tend to dominate much of our contemporary debate over the appropriate nature of our society: Marxism and liberalism. These two philosophies, in fact, tend to dominate much of the thinking of the societies that make up the modern world. The democratic and capitalist nations mainly adhere to the tenets of liberalism, while the socialist and communist nations primarily adopt the tenets of Marxism.

It is appropriate, therefore, for us to showcase in this chapter on society two thinkers—Karl Marx and John Rawls—who present and argue for the principles underlying these two dominant social philosophies. The writings of Marx are the origins of those social philosophies that call themselves "Marxist," while John Rawls is considered by many to have articulated the central principles of modern liberalism. Examining the views of these two major modern thinkers will enable us to more clearly understand what is at stake in current debates over what our society should be like.

MARX

On several occasions in this chapter and elsewhere in our study, we have alluded to Karl Marx. So seminal a social philosopher of the modern age is Marx, and so widely misunderstood, that we will focus on him in this showcase.

Karl Marx was born in 1818 in Trier in the Rhineland to Jewish parents who, faced with anti-Semitism, turned Lutheran. After completing his course of studies at the gymnasium in Trier, Marx went on to study at the universities of Bonn and Berlin.

When Marx entered the University of Berlin in 1836, the dominant intellectual influence throughout Germany and at the university was the philosophy of Georg Hegel (1770–1831). Central to Hegel's thought was that reality is not fixed and static, but changing and dynamic. Life is constantly passing from one stage of being to another; the world is a place of constant change. But Hegel did not believe the change itself is arbitrary. On the contrary, he thought it proceeds according to a well-defined pattern or method, termed a *dialectic*.

The idea of the dialectic is that reality is full of contradictions. As reality unfolds, the contradictions are resolved and something new emerges. The procedure of the dialectical method can be represented as follows:

> Thesis: assertion of position or affirmation
>
> Antithesis: assertion of opposite position or negation
>
> Synthesis: union of the two opposites

The Hegelian **dialectic** presumably expresses the process of development that Hegel believed pervades everything. By this account, there is only one reality: Idea. The only thing that is real is the rational; the Idea is thought itself thinking itself out. The process of thought thinking itself out is the dialectic.

In thinking itself out, thought arrives at the main antithesis to itself: inert matter. At this point Idea objectifies itself in matter: It becomes Nature, or, for Hegel, the creation of the world. Life is the first sign of synthesis. Thought reappears in matter, organizing plants and displaying conscious instinct in animals. Ultimately, thought arrives at self-consciousness in human beings. The dialectic continues through human history.

In order to understand a society or culture, therefore, it is crucial to recognize the dialectical process that is operating. Each period in the history of a culture or society has a character of its own. This character can be viewed as a stage in the development from what preceded it to what follows it. This development proceeds by laws that basi-

Karl Marx: "What constitutes the alienation of labor? First, that the work is *external* to the worker, that it is not part of his nature; and that, consequently, he does not fulfill himself in his work but denies himself, has a feeling of misery rather than well-being, does not develop freely his mental and physical energies but is physically exhausted and mentally debased."

cally are mental or spiritual. In effect, a culture has a personality of its own, which largely accounts for its development. Indeed, by Hegel's reckoning, the whole world or all of reality can be identified with a single character or personality—with what Hegel variously called *the Absolute, world self,* or *God* (taken in a pantheistic sense). All of human history, then, can be viewed as the progressive realization of this Absolute Spirit that is the synthesis of the thesis, Idea thinking itself out, with the antithesis, Idea spread out into Nature.

While at the University of Berlin, Marx read Hegel's complete works. He was drawn to a revolutionary aspect of Hegel's philosophy, namely, that history moves through a dialectical process of development. Marx also joined the Berlin Club of Young Hegelians, but soon became convinced that

philosophy alone was inadequate to change the world. What was needed was social and political action.

After completing his doctoral dissertation in 1841, Marx turned to socialistic journalism, taking an editorial position in 1842 at the *Rheinische Zeitung (Rhineland Gazette)*. In this position, Marx became familiar with the social problems of the day and deepened the social orientation of his thought. Soon he became editor-in-chief of the newspaper and took it in a radical direction, conducting a campaign against Christian religion and the Christian state. As a result, the newspaper was shut down by the state censor in March 1843.

The suppression of the *Rheinische Zeitung* marked a new period in Marx's intellectual development, during which he began to formulate his materialistic concept of history and eventually became a communist. Also during this time, which he spent in Paris, Marx turned to a critical examination of Hegelian thought, and in 1843 published an article on the subject: "Introduction to the Critique of Hegel's Philosophy." The article portrayed religion as an illusion resulting from the fact that the world is alienated and estranged from its real nature. Total revolution, Marx argued, is necessary to turn and emancipate society from this condition. Marx's critique of Hegel was significantly influenced by the work of Ludwig Feuerbach.

In his *Essence of Christianity* (1841), Feuerbach had tried to show that Hegel's idealism was wrongheaded in that it had succeeded in eliminating physical reality. By contrast, Feuerbach held that philosophy is the science of reality, which consists in physical nature. Part of the illusion Feuerbach saw in Hegel was Hegel's belief in Absolute Spirit or God progressively realizing itself in history. In fact, according to Feuerbach, the ideas of religion are produced by human beings as a reflection of their own needs. Because individuals are dissatisfied or "alienated" in their practical lives, they need to believe in illusions such as those fostered in Hegelian philosophy. Thus, metaphysics is no more than an "esoteric psychology"; it is the expression of feelings within ourselves rather than truths about the universe. In particular, religion is the expression of alienation. Individuals can be freed from the illusions of religion only by realizing their purely human destiny in this world.

Feuerbach's influence on Marx was such that Marx grew convinced that dialectical philosophy could avoid idealism by starting from human reality rather than from an ideal Absolute Spirit. Also, it could avoid mechanistic materialism by taking the concrete nature of the human being as its initial principle.

While his reading of Feuerbach did alter Marx's view of Hegel, Marx nevertheless did preserve Hegel's notion of historical development and of alienation. These he wove into his own materialist concept of history. Like Hegel, Marx saw historical development operating in things, but it was not spiritual, rather material in character. The key to all history lay not in the individual's idea, but in the economic conditions of his or her life. Again, while culling Hegel's notion of alienation, Marx did not see it as metaphysical or religious in nature, but social and economic. Marx's view of alienation can be found in his "Economic and Philosophic Manuscripts" (1844). His materialistic concepts of history can be found in various works of the same period: *The Holy Family* (1845), *The German Ideology* (1846), and *The Poverty of Philosophy* (1847).

Until recently, Marx was best known as the author of *Das Kapital* (1867) and the *Communist Manifesto* (1848), which he coauthored with friend and collaborator Friedrich Engels. Today, largely as a result of the publication of his early writings, the philosophical aspect of Marx's work has caught scholars' attention. Indeed, it is now thought that Marx's later writings cannot be fully understood and interpreted without reference to his earlier works, especially "Economic and Philosophic Manuscripts" and *The German Ideology*.

View of History

Distinctive in Marx's understanding of the world as a whole is his interpretation of history. Marx was firmly convinced that he had discovered a scientific method for studying the history of human societies, that eventually there would be a single science that would include the science of mankind along with natural science. Accordingly, he held that there are universal laws behind historical change. Just as we can predict things like eclipses, we can predict the future large-scale course of history from a knowledge of these laws. Just as physicists aim to uncover the natural laws of the universe, so Marx believed he was laying bare the economic laws of modern society, the material laws of capitalist production. These laws, presumably, are working with iron necessity toward inevitable results.

Like Hegel, Marx held that each period in each culture has its own character and personality. Therefore, the only true universal laws in history are those concerned with the process of development whereby one stage gives rise to the next. He viewed this developmental process as roughly divided into the Asiatic, the ancient, the feudal, and the "bourgeois" or capitalist phases. When conditions are right, said Marx, each stage must give way to the next. Ultimately, capitalism will give way to communism. Writing with Engels in the *Communist Manifesto*, Marx puts it this way:

> The history of all hitherto existing society is the history of class struggles.
> Freeman and slave, patrician and plebian, lord and serf, guild-master and journeyman, in a word, oppressor and oppressed, stood in constant opposition to one another, carried on an uninterrupted, now hidden, now open fight, a fight that each time ended, either in a revolutionary re-constitution of society at large, or in the common ruin of the contending classes.
> In the earlier epochs of history, we find almost everywhere a complicated arrangement of society into various orders, a manifold gradation of social rank. In ancient Rome we have patricians, knights, plebians, slaves; in the middle ages, feudal lords, vassals, guild-masters, journeymen, apprentices, serfs; in almost all of these classes, again, subordinate gradations.
> The modern bourgeois society that has sprouted from the ruins of feudal society, has not done away with class antagonisms. It has but established new classes, new conditions of oppression, new forms of struggle in place of the old ones.
> Our epoch, the epoch of the bourgeoisie, possesses, however, this distinctive feature; it has simplified the class antagonisms. Society as a whole is

more and more splitting up into two great hostile camps, into two great classes directly facing each other: Bourgeoisie and Proletariat.[22]

Marx believed not only that there are universal laws operating in history but that these laws are economic in nature. Moreover, there is a causal connection between the economic structure and everything in society such that the mode of production of material life determines the general character of the social, political, and spiritual processes of life. In a word, the economic structure is the real basis by which everything else about society is determined.

Marx's view of history, then, can be characterized as having two main features. First, there are universal laws operating behind historical change. Second, these supposed laws of history are economic in nature. Based on this view of history, Marx predicts that capitalism will become increasingly unstable economically. The class struggle between the *bourgeoisie* (ownership class) and *proletariat* (working class) will increase, with the proletariat getting both poorer and larger in number. The upshot will be a social revolution: The workers will seize power and eventually institute the new communist phase of history.

View of Human Nature

Related to Marx's view of history is his view of human nature, which we alluded to in Chapter 2. Apart from some obvious biological factors, such as the need to eat, Marx denies that there is any such thing as an essential human nature, that is, something that is true of every individual at all times everywhere. He does allow, however, that humans are social beings, that to speak of human nature is really to speak in terms of the totality of social relations. Accordingly, whatever any of us does is a social act, which presupposes the existence of other people standing in certain relations to us. In short, everything is socially learned.

The social influence is especially apparent in every activity of production. Producing what we need to survive physically is a social activity: It always requires that we interact and cooperate with others. Given Marx's account, it follows that the kind of individuals we are and the kinds of things we do are determined by the kind of society in which we live. In other words, for Marx it isn't the consciousness of individuals that defines their beings, but their social being which determines their consciousness. In commenting incisively on this point, professor of philosophy Leslie Stevenson has written:

> In modern terms, we can summarize this crucial point by saying that sociology is not reducible to psychology, i.e., it is not the case that everything about men can be explained in terms of facts about individuals; the kind of society they live in must be considered too. This methodological point is one of Marx's most distinctive contributions, and one of the most widely accepted. For this reason alone, he must be recognized as one of the founding fathers of sociology. And the *method* can of course be accepted whether or not one agrees with the particular *conclusions* Marx came to about economics and politics.[23]

Professor Stevenson goes on to point out that, despite Marx's denial of such a thing as individual human nature, Marx is prepared to offer at least one generalization about human nature. It is that humans are active, predictive beings who distinguish themselves from other animals by the central, overriding fact that they produce their own means of subsistence. Indeed, according to Marx, it is not only natural for humans to work for their livings but *right* as well. Thus, by Marx's account, the life of productive activity is the right one for humans.

Granted it is proper for humans to work for their living, what may be said about the product of that work? Like Locke before him, and numerous thinkers after him (including Rawls and Nozick), Marx thought that individuals have a legitimate claim to the product of their own labor. But Marx rejects the notion that they are entitled to

---

22. Karl Marx and Friedrich Engels, *Communist Manifesto*, trans. Samuel Moore (Chicago: Regnery, 1969).

23. Leslie Stevenson, *Seven Theories of Human Nature* (New York: Oxford University Press, 1974), 54.

own property that they have not personally produced. Neither is property ownership licit when it functions to enrich the already affluent at the expense of other people, thereby forcing these people to work without benefit of the products of their labor. But this, according to Marx, is precisely what capitalism encourages: the exploitation of the large working class (proletariat) at the hands of the affluent few who own the means of production (bourgeoisie). Again, here are Marx and Engels writing on this subject in the *Communist Manifesto:*

The bourgeoisie, wherever it has got the upper hand, has put an end to all feudal, patriarchal, idyllic relations. It has pitilessly torn asunder the motley feudal ties that bound man to his "natural superiors," and has left remaining no other nexus between man and man than naked self-interest, callous "cash payment." It has drowned the most heavenly ecstasies of religious fervor, of chivalrous enthusiasm, of philistine sentimentalism, in the icy water of egotistical calculation. It has resolved personal worth into exchange value, and in place of the numberless indefeasible chartered freedoms, has set up that single, unconscionable freedom—Free Trade. In one word, for exploitation, veiled by religious and political illusions, it has substituted naked, shameless, direct, brutal exploitation.

The bourgeoisie has stripped of its halo every occupation hitherto honored and looked up to with reverent awe. It has converted the physician, the lawyer, the priest, the poet, the name of science, into its paid wage-laborers.

The bourgeoisie has torn away from the family its sentimental veil, and has reduced the family relation to a mere money relation.

The bourgeoisie has disclosed how it came to pass that the brutal display of vigor in the Middle Ages, which Reactionists so much admire, found its fitting complement in the most slothful indolence. It has been the first to show what man's activity can bring about. It has accomplished wonders far surpassing Egyptian pyramids, Roman aqueducts, and Gothic cathedrals; it has conducted expeditions that put in the shade all former Exoduses of nations and crusades.

The bourgeoisie cannot exist without constantly revolutionizing the instruments of production, and thereby the relations of production, and with them the whole relations of society. Conservation of the old modes of production in unaltered form, was, on the contrary, the first condition of existence for all earlier industrial classes. Constant revolutionizing of production, uninterrupted disturbance of all social conditions, everlasting uncertainty and agitation distinguish the bourgeois epoch from all earlier ones. All fixed, fast-frozen relations, with their train of ancient and venerable prejudices and opinions, are swept away, all new-formed ones become antiquated before they can ossify. All that is solid melts into air, all that is holy is profaned, and man is at last compelled to face, with sober senses, his real conditions of life, and his relations with his kind.

The need of a constantly expanding market for its products chases the bourgeoisie over the whole surface of the globe. It must nestle everywhere, settle everywhere, establish connections everywhere.

The bourgeoisie has through its exploitation of the world-market given a cosmopolitan character to production and consumption in every country. To the great chagrin of Reactionists, it has drawn from under the feet of industry the national ground on which it stood. All old-fashioned national industries have been destroyed and are daily being destroyed. They are dislodged by new industries, whose introduction becomes a life and death question for all civilized nations, by industries that no longer work up indigenous raw material, but raw material drawn from the remotest zones; industries whose products are consumed, not only at home, but in every quarter of the globe. In place of the old wants, satisfied by the productions of the country, we find new wants, requiring for their satisfaction the products of distant lands and climes. In place of the old local and national seclusion and self-sufficiency, we have intercourse in every direction, universal interdependence of nations. And as in material, so also in intellectual production. The intellectual creations of individual nations become common property. National one-sidedness and narrow-mindedness become more and more impossible, and from the numerous national and local literatures there arises a world-literature.

The bourgeoisie, by the rapid improvement of all instruments of production, by the immensely facilitated means of communication, draws all, even the most barbarian, nations into civilization.

The cheap prices of its commodities are the heavy artillery with which it batters down all Chinese walls, with which it forces the barbarians' intensely obstinate hatred of foreigners to capitulate. It compels all nations, on pain of extinction, to adopt the bourgeois mode of production; it compels them to introduce what it calls civilization into their midst, i.e., to become bourgeois themselves. In a word, it creates a world after its own image.

The bourgeoisie has subjected the country to the rule of the towns. It has created enormous cities, has greatly increased the urban population as compared with the rural, and has thus rescued a considerable part of the population from the idiocy of rural life. Just as it has made the country dependent on the towns, so it has made barbarian and semi-barbarian countries dependent on the civilized ones, nations of peasants on nations of bourgeois, the East on the West.

The bourgeoisie keeps more and more doing away with the scattered state of the population, of the means of production, and of property. It has agglomerated population, centralized means of production, and has concentrated property in a few hands. The necessary consequence of this was political centralization. Independent, or but loosely connected provinces, with separate interests, laws, governments and systems of taxation, became lumped together in one nation, with one government, one code of laws, one national class-interest, one frontier and one customs-tariff.

The bourgeoisie, during its rule of scarce one hundred years, has created more massive and more colossal productive forces than have all preceding generations together. Subjection of Nature's forces to man, machinery, application of chemistry to industry and agriculture, steam-navigation, railways, electric telegraphs, clearing of whole continents for cultivation, canalization of rivers, whole populations conjured out of the ground—what earlier century had even a presentiment that such productive forces slumbered in the lap of social labor?[24]

According to Marx, the result of bourgeois exploitation is alienation, a key concept in his political and social philosophy.

---

24. Marx and Engels, *Communist Manifesto*.

Concept of Alienation

Marx borrowed his notion of alienation from Hegel and also from Feuerbach. For Hegel alienation has its roots in a distinction between a subject and supposedly alien object. For Marx, the human can be considered the subject; and Nature, that is, the human-created world, can be viewed as object. Humans are alienated from Nature, from the world and the social relations they create. What is the cause of this alienation? Marx is rather fuzzy about this. At one point he traces the roots of the alienation to the ownership of private property. Elsewhere he says that private property is not the cause but the effect of alienation. Whether private property is a cause or effect of alienation, one thing is evident: Marx associates alienation with economics, with the ownership of private property. Specifically, alienation consists of individuals not fulfilling themselves in work. Rather, because the work is imposed on them as a means of satisfying the needs of others, they feel exploited and debased. What about workers who are paid handsomely for their efforts? Nevertheless, says Marx, they remain estranged. Insofar as the fruits of their labor are enjoyed by someone else, the work ultimately proves meaningless to them. In the following selection from his "Economic and Philosophic Manuscripts" (1844), Marx summarizes his notion of alienation as the separation of individuals from the objects they create, which in turn results in separation from other people and ultimately from oneself.

> We shall begin from a *contemporary* economic fact. The worker becomes poorer the more wealth he produces and the more his production increases in power and extent. The worker becomes an ever cheaper commodity the more goods he creates. The *devaluation* of the human world increases in direct relation with the *increase in value* of the world of things. Labor does not only create goods; it also produces itself and the worker as a *commodity*, and indeed in the same proportion as it produces goods. . . .
>
> All these consequences follow from the fact that the worker is related to the *product of his labor* as to an *alien* object. For it is clear on this presupposition that the more the worker expends himself in work the more powerful becomes the world of

objects which he creates in face of himself, the poorer he becomes in his inner life, and the less he belongs to himself. It is just the same as in religion. The more of himself man attributes to God the less he has left in himself. The worker puts his life into the object, and his life then belongs no longer to himself but to the object. The greater his activity, therefore, the less he possesses. What is embodied in the product of his labor is no longer his own. The greater this product is, therefore, the more he is diminished. The *alienation* of the worker in his product means not only that his labor becomes an object, assumes an *external* existence, but that it exists independently, *outside himself*, and alien to him, and that it stands opposed to him as an autonomous power. The life which he has given to the object sets itself against him as an alien and hostile force. . . .

The worker becomes a slave of the object; first, in that he receives an *object of work*, i.e., receives *work*, and secondly, in that he receives *means of subsistence*. Thus the object enables him to exist, first as a *worker*, and secondly, as a *physical subject*. The culmination of this enslavement is that he can only maintain himself as a *physical subject* so far as he is a *worker*, and that it is only as a *physical subject* that he is a worker. . . .

What constitutes the alienation of labor? First, that the work is *external* to the worker, that it is not part of his nature; and that, consequently, he does not fulfill himself in his work but denies himself, has a feeling of misery rather than well-being, does not develop freely his mental and physical energies but is physically exhausted and mentally debased. The worker, therefore, feels himself at home only during his leisure time, whereas at work he feels homeless. His work is not voluntary but imposed, *forced labor*. It is not the satisfaction of a need, but only a *means* for satisfying other needs. Its alien character is clearly shown by the fact that as soon as there is no physical or other compulsion it is avoided like the plague. External labor, labor in which man alienates himself, is a labor of self-sacrifice, of mortification. Finally, the external character of work for the worker is shown by the fact that it is not his own work but work for someone else, that in work he does not belong to himself but to another person. . . .

We arrive at the result that man (the worker) feels himself to be freely active only in his animal functions—eating, drinking and procreating, or at most also in his dwelling and in personal adornment—while in his human functions he is reduced to an animal. The animal becomes human and the human becomes animal.

Eating, drinking and procreating are of course also genuine human functions. But abstractly considered, apart from the environment of human activities, and turned into final and sole ends, they are animal functions.

We have now considered the act of alienation of practical human activity, labor, from two aspects: (1) the relationship of the worker to the *product of labor* as an alien object which dominates him. This relationship is at the same time the relationship to the sensuous external world, to natural objects, as an alien and hostile world; (2) the relationship of labor to the *act of production* within *labor*. This is the relationship of the worker to his own activity as something alien and not belonging to him, activity as suffering (passivity), strength as powerlessness, creation as emasculation, the *personal* physical and mental energy of the worker, his personal life (for what is life but activity?), as an activity which is directed against himself, independent of him and not belonging to him. This is *self-alienation* as against the above-mentioned alienation of the *thing*.[25]

Marx goes on to infer yet a third aspect of estranged labor from the preceding two: the estrangement of the individual from the species itself. But this needn't concern us here.

In Marx's view, when workers are alienated they cannot be free. Yes, they may have the political and social freedoms of speech, religion, and governance that classical liberals delineate. But even with these freedoms that guarantee noninterference, individuals still are not free; for freedom from government interference and persecution are not necessarily guarantees of freedom from economic exploitation. And it is for this kind of freedom, freedom from alienation, that Marx and Engels feel such passion.

---

25. Karl Marx, "The Economic and Philosophic Manuscripts of 1844," in *Karl Marx: Early Writings*, trans. T. B. Bottomore (Copyright © T. B. Bottomore, 1963). Used with permission of McGraw-Hill Book Co.

Sense of Freedom

How can humans be free of alienation? To begin with, they must recognize that the key to freedom and the lack of it lies in economics. Therefore, humans must return to a "natural" state in which they and their labor are one. This natural state is similar to Rousseau's in the sense that it recognizes the corrupting influence of society and calls for a conception of the state that will allow humans to be unselfish and nondestructive. But don't misunderstand. Marx is not advocating the end of work. On the contrary, he holds that work is humanizing, ennobling. Thus, he is urging people to liberate themselves from alienated work. Without this kind of freedom, which is basically a freedom from material need, other freedoms are a sham.

Basically Marx prescribes a fairer distribution of wealth as a means for combating alienation and insuring freedom. For Marx justice requires that the means of production be owned by everyone. In unvarnished terms, in part this means no ownership of property except for those products a person makes directly. It also means an end to the worker/owner distinction, thereby making everyone a laborer who shares in the benefits of his or her labor. Specifically, Marx calls for nationalization as a way of attaining freedom from alienation—nationalization of land, factories, transport, and banks. But insofar as Marx presumably believes that (1) the State is the basis of all social ills, and (2) nationalization evidently will exacerbate this by concentrating power in the hands of the State, it isn't at all clear how such institutional changes could effect freedom. This observation has led Leslie Stevenson to suggest that we understand Marx as saying "at least in his early phase, that alienation consists in the lack of community. In other words, since the State is not a real community, individuals cannot see their work as contributing to a group of which they are members. It would follow that freedom from alienation would be won by decentralizing, not nationalizing, the State in genuine communities or 'communes.' These entities would be characterized by the abolition of money, specialization, and private property."[26] Indeed, it may be this community element of Marx's vision that explains why Marx continues to win and hold followers. After all, it is difficult to disagree with such ideas as a decentralized society in which individuals cooperate in communities for the common good, technology is harnessed and directed for the interest of all, and the relationship between society and nature is harmonized. At the same time, Marx gives no good reason for assuming that the communist society will achieve any of these ideals. In fact, if the history of Russia since the revolution is any indication, quite the opposite seems the case.

RAWLS

About one-third of the world's population today lives in societies that claim to be based on the socialist views proposed by Marx. Much of the rest of the world lives in societies that by and large follow a philosophy termed *liberalism*. Liberalism has its roots in the individualism of John Locke and of John Stuart Mill. At the heart of early liberalism was the view that the best society is the one in which individuals are left free to puruse their own interests and fulfillment as each chooses. As Mill argued, the only restraints to which adult individuals should be subject are those necessary to keep one individual from harming others.

Contemporary liberalism has retained this fundamental commitment to individual liberty but has added to it an awareness of the extent to which economic realities can indirectly limit an individual's liberty. The choices of a poor person, for

---

The path of freedom is blocked much more by those who wish to obey than by those who desire to command.

M. D. PETRE

---

26. Stevenson, *Seven Theories of Human Nature*, 58.

example, are much restricted by that person's poverty, whereas wealth and property endow the rich with choices and power that are not available to the poor. Contemporary liberalism, therefore, has tended to incorporate the view that individuals can be constrained to provide economic support for the poor through welfare programs. Contemporary liberalism has also tended to accept the view that individuals should be given some protection against the economic power of the wealthy through laws that protect the worker. Undoubtedly, these contemporary modifications of liberalism have been greatly influenced by Marx. To a large extent, in fact, contemporary liberalism is the response capitalist societies have made to Marx.

Perhaps the best representative of contemporary liberalism is John Rawls, a philosopher who teaches at Harvard University. In his now classic work, *The Theory of Justice*, Rawls presents a brilliant and often passionate argument in support of contemporary liberalism. Many philosophers hold, in fact, that the modern world is faced with a fundamental choice between two kinds of societies: the kind of socialist society advocated by Marx or the kind of liberal society advocated by Rawls.

Rawls was born in 1921 and received his doctorate in philosophy from Princeton University in 1950. From 1953 to 1959 he taught at Cornell University and then moved to Massachusetts Institute of Technology, where he taught from 1960 to 1962. Since 1962 he has been teaching philosophy at Harvard University.

For Rawls the most important question to ask about a society is the question: Is it just? The laws and institutions of a society must embody justice, or they must be reformed.

> Justice is the first virtue of social institutions, as truth is of systems of thought. A theory however elegant and economical must be rejected or revised if it is untrue; likewise laws and institutions no matter how efficient and well-arranged must be reformed or abolished if they are unjust. Each person possesses an inviolability founded on justice that even the welfare of society as a whole cannot override. For this reason justice denies that the loss of freedom for some is made right by a greater good shared by others. It does not allow that the

sacrifices imposed on a few are outweighed by the larger sum of advantages enjoyed by many. Therefore in a just society the liberties of equal citizenship are taken as settled; the rights secured by justice are not subject to political bargaining or to the calculus of social interests. The only thing that permits us to acquiesce in an erroneous theory is the lack of a better one; analogously, an injustice is tolerable only when it is necessary to avoid an even greater injustice. Being first virtues of human activities, truth and justice are uncompromising.[27]

If we are to analyze the justice of society, Rawls claims, we must look not at the particular actions of individuals, but at its basic political, economic, and social *institutions*. Like Marx, Rawls acknowledges that social relationships have a deep and profound effect on the individual's sense of fulfillment. A society's institutions are what primarily determine what we can do and what our lives as individuals will be like. From the very beginning they favor some of us and hamper others.

> Many different kinds of things are said to be just and unjust: not only laws, institutions, and social systems, but also particular actions of many kinds, including decisions, judgments, and imputations. We also call the attitudes and dispositions of persons, and persons themselves, just and unjust. Our topic, however, is that of social justice. For us the primary subject of justice is the basic structure of society, or more exactly, the way in which the major social institutions distribute fundamental rights and duties and determine the division of advantages from social cooperation. By major institutions I understand the political constitution and the principal economic and social arrangements. Thus the legal protection of freedom of thought and liberty of conscience, competitive markets, private property in the means of production, and the monogamous family are examples of major social institutions. Taken together as one scheme, the major institutions define men's rights and duties and influence their life-prospects, what they can expect to be and how well they can hope

---

27. John Rawls, *A Theory of Justice* (Cambridge, Mass.: Harvard University Press, 1972), 3–4. Reprinted by permission of Harvard University Press. © 1971 by the President and Fellows of Harvard College. All rights reserved.

to do. The basic structure is the primary subject of justice because its effects are so profound and present from the start. The intuitive notion here is that this structure contains various social positions and that men born into different positions have different expectations of life determined, in part, by the political system as well as by economic and social circumstances. In this way the institutions of society favor certain starting places over others. These are especially deep inequalities. Not only are they persuasive, but they affect men's initial chances in life; yet they cannot possibly be justified by an appeal to the notions of merit or desert. It is these inequalities, presumably inevitable in the basic structure of any society, to which the principles of social justice must in the first instance apply. These principles, then, regulate the choice of a political constitution and the main elements of the economic and social system. The justice of a social scheme depends essentially on how fundamental rights and duties are assigned and on the economic opportunities and social conditions in the various sectors of society.[28]

But what are the principles and rules that should govern our social institutions? What principles, guidelines, and formulas should we follow when designing our institutions if those institutions are to be just? Rawls argues that in order to discover what just institutions should be like, we should engage in a kind of imaginary experiment. Imagine, he says, that before people formed a society, they could all gather together in a large meeting. And suppose that at this imaginary first meeting (or "original position") no one knew what place each person would have in their future society. Suppose no one knew whether he or she would turn out to be rich or poor, owner or worker, ruler or ruled. In fact, suppose that no one knew even whether he or she would turn out to be male or female, intelligent or stupid, healthy or sick, strong or weak, black or white. Suppose, that is, that everyone at this original meeting is "behind a veil of ignorance," where no one knows what each will be like in the future society.

Suppose, then, that the people at this original

meeting had to choose the basic rules or principles that would govern their future society. Clearly, Rawls says, the parties in such an original position will have to be perfectly fair to everyone in their future society, since no one knows who he or she may turn out to be. In such a situation, a person would not choose principles that would favor whites over blacks, since in their future society that person might turn out to be black. Nor would a person choose principles that favor the rich over the poor since the person might turn out to be poor. In short, the "veil of ignorance" forces everyone in this hypothetical or imaginary meeting to choose principles that will be perfectly just to everyone.

Thus we are to imagine that those who engage in social cooperation choose together, in one joint act, the principles which are to assign basic rights and duties and to determine the division of social benefits. Men are to decide in advance how they are to regulate their claims against one another and what is to be the foundation charter of their society. Just as each person must decide by rational reflection what constitutes his good, that is, the system of ends which it is rational for him to pursue, so a group of persons must decide once and for all what is to count among them as just and unjust. The choice which rational men would make in this hypothetical situation of equal liberty, assuming for the present that this choice problem has a solution, determines the principles of justice.

In justice as fairness the original position of equality corresponds to the state of nature in the traditional theory of the social contract. This original position is not, of course, thought of as an actual historical state of affairs, much less as a primitive condition of culture. It is understood as a purely hypothetical situation characterized so as to lead to a certain conception of justice. Among the essential features of this situation is that no one knows his place in society, his class position or social status, nor does any one know his fortune in the distribution of natural assets and abilities, his intelligence, strength, and the like. I shall even assume that the parties do not know their conceptions of the good or their special psychological propensities. The principles of justice are chosen behind a veil of ignorance. This ensures that no one is advantaged or disadvantaged in the choice

---

28. Ibid., 7.

of principles by the outcome of natural chance or the contingency of social circumstances. Since all are similarly situated and no one is able to design principles to favor his particular condition, the principles of justice are the result of a fair agreement or bargain. For given the circumstances of the original position, the symmetry of everyone's relations to each other, this initial situation is fair between individuals as moral persons, that is, as rational beings with their own ends and capable, I shall assume, of a sense of justice. The original position is, one might say, the appropriate initial status quo, and thus the fundamental agreements reached in it are fair. This explains the propriety of the name "justice as fairness": it conveys the idea that the principles of justice are agreed to in an initial situation that is fair. The name does not mean that the concepts of justice and fairness are the same, any more than the phrase "poetry as metaphor" means that the concept of poetry and metaphor are the same.[29]

Rawls then argues that the imaginary parties to this original position would not choose utilitarian principles. Utilitarian principles, Rawls claims, sometimes require some people to suffer losses for the sake of maximizing society's utility. Clearly, a person in the original position would not agree to this since that person might turn out to be one of the people forced to suffer losses. Instead, Rawls claims, the parties to the original position would settle on two alternative principles of justice. First, they would choose the principle that everyone in society must have equal political rights and duties. Second, they would choose the principle that the only economic inequalities that are justified are those that are required to make everyone better off by serving as incentives. These two kinds of principles, Rawls holds, would be chosen by people in the original position who do not know their particular natural endowments and social circumstances.

In working out the conception of justice as fairness one main task clearly is to determine which principles of justice would be chosen in the original position. To do this we must describe this situation in some detail and formulate with care the problem of choice which it presents. These matters I shall take up in the immediately succeeding chapters. It may be observed, however, that once the principles of justice are thought of as arising from an original agreement in a situation of equality, it is an open question whether the principle of utility would be acknowledged. Offhand it hardly seems likely that persons who view themselves as equals, entitled to press their claims upon one another, would agree to a principle which may require lesser life prospects for some simply for the sake of a greater sum of advantages enjoyed by others. Since each desires to protect his interests, his capacity to advance his conception of the good, no one has a reason to acquiesce in an enduring loss for himself in order to bring about a greater net balance of satisfaction. In the absence of strong and lasting benevolent impulses, a rational man would not accept a basic structure merely because it maximized the algebraic sum of advantages irrespective of its permanent effects on his own basic rights and interests. Thus it seems that the principle of utility is incompatible with the conception of social cooperation among equals for mutual advantage. It appears to be inconsistent with the idea of reciprocity implicit in the notion of a well-ordered society. Or, at any rate, so I shall argue.

I shall maintain instead that the persons in the initial situation would choose two rather different principles: the first requires equality in the assignment of basic rights and duties, while the second holds that social and economic inequalities, for example inequalities of wealth and authority, are just only if they result in compensating benefits for everyone, and in particular for the least advantaged members of society. These principles rule out justifying institutions on the grounds that the hardships of some are offset by a greater good in the aggregate. It may be expedient but it is not just that some should have less in order that others may prosper. But there is no injustice in the greater benefits earned by a few provided that the situation of persons not so fortunate is thereby improved. The intuitive idea is that since everyone's well-being depends upon a scheme of cooperation without which no one could have a satisfactory life, the division of advantages should be such as to draw forth the willing cooperation of everyone taking part in it, including those less well situ-

29. Ibid., 11–13.

ated. Yet this can be expected only if reasonable terms are proposed. The two principles mentioned seem to be a fair agreement on the basis of which those better endowed, or more fortunate in their social position, neither of which we can be said to deserve, could expect the willing cooperation of others when some workable scheme is a necessary condition of the welfare of all. Once we decide to look for a conception of justice that nullifies the accidents of natural endowment and the contingencies of social circumstance as counters in quest for political and economic advantage, we are led to these principles. They express the result of leaving aside those aspects of the social world that seem arbitrary from a moral point of view.[30]

Rawls later elaborates his principles in more detail. The two principles of justice that would be chosen, he writes, can be formulated as follows: "First: each person is to have an equal right to the most extensive basic liberty compatible with a similar liberty for others. Second: social and economic inequalities are to be arranged so that they are both (a) to the greatest benefit of the least advantaged and (b) attached to offices and positions open to all under conditions of fair equality of opportunity.[31]

According to Rawls, the parties to the original position would choose the first principle, which requires equal political freedoms for everyone, because each person would want to at least be equal to everyone else in the political sphere. However, he claims, the parties would agree to allow social and *economic* inequalities if such "inequalities set up various incentives which succeed in eliciting more productive efforts" from people. For example, allowing higher wages for some people can spur them on to produce more goods, and this added productivity will work to everyone's benefit. But the parties to the original position will each want to have an equal chance at these more lucrative positions. Consequently, they will insist that these positions be "open to all under conditions of fair equality of opportunity." Moreover, the parties to the original position will want to protect themselves in case they turn out to be among the "least

advantaged." So they will agree that the benefits produced by allowing inequalities should be used to protect the least advantaged.

Rawls's two principles, then, are the principles that anyone—ourselves included—would choose if they were in the original position behind the "veil of ignorance." And since the original position requires us to be absolutely fair and just, these two principles are themselves just and express what justice requires of us.

And what does justice require of us according to Rawls? Certainly not the kind of socialist state advocated by Marx in which individuals are not free to own and exchange private property; in which all land, factories, transport, and banks are nationalized and controlled by the state; and in which free markets are prohibited. Nor does justice require an absolute equality. Instead, Rawls argues, justice requires freedom and merely *political* equality. In particular, justice requires freedom from the interference of the state, and it allows (although it does not *require*) private property and free markets. Justice also allows *economic* inequalities, while it requires that the state must provide adequate welfare programs for the poor and the disadvantaged.

In short, justice requires and allows more or less what Western social, economic, and political institutions require and allow. This is perhaps not surprising, since Rawls's philosophy is intended to defend Western liberal ideals. It is, perhaps, the most powerful alternative to contemporary Marxism and the most powerful contemporary defense of liberalism.

QUESTIONS

1. In your own words, explain what the bourgeoisie is and how it developed. Does the bourgeoisie exist today? Explain.

2. To what extent does Marx's concept of alienation apply to modern workers? To what extent does it apply to the modern college student? How would Marx analyze the contemporary trend toward careerism among today's college students (that is, the trend to see a college education as preparation for a job or a career instead of as a humanizing and liberating activity)?

30. Ibid., 14–15.
31. Ibid., 60, 83.

3. Explain in your own words what Rawls's "original position" is and why it is supposed to show us the meaning of justice. Do you agree that using the original position is an adequate way of determining what justice requires? Why? Do you think that Rawls's two principles of justice are adequate? Why?

4. How do Rawls's views about society differ from Marx's? What assumptions do you think Marx and Rawls make that lead each of them to such different conclusions?

5. What do you think Rawls would say about the justice or injustice of making pornography illegal? About making drugs such as marijuana and cocaine illegal? About nationalizing businesses? About the international problem of poverty?

ALDOUS HUXLEY

Brave New World

What will be the relationship between the individual and the state? On the basis of current trends, can we anticipate what the future holds for a highly industrialized society such as our own?

Numerous literary works have attended to these questions. Perhaps the best known and most widely read is Aldous Huxley's Brave New World. *The theme of this futuristic novel is how the advancement of science affects humans. Specifically, the work is about a group of people who achieve social stability by revolutionizing human control and conditioning with scientific means. As Huxley himself pointed out,* Brave New World *is a warning that unless science is used as a means to the end of producing a race of free individuals rather than as the end to which humans are the means, we invite totalitarian regimes to satisfy society's need for efficiency and stability.*

Totalitarian—there's a word that makes Western liberals shudder. Huxley's Brave New World *is surely a totalitarian state, for one would have to travel far, inside as well as outside fiction, to find a more ruthless concentration of power. And yet, no one can deny that totalitarianism has appeal to people of good will; its success hinges on its offering refuge to the beleaguered, hope to the despairing, and faith to the disillusioned. To dismiss totalitarianism as irrational, undemocratic, or unequal is to misunderstand it. Proponents have argued that totalitarianism's technically advanced scientific management and bureaucratic custodianship of cultural life are consummately rational, that its popular foundations are in the philosophy of such Western liberal darlings as Rousseau, and that the elimination of all associative groups— religious, academic, economic, and artistic—is for the purpose of advancing equality.*

You must avoid the temptation to dismiss the Brave New World *with ridicule and name calling. It is an extension (some might say an aberration) of the historical movement toward the superstate that took root in the liberalism of the eighteenth and nineteenth centuries. What's needed is an alternative that accounts for human nature and cultivates individuality more effectively. After all, those who manage the* Brave New World *are fervent in their conviction that they are fostering a society that will satisfy human wants and needs and will emancipate individuals from the shackles imposed by the petty groups that claim them.*

The selection that follows shows the regime in operation. It describes the conditioning of eight-month-old babies. In reading the selection, be alert to the seemingly utilitarian justification for the conditioning: In the long run, such conditioning will best serve the interests of all.

SOURCE: Aldous Huxley, *Brave New World* (Copyright 1932, © 1960 by Aldous Huxley). Reprinted by permission of Harper & Row, Publishers, Inc., and Mrs. Laura Huxley and Chatto & Windus Ltd.

Mr. Foster was left in the Decanting Room. The D.H.C. and his students stepped into the nearest lift and were carried up to the fifth floor.

"Infant Nurseries. Neo-Pavlovian Conditioning Rooms," announced the notice board.

The Director opened a door. They were in a large bare room, very bright and sunny; for the whole of the southern wall was a single window. Half a dozen nurses, trousered and jacketed in the regulation white viscose-linen uniform, their hair aseptically hidden under white caps, were engaged in setting out bowls of roses in a long row across the floor. Big bowls, packed tight with blossoms. Thousands of petals, ripe-blown and silkily smooth, like the cheeks of innumerable little cherubs, but of cherubs, in that bright light, not exclusively pink and Aryan, but also luminously Chinese, also Mexican, also apoplectic with too much blowing of celestial trumpets, also pale as death, pale with the posthumous whiteness of marble.

The muses stiffened to attention as the D.H.C. came in.

"Set out the books," he said curtly.

In silence the nurses obeyed his command. Between the rose bowls the books were duly set out—a row of nursery quartos opened invitingly each at some gaily colored image of beast or fish or bird.

"Now bring in the children."

They hurried out of the room and returned in a minute or two, each pushing a kind of tall dumbwaiter laden, on all its four wire-netted shelves, with eight-month-old babies, all exactly alike (a Bokanovsky Group, it was evident) and all (since their caste was Delta) dressed in khaki.

"Put them down on the floor."

The infants were unloaded.

"Now turn them so that they can see the flowers and books."

Turned, the babies at once fell silent, then began to crawl towards those clusters of sleek colors, those shapes so gay and brilliant on the white pages. As they approached, the sun came out of a momentary eclipse behind a cloud. The roses flamed up as though with a sudden passion from within; a new and profound significance seemed to suffuse the shining pages of the books. From the ranks of the crawling babies came little squeals of excitement, gurgles and twitterings of pleasure.

The Director rubbed his hands. "Excellent!" he said. "It might almost have been done on purpose."

The swiftest crawlers were already at their goal. Small hands reached out uncertainly, touched, grasped, unpetaling the transfigured roses, crumpling the illuminated pages of the books. The Director waited until all were happily busy. Then, "Watch carefully," he said. And, lifting his hand, he gave the signal.

The Head Nurse, who was standing by a switchboard at the other end of the room, pressed down a little lever.

There was a violent explosion. Shriller and ever shriller, a siren shrieked. Alarm bells maddeningly sounded.

The children started, screamed; their faces were distorted with terror.

"And now," the Director shouted (for the noise was deafening), "now we proceed to rub in the lesson with a mild electric shock."

He waved his hand again, and the Head Nurse pressed a second lever. The screaming of the babies suddenly changed its tone. There was something desperate, almost insane, about the sharp spasmodic yelps to which they now gave utterance. Their little bodies twitched and stiffened; their limbs moved jerkily as if to the tug of unseen wires.

"We can electrify that whole strip of floor," bawled the Director in explanation "But that's enough," he signalled to the nurse.

The explosions ceased, the bells stopped ringing, the shriek of the siren died down from tone to tone into silence. The stiffly twitching bodies relaxed, and what had become the sob and yelp of infant maniacs broadened out once more into a normal howl of ordinary terror.

"Offer them the flowers and the books again."

The nurses obeyed; but at the approach of the roses, at the mere sight of those gaily-colored images of pussy and cock-a-doodle-doo and baa-baa black sheep, the infants shrank away in horror; the volume of their howling suddenly increased.

"Observe," said the Director triumphantly, "observe."

Books and loud noises, flowers and electric shocks—already in the infant mind these couples were uncompromisingly linked; and after two hundred repetitions of the same or a similar lesson would be wedded indissolubly. What man has joined, nature is powerless to put asunder.

"They'll grow up with what the psychologists used to call an 'instinctive' hatred of books and flowers. Reflexes unalterably conditioned. They'll be safe from books and botany all their lives." The Director turned to his nurses. "Take them away again."

Still yelling, the khaki babies were loaded on to their dumbwaiters and wheeled out, leaving behind them the smell of sour milk and a most welcome silence.

One of the students held up his hand; and though he could see quite well why you couldn't have the lower-caste people wasting the Community's time over books, and that there was always the risk of their reading something which might undesirably decondition one of their reflexes, yet . . . well, he couldn't understand about the flowers. Why go to the trouble of making it psychologically impossible for Deltas to like flowers?

Patiently the D.H.C. explained. If the children were made to scream at the sight of a rose, that was on grounds of high economic policy. Not so very long ago (a century or thereabouts), Gammas, Deltas, even Epsilons, had been conditioned to like flowers—flowers in particular and wild nature in general. The idea was to make them want to be going out into the country at every available opportunity, and so compel them to consume transport.

"And didn't they consume transport?" asked the student.

"Quite a lot," the D.H.C. replied. "But nothing else."

Primroses and landscapes, he pointed out, have one grave defect: they are gratuitous. A love of nature keeps no factories busy. It was decided to abolish the love of nature, at any rate among the lower classes; to abolish the love of nature, but *not* the tendency to consume transport. For of course it was essential that they should keep on going to the country, even though they hated it. The problem was to find an economically sounder reason for consuming transport than a mere affection for primroses and landscapes. It was duly found.

"We condition the masses to hate the country," concluded the director. "But simultaneously we condition them to love all country sports. At the same time, we see to it that all country sports shall entail the use of elaborate apparatus. So that they consume manufactured articles as well as transport. Hence those electric shocks."

"I see," said the student, and was silent, lost in admiration.

There was a silence; then, clearing his throat, "Once upon a time," the Director began, "while our Ford was still on earth, there was a little boy called Reuben Rabinovitch. Reuben was the child of Polish-speaking parents." The Director interrupted himself. "You know what Polish is, I suppose?"

"A dead language."

"Like French and German," added another student, officiously showing off his learning.

"And 'parent'?" questioned the D.H.C.

There was an uneasy silence. Several of the boys blushed. They had not yet learned to draw the significant but often very fine distinction between smut and pure science. One, at last, had the courage to raise a hand.

"Human beings used to be . . ." he hesitated; the blood rushed to his cheeks. "Well, they used to be viviparous."

"Quite right." The Director nodded approvingly.

"And when the babies were decanted . . ."

" 'Born,'" came the correction.

"Well, then they were the parents—I mean, not the babies, of course; the other ones." The poor boy was overwhelmed with confusion.

"In brief," the Director summed up, "the parents were the father and the mother." The smut that was really science fell with a crash into the boys' eye-avoiding silence. "Mother," he repeated loudly rubbing in the science; and, leaning back in his chair, "These," he said gravely, "are unpleasant facts; I know it. But then most historical facts *are* unpleasant."

He returned to Little Reuben—to Little Reuben, in whose room, one evening, by an oversight, his father and mother (crash, crash!) happened to leave the radio turned on.

("For you must remember that in those days of gross viviparous reproduction, children were always brought up by their parents and not in State Conditioning Centers.")

While the child was asleep, a broadcast program from London suddenly started to come through; and the next morning, to the astonishment of his crash and crash (the more daring of the boys ventured to grin at one another), Little Reuben woke up repeating word for word a long lecture by that curious old writer ("one of the very few whose works have been permitted to come down to us"), George Bernard Shaw, who was speaking, according to a well-authenticated tradition, about his own genius. To Little Reuben's wink and snigger, this lecture was, of course, perfectly incomprehensible and, imagining that their child had suddenly gone mad, they sent for a doctor. He, fortunately, understood English, recognized the discourse as that which Shaw had broadcasted the previous evening, realized the significance of what had happened, and sent a letter to the medical press about it.

"The principle of sleep-teaching, or hypnopaedia, had been discovered." The D.H.C. made an impressive pause.

The principle had been discovered; but many, many years were to elapse before that principle was usefully applied.

"The case of Little Reuben occurred only twenty-three years after Our Ford's first T-Model was put on the market." (Here the Director made a sign of the T on his stomach and all the students reverently followed suit.) "And yet . . ."

Furiously the students scribbled, *"Hypnopaedia, first used officially in A. F. 214. Why not before? Two reasons. (a) . . ."*

"These early experimenters," the D.H.C. was saying, "were on the wrong track. They thought that hypnopaedia could be made an instrument of intellectual education . . ."

(A small boy asleep on his right side, the right arm stuck out, the right hand hanging limp over the edge of the bed. Through a round grating in the side of a box a voice speaks softly.

"The Nile is the longest river in Africa and the second in length of all the rivers of the globe. Although falling short of the length of the Mississippi-Missouri, the Nile is at the head of all rivers as regards the length of its basin, which extends through 35 degrees of latitude . . ."

At breakfast the next morning, "Tommy," someone says, "do you know which is the longest river in Africa?" A shaking of the head. "But don't you remember something that begins: The Nile is the . . ."

"The-Nile-is-the-longest-river-in-Africa-and-the-second-in-length-of-all-of-the-rivers-of-the-globe . . ." The words come rushing out. "Although-falling-short-of . . ."

"Well now, which is the longest river in Africa?"

The eyes are blank. "I don't know."

"But the Nile, Tommy."

"The-Nile-is-the-longest-river-in-Africa-and-second . . ."

"Then which river is the longest, Tommy?"

Tommy bursts into tears. "I don't know," he howls.)

That howl, the Director made it plain, discouraged the earliest investigators. The experiments were abandoned. No further attempt was made to teach children the length of the Nile in their sleep. Quite rightly. You can't learn a science unless you know what it's all about.

"Whereas, if they'd only started on *moral* education," said the Director, leading the way towards the door. The students followed him, desperately scribbling as they walked and all the way up in the lift. "Moral education, which ought never, in any circumstances, to be rational."

"Silence, silence," whispered a loudspeaker as they stepped out at the fourteenth floor, and "Silence, silence," the trumpet mouths indefatigably repeated at intervals down every corridor. The students and even the Director himself rose automatically to the tips of their toes. They were Alphas, of course, but even Alphas have been well conditioned. "Silence, silence." All the air of the fourteenth floor was sibilant with the categorical imperative.

Fifty yards of tiptoeing brought them to a door which the Director cautiously opened. They stepped over the threshold into the twilight of a shuttered dormitory. Eighty cots stood in a row against the wall. There was a sound of light regular breathing and a continuous murmur, as of very faint voices remotely whispering.

A nurse rose as they entered and came to attention before the Director.

"What's the lesson this afternoon?" he asked.

"We had Elementary Sex for the first forty minutes," she answered. "But now it's switched over to Elementary Class Consciousness."

The Director walked slowly down the long line of cots. Rosy and relaxed with sleep, eighty little boys and girls lay softly breathing. There was a whisper under every pillow. The D.H.C. halted and, bending over one of the little beds, listened attentively.

"Elementary Class Consciousness, did you say? Let's have it repeated a little louder by the trumpet."

At the end of the room a loudspeaker projected from the wall. The Director walked up to it and pressed a switch.

" . . . all wear green," said a soft but very distinct voice, beginning in the middle of a sentence, "and Delta Children wear khaki. Oh no, I don't want to play with Delta children. And Epsilons are still worse. They're too stupid to be able to read or write. Besides they wear black, which is such a beastly color. I'm *so* glad I'm a Beta."

There was a pause; then the voice began again.

"Alpha children wear grey. They work much harder than we do, because they're so frightfully clever. I'm really awfully glad I'm a Beta, because I don't work so hard. And then we are much better than the Gammas and Deltas. Gammas are stupid. They all wear green, and Delta children wear khaki. Oh no, I *don't* want to play with Delta children. And Epsilons are still worse. They're too stupid to be able . . ."

The Director pushed back the switch. The voice was silent. Only its thin ghost continued to mutter from beneath the eighty pillows.

"They'll have that repeated forty or fifty times more before they wake; then again on Thursday, and again on Saturday. A hundred and twenty times three times a week for thirty months. After which they go on to a more advanced lesson."

Roses and electric shocks, the khaki of Deltas and a whiff of asafoetida—wedded indissolubly before the child can speak. But wordless conditioning is crude and wholesale; cannot bring home the finer distinctions, cannot inculcate the more complex courses of behavior. For that there must be words, but words without reason. In brief, hypnopaedia.

"The greatest moralizing and socializing force of all time."

The students took it down in their little books. Straight from the horse's mouth.

Once more the Director touched the switch.

" . . . so frightfully clever," the soft, insinuating, indefatigable voice was saying. "I'm really awfully glad I'm a Beta, because . . ."

Not so much like drops of water, though water, it is true, can wear holes in the hardest granite; rather, drops of liquid sealing-wax, drops that adhere, incrust, incorporate themselves with what they fall on, till finally the rock is all one scarlet blob.

"Till at last the child's mind *is* these suggestions, and the sum of the suggestions *is* the child's mind. And not the child's mind only. The adult's mind too—all his life long. The mind that judges and desires and decides—made up of these suggestions. But all these suggestions are *our* suggestions!" The Director almost shouted in his triumph. "Suggestions from the State." He banged the nearest table. "It therefore follows . . ."

A noise made him turn round.

"Oh, Ford!" he said in another tone, "I've gone and woken the children."

QUESTIONS

1. What is meant by the statement "What man has joined, nature is powerless to put asunder"? Do you think this observation is consistent or inconsistent with the philosophy of individualism that arose in the eighteenth and nineteenth centuries?

2. Why are the Deltas conditioned to dislike books? Flowers? Every state has numerous ways to condition its members and, in fact, uses them. Where would you draw the line between justifiable and unjustifiable state conditioning of citizens?

3. Could the Brave New World in any way be characterized as classically liberal? Would it violate any of classical liberalism's enabling assumptions?

4. Could the Brave New World in any way be characterized as classically conservative? Would it violate any of classical conservatism's enabling assumptions?

5. Does any social contract operate in the Brave New World? If so, how would you describe it?

6. Would people in Rawls's original position be likely to agree to live in the Brave New World?

7. What does the Director mean when he says: "Moral education . . . ought never . . . to be rational"? Would you consider this a departure from the classical philosophy of individualism or a natural extension of it?

SUGGESTIONS FOR FURTHER READING

Avineri, Shlomo. *The Social and Political Thought of Karl Marx*. New York: Cambridge University Press, 1968. Many people still consider this the best introduction to Marx's thought.

Dworkin, Ronald. *Taking Rights Seriously*. Cambridge, Mass: Harvard University Press, 1978. This is both a challenging and interesting book on a variety of social issues by an avowed liberal.

Golding, William. *Lord of the Flies*. New York: Capricorn Books, 1959. Golding creates a "state of nature," then portrays the attitudes and behavior of a handful of innocents who find themselves a part of it. A disturbing portrayal of the darker side of human nature.

Hartman, Robert H., ed. *Poverty and Economic Justice*. New York: Paulist Press, 1984. In this paperback Hartman brings together the major ethical positions on problems of poverty.

Held, Virginia. *Property, Profits and Economic Justice*. Belmont, Calif.: Wadsworth, 1980. This collection of readings from Locke and Smith down to the present examines the corporation as a social invention.

Kaufman, Arnold S. *The Radical Liberal: The New Politics in Theory and Practice*. New York: Simon & Schuster, 1968. Kaufman argues for fundamental liberal values while advocating actively bringing about radical social change. He argues for the "politics of radical pressure" with respect to black power, education, and foreign affairs.

Machiavelli, Niccolo. *The Prince*. Translated by C. Detmold. New York: Airmont, 1965. This classic about political machinations is essential reading for anyone interested in political philosophy.

Marcuse, Herbert. *One-Dimensional Man: Studies in the Ideology of Advanced Industrial Society*. Boston: Beacon Press, 1964. This is an attack on the alienation and dehumanization of humankind in "advanced" technological societies. Marcuse argues that, rather than being used to enslave humans, science and technology could be used to liberate human capacities.

Schell, Jonathan. *The Fate of the Earth*. New York: Knopf, 1982. This disturbing book began the current debate on the moral issue of nuclear war.

Sterba, James P., ed. *The Ethics of War and Nuclear Deterrence*. Belmont, Calif.: Wadsworth, 1985. In this paperback anthology, Sterba brings together some of the best writers on war in general and on nuclear war in particular.

Walzer, Michael. *Just and Unjust Wars*. New York: Basic Books, 1977. This is a challenging book on a pressing social problem: the justice of war.

Wolfe, Tom. *The Pump House Gang*. New York: Bantam, 1965. Perhaps America's leading satirist, Wolfe has written a highly entertaining and ironic collection of essays that deal largely with the problem of increased self-involvement in contemporary society.

Wolff, Robert Paul. *Understanding Rawls*. Princeton, N.J.: Princeton University Press, 1975. This is a difficult but useful short paperback that summarizes and criticizes the central ideas of Rawls.

Glossary

Some of these terms are not used in the text but are included because they are part of the philosopher's working vocabulary. In many instances these terms carry nuances that are unmentioned here. Every attempt has been made to be concise without being misleading.

A

abstraction the mental power of separating one part of an entity from its other parts or of inferring the class from the particular instance

accidental characteristic a characteristic that is not necessary to make a thing what it is; an accompanying characteristic

act utilitarianism in normative ethics, the position that an action is moral if it produces the greatest happiness for the most people

aesthetics the branch of philosophy that studies beauty, especially in the arts

agnosticism a claim of ignorance; the claim that God's existence can be neither proved nor disproved

analogy a comparison; when you reason from analogy, you conclude that because two or more entities share one aspect, they share another as well

anarchism the theory that all forms of government are incompatible with individual and social liberty and should be abolished

animism the belief that many spirits inhabit nature

anthropomorphism the attributing of human qualities to nonhuman entities, especially to God

antinomy used by Immanuel Kant to refer to contradictory conclusions arrived at through valid deduction

a posteriori pertaining to knowledge stated in empirically verifiable statements; inductive reasoning

a priori pertaining to knowledge that is logically prior to experience; reasoning based on such knowledge

atheism denial of theism

atman the Hindu idea of the self after enlightenment; the concept of no self

authority a common secondary source of knowledge; a source existing outside the person making the claim that the person uses as an expert source of information

avidya in Buddhism, the cause of all suffering and frustration; ignorance or unawareness that leads to clinging

axiology the study of the general theory of values, including their origin, nature, and classification

axiom a proposition regarded as self-evident or true

B

behaviorism a school of psychology that restricts the study of human nature to what can be observed rather than to states of consciousness

Brahman the Hindu concept of an impersonal Supreme Being; the source and goal of everything

C

categorical imperative Immanuel Kant's ethical formula: act as if the maxim (general rule) by which you act could be willed to become a universal law; the belief that what is right for one person is also right for everyone in similar circumstances

catharsis a purging or cleansing of the emotions; used by Aristotle to describe the purifying of the audience through emotional involvement in a play

causality, causation the relationship of events or of cause and effect

cause whatever is responsible for or leads to a change, motion, or condition

classification the process of grouping like things

cognition the acquiring of knowledge of something; the mental process by which we become aware of the objects of perception and thought

coherence theory a theory contending that truth is a property of a related group of consistent statements

common sense the way of looking at things apart from technical or special training

common-sense realism the epistemological position that does not distinguish between an object and an experience of it

concept a general idea, distinguished from a *percept*, which we have upon experiencing particular entities; thus, we can have a percept when we see particular citizen John Smith, but we have a concept of man, a universal unexperienced entity

conditioned genesis the Buddhist formula consisting of twelve factors that summarize the principles of conditionality, relativity, and interdependence

consequentialist theory in ethics, the position that the morality of an action is determined by its nonmoral consequences

contingent an entity that may be and also may not be

contract theory in social philosophy, the doctrine that individuals give up certain liberties and rights to the state, which in turn guarantees such rights as life, liberty, and the pursuit of happiness

correspondence theory a theory contending that truth is an agreement between a proposition and a fact

cosmology the study of the universal world process—the process by which the world unfolds and evolves

critical philosophy the analysis and definition of basic concepts and the precise expression and criticism of basic beliefs

D

deduction the process of reasoning to logically certain conclusions

defining characteristic a characteristic in whose absence a thing would not be what it is

deism a widespread belief in the seventeenth and eighteenth centuries in a God who, having created the universe, remains apart from it and administers it through natural laws

denotation a definition that is a verbal example of what a word signifies

designation a definition consisting of the defining characteristics of a word

determinism the theory that everything that occurs happens in accordance with some regular pattern or law

dharma in Buddhism, the doctrine whereby self-frustration is ended; the Eightfold Path

dialectic in general, the critical analysis of ideas to determine their meanings, implications, and assumptions; as used by Hegel, a method of reasoning used to synthesize contradictions

disanalogy a difference between compared things that lessens the likelihood of an analogical conclusion

divine command theory a single-rule, nonconsequential normative theory that says we should always do the will of God

dualism the theory that reality is composed of two different substances, so that neither one can be related to the other; thus: spirit/matter, mind/body, good/evil

duty theory in ethics, the position that the moral action is the one that conforms with obligations accrued in the past, such as the obligations of gratitude, fidelity, or justice

E

eclecticism the practice of choosing what is thought best from various philosophies

egoism a consequentialist ethical theory which contends that we act morally when we act in a way that promotes our own best long-term interests

emergence, emergent evolution the view that, in the development of the universe, new life forms appear that cannot be explained solely through analysis of previous forms

emotivism the metaethical position that ethical statements primarily express surprise, shock, or some other emotion

empathy a psychological and aesthetic designation of the attitudes, reactions, and feelings that we experience when we identify with another person or object

empiricism the position that knowledge has its origins in and derives all of its content from experience

entelechy a nonmaterial power, vital force, or purpose that permits a form to come to realization

entitlement theory a theory of social justice contending that individuals are entitled to the holdings that they have acquired without harming anyone in the process

epiphenomenalism the view that matter is primary and that the mind is a secondary phenomenon accompanying some bodily processes

epistemology the branch of philosophy that investigates the nature, sources, limitations, and validity of knowledge

essence that which makes an entity what it is; that defining characteristic in whose absence a thing would not be itself

ethics the branch of philosophy that tries to determine the good and right thing to do

eudaemonism the view that the goal of life is happiness—that is, a complete, long-lived kind of well-being; from the Greek *eudaimonia*, "happiness"

existence actuality

existentialism a twentieth-century philosophy that denies any essential human nature; each of us creates our own essence through free action

extrasensory perception experiences outside normal sensory activity, as in telepathy

F

fallacy an incorrect way of reasoning; an argument that tries to persuade psychologically but not logically

false dilemma an erroneous bipolarity resulting from the existence of positions between the two presented

fatalism the view that events are fixed, that humans can do nothing to alter them

finite limited

formalism in ethics, the view that moral acts follow from fixed moral principles and do not change because of circumstances

free will the denial that human acts are completely determined

G

Gestalt a psychological view that the whole is not just the sum of its parts

Golden Rule the ethical rule that holds: Do unto others as you would have them do unto you

H

hard determinism the doctrine that every event has a cause that entails the denial of moral freedom

hedonism the view that pleasure is intrinsically worthwhile and is the human's good

humanism the view that stresses distinctly human values and ideals

human nature what it essentially means to be of our species; what makes us different from anything else

hypothesis in general, an assumption, statement, or theory of explanation, the truth of which is under investigation

I

idealism in metaphysics, the position that reality is ultimately nonmatter; in epistemology, the position that all we know are our ideas

ideational theory the theory of word meaning that stresses the emotional impact of words

identity theory the theory that mental states are really brain states

immanent indwelling, within the process, as God is frequently thought to be in relation to His creation

immortality the belief that the self or soul survives physical death

indeterminism the view that some individual choices are not determined by preceding events

individualism the social theory that emphasizes the importance of the individual, his or her rights, and independence of action

induction the process of reasoning to probable explanations or judgments

inference a conclusion arrived at inductively or deductively

infinite unlimited

infinite regress the causal or logical relationship of terms in a series that logically has no first or initiating term

informal fallacies common argumentative devices used to persuade emotionally or psychologically, but not logically

innate ideas ideas that, according to some philosophers, such as Plato, can never be found in experience but are inborn

instrumentalism synonymous with John Dewey's pragmatism; the view that emphasizes experience and interprets concepts, beliefs, and attitudes as ways in which an organism adjusts to its environment

interactionism the theory that the mind and the body interact, originally associated with Descartes

intuition a source of knowledge that does not rely on the senses or reason but on direct awareness of something

J

judgment asserting or denying something in the form of a proposition

K

karma the Hindu law of sowing and reaping; determines what form and circumstances we assume in each reincarnated state

L

laissez-faire in economics, politics, and social philosophy, the concept of government noninterference

language an aspect of human behavior that involves the use of vocal sounds and corresponding written symbols in meaningful patterns to formulate and communicate thoughts and feelings

linguistic analysis a contemporary form of analytic philosophy claiming that philosophical problems are partially language problems; the purpose of philosophy is to dissolve, not resolve, problems by a rigorous examination of language

logic the branch of epistemology that studies the methods and principles of correct reasoning

logical empiricism (positivism) a contemporary form of analytic philosophy that contends meaning is the most important feature of philosophical discourse; there are two kinds of epistemological meaning: (1) that expressed in analytic statements—that is, formal meaning that can be verified by logic and syntax; and (2) empirical—that is, factual meaning that can be verified by sense data

logical positivism the philosophical school of thought that would restrict meaningful propositions to those that can be empirically verified or to those that state relationships among terms

logos the term used by classical philosophers to describe the principle of rationality or law that they observed operating in the universe

M

materialism the metaphysical position that reality is ultimately composed of matter

maximin principle the social theory of justice which contends that inequality is allowable only insofar as it improves the lot of the worst off in a society

maya in Buddhism, the world of illusion

mechanism the view that everything can be explained in terms of laws that govern matter and motion

meliorism from the Latin meaning "better"; the view that the world is neither all good nor all bad, but can be improved through human effort

mentalism the view that mind or idea is all that exists

metaethics the study of the meanings of ethical words and of the sentences in which they appear

metaphysics the branch of philosophy that studies the nature of reality

metempsychosis the belief that upon physical death the soul can migrate into another body

monism the view that reality is reducible to one kind of thing or one explanatory principle

monotheism the belief in a single God

morals the conduct or rule of conduct by which people live

mysticism the philosophy of religion contending that reality can be known only when we surrender our individuality and experience a union with the divine ground of all existence

N

naive realism the view that the world is as we perceive it to be

naturalism a view of ethics that rejects supernatural principles and maintains that morality can be explained only in terms of scientifically verifiable concepts

natural law a pattern of necessary and universal regularity holding in physical ratio; a moral imperative, a description of what ought to happen in human relationships

necessary condition a way to refer to cause; for example, when B cannot occur in the absence of A, A is said to be a necessary condition of B

new realism the view that the world is as we perceive it to be

nihilism the view that nothing exists, that nothing has value; the social view that conditions are so bad that they should be destroyed and replaced by something better

nirvana in Buddhism, enlightenment that comes when the limited, clinging self is extinguished

nominalism the view that only particular entities are real and that universals represent detectable likenesses among particulars

nonconsequentialist theory in ethics, the position that the morality of an action is determined by more than just its consequences

nonnaturalism the metaethical position that ethical statements defy translation into nonethical language

nonnormative ethics the scientific or descriptive study of ethics; or the study of ethical terms, including the notion of moral justification

normative ethics the branch of ethics that makes judgments about obligation and value

O

objective a term describing an entity that has a public nature independent of us and our judgments about it

objective idealism the position that ideas exist in an objective state, associated originally with Plato

objective relativism the value theory which contends that values are relative to human satisfaction but that human needs and what satisfies them are open to empirical examination

obligation that which we must or are bound to do because of some duty, agreement, contract, promise, or law

omnipotent all-powerful

omnipresent being everywhere at once

omniscient all-knowing

ontology a subdivision of metaphysics; the theory of the nature of being and existence

ostensive definition a definition that consists of an instance of a word's denotation

P

panentheism the belief that God is both fixed and changing, inclusive of all possibilities

pantheism the belief that everything is God

parallelism the theory that physical and mental states do not interact but simply accompany each other

parapsychology the school of psychology that studies extrasensory powers

paternalism the view that government may legitimately decide what is in the best interests of adult citizens, just as a parent may legitimately decide what is in the best interests of the child

perception the act or process by which we become aware of things

phenomenalism the belief, associated with Kant, that we can know only appearances (phenomena) and never what is ultimately real (noumena); that the mind has the ability to sort out sense data and provide relationships that hold among them

phenomenology the philosophical school founded by Edmund Husserl which contends that being is the underlying reality, that what is ultimately real is our consciousness, which itself is being

philosophy the love and pursuit of wisdom

pluralism the view that reality consists of many substances

polytheism belief in many gods

positivism the view that only analytic and synthetic propositions are meaningful

postulate a presupposition used as a basis for establishing a proof

pragmatism the philosophical school of thought, associated with Dewey, James, and Peirce, that tries to mediate between idealism and materialism by rejecting all absolute first principles, tests truth through workability, and views the universe as pluralistic

prajñā in Zen Buddhism, transcendental wisdom

predestination the doctrine that every aspect of our lives has been divinely determined from the beginning of time

prima facie duties according to Ross, duties that generally obligate us but may not in a particular case because of circumstances

primary qualities according to Locke, qualities that inhere in an object: size, shape, weight, and so on

probability the likelihood of an event's happening or of a statement's being true

proposition a true or false statement

R

rationalism the position that reason alone, without the aid of sense information, is capable of arriving at some knowledge, at some undeniable truths

realism the doctrine that the objects of our senses exist independently of their being experienced

reason the capacity for thinking reflectively and making inferences; the process of following relationships from thought to thought and of ultimately drawing conclusions

referential theory a theory of word meaning which contends that words refer to things

relativism the view that human judgment is conditioned by factors such as acculturation and personal bias

religious belief in its broadest sense, the belief that there is an unseen order and that we can do no better than to be in harmony with that order

representative realism the position, associated with Locke, that distinguishes between an object and one's experience of it

right in ethics, act that conforms to moral standards

rights those things to which we have a just claim

rule utilitarianism the normative ethical position which contends that we should act so that the rule governing our actions produces the greatest happiness for the most people

S

samsara in Buddhism, the round of birth and life

scientific method a way of investigation based on collecting, analyzing, and interpreting sense data to determine the most probable explanation

secondary qualities according to Locke, qualities that we impose on an object: color, smell, texture, and so on

self the individual person; the ego; the knower; that which persists through changes in a person

self-determinism the view that holds that our actions are determined, but not solely, by external forces or conditions

semantics the study of the relationship between words and reality, including their linguistic forms, symbolic nature, and effects on human behavior

sense data images or sense impressions

situation ethics according to Joseph Fletcher, the doctrine that contends that the moral action produces the greatest amount of Christian love (*agape*)

skepticism in epistemology, the view that varies between doubting all assumptions until proved and claiming that no knowledge is possible

social philosophy the application of moral principles to the problems of freedom, equality, justice, and the state

soft determinism a view that attempts to reconcile freedom and responsibility with determinism

solipsism an extreme form of subjective idealism, contending that only I exist and that everything else is a product of the subjective consciousness

soul the immaterial entity that is identified with consciousness, mind, or personality

subjective that which refers to the knower; that which exists in the consciousness but not apart from it

subjective idealism in epistemology, the position that all we ever know are our own ideas

substance that which is real; essence; the underlying ground in which properties inhere; that which exists in its own right and depends on nothing else

sufficient condition a way to refer to cause; A is said to be a sufficient condition of B if, without exception, whenever A occurs B occurs

T

tautology a statement whose predicate repeats its subject in whole or in part

teleology the view that maintains the reality of purpose and affirms that the universe either was consciously designed or is operating under partly conscious, partly unconscious purposes

telepathy in ESP, the name given to the phenomenon of thought transfer from one person's mind to another's without normal means of communication

theism the belief in a personal God who intervenes in the lives of His creation

theology the rational study of God, including religious doctrines

totalitarianism the political view that the state is of paramount importance

U

universal that which is predictive of many particular entities; thus, "woman" is a universal, since it is predictive of individual women

utilitarianism in ethics, the theory which contends that we should act in such a way that our actions produce the greatest quantity of happiness or pleasure

V

validity correctness of the reasoning process; characteristic of an argument whose conclusion follows by logical necessity

value an assessment of worth

verification the proving or disproving of a proposition

vitalism the view that there is in living organisms an entelechy, or life principle, that provides purpose or direction

Art Credits

Index